# Instructor's Ma
# Test Bank

to accompany

# International Marketing

## Eleventh Edition

Philip R. Cateora
*University of Colorado*

John L. Graham
*University of California, Irvine*

Test Bank prepared by
Ronald L. Weir
*East Tennessee State University*

McGraw-Hill Irwin

Boston Burr Ridge, IL Dubuque, IA Madison, WI New York San Francisco St. Louis
Bangkok Bogotá Caracas Kuala Lumpur Lisbon London Madrid Mexico City
Milan Montreal New Delhi Santiago Seoul Singapore Sydney Taipei Toronto

*McGraw-Hill Higher Education*
*A Division of The McGraw-Hill Companies*

Instructor's Manual/Test Bank to accompany
INTERNATIONAL MARKETING
Cateora and Graham

Published by McGraw-Hill/Irwin, an imprint of the McGraw-Hill Companies, Inc., 1221 Avenue of the Americas, New York, NY 10020. 

2 3 4 5 6 7 8 9 0 HAM/HAM 0 9 8 7 6 5 4 3 2 1

ISBN 0-07-244875-X

www.mhhe.com

# CONTENTS

## INTRODUCTION

The tenth edition of *International Marketing* is designed to serve as the text for a first course in international marketing. The field of international business abounds with courses titled international business, international trade, export trade, global marketing, international marketing management, and international marketing all of which are courses for which the tenth edition of *International Marketing* is appropriate. Any international business or marketing course which emphasizes the cultural/environmental aspects of international trade and stresses the integration of culture and marketing functions can use this text effectively.

Since many schools offer only one course in the international field, we have included information in the Instructor's Manual that goes beyond the traditional text bank and answers to end-of-chapter questions. Be sure to look for:

**INTERNET TIPS**
**STUDENT PROJECTS**
- **DEBATES**
- **COUNTRY NOTEBOOK**
- **GUIDE FOR INTERNATIONAL MARKETING PLAN**
- **USING COMPUTER-BASED DATA IN MARKETING PLANS**
- **DEVELOPING CULTURAL AWARENESS**

**DESCRIPTIONS OF SOFTWARE AND DATABASES FOR INTERNATIONAL BUSINESS**
**CURRENT LIBRARY INFORMATION SOURCES**
**VIDEO AND FILMS (ANNOTATED)**
**TRANSPARENCY MASTERS FOR TEXT MATERIAL**
**MAPS - 35 TRANSPARENCY MASTERS**
**COMPUTERIZED TEST BANK**
**NOTES FOR END-OF-CHAPTER QUESTIONS**
**TEACHING SUGGESTIONS FOR EACH CHAPTER**
**NOTES FOR CASES**

Plan to examine the Instructor's Manual carefully, it is an important source of information, tips, projects, and suggestions designed to assist you in teaching international marketing. Many of the class projects have been developed by professors who have allowed us to include them for the benefit of others. If you have projects, teaching tips and other teaching suggestions that you use and would like to share, please pass them along.

Philip R. Cateora
University of Colorado, Boulder

John L. Graham
University of California—Irvine

## DON'T OVERLOOK THESE FEATURES IN THE INSTRUCTOR'S MANUAL

**INTERNET TIPS**

**STUDENT PROJECTS:**

(All classroom tested)

- Developing Cultural Awareness (Student project designed to enhance cultural awareness.)
- Notes and guidelines for Case Development (Student-generated case project.)
- Student Debates (Organizing an in-class debate, evaluation forms, case and topic suggestions.)
- Notes on "The Country Notebook-A Guide for Developing a Marketing Plan"—using supplemental materials in International Marketing. (Description of project, country selection, product selection, grading methods, assignment schedule, and answers to questions often asked about the project.)
- Using Computer-Based Country Data Sources to develop an international marketing plan for a region or set of countries. (Description of project, data bases—PC-Globe and CORE, and course syllabus.)

**SOFTWARE AND DATABASES FOR INTERNATIONAL MARKETING:**

(Description, addresses, telephone numbers for)

- PC-Globe (Data, maps, graphics for 177 countries.)
- CORE (Company Readiness to Export)
- GETI ONE (An export trading company tutorial.)
- Export to Win (An interactive tutorial on exporting.)
- Canadplan (An advertising and sales promotion simulation game)
- Barnga (A simulation game on cultural clashes)
- Flash Facts (Information on fax available from the Department of Commerce Country Desks)

**LIST OF CURRENT SOURCES FOR:**

- Statistical data
- Retail market data
- Culturgrams
- International Advertising Rates and more.

**ANNOTATED LIST OF CURRENT FILMS AND VIDEOS:**

(prices, telephone numbers, addresses)

**TRANSPARENCY MASTERS FOR:**

- Maps (All maps in the text plus additional countries and/or regions.)
- Key exhibits in text
- Additional exhibits not in text
- Lists of topics, concepts, etc.

**AND OF COURSE:**

- A computerized test bank.
- Notes for end-of-chapter questions
- Teaching suggestions for each chapter
- Notes for cases

# PART I
# GENERAL TEACHING SUGGESTIONS

## A. NOTES ON USING THE INTERNET

1. What is a URL?

URL stands for Uniform Resource Locator. It is the address of a given Website or homepage. For example, the URL for Wal-Mart is http://www.wal-mart.com. This URL has two parts: http:// is referred to as the prefix, it indicates that this address points to an HTML-encoded document (http stands for Hypertext Transport Protocol).[1]

The next part of the URL, www.wal-mart.com, is the name of the *computer, host or server* where this document is stored. Another term for this label is the *domain name.* A domain name generally has three parts, which are separated by a period (.) that is referred to as a "dot". The three parts include, www (World Wide Web); a name (an abbreviation of a company name such as Levi in this example or some specially created name), and an organizational designation, com, which stands for commercial organization. Other organizational designations are:

COM Commercial organization
EDU Educational and research institution
GOV Government agencies
MIL Military agencies
NET Major Network support centers
ORG Other organizations (For example, the URL for the OECD,
INT International organizations

A URL will often have additional parts after the domain name. These additional parts direct the computer to specific locations within an address or Web page. For example http://www.wal-mart.com/stores/graduation/college.html will take you to Wal-Mart's on-line store (stores) and within that to the section that offers suggestions for graduation presents (graduation) and then to selections for college graduates (college.html). You can also get to the same location by using only the domain name (http://www.wal-mart.com) and then, when you are within the homepage, following the guides to the location you are seeking. This last point is especially important to remember since addresses for specific locations within an address are often changed, updated, or eliminated. When that happens you will get a message that the specific site cannot be opened. When this occurs, drop all the parts of the address except the domain name (in our example that would be http//www.wal-mart.com). This will get you into the homepage from which you can search for the information or section you want. You might want to try http://www.wal-mart.com/stores/graduation/college.html and see what happens. Since this is a seasonal promotion within Wal-Mart's e-store, there is a good chance that this address will not access this specific location.

2. Are there specific designations for URLs in foreign countries?

Besides the designations cited above, there are designations for foreign countries. For example, http://www.transparency.de/ is the URL for Transparency International, a not-for-profit, non-governmental organization to counter corruption in international business transactions, which is located in Germany (de).

A few country designations are:

| | | |
|---|---|---|
| AR Argentina | | AT Austria |
| AU Australia | | BR Brazil |
| CA Canada | | DE Germany |
| ES Spain | | FR France |
| HK Hong Kong | | JP Japan |
| MX Mexico | | UK United Kingdom |

Some companies may have several different domain locations. For example, Hertz has specific locations in the United States (http://www.hertz.com) and in other countries such as Brazil (http://www.hertz.com.br); and Mexico (http://www.hertz.com.mx). Companies not in the United States such as El Corte Ingles, a major department store in Spain, will often have a domain name such as (http://www.elcorteingles.es).

3. What do I do when I get a message such as: "Cannot open the Internet site. A connection with the server could not be established?"

   a. Check to be sure that you have entered the exact URL. An extra space, period, letter, misspelling or an omission of something will result in failure to connect. The URL must be entered exactly.

   b. If the problem is not the result of one of the points mentioned above (a) and the URL includes specific locations within the site such as http://www.wal-mart.com/stores/graduation/college.html, the specific location within the homepage of Wal-Mart may have been deleted or renamed – in other words, it no longer is at the address you entered. In this case, drop everything from the URL except the domain name (http://www.wal-mart.com) and search for the location once you have entered the homepage.

4. What does it mean if I type a URL and get a site other than the one I typed?

   When this happens you have either used the wrong organization designations, for example used (*com*) when you should have used (*org*); or, you have misspelled the name of the host. Check to be sure that you have spelled everything correctly and the organization designation is correct.

5. Throughout the text we have included Internet sites in the footnotes and in the body of the text. In addition to those citations, are others:

   http://www.mhhe.com/cateora—home page for ***International Marketing.*** Visit the site for updates on Web sites and other information.

## B. USEFUL INTERNET LINKS

The following Internet Links should be included in your Internet Bookmarks. There are many others but these seem to be especially useful.

### 1. Indiana University CIBER's Web Link

IU CIBER's pedagogy links groups together several Web sites which should prove useful for teaching international business or internationalizing your business courses. This page can be accessed at: http://pacioli.bus.indiana.edu/ciber/ciber.htm.

The CIBERs around the country are good sources of online information and help

---

[1] Other prefixes used on the Internet include *ftp://; file://; gopher://; and telnet://.* These prefixes will not be discussed here since these notes focus only on World Wide Web documents.

- CIBERweb This Web site links all of the CIBERs from around the U.S.
- IU CIBER
- Pedagogy newsletters Trying to catch up on recent international business teaching resources? Read the current and back issues for news and reviews.
- Info Express Do you need teaching resources for a specific international topic? Let our info-express wizards compile a list of relevant resources for you. Don't forget, express means speedy delivery! Have our GAs work for you.
- Pedagogy Workshops Curious about how those games and simulations operate in real life? Come to the summer workshop and test drive them yourself. You will also get the latest in effective teaching with videos and cases. So much information in so little time for so little money!
- MSU Ciber This site is wonderful beyond belief. This site links together international business and country information Web sites in an easy to use and logical format. The site also provides a search engine as well. Don't miss this site!

**Here are some resources you should find useful in preparing to teach international business courses:**

- Pointcast This free software program will assist you in keeping up with news and events from around the world. This program gathers news and information from many sources and presents it to you in a logical and useful format. The program provides a wonderful screen saver.
- City Net This Web site is a gold mine of country information. The site is set up with an easy to use graphical interface. All you have to do is to point and click on the country about which you would like more information. A nice resource for students and instructors. Let's go to Germany.
- Syllabus Magazine This magazine provides the latest developments in multimedia technology which can be used in teaching. You can read the issue online or sign up for a free subscription. There are frequent articles regarding the classroom use of internet resources.
- Business Presenter's Home Page Tired of one boring student presentation after another? Send your students here. There are plenty of links which should help students prepare and deliver solid presentations. Great tips and checklists. You might find something useful as well!
- Modern Video Looking for free videos, which can be kept, on various international business topics? Try this site. Topics range from doing business in Japan to the benefits of free trade.
- Vanderbilt News Archives This site provides an archive of television news broadcasts. You can put together a custom video on virtually any international business topic.
- ECCH Case Clearinghouse
- HBS Cases A well known source for international cases and videos.

**Wondering how other professors are using internet resources in their international business courses? Here are some examples:**

- World Lecture Hall This site provides online syllabi for business courses. Many of these courses have integrated Web-based materials. It can be a good source of information. Don't be surprised if you find a number of outdated links.
- Indiana University D301 - International Business This is an example of an award-winning international business course taught entirely online. This is a trend in distance education.
- Socrates This site can provide the benefits of the information age in your classroom.

An important new initiative of the IU CIBER will fill a void of long standing: the very limited availability of international case materials by American professors not at Harvard. There is significant teaching material that fits this category, some of it spawned by CIBERs across the US. Properly publicized and distributed, this material can add greatly to the repertoires of professors everywhere.

For this reason, the IU CIBER has created a case clearinghouse that solicits, reviews, edits, formats, and publicizes cases, and, in alliance with the European Case Clearing House (ECCH) at Babson College, distributes them as the CIBER Case Collection. The IU CIBER is also developing teaching notes for suggested modules of cases and manuals for such innovations as the IU Global BizQuiz.

2. **CIBERweb** provides links to all the CIBERs around the U.S.

   CIBERweb has recently gone through a transformation. Not only has the design of the site been updated, but you will find many new features that will help you top get the most out of the Centers. Please feel free to browse through the contents of this site.

   This site offers links to other CIBERS as well as a service that allows you to get the information that you need quickly. CIBERweb is a service that will show you only the information that is of interest to you. All that you need to do is register for a *free* account. Then tell us some of your interests in International Business, and you will be presented with your CIBERweb page.

   Visit this site at: http://ciber.centers.purdue.edu.

**COURSE OUTLINES AND TEACHING MATERIALS DEVELOPED FOR INTERNAIONAL BUSINESS**

This site focuses mostly on international business although there are several international marketing sources reviewed. In addition there are links to a variety of Universities. The site includes:

A. Innovative Teaching Resources
B. Course Outlines or Syllabi
C. Readings, Reference Lists and Conference Proceedings
D. International Business Curriculum Designs
E. Working Paper Series

Visit the following for complete details on these topics:
http://www3.mgmt.purdue.edu/CIBER/Publications/CIBER-RESOURCE-HANDBOOK/1.htm.
NOTE: THIS ADDRESS IS CASE SENSITIVE.

3. **J GUIDE Stanford Guide to Japanese Information Resources**

   The following topics are included at this site:

   References; Indices and Guides; Business, Economics, and finance; Language and Culture; Politics and Government; History and Geography; and various other topics.

   Visit: http://fuji.stanford.edu/jguide/

4. **LANIC - Latin American Network Information Center**

   This site of The University of Texas provides an extensive source of information on Latin America and lists itself as the most complete library of Latin American Studies on the Web.

   There is a Country Directory and Subject Directory. Some of the subjects include Statistics; Trade; Newspapers; Reference; Economy; History, Libraries and many more. Visit the home page at: http://www.lanic.utexas.edu .

5. **UNESCO (United Nations Educational, Scientific and Cultural Organization)**

   UNESCO provides information that a student can use in projects, class assignments, and other research efforts. Includes topics on : Publications; Statistics; UNESCO partners; Information services; and, Current events. Visit this site at: http://www.unesco.org.

## C. COURSE ORGANIZATION PLANS

**International Marketing** is designed for an introductory course in international marketing. The author suggests the following assignment schedule for 10-week or 15-week periods. The topical description may be used with an instructor's class outline. When cases, term projects, or other instructional material are used, they can easily be included in the proposed assignment schedules.

**Assignment Schedule for 15 Weeks**

| Week | Chapter(s) |
|---|---|
| 1 | 1, 2 |
| 2 | 3 |
| 3 | 4 |
| 4 | 5 |
| 5 | 6 |
| 6 | 7, 8 |
| 7 | 9, 10 |
| 8 | 11 |
| 9 | 12 |
| 10 | 13 |
| 11 | 14, 15 |
| 12 | 16 |
| 13 | 17 |
| 14 | 18 |
| 15 | 19 |

**Assignment Schedule For 10 Weeks**

| Week | Chapter(s) |
|---|---|
| 1 | 1, 2 |
| 2 | 3 |
| 3 | 4, 5 |
| 4 | 6, 7 |
| 5 | 8, 9 |
| 6 | 10, 11 |
| 7 | 12, 13 |
| 8 | 14, 15 |
| 9 | 16, 17 |
| 10 | 18 |
| | 19 |

## D. SAMPLE SYLLABUS FOR A 15-WEEK SEMESTER MEETING TWO DAYS PER WEEK

This syllabus includes both the country notebook project. (See "The Country Notebook—A Guide for Developing a Marketing Plan," text, p. 610 and the "Current Readings and Class Reports,"—G–1 project described on page 9 of this manual.)

Mk 4100
SPRING 20___
T.TH. 1100 – 1215

| DATE | TOPIC | ASSIGNMENT*** CATEGORY | CHAPTER |
|---|---|---|---|
| Th. Th | Introduction | A | 1 |
| T | Global Marketing | A | 2 |
| Th | Geography / History | B | 3 |
| | Country / Team Selection* * | | |
| T | Culture | C | 4 |
| Th | **Trade With China/Current Prospects*** | | 4 |
| T Feb. | No class – Team Meetings | | |
| Th | Business Customs | D | 5 |
| T | Political Vulnerability | A | 6 |
| Th | Legal Systems | B | 7 |
| T | Intellectual Property Rights | C | 7 |
| Th | Culture Paper Due & Oral reports | | |
| T | Hour Exam – Chapters. 1–7 | | |
| Th | Marketing Research | D | 8 |
| T March | **Expansion Of NAFTA*** | | |
| Th | Emerging Markets | A | 9 |
| T | Regional Market Groups | B | 10 |
| Th | Strategic Marketing | C | 11 |
| T | Collaborative Relationships | D | 11 |
| T | Developing Consumer Products | B | 12 |
| | SPRING BREAK | | |
| Th | Industrial Products | C | 13 |
| T. April | Hour Exam Chapters.8 – 14 | | |
| T | Distribution Systems | D | 14 |
| Th | **Accessing Japanese Distribution*** | | |
| Th | Export Mechanics | A | 15 |
| T | Economic Paper Due & Oral Reports | | |
| Th | Global Advertising | A | 16 |
| T | Cross-Country Negotiations | B | 17 |
| Th | Pricing | C | 18 |
| T | Negotiations | D | 19 |
| Th | Last Class Day – ALL PAPERS DUE | | |
| T May | **Final Exam** | | |

*** (Note to Professor) See E–1, page 6 of Instructor's Manual for discussion of Assignment Groups.
** (Note to Professor) See F, page 17 of Instructor's Manual for discussion of Country / Team Assignment.
*Special Lectures
TEXT: Cateora, Philip, *International Marketing*, 9th Edition, Richard D. Irwin, 1996

**NOTE:**

A. AN EXAMINATION WILL BE GIVEN EACH FRIDAY. No make-up exam will be given. If an exam is missed for a reason acceptable to the professor, the final exam value will be increased to include value of missed exam. Permission to miss an exam will rarely be given and then only for the most unusual cases.

B. Dates for examinations, class presentations, and assignments will not be changed. Please schedule your personal absences so as not to conflict with your active participation.

C. Class participation includes attendance, assigned topics, participation in class discussions, and all papers assigned. Regular attendance is expected.

D. All papers are due on date assigned. A late penalty will be assessed for unexcused late papers.

Four weekly exams 100 pts.; Five weekly assignments 50 pts.; class participation 15 pts.; final exam 35 pts.; Total 200 pts. PLUS AND MINUS GRADE WILL BE GIVEN.

NOTE: Weekly topic assignments will be graded as PASS/FAIL. *All papers* must bc submitted and receive a grade of Pass to earn the 50 points for this assignment. All papers graded FAIL can be resubmitted until a grade of PASS is received. In other words, do your assignment and receive 50 points toward your final grade.

**Suggested Business Journals**

Advertising Age International
Business America
Business Asia
Business China
Business Eastern Europe
Business Europe
Business Horizons
Business International
Business Latin America
Business Week
Europe
Financial Times
Forbes
Fortune
Harvard Business Review
International Management
Journal of International Business
Journal of International Marketing
Wall Street Journal
Trade & Culture
International Business
and others.

**GRADES:**

Two hour exams 300 pts.; term project 350 pts.; class participation 100 pts.; five briefs of current articles 50 pts.; final exam 200 pts.; Total 1000 pts. PLUS AND MINUS GRADES WILL BE GIVEN.

Term Project Grade Allocation (350 pts. Total)
Culture Paper 75 pts.
Economic Paper 75 pts.
Marketing Plan 200 pts.

## E. SUGGESTIONS FOR TEACHER'S FILES

Most international marketing teachers find that the wealth of materials about international business and international affairs all but overwhelms them unless they have a systematic filing system. I suggest that a file of articles, pamphlets, sample forms and documents can help the professor interject notes of realism and tangibility to discussions and lectures. The file will also provide factual materials and article materials worthy of comment at the professor's fingertips when making class preparations.

A simple but effective way to integrate the filing system and the teaching activity is to set up a file folder for each chapter of the book and to sort materials gathered only at such time as they become cumbersome. Natural divisions following the professor's interest patterns will later suggest themselves. By utilizing the chapter outline as a filing guide, different materials needed on a given topic will be readily available to the professor. Additional topics which may not be covered by the book but which the instructor may want to introduce can be accommodated into the filing system simply by adding a few additional categories. The text outline is essentially functional in nature and should accommodate most materials.

## F. CLASSROOM PROJECTS

A few general comments about various types of classroom activities which may be applied to the course as a whole or which may relate to any or all of the chapters may be useful. The suggestions below are merely indicative of the types of things which an instructor may do to gain heightened student involvement and impart maximum interest to his course.

1. **Outside speakers**, judiciously used, often can add spice and realism to an international course. It is suggested that excessive reliance not be placed on outside speakers because, in general, the content of their remarks cannot be controlled and integrated as fully as most instructors desire. However, as many as four to six speakers can be successfully integrated into a course. It is suggested that several different types of speakers be utilized. Two major categories of speakers would be foreign persons and businessmen or government officials with foreign involvements.
2. **Foreign students** add a strong cultural note and can also provide specific information about their country and its business involvements. An *ambassador* or other *diplomatic representative* of a foreign country can often be counted on for a visit. If foreign students are enrolled in the class, they may act in a sense as "experts in residence" and provide continuing information for the class, if they are drawn out. *Businessmen* or *government officials* representing large and small firms or export or foreign operations can add several other kinds of viewpoints. Very often, *U.S. Department of Commerce* officials are cooperative not only in speaking themselves, but in providing names of local businessmen with foreign involvements. Many cities have *export trade clubs* or other associations composed of people with international business. Such groups are usually willing to provide speakers or develop entire programs for international classes.
3. **Student participation.** Reports and other types of student contributions in the classroom can increase involvement significantly and can provide discussion information and materials to supplement those given by the instructor. We have had considerable success in using students as specialists in either *functional or geographic areas.* Each student may be assigned a different topic and make it his responsibility to read and otherwise learn as much about that topic as possible. He/She can then participate with the instructor in presenting the functional area materials within the subject areas considered in the course. Such functional area specialists can also provide information throughout the course which will give a stronger interrelationship. As an example, one student may specialize on the legal aspects of marketing and be able to

contribute legal information when discussions are under way concerning advertising, import restrictions, pricing, or any of the other marketing areas.

4. **Country specialization** calls for the student to absorb all the material he /she can about a given assigned country. Various students will then be in a position to provide information relative to marketing in different parts of the world. Thus, when a discussion of advertising, say, is in progress, one student can tell what he knows about advertising in Australia; another, advertising in Egypt; another, advertising in Germany; and so on. Students enjoy both types of participation, and it gives them a heightened sense of awareness of the problems associated either functionally or geographically in international marketing.

   Another technique that is sometimes useful is to attempt to gain a *depth exposure* to a specific country. In such an instance, everyone in the class studies the same country or the same two or three countries. The instructor should make a special effort to have adequate library materials on hand about the country or countries and line up speakers from those countries or who have had experience in those countries. With an information base of this sort, the class can intelligently venture into such areas as national policy, cultural barriers, and can even develop in-depth studies oriented around marketing products into that country. Sometimes an interesting variation can be found by assigning different students or groups of students to *different types of products* which might encounter different problems even within a given country.

## G. STUDENT PROJECTS

In order to build involvement and expertise among students, a number of activities can be undertaken. All have been used by the authors and found beneficial in varying degrees.

### 1. Current Reading and Class Reports

An important objective when we teach a basic course is to introduce and encourage students to read current business periodicals and journals. Their interest in the course increases when they read current articles which relate to class material about what is happening in the business world. In order to achieve this objective, we have developed a class project that is relatively painless for the students, gets them reading current business journals, and keeps us updated on current happenings as well. This project works so well we adapted it to international topics when we internationalized the basic course.

We have found this to be one of the most successful projects we have ever used in the basic course and further, student reaction has been very positive. It is a relatively painless way to get the students to read more about marketing and especially international marketing.

**The Assignment**

The assignment is simple to do. Each student is asked to find an article in a current periodical (described as no more than one-year old) on an assigned topic with international application. They are to read the article and summarize it in the equivalent of one double-spaced typewritten page. They are also asked to include the title of the article, name of the periodical, date and page number. They are told they *may* be asked to give a brief report on the article during class. Each student's assignment is due at the beginning of class period on the day the topic is assigned.

**Frequency of Assignment**

To make the assignments worthwhile we believe each student should read no fewer than six articles. We also believe the articles should be spread throughout the semester. To facilitate this, we divide the class into groups (thirds, quarters, or fifths depending on the number of days during the term the class meets.) Each group is assigned a sequential letter. When a letter appears on the class syllabus each student with that letter knows he or she has a summarized international article due. This way one segment of the class each period is turning in an assignment and, depending on the starting and ending of the assignments, each student will do from 6 to 9 articles.

**Topic Assignment**

The topics assigned to each group parallel the topics of the text reading assignment and lecture. We pick very broad topics to give the student some leeway in article selection. For example, when discussing product, one assignment might be product life cycle, the next, product development, then brand names, etc. In each case, the topic is discussed in the assigned chapter and the students are expected to find an international article that addresses the topic assigned, e.g., product life cycle. We are not very rigid on the preciseness of the article topic selected since the goal is for students to find something with an international topic and sometimes it is difficult for them to find an article that fits exactly. Students are aware of their assignments for the entire term.

This is important since they need time to find the appropriate articles and, as discussed later, there is an added benefit to having them begin searching for articles at the beginning of the term.

**Source of Articles**

The students are permitted to find articles to summarize in any current periodical but not in a book. Textbooks or other books are excluded because there are one or two books from which they could get all their assignments. Further, if allowed to consult books, one of the major purposes of the assignments, i.e., getting them to read business periodicals, would be lost. Newspapers and popular magazines are allowed; however, most use business periodicals. Suggested sources include The *Wall Street Journal*, *Forbes*, *Business Week*, *Fortune*, *Business Horizons*, *Journal of Marketing*, *Advertising Age International*, *Journal of Retailing*, *Dun's Review* and other periodicals available in the library. They are also urged to consult the *Index to Business Periodicals* as another source of articles. Articles with international subjects appear in almost everything published.

**Grading**

These assignments are not graded. Instead, the assignment is a requirement of the course, i.e., they must complete it when assigned in order to fulfill the requirements of the course. Grading these assignments is difficult to do; the assignment is either correctly done or it is not, so it is either accepted or rejected. If the assignment is not done properly, we simply write "Redo" across the top and expect another one the next class period. At the beginning of the term there are about ten percent "redos" because the students do not understand the assignment. After the first few, most are correct with very few "redos." The students must resubmit the "redos" in order to get credit for them. The assignment is made as painless as possible to increase their enthusiasm.

**Using the Assignments in Class**

It is helpful to use the papers in class. This is done in two ways. Students are invited to volunteer international topics relevant to the current class discussion. They are also asked to give a brief summary of the article during class which is then incorporated into the topic of the lecture.

Once two or three day's assignments have been presented, we find we have several good examples that an be used in class to illustrate points. This is an important benefit of using this assignment, i.e., it provides the professor with an abundance of current examples to use in lectures where appropriate. It is frequently necessary to go to the original source to read further so it is essential to stress the importance of including the article, title, source, and so on when giving the assignment. Sometimes papers are returned when they do not give the proper citation and a redo is required in order to get credit for the assignment.

**Advantages of Assignment**

The several advantages of this assignment are:

- Students become familiar with business journals and periodicals.
- They begin thinking about marketing in an international context.
- There is always a segment of the class ready with topics for discussions.
- Interest in the course and international topics is enhanced since the assignment has relevancy to what is happening in business today, i.e., real examples.
- It provides the professor with an abundance of interesting and current examples to use in future classes.
- A hidden benefit is that the students read or at least scan many more topics than just the six or so they will use in class. By assigning the topics at the beginning of the term, many will begin looking for articles for their assignments and, as they do, they become aware of many different topics and are unconsciously expanding their exposure to current business topics.

See PART III, C, Sample Syllabus (for 15 weeks) for suggestions on integrating this project into the daily schedule.

**2. Student Organizations and Field Trips**

Before the establishment of our international business or international marketing club, we interjected international elements into the student marketing club program. These were well received and created considerable interest in the international program and provided the basis for forming the international club. If the international business or international marketing program is well developed and has a significant number of students, such a club may be beneficial.

Field trips can be entertaining and informative if they are used in moderation. We have found that one or at most two field trips per term are as many as can be beneficially absorbed. The best use of a field trip is generally an inspection of international facilities or a review of an international department. This may be supplemented by a speech by an executive of the company or facility being inspected.

**3. Developing Cultural Awareness**

The following student project, developed by James McCullough is an effective way of getting students to examine other cultures.

EXAMINING CULTURAL DIFFERENCES THROUGH FOREIGN STUDENT INVOLVEMENT IN INTERNATIONAL MARKETING PROJECTS

James McCullough, Department of Marketing, Washington State University

One of the more difficult problems in teaching American students about International Marketing is their lack of exposure to differing cultural environments. As a result, they lack the sensitivity necessary to effectively develop marketing plans for use in foreign markets and are unable to anticipate the problems likely to arise in conducting marketing research in a foreign country. Ideally, this ethnocentric perspective is tempered by foreign travel and study at a foreign university. For most students these options are neither economically nor academically feasible. Since many campuses in the United States have foreign student populations representing diverse ethnic backgrounds, it was felt that these students could be used to teach American students about the difficulties posed by cultural difference. This paper examines how foreign students were used as a vehicle for providing students of International Marketing with increased cultural sensitivity.

Research conducted at the University of Arizona indicated that unbiased and reliable consumer information about foreign markets could be obtained from foreign students if they were well informed on the products or market activities being studied and if the questions could be clearly explained to the respondents.

**Design of the Project**

After discussion of previous research and consideration of problems, a research project using international students was incorporated into the international marketing course. The project was designed to provide information about the differences that foreign students observed while shopping in the United States. Students were encouraged to develop the study along the lines they felt most appropriate as it was felt this was important in order to emphasize the problems of cultural differences.

**Conduct of the Study**

In order to obtain as much information as possible and to identify problems and constraints individual personal interviews were conducted. Students from a business class at the Center for English as a Second Language (CESL) were chosen as subjects and each student in the International Marketing class was assigned to conduct an interview. CESL students had previously been exposed to material on marketing in the United States and were provided a two-page outline of key marketing concepts.

While interviewers conducted the survey other American students observed the process and made notes for later class discussion. The interview took about 15-20 minutes to complete, following which each respondent-interviewer pair was interviewed to get their feedback on the activities.

**Learning Results and Conclusions**

American students conducting the interviews were surprised at the high level of cooperation since they believed that foreigners would be apprehensive about answering questions regarding their personal purchase patterns. This was not so, and the answers appeared to be sincere and honest. Although students were very cooperative, there were several problems encountered in conducting the survey. There seemed to be a problem with the wording of the questions, and some respondents had difficulty understanding the real meaning of the questions. The circumstances surrounding the interviews did not parallel actual buying situations causing some problems with understanding. Due to the small sample size significant conclusions could not be drawn. Some commonality of response was noted, however (Rodriguez et al., 1982).

This method of information gathering was educational and students learned rapidly that the use of foreign students as sources of information is not as easy as it appears. They tended to attribute this to their own failings, not to the foreign students, and rapidly recognized the need for improved planning and increased cultural understanding.

The value of the exercise lies in exposure to students of the problems inherent in cross-cultured research, without the need to travel to a foreign environment. Students learn to deal with the problem of operationalizing the stated objectives. They generally believe this is an easy task but found that was not true. Although they had definite goals and objectives, they found it extremely difficult to execute their ideas.

**4. Case Development**

Another beneficial activity which we have employed is requiring the students to visit firms with international business connections and write "Harvard style" cases. In general, we have found that it is preferable to have students write only one case per term so that they can gain adequate depth and information. If these cases are due by the middle of the term, they can then be reviewed by the instructor and the best of them can be used for classroom discussion. The following pages are from the student handout which we use in introducing the case-writing project.

Some Notes on Case Development as an
Educational Method
PURPOSE

Case analysis and presentation has become an almost standard tool of business education. It is used in nearly every type of business course and at every level of business education. Some schools and some professors use cases only infrequently while others use it as a primary pedagogical device. One can hardly assail the effectiveness of business cases and business education without immediate accusatives of academic heresy. It is not the intent of this item to debate the conventional use of cases; but rather to suggest an extension of the conventional technique to include the development of cases by undergraduate students.

The written case has several disadvantages. No matter how well written, the case lacks part of the dynamism, vitality, and immediacy of the actual business situation. A case of reasonable length inevitably must present the problem at hand in a rather straightforward manner—thus the student needs only to marshal the facts (often provided for him) and follow them to a logical decision (itself a difficult chore for some). As any businessman or consultant knows, the task of putting one's finger on the problem is often more crucial, or at least more difficult, than drawing conclusions once the problem and facts are known.

Some of the depth and impact of the business situation can be impressed on students by requiring them to develop business cases as part of their course work. Cases written by undergraduates tend to be unsatisfactory for classroom use when the writer is no longer present. Nevertheless, they impart numerous advantages to the case writer himself and to the class for which the case is written. Student-developed cases can be improved greatly by providing procedural instructions in the classroom. Tell students how to develop and write a business case. Individual class members not only write the cases, but also present them to the class and serve as source personnel in the class discussion. Instructors should carefully screen all cases before they are used in the classroom and, obviously, only the best should be utilized during class time.

This type of case-writing approach gives the individual student business contact and requires a rather perceptive probing and analytical investigation of the business on the part of the student. It helps him to realize that the common student complaint "this case doesn't have enough information" is not unique to written cases but it also inherent in business situations as well. The very process of contacting businessmen to find cases is rewarding for a student because many have no other opportunity to deal with managerial personnel until they are actually on the job market or on their first job.

**SOURCES**

Business cases can be developed from a variety of sources; common ones follow:

1. **Business firms.** Direct contact with business is by far the best source. Every type of business can provide case materials; and the nature and size of the business usually makes no difference. Successful, mediocre, or unsuccessful ventures all can provide useful data. In dealing with business firms, it seems wise to have the student talk to the highest officer he can reach. This will clear the way for permission to use the case. If the top man does not wish to work on the case himself but assigns a subordinate to work with the student, full cooperation can be expected. Sometimes when businessmen are reluctant to talk about their own business situation, it is good strategy to seek information about the competitors and

their problems. Any businessman will talk about his own problems while attributing them to other firms. Family and hometown sources are excellent because their distance from campus may provide insulation. One caution: students tend to make a beeline for the nearest acceptable case source. Businessmen, in general, are cooperative but are alienated by incessant pestering. The instructor is morally obligated to regulate the case-seeking visits of students. A list of companies (and officers) contacted for cases should be maintained. Students should receive the instructor's permission before contacting a given business firm.

2. **Published accounts of business problems.** Careful readership of business periodicals can provide good leads to case material and often enough information can be gleaned around which to base a good factual case. Use of published material requires considerable amounts of follow-up and some fairly clever research.

3. **Business client service firms** such as management consultants, lawyers, advertising agencies and accountants often are aware of clients' problems and can provide leads to clients or may be able to provide case information directly.

4. **Governmental and associations sources.**
Administrators in the small business administration and department of commerce often have contact with businessmen and are aware of their problems. The same is true of Chamber of Commerce and trade association officials who may be able to provide leads or case information.

## PROCEDURE

Two basic approaches may be used in seeking business cases. The first pinpoints a specific type of problem and attempts to isolate that type of problem in discussions with businessmen. The second approach may be called cold searching. In this instance the case writer is interested in any type of case within a broad general field: marketing, finance, accounting, retailing, etc. In this section marketing examples are utilized.

### Specific Problem Seeking

In seeking a specific problem the searcher must define the general area in which he wishes to work. In the marketing area he might be interested in problems concerning: pricing, channels, advertising, sales management, product development, packaging, etc. Having decided on his general area he should, by way of preparation, develop a series of hypothetical problem situations which he might logically expect to encounter. In pricing, for example, he might be concerned with pricing a new product, meeting price competition, modifying a price on an established product, meeting legal requirements relative to price, establishing the position of price authority in a business firm, etc. Thinking through possible problem areas will help the case writer spot problems in his discussion and forces him to think through the problem area more completely.

Reiterating this step then, the following steps provide a logical working procedure.

1. Define the area of emphasis and objectives and analyze that subject area in advance.
2. Undertake preresearch on the company and industry in question so the student will be able to approach the businessman intelligently.
3. Contact an officer in the company under whose jurisdiction the area of consideration falls. The writer should explain his purpose and objectives and seek cooperation of the businessman.

4. Define, for the respondent, the area of interest and specify the type of situation which is needed. (It may be useful to take along a case written about a well-known company for the businessman to pursue.)
5. Ask the businessman questions about the area in which a case is desired. There should be a general discussion of the possible situations within this general problem area. *Problems may be current, past or anticipated; solved or unsolved.*
6. Probe into all the possible case ideas that develop and determine which is the most promising.
7. Zero in on the idea with the most case potential. Attempt to secure all the information possible pertaining to that problem. Seek the types of information listed in the sections below.
8. Consult outside (library) sources which may provide information relevant to the situation at hand; or to the competitive situation, or to the general economic situation.
9. Draft the case.
10. Return the case to the businessman to recheck the facts and the sense of the case.
11. Make any necessary modifications and secure the businessman's permission to use the case either in disguise or actual form.

**General Search Case Hunting**

The cold search or open-minded seeking of some type of business case within a functional area would seem to be the easiest approach but often it is the most difficult. In this situation the case seeker discusses the general (in this case marketing) operation of the firm and may go in any direction following up leads in pricing, packaging, advertising or any other circumstances that seem promising. When such an approach is used the case writer must be unusually alert to clues which he may encounter. Both he and his respondent must have a fairly large amount of time for a general discussion as they seek a profitable area for specific discussion. In this type of situation he must gain the respondent's confidence and cooperation at a very early time. The steps the case writer follows then are essentially the same as those mentioned above except that the orientation will be more general and the case writer will have to provide more possible question areas. (Students should usually be assigned subject matter subareas with deadlines corresponding to special assignments.)

INFORMATION THAT SHOULD BE INCLUDED IN THE WRITTEN CASE

When written for classroom presentation, the case should include company background, product information, industry background, the problem situation itself and the facts bearing on the problem and questions.

**Company Background**

The case writer should seek and present pertinent information about the company's organization and objectives, the company's financial condition and its profitability, something about the personality of its key officers or the personnel in question in the case, and there should be some information about the company location as it is particularly relevant.

**Product Information**

Information should be presented concerning the specific product in question its relationship to the company's product line. The product mix should be reviewed, specifically as it pertains to the product's contribution to sales volume and profit. Information about the specific product as compared to competing products, a very straightforward description of the exact purpose and use of the product and, when necessary, something about production cost, production efficiency, volume and production capability.

**Industry Background and Competitive Situation**

The case writer should provide as much information as is pertinent about the structure of the industry, and its trends. He or she should probably mention the number of suppliers and their names, and something about the marketshare patterns, the degree and type of competition, and where the company fits in the competitive picture. It is often beneficial to indicate some of the competitors' advantages and disadvantages.

**Market Structure**

Basic information should be provided relative to the size, relative structure, and composition of the market for the product.

**Problem Situation Background**

The case writer should indicate how the problem arose, how important it is, and should provide a specific and precise definition of the problem or problems. The problem must have two or more sides or alternative solutions which are quite practicable. If a problem does not have two or more sides, it is not a problem but a foregone conclusion. Often a problem will have subproblems and these may or may not be identified in the case. In most cases they probably should be, but in some situations it is preferable to let the students discover the subproblem alternatives.

**Presentation of Facts Bearing on the Problem**

As much pertinent information as is possible should be given without giving away the solution. The facts may be drawn from the company itself or from the library research and other outside research on the problem. In many situations the facts provided by the company are not adequate and others should be marshalled for classroom use. Some presumptions on speculation may be included when absolutely necessary but such fiction must be clearly identified in the student's original paper. Double underlining such as this will be employed.

**Questions**

The case writer should provide questions which identify the main problem areas and sub- or related problem areas and may want to include questions related to the effects of possible solutions on other areas of the company's business operation.

**SOLUTION**

The case writer will benefit rather substantially if he is required to develop his own solution to the case. If possible, he should answer the question which he has posed and he should review the advantages and shortcomings of the main alternative solutions. In this way he will be best prepared to answer classroom questions and it may be that the process of working out the solution will force him to rethink and restructure his case. If the problem has been solved by the company, the solution should provide information pertaining to the method in which it was solved but should still consider other alternatives.

5. **Student Research**

We always use student term papers to supplement class work. They permit students experience, give them opportunity to develop their own thinking, and make a good presentation. Generally, we have used three types of paper: (1) those devoted to analyzing a country or a multinational group such as the European Union, and these may in turn be either general studies of the country or market or may be functionally specialized; (2) topical or functional papers which parallel the chapter outline of the book, each student being required to take a different topic or a different country, but sometimes a single topic is used; (3) product-marketing studies in which students are assigned the task of researching one market or the world market for a given product. Such studies may be set up on an export or on an international operations basis, or that decision may be left to the student. For students who are particularly lacking in any type of international exposure or contact, a meaningful effort sometimes may be to reverse the export situation and have the student export a product from a foreign country into the United States, analyzing U.S. customs, market barriers, pricing policies, as they would strike a foreigner.

In Part VI, Supplementary Material, p. 610 of the text is "The Country Notebook—A guide for Developing a Marketing Plan." The author has found this project to be very successful in getting students involved with foreign countries. Below (Part I - H, p. 21 of this instructor's manual) is a complete description and rationale for this student project. It is suggested that the Professor read "Notes on The Country Notebook—A Guide for Developing a Marketing Plan" (page 21 of the Instructor's Manual) if planning to use this project.

The project serves as a means to expand the student's cultural awareness as well as a vehicle to bring all the elements of the course together in one project. While this project requires an extensive amount of work on the part of the students, the majority of the class is very complimentary about the endeavor once it is completed.

**6. Student Debates***

Staged student debates can be a good way to encourage students to do further research on a specific international marketing topic, while also enhancing communication skills and encouraging class involvement in major issues. Students can be divided into teams assigned to a point or counterpoint position on one of a selected group of international marketing controversial issues. Ideally, students are assigned to a team based on preferences indicated at the start of the semester.

Each team is asked to research its topic thoroughly and to develop a position paper with an introduction, bullet points of the points and rebuttals the team believes should be made in the debate, and a conclusion. Students should be encouraged to take an extreme, not middle-of-the-road position for purposes of argument, and should be urged to use as many references and examples as possible in developing their position.

A debate can then be run in the classroom. A possible format for a 50-minute class is as follows (with the team winning a coin toss deciding whether to go first or second):

3 minutes – point introduction
3 minutes – counterpoint introduction
15 minutes – open debate between the two teams
15 minutes – structured questioning from the rest of the class, alternating between the teams
2 minutes – counterpoint conclusion
3 minutes – point conclusion
1 minute – counterpoint rebuttal

Students in the rest of the class should be encouraged to read information on the subject, and to actively participate by preparing and asking questions of the participating teams. Some of the cases provided in the book are useful as background for debate topics and can be assigned as class reading, as suggested below.

Students can also be given evaluation forms to fill out after each debate to determine 50% or some other portion of each team's debate grade, and to provide comments as feedback to the debating teams. Each team's total grade can be based 50% on the position paper and 50% on the debate performance. When participating in the grading of the debate, students in the rest of the class must be reminded not to be influenced by their personal point of view on the topic, but to

* This project was developed by Professor Kathy Frazer Winsted, Pace University.

judge the team only on their performance in the debate (including preparation, organization, analysis, persuasiveness, interest generated, and responses to questions).

It is also useful to start the next class period with discussion of the pros and cons of each of the positions and the class's resulting point of view. Generally, middle ground is called for, and there is rarely agreement on an "obvious" position.

Some possible debate topics with suggested background case readings and chapter tie ins include:

| | | |
|---|---|---|
| Cultural Impact on Marketing | Chapters 1, 4, 11 | Case 1–1, 1–2, 2–1 |
| Should Women Hold Multinational Management/Marketing Positions? | Chapters 5, 17 | Case 2–2, 4–16 |
| To Bribe or Not To Bribe? | Chapters 5, 6 | Case 2–3, 2–6 |
| Global Ads vs. Localized Ads | Chapter 16 | Case 4–12 |
| Social Responsibility and Ethical Behavior | Chapters 4, 5, 13 | Case 4–17, 4–18 |

Following are suggestions for evaluation forms (Exhibits 1 and 2) that can be used with the debates. I have found that having the students evaluate each debate keeps their interest active and it also gives excellent feedback to the group presenters.

Exhibit 1, *Evaluation of Group Debates* is to be returned to the professor.

Exhibit 2, *Evaluation of Debates,* will be returned to the group. Each student is to receive two copies, one for pro and one for con arguments. They are returned to the professor and, after the professor evaluates them, will be given to the group presenters.

**Exhibit 1**

EVALUATION OF GROUP DEBATES

YOUR NAME: ____________________________________________

DEBATE TOPIC:__________________________________________________________

POSITION:____________________________________

OVERALL GRADE (1-100):______________________

OPPOSITE POSITION:__________________________

OVERALL GRADE (1-100):____________________

**Exhibit 2**

EVALUATION OF DEBATES

DEBATE TOPIC: ____________________________________

POSITION:________________________________

OVERALL GRADE (1-100):_________________________

Please grade the debators for this position on a scale of 50 (F) to 100 (A+) for each of the characteristics shown, using the descriptions at either end as a guide. Please give this careful consideration, as 5% of each person's grade will depend largely on your evaluations. Please provide comments to the group in the comment blanks provided.

| | | | | | | | | | | | | |
|---|---|---|---|---|---|---|---|---|---|---|---|---|
| Very dull | 50 | 55 | 60 | 65 | 70 | 75 | 80 | 85 | 90 | 95 | 100 | Very interesting |
| Not at all persuasive | 50 | 55 | 60 | 65 | 70 | 75 | 80 | 85 | 90 | 95 | 100 | Very persuasive |
| Poorly organized | 50 | 55 | 60 | 65 | 70 | 75 | 80 | 85 | 90 | 95 | 100 | Well organized |
| Poorly informed | 50 | 55 | 60 | 65 | 70 | 75 | 80 | 85 | 90 | 95 | 100 | Very well informed |
| Poor analysis | 50 | 55 | 60 | 65 | 70 | 75 | 80 | 85 | 90 | 95 | 100 | Excellent analysis |
| Poor question responses | 50 | 55 | 60 | 65 | 70 | 75 | 80 | 85 | 90 | 95 | 100 | Excellent question responses |
| Bad overall debate | 50 | 55 | 60 | 65 | 70 | 75 | 80 | 85 | 90 | 95 | 100 | Terrific overall debate |

COMMENTS: ____________________________________________________________

THANK YOU.

PLEASE FOLD AND TURN IN ON THE DAY OF THE PRESENTATION.

## H. NOTES ON "THE COUNTRY NOTEBOOK—A GUIDE FOR DEVELOPING A MARKETING PLAN"*

One of the major challenges in teaching international marketing is getting the students to appreciate the importance of cultural adaptation in marketing programs. This is particularly difficult when the student's understanding of other cultures is limited. For many, the international marketing course is the first exposure to the study of other cultures. When the majority in a class lack cultural perspectives beyond those of the United States, it is difficult to get them meaningfully involved in a discussion of marketing issues from a multicultural perspective. Unless students acquire a minimal understanding of another culture early in the course, the opportunities for these students to fully appreciate the complexity of developing a marketing plan in a foreign market are reduced. There are a variety of ways to provide the students with this understanding. In the authors' opinion, the international marketing term project is one of the most effective.

*NOTE: This is a description of a project that uses "The Country Notebook—A Guide for Developing a Marketing Plan," which is in Part VI, page 610 in thc text, INTERNATIONAL MARKETING, Richard D. Irwin, 9th Edition, 1996. This section is taken from: Philip R. Cateora and Philip D. White, "Meeting the Challenge of International Marketing Education: The International Marketing Term Project," and Neil Beckwith et al (editors) 1979 *Educator's Conference Proceeding* Chicago, American Marketing Association, pp. 183-87.

### PROJECT OBJECTIVES

The learning objectives for the international marketing term project are fourfold. The first objective is to familiarize the student with the cultural environment of a country as the subject of the project and to facilitate cross-cultural understanding early in the semester. The second objective is to provide the students with the opportunity to prepare a marketing plan for a product which is being considered for marketing in a country they have selected. The project emphasizes the need to understand the environment as an essential step preceding the preparation of a marketing plan. The final two objectives of the term project are to effectively reinforce key concepts covered in this and other courses and to stimulate students to expand their learning horizons through the identification of materials required to complete the project.

### PROJECT OVERVIEW

The project requires that the student select a country and write a series of three or four papers, 15 to 20 pages each. The first paper is a general survey of the country's culture and is due one-quarter way into the term. The second, due halfway through the term, covers the economy of the country including a thorough analysis of the distribution and marketing systems. The third paper is a market audit and competitive analysis of a country market for a specific product. The fourth, due at the end of the term, has the students develop a preliminary marketing plan for a product under consideration for marketing in the country they have selected. The typical schedule of assignments is presented in Exhibit I. After the first paper is completed, it has been the authors' experience that the students begin making significant contributions about the cultural environment of their respective countries in class discussions. This represents substantial progress toward accomplishing the first learning objective.

## EXHIBIT I

### ASSIGNMENT SCHEDULE*

| | | |
|---|---|---|
| Week 2 | (a) | Students select countries subject to review and approval by the instructor. |
| | (b) | Assignment I—Guideline for a Cultural Analysis and Assignment II—Guideline for an Economic Analysis. (See Part VI, page 614 in Text for these guidelines) |
| Week 6 | | Culture Paper Due |
| Week 7 | | Return Culture Paper with comments, suggestions, etc. |
| Week 10 | | Economics Paper due |
| Week 11 | (a) | Return Economics Paper with comments, suggestions, etc. |
| | (b) | Provide information about the two products to be studied. |
| | (c) | Assignment III—Guideline for a Market Audit and Competitive Analysis and Assignment IV— Guideline for Preliminary Marketing Guide. (See Part VI, page 610 in Text for these guidelines) |
| Week 14 or 15 | | International Marketing Term Project due; Culture and Economics papers with revisions and the Market Audit and Marketing Plan as on consolidated paper. |
| Week 16 | | Complete grading of term projects. |

*Assuming a sixteen-week semester.

## COUNTRY AND PRODUCT SELECTION

Prior to assigning the project, the professor must take two important decisions. First, to what extent will the students be guided or constrained in the selection of their country. Second, which products are to be made available for marketing consideration.

### Selecting a Country

To achieve maximum interest and involvement, it is suggested that the student be permitted as much latitude as possible in selecting a country. The authors generally suggest that the students select a country in which they have some specific interest. While this is a general goal, there are some necessary constraints. The professor may want to direct the geographical orientation of the course by restricting choices to groups of countries, e.g., Europe, Latin America or Africa or economic considerations can be emphasized by limiting choices to developing countries. In those instances where there are students whose homes are other than the United States, it is recommended that they be required to study a country other than their own. It has been suggested that foreign students study the United States; however, the authors' experience has been that this is not effective in achieving the learning objectives of the project.

### Selecting a Product

While industrial products currently account for more than 50 percent of international trade, and their importance is appropriately stressed in class, the focus of this project is exclusively on consumer products. Two factors argue in favor of using consumer rather than industrial products. First, to maintain the cultural orientation of the project, consumer products offer more opportunities to focus on cultural adaptation than do most industrial goods. Second, since students generally know little about industrial products, too much effort is expended on gaining product knowledge instead of developing a marketing program where the emphasis should be.

As discussed in the section of the paper dealing with country selection, students have a lot of latitude in selecting the country that will serve as the focus of the project. Students typically select countries ranging from the most economically developed to the most recent developing nations. Therefore, it is advisable to have two products the students can select from for detailed marketing consideration. One product should be consistent with the needs of large numbers of consumers in developing nations while the second product should be of interest to consumers in industrialized countries. Meeting this requirement does not preclude either product from consideration for marketing in industrialized or developing nations.

Two additional factors should be considered. First, the product should have obvious cultural overtones to provide a strong cultural impact to the project. Second, the product should be one that students know something about. Products meeting these criteria and which have been used successfully in the past include: baby food, disposable diapers, powdered milk, contraceptive pills, high-protein diet supplements, prepared foods such as dry soups, portable washing machines, soft drink mix, children's toys, instant noodles, franchise outlets and early pregnancy tests.

There might be some possible merit in making more than two products available for students to choose from, but this increases the work for the instructor and complicates the choice for students. The objective is to provide at least two products that do not have any obvious disqualifying features and to force the students to make a selection so they can move into the market plan part of the analysis.

Alternatively, the instructor might select a product and assign this product to all the students. Given the diversity of countries typically selected, the one product alternative has some serious limitations. First, it makes product selection critical to the project and increases the possibility that students will decide they did not have a viable product to work with. Second, given the work involved, the option of having at least some choice seems to be appreciated.

Allowing students to select any product to study has not been successful in our minds either. A number of factors reduce the viability of this approach. Some students have difficulty selecting one product from the vast number of products which "could" conceivably be selected. For those students who have difficulty making a selection, this freedom become dysfunctional and frequently creates a substantial amount of anxiety. On the other hand, some students make a selection which is "fixed" in the sense that the product is already being marketed in their country or, conversely, is obviously inappropriate for that country. Our experience leads us to conclude that giving the student the option of selecting any product they choose substantially reduces the learning opportunity the project is designed to provide. Lastly, if each student selects different products to be studied, there is little or no basis for comparison across completed projects.

This can be an important ingredient in evaluating and grading the project, a topic which will be discussed in detail below.

Once the products have been selected by the instructor, it is necessary to provide information sheets to the students. Exhibit II is an example of the product information presented to the students in the past semesters; the data provided (Exhibit II) are generally limited to content information, product uses, preparations, and product costs. Most of this information can be found on or with the literature accompanying the product. In addition, a sample of each product is available for the student to examine.

Selection of the two products by the professor is of major importance. Even though the products are determined early in the semester, the students are not informed of the selection until the culture and economics papers have been completed. The product is given with the outline for Part III, "Guideline for a Market Audit and Competitive Analysis" (see page 614 in text). Students are told only that the product will be either a consumer durable or nondurable product. It has been the authors' experience that when product information is presented at the beginning of the project, the culture and economics papers are too narrowly focused on the product. This detracts from the learning objective of the culture and economics papers which are designed to provide the student with a broad and general cultural perspective.

## PROJECT COMPONENTS*

The international marketing term project is designed to provide the students with experience in analyzing a country's cultural and economic environment and experience in developing a marketing program for a specific product. The assignment consists of four parts: Part I is a cultural analysis of a country; Part II is an economic analysis of a country; Part III is a market audit and competitive analysis of a product in a country; and, Part IV is a complete marketing plan for one of the two products in the selected country.

### Guideline for Cultural Analysis—Part I

The approach taken in many international marketing courses is that of environmental adjustment. Before a marketing manager can determine if it is necessary to adjust to the environment or to determine what adjustments would be appropriate, it is necessary to understand the environment. This is particularly true of the culture of a country.

*Please see discussion in text, "The Country Notebook—A Guide for Developing a Marketing Plan," page 614, for more detailed discussion of each of the four parts of this project.

## EXHIBIT II

Product Fact Sheet

| | | |
|---|---|---|
| PRODUCT 1: | e.p.t.[TM] | In-home Early Pregnancy Test |
| Unit: | One (1) test | Cost: $4.00 each—in gross lots (includes c.i.f., taxes, and packaging) |

At last, an accurate early pregnancy test that women can do at home quickly, safely, and very easily. The e.p.t. In-home Early Pregnancy Test is a private little revolution any woman can easily purchase at her drugstore. It is highly accurate when used to detect pregnancy. A verified accuracy rate checked by doctors in clinical tests of hundreds of women.

You can do this easy pregnancy test yourself in the privacy of your home without waiting for appointments or delays. At last, early knowledge of pregnancy belongs easily to us all—right at home. It's simple, fast, and there is no risk; no physical danger whatever in doing it. A sample of your first morning urine is all that is needed to use e.p.t.

How e.p.t. works: As soon as you become pregnant, your body starts to produce a special hormone—HCG. Starting on the 9th day after the date you expected your menstrual period to begin, there should be sufficient concentration of HCG in your urine to give an accurate reading of pregnancy.

The e.p.t. In-home Pregnancy Test simply verifies whether or not this pregnancy hormone is present in your urine in sufficient quantity to detect pregnancy. That's all there is to it.

Before the 9th day *after* the day you expected your period to begin, there may not be enough of the pregnancy hormone in your urine. It is important that you wait until at least the 9th day before doing the test to obtain accurate test results. Consult your pharmacist for further information on e.p.t.

Test contains:

1. Glass test tube with rubber stopper containing reagent chemicals.
2. Clear plastic support with mirror to enable you to see the result without touching the box.
3. Plastic vial containing special purified water.
4. Lid (can be used to hold urine needed for the test).
5. Dropper with squeeze bulb.

Usage:

1. Collect a sample of your first morning urine. First, place 3 drops into the test tube which already contains the test chemicals; and, then add the contents of the plastic vial which contains purified water.
2. Press rubber stopper into test tube and shake vigorously for ten seconds.
3. Place test tube back in its original position in the holder and leave it *completely undisturbed* for 2 hours.
4. After 2 hours, if a dark brown donut-shaped ring is visible in the mirror under the test tube, it indicates that your urine contains the pregnancy hormone, and you can assume you are pregnant and should consult your doctor.

While students frequently encounter difficulties in obtaining cultural information, the problems almost always can be overcome in a satisfactory manner. The information suggested in the outline provided in Appendix I of the text deals with some of the key aspects of the culture and is relevant to the latter part of the project involving the development of the marketing plan. Throughout the culture paper, the students are encouraged to report the facts which they have identified and to analyze the facts in terms of likely marketing implications of such information.

As a final task in preparing the culture paper, the students are asked to write a two-page (maximum length) essay on "what it is like to be a citizen of" the country under study. The purpose of the essay is to force the students to reflect on the country's culture as a whole and to draw together their observations.

While completion of this part of the project does not constitute a complete job of acculturation, it does reinforce in the minds of the students the necessity of understanding the culture of the country in which they will be marketing products and the difficulty associated with attaining this understanding.

Guideline for Economic Analysis—Part II

The information asked for in the outline of the economics paper contained on page 613 of the text highlights the kind of information which is useful in understanding the economy of a country, particularly as it is related to marketing considerations. Of the different sections of the economics paper, those dealing with media and channels of distribution typically provide the most challenge for students in terms of finding the needed information. However, the information contained in these sections is also the most directly relevant to developing the marketing plan.

It should be noted that students sometimes argue and correctly so, that entire books could and have been written on the topics contained in the outline. The objective of covering these topics in this paper is not to have the students present a written report of all the information they have found on the subject, but, to have the student demonstrate an understanding of the material and highlight those points of particular significance from a marketing planning perspective.

Both the culture and economics papers have a limit of twenty (20) pages. Since most students find enough information to write substantially more than 20 pages, this forces the student to organize, analyze and then present only the most important material. Students can ask for a waiver of this limit if some exceptional reason exists and a length extension will be given. However, the trade-off between the increased amount of instructor time involved in reading longer papers versus the incremental information supplied clearly argues in favor of some reasonable page limit on these two papers.

Part III and Part IV below may be assigned as one paper. If this is done, the maximum length should be limited to 25 pages.

Guideline for a Market Audit and Competitive Analysis—Part III

Of the guidelines presented, this is the most product or brand specific. Information in the other guidelines is general in nature focusing on product categories, whereas the data in this one are brand specific and are used to determine competitive market conditions and market potential.

Two different components of the planning process are reflected in this guideline. Information in Parts II and III serves as the basis for an evaluation of the product/brand in a specific market country. Information in this guideline provides an estimate of market potential and an evaluation of the strengths and weaknesses of competitive marketing effort. The data generated in this step are used to determine the extent of adaptation of the company's marketing mix necessary for successful market entry and to develop the final step, the action plan.

The detailed information needed to complete this guideline will not necessarily be available without conducting a thorough marketing research investigation. Thus, another purpose of this part of the country notebook is to identify the correct questions to ask in a formal market study.

Guideline for a Preliminary Marketing Plan—Part IV*

In earlier presentations of this project, there were only three parts. What is now Part III, "A Guideline for a Market Audit and Competitive Analysis" was divided between Part II, "An Economic Analysis" and Part III, "The Marketing Plan." In the author's experience, students did not do an effective market audit and competitive analysis when the two papers were combined. Since creating a separate paper that focuses on a market audit and competitive analysis, the quality of the marketing plan has improved. Instead of having them submit four different papers, I have assigned the last two guidelines at the same time, which seems to work well.

After the students have completed the culture, economics and market audit papers, the emphasis of the project shifts to the second learning objective, that of preparing a marketing feasibility study or marketing plan for a specific product. Specific requirements for this part of the paper are found in the Appendix of the text.

In any study of the domestic market, it is essential that a thorough understanding of the situation confronting the firm be developed. The situation analysis usually is defined as consisting of the following topics: general information about the industry, competition and governmental controls along with information about the firm and the market. The information required varies in the amount of detail depending on the time and resources available for the situation analysis.

Marketing managers and researchers involved in the collection of information for situation analyses are well aware of the problems associated with identifying needed information. The availability of needed information is a substantial problem in the domestic market, and the problems intensify when trying to identify needed information for a foreign market. Since the sources of information available to students are primarily secondary, it is typically necessary to modify the requirements of the situation analysis for students trying to identify such information about a foreign market.

Two strategies are used to make this objective more attainable. The first is to select a product which is basically a new product. In this way, that part of the situation analysis which deals with the industry and competition is simplified. If a new or relatively new product is selected, then the students are asked to do an analysis of its innovativeness. This includes an analysis of the product in terms of the five characteristics which influence the rate of diffusion. This represents a trade-off with one type of analysis being substituted for another. However, given the information problems associated with identifying the needed information for the typical situation analysis, this is a reasonable departure.

The second strategy focuses on those pieces of information in the typical situation analysis which are still required. In developing a marketing plan for a product in an international market, it is necessary to have the necessary information or make an assumption about what the information would be in order to complete the situation analysis. Thus, some of the critical elements of the situation analysis are still included.

The remaining information that is a part of the situation analysis is information about the firm. Since this is not one of the central concerns in the development of the project, information about the firm is handled in two ways. First, the context of the project is that the parent company is organized in terms of profit centers. This is discussed in terms of the international department as a profit center and the foreign venture, whatever its ownership characteristics, as a profit center. Thus, the students are assigned the task of determining whether the product they have selected can be marketed profitably in that particular foreign market. Second, the students must specify an organizational form consistent with the countries' laws, but further background information about the firm is kept to a minimum so that the students can focus their attention on the marketing opportunity and problems associated with marketing the product in the country they have selected.

The structure of the project is such that the students are asked to prepare an analysis of the feasibility of marketing a product in the country they have selected. It should not be interpreted to mean that the approach taken in this project is product oriented. As noted above, the selection of the product involves a number of issues which are critical to the success of the project. Further, it is not uncommon for a United States firm to face the situation in which it has an established product and wishes to determine if there is a profitable opportunity to market the product in a foreign country.

QUESTIONS

The actual execution of this project invariably raises a number of questions. Some of the more important ones are considered, and our recommended responses are given.

1. **Why in "II Guideline for an Economic Analysis" and in "IV Guideline for A Preliminary Market Plan" is information on media and channels of distribution requested in both guidelines?**

   For both media and channels of distribution the reasoning is the same. In Guideline II, media information refers to the country as a whole, i.e., all the media available for a company to use, if it chooses. In Guideline IV, the media section refers to the specific choices your company will make from all media available in the country, i.e., your company's specific promotion mix. While there is some duplication here, the purpose of separating the two is to emphasize to the student that there exists, in every country, a set of available media, with costs, limitations, etc., and that when they develop a marketing plan, their promotional plan (Mix) will have to be developed from the media available. Media information in IV reflects the actual media plan you will use to achieve your marketing objectives. Guideline II is a macro approach to media whereas Guideline IV is a micro approach to media. The same is true for distribution channels, Guideline II reflects the entire distribution system (macro) whereas Guideline IV reflects the specific distribution plan (micro) your company will use to achieve your marketing goals and objectives.

2. **Should you assign the paper in three parts as suggested above or one paper to be submitted at the end of the term?**

   Our experience has been that the most effective procedure is to divide the paper into three parts. Although this increases the professor's grading time somewhat, it proves to be an effective device for getting the students involved very early in the semester. The natural difficulty of having the paper due at the end of the term is that many students will not begin working on the paper until the latter part of the semester. When this happens, the impact of the students gaining a cross-cultural perspective by researching their countries in the early part of the semester is lost. Further, the amount of work involved is large enough so that unless it is divided into three parts and submitted according to the schedule in Exhibit I, students' performance is low and complaining behavior is high.

3. **How do you grade the paper?**

   This paper is not easy to grade. However, some guidelines may make the task more manageable. At the beginning of the term, the students are informed of grading procedures for the papers. The first two papers are read by the instructor with comments in the margins but a grade is not assigned. In a supplement to the final paper, the students are given the opportunity to fill in the holes and correct any shortcomings that may exist in the earlier papers. This allows the professor to guide the students into areas of importance which they may have overlooked and it also enables the student to correct past errors.

The students are told that the project grade will be assigned after the last paper is read. One-half of the grade will be determined by the first two papers in terms of their adequacy and coverage. In determining this grade, the instructor may need to make some minor adjustments based on data availability. The remaining half of the grade is determined by the final paper. In grading the last paper (the marketing plan), several points are considered. Of major importance is how well information gathered in the cultural and economics papers is applied in developing a marketing program. In addition, the application of marketing concepts presented in lectures and text assignments as well as concepts learned in other marketing and business courses is considered in grading the last paper. The authors consider this last point important because, by expecting them to use all related marketing information and knowledge to complete the marketing plan, the third learning objective of reinforcing key concepts is accomplished.

4. **Do we have to market the product in the country?**

   This question always arises and is directly related to grading. The answer is, "No." Students do not have to market the product but a complete analysis of the country is required in either case. In making the assignment, the authors stress that the students have the option of recommending to market or not to market the product in the country. Either recommendation may be appropriate.

   When discussing the project, it is stressed that they should work as if they represent a large multinational company planning to expand operations to several new countries. Their task is to analyze and tentatively propose a marketing program for the company's product in one of the countries. Under those circumstances, the value of a decision not to market the product in the country is as important as a decision to market. In the authors' experience, about 20 percent of the students elect not to market their products. The only word of caution given to students who might elect not to market the product is to be certain that their market analysis is adequate and that they can justify their decision based on the data collected.

5. **How do you set the price for the student?**

   In all the situations, the price given the student includes all import taxes, transportation, etc., at two ports of entry to be designated by the student. This procedure is followed because we feel the time necessary to determine import taxes, transportation costs, etc., would be greater than the benefit derived from the exercise. We want the student to deal only with those pricing factors that occur after the product is imported. In most cases, the price given to the student is about 70 percent of the retail price in the United States.

6. **Do you have the students import the product?**

   As discussed above, the students are not required to get involved with import taxes, import restrictions, etc. The product is delivered to two ports of entry. The students are asked to assume that they represent a parent company in that country and are responsible for providing a preliminary analysis and tentative marketing program for the product in the country. They are not to concern themselves with where the product is manufactured or from where it is shipped. This procedure is followed so the emphasis will be on the marketing portion of the project rather than upon exporting or importing.

7. **What if there are import restrictions against the product in the country?**

   The students are told that if they do find that there are restrictions on importation of the product into the country, they are to ignore those restrictions and proceed as if those restrictions do not exist.

8. **Is information available?**

   The answer to this question is, "Yes." There is, however, some variation among countries as to the availability and quality of data. The instructor should take these variations into consideration when grading the projects. The students' library research both in breadth and scope will generally range beyond that necessary for typical business reports. Many will complain while doing this part of the project but when it is completed, most comment favorably about the extent to which the experience has broadened their familiarity with the university library and extended their learning horizons. We consider this to be a positive benefit of the project and fulfillment of the fourth learning objective.

### SUMMARY AND CONCLUSIONS

Clearly many issues are involved in the use of a project of this length and magnitude. Several of the key issues have been discussed in this paper. Performance expectations for both students and faculty are demanding. Yet, when everything is considered, it is our strong opinion that this project gives students a very worthwhile learning experience and an appreciation of international marketing which is increasingly essential for managers in today's international environment.

## I. SIMULATIONS

(1) CANADPLAN–An Advertising & Sales Promotion Simulation Game This simulation is appropriate for a senior level international marketing course or a masters level international marketing course.

**Basic Information**

1. The game is set in Canada and features a medium-size food company.
2. Students, working in teams, are required to produce advertising and sales promotion campaigns for two company products (a frozen microwaveable pizza and a reformulated, low-calorie chocolate bar).
3. Campaigns must be produced for both English-speaking and French-speaking Canada.
4. The simulation includes market, media and other information presented—51 tables and 13 exhibits. Player role profits and player's forms are also included.
5. A detailed Instructor's manual is available.
6. Software is available for both instructors and students.
7. The game teaches students to make management decisions, in an international setting, in a logical and sequential way.
8. Because of the fact that Canada is the United States' biggest trading partner at present, and because it is now a fellow member of the North American Free Trade area, it is vitally important that Americans learn something of the geography of Canada, e.g., where its chief cities are located, where the French-speaking market is located, etc. The game, which includes a map and extensive market data achieves this.

(2) Simulated international business negotiations can be quite useful in achieving a number of teaching objectives. Case # 4–5 involves a simulated buyer-seller negotiation between American and Japanese and Brazilian business people over the prices (and related issues) of an MRI machine for use in hospitals. The details of the case are supplied in the text and in a subsequent section of this Manual. The case relates to pricing, sales management, cross-cultural communication, and, of course, international negotiation. Indeed, international business negotiations are one of the fundamental activities of global commerce.

(3) INTOPIA - International Operations Simulation/Mark 2000 is a PC simulation of Global Business Strategy in the management game format. Participant executives or students range from

15 to 150. Complete details (22 pages) of this simulation are available on the Internet at: http://php.indiana.edu/~thorelli.

(4) Negotiations Simulation

**Foreign Investment Negotiations Simulation** is an exercise that simulates a negotiating simulation among several multinational corporations and the governments and local companies of four newly-industrializing countries of Asia and Latin America. The negotiations are concerned with the development of a high technology manufacturing industry in these countries, and may involve foreign direct investment, joint ventures, and technology transfer agreements. Complete details can be obtained from: Richard W. Moxon, 8215 N.E. 8th St., Bollevue, Washington, 98004. Tel: (206) 543-4587

(5) **International Trade and Investment Simulation**

This simulation teaches international trade and investment concepts in a highly interactive, realistic, and fun way. Participants are assigned to groups that assume the role of either a country government (in one of three countries), a multinational firm, or local consumers/workers. Country teams develop trade policy by determining tariff rates, setting tax policies, controlling natural resource use, and managing exchange rates through intervention in currency markets. Multinational firms attempt to produce and market a product. Firms can choose among any of the three countries to procure resources, manufacture, and market their products. Consumer/worker groups negotiate labor contracts and purchase products from firms.

**Order contact:**

Robert D. Stephens
Jerry Siefers
Department of Management, Room 650
School of Business
Indiana University
Bloomington, IN 47405

Tel: (812) 855-9200
E-mail: rdstephe@indiana.edu
jsiefers@indiana.edu

## J. EXPANDING THE SCOPE OF TEXT CASES AND OTHER CASE MATERIALS

1. Expanding Text Case Materials

The case material presented in the text can be used in a variety of ways. Many of the cases are designed primarily as discussion facilitators rather than comprehensive decision-making exercises. Those cases address issues relevant to international marketing/business and I believe are appropriate for an international marketing course or any other international business course.

Other cases are market problem oriented and can be used as short cases relying solely on the data presented in the case. However, if the professor is interested in assigning more comprehensive cases, the cases can be used with *The Country Notebook – A Guide for Developing a Marketing Plan*, p. 610 in the text. Instead of assigning a country and product as discussed in the section above Part I–F, I have assigned a case, e.g., Case 2–2 –Disney or some other product-oriented case, as the problem around which the international marketing term project is based. The depth and breadth of the case exercise can be further modified by omitting parts of the project. For example, I have found that the Medico-Devices, Inc. case (4-6) works well when I use only Parts III and IV—Guideline for a Market Audit and Competitive Market Analysis and the Guideline for a Preliminary Marketing Plan. Other times I have had the students analyze cases in the text using only one of the Guidelines. Experiment with using the Guidelines and the various text cases. You will find you can provide your students with a wide variety of educational experiences.

2. Other Sources of Case Material

   In addition to the cases in the text, you may want to adopt a case book. Some you might consider are:

   Robert D. Buzzell, John A. Quelch, Christopher A. Bartlett and Christopher R. Bartlett, *Global Marketing Management: Cases and Readings* (Reading, MA: Addison-Wesley, 1995)

   John A. Quelch (Editor), *Cases in Marketing Management and Strategy: An Asia-Pacific Perspective* (Englewoods Cliff, NJ: Prentice Hall, 1996)

   Robert T. Moran (Editor), David O. Braaten, John E. Jr. Walsh (Editor), *International Business Case Studies for Multicultural Marketplace (Managing cultural Differences* (Houston, TX: Gulf Publishing Company, 1994)

   Jean-Pierre Jeannet, Christopher Gale and Kamran Kashani, *Cases in International Marketing* (Englewoods Cliff, NJ: :Prentice Hall, 1994)

3. There are also a variety of case clearing houses. The most well known is:

   a. HBF, Case Services
      Harvard Business School
      Soldiers Field Post Office
      Boston Massachusetts 02163
      (617) 495-6117

      (formerly Intercollegiate Case Clearinghouse).

      A sample of the more recent bibliographies include:

      CASES AND OTHER MATERIALS FOR THE TEACHING OF BUSINESS ADMINISTRATION IN DEVELOPING COUNTRIES, COMPARATIVE INDEX

      CASES AND OTHER MATERIALS FOR THE TEACHING OF BUSINESS ADMINISTRATION IN DEVELOPING COUNTRIES, SOUTH AND SOUTHEAST ASIA

      CASES AND OTHER MATERIALS FOR THE TEACHING OF BUSINESS ADMINISTRATION IN DEVELOPING COUNTRIES, AFRICA AND THE MIDDLE EAST

      CASES AND OTHER MATERIALS FOR THE TEACHING OF BUSINESS ADMINISTRATION IN DEVELOPING COUNTRIES, LATIN AMERICA

      CASES AND OTHER MATERIALS FOR THE TEACHING OF MULTINATIONAL BUSINESS

      "Electronic Commerce on the World Wide Web," by Blake Ives and Sirkka Javenpaa.

      This case looks at the use of the Internet and the World Wide Web, precursors of the global data highway, for electronic commerce. In addition to a discussion and examples of electronic commerce, the case provides students with information about the Internet, WWW, and Web-browsers such as Mosaic as well as some knowledge of how to develop Web applications. The case contains many links to other servers and thus will be quite dynamic, but it can also be used in paper form. Thee is some information available for instructors.

Harvard Business School Publishing provides a collection of case studies. The complete line of over 7,500 Harvard business School cases studies, including teaching notes, case videos, and a selection of software ancillaries.

Also available from this site is a selection of quality cases from **Business Enterprise Trust; Design Management Institute; Stanford University; and, University of Western Ontario's Ivey School of Business.**

Choose to search in the "Cases" section of the online catalog found at: http://www.hbsp.harvard.edu/products/cases/collections.html

The material in this section of the Manual is intended to expand on the information resources detailed in the Appendix of Chapter 8 of the text. See that section of the text first.

b. International Business Case Bibliography, The Western Business School, The University of Western Ontario, London Ontario Canada. N6A 3K7. (519) 661-3208 FAX: (519) 661-3882 Case and Publications Services is the distributor for the teaching materials produced by The Western School of Business, The University of Western Ontario, as well as Canadian distributors for The Harvard Business School and Darden Graduate School of Business Administration, University of Virginia. The collection includes: Cases; Reprints; Working Papers; Catalogs; Videos; and Textbooks.

c. The European Case Clearing House (ECCH), ECCH at Babson Ltd., Babson College, Babson Park, MA 02157-0310, (617) 239-5884, Fax (617) 239-5885, or e-mail Carmichael@Babson.edu.
ECCH is one of the largest independent sources of management case material. It distributes cases from leading North American business schools including Harvard, Darden Graduate School, University of Virginia and University of Western Ontario. It also publishes cases on behalf of European schools including IESE in Spain, IMD in Switzerland, and INSEAD in France.

ECCH operates an on-line database of case abstracts, COLIS (Case On-Line Information System) which permits enquirers to search and identify items which meet user-specified criteria. For individuals seeking to augment or replace existing teaching materials, COLIS presents the most effective route for accomplishing what can often be a frustrating and time-consuming task. COLIS is available free of charge over the Internet. To access COLIS, telnet directly to:

*ECCH.babson.edu*
*At the prompt enter COLIS and hit return.*

Also available from ECCH AN ECCHO, the official newsletter of the European Case Clearing House. In addition to general news about ECCH, ECCHO lists new additions to the case collection.

d. Management Institute for Environment and Business, 1101 17th St., NW, Suite 502, Washington, DC 20036, (202) 739-0149, Fax (202) 833-6228

Management Institute for Environment and Business (MED) publishes an annotated bibliography of case materials. It includes videos, cases, and abstracts from a variety of sources that serves as a resource to enable faculty to incorporate business and environment case materials into business school curricula. For professors looking for a source of cases that focus on environmental issues, MEB is an excellent source.

MEB also publishes *EnviroLink*, a newsletter for educators in the field of business and the environment. Requests for information about MEB and to request to be placed on the mailing list for *EnviroLink* can be made to the address above.

## K. INFORMATION SOURCES

### 1. Statistical Data

There are many good sources of statistical data on foreign markets available in most libraries. A selected list of these sources, which cover most common needs and are generally available is included. This short, annotated bibliography on statistical data sources should by no means be considered complete: it is intended to provide general and historical data, the use of which will lead to additional sources.

(a) **United Nations Statistical Yearbook**

Published annually by the United Nations, New York, New York. About 700 pages.

This yearbook provides detailed historical statistics on virtually every aspect of world business.

Chapter headings include:

| | | | |
|---|---|---|---|
| 1. | Population | 12. | Transport |
| 2. | Manpower | 13. | Communications |
| 3. | Production Summary | 14. | Internal Trade |
| 4. | Agriculture | 15. | External Trade |
| 5. | Forestry | 16. | Balance of Payments |
| 6. | Fishing | 17. | Wages and Prices |
| 7. | Mining, Quarrying | 18. | National Accounts |
| 8. | Manufacturing | 19. | Finance |
| 9. | Construction | 20. | Public Finance |
| 10. | Energy | 21. | Social Statistics |
| 11. | Consumption | 22. | Education, Culture |

Data on all major countries and most minor ones are included under each of the above headings.

(b) **UNESCO Social Statistical Compendium**

Publisher:
Publishing Service
United Nations
New York, New York 10017

(c) **Organization for Economic Cooperation and Development (OECD)**

The OECD, a series of economic reports on its member nations. For information about OECD publications write:

OECD Publications and Information Center
Suite 700
2001 L Street NW
Washington, DC 20036
(202) 785-6323

(d) **European Marketing Data and Statistics**, London: Euromonitor Publications. Annual.

(e) **Consumer Europe**, London: Euromonitor Publications.

(f) **Statistical Yearbook for Latin America**, NY: United Nations. Annual, updated by **Statistical Bulletin for Latin America**, (Norlin, Govt Pubs).

(g) **Statistical Abstract of Latin America**, Los Angeles: UCLA.

(h) **The Markets of Asia/Pacific: Thailand, Taiwan, People's Republic of China, Hong Kong, South Korea, The Philippines, Indonesia, Singapore, and Malaysia**, London: The Asia Pacific Center, LTD, printed by NY: Facts on File, 1981-84.

(i) **Worldwide Economic Indicators**, N.Y.: Business International. Annual.

(j) **International Marketing Data and Statistics**, London: Euromonitor Publications. Annual.

(k) **Retail International**, 3 V. London: Euromonitor, 1983.

(l) **Retail Trade International** (annual), vol. II (Europe), vol. III (The Americas). (London: Euromonitor Publications Limited, 1981) Includes data on consumer purchase patterns by product and retail store type. Some prices, middleman markups, and retail store operating data.

(m) **International Marketing Data and Statistics**, Annual, (London: Euromonitor Publications Limited) and *European Market Data and Statistics,* (London: Euromonitor Publications Limited).

Includes data on living standards for all European countries as well as many other countries in the world. Included are such data as rooms per dwelling, persons per room, electric lighting, etc.

(n) **The Statesman's Year-Book**. A statistical and information guide to all countries and many of their provinces and territories. Updated regularly. Available through St. Martin's Press, 175 Fifth Avenue, New York, NY 10010

(o) **World Factbook**. An annual statistical publication of the Central Intelligence Agency. Available through National Technical Information Service, 5285 Port Royal Road, Springfield, VA 22162

(p) **World Development Report**. An annual statistical publication of the World Bank that discusses salient issues, provides economic analysis, and present data for developing countries. Available through World Bank Publications, 1818 H Street, NW, Washington, DC 20433

(q) **World Tables**. Statistical data on most countries, focusing on economic indicators and trends for the past 20 years. Available from World Bank Publications (see address in (p) above). The World Bank has a number of other excellent resources available for purchase. World Bank Publications will supply a free catalog.

**2. Bibliographies and Indexes**

(a) **The Economist Intelligence Unit** (formerly *Business International*, 111 West 57th Street, New York, NY 10019, (212) 554-0600.

The Economist Intelligence Unit (EIU) publishes weekly newsletters for managers in worldwide operations. It provides an overview of recent development; also focuses on specific problems of each country examined. News as it affects business relating to such topics as taxes, licensing, capital sources, politics, market indicators, and profitability; checklists and occasional statistical tables are all included in the various publications of EIU.

Publications include:

**Crossborder Monitor** (formerly *Business International) Business Asia, Business China, Business Eastern Europe, Business Europe, Business Latin America* and a variety of checklists such as *130 Checklists for Managing in Asia/Pacific* and specific reports such as *Hong Kong and 1997: Responding to Uncertainty.*

(b) **Sociological Abstracts**

Publisher:

Sociological Abstracts
73 Eighth Avenue
Brooklyn, New York 11215

(c) **Geographical Abstracts**

Publisher:

Geo. Abstracts, Ltd.
University of East Anglia
Norwich, NOR 88C, England

(d) **National Geographic Index**

Publisher

National Geographic Society
17th & M Streets, N.W.
Washington, D.C. 20036

(e) **Public Affairs Index Service Bulletin**

Publisher:

Public Affairs Information Service
11 West 40th Street
New York, New York 10018

(f) **Business Periodicals Index**

Publisher:

H..W. Wilson Co.
90 University Ave.
Bronx, New York 10452

(g) **Information Please Almanac**

Published annually by Simon & Schuster, New York, New York. About 900 pages.

This includes brief descriptions of the more notable geographic features of the world and maps of most areas of the world. There are also sections on world travel, the United Nations, and world history.

This section on world statistics lists the leading nations in natural resources, agriculture, and industry.

Also included are the dollar values of total imports and exports of the major countries. Population and education figures are also presented. The statistics section derives its summary tables from the *U.N. Statistical Yearbook.*

(h) **Global Guide to International Business**, by David Hoopes, New York. Facts on File, Inc.

(i) **Encyclopedia of Geographic Information Sources**, edited by Paul Wasserman, Detroit: Gale Research.

(j) **International Business Reference Sources**, by Cynthia C. Ryans, Lexington, Massachusetts: Lexington Books.

(k) **The Henry Holt International Desk Reference: A Guide to Essential Information Resources of the World's Major Trading Nations,** edited by Gary R. McClain, (New York: Holt, 1992)

(l) **JETRO** (Japan External Trade Organization) is a nonprofit, Japanese government-supported organization dedicated to promoting mutually beneficial trade and economic relationships between Japan and other nations. http://www.jetro.org.

This site includes the following topics:

- Publications
- Periodicals
- Videos (http://www.jetro.org/what4.html)
- Japanese Market Report Database (http://www.jetro.org/biz1.html)
- Government Procurement Database
- Potential Importer
- Practical Information on Business in Japan

**3. Information by Country**

(a) **The Japan Trade Center**

The Japan Trade Center, 725 Figueroa Street, Suite 1890, Los Angeles, California 90071, (213) 624-8855 will provide free of charge for most publications a wealth of information on Japan. They have several periodic publications giving information on marketing opportunities in Japan as well as special studies such as *China Newsletter* dealing in opportunities for trade with China. It is recommended that the teacher of international business contact the source at the address mentioned above for these publications. There is also Japan Trade Center offices in Chicago, New York, San Francisco, Houston, Atlanta and Denver.

The Japan Trade Center Publications are extensive. Below are the categories of publications with a sample of titles. There are many more titles than appear here. Interested professors should write their closest JETRO center and request an updated JETRO Publications List.

JETRO MARKETING SERIES

Included reports such as:

- Japan As an Export Market
- Doing Business in Japan
- Retailing in the Japanese Consumer Market
- Planning for Distribution in Japan
- Changing Lifestyles in Japan and others

JETRO BUSINESS INFORMATION SERIES

- Operating a Business in Japan
- Labor-Management Relations in Japan
- Japanese Corporate Decision Making and others

ACCESS TO JAPAN'S IMPORT MARKET SERIES and YOUR MARKET IN JAPAN SERIES

Comprehensive market studies for:

- Furniture
- Leisure and Sporting Goods
- Baby Products
- Cosmetics
- Food Processing Machinery and many, many others

NOW IN JAPAN SERIES

- Promotion of Small and Medium Enterprise in Japan
- Foreign Companies in Japan and others

EXPORTING TO JAPAN SERIES

- Japan's Tariff and Customs Procedures
- Japan's Distribution System
- Japan's Import System

SPECIAL ISSUES

- Japan
- Marketing and Distribution Strategies of Foreign Products
- Selling to Japan from A to Z and others

(b) **The World Almanac and Book of Facts**

Published annually by *The New York World Telegram,* New York, New York. About 900 pages.

This almanac includes capsulized descriptions of all foreign countries. These descriptions include:

1. Descriptive comments on form of government, population, monetary units, location, and general geographic characteristics.
2. Listings of principal resources and industries.
3. History and government of the countries.
4. Education and religion.
5. Defense.

Although all countries are included, there is considerably more detail on the major countries.

(c) Price, Waterhouse, & Co. DOING BUSINESS IN NY: Price, Waterhouse, & Co. Irregular.

(d) E & W INTERNATIONAL SERIES. NY: Ernst and Whinney. Irregular.

(e) Deloitte, Haskins, and Sells. INTERNATIONAL TAX AND BUSINESS SERVICE. NY: Deloitte, Haskins, and Sells. Irregular.

(f) **Worldmark Encyclopedia of Nations**

Publisher:

Worldmark Press, Inc.
Harper Brothers
New York, New York

(g) **Europa Yearbook**

Publisher:

Europa Publications Limited
18 Bedford Square
London, England

(h) **Country Profiles (Superseded the Former Area Handbooks) (country)**

Publisher:

Superintendent of Documents
U.S. Government Printing Office
Washington, D.C. 20402

(i) **Background Notes**. A publication of the U.S. Department of State that provides historical details, a map, and other valuable information about individual countries. The series is periodically updated. Available through the Superintendent of Documents, U.S. Government Printing Office, Washington, DC 20402.

(j) **The Economist Intelligence Unit**. (See 2 (a), page 51 above.)

**4. Cultural Information by Country**

(a) Intercultural Press, Inc.

The Intercultural Press, Inc. publishes books in the intercultural field. Recent texts include Survival Kit for Overseas Living, Multicultural Education, Women in Management Worldwide, China, Inc.: How to Do Business in China, The Asia Business Book, Good Neighbors: Communications With the Mexicans, and other intercultural texts and pamphlets. While these are not free, you may want to write Intercultural Press for a list of their bibliography as many of their publications would be good additions to your library. The address is:

Intercultural Press, Inc.
P.O. Box 700
Yarmouth, Maine 04096
(207) 846-5168
Fax (207) 846-5181
e-mail, intercultural@mcimail.com

(b) **CULTUREGRAMS**

A *Culturgram* is a four-page briefing designed specifically to introduce readers to the daily customs and lifestyles, as well as the political and economic structure, of a nation. Our goal is to present the people of a culture to the reader, thus encouraging understanding and appreciation between those of different nationalities. Ideal for educators, students, community leaders, businessmen and women, government representatives, and travelers, *Culturgrams* provide clear, concise information about daily life in a given nation. A glossary is also available containing information to help *Culturgram* readers use and understand the variety of terms found in the series.

The price of 1-5 Culturgrams is $2.00 or the entire set of 128 countries is $60.00 Culturgrams are available from:

Brigham Young University
David M. Kennedy Center for International Studies
P.O. Box 24538<R>Provo, Utah 84602-4538
(800) 528-6279

Each four-page *Culturgram* strives to offer readers an accurate view of a culture rather than focusing on statistical data. A number of other fine resources present national statistics, but few inform the reader about people on a personal level. In an effort to present the people of various cultures, the following topics are included in each *Culturgram*: More information about Culturgrams, Infograms, scholarly papers, journals, and books and ordering information can be accessed at: www.culturegrams.com

5. **Advertising Rates**

**International Advertising Rates:**

Frequently class projects require some knowledge of international advertising rates. INTERNATIONAL MEDIA GUIDE is one of the most comprehensive sources available for rate lists for business publications, newspapers, and consumer magazines. The complete set includes six volumes: *IMG Business Publications*—Europe, Latin America, Middle East/Africa, and Asia/Pacific

*IMG Newspapers Worldwide*
*IMG Consumer Magazines Worldwide.*

Available from: Directories International, Inc., 22 Elizabeth Street, South Norwalk, Conn. 06854, (203) 853-7880.

6. **Other Information**

(a) **ABI/INFORM. ABI/INFORM**, available in many college and university libraries, provides summaries of over 400,000 journal articles taken form over 800 business periodicals published in the U.S., Canada, the U.K., Western Europe, Australia, Hong Kong, and Japan. About a thousand new article summaries are added to the data base each week.

(b) **201 Checklist: Decision Making in International Operations** Published by the Economist Intelligence Unit, 111 West 57th Street, New York, NY 10019, (212) 554-0600

(c) **Europe Yearbook,** London. Annual.

(d) **Worldmark Encyclopedia of Nations.** 6th ed. NY: Harper and Row.

(e) **Exporters' Encyclopedia: World Marketing Guide**. (Export Documentation Handbook.) NY: Dun and Bradstreet. Annual

## L. FLASH FACTS

Flash facts is an automated information system provided by the Commerce Department for information concerning trade with several regions of the world. Included is information on doing business within each region or country, including such topics as tariffs, rules of origin, distribution, export techniques and marketing issues. This free service is available 24 hours a day, seven days a week, and sends information directly to your fax machine within a few hours (often just a few minutes). Information for different regions of the world can be reached from the following:

**Amerifacts, (202) 482-4464.**

Information on countries of the Western Hemisphere, available under *NAFTA FACTS*, for Mexico, United States and Canada; *OLA/C FACTS*, for Latin America and Caribbean countries; and *HAITI FACTS*, for Haiti.

**Eastern Europe Business Information Center (EEBIC)**, (202) 482-5745.

Categories include information on techniques to help U.S. companies export to Eastern Europe; sources of financing; U.S. government programs; specific export and investment opportunities in the region, updated each week; upcoming trade promotion events; information on specific East European countries (Albania, Bosnia-Hercegovina, Bulgaria, Croatia, Czech Republic, Estonia, Hungary, Latvia, Lithuania, Poland, Romania, Slovak Republic, and Slovenia); and recent issues of the *Eastern Europe Business Bulletin*.

**Office of the Pacific Basin**, (202) 482-3875 or 482-3646

Categories include general export information; regional information; country information (Australia, Cambodia, Indonesia, Korea, Laos, Malaysia, New Zealand, Philippines, Singapore, Taiwan, Thailand, and Vietnam). Documents in the Office of Pacific Basin Flash Facts range in length from one to seven pages.

**Business Information Service for the Newly Independent States (BISNIS)**; (202) 482-3145

Categories include U.S.—Newly Independent States trade statistics; current export an investment opportunities; upcoming trade events; World Bank and European Bank for Reconstruction and Development (EBRD) opportunities; export opportunities; BISNIS publications; country commercial overviews; and sources of government financing. The menu is updated approximately once a week.

**Offices of Africa, Near East, and South Asia**; (202) 482-1064

Categories for the Office of Africa include general information and country information (Nigeria and South Africa). For the Office of the Near East, categories include general information and country information (Algeria, Bahrain, Egypt, Iran, Iraq, Israel, Jordan, Kuwait, Lebanon, Libya, Morocco, Oman, Qatar, Saudi Arabia, Syria, Tunisia, United Arab Emirates, and Yemen). Categories for the Office of South Asia include general information and country information (Afghanistan, Bangladesh, Bhutan, India, Nepal, Maldives, Pakistan, and Sri Lanka).

## M. The National Trade Data Bank (NTDB)

Information on the latest opportunities, resources, and contacts is available on the NTDB CD-ROM. The NTDB contains a wealth of information. Do you need to know the cost of labor in Mexico? Which state sold Germany the most medical equipment last quarter and exactly how much? What the legal system and export regulations are in the Ukraine? The hottest trade prospects for China? You can get answers to these questions and access to over 18,000 market research reports, and you can get in touch with over 80,000 different trade contacts, through the NTDB.

The entire contents of NTDB's vast collection of trade information is available on CD-ROM. The CD-ROM is updated monthly and offers two search and retrieval software interfaces that allow you to find just the information you need, allowing you to search the full texts of over 200,000 different documents, including the new *Country Commercial Guides* from the International Trade Administration, the CIA's *World Factbook*, two years of *Business America* magazine, the Census Bureau's import and export statistics that are easily "exported" into any spreadsheet software, and 140 other programs from 26 federal agencies.

The NTDB continues to evolve, and is now offering a new method of access as an alternative to its traditional CD-ROM platform. In June 1994 the NTDB made its debut on the Internet, opening instant access to the NTDB on the World Wide Web (WWW), and taking advantage of the very latest in software technology. Instead of trying to understand the intricacies of Boolean searching, you could type, "how do I export computers to Brazil?" and the software will understand your natural language, search the database, and provide you with all the relevant information. Navigating through the information has never been more fast and easy.

Access to the NTDB, and other STAT<195>USA databases, on the Web is only $24.95 for three months of unlimited access, and $8.35 per month after that. You may access the NTDB by connecting to *www.stat-usa.gov* with a valid User ID; arrange for a User ID by calling the STAT •USA HelpLine. Access to the NTDB on the Internet can be arranged the same way. Call the STAT•USA HelpLine on (202) 482-1986, or fax (202) 482-2164, for more information or to place an order. The NTDB is also available for use at many Commerce Department District Offices, and at more than 1,000 Federal Depository Libraries.

## N. FILMS AND VIDEO CASSETTES

Films can provide a meaningful source of background information if used with some discretion. I have enclosed a list which may be used to give the student an exposure to different viewpoints. The films should be designed to give background and stimulate discussion rather than to impart specific knowledge.

**Note: Contact your Irwin representative to obtain the cassette of video cases produced for use with INTERNATIONAL MARKETING, 10th edition. See the Video Resource Guide that accompanies INTERNATIONAL MARKETING, 10th edition for a current list of videos.**

(a) Sources for Films:

1. **The Library of Congress Catalog: Motion Pictures and Filmstrips**, Washington, D.C.: Library of Congress.
2. **Educators Guide to Free Films,** Randolph, Wisconsin: Educators progress Service. These bibliographies are available in most libraries and contain principally the same information we have included.
3. For a reference volume of film rental sources for over 45,000 educational films write: Educational Films Locator

   Reed Reference
   121 Chanlon Road
   New Providence, NJ 07974
   (800) 521-8110

   There is a charge for this volume but most major libraries and many university libraries will have a copy.
4. JETRO has produced three new films which are now available for viewing and takeout loan at the Japan Trade Center.

   All JETRO films are in color, 16mm, with English soundtrack. For film information, please contact the Public Relations Section, Japan Trade Center of Los Angeles, 725 Figueroa Street, Suite 1890, Los Angeles, California 90017. (213) 624-8855 or the nearest JETRO office.

Below is a list of current films available from JETRO:

(b) General Introductions to Japan and its Culture

1. **WHERE IS THE REAL JAPAN?** (23 min.) A veteran Tokyo correspondent ponders Japan's contrasting cultural elements and the necessity of establishing harmony among them, with keen insights into life-styles, thought and behavior patterns, and future trends. A strikingly effective look at what Japan is all about today.

2. **UNDERSTANDING JAPAN** (25 min.) A graphic examination of the social and cultural fabric of the modern Japanese nation through the eyes of noted educators and journalists living in Japan.

3. **FOUR WOMEN, FOUR CHOICES** (28 min.) A look at the changing role of women in Japanese society and the economy. Four Japanese women from diverse social backgrounds are interviewed.

4. **U.S. TEACHERS TO JAPAN** (32 min.) In their own words, 10 Southern California teachers retell their experiences while touring Japan as guests of the Japan Business Association of L.A. Public schools, temples and gardens, a traditional tea ceremony and a visit with the Minister of Education are seen as the teachers themselves saw them.

5. **THE EMPEROR AND EMPRESS OF JAPAN** (30 min.) Commemorating the exchange visits of the Imperial Family and the President (Ford) of the U.S. in 1975, this film examines the history of Japan's Royal Family in both continuity and change through the ages.

6. **MONSHO FAMILY CREST OF JAPAN** (27 min.) In an exploration of the origins and development of the Japanese Family Crest as an element of traditional design, much is revealed about historical trends, family structure and aesthetic values.

7. **DESIGN–HUMAN LIFE AND MATERIAL THINGS** (17 min.) Japan's modern designers endeavor to combine traditional artistic qualities with the influences of imported cultures. What remains consistent despite change in the complex relationship between daily life and material objects, as seen in Japan's old towns as well as in her bustling metropolises.

8. **OUR HOME IS JAPAN** (15 min.) A look at daily life of two Japanese children, at home, at school and at play. The film is intended for young, school-age children who may identify with the protagonists.

9. **AIZU HOLIDAY** (25 min.) A city-bred schoolboy is awe-stricken by the natural beauty and serenity of the peaceful countryside when he visits his parents' birthplace of Aizu for the first time.

Nature and the Environment

10. **A BOY AND HIS RIVER** (20 min.) A schoolboy living in the outskirts of Tokyo ponders the past, present and future of the Tama River as it flows from the distant mountains to the crowded and polluted industrial plain and on to the Pacific Ocean.

11. **LIVE ON FOREVER–OZE PARK** (20 min.) This natural parkland, on one of Japan's most beautiful plateaus, was saved from encroaching development and the threat of a bisecting expressway through the efforts of a single conservationist. A classical example of the conflict between economic growth and environmental protection.

12. **THE SEA AND THE JAPANESE** (20 min.) The Japanese have always looked to the sea as a central aspect of their life and culture. Now, in addition to reaping from it a great

portion of their food supply, they are enthusiastically developing its mineral and other natural resources. Religious festivals still celebrate the sea while technologists struggle to eradicate pollution with the newest methods.

Business and Industry

13. **THE JAPANESE ECONOMY NOW** (25 min.) The Japanese economy is in transition. A huge trade surplus, the appreciation of the yen, the existence of structurally ailing industries, and unemployment are the main problems affecting the Japanese economy now. Through interviews and on-location footage, this film depicts these economic changes as well as the impact that they have had on the lives of the Japanese people.

14. **BRIDGES AND BARRIERS** (30 min.) American executives are interviewed to give their personal opinions of many of the difficulties that exist in doing business with the Japanese. Many of the social, cultural business differences are explored.

15. **KACHO–A DAY IN THE LIFE OF A SECTION CHIEF** (25 min.) An entertaining and instructive glimpse at one Japanese "middle manager's" professional and personal world, providing a realistic portrayal of a typical businessman's life-style as well as the inner workings of the commercial sphere.

16. **ON THE JOB TRAINING IN JAPAN** (20 min.) Employee education is continuous in Japan. Workers at all levels undergo training programs designed to advance them into more skilled positions, thereby contributing to personal welfare, company productivity and the national economy.

17. **DECISION MAKING IN JAPAN** (17 min.) Group consciousness and policy planning based on consensus have been noted as unique characteristics in Japanese organizations. Here they are seen in action, not only in typical companies but also in marriages and in everyday social life.

18. **KOJI–A YOUNG MECHANIC** (25 min.) A portrait of the pleasures and problems of a blue collar worker emerges from this look at Koji's relations with colleagues and family, dramatizing such special features of Japan's companies as life-time employment, seniority system, and the "sense of belonging."

19. **DOING BUSINESS IN JAPAN** (15 min.) Many foreign businessmen are baffled by the customs and practices of their Japanese counterparts on first acquaintance. Actual case studies of overseas businessmen dealing successfully in Japan illustrate how these puzzlements can be overcome.

20. **100 MILLION VARIED CONSUMERS** (25 min.) What do the Japanese want in food, clothes, and housing? When do traditional tastes prevail over the desire for the new and the modern? These are important concerns for the exporter contemplating Japanese markets or anyone curious about a unique, complex culture.

21. **JAPAN AND THE SUN** (25 min.) Ancient Japanese saw the sun as a goddess; today, scientists develop techniques to harness energy. The evolving role of the sun in Japanese life is seen in farming and fishing villages as well as in urban industrial centers.

22. **JAPAN IS YOUR MARKET** (20 min.) Successful Western businessmen relate their experiences in penetrating the Japanese consumer market. Actual case studies of both American and European businessmen are presented.

23. **TIME FOR THOUGHT IN TSUBAME** (21 min.) Since the beginning of the Meiji Period the Japanese have been noted for their ability to absorb Western technology. This film documents the transitions a small manufacturing community makes to meet the

challenge of foreign competition, rising value of the yen and changes in consumer demand.

24. **THE DOOR IS OPEN–JAPAN'S IMPORTS ON THE RISE** (20 min.) The Japanese market has never been more open, and more imports are becoming accessible to Japanese consumers. Focusing on the environment surrounding imports, this film questions department stores, large chain stores, small and large trading companies and manufacturers on their views of imports.

25. **PAST MEETS PRESENT IN MINDANI HAMLET** (30 min.) The traditional social structure and way of thinking that developed within the Japanese village are still underlying forces in current Japanese economic activity. This film visits an existing hamlet to study contemporary life-styles of its inhabitants.

26. **A DEPARTMENT STORE LOOKS ABROAD—IMPORTS PLAY AN IMPORTANT ROLE IN JAPAN'S RETAIL INDUSTRY.** (25 min.) This film focuses on the giant $400 billion retail market in Japan. Filmed at a leading department store which employs 13,000 people, the film shows buyers working to find and import attractive products from other countries.

27. **HUMAN AGE AND ROBOTS IN JAPAN** (27 min.) This film portrays various ways in which the industrial robot is being utilized in the Japanese workplace to make factory work less monotonous, less dangerous, and more productive. It begins with the simpler applications of robotics technology and ends with a discussion of possible future uses of industrial robots.

28. **JAPAN: OBSTACLES AND OPPORTUNITIES** The U.S.– Japan Trade Study Group was conceived to review some of the existing trade questions and rather than deal with non-tariff barriers, the U.S. – Japan Trade Study Group focuses more on potential markets in Japan that have not been fully explored by American exporters.

(c) JETRO Videotapes. All videotapes are 30 minutes and available in 3/4 format. Available from Japan Trade Center—see address above.

1. **HOW TO PENETRATE THE JAPANESE MARKET** 1980 The first part features an interview with Ben Fujita, the person responsible for the establishment and success of McDonald's in Japan. He gives his views on doing business in Japan, establishing joint ventures, marketing practices, and other aspects of being successful in the Japanese market. In the second part, a business consultant describes key factors which are important to the penetration of the Japanese market.

2. **WHY NOT LET THE SOGO SHOSHA SOLVE YOUR PROBLEMS** 1980 This film shows the extent and variation of activities of the Sogo Shosha. Due to their worldwide networks, broad business foundations and expertise, general trading firms are capable of handling the wide variety of complex problems associated with a diverse project base.

3. **HOW A JAPANESE COMPANY ACHIEVES HIGH PRODUCTIVITY–THE WAY TOYOTA DOES IT** 1982 A director of Toyota's production department explains some of the keys of Toyota's success. Two systems examined are "Just In Time" and "Selfmation." "Just In Time" is a concept that schedules the particular car parts to arrive at the exact time they are needed to avoid expensive warehousing costs. "Selfmation" describes the ability of any employee on the production line to halt production in order to correct any problem he discovers.

4. **NON-TARIFF BARRIERS** 1982 Two Americans and two Japanese representing the business and academic worlds debate the topic, "Japan should remove all non-tariff

barriers." The Americans focus on the need for further steps to reduce non-tariff barriers while the Japanese claim that other countries are asking too much from Japan and no one appreciates the steps already taken by the Japanese government.

5. **POINT MEN FOR FOREIGN BUSINESS IN JAPAN** 1982 Many U.S. exporters' failure to successfully penetrate the Japanese market can be explained in part by not being familiar with it. "Point Men" are business consultants who assist exporters in adapting their products to suit the needs of the Japanese consumer by stressing establishment through long term investment, quality of products, and after-sales service as key points to success.

6. **ARE THE JAPANESE REALLY UNIQUE?** 1982 Three scholars, two Japanese and one American, challenge the notion that Japan's economic success is due to certain cultural characteristics. The stereotype of Japanese lacking individualism, being group-oriented, and using consensus in decision-making are viewed here as simplifications that do not attempt to answer the questions of Japan's economic rise.

7. **KEYS TO SUCCESS IN THE JAPANESE MARKET** 1980 Three foreign executives in Japan detail how and why their companies have been successful in the Japanese market. Each looks at the actual market atmosphere for foreign goods and outlines the changes that are taking place as well as the pitfalls foreign investors and traders must avoid.

8. **COMMUNICATIONS GAP** 1981 Three businessmen from the U.S., Australia, and France discuss to what extent a communications gap exists between Japan and the rest of the world. Each offers different insights into the reasons for its existence, and how at different periods of time this has been both a help as well as a hindrance to Japan.

9. **VITALITY OF JAPAN'S SMALL BUSINESS** 1981 Small and medium size enterprises make up the largest segment of Japanese business, employing 80 percent of the workers and accounting for over 90 percent of the total firms. The many reasons they do well are creativity, sensitivity to the problems of other small and medium size companies and consumers, and high quality controls.

10. **ACCESSING THE JAPANESE MARKET** 1994 (23:15) Introduction to the various public and private agencies which provide support and assistance to potential overseas investors. Services in a number of areas, including financing, establishment, law, the Foreign Investment in Japan Development Corporation and other agencies.

11. **ACHIEVING SUCCESS** A Small American Business Exports to Japan – 1992 (26 min.) Examines the success of an American entrepreneur in the anti-corrosion device field. Describes why and how he entered the Japanese market, and how JETRO trade advisors provided assistance.

12. **FOREIGN CONPANIES IN JAPAN'S PROVINCES: THE KEY TO SUCCESS** 1995 (22 min.) Shows the numerous advantages foreign companies have when establishing Japan's rural countryside. Highlights five successful examples, with feedback and advice from the employees of those firms.

13. **GUIDE TO EXPORTING TO JAPAN** 1992 Consists of interviews with executives from foreign companies who have enjoyed success in Japan. The video reveals how they obtained access to the market and overcame unfamiliar business customs and other obstacles.

14. **GUIDE TO INVESTING IN JAPAN** 1993 Explains the importance of investing in Japan, the world's 2nd largest marketplace, and presents various suggestions and assistance available to foreign investors.

15. **JAPAN'S CHANGING DISTRIBUTION SYSTEM** 1995 (21:56) In-depth look at the changing distribution system in Japan, which has been profoundly affected by the new attitudes of the Japanese consumers. Topics covered include how price slashing, deregulation, changing consumer demand and the yen's appreciation have changed Japanese distribution strategies towards low cost distribution and increased foreign imports.

16. **JAPAN'S ECONOMY—The Road to Economic Growth** 1994 (21:13) Focus on markets where overseas companies are still engaging in successful business regardless of the downturn in the Japanese economy. Also provides an overview of the current Japanese economic situation, as well a brief history of the "bursting of the bubble economy". Additionally, highlight steps being taken by Japanese businesses and entrepreneurs to find profits in the current economy.

17. **THE KACHO—SECTION MANAGER: JAPANESE CORPORATE COMMUNICATIONS** 1996 Enhances the viewers' understanding of Japanese business, decision making and society by focusing on the activities of one *kacho*, or section chief, employed at a Japanese trading company. Besides introducing the pivotal role the kacho plays in Japanese corporate decision making, the section chief's life away from the company, including family life and leisure activities, are also brought to light.

18. **LIVING IN JAPAN** 1994 (30 min.) Foreign homemaker's view of living in Japan, and how they deal with the everyday challenges of life in a different culture, such as locating essential services and products like housing, clothing and medicine.

19. **MARKETING IN PRACTICE** 1995 (22 min.) A basic introduction to the Japanese approach to marketing. Includes fundamental points that will not only help a product break into the Japanese market, but will also provide the keys to success in the global market.

20. **THE NEWEST WAVES OF JAPANESE CONSUMERS** 1992 (12 min.) Imported quality goods play a significant role in Japan's newest wave of consumer spending. This video examines the tastes, preferences and the changing lifestyles of Japan's three main consumers: women, youth, and senior citizens.

21. **OUR SUCCESS STORIES** 1994 (30 min.) Four foreign businessmen explain first hand why they chose to invest in Japan, what obstacles they faced, and which business strategies they found most effective.

(d) ENTERPRISE SERIES. Video cassettes of Public Broadcast Series on business. Available at $99 each from: Learning Corporation of America, 108 Wilmot Road, Deerfield, Illinois 60015. 1-800/621-2131, (708) 940-1260. Fax (708) 940-3600.

Study guides containing detailed case synopses, commentaries, discussion questions, and bibliographies are available with each film free of charge. Contributing to these guides were professional business consultants working in cooperation with Enterprise.

1. **BOEING VS. THE WORLD (THE JET SET)** After a dramatic skid in the late 1960s, Boeing is back in the cockpit as world leader of the aircraft industry. However, it faces stiff competition from the European government-backed consortium, Airbus Industries. Will Boeing's fuel-efficient 767 fly higher than Airbus' A310 Code #EP122

2. **THE BUCK STOPS IN BRAZIL** Why do the world's largest banks continue to invest in Brazil, a country that already owes $70 billion it can never hope to repay even as its export revenue to debt ratio widens? A surprising look at international banking and specter of default. Harvard Business School advisor: Robert R. Glauber, Professor of Business Administration. Code #EP170

3. **THE COLONEL COMES TO JAPAN** When a quintessential American chain sets up shop in a markedly different culture, a host of unusual marketing challenges arises - as seen here in Kentucky Fried Chicken's entry into the Japanese fast-food market. Emmy Award Winner. Code #EP112

4. **THE DIAMOND GAME** This rare glimpse into the secretive gem business takes us from the DeBeers mines in South Africa to New York's "Diamond District," where "the special fun of this program lies in its scenes of bargaining . . . a ritual that is at least as old and as formal as Japanese wrestling." - The New York Times. Code #EP169

5. **HONG KONG DRESSES UP** S.T. King, truly the king of Hong Kong clothing manufacturers, makes much of what design-conscious Americans will be wearing this year. But what about the future? His "up market" strategy for offering fewer goods at higher quality to deal with quota restrictions gives an incisive look into planning within the freest of the free-market economies. Harvard Business School advisor: Michael Y. Yoshino, Professor of Business Administration. Code #EP177

6. **THE KYOCERA EXPERIMENT** "Theory Z" is put to the test in San Diego, where American employees of the Kyocera Company adjust to their owners' thoroughly Japanese brand of management—but not without tensions related less to production goals than to cultural differences in organizational style. Code #EP115

7. **THE NEW SPACE RACE** Seeking contracts to launch satellites, a host of U.S. and foreign companies are gambling enormous sums to share in this new billion-dollar industry. Will these companies become the IBMs and AT&Ts of the future—and will NASA regain its former control? Harvard Business School advisor: William E. Sasser, Jr., Professor of Business Administration. Code #EP175

8. **ONE MAN'S MULTINATIONAL** One out of every three pairs of shoes sold in the noncommunist world bears the name of Thomas Bata, followed here from his boardroom to his plants in Chile, Upper Volta, Sri Lanka, and Kenya. It's a fascinating portrait of a CEO-as-diplomat in a world where he finds capital and labor under dictatorships and democracies alike.

9. **ANATOMY OF AN EMBARGO** This program examines the political viability of economic sanctions. History suggests that economic policy does not successfully alter the political practices of a targeted nation. In fact, it often complicates that political climate. An evaluation of the embargo placed on U.S. banana imports from Nicaragua in 1985 illustrates the advantages and disadvantages of imposing economic restrictions. Order #5116M

10. **BILLION DOLLAR DAY** Big money, big risk and big profits—that's the nature of the Currency Exchange Market. Swift decision making, and carefully timed actions are essential to the currency trader. Visit New York, London and Hong Kong to see a day in the life of three different currency traders and watch as they gamble a combined total over one billion dollars! Order #4997M

(e) Cornet/MTI Film and Video. Each of these films is accompanied by a synopsis of the film, commentary and suggested questions for discussion. Order from: Cornet/MTI Films, 108 Wilmot Road, Deerfield, Illinois 60015. Telephone (800) 777-8100 (708) 940-1260.

1. **GERMAINE GREER'S SYDNEY** "This is a city where the poorest people can be millionaires. Where, for nothing, practically, you do the same things that in other countries you have to join select clubs to do, and pay enormous membership fees and qualify in all kinds of obscure ways." Before the publication of her first book, *The Female Eunuch*, Germaine Greer held teaching positions at the Universities of Sydney and Warwick. Since then, owing to the demands on her time as a writer/broadcaster, Dr. Greer has given up full-time teaching and accepts only lecture tours and visiting fellowships.

   1980–SCA–25 minutes–sale $475–rental $45.
   LC #80-701285

2. **TWO FACTORIES: JAPANESE AND AMERICAN** An American factory worker is apt to consider the job a necessary means to an end. To a Japanese, the job is an extension of personal life; the company, a surrogate parent. Filmed at the Sylvania plant in Batavia, N.Y., and a Matsushita Electric complex in Osaka, Japan; produced by John Secondari and Helen Jean Rogers for LCA. Reviews: Training Magazine, ALA Booklist, Landers.

   1974–EJS–22 minutes–sale $350–rental $35.
   LC #73-702233

3. **IT'S ALWAYS SO IN THE WORLD (URBAN COMMUNAL LIVING)** By participating in the life of one family, we see many aspects of urban life in China's largest city, Shanghai, and learn that the extended family—parents, children and grandparents living together—is an accurate reflection of communal society in China today. We meet the Sun family at home in Pengpu Village, one of Shanghai's new housing complexes, and follow each family member through the working day. As they work and play, the Suns discuss their social and political ideas, economic aspirations and hopes for the future, giving us a clear picture of contemporary life in China's greatest metropolis. Reviews: Landers, The New York Times.

   1980–SCA–28 minutes–sale $450–rental $40.
   LC #79-701738

4. **AFRICAN ODYSSEY: THE RED BICYCLE** Following the adventures of a bicycle in East Africa, this cleverly conceived film becomes an introduction to the realities of life in an underdeveloped nation, as the bicycle passes from owner to owner. Reviews: EFLA Sightlines, ALA Booklist, Landers, Film News. Award: CINE Golden Eagle.

   1971–EJ–13 minutes–sale $250–rental $25.
   LC #70-710045
   This video series on Japan by Coronet Films are all current and interesting.

5. **THE ELECTRONIC TRIBE** This fascinating overview chronicles the historical and cultural forces that have shaped the Japanese temperament to be especially adept at forming cohesive organizations and thinking collectively. Investigation reveals how this cultural distinction has translated to the highly efficient and effective Japanese factory system. In a personal exploration of the peoples of Japan, the focus is on the contrast between old and new, between a rural population closely adhering to ancient traditions

and customs, and a thoroughly modern urban population closely aligned to contemporary Western ideals and manners. Order #5844C-$125 (A specially edited School Version excluding approximately two minutes of inappropriate material has been made available for our customers. Order #5848C)

6. **THE SWORD AND THE CHRYSANTHEMUM** Of equal importance in today's Japanese culture are an aggressive corporate philosophy and the tranquil spiritual life of the artist-poet. Insightful investigation traces these conflicting, yet equally strong cultural behaviors to Japan's paradoxical history: ruthless Samurai and Ninja warriors, the ancient tea ceremony, and fascination with meticulous garden design. Rare and beautiful photography underscores the strong influences which define Japan's business behavior, her rigid social hierarchy and the easy acceptance of the new. Order #5845C-$125 (A specially edited School Version excluding approximately two minutes of inappropriate material has been made available for our customers. Order #5849C)
7. **THE LEGACY OF THE SHOGUNS** Detailing the 17th century traditions of hard work, discipline and rigid hierarchy that kept Japan a small isolated feudal country for centuries, this fascinating program explores the change in focus that inspired a brutal military power bent on world domination. Tracing the historical and cultural events to the fateful days of World War II, the logical evolution of Japan's aggressive race to the forefront of modern world economics is explored. Order #5846C-$125
8. **A PROPER PLACE IN THE WORLD** Beginning with an incisive look at the political and economic factors contributing to World II, this program moves rapidly to the post-war era, focusing on MacArthur's reform policies for Japan and how this tiny island nation managed to raise itself from the ashes to become a major economic force in less than fifty years. Japan's stock exchange now rivals that of Wall Street! Along with the rewards of economic success have come modern-day problems: over-industrialization, overcrowding, and an exceedingly fast-paced and competitive lifestyle. How Japan will continue to confront these problems, and how Japan is striving to find its own national identity—its "proper place in the world" —are the issues raised in this fascinating series finale. Order #5847C-$125

(f) **ADVENTURES IN THE CHINA TRADE** Director/Producer: McDonnell Douglas Corporation and the International Trade Administration, U.S. Department of Commerce. Dist. by National Audio Visual Center, National Archives & Records, 8700 Edgeworth Dr., Capital Heights, MD 20743-3701, (301) 763-1896, (800) 788-NAVC.

This film on China is unique in its emphasis on current economic development and international trade. It represents and appeals to American business interests. Although problems of capital, technology, energy, transportation, and negotiations in a different language and culture are presented, the tendency by 1981 for the People's Republic of China to retreat on joint ventures and the resulting dismay of American corporations are somewhat understated in the film. The value of "progress" for a developing China is assumed. A more critical treatment might stress the dangers for China of excessive reliance on foreign capital and Western culture. The production is of high quality technically, although it is not designed to be entertaining. Shots of airplanes, petro and hydro projects, a satellite-earth station, and a nuclear institute contrast with bikes and carts in Peking, tai chi exercises, and crowded street scenes in Shanghai. Although most appropriate for college and adult audiences concerned with international business and economics, high school and other audiences interested in other disciplines, such as traditional Chinese culture, could benefit.

(g) Aims Media Company. 9710 De Soto Ave., Chatsworth, CA 91311-4409–(818) 773-4300, (800) 367-24

**CHINA: AN OPEN DOOR PART I: AN AWAKENING GIANT** Using footage taken during President Nixon's historic visit to Peking and that taken by Russian, French, and Chinese photographers over the years, A.P. newsman John Roderick compiled this documentary. The film presents both an historical and a contemporary perspective of a nation that has just reopened its doors to the Western world. By the Associated Press.

Number 4519–20 minutes–$320 (Rental: $30) in color.

(h) Films, Inc., 5547 North Ravinswood, Chicago, Illinois 60640. (800) 323-4222

**INDIAN'S SACRED COWS** Some have said that the cow, protected from slaughter by the Hindu faith, will one day "eat India." However, this film investigates the importance of the domestic cattle to the Indian people, especially the Hindus.

The Hindu religion forbids its followers to kill cows or to eat their food. Cows are considered sacred. Many holy shrines are built to "Mother Cow." Cows are allowed to wander unharmed throughout the towns and cities. Hindus may consume the cow's milk and cheese. The cows produce over 800 million tons of manure each year. When the dung is dry, it is used as fuel. It burns with no odors as it produces methane gas. The remaining manure is used as fertilizer to help raise the wheat and rice so badly needed by the Indian people.

"India's Sacred Cows" also presents, in an absorbing way, how millions of Indians live and work in a country that is overpopulated and plagued by poverty.

Study guide available. 28 minutes–color–Sale $375–Rental $35.

(i) **CONTROLLING INTEREST: THE WORLD OF THE MULTINATIONAL CORPORATION** Shows the corporate expansion which has brought productive resources and economic decision making throughout the world under the control of a small number of giant multinational companies. Examines the corporation's search for cheap labor, causing exploitation of the new industrial work force in the Third World. Interviews major corporation executives.

C News, 1978, 45 min., color, #CSC 263. Order from: University of Utah, Instructional Media Services, 207 Milton Bennion Hall, Salt Lake City, Utah 84102, telephone (801) 581-6771.

(j) The World Bank. There are a series of films on development available from the World Bank. A complete list of their series and the films listed below can be obtained from: The World Bank, Audio-Visual Division, 1818 H. Street, N.W., Washington, D.C. 20433, telephone (202)458-1721. Of the eight films available through the World Bank, the following four seem appropriate if one wants to delve deeply in the problems of the developing countries.

Development: (a) "Development Is People," (b) "An Essay on Poverty," (c) "Reflections of the 21st Century," and (d) "30 Minutes at the World Bank."

1. **DEVELOPMENT IS PEOPLE** An insight into the real meaning of development for the less fortunate people of the world is given in this film. The documentary follows the struggle of the poor for improvement in their meager lives, often simply to exist, in a world of great disparity of income and opportunity. The presentation focuses on the poor—who they are and how they live. The World Bank's concern for their plight, their needs, and their hopes is woven through scenes of contemporary life in the developing world.

   The motion picture was originally produced as a multiscreen slide show of the same title. It uses split-screen techniques along with unique dissolve effects to animate its poignant message. Screen time: 13 minutes, 16mm color-sound motion picture, Rental fee: $15.

2. **AN ESSAY ON POVERTY** Of the two billion people who now inhabit the developing countries, over one billion live in conditions that degrade the very meaning of humanity. In the next 25 years, an estimated two billion will be added to these numbers. What is their future?

   This film explores the enormous problems of poverty in today's world, giving some insights into the crucial issues of development. Migration to urban areas, women's role in developing societies, progress being made in rural development, inequality in distribution of income, and lack of opportunity are all discussed in terms of their effects on the central objective of development—meeting the basic needs of the very poor.

   Finally, the responsibilities of both rich and poor countries are raised. What emerges is that severe poverty can be relieved and the challenge to do so cannot be ignored.

   Screen time: 24 minutes, 16mm color-sound motion picture, Rental fee: $20.

3. **REFLECTIONS OF THE 21ST CENTURY** Many of the world's food producers experience one crop failure every four years due to drought. With the growing population it is becoming more urgent than ever before. This film examines the world hunger problem, presenting the views of World Bank experts.

   The documentary looks to increasing the productivity of subsistence farmers as a solution to the possible food crisis. It addresses the need for improved agricultural methods, modern transportation, efficient marketing facilities, reliable water supplies, and education to meet this goal.

   Focusing primarily on Asia, Latin America, and Africa, the film suggests that we must help these farmers advance themselves beyond subsistence levels today—if our children are to be fed in the coming century.

   Screen time: 23 minutes, 16mm color-sound motion picture, Rental fee: $20.

4. **30 MINUTES AT THE WORLD BANK** Development is . . .

   "Growth . . . Any kind of movement of a people . . . Upwards . . ."

   "The process through which a given society is trying to achieve the goals that they have set for themselves."

   "The opportunity for choice—people have a choice they didn't have previously." These are some of the comments World Bank staff members make on the Bank's ultimate goal, development.

   The World Bank is owned by over 130 nations. It is a unique organization which transfers funds and technical assistance from its richer member countries to its poorer ones for specific projects designed to better the living conditions of the recipients' less fortunate people.

   Filmed at the World Bank's headquarters, the documentary presents the views of members of the Bank's multinational staff, who offer their own spontaneous opinions on what the Bank is, what its goals are, how it operates, and where its future lies.
   Screen time: 30 minutes, 16mm color-sound picture, Rental fee: $20.

(k) Chamber of Commerce of the U.S., Special Projects, 1615 H. Street N.W., Washington, D.C. 20062. (202) 463-5755. A set of three 35mm slides with audio tapes on exporting. One of the best presentations on world trade, its importance to the U.S. economy, and steps on "how to do it." $95.00 per set or $37.50 each.

World Trade (individual titles):

1. **THE CASE OF TWO-WAY TRADE–#6666**
2. **THE REAL WORLD OF EXPORTING: OPPORTUNITIES AND REALITIES #6667**
3. **EXPORT FOR PROFIT–#6668.**

(l) Going International. Professionally produced series of six films/videos and training guides. User's guides review the information in each film and include supplemental exercises and suggested resources. Each film has its own guide which can be purchased separately.

Available from: Copeland Griggs Productions, 2046 Clement Street, San Francisco, CA 94121. (415) 668-4200, FAX (415) 668-6004. Available for rental or purchase (3-day rental, $75 for non-profit purchase price noted on description).

1. **BEYOND CULTURE SHOCK** is specifically for the individual or family moving abroad. Experts explain the psychological phases of the adjustment process. U.S. and Canadian expatriate families describe their experiences and suggest strategies for overcoming culture shock. Spouses' and children's needs during relocation are given particular attention. This film offers practical suggestions for making living abroad an enriching adventure. 28 minutes $595 purchase.
2. **WELCOME HOME, STRANGER** focuses on the unexpected problems of returning home. Family members share how they overcame the difficulties of "reentry" into the workplace, community and school environments. Reentry is often the hardest part of an overseas experience and should not be ignored. 14 minutes. $395 purchase.
3. **BRIDGING THE CULTURE GAP** is an introduction to the challenges of traveling, living and working in a foreign culture. Colorful film from around the world powerfully illustrates fundamental concepts of culture, in theory and in practice. Interviews with experts and foreign nationals show the importance of cross-cultural awareness, giving audiences a new understanding of the impact of cultural differences on all international activities. 28 minutes. $595 purchase price.
4. **MANAGING THE OVERSEAS ASSIGNMENT** dramatically portrays communication problems anyone can experience in foreign situations. Examples of U.S. travelers in countries as diverse as Japan, Saudi Arabia, England, India and Mexico illustrate how cultural taboos and accepted standards of behavior differ around the world. Nationals of the featured countries and cross-cultural experts explain how travelers can adapt their communication skills and personal conduct to be more effective abroad. 29 minutes. $595 purchase price.
5. **WORKING IN THE USA** introduces all cultures to the realities of the U.S. workplace. The film facilitates communications, improves the foreigner's understanding of professional associates, reduces intercultural conflicts in the work force and helps increase productivity. Foreign nationals working in the United States talk about their experiences and share advice. Documentary footage shows specific situations which the foreign national will confront. 30 minutes. $695 purchase.
6. **LIVING IN THE USA** deals with the challenges foreigners face when relating to the United States. While giving an overview of the cultural diversity and vastness of the U.S.A., the film also highlights practical issues such as housing, banking, credit, schools, shopping and transportation. Exploring the importance of social activities and the making of friends, the film brings together personal and practical advice on how to adjust to life in the United States. 30 minutes. $695 purchase.

7. **GOING INTERNATIONAL: SAFELY** alerts the traveler to the variety of security problems that can interrupt a trip: crime, accident, illness, arrest, fire natural disaster and terrorism. The video shows how any traveler can reduce risk each step of the way: while planning a trip, at the airport, on the street, in a car, and in a hotel, home or workplace. Advice is given for what to do in the event of an emergency overseas. 30 minutes.

(m) Intercultural Press offers films and videos for sale or rental. Contact: Intercultural Press, Inc., P.O. Box 700, Yarmouth, Maine 04096. (207) 846-5168.

1. **COLD WATER** Noriko Ogami, Producer

   This video is about cross-cultural adaptation and culture shock. It is about diving into a new culture and having it feel—as one of the foreign students interviewed in the video put it—like a "plunge into cold water."

   The perceptions of 12 Boston University foreign students of their experiences in the U.S. are captured as each of the foreign students (plus one American student and three knowledgeable specialists in cross-cultural affairs) are interviewed about the experience of living and studying in a new culture.

   An excellent resource for any program wishing to help its participants better understand the cross-cultural adjustment process and the experience of being a foreigner in the U.S.

   Intercultural Press
   48 minutes, No. 875, 1987
   Formats: VHS 1/2", 3/4"U
   1-week preview/rental–$35
   Purchase–$125 Shipping–$7

2. **WORKING WITH JAPAN** This is a series of six videos that focus on a guide to business success in Japan. The two videos available now are listed below. Write Intercultural Press for information on these and other releases.

   For Westerners in either the preliminary stages of an association with a Japanese company or already involved in a business relationship, this new series provides invaluable guidance for building productive relations with the Japanese.

   Through the insights of distinguished businesspeople and educators, the viewer will gain an understanding of Japanese business culture and learn what to do and what to avoid when conducting business with the Japanese.

   **PREPARATION**

   This video covers critical differences in U.S.-Japan business and communication styles and common misconceptions about business in Japan. It includes practical advice in eight areas ranging from market research and strategic planning to support material and business cards and gifts. 47 minutes, No. 820/$395.

   **FIRST MEETING**

   This video takes an in-depth look at first meetings with Japanese and provides practical guidelines on appropriate conduct in these settings. The video demonstrates proper greetings and introductions, appropriate conversation topics and seating arrangements, the use of questions and effective communication strategies. 35 minutes, No. 821.

3. **CULTURAL DIVERSITY** At the Heart of Bull. Bull HN Information Systems.

   *I have found students of all levels consistently fascinated by the views presented in the video by their compatriots and their views presented by the French; even weak students have sought a deeper explanation for the cross-cultural difficulties evident. Apparently the video's documentation of gaps in mutual understanding in a real business setting strikes them as believable and compelling.*
   –Ruth L. Doyle, Central Missouri State University

   This video is designed to inform and assist people in dealing with ethnic and cultural diversity in the workplace. It will be useful for any company operating globally. It is also recommended for business school courses on global management.

   Originally developed by the Human Resources and Communication groups of Bull HN Information Systems, Inc., the video focuses specifically on cultural differences between French and Americans as seen from the perspective of Bull employees. It is a candid, fast-paced look at how employees from both cultures perceive themselves, one another, and the world around them.

   The 28-minute video is accompanied by a copy of *Understanding Cultural Differences: Germans, French and Americans,* by Edward T. Hall and Mildred Reed Hall, anthropologists who are well known for their studies of culture and intercultural relations. Additional copies of the book may be ordered from Intercultural Press. The price per additional book is $15.95 plus shipping.

   Intercultural Press, 28 minutes, No. D-877, 1992.

4. **HOW TO WELCOME BUSINESS GUESTS FROM JAPAN** Intercultural Business Center. This video shows the crucial protocols necessary to successful business dealings with the Japanese: appropriate greetings, business card exchange, the Japanese tea ceremony, and gift giving.

   Here are the keys to successful plant and company tours with your Japanese visitors and the rules for social interaction, including dining, drinking, and entertaining. Finally, you will discover the vital protocols for preparing, conducting and closing meetings and the necessary follow-ups.
   Intercultural Business Center, 30 minutes, No. 890,1990

5. **WEST MEETS EAST: IN JAPAN** *West Meets East: In Japan* is a training film introducing Japanese social and business etiquette to Western executives.

   As it follows a likable "every Westerner" through his interactions with the Japanese—in public, at work, and at a party given in his honor—this engaging video helps business travelers master the social skills necessary for building smooth working relationships in Japan.

   The comprehensive study guide which accompanies *West Meets East* provides more detailed information on such topics as public behavior, etiquette, gender roles in the Japanese business world, dealing with disagreement, and more. Intended for businesspeople, this video would also be helpful for exchange students and travelers visiting Japan.

   West Meets East Productions, 37 minutes, No. 880, 1992

6. **WORKING WITH JAPAN** A practical guide to Business Success. *Working with Japan* is a six-part video providing practical recommendations and instructions for managing business meetings, social situations, and negotiation sessions with Japanese counterparts.

Featured are interviewed with distinguished businesspersons and educators with extensive experience in Japan.

This series is for Western business executives who work with Japanese either in their home countries or in Japan. It is designed to benefit people with varying levels of experience, from those just beginning an association with a Japanese company to those already involved in a business relationship.

The videotapes, 25-35 minutes each, include supplementary booklets.

1. **PREPARATION—GROUNDWORK FOR SUCCESS** market research, quality assurance, strategic planning, team development, proper instructions, meeting arrangements, business cards, and gifts.
2. **FIRST MEETING—PRESENTING YOURSELF** introductions, building rapport, exchanging information, communicating effectively.
3. **NEGOTIATING—STRATEGIES THAT WORK—TAPE I** What to Expect: comparative negotiating styles, typical Japanese negotiating behaviors; Tape II–Strategies and Tactics: preparing, presenting, clarifying, persuading, reaching agreement.
4. **BUSINESS ENTERTAINING—THE ROLES OF HOST AND GUEST** extended business hours, recommendations for the guest, responsibilities of the host.
5. **WOMEN IN BUSINESS—OBSTACLES AND OPPORTUNITIES** establishing credibility, building relationships, working for Japanese companies.
6. **MANAGING THE RELATIONSHIP—KEYS TO LONG-TERM SUCCESS** people, products and services, conflicts, achieving global excellence.

Intercultural Training Resources, Inc., 1991

7. **DOING BUSINESS IN MEXICO** *Doing Business in Mexico* is a fast-paced, exciting excursion into the streets and the countryside of Mexico, and into the heart of the Mexican business community. A captivating viewing experience as well as a thorough training presentation, the video provides tips from top business executives augmented by concise summaries and striking graphics.

   The video focuses on making the right contacts to assure business success; building solid, long-term business relationships; making sure work is done right and on time; communication and understanding; proper etiquette; negotiation; and enjoying yourself.

   Big World, Inc., Format: VHS, 33 minutes, No. D-898, 1994

8. **COLD WATER** Noriko Ogami, Producer. This video is about cross-cultural adaptation and culture shock. It is about diving into a new culture and having it feel—as one of the foreign students interviewed in the video puts it—like a "plunge into cold water."

   Twelve Boston University foreign students share perceptions of their experiences in the U.S. as each of them (plus one American student and three knowledgeable specialists in cross-cultural affairs) are interviewed about living and studying in a new culture. One of the striking things about this video is the pace at which it moves—from student to student to specialist—one often answering the other's questions though they were all interviewed separately. An excellent resource for any program wishing to help its participants better understand the cross-cultural adjustment process and the experience of being a foreigner in the U.S.

*Cold Water* is useful in foreign student, refugee, or TA orientation programs; briefings for American personnel dealing with foreign students; and orientation for exchange students or Americans in study abroad programs and ESL or other courses in which cross-cultural interaction is a significant focus of study. A facilitator's guide by Louis Meucci accompanies the videotape.

Intercultural Press, 48 minutes, No. E-875, 1987

9. **WORKING WITH CHINA** From the producers of the popular *Working with Japan* series. *Working with China* is a six-part video providing practical recommendations and instructions for managing business meetings, social situations, and negotiation sessions with Chinese counterparts. Featured are interviews with distinguished businesspeople and educators with extensive experience in China.

   This series is for Western business executives who work with Chinese either in their home countries or in China. It is designed to benefit people with varying levels of experience, from those just beginning an association with a Chinese company to those already involved in a business relationship.

   The videotapes, 25-35 minutes each, include supplementary booklets. Titles available: *Succeeding in China; Building the Relationship; Negotiating* (opening moves); *Negotiating* (the middle game); *Negotiating* (closing the deal); and *Living and Traveling.*

   Still available: *Working with Japan* series. *Preparation–Groundwork for Success; First Meeting–Presenting Yourself; Negotiation–Strategies That Work*; two tapes; *Business Entertaining–The Roles of Host and Guest; Women in Business–Obstacles and Opportunities*; and *Managing the Relationship–Keys to Long-Term Success.*

   Interculture Training Resources, Inc., 1994

10. **WORKING TOGETHER**. Managing Cultural Diversity, based on the book by Dr. George F. Simons. This video-book program calls on experts to help viewers understand and respect people from other cultures, who reciprocate understanding and respect in return. It teaches viewers how to manage their minds, their words, and their unspoken language to become more effective in a multicultural environment. The Leader's Guide helps even inexperienced individuals conduct meaningful and sensitive discussions. Package includes videotape, 6 copies of the book, *Working Together*, and the Leader's Guide.

    Crisp Publications, 25 minutes, No. D-831, 1989

11. **NEW SKILLS FOR GLOBAL MANAGEMENT** Ben Kozuch, Jurgen Leschner and Stephen Rhinesmith. In this video presentation Stephen Rhinesmith, one of the foremost authorities on the human aspects of globalization, addresses managers regarding the new skills and mindsets required for effective global management: managing global competitiveness, managing complexity and conflict, managing multicultural teams, and managing adaptability.

    Rhinesmith takes us to organizations like AT&T, Grace Cocoa, KPMG Peat Marwick, and Siemens to look at how their executives manage globalization. To further enhance its training effectiveness, this 35-minute video is accompanied by the Leader' Guide with instructional notes, exercises, overhead masters, and an audio cassette.

    Multi Media Inc., 35 minutes, No. 895, 1993

(n) **ETHICS ISSUES IN INTERNATIONAL BUSINESS** The Ethics Resource Center's latest video addresses the special cultural, economic and legal issues involved in doing business in foreign countries, such as: marketing in culturally different environments, transferring technology and complying with the Foreign Corrupt Practices Act.

Some of the videos listed above plus a variety of other international marketing videos can be obtained from the following distributors (check their Web sites for details):

Big World
1350 Pine St. Suite 5
Boulder, CO 80302
1-800-682-1261
(fax) 1-303-444-6190
http://www.bwvideo.com
BigWorld@aol.com

Films for the Humanities & Sciences
PO Box 2053
Princeton, NJ 08543-2053
1-800-257-5126 or 1-609-275-1400
(fax) 1-609-275-3767
http://www.films.com

A particularly useful series is their Challenge to American (1994) in which the competitiveness of Japan, Germany, and the United States are compared (including educational systems, cultural differences, and business systems). Some of the material is dated, but even that is interesting from an historical perspective. For instance, the series ignores China, which seems quite silly from the viewpoint of the late 1990s.

Insight Media
2162 Broadway
New York, NY 10024-6620
1-800-233-9910 or 1-212-721-6316
(fax) 1-212-799-5309
http://www.insight-media.com

Meridian Resources Associates
1741 Buchanan Street
San Francisco, CA 94115
1-800-626-2047 or 1-415-749-2920
(fax) 1-415-749-0124
http://www.mera.com

Producers Media International
429 Santa Monica Blvd. Suite 450
Santa Monica, CA 90401
1-800-320-3313 or 1-310-393-7274
(fax) 1-310-393-4823
asia@producersmedia.com

Write:

Ethics Resource Center, Inc.
600 New Hampshire Avenue, NW
Washington, D.C. 20037
(202) 333-3419

(o) **DOING BUSINESS IN ASIA SERIES** A Northwest Airlines sponsored series of four videos includes Doing Business in: Japan, Hong Kong, Taiwan, and South Korea. Each film runs for approximately 60 minutes. Discussion Guides are available. Videos can be rented or purchased. There is also available a 15-minute tape of highlights from all four videos.

Write:

Doing Business in Asia
P.O. Box 68618
Indianapolis, IN 46268-2555
(800) 526-8926 Ext. 110

(p) **WEST MEETS EAST: IN JAPAN** This film is designed to introduce Japanese social and business etiquette to Western executives. This 37-minute film, together with its comprehensive study guide, identifies, illustrates, and explains the manners and customs essential to successful negotiations in the Japanese business world. A comprehensive 20-page study guide accompanies this video and provides more detailed information on mastering the social skills necessary for building smooth working relationships in Japan. Topics include:

A Summary of Relevant Japanese History
Attitudes of Japanese Towards Foreigners
Public Behavior on the Crowded Islands
The Bow Versus the Handshake
Etiquette in Japanese Interiors
Entertainment is Serious Business
Conversation with the Japanese
The Role of Drinking in the Japanese Business World
Notes on Table Manners
Polite Conduct Toward the Opposite Sex
Gender Roles in the Japanese Business World
The Foreign Female Executive in Japan
Business Dealings with the Japanese
Gaining the Sense of Group
The Ritual of Introductions
The Problem of Language and Communication
Dealing with Disagreement

Write:

Pyramid Film and Video
Box 1048
Santa Monica, CA 90406-1048
(800) 421-2034
In California - (310) 828-7577

(q) Other recommended films and video cassettes

The following additional films are suggested.

1. **EUROPE UNITED** a new 26-minute film, dealing with the enlarged European Community and its relation with the United States. It comes with a "teaching manual," suggesting discussion topics for students, civic groups, or professional organizations. Write European Community Information Service, 2100 M Street, NW, Washington, D.C. 20037.

2. **DOING BUSINESS IN JAPAN–NEGOTIATING A CONTRACT** a 35-minute 16mm color motion picture, detailing a contract negotiation between a team of American businessmen and a team representing a Japanese company. The film was produced under the auspices of the Business Council for International Understanding. This film provides a careful analysis of the negotiation process, exploring such complex elements as language and communication; cultural and pragmatic disparities of background; social setting and entertainment; use of interpreter; and a variety of other critical points essential to successfully doing business in Japan. It is designed to stimulate discussion and is accompanied by a Discussion Guide. It is ideal for effective use in preparing corporate executives for contract negotiations. The film focuses on a variety of other business relationships in any foreign country where language and cultural differences exist.

   Requests for prints: sale, rental, or audition – write: Vision Associates, Inc., 665 Fifth Avenue, Department E, New York, NY 10022. Purchase: $350 per print plus shipping. Rental: $75 per showing plus shipping.

3. **TAKING YOUR PRODUCT INTO THE JAPANESE MARKET** (1990). A comprehensive orientation to the Japanese business environment, designed to help Americans avoid common mistakes. A trainer's manual and user's manual are included. Supplementary materials available. 150 minutes. Available from QCI International, 1350 Vista Way, P.O. Box 1503, Airport Industrial Park, Department 1030, Red Bluff, CA 96080-1335, (916) 527-6374, (800) 527-6970.

4. **CHINA BUSINESS BRIEFING** A profile of Chinese business techniques noted for their efficiency and productivity. Supplementary materials available. 75 minutes. Available from Direct Cinema Limited, P.O. Box 10003, Santa Monica, CA 90410, (310) 396-4774, (800) 525-0000

5. **THE JAPAN SERIES** (1990) The development of Japan into a world economic power is examined through its history, culture and people. Six titles in the series: 1. Geography; 2. History; 3. Industry; 4 Society; 5. Daily Life; and 6. Farming and Fishing. Available from United Learning Inc., 6633 W. Howard Street, P.O. Box 48718, Niles IL 60714, (708) 647-0600 (800) 424-0362.

6. **DOING BUSINESS IN ASIA** Four-part series covering the cultural and psychological factors involved in U.S./Asian business relationships. Available from Doing Business in Asia, P.O. Box 68618, Indianapolis, IN 46268-2555, (800) 526-8926.

7. **GLOBAL DUMPING GROUP** PBS *Frontline* investigates the U.S. shipping of toxic waste to third world countries with fewer dumping regulations, sometimes for profit. Supplementary materials available. 58 minutes and *The Global Dumping Ground: International Traffic in Hazardous Waste.* PBS *Frontline* report examines the problem of exporting hazardous waste to countries with less-stringent regulations on disposal. Supplementary materials available. 60 minutes. Both available from The Video Project, 5332 College Avenue, Ste. 101, Oakland, CA 94618, (510) 655-9050, (800) 4-PLANET.

8. **FRONTLINE: LOSING THE WAR WITH JAPAN** Discussion on the Japanese challenge to American business. 86 minutes. Available from University of Washington Educational Media Collection, Kane Hall, DG-10, Seattle, WA 98195, (206) 543-9909.

9. **HOW TO DO BUSINESS IN JAPAN: WITHOUT LOSING YOUR FACE** Learn the subtleties of Japanese culture and how to successfully conduct business in that market. Includes footage of business situations in Japan, and captioned Japanese phrases. 75 minutes. Available from Books In Motion, E. 9212 Montgomery, Ste. 501, Spokane, WA 94206 (509) 922-1646.

10. **INTERNATIONAL OPERATIONS** A Canadian Supermarket chain opens store in Paris. This program shows the impact of the store on shoppers, employees, and other local merchants. 29 minutes and *Managing the Overseas Assignment.* Trying to complete a business deal and figure out foreign customers can be a tricky maneuver to pull off. Key issues are covered. 30 minutes. Both available from National Film Board of Canada, 1251 Avenue of the Americas, 16th Floor, New York, NY 10020-1173, (212) 596-1770, (800) 542-2164.
11. **JAPAN: ECONOMIC WORLD POWER** Informative study of the Japanese economy surveys the lives of businessmen and their families. Visits the Nissan and Mitsubishi conglomerates, pointing out that economic success is the product of many factors, including high standards of quality, an employee's loyalty to the company, automation, and exports. Includes guide. Supplementary materials available. 15 minutes. Available from Britannica Films, 310 South Michigan Avenue, Chicago, IL 60604, (312) 347-7000, (800) 554-9862.
12. **JAPAN 2000**. A look at some of the things that the Japanese do to make their products inexpensive and of high quality. 30 minutes. Available from Great Plains National (GPN), 1800 N. 33rd Street, Box 80669, Lincoln, NE 68501-0669, (402) 472-2007, (800) 228-4630

(r) World Bank Electronic Media Products And Services

The World Bank Group provides a film and video unit library that consists mostly of documentary and informational films/videos. For information on what is available and ordering information visit: http://www.worldbank.org/globallinks/index.htm

For ordering information, please contact Craig Hobbs of the Film and Video Unit at (202) 473-2149.

1. **SOUTH AFRICA: AFTER THE MIRACLE** An in-depth exploration of the economic issues that confronts the new government of South Africa as it attempts to deal with the legacy of apartheid. Includes interviews with Nelson Mandela, Fredrick de Klerk and many others.

   Video, 1994 • 58 minutes • English • Documentary
   0586 • $19.95

2. **THE BUSINESS OF SERVICE**

   Video, 1994 • 8 minutes • English, French, Spanish • Informational
   0157 • $9.95

3. **Investing in People** East Asia's "miracle" economies are delivering better lives for millions of people. Yet millions of others—especially those in rural areas—are still trying to escape poverty and environmental degradation. For some of them an even greater miracle may be starting to emerge in places where development assistance is going straight to the people.

   It is increasingly clear that development is most effective when the beneficiaries of a project are closely consulted with and involved. This video—a visually stunning new documentary—shows how dramatic the results can be. In three corners of East Asia—the huge and desolate Loess Plateau of China, the rugged mountains of Java and the islands of the central Philippines—communities are transforming the quality of their lives through their own efforts.

Video, 1996 • 38 minutes • English • Documentary
1121 • $19.95

4. **FUNDAMENTALISM IN THE MIDDLE EAST** Religious fundamentalism manifests itself in many ways in many parts of the world. Extremism and terrorism are also found in many different societies. Currently, several governments in the Middle East and North Africa are struggling with militant forms of Islamic extremism. But what are the root causes of religious and political extremism? What role does it play in the competing social forces in these countries?

   In this panel discussion, a distinguished group of Arab experts explore religious fundamentalism and how it relates to social change, social transformation, cultural identity and economic development. The views expressed are clearly those of the participants and do not in any way represent the position of the World Bank, or any of its affiliated organizations.

   Video, 1997 • 50:08 minutes • English • Panel Discussion
   1131 • $14.95

5. **SOCIAL ISSUES** Today the world is in the throes of powerful forces that are creating currents of globalization and homogenization as never before. Markets are being integrated, capital flows are being created, cultural icons are being determined across the boundaries of states and continents. Material well-being is growing, and in most indicators, people are better off than they were a generation ago. And yet, in practically every society there is a profound sense of loss; there is a sense of anomie; there is a sense even bordering on despair.

   In this panel discussion, a distinguished panel of experts examine some of the problems confronting societies all over the world, especially those in developing countries.

   Video, 1997 • 29:42 minutes • English • Panel Discussion
   1132 • $14.95

(s) University of Washington Business School' s Instructional Resources Office

This site provides a good source of videos, simulations, and cases. Visit the homepage at: http://depts.washington.edu/%7Eir/material.html#intmater

Among the Videos available are:

**International Business Teaching Materials**

Videos

1. **BREAKING BARRIERS: FOREIGN COMPANIES THAT SUCCEED IN JAPAN** This video documents how several foreign companies have managed to enter the Japanese market and prosper. Looking specifically at Kentucky Fried Chicken and Wella Cosmetics, the video explores how these foreign companies managed to compete successfully away from their home markets. Interviews with Japanese and non-Japanese executives illuminate the obstacles foreign companies encounter and what it takes to overcome them.

   1987 – 30 min.

1. **BUSINESS ETHICS** three vignettes produced by the University of Michigan School of Business.
   a. "The Great Whale Hydro-Electric Project: A Question of Power" Explores the controversy about constructing a dam in Quebec, including Cree and Inuit opposition to the destruction of habitat and wildlife.
   b. "Your Job or Mine: Green Giant's Decision to Move to Mexico." Examines who benefits and who suffers when a Green Giant plant moves from the Salinas Valley in California to Mexico.
   c. "Violence on Television: The Impact Upon Society." Explores whether the market for violence leads producers to create programs that promote real life violence.
2. **DOING BUSINESS IN ASIA: HONG KONG** Yue-Sai Kan, Asian expert and television broadcaster, shows how a competitive laissez-faire market has co-existed with Chinese traditions. Case studies include Citibank, Regent International Hotels, and Diane Freis, Ltd.

   1990 – 30 min.
3. **DOING BUSINESS IN ASIA: JAPAN** Yue-Sai Kan, Asian expert and television broadcaster, discusses the complexities of the business world in Japan, including the demand for quality and the intricacies of business and social practices. Includes case studies of Coca-Cola and Estee Lauder.

   1990 – 30 min.
4. **DOING BUSINESS IN ASIA: SOUTH KOREA** Yue-Sai Kan, Asian expert and television broadcaster, discusses how to overcome cultural barriers in Korea. Includes case studies of IBM, Litton, and Hobsen's Ice Cream.

   1990 – 30 min.
5. **DOING BUSINESS IN ASIA: TAIWAN** Yue-Sai Kan, Asian expert and television broadcaster, explains why Taiwan is one of the best countries in Asia in which to do business. Includes case studies of Toys 'R' Us, Avon, and General Electric.

   1990 – 30 min.
6. **EUROPEAN UNION**

   Segments produced 1988 – 1997

   5 videos:

   Video #1 –**An Evolving Union: Jean Monnet, Father of Europe** – 12 min., 1992 and Beyond – 12 min., EU Enlargement – East/Central Europe – 4 min., Who Runs the Union? – 10 min.

   Video #2 –**Economic Challenges: One Currency for Europe** – 9 min., Europe at the Millennium – 22 min., Environment at the Center of EU Policy – 12 min., Eurobiz – 17 min.

   Video #3 –**Transatlantic Relations: Extraordinary Partners – The EU and the US** – 27 min., Ties & Tensions – EU-US Relations in the Next Century – 26 min.

   Video #4 –**Europe and the World: PHARE – The EU AID Program for Eastern Europe** – 22 min., ECHO – 12 min., From Yaounde to

Mauritius – A History of the Lome Convention – 5 min., Refugees in Central America – 13 min.

Video #5 –**European ABC: European ABC – The European Union** – 6 min., The Institutions – 6 min., The Single Currency – 4 min., External Relations – 4 min.

7. **FORGING THE INTERNATIONAL PARTNERSHIP** Overview of the joint venture between Corning and Samsung and how the companies learned to resolve cross-cultural conflicts.

   1995 – 20 min.

8. **GLOBALLY SPEAKING: SKILLS AND STRATEGIES FOR SUCCESS WITH ASIA, #3 - TEAM FORMATION** Meeting scenarios that illustrate difficulties in intercultural teamwork.

   1997 – 30 min.

9. **GOING INTERNATIONAL, PART 1, BRIDGING THE CULTURE GAP** An introduction to the challenges of living and working in a foreign culture. Foreign footage takes you to countries all around the world. The film shows the importance of cross-cultural skills and prepares individuals for cultural adjustment and effectiveness in a foreign environment.

   1983 – 30 min.

10. **GOING INTERNATIONAL, PART 2, MANAGING THE OVERSEAS ASSIGNMENT** This video portrays specific problems Americans might have doing business in Japan, Saudi Arabia, England, India, and Mexico. Cultural taboos and accepted standards of business behavior are explained by foreign nationals of the host countries. Strategies for improving personal performance in foreign business situations are described.

    1983 – 30 min.

11. **GOING PLACES: DISTRIBUTION CHANNELS - THE INTERNATIONAL MARKET** This video explores methods for foreign distribution by small businesses. It explains the importance of understanding foreign customs, discusses domestic and international distribution procedures, and details factors to consider when selecting an overseas distribution channel.

    1991 – 30 min.

12. **INSIDE THE GLOBAL ECONOMY** This series presents the principles of international economics using on-location documentary case studies, news and archival footage, and commentary from distinguished international economists.

    1995 – 13 one-hour programs on 7 cassettes.

    Program #1 Trade – An Introduction: Why do nations trade?

    IBM's move to Japan is featured.

    Program #2 Protectionism – Impediments to trade and the driving forces behind protectionism.

    Program #3 Trade Policy – Countries strengthen their competitive advantage through subsidies and regulatory policies.

| | |
|---|---|
| Program #4 | Trade Liberalization and Regional Trade Blocs: Compares the post-WWII trade liberalization with GATT and the Canadian-U.S. Free Trade Agreement. |
| Program #5 | Labor and Capital Mobility: The U.S.-Mexico maquiladora program exemplifies the trans-border labor force. |
| Program #6 | Multinational Corporations: Features Smith-Corona and Brother. |
| Program #7 | Fixed vs. Floating Exchange Rates: The case of Caterpillar and Komatsu shows the potential effects of exchange rates. |
| Program #8 | Managing Currencies and Policy Coordination: The limits to government intervention in foreign exchange markets. |
| Program #9 | Exchange Rates, Capital Flight, and Hyperinflation: Factors affecting exchange rates in Argentina and Mexico. |
| Program #10 | Developing Countries: South Korea and Sri Lanka illustrate different development strategies. |
| Program #11 | Economies in Transition The transformation of former Communist countries into free-market economies. |
| Program #12 | Environment: Considers whether free-trade and environment preservation can be compatible. |
| Program #13 | The Evolving World Economy: What is the new path to prosperity in world trade? |

13. **INTERNATIONAL BUSINESS PRACTICES: HIDDEN DIMENSIONS** This video explores cultural assumptions about space, time, and information in international business. Anthropologist Edward T. Hall looks at offices in Japanese and American corporations and explains how culture influences communication and business transactions.

    1996 – 62 min.

13. **MACNEIL LEHRER NEWSHOUR**

    Two features:

    a. the NAFTA treaty controversy, including substantial excerpts from the Gore-Perot debate

    b. "China in Transition: Risks for Foreign Investors," one part of a three-part report.

    1993 – 57 min.

14. **PACIFIC LINK: A HALF CENTURY OF U.S./JAPAN ECONOMIC TIES. NIGHTLY BUSINESS REPORT, SPECIAL EDITION** An overview of U.S.-Japan economic relations from 1945, the end of World War II, to 1995.

    1995 – 26 min.

15. **PACIFIC TRIANGLE. NIGHTLY BUSINESS REPORT, SPECIAL EDITION** A look at China's growing economic power and what it means for Japan and the United States.

    1997 – 27 min.

16. **RETAILING IN EUROPE** This program contrasts Western Europe with the United States to examine how social and cultural differences affect retailing. Interviews with European consumers and authorities on international retailing illuminate how the systems differ. The program also considers the implications of EC (European Community) and EFTA (European Free Trade Association) economic programs for retailers.

1992 – 22 min.

# PART II
# INSTRUCTOR'S NOTES ON TEXT CASES

## CASE GUIDE — CHAPTER

| CASE | 1 | 2 | 3 | 4 | 5 | 6 | 7 | 8 | 9 | 10 | 11 | 12 | 13 | 14 | 15 | 16 | 17 | 18 | 19 |
|---|---|---|---|---|---|---|---|---|---|---|---|---|---|---|---|---|---|---|---|
| 1–1 Lost in Translation: AOL's Assault on Latin America Hits Snag in Brazil | X | | | X | X | | | | | | X | X | | | | | | | |
| 1–2 Unilever and Nestlé – Analysis | X | | | X | | | | | | | | X | | | | | | | |
| 1–3 Nestlé – The Infant Formula Incident | | X | X | X | X | | | X | | | X | X | | | | X | | | |
| 2–1 The Not-So-Wonderful World of EuroDisney | | | | X | | X | X | X | | | X | | | | | | | X | |
| 2–2 Instructors Notes: Dealing with an Unexpected Bureaucratic Delay | | | | | X | | | | | | | | | | | | | | X |
| 2–3 Starnes-Brenner Machine Tool Company – To Bribe or Not to Bribe | | | | | X | | X | | | | | | | | | | | | |
| 2–4 When International Buyers and Sellers Disagree | | | | | | | X | | | | | | | | X | | | | |
| 2–5 Instructor's Notes: How Companies React to Foreign Corruption | | | | | X | | | | | | | | | | | | | | |
| 2–6 Coping with Corruption in Trading with China | | | | | X | X | X | | | | | | | | | | | | |
| 3–1 Asian Yuppies – Having It All | | | | | | | | | X | | | X | | | | | | | |
| 3–2 Instructor's Notes: Developing a European Web Site for Levi's | | | | | | | | | | | | X | | X | | X | | | |
| 3–3 Konark Television India | | | | | | | | | X | | | X | | X | | | | | |
| 3–4 Swifter, Higher, Stronger, Dearer | | | | | | | | X | | | X | | | | | | | X | X |
| 4–1 Global Strategies – What Are They? | X | X | | | | | | | | | X | | | | | | | | |
| 4–2 Tambrands – Overcoming Cultural Resistance | | | | X | | | | | | X | X | X | | | | | | | |
| 4–3 Instructor's Note: Pricing a Product in Multiple Country Markets | | | | X | | | | | | | | | | | | | | X | |
| 4–4 Blair Water Purifiers India | | | X | | | | X | X | | | X | | X | | | | | | |
| 4–5 Sales Negotiations Abroad for MRIs | | | | | X | | | | | | | | | | | | | X | X |
| 4–6 Tough Decisions at Boeing | | | | | | | | | X | | X | X | X | | | | | X | |
| 4–7 National Office Machines – Motivating Japanese Salespeople: Straight Salary or Commission? | | | | X | X | | | | | | | | | | | | X | | |
| 4–8 Alan AeroSpace | | | | | | | | | | | | | | | | | | | X |
| 4–9 AIDS and Condoms | X | | | X | | | | X | X | | | X | | X | | | | | |
| 4–10 Making Social Responsibility and Ethical making Decisions: Selling Tobacco to Third-World | | | | | X | | | | X | | X | | | | | | | | |

*There are three suggestions on using case 4–15. (1) Have the students prepare the case in conjunction with the discussion of ethics and social responsibility in Chapter 5; (2) In a two stage approach, have the students prepare the case early in the semester after or during discussion of culture (Chapter 4) and business customs (Chapter 5) and then toward the end of the course after Chapter 17. Have them compare early recommendations with later recommendations. Discuss how attitudes have changed; (3) Have the students prepare the cases at the end of the semester after all text chapters have been read and discussed.

## Case 1 – An Overview

1-1 Lost in Translation: AOL's Assault on Latin America Hits Snags in Brazil
1-2 Unilever and Nestlé – Analysis
1-3 Nestlé – The Infant Formula Incident

## Case 2 – The Cultural Environment of Global Marketing

2-1 The Not-So-Wonderful World of EuroDisney
2-2 Instructor's Notes: Dealing with an Unexpected Bureaucratic Delay
2-3 Starnes-Brenner Machine Tool Company – To Bribe or Not to Bribe
2-4 When International Buyers and Sellers Disagree
2-5 Instructor's Notes: How Companies React to Foreign Corruption
2-6 Coping with Corruption in Trading with China

## Case 3 – Assessing Global Market Opportunities

3-1 Asian Yuppies – Having It All
3-2 Instructor's Notes: Developing a European Web Site for Levi's
3-3 Konark Television India
3-4 Swifter, Higher, Stronger, Dearer

## Case 4 – Developing global Marketing Strategies

4-1 Global Strategies – What Are They?
4-2 Tambrands – Overcoming Cultural Resistance
4-3 Instructor's Notes: Pricing a Product in Multiple Country Markets
4-4 Blair Water Purifiers India
4-5 Sales Negotiations Abroad for MRIs
4-6 Tough Decisions at Boeing
4-7 National Office Machines – Motivating Japanese Sales people: Straight Salary or Commission?
4-8 Alan AeroSpace – Communications Satellite Sales to Japan
4-9 AIDS, Condoms, and Carnival
4-10 Making Socially Responsible and Ethical Marketing Decisions: Selling Tobacco to Third-World Countries*

# CASE 1
# AN OVERVIEW

1-1 Lost in Translation: AOL's Assault on Latin America Hits Snags in Brazil
1-2 Unilever and Nestlé – Analysis
1-3 Nestlé – The Infant Formula Incident

## Case 1–1 Lost in Translation: AOL's Assault on Latin America Hits Snags in Brazil

1. We see most of AOL Brazil's problems as being of the controllable nature:

   a. Product quality – the initial CD-ROMs distributed "accidentally" included rock music and unexpected upgrades to browsers; both making users dissatisfied.

   b. The company did not act fast enough to secure the AOL.com.br domain site earlier on and then spoiled negotiations with the owner with their attorney-led approach.

   c. The brand name itself – America On Line/AOL – does not have the cache in Latin America that it does in the USA. One is reminded of the early problems USA Today had in Canada.

   d. Unlike the US market, AOL is not the pioneer in most Latin American countries. UOL and other "local" competitors are backed by phone companies and include strong content. Both this competitive factor and c. above, have yielded AOL's early market forecasts unreasonable.

   e. The choice of a Venezuelan partner for all of Latin America was a bad one. Certainly the Brazilian market is large enough and culturally distinct enough (Portuguese spoken is only the obvious dimension of cultural diversity) to warrant a separate entry strategy and/or tactic. AOL also appears to have suffered from both bad advice and lack of control given the JV entry strategy as implemented.

   f Its initial ad campaign was tremendously ethnocentric, emphasizing "biggest and best;" although the new "ease of use" approach may work better.

   g. Finally, the negotiations with UOL also seem to have been mismanaged as the firm was distracted with bigger fish in the US, that is, Time Warner, etc.

   h. Finally, perhaps on the "uncontrollable factors" might be the strong competition from UOL and the free service providers. Also, UOL insider status seems to have made a difference in AOL's success in Brazil.

2. Separate entry strategies were clearly warranted for the Brazilian market (large size and cultural distinctiveness). A range of options might have been considered from simply licensing technology to UOL (or some similar Brazilian partner) to purchasing UOL. The advertising campaign should also have been adapted avoiding the ethnocentric "AOL" and "biggest and best."

3. The fundamental mistake made by AOL in Brazil seems to be the assumption that a "business model" that works in the US can be used with little adaptation to Brazil. The company must step back and consider which aspects of its services technologies and marketing practices are readily exportable and which require adaptation to the local environment. Key to future successes avoiding problems down the road will be partnering with local companies or talent to take advantage of AOL's comparative advantages in this new major market. Finally, one might question another fundamental assumption of the AOL's corporate strategy. That is, is "torrid subscriber growth" in foreign markets really necessary for the firms future profitability? If so, this does not bode well for the long-term health of the company.

## Case 1–2 Unilever and Nestlé – An Analysis

This case is designed to engage students in searching on the Internet and to illustrate how two international companies that market worldwide, are very different on many dimensions. These two excerpts from the company statements will give the instructor the different philosophies and approaches of these two companies.

**Nestlé**

Nestlé is The World's Largest Food Company. Only two percent of sales are generated in Switzerland, our country of origin, and our management and staff reflect a truly international outlook. As a Company, we do not believe in mission statements, because one would either be so general as to become meaningless, or so specific that it wouldn't be applicable or relevant everywhere—we would like to offer a set of principles that will provide insight into the Company's attitudes and culture.

At Nestlé, we try to take the mentality and customs of individual countries into account, but there are some general guidelines that we apply everywhere. Those include:

- A positive attitude toward work
- A pragmatic, realistic approach to doing business
- An open-minded approach to the world
- A minimal number of systems and written guidelines
- A personal style of management
- An atmosphere of mutual trust
- An avoidance of showing off, windy rhetoric and hypocritical remarks
- An emphasis on practical experience and on the setting of good examples

Switzerland is home to Nestlé's Swiss subsidiary, its international headquarters and the registered office of Nestlé's holding company, but Nestlé does not regard its Swiss headquarters as the center of the universe. Decentralization is a basic principle of Nestlé. Our policy is to adapt as much as possible to regional circumstances, mentalities and situations. By decentralizing operational responsibility, we create strength and flexibility and are able to make decisions that are better attuned to specific situations in a given country. Policies and decisions concerning personnel, marketing and products are largely determined locally. This policy creates stronger motivation for Nestlé's executives and employees and a greater sense of identification with Nestlé's business. It is not Nestlé's policy to generate most of its sales in Switzerland, supplemented by a few satellite subsidiaries abroad. Nestlé strives to be an "insider" in every country in which it operates, not an "outsider."*

* http://www.nestle.com

**Unilever**

"Our purpose in Unilever is to meet the everyday needs of people everywhere—to anticipate the aspirations of our consumers and customers and to respond creatively and competitively with branded products and services which raise the quality of life. Our deep roots in local cultures and markets around the world are our unparalleled inheritance and the foundation for our future growth. We will bring our wealth of knowledge and international expertise to the service of local consumers—a truly multi-local multinational. Our long-term success requires a total commitment to exceptional standards of performance and productivity, to working together effectively and to a willingness to embrace new ideas and learn continuously. We believe that to succeed requires the highest standards of corporate behavior towards our employees, consumers and the societies and world in which we live. This is

Unilever's road to sustainable, profitable growth for our business and long-term value creation for our shareholders and employees.

Unilever is one of the most international companies in the world. The number of products in two main categories, Foods and Home and Personal Care, is vast. Unilever sells over a thousand brands, many of which are market leaders—in a country, in a geographic region or in the world.

The sales generated by its brands put Unilever among the top industrial companies in the world. Consequently Unilever has the financial strength to fund the investment in new markets and the development of existing businesses that drive its growth. The impetus of the last three years has seen it establish operating companies in Bolivia, Cuba, Israel, Lebanon, Nepal, Paraguay, Peru, Romania, Russia, Vietnam and Zambia."

Unilever is successful because consumers have learned that they can rely on the quality, efficiency and safety of its products. Unilever's care for customers and consumers is reflected not only in the products it provides, but in the way it provides them. For example, it believes that a fundamental part of being successful is having a sound environmental policy. This is increasingly expressed in the way Unilever designs and makes its products.

International in a local way

Unilever describes itself as 'international,' not 'global,' because it does not attempt to enter all markets with the same product. Half of Unilever's business is in food, where it is often essential to take a local view. Only a few products—like ice cream, tea and olive oil—successfully cross national or regional borders. Similarly, in detergents, the formulation Unilever sells in South Africa will differ from the one in France, because washing habits, machines, clothes and water quality are all different. Personal wash products, on the other hand, need to vary less, so there are strong international brands like Lux and Dove. The Unilever portfolio includes a balanced mix of local, regional and international brands which take account of the differences as well as the similarities in consumer needs.

Unilever is essentially a local company in all of the countries in which it operates. It remains close to the local market and its day-to-day operations are organized accordingly. Few international companies have such a decentralized style, with just 7% expatriate managers as the norm. Furthermore, expatriates come from many countries, exerting an internationalizing influence across the business.

There is a common Unilever approach to safety standards and personnel policies, whatever the country. In contrast, Unilever's attention to customers and consumers is explicitly local. Consequently, innovation can happen everywhere, not just at the center. Some of these initiatives later travel the world: for example, Magnum ice cream came from Germany, while Organic shampoo was developed in France and Thailand." *

* http://www.unilever.com

The statements above are taken from the Web pages of these two companies. Class discussion can focus on the different orientations, i.e., global versus international company. Do the two have the same philosophy or are they vastly different?

To expand the discussion, have a group of students study the Web pages of a U.S. company like General Foods, Campbell or some other international food company and discuss differences in philosophy among the three.

## Case 1–3 Nestlé – The Infant Formula Incident

### Summary of Case and Results

In response to a pamphlet entitled "Nestlé Kills Babies," published in 1974 by the Swiss consumer/activist group, *Arbeitsgruppe Dritte Welt,* Nestlé Alimentana filed a four-count libel suit against members of the organization. The pamphlet was a reprint of an earlier one entitled "Bottled Babies," published by a similar British group. Both alleged that false advertising had prompted mothers in LDCs to use infant formula instead of breast feeding, and consequently caused the deaths of thousands of children. However, the original pamphlet had not mentioned Nestlé or any of the other companies by name, and thus did not raise the issue of libel.

Three of the charges, which Nestlé subsequently withdrew, related to allegations made in the pamphlet about Nestlé's promotional methods in LDCs. The fourth charge, which led to a judgment against thirteen members of the group in June 1976, focused on the defamatory title "Nestlé Kills Babies."

In his decision, the judge stated that the cause behind the injuries and deaths was not Nestlé's products; rather, it was the unhygienic way they were prepared by end-users. Although Nestlé won its case, the firm's victory was diluted by (1) having to pay one third of the court costs and (2) being told by the judge to change its marketing methods to prevent further misuse of its products. The defendants were ordered to pay $120 each in damages to Nestlé and two thirds of court costs.

### Suggestions

Companies selling consumable products (foods, beverages, pharmaceuticals) to LDCs have long recognized the need to adapt their promotional techniques to their consumers who are, by and large, poor and illiterate. In recent years, one particular group of food producers—those firms making infant formula and other milk products—has come under severe attack by various religious, consumer and governmental organizations. Criticism focuses on two issues: (1) that companies allegedly use false advertising to induce mothers to substitute formula for their own milk, and (2) that firms are directly responsible when misuse of their products results in illness or death. The assault was dramatized in the recent Swiss case involving Nestlé Alimentana.

The responses of milk product manufacturers have ranged from writing corporate policies on LDC marketing to organizing industry councils and holding meetings with pressure groups. But most significantly, companies have altered marketing practices in ways that other firms making consumable items should find instructive. These changes include

**Tightening up direct selling methods.** A common practice is to have "mother-craft nurses," —local women who may be nurses, dietitians or midwives—visit clinics and homes to encourage doctors and consumers to use infant formula. Critics charge that these women are often unqualified to speak on nutrition and that they distort facts to make formula feeding more attractive than breast feeding. As a result, many firms now forbid representatives from discouraging breast feeding and demand that they go to clinics and homes only if invited or sent by a family doctor.

**Stressing nutritional training.** Firms are improving the nutritional instruction given to representatives. In addition, promoters are providing consumers with educational presentations, including seminars, films and brochures.

Such training not only combats misuse of products, but also benefits the manufacturer. For example, one corporation whose sales representatives in Indonesia conducted local demonstration on uses of a condensed-milk product found that the presentations accomplished several aims: (1) alerted the representative to problems people had in preparing and using the product, (2) served as a rough test market for the product and (3) helped to bolster the firm's image.

**Controlling distributors' promotional activities.** Manufacturers selling milk products through distributors have often given them free rein over local advertising. Some corporate executives worry about becoming too closely associated with distributors' advertising, fearing possible liability for erroneous claims made by distributors. However, such liability would be difficult to avoid in any situation involving a company's trademarks and products. A few firms, recognizing this, are currently monitoring all new promotional campaigns of distributors.

**Curtailing mass media advertising.** Several corporations that formerly advertised infant formula on TV, radio, billboards and newspapers are now relying solely on sales representatives.

**Improving labeling and directions for use.** Some firms have revised package instructions to ensure safety. For example, Wyeth Laboratories' X S-26 formula labels include the following: (1) comprehensive, easy-to-follow directions on preparing and storing the product (vital in areas lacking refrigeration and/or clean water), (2) a "suggested feeding table" giving the amount of formula and frequency of feedings according to an infant's weight and age, (3) a statement in bold type stressing the importance of following directions carefully and (4) a statement on the preferability of breast feeding newborn babies and the proper role for prepared formula in an infant's feeding.

**Developing promotional/instructional materials to help low-literacy users.** The International Council of Infant Food Industries, formed in 1975, is studying ways to improve communication methods for use in areas of high illiteracy. Possibilities include cartoons, pictures, radio programs and even sound trucks. (Use of new informational materials would be subject to approval of local authorities.)

### Price of Social Responsibility

For some firms, the cost of maintaining ethical standards is high. One large food company actually closed down its milk-processing plant in Pakistan because pasteurization laws were not being enforced, and local firms selling unpasteurized milk were gaining a competitive edge. Additionally, the quality of the firm's product was tarnished by local consumers who frequently diluted the milk with polluted stream water to "stretch" it for their own use or for resale.

In light of these problems, and others—such as the high cost of marketing and training, and the relatively low sales volume—some companies have contemplated withdrawing these products from LDC markets. However, the market potential for milk products in these countries is strong because of increasing populations and rising standards of living. In addition, the growing role of women in the labor force is creating a greater need for infant formulas. Thus, it appears that firms will remain in these markets.

### Notes to Instructors

The following considerations should be examined by the case discussants

1. The infant formula food was successful in certain countries and very detrimental in others. (Basically, the answer is in the controlled use by educated missionaries.) This may also indicate that reasonable use of the formula food and full use by medical and religious groups might be an answer, with monitored introduction to other areas. Education is a must.
2. The boycott groups are well organized and use modern political pressure. In addition, they are getting strong media coverage.
3. Nestlé is being isolated as the major contributor to this problem.

4. Nestlé is considered a non-American company, and therefore, U.S. government loyalty may begin to wane.
5. The longer the controversy carries on, the more costly the settlement will be.
6. The cross-cultural aspects of product introduction and communication activities must be better planned and monitored.
7. Corporate responsibility is not only what is defined by industry, but what is perceived by consumers.
8. Strong external affair (outside public relations activities) programs must be closely coordinated and monitored by the Nestlé headquarters.

**Update**

The Nestlé infant formula controversy continues after more than twenty years. In a 1984 agreement with the International Nestlé Boycott Committee, Nestlé agreed to cease distribution of free and low-cost formula in developing countries, except in need.

However, one Nestlé Infant Formula Audit Commission (NIFAC) alleges that a study conducted in 1989 in Mexico revealed that Institutions can have as much formula as they want and in many cases it [formula] is given to 100 percent of the children in developing countries.

Nestlé claims it provides only small amounts of free and low-cost formula. Further, their sales of infant formula in developing countries is less than 1% of $46.3 billion 1990 sales. The problem according to Nestlé, is that when Nestlé stopped giving out free formula rival infant-formula makers increased their free distribution. For example, when Nestlé stopped free formula in Thailand in 1988, rival companies filled the void.

In 1991, Nestlé announced it would stop all free and low-cost give aways in developing countries except for the limited number of infants who need it.[1]

Just after Nestlé's commitment to stop formula give aways in developing countries, American Home Products, the second largest infant formula marketer, unveiled a plan to stop providing free and low-cost infant formula to developing countries as well.

Nestlé and American Home have been under mounting pressure for defying the World Health Organization (WHO) guidelines by dumping large quantities of free and low-cost formula. In 1988, a Minneapolis-based adversary group launched a worldwide boycott against both companies. The companies say they have been in full compliance with the WHO code but that hospital administrators interpret in need broadly and provide free and low-cost formula on request. The boycott has now spread to 16 countries.

This step by the two companies is seen by some as an industry trend while others are more skeptical. In December 1991, *Advertising Age* reported that Nestlé began a series of advertisements advising women to breast-feed. Targeted at poor women who get free formula from the government, Nestlé has nothing to lose since they have no government contracts. The director of public affairs for Nestlé, said the new campaign is meant to promote breast-feeding to an undereducated audience.[2] In the long run, they may gain if this advertising campaign helps polish their tarnished image.

---

[1] Alix M. Freedman, to Curtail Infant Formula In Third World, *The Wall Street Journal*, January 30, 1991, A1.

[2] Bradley Johnson, Ads Pitch Breast-Feeding, Advertising Age, December 2, 1991, p. 40 and Vital Signs: A Medical Renegade Stands the System on Its Head; The Boycott Is Back, Health/Pac Bulletin, Fall 1990, V.20, No. 3 p. 42.

However, in another controversy, Nestlé has been accused of raising the specter of AIDS as a justification for bottle-feeding when the head of public relations at Nestlé UK told schoolchildren that the spread of AIDS in many African countries meant that mothers who are HIV positive "can't then breast-feed because the baby will then run the risk of getting AIDS." A few days later, the media reports were described as misleading and, further, Nestlé was not seeking to give the impression that HIV-infected mothers should not breast-feed.

In response to an editorial critical of Nestlé's alleged position on HIV and breast-feeding that appeared in an issue of a newsletter produced by a Nestlé shareholders' association, a Nestlé vice president said that the association represented only about 100 out of the 100,000 shareholders and has no claim whatever to speak for Nestlé. He said the company is in full agreement with the official WHO recommendations which note that the large majority of babies breast-fed by HIV-infected mothers do not become infected through breast milk and which emphasizes that where the primary causes of infant deaths are infectious diseases and malnutrition, breast-feeding should remain standard advice.

Regarding question 5 in the text, it will be quite important for Nestlé to cooperate with the local health and government officials IN EACH COUNTRY SEPARATELY in order to determine the best approach to handling the AIDS/infant formula problem. Each country has its own set of problems and circumstances and any promotional/advertising programs should be developed with much care. LOCALIZATION will be key.

**Films Available**

1. The most complete discussion of the Nestlé infant formula controversy is now available in a CD-ROM format from the Council for Ethics in Economics, 125 E. Broad Street, Columbus, OH 43215–3605, (614) 221–8661, FAX (614) 221–8707, www.businessethics.org.
2. **Into the Mouths of Babes** (CBS News, color, 35mm) is available through the National Council of Churches, Room 860, 475 Riverside Drive, New York, New York 10015. It is likely that a local chapter of INFACT, or a local third World Resources Center, will have a copy.
3. **Bottle Babies** (Dir. Peter King, Teldok Films, 1975 color, 26 min.) is the film mentioned in the case which heightened awareness of the issue. It is obviously oriented "against" the companies.

Some current articles on this controversial subject that the Professor may want to have students read in preparation for this case discussion are:

1. "Tailors Marketing of Infant Formula to Meet WHO Code Demands," *Business International,* April 30, 1982.
2. James C. Baker, "The International Infant Formula Controversy: A Dilemma in Corporate Social Responsibility," *Journal of Business Ethics,* #4, 1985, pp. 181–190.
3. Thomas V. Greer, "The Future of the International Code of Marketing of Breast-milk Substitutes: The Socio-Legal Context," *International Marketing Review,* Spring/Summer 1984, pp. 33–41.
4. Two publications available from the company are excellent. They are: "The Dilemma of Third World Nutrition," updated, 1985 and "The Role of Infant Formula in Developing Countries: The Resolution of a Conflict," 1985. Both of these are available from: Coordination Center for Nutrition, Inc. 1025 Connecticut Avenue NW, Suite 707, Washington, DC 20036–(212) 775–0180.
5. Alix M. Freedman, To Curtail Infant Formula In Third World, The Wall Street Journal, January 30, 1991, A1.
6. Alex M. Freedman, American Home Infant-Formula Giveaway to End, The Wall Street Journal, February 4, 1991, p. B4.g
7. Bradley Johnson, Ads Pitch Breast-Feeding, Advertising Age, December 2, 1991, p. 40 and Vital Signs: A Medical Renegade Stands the System on Its Head; The Boycott is Back, Health/Pac Bulletin, Fall 1990, V. 20, No. 3, p 42.
8. Prakash Sethi, Multinational Corporations and the Impact of Public Advocacy on Corporate Strategy; Nestlé and the Infant Formula Controversy (Norwell, MA: Kluwer Academic Publications, 1994)
9. If you are able to show one of the videos above an excellent contemporary article arguing in favor of Nestlé and the other infant formula makers is "The Corporation Haters," by Herman Nickel, *Fortune*, April 17, 1980. The combination of reading this article then viewing the video makes for the liveliest class discussions.
10. We also recommend a series of articles on the topic in the Journal of Macromarketing, Spring and Fall 1988 and Spring 1988. The academic arguments in the Fall 1988 are perhaps the most interesting: Mary C. Gilly and John L. Graham, "A Macroeconomic Study of the Effects of Promotion on the Consumption of Infant Formula in Developing Countries" (Spring 1988); Jean J. Boddewyn, "Comments on Gilly and Graham's Study" (Fall 1988); Bill Meade,

"Comments on Gilly and Graham's Study," (Fall 1988); and Graham and Gilly's "Rejoinder" (Spring 1989). These articles are also part of Meloan and Graham's International & Global Marketing Concepts and Cases, Irwin-McGraw-Hill (1998 and 1995).

11. Barry Meier, "Anglicans Mull New Step on Baby Formula," *New York Times*, 3/3/97, page 8, column 4.
12. "Mother's Dilemma: A Special Report," *New York Times*, 6/8/97, business/financial desk. This article provides more information on the HIV aspect of the infant formula problem.
13. Finally, see http://www.nestle.com/html/a.html.

**Back to the bottle?**

NAIROBI

MULTINATIONAL food companies have long been under attack for pushing milk powder at mothers who do not need it and cannot afford it. But the anti-bottle-feeding lobby is now in a quandary. Evidence is growing that around half the 3.8 million children infected with HIV contracted the infection at their mothers' breast.

In rich countries, HIV-infected women can be told to bottle-feed their babies. But the problem is more complicated in the developing world, where over 90% of child infections occur. The risks of bottle-feeding remain—breast-milk protects infants from all manner of other infections—and so does the cost.

Moreover, in even the most heavily infected areas, 70% of mothers do not carry the virus and, for them, breast-feeding is still by far the best option. The difficulty is that the vast majority of pregnant women in the developing world have no idea whether or not they are infected. Promoters of breastfeeding worry that large numbers of healthy women will switch to bottle-feeding just in case. Others fear that if bottle-feeding becomes a badge of infection, even women who know they are infected will continue to breastfeed to avoid being stigmatized.

Many of them have no alternative. Even where mothers have access to clean water to prepare artificial milk, a year's supply of powdered milk can cost over $700, more than the GNP per head in some heavily infected countries. Ironically, the cost is pushed up by high taxes, imposed to discourage bottle-feeding.

A few countries, such as Thailand, offer testing to all pregnant women, and give those who are HIV-infected free milk powder. But in Africa, where a woman is likely to be pregnant three times as often as in Thailand and where HIV infection ranges up to 25% of the population against Thailand's 2%, that solution is an expensive and distant dream.

# CASE 2
# THE CULTURAL ENVIRONMENT OF GLOBAL MARKETING

## Case 2–1 The Not-So-Wonderful World of EuroDisney

### Summary

This case tells the story of the planning, construction and early days of management of a new Disney theme park in France, Euro Disneyland ("EuroDisney"). Details are given on the background to the project and the expectations of success. Real-life results did not meet expectations. Problems were encountered requiring extensive adaptation of both strategy and tactics by EuroDisney's management. Eventually the parent company, The Walt Disney Company ("Disney") had to step in to organize a financial bail-out. Reasons for the poor performance of EuroDisney are suggested in the case, along with some implications for the future of the ambitious new theme park.

### Use of the Case and Teaching Objectives

The case is appropriate for use in both undergraduate and graduate international marketing classes. End-of-case questions are provided as a focus for class discussions.

The case allows the instructor to explore in considerable depth aspects such as:

- the role of environmental factors in shaping international marketing strategies;
- the impact of ethnocentric thinking on overseas investments;
- the need for adaptation (versus the desire for standardization) of company marketing policies abroad;
- market forecasting and assumptions about consumer response to foreign products and services;
- cultural conflicts between buyers and sellers; and
- issues involved in developing international marketing strategies, tactics and policies.

### Answers To Questions

1. What factors contributed to EuroDisney's poor performance during its first year of operation? Three types of factors can be identified from the case: (i) managerial errors of judgment; (ii) elements of consumer response; and (iii) environmental factors.

   (i) Students will easily be able to identify from the case a list of managerial errors relating to over-ambitious forecasts and real-estate investments, expensive or inappropriate park design and construction, flawed initial marketing, pricing, staffing, and park management policies.

   (ii) Disney management expected some 50% of park attendance to include French visitors. The French people in general proved to be reluctant in their response to this example of "Americana" in Europe. EuroDisney's management seriously underestimated negative attitudes among the French. Visitors of other nationalities were also unwilling to pay the high prices of EuroDisney or to stay more than one or two days (instead of the expected three days). Clearly, perceptions of the park's benefits among tourists differed from those of the American managers.

   (iii) In summer 1992, transatlantic airfare wars and currency swings made it cheaper to go to DisneyWorld in Florida than to EuroDisney in France, for many European tourists. Perhaps EuroDisney's management could not be expected to foresee such eventualities, but they should have planned for seasonal variations in attendance related to the poor winter weather of northern Europe. Also, better environmental monitoring would have alerted management to the approaching recession, which hit the whole of Europe in the late 1980s and persisted into the early 1990s.

2. To what degree do you consider that these factors were (i) foreseeable and (ii) controllable by either EuroDisney or the parent company, Disney?

   The narrative in the case makes it clear that managers and planners involved in the EuroDisney project were infected with over-confidence, led by Disney's "dynamic duo," chairman Eisner and president Wells. Both of these two had achieved significant successes for the company in previous years, and seemed to believe that their judgment was infallible: hence the grandiose real estate development plans, the ambitious financing, and rigid imposition of the "Disney way" of doing things in Europe.

   Students can debate how far Disney's management should be held responsible for being blind-sided to environmental events and being insensitive to cultural differences. Probably a lot of the early missteps can be attributed to poor judgment, particularly as corrections in strategy and tactics were made after the first year of operation. More marketing research in France and better environmental scanning would have helped make some of the unfortunate events at least foreseeable, if not entirely controllable.

3. What role does ethnocentrism play in the story of EuroDisney's launch?

   This question is a little more subtle than it might appear at first glance. For example, students may rush to judgment and say that "EuroDisney's managers should have known.. . . but it would be prudent to discuss separately the quality of management's decisions versus the nature of the product and the need for standardization across world markets.

   Disney's "product" is grounded in American life, culture, and entertainment traditions. Thus the question of how far to standardize or adapt the product offering overseas must be set in the context of its country-of-origin effect. In other words, to make EuroDisney completely "French" (by adapting to the local market) would have undermined the whole selling proposition.

   However, ethnocentrism does appear to have clouded management's judgment. It certainly played a role in the unwillingness of Disney's managers to even consider the need for some adaptation in Europe when marketing such an all-American product.

4. How do you assess the cross-cultural marketing skills of Disney?

   Based on a SWOT analysis (Strengths and Weaknesses, Opportunities and Threats) of the new theme park, one would probably conclude that the EuroDisney experience was an initial cross-cultural marketing failure, due primarily to rigid imposition of Disney rules and unwillingness to consider adaptations. After the first year of operations, greater sensitivity was shown and numerous small but important changes were made in marketing, operating and staffing policies.

5. a. Do you think success in Tokyo predisposed Disney management to be too optimistic in their expectations of success in France?

   Yes. The outstanding success of Tokyo Disneyland must certainly have given Disney's management the impression that managing theme parks overseas did not present any major problems. However, the false assumption was made that all foreigners would respond favorably to "Americana." The Japanese people visit America in great numbers and spend extravagantly, once here. They share a common fascination with the American way of life, fashions, and style of entertainment (such as MTV and movies).

   In contrast, Europeans are much more independent and value deeply their own cultural habits and traditions. There are pockets of active dislike of America among Europeans, left over from the 1960s when American firms were investing heavily in Europe. Greater research of the French market might have revealed some of these differences to Disney's management. Certainly when Eisner was pelted with eggs in Paris, he should have suspected that market entry might not be that easy.

5. b. Do you think the new theme park would have encountered the same problems if a location in Spain had been selected?

   The answer to this question depends on answers to earlier questions insofar as one is willing to sympathize with EuroDisney managers' mistakes or one is led to censor their lack of insight, sensitivity, and basic information about the French market. If one believes that uncontrollable variables affecting the economy (e.g., recession, currency swings) were largely responsible for EuroDisney's troubles, then these problems would also have been encountered in the Spanish market at that time. However, if one believes that many of EuroDisney's problems were the result of poor marketing practice, then it is possible that the same mistakes would have been made, regardless of the location. Alternatively, Disney's managers may have done better research in Spain and achieved a deeper understanding of this less familiar market.

   If one argues that EuroDisney's problems were primarily due to environmental factors such as poor weather in the off-season, then clearly Spain, with its Mediterranean climate, would have been a better choice of location. Nevertheless, Disney's management decision to pursue a market skimming policy to earn a fast return, might have led to poor attendance levels in Spain too.

6. Disney's entry strategy for Japan minimized risk and control. Their strategy for Europe was the opposite. The firm has been satisfied with neither. Having most recently been burned in Europe, the company's approach in China is much more like the Japanese model, letting the Chinese take the greater part of the risk (investment in hotels, etc.) and control. The company should recognize that each major expansion into country X will demand a unique approach and a new assessment of the potential risks and returns. Indeed, one would predict that ultimately Disney will be dissatisfied with the structure of the Hong Kong deal feeling perhaps that their return might have been greater had their commitment been less conservative in reaction to the bad experiences in France.

7. This question should lead to a lively discussion. Key factors of course will be population, per capita income, climate, and familiarity with Disney. Thinking out to the year 2010, potential sites might include:

   a. San Antonio, Texas
   b. Rio de Janeiro, Brazil or Buenos Aries, Argentina (Michael Eisner mentioned Latin America in his 1998 letter to investors) and President Bush is now promoting an American Free Trade Area to include both North and South America.
   c. Singapore/Malaysia area
   d. Bombay, India
   e. Southern Spain – likely to cannibalize from Paris Disneyland
   f. The Black Sea area, Sevastapol in the Ukraine

8. The experiences of American, Tokyo, and now Paris will help of course. But no matter what the new location, new and unforeseen financial and operational problems should be expected. Class members who are from or who have visited potential new locations might provide interesting insights regarding the feasibility of Disney expanding.

**References**

Further reading on subsequent events at Disneyland Paris and other actions taken by The Walt Disney Company is suggested below:


DeGeorge, Gail and Ronald Grover (1994), "Reanimating DisneyWorld," *Business Week*, (December 5), 41.

Dwyer, Paula (1994), "Is Disney Headed for the Euro-Trash Heap?" *Business Week*, (January 24), 52.

Grover, Ronald and Gail DeGeorge, "Theme-Park Shootout, A Host of New Competitors Has Disney Building Like Crazy," *Business Week*, 4/6/98, pages 66–67.

Longman, Phillip J. "No Sex S'il Vous Plait. We're Club Med, Can Disneyfication Save the French Resort?" *U.S. News & World Report*, 9/8/97, pages 46–47

Marcial, Gene G. (1994), "Could These Cats Pounce on Mickey?" *Business Week*, (December 5), 92.

Solomon, Jolie, Andrew Murr and Daniel McGinn (1994), "Disney: A Sudden Surrender in Virginia" *Newsweek*, (October 10), 46.

Toy, Stewart (1995), "Mickey Goes To Charm School, *Business Week*, (February 13), 8.

## Case 2–2 Instructor's Notes: Dealing with an Unexpected Bureaucratic Delay

Management eventually decided to abandon the project, while continuing to pursue another operation elsewhere in the country.

Payment, in this example, would have been illegal under the Foreign Corrupt Practices Act (FCPA) and its equivalents in countries that have ratified the Organization for Economic Cooperation and Development's (OECD) Convention Against International Bribery. Moreover, once the company had shown a willingness to pay, it might well have faced further demands as the project progressed. The decision to drop the project, though deeply frustrating, was the only sensible and legal option.

The company claimed organizational difficulties and thus managed to withdraw without causing embarrassment on either side. It had invested considerable time and effort in getting to know the country, the local market, and senior officials. It still hopes to recoup some of this investment from future projects. Having shown a determination to resist blackmail, it is less likely to receive further demands, but operating conditions will continue to be tough. International companies are under constant pressure to go along with bribery demands in many countries. Those hoping to operate ethically and legally worldwide must be prepared to withstand such pressures.

At the heart of the commercial corruption debate is a disparity between global principles and local practice. Few business people actively condone corruption, but it still occurs, and even some of the largest corporate names have been involved. Corruption occurs, in part, due to local power structures. For example, some regions give politicians or poorly paid government officials power over whether commercial projects succeed or fail. If commissions are regarded as customary or law enforcement is inadequate, local authorities can use this power to demand payment from commercial clients.

In theory, companies do not need to pay, and an increasing number of major corporations refuse outright. But many succumb. The most common justification is the pressure of competition.

In a recent survey of U.S. and European business directors, respondents were asked about the impact of bribery on their projects. Nearly 60 percent thought that companies that did not pay bribes lost international contracts. In an era of heightened competition, pragmatists have argued that paying bribes is an unavoidable part of doing business in certain countries. If they fail to comply, they will lose out to unscrupulous rivals.

It is now more generally understood that corruption impedes economic development. Partly for that reason, corruption is now firmly on the agenda of the World Bank, the International Monetary Fund, and the regional development banks. There is a general trend towards tighter enforcement of existing domestic laws against bribery. Similarly, the OECD convention against transnational bribery has made it easier to prosecute offenders for bribes paid abroad. Nongovernmental organizations (NGOs), most notably Transparency International, have launched campaigns against corruption, and these have been well publicized in the international press.

While corruption may seem endemic to international business, there is growing pressure for change from several different quarters. For example, in countries ranging from Pakistan to Indonesia and South Korea, there has been a domestic political backlash against corruption. Political leaders associated with graft have been humiliated and sometimes driven from power.

## Case 2–3 Starnes-Brenner Machine Tool Company–To Bribe or Not to Bribe

Several questions should be emphasized in the case; the question of ethics, the question of self-reference criterion and a more important question of what role should the marketer play; how much should they try to change the system and how much should they try to become a part of the system. A strong point should be made that in a country where bribery is part of the way of doing business, there is an identifiable system of how much bribes are made, how much for different activities, when paid and to whom paid. One retired British executive once graded bribes as: 5% of $200,000 will be interesting to a senior official below the top rank, while 5% of $200 million justifies the serious attention of the head of state.[1] Anyone being sent to a country where bribery is an important aspect of doing business should be well versed on the system of bribery in the country and be prepared to deal with it effectively.

**Pertinent Facts**

The Latin American sales effort of Starnes–Brenner Machine Tool Company of Iowa City, Iowa centers around a one-man operation in Latino. The company is changing its international marketing emphasis and is going to act more aggressively as an international firm. A new salesman is going to replace the Latino representative who is retiring. During the training period the new man who is a company man from the U.S., is introduced to the role bribery plays in doing business in Latin America. He questions the ethics of the practice and the rationality of it as a means of doing business profitably. The retiring representative points out that the firm in Latino, in addition to making a profit, is stimulating the economy of the country and that since bribery is a recognized means of doing business it is stimulating to the economy of Latino. He proposes that ethics will rise with an increase in the standard of living.

Bribery persists as a problem the world over. In China, many of the Republics of the former USSR, and elsewhere, the business person is confronted with the decision to bribe or not to bribe. The instructor may want to have the students review the section on Business Ethics in Chapter 5 before attempting this case. It may be useful to have them examine the case without using the decision tree for ethical and socially responsible decisions (Exhibit 5–4) and then to review the case using the decision tree. The advantage of using the decision tree is to help them focus their thinking on the consequences of their decisions.

One of the purposes of this case is to explore all the ramifications of bribery. A point raised in the case concerned bribery in the U.S. The attitude presented is that all others engage in wholesale bribery but that Americans are somehow above it all, except for isolated cases. Two articles that address issues of bribery both in the United States and elsewhere are recommended before discussion of this case. See "The Destructive Costs of Greasing Palms," *Business Week*, December 6, 1993, p.133–138 and Daniel B. Moskowitz, "Taking Aim at Bribes Overseas," *International Business*, February 1994, p. 110.

An excellent review of the present state of bribery around the world and international attempts to curtail the activities can be found in "Bye-bye To Bribes: The Industrial World Takes Aim at Official Corruption," *U.S. News & World Report*, December 22, 1997.

[1] Robert Keatley, "U. S. Campaign Against Bribery Faces Resistance from Foreign Governments, " *The Wall Street Journal*, February 4, 1994, p. A-10.

## Case 2–4 When International Buyers and Sellers Disagree

### Pertinent Facts

The disagreement is that a West German importer bought pork livers from a U.S. supplier. The buyer was expecting 100 percent male pig livers, but got 45 percent sow livers which the Germans consider inferior to the male pig liver.

The German firm had to dispose of the sow livers at a reduced price and wants the U.S. supplier to reduce his price accordingly on the sow livers.

The U.S. supplier refused to pay the $1,000 requested.

### Comments

Insofar as contract law is concerned, the crux of the problem seemed to be whether the phrases "customary merchantable quality" referred to standards in the United States, where the meat originated, or in the country to which it was exported. Many other firms in the industry awaited the arbitrator's decision because, while arbitral awards do not constitute binding precedents as such, they do provide some guidelines for the future.

The American Arbitration Association upheld the American exporter. The arbitrator found that, although there was some tendency in the U.S. for packers to distinguish between male pork livers and pork livers from sows, the practice was not so widespread as to constitute an implied term of the contract. If the German buyer wanted no sow livers included in the shipment, he should have stated so when the contract was made.

## Case 2–5 Instructor's Notes: How Companies React to Foreign Corruption

Risk vs. reward. Though considered a reality of doing business in some countries, corruption poses significant risks. When companies pay bribes, they do so in the hope of securing some special benefit and because they believe, usually incorrectly, that they have no choice. However, by paying, companies lose control. For example, if a company pays once, it will receive more demands. This applies both to simple grease payments for expedited work and to grand corruption engineered to secure contracts.

If the company does not get what it paid for, it is in no position to complain. There is no source of legal redress because the company has broken the law. Moreover, the company becomes vulnerable to various forms of blackmail. And, if the company enters into a corrupt relationship and then tries to suspend outstanding payments, it may face a variety of different threats, including the threat of violence.

For example, a Western company was operating in the former Soviet Union. A local manager paid regular bribes to authorities to secure a reduction in taxes. The regional director found out and, because of the company's high standards, promptly fired the manager. However, this did not solve the problem. A local mafia group, which was working with the tax inspectors, issued a series of death threats to the chief accountant. If the accountant revealed what had been happening, the thugs warned, he would be killed. The company was advised by its consulting firm to investigate the source of the threats and contact the officials to whom the tax inspectors reported. The company resolved the issue with the government in secret negotiations.

Preventing such corrupt practices requires a clear company policy. Most major international companies have codes describing their business principles, and these typically include a clause prohibiting bribery. However, experience shows that such codes will have little impact unless senior management actively supports them. Management must ensure that the policy is understood at all levels of the company. Furthermore, to successfully implement an anticorruption policy, businesses must police and support the ranks of managers, limit the use of middlemen, and communicate the policy to the company's subsidiaries.

In a survey of the business development directors of 50 American and 50 European companies, respondents were asked to identify the tiers of management most likely to be involved in corruption, distinguishing between senior management such as divisional directors, locally-based country managers, middle managers, and junior staff. The results of the survey indicated that locally-based managers were most likely to be involved in corruption, middle managers were next in line, and junior staff came last.

In some cases, middle-ranking executives may be more exposed because they are working in regions where corruption is systemic, but the problem goes deeper than that. All too often, country managers complain that they receive mixed messages from their superiors. They are told that they should observe the company code at all times, but they are most likely to gain promotion if they bring in more business. They may receive polite sympathy if they lose a contract because a competitor pays a bribe, but they will be rewarded for success, not failure. The implied message is that winning the contract is the overriding goal.

Many companies also face tension between the need to enforce corporate policy from the center and the desirability of a high degree of local autonomy. Corporate headquarters is often particularly reluctant to intervene in a local office that is making profits. The well established and apparently successful local manager who flouts corporate guidelines is, therefore, a common phenomenon.

Such comments show that codes of conduct are not sufficient on their own. If a policy is to be effective, companies will need to establish a broad network of support. First, middle managers are more likely to support codes of conduct if they are involved in drafting them. Statements of principle will be of limited value unless they reflect practical experience.

It is essential to train expatriate managers before they are posted to regions where corruption is systemic. Executives are much less likely to succumb to bribery demands if they are well versed in the principles of resistance. Finally, companies must encourage clear lines of communication based on trust. Managers need to feel confident that they can share ethical problems with their superiors. Where there is a genuine dilemma, the company is much more likely to find an acceptable solution if it draws on the expertise of both local managers and their head office superiors.

---

Source: John Bray, "The High Road to Profits," *Security Management*, April 2000, p. 46+. Also visit: www.oecd.org/subject/bribery/, www.crg.com and www.transparency.de for additional information.

## Case 2–6 Coping With Corruption in Trading With China

This is a good case to explore the broad issues of ethical, legal, and unethical decisions. While some of these examples are blatant misuses of power (the extortion cases) some are minor but nevertheless unethical. Reality may dictate the necessity of paying but students should realize that some moral codes would dictate that they not pay. Others may just wink at the issues. Each student must decide his or her own moral standards. On a strictly legal basis, most of the activities would be considered illegal.

1. All the bribes, payments or favors mentioned in the case would be illegal under the FCPA. The one exception may be a trip or payment that simply ensures that the official does what he or she is supposed to do. The case of the PRC bank official that refused to issue a letter of credit until he was invited on a trip is obviously a case of extortion on the part of the official but whether or not it would be considered as illegal under the FCPA is questionable. Would a trip be considered a small payment? That may be an issue that cannot be answered outside of a court.
2. All requests for payments by an official who has the authority to deny a sale is considered as extortion. Some examples in the case are:

   Trips built into cost of machines – extortion.

   Trip in exchange for a letter of credit – extortion

   Overseas education for children – extortion

   Cash payments for sales – extortion

   Dismantle the products for inspection if trips are not offered – extortion

   All offers to an official to have the official break his/her country's laws are considered subornation. Some examples of subornation in the case are:

   Purchase black market import and export licenses – subornation

   Paying customs officials in a southern province to reduce the dutiable value of imports – subornation
3. All are illegal under the FCPA with the possible exception of the one lubrication payment that was paid to ensure that the official carried out his/her official responsibility.
4. Even if the FCPA did not exist, such behavior outlined in the case would be unethical. It hurts the country in the long run, adds to illegal behavior, increases prices for the benefit of officials only, and, in general, is corrupt.
5. Yes, there is reason to hope that the large MNCs will change their behavior. At this writing already bills to comply with the OECD treaty have been submitted to legislators in Germany, the Czech Republic, Belgium, and Japan. Also, in China it will be particularly interesting to see who influences whom – that is, will more direct contact with the relatively "clean" Hong Kong system (Transparency International rated #18) help "clean up" the larger China system (TI rated #41), or vice-versa?
6. A variety of actions are possible. Some of those are:
   a. Pay the bribe – illegal and unethical with all the associated ramifications
   b. Report the requested bribe to person's superior
   c. Report the requested bribe to a local enforcement agency
   d. Report the requested bribe to a local news agency

e. Negotiate legal alternatives such as paying for community improvements

f. Check with local expert or partner

g. Usually students can come up with a list of more than a dozen alternatives, some of them humorous

A study on the effects of corruption on administration performance by the World Bank and others made the following estimates on what corruption costs.

**What Corruption Costs Around the World**[2]

| **Corrupt Activity** | **Economic Cost** |
|---|---|
| government bureaucrat accepts "speed" money to issue licenses | 3% to 10% premium above licensing fee |
| Organized crime, with sanction of local officials, controls and sets prices in markets | Goods sell at 15% to 20% premium |
| Tax collectors permit underreporting of income in exchange for a bribe | Income tax revenues reduced by up to 50% |
| Government officials order expensive capital goods, or overpay or over-invoice for public works, in exchange for kickbacks | Goods and services priced 20% to 100% higher than necessary |

The professor may have the students read the following in preparation for the case discussion. Certainly have the students visit the Transparency International Web site referenced in the book.

Shengliang Deng, A New Look At Ethics in International Business, *The International Executive*, Vol. 34, No. 2, March/April 1992, pp. 151–162.

PRC Trade – "Where for Some Payoffs Are a Way of Life," *Business Asia*, June 24, 1991, pp. 216–217.

"The Destructive Costs of Greasing Palms," *Business Week*, December 6, 1993, p. 136.

Daniel B. Moskowitz, "Taking Aim At Bribes Overseas," *International Business*, February 1994, p. 110 – 13i

"The Gloves are Coming Off In China," *Business Week*, May 15, 1995, pp.60–61.

[2] Sources: Robert Klitgaard, *Controlling Corruption* (University of California Press, 1991); World Bank, *The Effects of Corruption on Administrative Performance*, and "The Destructive Costs of Greasing Palms, "*Business Week*, December 6, 1993, p. 136.

# CASE 3
# ASSESSING GLOBAL MARKET OPPORTUNITIES

3-1 Asian Yuppies – Having It All
3-2 Instructor's Notes: Developing a European Web Site for Levi's
3-3 Konark Television India
3-4 Swifter, Higher, Stronger, Dearer

## Case 3–1 Asian Yuppies–Having It All

### Synopsis

This short case presents a profile of Asian Yuppies in five countries, namely Hong Kong, Singapore, South Korea, Taiwan, and Thailand. Along with some demographic data, information is given about the brand preferences and shopping habits of young people in these markets. Although not wealthy by U.S. standards, Asian Yuppies constitute a very viable, growing segment in their own terms. Case questions address market segmentation issues leading to a discussion of appropriate marketing strategies.

### Teaching Suggestions

An important element in this case is to confer upon students some familiarity with the geography of the Pacific Rim. Attention should be paid to the relative distance between each market (or the relative proximity), a factor which will impact the choice of marketing strategy. Also relevant is some reference to the cultural environment focusing upon languages spoken in these countries, values and lifestyles. It is useful here to remind students of the increasing homogenization of world markets, particularly among the young where Westernization is very popular. Levitt's globalization thesis is very relevant here.

In order for students to answer the questions effectively, the instructor should remind them of the various bases for market segmentation (geographic, demographic, psychographic, and product-related), along with the differences between strategies of market concentration or multi-segment marketing. Market concentration or niche marketing relies upon serving one segment across a number of countries. A multi-segment strategy presupposes that the company will offer a line of differentiated products to a number of segments either within a country or across several countries.

If students conclude that Yuppies in the five markets are overwhelmingly similar in their consumer behavior, then a standardized concentration strategy featuring a global brand-name product will be appropriate. However, more realistically, students should be led to recognize that there exist some important differences in demand both within and between countries. Although wants and needs may be similar, buying power based on income differs notably between segments of young people. A hint of this is given in the case by the references to the cheaper products, Secret and Scoupe, designed to meet the needs of less affluent, but equally fashion-conscious young consumers.

Useful background information and ideas for the instructor on the global upscale market can be found in the following reference which identifies three segments of upscale consumers: the truly affluent, conspicuous consumers, and indulgers.

### Discussion of Case Questions

1. Asian Yuppies appear to be very similar in age, lifestyle, and values across national boundaries in Pacific Rim countries, with shared preferences for brand-name, high-touch products. The key difference between members of the "Yuppie" lifestyle is their ability to buy, i.e., income. Therefore, demographic segmentation based on income, along with geographic and psychographic segmentation will allow the marketer to identify large segments of consumers across the five nations who have similar buying power and lifestyles. Products can then be developed to satisfy this homogeneous demand. Alternatively, a company might examine the benefits associated with its current product offering and then seek out the consumer segment whose needs can be satisfied by this product.
2. Given that there exists an easily identifiable "Yuppie" segment in each of the five countries, marketers have the opportunity to implement a global marketing strategy by focusing on this

well-defined market segment. If the company is small or just entering the Asian market, it may wish to use a strategy of concentration on key markets in order to establish a presence. Larger companies with more resources and a full product line will be better positioned to serve several segments across several geographic markets at one time. For example, it is possible to sell a high price brand-name item to the truly affluent Yuppies in several countries, alongside a cheaper version targeted to the Yuppie emulators who are less wealthy.

**Outlook For The Future**

Reference is made in the case to the expected demographic growth in the Pacific Rim countries. Sheer numbers of consumers, whether or not they are "truly affluent" or merely "indulgers," argue in favor of serious study of market opportunities in the region. Synergy will be achieved by using effective market segmentation as a basis for developing a multi-segment global marketing strategy.[1]

**ASIAN YUPPIES – WHAT THEY MAKE, WHAT THINGS COST**

| **Earnings** | **Hong-Kong** | **Singapore** | **Seoul** | **Taipei** | **Bangkok** |
|---|---|---|---|---|---|
| Annual Income – 32 year-old banker | $35,000 | $32,000 | $31,000 | $18,000 | $12,000 |
| Per Capita Gross Domestic Product | 10,000 | 11,000 | 5,000* | 7,300* | 1,200* |
| **Prices** | | | | | |
| Two-Bedroom Apartment within an hour's commute | 200,000 | 240,000 | 140,000** | 230,000 | 50,000 |
| BMW | 45,000 | 49,000 | 49,000 | 51,000 | 43,000 |
| Gold Wristwatch | 5,000+ | 5,000+ | 5,000+ | 5,000+ | 5,000+ |
| Large Refrigerator | 1,250 | 1,700 | 1,950 | 1,150 | 2,400 |
| Sony Audio-visual Laser Disk player | 530 | 530 | NA | 680 | 730 |
| Remy Martin VSOP Cognac | 27 | 43 | 140 | 60 | 60 |
| Ralph Lauren Men's Polo Shirt | 40 | 50 | 55 | 60 | 60 |
| Round of Gold on Weekdays | 70 | 53 | 64 | 62 | 15 |
| Dinner for Two at a Trendy Restaurant | 80 | 80 | 55 | 60 | 35 |

*Figures are for South Korea, Taiwan, and Thailand

**First-time buyers often pay less under a government lottery.

[1] Amine, Lyn S. (1992), "Global Marketing to Upscale Consumers The Need for Segmentation," in *The Globalization of Consumer Markets*, edited by Salah S. Hassan, Haworth Series on International Business Binghampton, NY.

## Case 3–2 Instructor's Notes: Developing a European Web Site for Levi's

This case will require that students gather information from the Internet and be as involved as the Instructor wants. While the technical design of a Web site is not suggested, the response to this case covers marketing strategy, issues and questions related for one, two, or three possible Web strategies. Issues that may be addressed are:

1. How rapidly is e-commerce growing in Europe?
2. Will a Web site provide any solution to the parallel market problem?
3. What are the main issues such as language, pricing for different country markets, service fulfillment, and so on, that must be addressed in the development of a Web site?
4. Should high-tech fitting systems in stores be established so that a customer can get scanned in a retail store, store the measurements on the Web, and, when a customer wants to order, use the stored measurements.

The company has devised a three-point plan to address its decline in Europe. Phase one is improving store presentation and stock flow. Its new retailing concept is based on extensive research and embraces a wealth of detail related to buying a pair of Levi's jeans. Out go the wood and Americana formerly seen in Levi's stores and concessions. In comes a modern, energetic look epitomized by the Levi's London store on regent Street. Levi's is also taking charge of its own logistics in retail stores where it operates concessions in order to better manage stock.

Phase two of Levi's revival plan has been new product innovation, seen most visibly in the new range of Engineered Jeans.

Phase three is improved advertising that describes product attributes more clearly. This includes ads featuring Engineered Jeans.

Early evidence suggests Levi's has managed to turn things around but it still must learn how to make money selling in the new shopping mall, the Internet.

See also:

Ernest Beck, "Levi's Takes An International Approach With Its New Marketing Pitch in Europe," *The Wall Street Journal,* September 5, 2000, p. B13

## Case 3–3 Konark Television India

### Synopsis

Konark Television is a major manufacturer of black and white and color television sets in India. The primary issue in the case concerns Konark's distribution objectives and its distribution strategy to compete in a highly competitive industry that is facing an imminent shakeout. Moreover, the state government of Orissa has just announced that Konark will no longer enjoy a state sales tax exemption, making the retail price of Konark sets the same as retail prices for larger competitors.

To resolve the issues in the case, students need to undertake analyses of the company's consumers, competitors, and dealers. They need to analyze the company's internal strengths and weaknesses. They should be asked to make strategic and tactical recommendations. The case is complex and full of learning possibilities.

### Teaching Objectives

The case can be used to meet several teaching objectives. Students should learn that:

1. Typical channel of distribution decisions for a manufacturer in an international setting include choosing market areas, identifying and selecting wholesalers and dealers, motivating wholesalers and dealers, managing conflict, and controlling wholesalers and dealers.
2. Almost all members of an international channel of distribution desire to gain power and to achieve some degree of control over channel activities.
3. A multichannel strategy often increases a manufacturer's control over dealers and wholesalers. However, the strategy must be executed carefully or it will increase channel conflict.
4. To develop a distribution strategy requires that the firm first have distribution objectives.

### Teaching Suggestions

Given the complexity of the case, Konark Television India should be assigned in the latter half of the course, particularly after students feel some sense of competence in analyzing cases. The Indian setting has not been troublesome at all, given the description of consumers in the primary segment in the case section headed *"Indian Consumers."*

The case can be used for discussion or testing purposes. A class period of 75 minutes minimum is needed. Discussion begins well when the instructor reads the following two paragraphs taken from a visitor's letter (written in India in 1989 to friends in the U.S.):

I awoke about 9:00 a.m. on Sunday in Dr. Nayak's house, still suffering from what seemed like terminal jet lag. The din outside my bedroom was incredible. On opening the door, I saw a room filled with 16 people! All were focused intently on the TV, which appeared to be playing a melodrama set in ancient India. Later that day I learned that the people in the room consisted of the cook and his family, the sweeper and two friends, Dr. Nayak's family, plus Dr. Nayak's next door neighbors. The program was *"Ramayana,"* a religious epic in serial form.

Next Sunday, I went for a walk at about the same time. About a mile from the house I came upon a village near a river. Here the same scene was repeated but on a much larger scale. There must have been a hundred people in an open area watching the same program on a TV placed on a shaded stand. No one so much as glanced at me as I went by. "This program is like the Super Bowl," I thought, "except that its share is twice as high!"

This start begins discussion in an interesting manner and emphasizes a point in the case that there is, indeed, much latent demand for TVs in India. Discussion then can proceed along lines suggested by questions presented in the next section. A typical class session might cover three or four of these questions; the balance could be used as a follow-up written assignment or as an in-class exam.[2]

**Areas for Discussion/Analysis**

A. **Describe the influence of governmental policy on Konark's marketing strategy.**

On the surface, the case seems to represent a company focussing only on its domestic market. Thus, students usually begin their comments by noting the "normal" influences of a national government on business activities inside its borders. They describe such things as the Indian government's attitude toward the industry as a luxury industry and "capable of bearing heavy taxes." They note the high import duties placed on component parts brought into the country and the heavy excise taxes levied on assembled sets. They might guess at a balance of payments problem, a lack of hard currency, and a limited ability of Indian TV sets to compete in world markets as consequences of government policy.

Yet in another sense, the case illustrates a typical international setting. Students should recognize that Konark faces a bewildering set of economic conditions, regulations, restrictions, languages, and governments as it moves from one Indian state to another. An earlier presentation on the political, social, and economic conditions in India would heighten this realization. Alternatively, the Instructor might assign the U.S. State Department's "Background Notes on India" as required reading before students discuss the case. This brief note is sufficient to give students an understanding of conditions in India, and costs only $1. Students should conclude that Konark is really "exporting" its TV sets to other Indian states, given these states' great diversity and their sales tax policies favoring the production of sets inside their borders.

B. **Describe the buying process from the consumer's perspective.**

This question is important from the standpoint of having students understand consumers in a (very) foreign culture and economy. Yet, students should conclude that upscale consumers in India are more similar to upscale consumers in the U.S. than they are to lower class Indians!

The buying process for an expensive consumer durable consists of a series of steps: problem recognition, information search, alternative evaluation and decision, purchase, post-purchase outcomes. Student discussion might proceed as follows.

According to the case, the target market presently consists of "affluent middle and upper social classes," some 100 to 200 million Indians. (Once this segment begins to mature, Konark might target a much larger segment consisting of middle market consumers.) Almost every household in the target segment is aware of television and desires at least one set. Problem recognition can be stimulated by TV advertising in various media, dealer promotions, group viewing in a neighbor's house, shipping visits to a dealer, etc. The product is likely a status symbol.

Prospective buyers will actively search for information. Marketer dominated sources include advertisements and dealers. Consumer dominated sources consist of opinion leaders via word of mouth. Students should deduce that first time buyers are especially careful shoppers who find it difficult to compare technical merits of this rather complex product (much like first time buyers of home computers in the U.S.). Instead, these buyers will rely greatly on the advice of a trusted friend or salesperson. Most buyers want to bargain with the salesperson to get a good price.

Once purchased, the TV set will be carefully placed in a sitting room. Invited guests as well as domestic help will stare at the device and take pleasure in its performance. Within a few months, a large external

[2] These teaching notes were prepared by Professor James E. Nelson, University of Colorado at Boulder.

antenna or VCR may be added to improve the viewing experience. Later, the household may add a second TV.

To complete the consumer analysis, the instructor might summarize the situation as follows:

"The market is immense and growing. The purchase is important to the buyer in economic and social terms. Buyers often shop around and compare alternatives; they have difficulty evaluating technical aspects of the product and must rely on opinion leaders and dealers for much information. They like to negotiate a fair price."

C. **How would you assess the competition?**

Level of competition in the industry is intense. The industry is expected to shrink from over 140 manufacturers to just 20 or 30. Because TVs are the early stages of the product life cycle, competitors are racing to stimulate primary demand and to establish brand awareness. Competitors quickly need to develop a large dealer network—to sell the product and to assure consumers that service is both available and convenient. They need to find dealers before dealers agree to carry a competing line or two.

Competition is probably equally intense in terms of advertising. Only the "big boys" can afford large budgets with the result that smaller firms will soon disappear. Most advertising budgets are spent in the print media. (Why advertise TV's to non-owners using the TV medium?) Product features probably are a less intense basis of competition. Most products marketed by major competitors have similar features: differences in quality and performance are "difficult for consumers to recognize." Style and appearance are important for color sets.

Students should spend a few minutes discussing price competition. They should conclude that price is to some degree unimportant for color TVs as long as it is within an acceptable range. Of course, every buyer would like to save Rs. 500 on the purchase but Rs. 500 is typically less than 5% of the total price. Besides, the ability of the buyer to obtain, say, a Rs. 300 reduction from list price via bargaining may be more satisfying than to pay a comparable full price. Price is a more important consideration in buying a black and white set.

D. **How effective are the Konark showrooms?**

The effectiveness of Konark's showrooms can be examined in qualitative and quantitative terms. From a qualitative perspective, a good retail outlet should display numerous models that are produced by two or more manufacturers. (However, Konark does not permit its dealers to carry competing products.) Consumers want to compare performance, prices, and styles. Consumers need assurance on operation, service, and warranty because the price of a TV set is high relative to income and because friends and neighbors will be viewing. Consumers want to bargain with the dealer to get a fair price.

Now, Konark showrooms can do only some of these things. Showrooms cannot stock and sell competing TV sets; nor can they bargain on price. However, showrooms can display a full line of Konark products and can provide much better education and "push" than a dealer. They can collect marketing research information about consumers' likes and dislikes. They also can help Konark management understand dealer problems and complaints. Showrooms probably are a sore point with some dealers because they represent lost sales and a threat to the dealer's ability to continue to carry the line. Showrooms shift some channel power back to Konark. (A parallel in the U.S. that most students will recognize are the growing numbers of outlet malls/stores for fashion and other goods.) On balance, students should conclude that Konark showrooms compete with Konark dealers to some degree, particularly when showrooms are located close to dealers.

From a quantitative perspective, students need to analyze financial data for the showrooms. A statement in the case permits an estimate of Konarks' sales for 1990 at Rs. 800 million and 333,500 units. Half of these amounts—Rs. 400 million and 167,000 units—come from the home state of Orissa where the 10 showrooms are located. The showrooms account for only 5% of Orissa sales or Rs. 20 million and 8,350 units. The showrooms incur a total cost to Konark of Rs. 1.0 million, an amount that Konark would not pay if these units were sold instead through the state's 250 dealers. The dealers receive an average margin of Rs. 320 per set. Thus, if dealers had sold these units, Konark would have given up a total margin of 8,350 units x Rs. 320 or Rs. 2.6 million. This amount is much more than Konark's cost for the showrooms. However, Konark also ties up its capital in showroom inventory and it may incur hidden costs in the form of additional overhead.

E. **Recommend elements of Konark's distribution strategy.**

Students usually plunge headlong into a discussion on this topic. They start to describe selective coverage strategy, complete with Konark-owned showrooms and a few branch offices in distant states. They are eager to expand into new market areas because a strategic window is open. All these suggestions are good but poorly timed.

That is, early into this discussion the instructor might call for a time out with a comment like, "While I agree with much of what we've just heard, I'm uneasy because we seem to have the cart before the horse here. That is, we're discussing distribution strategy when we don't even have a good idea on distribution . . .?" The missing topic is *objectives.* Students should be pressed to identify several distribution objectives for Konark. Examples include:

- Improve the quality and size of Konark's dealers.
- Reduce the number of Konark's dealers.
- Improve dealer cooperation; reduce channel conflict.
- Expand the dealer network into one new state each year.
- Gain more control over the dealers.

Once Konark knows what it wants to accomplish with its channel of distribution, it can devise a distribution strategy.

Konark's distribution strategy should be based on large, healthy dealers. In general, large dealers when compared to small dealers can carry more inventory from which buyers may choose; they can be reached more efficiently; they can be better trained to sell and service Konark products; they can be more highly and easily motivated because Konark sales are substantial; they have a better image; they are easier for consumers to find; they make cooperative advertising more effective. Most importantly a smaller number of larger dealers should be easier for Konark to control.

The distribution strategy should include a few Konark showrooms. Showrooms are profitable and help keep dealers in line. However, too many showrooms will make dealers nervous and resentful because of sales perceived to be lost to the showrooms. Probably the best strategy here is to promise dealers that Konark will never: have more than one showroom for every 30 or so dealers; locate showrooms within an existing dealer's sales area; permit showroom salespeople to bargain on price.

Students should undertake an analysis of the branch office vs. independent distributor issue. Disregarding the home state of Orissa, Konark has eight branch offices that will account for about Rs. 240 million in Konark sales revenue in 1990 and three independent distributors that will total about Rs. 160 million. (The single branch office in Orissa accounts for the other Rs. 400 million in Konark revenue and should be considered outside the present analysis.) If the eight branches were replaced by eight distributors, Konark would pay a 3% margin on the Rs. 240 million or Rs. 7.2 million. In contrast, the cost of operating the eight branch offices is given at about Rs. 10 million. Thus, it would seem to be to Konark's advantage to replace branches with distributors. Distributors also would accept risk of loss and may spread some of their overhead over products supplied by other manufacturers.

However, students should also present qualitative arguments in support of the branches. Branches offer much more control than do distributors. Branches probably provide better service and repair; production personnel at the branches should be better trained and should assemble sets having fewer defects. Finally, branches permit Konark to be one step closer to dealers and to better understand conditions in the field. On balance, Konark would be well advised to keep their existing branches but perhaps control their expenses more effectively to bring branch office costs more in line with distributor margins.

The instructor might end this discussion by posing a question raised at the very end of the case, "How does this distribution strategy combat the loss of the sales tax exemption in Orissa? This loss means a 'level playing field' as far as Konark and the larger national competitors are concerned." The answer is that all aspects of the new distribution strategy help combat the loss of the exemption. However, students ought to conclude that the burden of combating the loss should be limited not just to distribution. Instead, Konark's entire *marketing and business* strategy must be examined in a total effort to compete.

F. **What short-term actions would you have Konark take to motivate and control its dealers?**

Short-term actions should be consistent with Konark's distribution objectives and strategy and should accomplish one or more of several things: Dealers must be motivated, trained, rewarded, and controlled. Once recognition of this objective is achieved, the instructor might divide students into groups of three or four and give them 15 minutes to come up with a list of specific actions.

Actions to motivate dealers can be either positive or negative in terms of reinforcement. The bulk of Konark activities probably should be oriented toward the first category. Reinforcements themselves can be either monetary or nonmonetary. For example, sales contests can be structured so that winners receive money, recognition, and praise. Quotas, when met, can result in gifts, travel, framed certificates, or mention in a newsletter. Sales meetings can recognize salespeople or dealers that have met quarterly sales objectives set by Konark. A "mystery shopper" program might be started to recognize and reward outstanding performance.

Dealer personnel can be trained by capable Konark field representatives on successful sales techniques, Konark product knowledge, and competitors' products. Personnel can be trained on service procedures and dealers shown how to make money on service activities. Training can be conducted at dealer facilities or at Konark headquarters.

Dealers must be adequately rewarded. Students readily understand that the very nature of a retail margin means that it is "incentive compensation" —the more you sell, the more you earn. However, Konark also should devise one or more short-term programs each year that reward in the form of bonuses or free goods. And, again, not all rewards in short-term programs have to be monetary or economic based. Praise, recognition, and extra support often can be as effective as cash.

Students should recognize that some negative or punishment activities also will motivate Konark dealers. If one or two dealers lose the Konark line for failing to live up to the terms and conditions identified in case Exhibit 2, then remaining dealers will take note and perhaps change their own behaviors. Remaining dealers must understand why Konark took such actions and should recognize the behaviors exhibited by the dropped dealers as unacceptable.

Actions to control dealers are perhaps the most difficult to devise and execute. Dealers are, after all, independent businesses. To develop some control over dealers, Konark should begin by making its expectations about dealer performance absolutely clear. Expectations can be communicated by the "Terms and Conditions" document, visits to individual dealers, newsletters, sales meetings, objectives and quotas imposed on dealers, and informal conversations. Konark can achieve control most likely through the use of reward power and expert power. It probably cannot achieve control via coercion until sales of Konark products become so important to a dealer that a threat to pull the line away will be seen as substantive.

**Summary**

In summary, the Instructor might present the learning objectives that began this note, to the extent that discussion relevant to the objectives actually took place in the classroom. The instructor might also draw parallels between the case and conditions in the West. Many high-tech products (e.g., personal computers, home security systems, home entertainment centers, video camcorders) face similar conditions with respect to first-time buyers as Konark. Many manufacturers employ multichannel strategies (e.g., IBM Product Centers vs. IBM sales at Sears; Sony Gallery of Consumer Electronics in Chicago vs. their normal channels).

Finally, the instructor could use the case as a springboard to discuss the issue of marketing LDCs. Just how different is it than marketing in developed countries? Should multinational firms in developed countries target selected LDCs or should they instead restrict efforts to the "Triad Markets" (U.S., Europe, and Japan) where cultures, life styles, business practices, and economies are so similar?

## Case 3–4 Swifter, Higher, Stronger, Dearer

There are several juicy topics addressed in this case—three are perhaps most useful. One is the growing importance of services and entertainment in international trade. Another is the fascinating interaction of professional athletics institutions and global communications companies. The case is also useful as a context for setting up international negotiations simulations for classroom play.

1. The pricing approach Peter Ueberroth used for pricing the 1984 Los Angeles Olympic broadcast rights makes sense here. He set up a bidding scheme in the U.S. pitting ABC, NBC, and CBS against one another. ABC bid highest and agreed to pay $250 million to broadcast the 1984 Olympics to Americans. Ueberroth then turned his attention to Japan. He reasoned that Japan population was about half that of the United States and Japan at the time had a per capita income about equal to the U.S. He also knew that Japanese consumers had more color televisions per capita that Americans. Finally, the value of the Games varies according to the relative time zone and the associated convenience for TV viewers. Based on all these factors his first offer to the Japanese was $90 million. A similar calculus might be used for each of the five markets listed in question #1.

2. The key factor in these kinds of negotiations is what Fisher and Ury[3] call the BATNA, that is, the Best Alternative to a Negotiated Agreement. That is, in 1984 Ueberroth had three alternatives in the U.S.—ABC, NBC, and CBS. Because of that market structure, one seller and three buyers, he was able to extract the maximum "rents" for the 1984 games. However, in Japan he negotiated with only one customer, a consortium of Japanese network lead by NHK. Thus, he was only able to extract about $20 million from the Japanese because he had no other good alternative except not selling the broadcast rights at all.

   So the class might be broken up into several groups for simulated negotiations. Having read the case they should be prepared. You might allow one class session (say 60–90 minutes) for the teams to prepare for the negotiations, another class session for the actual negotiations, and a third for comparisons of outcomes and feedback.

   You might break up a class of 36 students into the following teams:

   A team of 3 IOC representatives negotiating with a team of 3 NHK (Japanese) reps

   A team of 3 IOC with a team of 3 Chinese

   A team of 3 IOC reps with three teams (of two each) of Australian reps, each representing a different TV network

   A team of 3 IOC reps with a team of 3 EU reps (they also formed a consortium in past negotiations)

   A team of 3 IOC reps with three teams (of two each) of Brazilian reps, each representing a different TV network

   These are of course just guidelines, but this set up does work quite well. The teams selling to the Australians and Brazilians need not be given specific instructions to or how to set up a bidding process. It's actually more interesting to let them think it through and organize it themselves.

3. The Scottish Claymores make a nice hypothetical pricing problem including other investment criteria. Currently all the WFL teams are jointly owned by the NFL and Fox, and there are now no current plans to sell the teams to individual owners as in the States. However, such a sale is certainly within the realm of possibility given the dynamic nature of the global entertainment and

[3] Roger Fisher and William Ury, *Getting to Yes*, New York: Penguin, 1980.

communications industries. Pertinent information includes population, income, TV viewing habits, and interest in American football in the European countries. The attached article from the Washington Post provides crucial recent information that you may or may not wish to provide for your students. The prices of recent sales of NFL teams have run between $500 – $800 million. All things considered perhaps, $50 million makes sense for the Claymores as a long-term investment.

**Useful References**


Echikson, William "Making the Games Run on Time," *Business Week*, 2/9/98, pages 66–68.

Hamilton, David P. "Winter Olympics 1998: Made in Japan? Not for Home Team," *Wall Street Journal*, 2/18/98, page A6.

Hyman, Mark "Putting the Squeeze on the Media," *Business Week*, December 11, 2000, page 75.

Peers, Alexandra "Winter Olympics 1998: Salt Lake's Mission: Go One Better, and Do It Cheaper, Than Nagano," *Wall Street Journal*, February 20, 1998.

# CASE 4
# DEVELOPING GLOBAL MARKETING STRATEGIES

4-1 Global Strategies – What Are They?
4-2 Tambrands – Overcoming Cultural Resistance
4-3 Instructor's Notes: Pricing a Product in Multiple Country Markets
4-4 Blair Water Purifiers India
4-5 Sales Negotiations Abroad for MRIs
4-6 Tough Decisions at Boeing
4-7 National Office Machines – Motivating Japanese Sales people: Straight Salary or Commission?
4-8 Alan AeroSpace – Communications Satellite Sales to Japan
4-9 AIDS, Condoms, and Carnival
4-10 Making Socially Responsible and Ethical Marketing Decisions: Selling Tobacco to Third-World Countries*

## Case 4–1 Global Strategies – What Are They?

1. The response to this question will vary depending on the way a student evaluates the information and their interpretation of global.

2. Selective Contestability.

   Just as companies possessing a certain set of technologies and business competencies choose particular market segments to concentrate on, a global company can be selective about the countries in which it operates.

   Many small, high-technology companies and luxury good manufacturers do just that. They compete where there is adequate demand to justify the investments needed to access the market; they focus their investments to achieve critical mass only in those markets they are interested in.

   The important thing is that they can and are prepared to contest any and all markets should circumstances warrant. They constantly scour the world for market openings, they process information on a global basis, and they constitute a "potential" threat even in places they have not yet entered.

   Markets where such contestability exists, as a corollary, start to behave almost as if the company had already entered – provided, of course, the threat of entry is a credible one. This explains why telecom markets the world over are so fiercely competitive from the day they are no longer government or private monopolies. The handful of international players in the equipment business are not only waiting in the wings but have products that conform to international standards and resources they can deploy for market access as soon as opportunity arises.

3. Below are excerpts taken from the homepage of the companies.

   **Nestlé:**

   In a world of endless diversity, there is one activity that almost everyone shares. No matter where you go, you'll find people of all ages, from every social class, and representing every religion and ethnic group enjoying some Nestlé food or drink product. Our products (more than 8,500 in all) are sold in more than 100 countries, and they bring pleasure to millions of people. Whether it's ready-to-eat meals, instant coffee, chocolate bars or mineral water, Nestlé products are enjoyed around the world.

   Meeting the needs and desires of a diverse and ever-changing world requires respect for and knowledge of local values and desires. To achieve that, Nestlé has made decentralization a basic principle. We have offices, factories and research centers throughout the world. It is our policy to adapt as much as possible to local customs and circumstances while allowing decisions about products, marketing and personnel to be made at the local level.

   Nestlé is The World's Largest Food Company. Only two percent of sales are generated in Switzerland, our country of origin, and our management and staff reflect a truly international outlook. As a Company, we do not believe in mission statements, because one would either be so general as to become meaningless, or so specific that it wouldn't be applicable or relevant everywhere—we would like to offer a set of principles that will provide insight into the Company's attitudes and culture.

   At Nestlé, we try to take the mentality and customs of individual countries into account, but there are some general guidelines that we apply everywhere. Those include:

   Employees, people and products are more important at Nestlé than systems. Systems and methods, while necessary and valuable in running a complex organization, should remain are sold in more than 100 countries, and they bring pleasure to millions of people. Whether it's ready-to-eat meals, instant coffee, chocolate bars or mineral water, Nestlé products are enjoyed around the world.

Meeting the needs and desires of a diverse and ever-changing world requires respect for and knowledge of local values and desires. To achieve that, Nestlé has made decentralization a basic principle. We have offices, factories and research centers throughout the world. It is our policy to adapt as much as possible to local customs and circumstances while allowing decisions about products, marketing and personnel to be made at the local level.

Nestlé is The World's Largest Food Company. Only two percent of sales are generated in Switzerland, our country of origin, and our management and staff reflect a truly international outlook. As a Company, we do not believe in mission statements, because one would either be so general as to become meaningless, or so specific that it wouldn't be applicable or relevant everywhere—we would like to offer a set of principles that will provide insight into the Company's attitudes and culture.

At Nestlé, we try to take the mentality and customs of individual countries into account, but there are some general guidelines that we apply everywhere. Those include:

Employees, people and products are more important at Nestlé than systems. Systems and methods, while necessary and valuable in running a complex organization, should remain managerial and operational aids but should not become ends in themselves. It is a question of priorities. A strong orientation toward human beings, employees and executives is a decisive, if not the decisive, component of long-term success.

Our focus is on products. The ultimate justification for a company is its ability to offer products that are appealing because of their quality, convenience, variety and price—products that can stand their ground even in the face of fierce competition.

Nestlé makes clear a distinction between strategy and tactics. It gives priority to the long-range view. Long-term thinking defuses many of the conflicts and contentions among groups—this applies to employment conditions and relations with employees as well as to the conflicts and opposing interests of the trade and the industry. Of course, our ability to focus on long-term considerations is only possible if the company is successful in the struggle for short-term survival. This is why Nestlé strives to maintain a satisfactory level of profits every year.

Switzerland is home to Nestlé's Swiss subsidiary, its international headquarters and the registered office of Nestlé's holding company, but Nestlé does not regard its Swiss headquarters as the center of the universe. Decentralization is a basic principle of Nestlé. Our policy is to adapt as much as possible to regional circumstances, mentalities and situations. By decentralizing operational responsibility, we create strength and flexibility and are able to make decisions that are better attuned to specific situations in a given country. Policies and decisions concerning personnel, marketing and products are largely determined locally. This policy creates stronger motivation for Nestlé's executives and employees and a greater sense of identification with Nestlé's business. It is not Nestlé's policy to generate most of its sales in Switzerland, supplemented by a few satellite subsidiaries abroad. Nestlé strives to be an "insider" in every country in which it operates, not an "outsider."

The public's sense of the power and size of a corporation is often inaccurate, for a company's power is limited by a host of factors including legislation, competition, regulatory bodies and publicity. From a business point of view, it is desirable for a firm to achieve the size best suited to a specific industry or mode of production. To be competitive internationally and make significant investments in research and technology, a larger company has an advantage. From a strictly organizational point of view, flexible, simple structures work best and excessively large units should be avoided whenever possible. In both respects Nestlé has a natural advantage: Although it is a big company, it is spread out over many countries and each of Nestlé's factories has its own management and responsibility.

Nestlé is probably unique in the food industry in having an integrated research and development program that engages in applied and basic research in the fields of human physiology, health, nutrition and raw materials. Our research and development program gives us the capacity to create new types of products that we cannot even imagine today, especially in the critical area where preventive medicine and food products overlap. In addition, as concern for the environment grows, research will play an important role in overcoming environmental problems. For Nestlé, this is particularly important in packaging. Concern for the effects of packaging on the environment is forcing us to look for new solutions and to consider their interaction with our biological product—food.

**Procter & Gamble:**

At Procter & Gamble, we work hard to understand consumers. In fact, P&G has long been on the leading edge of consumer research. We were one of the first companies in the world to hire full-time professionals to study consumer needs. We pioneered many of the research techniques that are now widely used across industry. And today, we interact with more than seven million consumers a year worldwide as we ask ourselves the questions that have motivated us for decades: "What can we learn and what can we do to make people's lives better?"

- ***We get to know our newest consumers.*** P&G conducted the first in-depth consumer studies ever in markets like China and Eastern Europe. The knowledge we achieved as a result enabled us to meet consumer needs from the beginning – and establish our brands as market leaders early on.
- ***We have a world of ideas.*** We compare what we know from one country to the next. In global categories such as Laundry and Hair Care, we're able to meet the needs that consumers everywhere have in common, as well as those needs which are unique to individual markets.
- ***We benefit from our experience.*** We've been gathering consumer feedback for more than 70 years – and consumers everywhere benefit from these decades of experience, which contribute to the quality of our products today and help us anticipate consumer needs in the years ahead

Since we introduced Ivory soap in 1879 – one of the world's first advertised brands – Procter & Gamble has been on the leading edge of marketing innovation. We pioneered many of the approaches that have become marketing fundamentals in every part of the world, from advertising and product sampling to concepts like brand and category management. Most important, we continue to strive for marketing leadership in every part of the world where our brands are sold.

- ***We get the word out.*** P&G advertising has always demonstrated why our products are better, and we continue to rely on advertising as the principal way to reach consumers. With more than $3 billion in annual spending, we are one of the world's largest advertisers.
- ***We help consumers try us out.*** We are reaching the doorsteps of consumers from China to the Czech Republic. Each year, we provide hundreds of millions of free product samples to consumers around the world – because we know that the best test of our products is the toughest use of our products, by real people solving real problems.
- ***We're there at the beginning.*** There are many moments in consumers' lives when they reach for a P&G product the first time: the birth of a first child, the move into a first

home, the first steps into adulthood. From Pampers' parenting programs to our new-homeowner program, we make these moments easier by ensuring that our brands are there, with information and product samples.

More than 51,000 P&G people work in more than 140 plants in nearly 50 countries making more than 30,000 products – year after year. And we are all focused on one clear objective: to provide the world's consumers with the best value that we can.

For us, value is a simple equation. When we provide the highest quality possible at the most affordable price, we know we're delivering the value that consumers expect and deserve. Our global Product Supply organization – which includes Manufacturing, Engineering, Purchasing and Logistics – is a key element in our value strategy. By making and shipping high-quality products in the safest, most efficient way we can, the men and women of Product Supply truly help make every day better for consumers around the world.

- ***We deliver the same high quality everywhere.*** We invest heavily to ensure that our plants in every part of the world operate at the same high-quality standard. This is true of our oldest plants – such as Ivorydale in Cincinnati, USA – to our newest, such as our food facility in Mechelen, Belgium. It is also true of sites we acquire, like our laundry plant in Novomoskovsk, Russia.

For an interesting discussion of this topic see: Bruce Kogut, "What Makes a Company Global?" *Harvard Business Review*, January/February 1999, p. 165.

## Case 4–2 Tambrands – Overcoming Cultural Resistance

This case may be too **DELICATE** for some students. The Instructor is advised to take this into consideration before assigning this case. However, it is a real live case and P&G is having success with promotions and it is gaining market share. The company said unit-volume growth rose 8%, adding that acquisitions—especially the $1.85 billion purchase of the Tambrands Inc., the maker of Tampax tampons—contributed 2% to P&G's unit volume growth in the quarter.

In Asia, unit volume was flat, which the company blamed on the region's economic crises. Asian sales fell 5%, while net earnings slid.

Among the problems P&G face with increasing its share of market globally are the cultural issues. Perspective can be gained by reviewing the cultural issues that still exist in the United States.

Here are some examples:

> So here it is. Again. That time of the month. If you're like the majority of American women, your most pressing concern is keeping your menstrual period hush-hush. You're not about to grab a tampon out of your purse and walk to the bathroom twirling it nonchalantly between your fingers.
>
> In fact, you probably schlep your whole briefcase to the restroom just to be discreet about it. And if you're like my mom, you have hidden that tampon in a pretty little plastic container inside your handbag, just in case anyone happens to peek. But wait a minute. It's 1998. We hear almost as much about condoms as we do about cappuccino. "Safe sex" is a buzz phrase. So why don't we talk openly about menstruation? As the century draws to a close, societal attitudes toward menses seem to be changing. Whether that's good news or bad depends upon whom you ask.
>
> "I truly think we're in a new era of openness about it, just based on the advertising alone," says Barbara Czerwinski, an associate professor of nursing at the University of Texas-Houston Health Science Center. Czerwinski studies women's health-care practices and serves on the board of the Museum of Menstruation. The what? Yes, Virginia, there really is a Museum of Menstruation. Harry Finley, 55, a graphic designer, opened the archive in July 1994. And though MUM, as it's called, fits neatly in the paneled basement of Finley's Maryland home, it has received a great deal of attention from major media outlets and academics.
>
> Skip to March 1997 and the Canadian release of the documentary "Under Wraps: A Film About Going With the Flow." It took four years before Vancouver-based Penny Wheelwright and Teresa MacInnes amassed the cash to make the slick 56-minute film.
>
> There's more literature, more grass-roots activism and more advertising surrounding menstruation than ever before, but a cloak of secrecy, shame and squeamishness continues to keep it out of public dialogue. The stigma attached to menstruation dates back to humankind's earliest days. In the Bible, the Old Testament book of Leviticus warns against contact with a menstruating woman: ". . . and whoever toucheth her shall be unclean until the even." Religious Jewish women still immerse themselves in a ritual bath following their periods each month. Many ancient cultures, and some modern ones, forbid a menstruating woman to touch food, plants, men and even herself, lest the powerful and strange forces causing the woman to bleed harm those things around her. Other societies beat, isolate or perform female circumcision on a girl upon her first period, called menarche. It's no wonder women take pains to hide their bleeding.
>
> ". . . he grew up in an Irish Catholic home with six sisters. "I never knew that anyone was menstruating in my house," he says. "It was totally secretive. It was dirty. It was not proper to show or talk about or admit to. "In my mother's generation it was looked upon as 'the curse,' he adds.

"That's a pretty negative concept. To turn something so beautiful and powerful into something so evil is pretty devastating."

Kotex marketed the first successful disposable pad in 1921; it was 22 inches long. Before that, women devised their own protection from cloths and wore rubber aprons underneath their skirts. Tampax introduced the tampon in 1936, touting it as "a comfort never known before." The inventor of Tampax, Dr Earle Haas, received no monetary rewards for his efforts, although the London Sunday Times named him one of the "1000 Most Important People of the 20th Century". (In fact, women have used a variation of tampon since ancient times. Egyptians used softened papyrus and Romans used wool.) Dr Haas sold the patent to businesswoman and physician Gertrude Tenderich. She had a few problems with American religious groups who feared that Tampax would encourage young women to masturbate.

Undeterred, Gertrude hired registered nurses to give lectures, sent women door-knocking and took on a smart partner. A full-page, four-color ad in the American Weekly depicted young women dancing, playing tennis etc. and demonstrated that with internal protection a modern menstruating woman could be active.

Next is an article that discusses the issues P&G faces and additional examples of how they are facing the issues.

> Consumer products giant Procter & Gamble launched a Web site for teenage girls with information on puberty and relationships and little dancing tampons at the bottom of the main page. The Web site, www.beinggirl.com, was designed with the help of an advisory board of teenage girls, P&G said.
>
> Sara Nathan, Levi's to Launch "Cool" Ad Campaign," USA Today, July 27, 2000, pp. 01B.
>
> Near the beginning of this century the Johnson and Johnson company produced the first commercial disposable pad. It was made of cotton covered with gauze, but the retail industry shunned the product.
>
> According to the book, The Curse: A Cultural History of Menstruation, this happened because "turn-of-the-century morality prevented advertising these 'unmentionables.'" The pads did not reach many women and were eventually withdrawn from the market.
>
> It was only after the First World War had ended that another company, Kimberly Clark, was prepared to once again try to market a feminine napkin. They decided to do this after it was learned that some resourceful Red Cross nurses had replaced obnoxious menstrual rags with Cellucotton, the surgical material the company had supplied to dress war wounds.
>
> In 1920, after intensive research and market testing, the company succeeded in producing a viable consumer product for women. The first napkins, bulky by today's standards, sold for 60 cents for 12 pads packaged in a "hospital blue" box. A customer didn't even have to request the product by name; all she had to do was put her money in a box near a pile of the unmarked packages and walk out of the store.
>
> Almost immediately the product was the center of controversy. Many drug and department stores refused to stock the Kotex pads. One Woolworth store in San Francisco was forced by a men's organization to take down a window display of the sanitary pads.
>
> Media outlets were aghast at the idea of advertising a product associated with something that was regarded as a "hush-hush" subject. Ladies Home Journal was the first magazine willing to accept an ad for sanitary pads, but this was done with the understanding euphemisms and great discretion would be paramount. Later, magazine publishers felt somewhat reassured when some ads stressed that women doctors had played a role in design improvements.

About the same time Kimberly Clark was pioneering its first sanitary pad, a young man on its staff was experimenting with a bizarre-looking device—a condom in which he had punctured holes and filled with the same material used in the pads.

He was thrilled with his innovative achievement, which he contended could be used by menstruating women. His father, Dr. George H. Williamson, who was Kimberly Clark's first medical consultant during the development of the sanitary pad, was shocked by his son's creation.

He said, "Never would I put such a strange article inside a woman." He also warned that marketing such a product would be a legal nightmare. "Don't discuss this with anyone because some damn fool will want to put it on the market and you'll be in trouble!"

But clever ideas seldom disappear and, 10 years later, another company bought the patent for a tampon prototype from a woman who claimed her device would be "a different method of taking care of menstruation." Given the name Tampax, the new feminine product was also destined to generate widespread outrage.

Any woman contemplating using the new product was warned that tampons could rupture a virgin's hymen. From church pulpits, clerics denounced tampons as an evil invention associated with abortion, masturbation and defloration.

But most women ignored this propaganda. They quickly educated themselves about the medical implications of using tampons and efforts to convince them to shun the product were doomed.

Today, many products designed for "women only" are available. Tampons, of course, experienced terrible press in the 1980s after a number of cases of toxic shock syndrome were traced to improper use of a particular type made of a super-absorbent material. These days, tampons are considered safe as long as users follow the manufacturers' instructions.

In recent years, a "menstrual cup" product has also found favor with many women. This device, which fits low in the vagina where it collects the menstrual flow, is now available in both single use and reusable versions.

The reusable type, which requires only a thorough washing after each use, is promoted as being "environmentally friendly." One brand, called The Keeper, which is priced under $60, can be reused for as long as 10 years. But menstruation and its impact on women still continues to present medical challenges.

In the 1970s, a feminist group in Los Angeles concluded it was time to find a way to eliminate menstruation, and several members of the organization developed a technique called menstrual extraction. Those who had supported the initiative were ecstatic about the significance of the procedure. They claimed the simple extraction method done by the woman herself or a friend could reduce the duration of menstruation from a few days to a matter of minutes.

In spite of feminists' insistence that menstrual extraction was safe and liberating, the procedure soon created a great deal of controversy. Many American doctors raised serious medical concerns about a woman or other lay person using a primitive suction method to remove the entire menstrual flow from a uterus (the procedure was also suspected as being a means of performing a very early abortion).

Those who have endorsed menstrual extraction contend it is no more traumatic than having an IUD inserted. What they fail to acknowledge is, given the choice, most women would probably prefer to experience their monthly menstrual period rather than face the risk of infection and tissue damage that many physicians insist could result from menstrual extraction.

Dorothy Grant is a freelance writer in Halifax.

Dorothy Grant, *From fig leaf to the 'sanitary napkin.'* Vol. 3 5, Medical Post, 04/06/1999

The first site is to be aimed at European teenagers, promoting products such as Clearasil, Sunny Delight and Tampax. Another example, Escobar says, is a site for young parents based around a trusted baby product brand, involving parenting advice, the opportunity to e-mail a pediatrician and a chat room for young mothers.

Procter & Gamble, to step up its Internet activity will give the World Wide Web a boost as a marketing medium. P&G has always been an early and aggressive adopter of new media, dating back to radio and television.

According to Kim Escobar, director of Euro RSCG Interactive, the agency that has been asked to develop the first European site for P&G, the opportunity presented by the Internet is twofold: to develop an interactive marketing device that allows for communication with customers; and to generate direct sales from the Web and make savings on promotional literature.

"High-tech companies have done a lot of work in this area but have a much easier model to work from because high-tech products are much more of a considered purchase," she says. "For a general fast-moving consumer-goods client you are seeking to build a branding relationship. There is not a clean-cut model for how you do that, so we are seeing a lot of experimentation. No one has the answer; it is just the same as when people started to use television to advertise products."

P&G's idea is to attract consumers to interactive sites that will be of interest to particular target groups, with the hope of developing deeper relationships with consumers.

---

Ed Shelton, "P&G to Seek Web Friends, The European, November 16, 1998, p. 18.

## Case 4–3 Instructor's Notes: Pricing a Product in Multiple Country Markets

To try to lessen price differentials, Kilburg tries to help distributors reduce their costs by offering reduced prices for bulk orders. This also allows them to save on shipping costs and on clearance fees. (Since clearance fees are a fixed amount regardless of the size of the shipment, it is more economical to send a quantity of time indicators than to send them one or two at a time.) In addition, by loading distributors up with inventory, it encourages them to move the product, which is better accomplished at lower prices. Lower prices mean there is less room for significant price differences between distributors. Plus, since distributors have minimum purchase requirements, they are contractually forced to price the product so that it will sell.

Kilburg also tries to get distributors to work together to share leads and business. He says he doesn't try to police them, because that is a violation of the trust built within each relationship (and could be a violation of antitrust laws as well, in Europe; for example, while exclusive distributors may, in certain cases, be restricted from soliciting business outside their country territory, they may not be restricted from filling unsolicited orders which now often come via the Internet, see below). "If you have to resort to a piece of paper to enforce your relationship, there's something wrong with the relationship to begin with," Kilburg reasons.

The Internet has only increased the problem of price differentials. Geochron has links on its Web site to all its foreign distributors in 46 countries. From this Web site, any customer with Internet access can shop around for a time indicator. To prevent too much shopping between countries, Kilburg asks his distributors not to post their prices on the site, and this strategy usually works. But because the time indicator is not considered by most an "impulse" buy, customers are more likely to shop around before purchasing. While price shopping frustrates distributors, it does help keep the prices within a narrower range.

Kilburg has also attacked price differentials by altering the clock for different territories. The time indicator may be slightly changed in its appearance, there may be an alternate color scheme, or the design of the product housing may be varied. Other alterations can be ordered. For example, Geochron has signed a contract with a company in China to distribute time indicators that have specific political boundaries that the Chinese government felt should be displayed on it.

Geochron does not use its minimum purchase requirements as a hammer to force lower prices, though. The market in each territory can only bear so much, and some of the distributor's costs cannot be lowered (e.g., tariffs, or a layered distribution system). As Kilburg says, "There is no point in having a built-in contract that's doomed to failure." His advice to the exporter? Keep good relations between you and your distributors. Make sure they keep good relations with each other and you. Many pricing and other problems can be attributed to growing pains, as they were with Geochron. Finally, remember that "Everything always comes back to haunt you, so you might as well do it the right and honest way to start with."

Visit also www.geochron.com.au and www.geochronusa.com.

## Case 4–4 Blair Water Purifiers India*

### Synopsis

Blair Company is a small U.S. manufacturer (1996 sales expected to be $400 million) of products designed to make water safe and palatable for human consumption. The company is considering entering the Indian market for home water purifiers with its "Delight" purifier. According to Blair Company Engineers, the Delight purifier should outperform anything currently on the market.

Students face the primary issue of whether or not Blair Company should enter the market. However, before they can answer "yes" or "no," students should consider mode of entry (license, joint venture, acquisition) and examine advertising, pricing, and channels possibilities. Students must undertake both qualitative and quantitative analyses to arrive at a good decision.

### Teaching Objectives

Teaching objectives for the case appear below.

1. Develop an awareness of global marketing issues and opportunities.
2. Understand the nature of a marketing opportunity in a less developed country (LDC).
3. Compare licensing arrangements, joint ventures, and acquisition as strategies to enter foreign markets.
4. Analyze a complex marketing opportunity in qualitative and quantitative terns and take a reasoned position.
5. Explore the nature of a strategic international alliance.

The instructor might take a moment or two at the end of the class period to present these objectives to students, as a way to conclude discussion.

### Teaching Suggestions

The case may be used either for classroom discussion or testing. A class period of 90 minutes minimum is necessary to resolve case issues via discussion. The following questions may be asked.

### Areas for Discussion/Analysis

A. Compared to a developed country like the U.S or Germany. what is different about marketing in a less developed country? What is the same?

   Students will find it easy to identify differences in marketing between developed countries and LDCs. The two types of countries show marketing environments that differ in every fundamental aspect—political, technological, social, competitive, and economic. Infrastructure in LDCs is less advanced than in developed countries, making communication, movement of goods and money, and change more difficult. Compared to a developed country, rural and urban consumers in LDCs will show greater contrasts in income and lifestyles. Governments and people in LDCs fear or mistrust multinational corporations and even smaller foreign companies; governments may limit the company's ability to remove profits. LDCs offer far greater potential for rapid growth in many product categories (e.g., automobiles, telephones, household appliances) than do developed countries.

---

* Teaching Notes prepared by Professor James E. Nelson, University of Colorado at Boulder.

After these and other relevant points come out in discussion, the instructor can turn to marketing similarities between developed countries and LDCs. After perhaps an awkward silence, someone might volunteer that good marketing strategy in LDCs still must consider consumers, competitors, and environments in a creative fashion. Marketers still must attempt to satisfy consumers while accomplishing organizational objectives. Marketers still must develop strategic alternatives, analyze each in a detailed fashion, and then choose one to implement. In short, after a few minutes of thought, students might conclude that differences in marketing between developed countries and LDCs are more ones of detail and degree rather than ones of principle and procedure.

B. How attractive is the Indian market for home water purifiers?

This is a good question to continue the discussion. The topic matter is important, the analysis complex, and the answer neither obvious nor unanimous among students. Students might note the following:

The Indian market for home water purifiers is attractive for several reasons. The market is huge and growing—see case Exhibit 1. Moreover, if the market could be expanded to India's rural areas, forecasts in Exhibit 1 would increase by some six to ten times (Chatterjee estimated that "existing manufacturers were reaching only ten to fifteen percent of the entire population." In addition, India's extremely low wage rates and central location offer the possibility of export sales to a number of nearby LDCs. Indian consumers are aware of problems with their water quality and are favorably disposed to Western products in general. The Indian government is actively seeking foreign investment into the economy. Water filters and purifiers currently on the market appear inferior to Blair Company's Delight purifier. India represents almost a prototypical case with respect to Blair Company's goal of thriving in LDCs (case's first paragraph). Finally, as will be seen in C. below, India can be entered with relatively little investment of Blair Company resources.

The Indian market for home water purifiers is unattractive for these reasons. India is a large, complex, far away nation considerably removed from Blair Company's established "comfort zone" of countries whose business practices and cultures are much more Westernized. The market may be mature with its numerous established competitors, who will not look the other way should Blair Company enter. The Indian government may reverse its position regarding the attractiveness of foreign investment.

C. Compare the three modes of market entry available to Blair Company in India.

Joint Working Arrangement or License. The joint working arrangement or license mode of entry represents relatively low risk: Blair Company would invest almost nothing and would occupy a very low political profile. Likely the product could be placed quickly on dealers' shelves and royalty payments soon would flow to Blair Company. However, Blair Company would have limited control over product quality and nothing at all to say about the nature and level of marketing activities. Blair Company would establish no brand awareness among consumers and develop no trade relationships among channel members. It would learn little about consumers, competitors, and business practice in India.

Breakeven quantities for the joint working arrangement or license depend on the hiring of an Indian national who would manage the arrangement. Annual fixed costs before hiring this individual are given in the case as $40,000; fixed costs after hiring drop to $15,000. The average royalty paid to Blair Company in both cases is given as Rs.300. For breakeven quantities, we have:($40,000 x 35)/Rs.300 = 4,667 units before hiring the Indian manager, and ($15,000 x 35)/Rs.300 = 1,750 units after.

These quantities can be compared to market forecasts for 1998 or 1999 (the expected first year of operation) in case Exhibit 1 to estimate necessary market shares. Using the "realistic scenario," forecasts from Exhibit 1, we have for 1998, 1,750 units/430,000 units = 0.4 percent of the market and

4,667 units/430,000 units = 1.1 percent. Both percentages are based on nation-wide demand. If the licensee restricts operations to just two regions (market potentials shown in case Exhibit 5), the same market shares for 1998 would be 1,750/55,000 or 3.2 percent and 4,667/55,000 or 8.5 percent. Some students may want to recover the $25,000 cost of the field study in the first year or two of operations and their breakeven quantities and share percentages will be a bit higher.

Students also might examine the upside aspect of licensing. Suppose that Blair Company actually achieves a 10 or a 20 percent market share in 1998. Using the same realistic scenario forecasts from Exhibit 1, profits for a 10 percent share of the national market would be (.10)(430,000 units)(Rs.300) – ($15,000)(Rs.35) = Rs12.375 million or approximately $354,000. For a 20 percent share, profits would be (.20)(430,000 units)(Rs.300) – ($15,000)(Rs.35) = Rs.25.275 million or approximately $722,000. If operations focus only on two regions, profits for 10 and 20 percent market shares reduce to Rs.1.125 million and Rs.2.775 million, respectively ($32,140 and $79,285).

On balance, the joint working arrangement looks extremely attractive—little is at risk and the opportunity is present for huge rewards—if Blair Company can find and motivate a licensee.

*Joint Venture.* When Blair Company partners with an Indian firm, the resulting joint venture will occupy a more visible position in the political arena and place more capital at risk (in the form of investments and annual fixed costs). Another concern is that Blair Company may find it difficult to find and convince an Indian firm to commit to the partnership. Blair Company also may find it difficult to establish day-to-day work rules, policy, and strategic direction with the partner. Still other potential thorny issues include the distribution of profits versus their reinvestment, transfer of technology, access to dealers, and product research and development, all possibly leading to mistrust and early dissolution of the joint venture.

On the plus side, the biggest gain that Blair Company realizes with a joint venture entry is increased control over all business activities, including procurement, production, finance, marketing and distribution. Blair Company also can take advantage of the Indian partner's expertise in these activities. (As one expert put it, "An international joint venture essentially reduces to a race between the two partners to see which one can learn the most from the other in the least amount of time.") And, while political and economic risks are increased, these risks will be shared between the two partners. However, so too, will be the rewards.

The amount at economic risk for a joint venture depends on operational scope, as shown in case Exhibit 5. Exhibit 5 also shows that annual fixed costs depend on whether the entry strategy will use dealers or a direct salesforce. Unit contribution margins depend as well on the choice between dealers and a direct salesforce and further on whether a skimming or a penetrating price strategy will be used. Estimated unit contribution margins for the channel and price options can be found in the case's last section and are summarized below:

| | **Channel Strategy** | |
|---|---|---|
| Price Strategy | Dealers | Direct Salesforce |
| Skimming | Rs.650 | Rs.500 |
| Penetrating | Rs.300 | Rs.200 |

Essentially, Chatterjee has figured for the skimming strategy that Rs.1050 are available to cover unit contribution, plus either the dealer's margin (Rs.400) or the salesman's commission (Rs.550). For the penetrating strategy, he has allowed Rs.600 to cover unit contribution, plus either the dealer's margin (Rs.300) or the salesman's commission (Rs.400). Thus, in both pricing strategies, the dealer margin per unit is less than the direct salesforce's commission per unit. The dealer option also ties up less money in inventory and incurs lower inventory carrying costs.

Beyond the four contribution margins above, student calculations for breakeven are complicated by the need to estimate advertising and promotion expenditures (next to last paragraph in the case). Chatterjee thinks that Eureka Forbes will spend about Rs.1 million in 1996 on advertising for Aquaguard and that Ion Exchange will spend a total of "around Rs.3 million" for all marketing activities associated with ZERO-B. Given this meager information, most students will estimate annual advertising and promotional expenditures somewhere between Rs.500,000 and Rs.2 million and recognize that their calculations are quite crude. More skillful students may include a return on investment in their breakeven calculations, applying an annual target return of around 20 to 25 percent to investments shown in case Exhibit 5.

Because students will use different estimates for advertising and promotion expenditures and different rates for ROI (including 0.0), classroom discussion will produce a range of Breakeven quantities and market share percentages. At the end of discussion, some students will be uncomfortable with the absence of a single, agreed upon answer. The case is purposely vague in terms of permitting a single answer, for two reasons. First, the opportunity itself is known to Blair Company only to the precision described in the case (indeed, many at Blair Company would hold that the case is much too exact and that more ambiguity, not less, actually characterizes the situation). Second, the case should be assigned very late in most courses, at a time when students should recognize that interesting marketing phenomena almost never are known to the penny or the paisa and that the whole idea of Breakeven analyses is for students to demonstrate their analytical judgment.

Shown following are data from case Exhibit 5, along with estimates for a 20 percent return on investment, estimates for expenditures on advertising and promotion, unit contribution margins for the various distribution and pricing options as given in the case, and resulting Breakeven quantities. Student results will differ based on their assumptions for ROI and expenditures for advertising and promotion.

**Operational Scope**

| | Two Regions | Four Regions | National Market |
|---|---|---|---|
| 1998 Market Potential | 55,000 units | 110,000 units | 430,000 units |
| Initial Investment (Rs.000) | 4,000 | 8,000 | 30,000 |
| 20% Return on Initial Investment (Rs.000) | 800 | 1,600 | 6,000 |
| Advertising and Promotion (Rs.000) | 500 | 1,000 | 2,000 |
| Analysis for Dealer Channels | | | |
| Fixed Overhead(Rs.000) | 4,000 | 7,000 | 40,000 |
| Total Fixed Costs (Rs.000) | 5,300 | 9,600 | 48,000 |
| Skimming Unit C.M. (Rs.) | 650 | 650 | 650 |
| Skimming Breakeven Q | 8,155 units | 14,770 units | 73,850 units |
| Penetrating Unit C.M. (Rs.) | 300 | 300 | 300 |
| Penetrating Breakeven Q | 17,670 units | 32,000 units | 160,000 units |
| Analysis for Direct Salesforce | | | |
| Fixed Overhead (Rs.000) | 7,200 | 14,000 | 88,000 |
| Total Fixed Costs (Rs.000) | 8,500 | 16,600 | 96,000 |
| Skimming Unit C.M. (Rs.) | 500 | 500 | 500 |
| Skimming Breakeven Q | 17,000 units | 33,200 units | 192,000 units |
| Penetrating Unit C.M. (Rs.) | 200 | 200 | 200 |
| Penetrating Breakeven Q | 42,500 units | 83,000 units | 480,000 units |

Students should compare Breakeven quantities above with the three estimates of market size, shown on the first line above and in case Exhibit 5. The range for Breakeven market share is (14,770 units)/(110,000 units) = 13.4 percent for the skimming price and dealer channel combination to (480,000 units)/(430,000 units) = 111.6 percent for the penetrating price and direct salesforce combination.

When these or similar numbers have been placed on the board, the instructor can ask for a summary interpretation. A good activity at this point is to stop discussion and give the class three to five minutes to jot down their interpretations. When time is up, class members can be polled. These sorts of ideas should arise.

1. The penetrating price and direct salesforce combination should be rejected out of hand.
2. Breakeven quantities for the skimming price and direct salesforce combination are about the same as the penetrating price and dealer channel combination.
3. Breakeven quantities for the skimming price and dealer channel are the smallest.
4. Contribution margins for all combinations using penetration pricing make licensing a preferred alternative.
5. Licensing is a preferred alternative if actual sales quantities stay small.

On this last point, one or two students may see a way to compare the economic aspects of licensing with a joint venture. Students can calculate critical values for quantities such that sales below these levels make licensing look more attractive than a joint venture and that sales above which make the reverse true. The calculations actually are quite simple. From the two region, dealer channel, skimming price data from case Exhibit 5, we can write an equation where the left side represents total contribution for licensing and the right the total contribution for a joint venture. We have [(Rs.300)(Q) – (Rs.15,000)] = [(Rs.650)(Q) – (Rs.4,500,000)], and Q = 12,814 units. For the four region, dealer channel, skimming price data, we have [(Rs.300)(Q) – Rs.15,000)] = [(Rs.650)(Q) – (Rs.8,000,000)], and Q = 22,814 units. For the entire national market, dealer channel, skimming price data, we have [(Rs.300)(Q) – Rs.15,000)] = [(Rs.650)(Q) – (Rs.42,000,000)], and Q = 119,957 units. All three calculations assume that Blair Company would receive 100 percent of the contribution and such is the case only for licensing. If Blair Company were to receive just half of the contribution (as might be stipulated in the joint venture agreement), then the three critical quantities above would double.

Finally, one or two students may comment on the idea that a lot of time is being spent on "crunching numbers" and that many other considerations need to be discussed. Besides, they might argue, Blair Company seems a bit old fashioned here—shouldn't a target segment and market demand drive cost such that the final product meets market expectations rather than existing price levels? This is an excellent point that the instructor should be prepared to stress before moving on.

Discussion now might shift to qualitative concerns: What else can be said regarding Blair Company's choice between skimming and penetrating price strategies? Skimming is an excellent way to "feel out" demand and to learn about the market as events take place. In addition, some Indian consumers probably associate price with quality and others exhibit inelastic demand. Skimming permits Blair Company to field a large salesforce and to control customer contact. Skimming encourages competitors to enter or to stay in the market. On the other hand, a penetrating strategy would permit Blair Company to realize economies of scale and experience curve effects more quickly. These efficiencies will enlarge the market and may pave the way for the joint venture to enter India's rural market. Finally, a penetrating strategy will discourage competitors from entering or staying in the market.

What else might be said regarding Blair Company's choice between using dealers or using a direct salesforce? Dealers are attractive because they take title and possession of goods, thereby reducing economic risk to the joint venture. Dealers may provide service for damaged or old units; they will stock and sell related products. Both activities offer convenience to consumers. Dealers already are in place and can begin sales of Delight Purifiers almost immediately. Dealers offer instant credibility and image, if they are chosen and trained properly. Dealers know their customers and trading areas. very well. Dealers are independent businesses, not under the thumb of the joint venture's managers. In contrast, the direct salesforce can be more easily trained, motivated, and controlled. Moreover, many consumers will need an education about the product category that a salesforce can best supply. Like life insurance, the product may be such that it needs to be pushed. However, a direct salesforce represents a huge investment and large fixed costs—should the market contract for any reason, the joint venture may not produce a profit. A large salesforce would be difficult to manage and control. A disgruntled salesman would reflect poorly on the joint venture, not the independent dealer.

*Acquisition*. The acquisition mode of entry represents the greatest political risk to Blair Company. The resulting operation, even if it is given an Indian name, will be known to politicians and social activists as a U.S. (ferengi) owned and managed operation. Thus, it will be vulnerable to the sorts of difficulties recently encountered by such U.S. firms as Cargill, Enroll, MacDonalds, and KFC.

In terms of economic risk, the acquisition mode of entry probably will have greater exposure than a joint venture (and certainly greater exposure than licensing). However, the case points out that the amount of investment actually may be lower for acquisition than a joint venture entry because it depends on exactly what will be acquired. For example, Blair Company might buy only a medium sized manufacturing facility, not an entire company, and the investment could be less than that for a joint venture. About the best that students can do here is to recognize these ideas and move on. The case simply lacks sufficient information for a more complete economic analysis.

D. What should Chatterjee recommend to Blair Company regarding the opportunity in India?

This is the most interesting question in the Note. Unfortunately, given the depth and breadth of preceding discussion, many classes will lack sufficient time to attack this question. In such cases, however, the question makes an excellent take home quiz or extra credit assignment. The question has essentially two answers.

One is for Chatterjee to recommend that Blair Company forget about India for the time being. Mostly this position is based on the idea that India is simply too exotic and that "there is too much at risk." Before leaving this answer, the instructor should tease out just what students mean. Clearly, India represents a major challenge to Blair Company's International Division and other LDCs may be easier to enter and offer greater opportunities. However, initial investments and annual fixed costs for the joint working arrangement in India are so small as to be negligible to Blair Company. Still, a troubled joint venture in India might tie up managers at Blair Company and represent a hidden opportunity cost.

The other answer is more adventuresome and would have Chatterjee recommend market entry, either via a joint working arrangement or a joint venture. Licensing is the easier answer and students see it as essentially a no risk decision. Licensing has economic advantages, particularly if initial sales levels are small. Licensing is consistent with Blair Company's present level of international expertise; it lets Blair Company start small and learn to walk before it learns to run. Many students reason that Blair Company's operation in India will be that of a single product firm whose product has never seen a moment's use in the field—in India or in any other country. How could the company consider investing even a small amount of resources in a joint venture with such (in)experience? What joint venture partner in India would see Blair Company as attractive, given the lack of a track record?

Students favoring a joint venture take a longer-term view. After all, they reason, many well-managed firms selling consumer durable goods recently have entered India. The market is huge, labor costs low, and political and economic risk of reasonable magnitudes. Why not enter with a joint venture? Blair Company managers undoubtedly will make some mistakes but they should try to learn from these mistakes and avoid repeating them. A vigorous entry now may deter one or more other entrants from entering in the very near future.

As should be obvious, the choice between licensing and a joint venture entry has no right answer. Perfectly legitimate positions may be taken on either side, depending on the students' tolerance of risk and decision horizon. Students who are risk averse and short-term oriented should favor licensing. Students who are risk tolerant and long-term oriented should choose the joint venture. The most important point for students to recognize is not "Any answer will do" but rather that "Both positions have strengths and weaknesses that must be understood before managers can make a good decision."

Regardless of mode of entry, operations in India probably should use a skimming price strategy. Skimming offers the lowest breakeven quantities. It permits the use of a large (or a small) salesforce. Most importantly, skimming generates cash for a variety of strategic purposes, all relevant to Blair Company operations in India. Cash will be needed to educate consumers via advertising and promotion and to attract, train, and support dealers (should the dealer option be chosen over the direct salesforce). Cash will be needed to expand market areas from two regions to four, from four regions to the entire nation, and, finally, to rural areas where market potential is huge. Cash also will be needed for new product development, to expand the Delight product line, and to add new lines. Line extensions will be needed when geographic expansion slows because sales increases cannot easily come from increased usage of the Delight purifier among existing owners.

Regardless of mode of entry, operations in India probably should emphasize a dealer network based on reasons outlined in part C. of this Note. Still, some large urban areas may use a direct salesforce who can prospect their neighborhoods and sell, deliver, and service products. The salesforce also can educate new users (and nonusers) and collect payments, if units are sold via hire purchase. Finally, the limited use of a direct salesforce or a factory owned retail outlet system may help Blair Company control dealers, much like the role of factory outlet stores in the U.S.

**Summary**

In summary, India seems a very nice fit for Blair Company's international goals. However, the company decided to enter Brazil first, via a joint venture. The company chose Brazil largely because of geographic proximity—Brazil lies only two time zones and just a few thousand miles away from Blair Company headquarters. If things go well in Brazil, Blair Company then will enter Argentina—again because of proximity (and similarity with Brazil). India has been put on the "back burner" for the time being.

Students usually are disappointed to hear this. However, managers at Blair Company received favorable reports on the markets for water purifiers in all four countries mentioned in the case—Argentina, Brazil, India, and Indonesia. Political concerns ruled out Indonesia for market entry but the company still faced a difficult choice. The Indian market (not counting the rural areas) was bigger than Brazil and Argentina combined. However, managers viewed India as too challenging, beyond their capabilities to understand and to perform well in. Still, Chatterjee and a few other managers at Blair Company believed that a license arrangement to enter India would have been a better decision.

A good way of ending the class is to distribute the attached snapshot of Singer Company's view of emerging markets. This brief description (taken from Singer's Web site at http://www.singer-nv.com/sing3O5.htm) illustrates why emerging markets are so attractive to many companies and how one company is able to take advantage of the opportunity. Alternatively, the snapshot could be distributed (or the Web site identified) earlier, when making the case assignment.

## THE SINGER N.V. COMPANY

### The Vast Potential of Emerging Markets

Singer is directly participating in the rising living standards of the rapidly developing economies of the emerging markets. Growth rates in Asia, Latin America and Africa will exceed those of all other regions for at least the next decade. Asia is the fastest growing region in the world and will continue to be the most dynamic element in the world economy in the next generation. Most countries have learned how to tame the hyperinflation that hampered growth in Latin America, while the political changes in South Africa have produced a free-world economy. Opportunity in the developing world will proliferate for years to come.

A critical strategy of Singer is to enter new markets as quickly as they open. As a market opens to commerce, one of the first consumer durable items purchased is a sewing machine, frequently on Singer's installment plan, usually the only source of consumer credit in the country. As our distribution infrastructure is built and the installment debt is repaid, the customer has the opportunity to buy Singer consumer durables for the home or trade up to a sewing machine with more features. As economies improve, more consumers are able to afford our sewing machines and consumer durable products.

These emerging markets have been a significant source of growth for our company. In the last five years, sales in Asia, Latin America and Africa have risen 85 percent. These markets contributed 65 percent of operating earnings in 1991; now they produce 79 percent. Earnings have risen 72 percent in the emerging markets in the last five years.

What is the formula to succeed in these high-growth economies?

- Invest in a large retail network (Singer has almost three-quarters of its 1,500 retail stores in these regions).
- Maximize this distribution network by selling not only sewing machines, but an increasing percentage of consumer durables for the home.
- Emphasize installment sales, which are a powerful stimulus to purchase. In most markets, installment sales are a potent competitive advantage.
- Tailor distribution to each market. For instance, Singer is constructing a 15,000 square foot megastore in Sri Lanka, which will be the largest store in the country. Meanwhile, we are deploying thousands of canvassers (door-to-door salespersons) throughout rural Thailand by foot, motorcycle or boat to sell and deliver products and collect monthly payments. The Company's broad distribution system, spanning 80 developing countries on three continents, consists of:
    - 18,200 door-to-door salespersons (most of them in Thailand)
    - 1,080 retail stores operated by the Company and its affiliates.

A wholesale network of 30,500 retail stores operated by independent dealers and mass merchants, as well as independent distributors.

Featured on the next page are three highly successful markets: Thailand, Brazil and Sri Lanka. Later (in the New Markets section) close-ups are provided of three markets we have entered only recently that represent vast potential: China, India and South Africa.

**Thailand**

- 1995 Gross National Product growth: 8.7%
- Population 61.3 million
- Singer distribution network:
  - 303 retail stores
  - 9 independent dealers
  - 12,894 canvassers

The country achieved outstanding economic growth with high levels of capacity utilization in 1995 despite the worst flooding in 25 years. Vigorous activity should continue, according to Thailand's finance minister. Sound economic management, a high savings rate and abundant natural and human resources should continue to lay a firm foundation for the economy.

With sales of over $300 million, Thailand is Singer's largest market. The Company's 48 percent-owned operating affiliate has by far the most extensive distribution of any country in terms of the number of stores and canvassers. Eighty percent of the country is considered rural, necessitating the large number of canvassers who work out of the stores. Staffing the distribution system has made the Company the second-largest employer in the country.

Singer has the largest distribution network in Thailand for consumer durables and has the largest market share in major appliances such as refrigerators, freezers and washing machines. It has the second largest market share in the country of televisions and stereos. Eighty-four percent of sales are made on the installment plan and the Company has 770,000 installment accounts.

**Brazil**

- 1995 Gross National Product growth: 5.5%
- Population: 158 million
- Singer distribution network:
  - 79 retail stores
  - 5,332 independent dealers, mass merchants, chain stores and department stores

After years of rampant hyperinflation and currency volatility, the economy has stabilized and is growing rapidly. The continuing success of the Real Plan and its impact on the economy allow rapid growth in per capita income and forces massive productivity improvements in the corporate sector. "This is the best macro-economic political situation for Brazil in the last 30 to 40 years" – Banco Norchem F.A., Chemical Bank's investment banking affiliate in Brazil.

Singer Brazil's sales more than doubled in 1994, from $74 million to $169 million. Sales rose another 42 percent in 1995 to $240 million. Earnings have doubled in the last two years. During this period Brazil's huge sewing machine market has grown by 50 percent, while Singer has maintained a market share of over 60 percent.

The Company has benefited from its heavy investment in retail stores. There were no retail operations in 1990. Now there are 79 stores, including 20 opened in 1995; 10 more will open their doors in 1996. Sales grew more than 30 percent in many stores last year. Several stores will have sales of more than $2 million per store in 1996. Installment sales were 49 percent of total sales.

The retail operations have produced brisk consumer durable sales, which now are half of total sales. Televisions and stereos are the top revenue generators, and the Company is a well-known distributor of major home appliances. Outside of the United States, Singer sells more furniture in Brazil than in any other country.

Significant revenues also are generated in Brazil by Singer's largest sewing machine manufacturing facility, which provides products to many parts of the world.

**Sri Lanka**

- 1995 Gross National Product growth 55%
- Population: 18 million
- Singer distribution network:
  - 81 retail stores
  - 499 mass merchants
  - 114 independent dealers

The economy has been growing in excess of five percent for several years and is forecast to continue to grow steadily. Per capita income is growing at near double-digit rates.

Singer continues to aggressively open retail stores and enlist consignment dealers to reach a population that is mostly rural. A majority of these new stores will be opened in rural agricultural towns where there is little or no competition. A three-year plan calls for increasing the distribution network by 40 percent.

Sales and operating income grew 14 percent in 1995; sales will surpass $50 million in 1996. The Company maintained its high share of the consumer durable products market, as sales of kitchen ranges rose over 40 percent and electronics over 60 percent. Furniture is currently the fastest-selling product, necessitating an expansion in manufacturing capacity.

## Case 4–5 General Medical MRI International Negotiation Simulation*

Negotiation is the most frequently used means of resolving conflicts between organizations. Particularly in international industrial marketing, when "big-ticket" and/or high technology products are involved, sales are most often negotiated. Yet principles of effective negotiation and negotiation skills are seldom part of the curriculum in business schools. The General Medical MRI Negotiation Simulation (GM/MRI) has been developed specifically to provide a context for experiential learning and practical discussion of international business negotiations. Through the simulation and associated debriefing, participants are familiarized with the complex bargaining issues, strategies, and pressures typical of relationships between industrial firms in the global market place.

The presentation of the (GM/MRI) Negotiation Simulation to follow is divided into five parts. First, the simulation is briefly described. Next, instructions for participation and administration are detailed. Third, instructions for debriefing are outlined. Fourth, variations in the use of the game are suggested. The last section, the Appendix, consists of the student materials for both the Japanese and Brazilian versions.

### A Brief Description Of The Simulation

The simulation and debriefing can be accomplished during a four-hour period. Two two-hour sessions are ideal. The GM/MRI Negotiation Simulation involves a final sales negotiation between two industrial concerns, one U.S. and the other a Japanese hospital group. The product is a $1.5 million Magnetic Resonance Imaging (MRI) System for installation in a Tokyo hospital. A second version of the simulation regards a similar Brazilian client – details are provided in the Appendix.

Six representatives of three firms are participating in the discussions: (1) a Sales Representative, a Regional Sales Manager, and a Product Sales Specialist from General Medical, Inc.; (2) the Radiology Department Manager, Chief Radiologist, and CFO of Ichikawa Hospitals. Each participant has somewhat different (and in some cases conflicting) personal and professional motives regarding the deal.

Previous to the negotiation, General Medical has submitted a price quotation for the MRI System, including several product options and General Medical standard terms and conditions. The Ichikawa Hospitals CFO has established certain purchasing objectives that would require substantial concessions from General Medical. Both sides are supplied with similar amounts of information about various environmental constraints (e.g., time schedules, market conditions, etc.). Additionally, each side has been instructed to come to an agreement during this meeting. The final agreement will consist of a completed purchase agreement, signed by representatives of both companies.

### Instructions for Participants

There are six roles to be played in the simulation (see the Appendix): three for the General Medical sales team and three for the Ichikawa Hospitals purchasing team. Groups of six students (smaller groups also work) are given the appropriate materials, and the three General Medical representatives are sent to a different location to plan bargaining strategies. The role-playing instructions are self-explanatory; however, a few questions of clarification should be anticipated. The Ichikawa Hospitals roles include a set of special cultural/behavioral instructions. The General Medical team is instructed to return at the end of 30 minutes (30 minute time limit for negotiation preparations) and begin the sales discussions.

The bargaining session is limited to one hour. If facilities allow, private intra-team conferences are permitted. In any case, the 60-minute time limit for bargaining is strictly adhered to. The simulation is complete when the final contract terms are specified and approved by the appropriate representatives of both firms (the form is included in the General Medical sales representative's materials). Usually bargaining is concluded very near the end of the time limit, and very often no agreement is reached. The simulation is designed to be a difficult negotiation. The purpose is not so much to compare outcomes, but instead the focus of classroom discussions should be negotiation PROCESSES. The simulation has been designed to provide an hour or so of negotiation interaction. Often students will ask for just "10 more minutes." However, that "10 more minutes" almost always turns into another 30, 40, or 50.

**Debriefing Instructions**

The simulation debriefing can be accomplished in approximately two hours and consists of three parts: (1) written student evaluation of the negotiations; (2) instructor-led class discussion; and (3) student discussion of the negotiation within the six-person groups.

Two forms should be prepared for evaluation of the negotiation by students. One is a negotiator evaluation form. Each participant is instructed to evaluate the performance of one member of the opposing team. The form consists of twelve dimensions of negotiator skills to be rated and includes room for brief comments. The twelve five-point items are: (1) well prepared/unprepared; (2) high aspirations/low aspirations; (3) good listener/poor listener; (4) asks good questions/doesn't ask good questions; (5) makes powerful arguments/makes weak arguments; (6) quick to respond/slow to respond; (7) honest/deceptive; (8) exploitative/accommodating; (9) patient/impatient; (10) avoids concessions/readily makes concessions; (11) creative/not creative; and (12) would be interested in working with person again/would not. On the second form the students are asked to comment on both negotiation teams' performance. The group evaluation form is much less structured and asks for general comments about "strong points" and "weak points." The forms require about 10 to 15 minutes to complete and should be filled out immediately after completion of the negotiation.

The instructor-led discussion includes four topics: (1) a comparison of the various groups' results, including disclosure of the purchasing objectives and a discussion about the reasons if no agreement is reached; (2) a description of the different and conflicting motives for each of the six roles; (3) possible effective bargaining strategies for each side; and (4) the special cultural nuances of the Japanese negotiation style. The Ichikawa Hospitals purchasing objectives should be disclosed first, followed by comparison of bargaining outcomes among student groups. However, it is important to point out during the discussion that any evaluation of negotiation outcomes is in itself a difficult task and very much dependent on one's point of view. Any deviations from standard terms and conditions or price or purchasing objectives almost always requires explanation once representatives return to their respective headquarters.

Following the comparison of results, the individual motives of each role should be shared with the group. For example, the Ichikawa Hospitals Radiology Department Manager wants the X2001 Software Package options, while the Chief Radiologist thinks that the X2001 is an unnecessary frill. All such individual motives should be revealed to the group. It should be pointed out to the students that such contrary personal and professional goals are typical of industrial sales negotiations.

The next topic to be discussed during the instructor debriefing is possible bargaining tactics. The list below is not intended to be exhaustive, but exemplary only.

The last topic of discussion is cultural influences on bargaining styles. The General Medical side should be asked if they noticed anything different or unusual about the Ichikawa Hospitals team's negotiation style. Their feelings and responses can be reported. Then the Japanese or Brazilian cultural instructions can be revealed.

### *General Medical Tactics*

The following are a few of the more important bargaining tactics which the General Medical team might have employed during the simulation.

1. *Market research at the negotiation table.* Initially maximize questions and carefully sound out the buyer's position. Get them to make a counter offer.
2. *Break and reconsider your strategy.* Once you are certain of the buyer's position and priorities, break for a private "strategy adjustment," given the new information.
3. *Raise your price.* "Things have changed since we prepared the quote." "If this seems too risky you may want to add, "...but we'll leave the price as it is." The ethics of such a tactic should be discussed. This is not a recommended strategy, but students should be aware of its use by others.
4. *Avoid concessions.* Avoid making any further commitments or concessions until you understand the full picture. "I can't say for certain until we've discussed the other issues."
5. *The mouthpiece routine.* Let the sales representative do the talking. This gives the sales manager the opportunity to change things and correct mistakes if necessary.
6. *Creativity.* Suggest concessions on issues not listed – future purchases, for example.
7. *Use all the time.* Make no concessions until near the end of the bargaining session.

### *Purchasing Team Tactics*

The following bargaining tactics might have been used by the purchasing team.

1. *Why so high?* Have the General Medial side explain "why" on every item in the quotation. Explore for weak points.
2. *Break, then reconsider your strategy.*
3. *No counter-offer.* Avoid making a counter-offer if possible. Your first offer is your first concession and it set limits on your profits from the deal.
4. *Start low.* If the other side forces a counter-offer, then start lower than your purchasing objectives. If you start with your listed price there is no room for the necessary compromise and no way to achieve your goals.
5. *Use all the time.*
6. *Good guy/bad guy routine.* Don't settle the X2001 software package issue ahead of time. Let the Chief Radiologist weaken General Medical's position.
7. *Creativity.*

Usually 45 minutes is adequate to accomplish this second part of the debriefing.

The final step in the debriefing includes discussion of the various students' evaluation forms within the groups of six. Each student reads his/her comments about the group and then the six amplify, clarify, or disagree. Sharing the information from the group evaluation forms serves as an excellent discussion stimulus. Following this group discussion, each person is given his/her individual evaluation form to review. Here again, the students usually ask questions and clarify the other's ratings of their own negotiation performance. Ordinarily this second step in the debriefing can be accomplished in about 30 minutes.

## Variations in Usage and Structure of the Simulation

There are a number of ways in which the GM/MRI Negotiation Simulation might be changed. Below are listed just a few of the possibilities.

*Smaller groups*. The simulation is ideally conducted with groups of six students. However, groups of five (the Radiology Department Manger's information is given to the Ichikawa Hospitals CFO) or four (and the General Medical Product Sales Specialist's information is given to the General Medical sales manger) also work well.

*Use of videotaping facilities*. The availability of videotaping facilities dramatically enriches the GM/MRI Negotiation Simulation experience. Each bargaining session would be videotaped. Following completion of the evaluation forms, each student would be required to review the taped negotiation and "correct" his or her evaluations. Such an exercise allows the students to view themselves as others do. Moreover, our limited capabilities of perception and memory are demonstrated by contrasting the recollections of events to the "reality" of the videotape. Videotaping also allows the instructor the opportunity to view and evaluate the performance of each team, even when several simulations are conducted simultaneously. The videotapes might be used during the debriefing to demonstrate successful or unsuccessful tactics. Finally, students absent from class on the day of the simulation might be required to view one of the tapes and fill out the evaluation forms. Such an assignment would enrich their participation in the instructor's debriefing.

# APPENDIX

## STUDENT MATERIALS

Each of the six role descriptions requires a different set of support documents. See the bottom of each for a list.

### 1. Materials for the Japanese (client is Ichikawa Hospitals) version of the simulation.

## GENERAL MEDICAL PRODUCT SALES SPECIALIST (J)

You will be playing the role of a Product Sales Specialist working for General Medical, Inc. (GMI), a manufacturer of a broad line of medical instruments and equipment. You have been selected by your firm to participate in negotiations with representatives of Ichikawa Hospitals, a chain of nine hospitals headquartered in Tokyo, Japan regarding their purchase of a model 2000 MRI. A price quotation for the basic system and associated product options is attached.

As a member of the Technical Sales Support Department of your firm, you are very interested in communicating to the client personnel the advantages of the options listed. It has been the experience of those in your department that when GMI supplies such options, fewer operational difficulties are encountered during installation and use of the system. Service contracts have proven advantageous in avoiding warranty work possibly caused by improper servicing by client personnel. GMI is recognized in the industry as the leader in providing cutting-edge technology and user-friendly MRI systems.

Both the TOF Angiography and the Flow Analysis options will be appropriate for cardiovascular work done at Ichikawa Hospitals. The X2001 Software Package you are particularly proud of since you advised GMI engineering staff on its development. It provides much faster and more flexible manipulation of the images and has wonderful ease of use qualities. However, since the package is new there may still be bugs to worked out. Ichikawa Hospitals is also the first foreign client to which it has been offered, so the price quoted for this option is relatively low.

You have thirty minutes to plan bargaining strategies with other members of your negotiation team. Feel free to use part or all of the information provided above in shaping your strategies. Create additional arguments to bolster your position if you so desire. It is important that you play the assigned role to the best of your abilities in order to maximize the learning of all participants. Although you can exchange information from these forms, please do not exchange forms with the other members of your negotiation team. You will have one hour to reach an agreement with the representatives of Ichikawa Hospitals. You may make notes on these forms and ask questions if clarification of the instructions is needed.

(attach price quotation)

## GENERAL MEDICAL REGIONAL SALES MANAGER (J)

You will be playing the role of a regional sales manager for General Medical, Inc. (GMI), a manufacturer of a broad product line of medical instruments and equipment. You will be heading up a team of GMI representatives in the final sales negotiations for a $1.5 million magnetic resonance imaging system (MRI) for Ichikawa Hospitals, a chain of nine hospitals headquartered in Tokyo, Japan. Your salesperson has been conducting preliminary sales and technical discussions. During this final session with the client personnel you will be expected to make the necessary decisions to conclude the agreement with Ichikawa.

This contract is particularly important for your firm because so far, sales of MRIs in the Japanese market have been dominated by Japanese competitors. The sale to Ichikawa Hospitals, a well-respected general hospital chain will be a crucial "foot in the door" in this increasingly important market. The opportunity to sell the X2001 Software Package, a brand new one for General Medical, is also important because the firm has had little experience with Japanese medical personnel using its advanced operating systems in English.

Your sales person has already submitted a price quotation to Ichikawa (see the attached copy). Company policy allows up to a 10 percent price reduction at your discretion. Any further reduction in price will require substantial justification on your return to headquarters. Additionally, a large part of your annual compensation depends on achieving profit objectives established at headquarters. Finally, according to market research, GMI's competitors have recently raised prices on comparable products, thus making your bid very attractive.

Recently, several customers have requested an arbitration clause as part of the terms and conditions. Your legal department feels that such clauses are not necessary. Indeed, in the past when GMI and client disagreements have gone to arbitration by a third party, GMI has consistently lost out. Thus, the legal department has asked you to actively avoid arbitration clauses of any sort.

Finally, the Japanese are likely to request to pay in yen. Your financial people have a strong bias against customers forcing currency risks on GMI and have asked you to ensure the contract be written in American dollars.

You have thirty minutes to plan bargaining strategies with other members of your negotiation team. Feel free to use part or all of the information provided above in shaping your strategies. Create additional arguments to bolster your position if you so desire. It is important that you play the assigned role to the best of your abilities in order to maximize the learning of all participants. Although you can exchange information from these forms, please do not exchange forms with the other members of your negotiation team. You will have one hour to reach an agreement with the representatives of Ichikawa Hospitals. You may make notes on these forms and ask questions if clarification of the instructions is needed.

(attach price quotation)

## GENERAL MEDICAL SALES REPRESENTATIVE (J)

You will be playing the role of a sales representative of General Medical, Inc. (GMI), a manufacturer of a broad product line of medical instruments and equipment. You have arranged a meeting between representatives of your company (your sales manager, a product sales specialist, and you) and the representatives of your client firm, Ichikawa Hospitals, a chain of nine hospitals headquartered in Tokyo, Japan. There will be three Ichikawa Hospitals personnel attending the meeting—the Radiology Department Manager, the Chief Radiologist, and the CFO. The purpose of this meeting is to negotiate the final details of a contract you have been working on during the last six months. This particularly contract is personally important to you because it will push your sales performance for the year into the bonus area.

You have submitted, with headquarters' approval, a price quotation to the client (a copy is attached). Most of your clients, particularly those in foreign countries, ask for substantial price reductions below original quotes. You have the opportunity to "trade off" hardware price for other favorable terms and conditions which are part of the standard agreement. GMI's standard terms and conditions are listed as part of the attached price quotation. In the past you have found that sticking to the standard warranty is considered most important by your headquarters. Particularly when installations are located in new markets, costs of labor and warranty work can be extremely unpredictable.

The product options specified by the client are not particularly important to you. You are very concerned that an agreement be reached for the basic system, as it dramatically affects your annual bonus. However, the product extras have no effect on your performance evaluation or compensation.

Your Ichikawa Hospitals counterparts have been hinting that an agreement written in yen is preferable. The yen has been depreciating recently, so this may be a problem in the discussions.

You have thirty minutes to plan bargaining strategies with other members of your negotiation team. Feel free to use part or all of the information provided above in shaping your strategies. Create additional arguments to bolster your position if you so desire. It is important that you play the assigned role to the best of your abilities in order to maximize the learning of all participants. Although you can exchange information from these forms, please do not exchange forms with the other members of your negotiation team. You will have one hour to reach an agreement with the representatives of Ichikawa Hospitals. You may make notes on these forms and ask questions if clarification of the instructions is needed.

The terms of the final contract will be recorded on the attached contract and signed by representatives of both companies.

(attach price quotation, blank contract)

## ICHIKAWA HOSPTIALS CHIEF FINANCIAL OFFICER (J)

You will be playing the role of the Chief Financial Officer for Ichikawa Hospitals, a chain of nine general hospitals headquartered in Tokyo, Japan. You are working with your medical staff in the final negotiations for a Magnetic Resonance Imaging (MRI) system for installation in your central Tokyo hospital being offered by an American company, General Medical, Inc. (GMI). A sales representative at GMI has submitted a bid ($1.5 million) for the system that may or may not be the best solution to your purchasing problem.

You consider the price quoted by GMI to be out of line with local Japanese manufacturers. Indeed, one of your college classmates working for Onzo Electric says his company will beat any price GMI offers. You recognize that GMI's products are superior, but you also know that GMI is trying to break into the Japanese market and should be willing to make substantial price concessions.

Of the terms and conditions included in the initial bid, you feel that three are critical. First, in recent months GMI has had difficulty meeting delivery dates. Therefore, the late delivery penalty will be an important issue during the discussions. Second, you believe that it is imperative that your vendors bear the risk of currency fluctuations, and therefore the agreement should be written in yen, not dollars. Indeed, latest forecasts are for the yen to decline during the upcoming year.

Your firm wishes to stay as far away as possible from American-style legal disputes, so you see a third party arbitration clause as an essential part of the contract.

Another issue of concern is an internal lack of harmony between your Radiology Department Manager and the Chief Radiologist. The latter has little interest in the X2001 Software Package—he sees it as an unnecessary and potentially unreliable frill. The Department Manager sees its purchase as an opportunity to aid in the development of similar products which might be sold throughout Japan.

Finally, the Chief Radiologist has asked you to consider buying two systems, the second to be installed in your central Yokohama hospital. Even though you are not sure about even one GMI system, you have included a second one in the Purchasing Objectives you've supplied the others on your negotiation team.

You have thirty minutes to plan bargaining strategies with other members of your negotiation team. Feel free to use part or all of the information provided above in shaping your strategies. Create additional arguments to bolster your position if you so desire. It is important that you play the assigned role to the best of your abilities in order to maximize the learning of all participants. Included in your materials will be some special instructions about "acting" Japanese. Have fun with these—try to make your portrayal as realistic as possible. Although you can exchange information from these forms, please do not exchange forms with the other members of your negotiation team. You will have one hour to reach an agreement with the representatives of General Medical, Inc. You may make notes on these forms and ask questions if clarification of the instructions is needed.

(attach price quotation, purchasing objectives, negotiation style instructions)

## ICHIKAWA HOSPITALS CHIEF RADIOLOGIST (J)

You will be playing the role of the Chief Radiologist at the central Tokyo location of Ichikawa Hospitals, a chain of nine general hospitals headquartered in your building. You are representing your fellow physicians and working with your administrative counterparts in the final negotiations for a Magnetic Resonance Imaging (MRI) system being offered by an American company, General Medical, Inc. (GMI). A sales representative at GMI has submitted a bid ($1.5 million) for the system and you are quite interested in getting this advanced equipment as soon as possible.

You consider the General Medical MRI to be a far superior product to any currently available from Japanese suppliers. Its speed and ease of use characteristics will not only result in increased operational efficiency at your hospital, but some of the newer cardiovascular imaging product options will help you provide a new, higher level of care to your older patients. You are, however, quite skeptical about the value of the "experimental" X2001 Software Package option. You know from discussions with your colleagues at international medical conventions who are most familiar with GMI's products that new software packages always have bugs. Indeed, such bugs have "brought down" the whole system previously. You would prefer to use the standard software, and not take a chance with the X2001.

Elatedly, you prefer that GMI train your own people to service the system. That would make the service contract unnecessary and you don't trust GMI to provide timely service in Japan anyway.

Finally, your fellow radiologists in Yokohama are also urging you to order a second MRI for their central hospital. You mentioned it to your CFO previously, but s/he seemed quite distracted at the time. However, a second system is included in the Purchasing Objectives the CFO has given you (see attached).

You have thirty minutes to plan bargaining strategies with other members of your negotiation team. Feel free to use part or all of the information provided above in shaping your strategies. Create additional arguments to bolster your position if you so desire. It is important that you play the assigned role to the best of your abilities in order to maximize the learning of all participants. Included in your materials will be some special instructions about "acting" Japanese. Have fun with these—try to make your portrayal as realistic as possible. Although you can exchange information from these forms, please do not exchange forms with the other members of your negotiation team. You will have one hour to reach an agreement with the representatives of General Medical, Inc. You may make notes on these forms and ask questions if clarification of the instructions is needed.

(attach price quotation, purchasing objectives, negotiation style instructions)

## ICHIKAWA HOSPITALS RADIOLOGY DEPARTMENT MANAGER (J)

You will be playing the role of the Radiology Department Manager for Ichikawa Hospitals, a chain of nine general hospitals headquartered in Tokyo, Japan. You are working with your CFO and the senior Radiologist on your medical staff in the final negotiations for a Magnetic Resonance Imaging (MRI) system for installation in your central Tokyo hospital. A sales representative of the American Company, General Medical, Inc. (GMI) has submitted a bid for the system preferred by your medical staff. Surprisingly, the CFO has also listed a second MRI for installation at your central Yokohama hospital in her/his Purchasing Objectives (see attached).

You know your CFO is primarily interested in saving money. From your talks with the senior Radiologist you know there is a strong bias against including the X2001 Software Package option. Its reliability is the main objection. However, you see obtaining this state-of-the-art software as the key to an important business opportunity for Ichikawa Hospitals. You and your staff hope to work with the Ichikawa Hospitals radiologists (particularly the younger ones) and GMI in developing Japanese language software for MRIs and a variety of other medical imaging instruments. Japanese manufacturers have been generally lagging behind the Americans in software development, and you see this as a big future opportunity for developing products for the entire Japanese health care market. You are quite concerned that the X2001 was not included on the Purchasing Objectives distributed by the CFO.

Finally, you would prefer to have GMI provide service for the systems. You feel the more contact with the GMI technical personnel the better, given your long-term objectives.

You have thirty minutes to plan bargaining strategies with other members of your negotiation team. Feel free to use part or all of the information provided above in shaping your strategies. Create additional arguments to bolster your position if you so desire. It is important that you play the assigned role to the best of your abilities in order to maximize the learning of all participants. Included in your materials will be some special instructions about "acting" Japanese. Have fun with these—try to make your portrayal as realistic as possible. Although you can exchange information from these forms, please do not exchange forms with the other members of your negotiation team. You will have one hour to reach an agreement with the representatives of General Medical, Inc. You may make notes on these forms and ask questions if clarification of the instructions is needed.

(attach price quotation, purchasing objectives, negotiation style instructions)

**Price Quotations**

| | |
|---|---|
| Deep Vision 2000 MRI (basic unit) | $1,200,000 |
| Product options: | |
| • 2D and 3D Time-of-flight (TOF) angiography for capturing fast flow | 150,000 |
| • Flow analysis for quantification of cardiovascular studies | 70,000 |
| • X2001 Software Package | 20,000 |
| Service contract (2 years normal maintenance, parts, and labor) | 60,000 |
| Total price | $1,500,000 |

**Standard Terms and Conditions**

| | |
|---|---|
| Delivery | 6 months |
| Penalty for late delivery | $10,000/month |
| Cancellation charges | 10% of contract price |
| Warranty (for defective machinery) | parts, one year |
| Terms of payment | COD |

**Ichikawa Hospitals Purchasing Objectives (J)**

| | | |
|---|---|---|
| **Two (2)** Deep Vision 2000 MRIs | | 226 million yen |
| 2D and 3D TOF Angiography (2) | | 28 million yen |
| Flow Analysis (2) | | 13 million yen |
| Service Contract (3 years) | | 11 million yen |
| | TOTAL PRICE | 278 million yen |

---

| | |
|---|---|
| Delivery | 3 months |
| Penalty for late delivery | $12,000/month |
| Cancellation charges | 2% of contract |
| Warranty | parts and labor, 2 years |
| Terms of payment | 4 equal payments:<br>1st at delivery,<br>2nd at start-up,<br>3rd and 4th at 90-day intervals |
| Third Party Arbitration Clause | included |

**Final Contract (J)**

Deep Vision 2000 MRI
Product Options (circle those selected)

Angiography
Flow analysis
X2001 Software

TOTAL Price $ ____________

Service Contact (list conditions)

______________________________

______________________________

Price $ ____________

______________________________________________________________

Terms and conditions ______________

Delivery ______________

Penalty ______________

Cancellation Charges ______________

Terms of Payment

______________

______________

Warranty Parts _____ Labor _____ Years _____

Arbitration clause Yes _____ No ____

______________________________________________________________

Signatures

______________________________ ______________________________

Ichikawa Hospitals Representative General Medical, Inc. Representative

## JAPANESE NEGOTIATION STYLE INSTRUCTIONS

The simulation becomes much more interesting for everyone if a little culture is brought into the game. Please try to incorporate the following three aspects of Japanese negotiation style into your behavior at the negotiation table.

1. Emphasize asking QUESTIONS. Even when they answer, ask the same question in another way.
2. Deliberately allow SILENT PERIODS.
3. Don't settle any issues until the end. It is OK for you to bring up issues again later in the negotiation, even if the other side thinks they were settled.

# APPENDIX

## STUDENT MATERIALS

2. **Materials for the Brazilian (client is Corcovado Hospital) version of the simulation.**

## GENERAL MEDICAL PRODUCT SALES SPECIALIST (B)

You will be playing the role of a Product Sales Specialist working for General Medical, Inc. (GMI), a manufacturer of a broad line of medical instruments and equipment. You have been selected by your firm to participate in negotiations with representatives of Corcovado Hospital, a large private hospital located in Rio de Janeiro, Brazil regarding their purchase of a model 2000 MRI. A price quotation for the basic system and associated product options is attached.

As a member of the Technical Sales Support Department of your firm you are very interested in communicating to the client personnel the advantages of the options listed. It has been the experience of those in your department that when GMI supplies such options, fewer operational difficulties are encountered during installation and use of the system. Service contracts have proven advantageous in avoiding warranty work possibly caused by improper servicing by client personnel, and they are quite profitable as well. GMI is recognized in the industry as the leader in providing cutting-edge technology and user-friendly MRI systems.

Both the TOF Angiography and the Flow Analysis options will be appropriate for cardiovascular work done at Corcovado Hospital. The X2001 Software Package you are particularly proud of since you advised GMI engineering staff on its development. It provides much faster and more flexible manipulation of the images and has wonderful ease of use qualities. However, since the package is new there may still be bugs to be worked out. Corcovado Hospital is also the first foreign client to which it has been offered, so the price quoted for this option is relatively low. There have been some questions asked about the very new (not yet approved by the FDA in the U.S.) Probe Spectroscopy option for head studies. You are personally reluctant to push this product in foreign countries ahead of its U.S. approval. However, others in the company don't feel that way.

You have thirty minutes to plan bargaining strategies with other members of your negotiation team. Feel free to use part or all of the information provided above in shaping your strategies. Create additional arguments to bolster your position if you so desire. It is important that you play the assigned role to the best of your abilities in order to maximize the learning of all participants. Although you can exchange information from these forms, please do not exchange forms with the other members of your negotiation team. You will have one hour to reach an agreement with the representatives of Corcovado Hospital. You may make notes on these forms and ask questions if clarification of the instructions is needed.

(attach price quotation)

## GENERAL MEDICAL REGIONAL SALES MANAGER (B)

You will be playing the role of a regional sales manager for General Medical, Inc. (GMI), a manufacturer of a broad product line of medical instruments and equipment. You will be heading up a team of GMI representatives in the final sales negotiations for a $1.5 million magnetic resonance imaging system (MRI) for Corcovado Hospital, a large private hospital located in Rio de Janeiro, Brazil. Your salesperson has been conducting preliminary sales and technical discussions. During this final session with the client personnel you will be expected to make the necessary decisions to conclude the agreement.

This contract is particularly important for your firm because so far, sales of MRIs in Latin America have faced tough competition from Japanese firms. The sale to Corcovado Hospital, one of the most respected private hospitals in the country, would be a crucial competitive coup in this increasingly important market. The opportunity to sell the X2001 Software Package, a brand new one for General Medical, is also important because the firm has had little experience with foreign medical personnel using its advanced operating systems in English.

Your sales person has already submitted a price quotation to Corcovado (see the attached copy). Company policy allows up to a 10 percent price reduction at your discretion. Any further reduction in price will require substantial justification upon your return to headquarters. Additionally, a large part of your annual compensation depends on achieving profit objectives established at headquarters. Finally, according to market research, GMI's competitors have recently raised prices on comparable products, thus making your bid very attractive.

Recently, several customers have requested an arbitration clause as part of the terms and conditions. Your legal department feels that such clauses are not necessary. Indeed, in the past when GMI and client disagreements have gone to arbitration by a third party, GMI has consistently lost out. Thus, the legal department has asked you to actively avoid arbitration clauses of any sort.

Finally, the Brazilians are likely to request to pay in *reals*. Your financial people have a strong bias against customers forcing currency risks on GMI and have asked you to ensure the contract be written in American dollars.

You have thirty minutes to plan bargaining strategies with other members of your negotiation team. Feel free to use part or all of the information provided above in shaping your strategies. Create additional arguments to bolster your position if you so desire. It is important that you play the assigned role to the best of your abilities in order to maximize the learning of all participants. Although you can exchange information from these forms, please do not exchange forms with the other members of your negotiation team. You will have one hour to reach an agreement with the representatives of Corcovado Hospital. You may make notes on these forms and ask questions if clarification of the instructions is needed.

(attach price quotation)

## GENERAL MEDICAL SALES REPRESENTATIVE (B)

You will be playing the role of a sales representative of General Medical, Inc. (GMI), a manufacturer of a broad product line of medical instruments and equipment. You have arranged a meeting between representatives of your company (your sales manager, a product sales specialist, and you) and the representatives of your client firm, Corcovado Hospital, a large private hospital in Rio de Janeiro, Brazil. There will be three Corcovado Hospital personnel attending the meeting—the Radiology Department Manager, the Chief Radiologist, and the CFO. The purpose of this meeting is to negotiate the final details of a contract you have been working on during the last six months. This particularly contract is personally important to you because it will push your sales performance for the year into the bonus area.

You have submitted, with headquarters' approval, a price quotation to the client (a copy is attached). Most of your clients, particularly those in foreign countries, ask for substantial price reductions below original quotes. You have the opportunity to "trade off" hardware price for other favorable terms and conditions which are part of the standard agreement. GMI's standard terms and conditions are listed as part of the attached price quotation. In the past you have found that sticking to the standard warranty is considered most important by your headquarters. Particularly when installations are located in new markets, costs of labor in warranty work can be extremely unpredictable.

In your last conversation with the Chief Radiologist at Corcovado he mentioned an interest in GMI's new Probe Spectroscopy option (list price = $50,000) for head studies, which hasn't yet received FDA approval. However, the product options specified by the client are not particularly important to you. You are very concerned that an agreement be reached for the basic system, as it dramatically affects your annual bonus. However, the product extras have no effect on your performance evaluation or compensation.

Your Corcovado Hospital counterparts have been hinting that an agreement written in *reals* is preferable. The *real* has been depreciating recently, so this may be a problem in the discussions.

You have thirty minutes to plan bargaining strategies with other members of your negotiation team. Feel free to use part or all of the information provided above in shaping your strategies. Create additional arguments to bolster your position if you so desire. It is important that you play the assigned role to the best of your abilities in order to maximize the learning of all participants. Although you can exchange information from these forms, please do not exchange forms with the other members of your negotiation team. You will have one hour to reach an agreement with the representatives of Corcovado Hospital. You may make notes on these forms and ask questions if clarification of the instructions is needed.

The terms of the final contract will be recorded on the attached contract and signed by representatives of both companies.

(attach price quotation, blank contract)

**CORCOVADO HOSPTIAL CHIEF FINANCIAL OFFICER (B)**

You will be playing the role of the Chief Financial Officer for Corcovado Hospital, a large private hospital located in Rio de Janeiro, Brazil. You are working with your medical staff in the final negotiations for a Magnetic Resonance Imaging (MRI) system for installation in your hospital being offered by an American company, General Medical, Inc. (GMI). A sales representative at GMI has submitted a bid ($1.5 million) for the system that may or may not be the best solution to your purchasing problem.

You consider the price quoted by GMI to be out of line with their Japanese competitors. Indeed, a good friend working for Hokkaido Electric says his company will beat any price GMI offers. You recognize that GMI's products are superior, but you also know that GMI is trying to beat the Japanese and should be willing to make substantial price concessions.

Of the terms and conditions included in the initial bid, you feel that three are critical. First, in recent months GMI has had difficulty meeting delivery dates. Therefore, the late delivery penalty will be an important issue during the discussions. Second, you believe that it is imperative that your vendors bear the risk of currency fluctuations, and therefore the agreement should be written in *reals*, not dollars. Indeed, latest forecasts are for the *real* to decline during the upcoming year.

Your firm wishes to stay as far away as possible from American-style legal disputes, so you see a third party arbitration clause as an essential part of the contract.

Another issue of concern is an internal dispute between your Radiology Department Manager and the Chief Radiologist. The latter wishes to order two MRI systems right away, and argues that the current patient load justifies the aggressive purchasing. The Department Manager prefers to see how this first GMI purchase works out before committing to a second system.

You have thirty minutes to plan bargaining strategies with other members of your negotiation team. Feel free to use part or all of the information provided above in shaping your strategies. Create additional arguments to bolster your position if you so desire. It is important that you play the assigned role to the best of your abilities in order to maximize the learning of all participants. Included in your materials will be some special instructions about "acting" Brazilian. Have fun with these—try to make your portrayal as realistic as possible. Although you can exchange information from these forms, please do not exchange forms with the other members of your negotiation team. You will have one hour to reach an agreement with the representatives of General Medical, Inc. You may make notes on these forms and ask questions if clarification of the instructions is needed.

(attach price quotation, purchasing objectives, negotiation style instructions)

## CORCOVADO HOSPITAL CHIEF RADIOLOGIST (B)

You will be playing the role of the Chief Radiologist at Corcovado Hospital, a large private hospital in Rio de Janeiro. You are representing your fellow physicians and working with your administrative counterparts in the final negotiations for a Magnetic Resonance Imaging (MRI) system being offered by an American company, General Medical, Inc. (GMI). A sales representative at GMI has submitted a bid ($1.5 million) for the system and you are quite interested in getting this advanced equipment as soon as possible.

You consider the General Medical MRI to be a far superior product to any currently available from other suppliers including the Japanese. Its speed and ease of use characteristics will not only result in increased operational efficiency at your hospital, but some of the newer cardiovascular imaging product options will help you provide a new, higher level of care to your older patients. You also are quite keen on adding GMI's new Probe Spectroscopy option for head studies (list price = $50,000). It may not yet be approved by the FDA in the U.S., but this is not an obstacle in Brazil.

Finally, your fellow radiologists are also urging you to order a second MRI. Patient load and quality of care more than justify the extra expense. You mentioned it to your CFO previously, but s/he seemed quite distracted at the time. However, a second system is included in the Purchasing Objectives the CFO has given you (see attached).

You have thirty minutes to plan bargaining strategies with other members of your negotiation team. Feel free to use part or all of the information provided above in shaping your strategies. Create additional arguments to bolster your position if you so desire. It is important that you play the assigned role to the best of your abilities in order to maximize the learning of all participants. Included in your materials will be some special instructions about "acting" Brazilian. Have fun with these—try to make your portrayal as realistic as possible. Although you can exchange information from these forms, please do not exchange forms with the other members of your negotiation team. You will have one hour to reach an agreement with the representatives of General Medical, Inc. You may make notes on these forms and ask questions if clarification of the instructions is needed.

(attach price quotation, purchasing objectives, negotiation style instructions)

## CORCOVADO HOSPITAL RADIOLOGY DEPARTMENT MANAGER (B)

You will be playing the role of the Radiology Department Manager for Corcovado Hospital, a large private hospital in Rio de Janeiro, Brazil. You are working with your CFO and the senior Radiologist on your medical staff in the final negotiations for a Magnetic Resonance Imaging (MRI) system for installation in your hospital. A sales representative of the American company, General Medical, Inc. (GMI) has submitted a bid for the system preferred by your medical staff. Surprisingly, the CFO has also listed a second MRI in her/his Purchasing Objectives (see attached).

You see buying two MRIs now as a big potential problem. Although GMI has a wonderful reputation, you do not know any of their personnel well. A new GMI sales representative seems to call on you every six months. Your preference is to perhaps buy one system and use it for at least six months before buying another. That would give your financial and technical staff some time to get to know the GMI people. You will be the person responsible for coordinating servicing and repair of the system, and if things don't work efficiently with GMI, you are the one that gets blamed.

Finally, you're very much against any risky new product features like the X2001 Software Package. New systems are notorious for bugs that can cause major system failures, and you don't trust GMI to repair/service the product in a timely manner. Indeed, great service has been the best part of the long relationship Corcovado Hospitals has enjoyed with Hokkaido Electric, a Japanese maker of a variety of medical instruments and systems. Clearly GMI now produces the best product, but their reputation for after-sales services is spotty.

You have thirty minutes to plan bargaining strategies with other members of your negotiation team. Feel free to use part or all of the information provided above in shaping your strategies. Create additional arguments to bolster your position if you so desire. It is important that you play the assigned role to the best of your abilities in order to maximize the learning of all participants. Included in your materials will be some special instructions about "acting" Brazilian. Have fun with these—try to make your portrayal as realistic as possible. Although you can exchange information from these forms, please do not exchange forms with the other members of your negotiation team. You will have one hour to reach an agreement with the representatives of General Medical, Inc. You may make notes on these forms and ask questions if clarification of the instructions is needed.

(attach price quotation, purchasing objectives, negotiation style instructions)

## Price Quotations

| | |
|---|---|
| Deep Vision 2000 MRI (basic unit) | $1,200,000 |
| Product options: | |
| 2D and 3D Time-of-flight (TOF) angiography for capturing fast flow | 150,000 |
| Flow analysis for quantification of cardiovascular studies | 70,000 |
| X2001 Software Package | 20,000 |
| Service contract (2 years normal maintenance, parts, and labor) | 60,000 |
| Total price | $1,500,000 |

## Standard Terms and Conditions

| | |
|---|---|
| Delivery | 6 months |
| Penalty for late delivery | $10,000/month |
| Cancellation charges | 10% of contract price |
| Warranty (for defective machinery) | parts, one year |
| Terms of payment | COD |

## Corcovado Hospitals Purchasing Objectives (B)

| | | |
|---|---|---|
| **Two (2)** Deep Vision 2000 MRIs | | 2,000,000 reals |
| 2D and 3D TOF Angiography (2) | | 240,000 reals |
| Flow Analysis (2) | | 110,000 reals |
| Service Contract (3 years) | | 97,000 reals |
| | TOTAL PRICE | 2,477,000 reals |

---

| | |
|---|---|
| Delivery | 3 months |
| Penalty for late delivery | $12,000/month |
| Cancellation charges | 2% of contract |
| Warranty | parts and labor, 2 years |
| Terms of payment | 4 equal payments:<br>1st at delivery,<br>2nd at start-up,<br>3rd and 4th at 90-day intervals |
| Third Party Arbitration Clause | included |

**Final Contract (B)**

Deep Vision 2000 MRI
Product Options (circle those selected)

Angiography
Flow analysis
X2001 Software

TOTAL Price $ ____________

Service Contact (list conditions)

______________________________

______________________________

Price $ ____________

______________________________________________________________

Terms and conditions ____________

Delivery ____________

Penalty ____________

Cancellation Charges ____________

Terms of Payment

______________

______________

Warranty Parts ___ Labor ____ Years ____

Arbitration clause Yes ____ No ____

______________________________________________________________

Signatures

______________________________ ______________________________

Corcovado Representative General Medical, Inc. Representative

## BRAZILIAN NEGOTIATION STYLE INSTRUCTIONS

The simulation becomes much more interesting for everyone if a little culture is brought into the game. Please try to incorporate the following three aspects of Brazilian negotiation style into your behavior at the negotiation table.

1. Do not talk about business directly during the first 10 minutes of the game. Sports, the weather, the world economy are all OK. But, during the first 10 minutes if the other side brings up business, you change the subject.
2. Try to INTERRUPT your counterparts frequently.
3. Periodically reach across the table and pat your counterpart's arm when you say something friendly.

## Case 4–6 Tough Decisions for Boeing

Boeing's biggest problem isn't Airbus; instead it's managing the volatility inherent in the industry. The mismanagement of this volatility reflected in huge and continuing production bottlenecks is eating the firm's profits this year, at a time when the firm should be hugely profitable.

1. Boeing has now begun development of a new "near-the-speed-of-sound" jet liner and has dropped plans to respond directly to the Airbus A380. The new "Sonic Crusier" or 20XX will have a delta shaped wing, fly about 20% faster than current commercial jets (excluding the Concorde), and hold about 200 passengers. The increased speed will shave about one hour from a trans-continental American flight. Airbus has received orders for 66 380s as of March 2001 while Boeing has received no new orders for its stretch version of the 747 that will seat 500-plus passengers. For details see Laurence Zuckerman, "At Near the Speed of Sound, Boeing Tries to Leave Airbus Behind," International Herald Tribune (from the New York Times), March 31–April 1, 2001, page 1.

2. BA's published price estimates are about $34 million per jet. Assuming BA is looking for the lowest capacity 737–300 which Boeing lists at $45 million to $55 million the negotiations are going to be tough. Pricing for the big BA business should reflect the huge backlog the firm already has. That means high prices, perhaps even above the $45 million mark. Airbus won't be able to fill all those orders. Moreover, given the current duopoly circumstance, Airbus will probably follow the Boeing's prices up.

3. Key will be raising prices during the boom. Pricing should be very flexible and reflect the notion that each new order has to "compete" for a space in Boeing's strapped production line. Being tough on cancellation fees in contracts will also be important because order cancellations are inevitable when the bust arrives. Maximize overtime in labor and avoid expanding the labor force. Likewise, resist the temptation to add capacity to meet current demand. Keep the product line broad and international production ventures warm, both will be important during an industry downturn.

All the recommendations are controversial and go against the conventional market share dogma of recent decades. We hope that such ideas stimulate useful discussions of the material in Chapter 13.

Associated articles:

Henry Chu, "Asian Clouds Cast a Shadow Over Boeing Flight Path," *Los Angeles Times*, February 15, 1998, p. D1.

Charles Goldsmith, "British Airways Seeks Airbus, Boeing Bids for Jets," *Wall Street Journal*, February 24, 1998, p. A16.

Stanley Holmes, "Boeing Will Likely Phase Out MD-80 and MD-90 Jet Production Lines," *Knight-Ridder Tribune Business News*, October 1, 1997.

Karen Kaplan, "737 Retrofit Has Boeing in Tailspin," *Los Angeles Times*, April 23, 1998, pp. D3 and D15.

Mike Maharry, "Market Analysts Foresee Brighter Times for Boeing," *Knight-Ridder Tribune Business News*, February 24, 1998.

## Case 4–7 National Office Machines – Motivating Japanese Salespeople: Straight Salary or Commission?

The problem of changing management methods and also motivating salesmen in another culture is highlighted in this particular case. The entire Japanese system, their basis for motivation, is so different from the U.S. method and system that major problems can arise in changing the basis for compensation. Several questions should be emphasized. Should a firm change its method of operation to blend more closely with the Japanese, since to change the Japanese culture is such a difficult problem? Or should the U.S. firm force a change in motivation methods because it realizes that Japanese culture is already changing? Problems associated with running a dual system between the old and the new should be highlighted and the very serious question of whether or not the Japanese will ever change their system should be pinpointed. There has been much written on the subject. The following piece may provide interesting background.

I don't think Japan is as westernized as is widely thought. Those who believe this are looking only at the surface of life, not at the essence of Japanese culture.

To be sure, many international conference halls and hotels of Japan seem totally westernized, as do the meetings that go inside them. But if there were an x-ray machine with which we cold look into people's minds, I believe many Japanese thoughts and feelings would seem "odd" and "fantastic" from a western point of view. For example, we'd find the Japanese quite at home with various gods and several religions. He thinks nothing of being married in a Christian church, praying at a Shinto shrine on New Year's Day, and holding funerals and memorials for ancestors according to Buddhist rites. This multi-layered, pluralistic thinking and living is basic to Japanese culture.

Consider also the daily life of the Japanese. It looks very westernized, but is a surface phenomenon. I, for instance, look very westernized in my suit and tie, but once I go home I take them off end get back into the traditional kimono. The same is true of food. Although I eat western food quite often, I haven't given up Japanese food. In effect, a layer of westernization has been added to the existing layers in the Japanese mind.

In trying to make Japanese culture comprehensible to international society, Japanese scholars and intellectuals tend to emphasize Japan's homogeneity with western cultures—just as the Rolumeikan party-goers did. But it is misleading to extend western terms to the underlying principles that unify, organize, and actually operate science, technology, industry and the economy. Japan's culture may be in many of its forms similar to Europe's and America's, but in nature and spirit it is very different.

The cultural legacy of the *samurai* and the *han* system lives in many areas of Japan's economy. In the large industries of modern Japan, for example, the executives are the lords or *samurai* of modem *hans*. In fact, some of the titles for officials such as *juyaku* and *torishimariyaku* from the days of the *han* system are still in use in today's companies.

The relationship between the *samurai* and his *han* was one of hereditary employment, as a general rule. Employment in modern Japanese companies is no longer hereditary but it is in general lifetime. Just as the relationship between the *samurai* and his *han* was marked by a deep loyalty, the same spirit continues today in Japanese enterprises, and the ethics and esthetics of the old order remain.

Nor did the influx of western people and ideas after World War II change Japan. For example, many people at one point thought the lifetime employment and seniority systems in Japan would be abolished as old-fashioned left-overs of feudalism. Not only did they continue, but in a sense they became even more developed. The lifetime employment system doesn't exist in a vacuum. It exists in a society which has a long history.

When Westerners study Japanese culture they sometimes think of it as mystical, beyond the intellect. There is, however, nothing particularly mystical about Japanese culture. It can be explained logically. But the premises are different than those of western logic. The first premise in the Japanese esthetics of behavior is concealing the self. From a Japanese viewpoint, western culture appears to be developed on the principle of being conspicuous. As in other East Asian countries self-assertion is not a virtue in Japan.

In general, human economic activities are based on the desire for wealth. While the Japanese have nothing against making money, it is rather the fascination or absorption in the activity itself that drives the Japanese. They like the planning, the running around, the whole process, the flurry and excitement of it all. Being immersed in and "drinking up" the various activities of business, produces in them a kind of aesthetic intoxication in which they revel. This, I believe, is the motivating power behind the spirited economic activities of the Japanese.**

The excerpt represented above reflects what many see as the traditional Japan of the past. Japan is changing, albeit not overnight, but nevertheless changing. Contrast the piece above with the Japan of the future as revealed by excepts from several current articles.

In a country famous for corporate loyalty, "lifetime" employees suddenly are harkening to the headhunter's call. Many are beginning to change jobs in return for better pay, greater opportunity and a chance to participate in a different management style. Some Japanese companies reduce jobs and tighten their belts—Japanese workers are thinking about their careers differently. People are beginning to sense the bottleneck in the promotional system much earlier than before. In Tokyo, many Japanese are sensing that their future course as a corporate employee won't be like the ones they have seen with their fathers. Indeed, more than 30% of businessmen in the Tokyo metropolitan area said they were inclined to change jobs in 1992, up from 25.4% in 1991.

In the future, analysts say, the headhunting trend may even extend to huge Japanese companies which will eventually switch to traditional, seniority-based promotion system to one based more on ability and performance. Even so, job-hopping is still not easy. Breaking the news to his wife and family was tough, said one executive. Most Japanese wives are still used to the idea that the job lasts through life. My wife had to speak to her parents. And my sister screamed at me and called me names, like when we were children. (Jenify Coddy, "Headhunting in Japan Gains Respectability," *The Wall Street Journal*, July 6, 1994, p. B–1.)

Lifetime employment, promotion through seniority and single-minded company unions—are the foundations of Japanese management crumbling? Evidence seems to point toward significant trends in that direction. Younger employees want to be promoted on merit not on age or seniority, and they are less likely to see themselves staying at the same company for life. Under these growing pressures, trade unions may have to re-invent their role. (Robert Heller, David Kilburn, Peggy Salz-Trautman, and John Thachray, "The Manager's Dilemma—What's In Store For Management," *Management Today*, January 1994, pp. 4248.)

The Japanese worked an average of 1,904 hours in 1994, down from 2,111 hours in 1988 and way down from a peak of 2,432 in 1960, according to the Ministry of Labor.

---

** Tadeo Umesao, "What Makes Japan Run," Atlas World Press Review, May 1977, pp. 27-30

Comparable American figures (blue collar manufacturing workers only), the Japanese Labor Ministry estimated that Japanese employees put in 2,017 hours in 1992, compared with 1,957 for American workers. But by 1994, the Japanese figure had dropped to about 1,960 while American work hours had risen by about 2.4 percent.

The company and their private lives are two separate things. They look for employers who will make full use of their abilities and provide opportunities. They are less inclined to be pegged into whatever slot pleases the personnel department and more inclined to change jobs if they sense more opportunity. (David Kilburn, "The Sun Sets on Japan's Lifers," *Management Today*, September 1993, pp. 4447.)

**Pertinent Facts**

National Office Machines of Dayton, Ohio entered into a joint venture with Nippon Cash Machines in Tokyo, Japan (N.A.B.M.C.). NCM is the oldest cash register manufacturer in Japan. But they have been steadily losing their market share.

There are 14 other manufacturers of Office/EDP equipment in Japan, including other American and foreign firms. The venture calls for doubling the sales force to 42 salesmen. U.S. personnel will man the supervisory positions for an indeterminate time.

One of the major problems facing the firm is the compensation and motivation of the expanded sales force. The traditional Japanese program is presently in use. Under this plan a man is hired until death on a straight salary, no bonus or incentive plan; at retirement he is given either a pension or a retirement sum, which is sufficient to retire on.

Use of an American plan centered around bonuses and incentives, while on the surface it appears good, runs into the serious problem of acceptance in the very tradition-oriented Japanese work force. In addition to the job for life concept the labor force also receives many benefits similar to an enlisted man in the U.S. Army (housing, PX, medical).

If the more American plan could be sold to the labor force, the problem of implementing it would still be considerable due to the nature of the market system in Japan. Essentially, retailers do business with those wholesalers or manufacturers whom they perceive themselves as owing favors to. Competition means very little to them. Therefore, it is questionable whether salesmen could break down the ties necessary to secure new sales if the compensation plan was instituted.

**Comments on NCR in Japan**

A pioneer in the development of commission selling in Japan, NCR has some 600 salesmen "on quota"—with most of them in the running for top salesmen honors. "The Commission system is considered as important an incentive there as in the United States and elsewhere," a company spokesman said. "Japanese NCR personnel currently in Dayton for sales seminars are of the opinion that the commission approach is becoming more and more popular in their country."

The NCR commission system has been widely studied in Japan. A number of Japanese firms have modeled plans directly on NCR's. In the past 10 years, NCR sales of EDP equipment, cash registers, accounting machines, and other office machines has quadrupled.

Xerox has approached the same problem in Japan (i.e., the custom of providing personal monetary incentives to salesmen); they created group norms and sales goals as team objectives. Salesmen collected regular salaries and benefits but teams that exceeded targets received extra payments and bonuses given all personnel twice annually. This system works very effectively for Fuji Xerox.

**Other Sources**

The professor may want to have students review the following articles for a discussion of changing trends in employment and human resource management in Japan:

"Japan's New 'Gamblers,'" *World Press Review*, November 1991, p. 46. This article addresses changes in employment, recruiting, risk taking and the demise of the ringi system in Japanese firms.

Another report on changes in employment traditions is found in Jenny C. McCune, "Japan Says Sayonara to Womb-to-Womb Management," *Management Review*, November 1990, pp. 12–16.

Stress in employment is chronic in Japan. Many believe it leads to Karoishi—sudden death by a heart attack or stroke by overwork—which kills an estimated 10,000 Japanese each year. More on this can be found in Karen L. Miller, "Now, Japan is Admitting It: Work Kills Executives," *Business Week*, August 2, 1992, p. 35.

Ken Goldstein, "Japan in Ferment," *Across the Board*, April 1994, pp. 51–52.

F.J. Logan, "Executive Recruitment, Japanese Style," *Across the Board*, September 1990, pp. 24 28. Although some things in human resource management are changing as indicated in the earlier articles, other processes remain the same. Such is the case of the elaborate system some companies employ in recruiting discussed in this article.

Lea Nattalia, "The Life of A Salaryman," *Manitoba Business*, July–August 1994, p. 46.

John L. Graham, Shigeru Ichikawa, and Yao Apasu, "Managing Your Sales Force in Japan and the United States," *Euro-Asian Business Review*, January 1987 and reprinted in Taylor Meloan and John L. Graham, *International & Global Marketing, Concepts and Cases*, Irwin/McGraw-Hill, 1998.

R. Bruce Money and John L. Graham, "Salesperson Performance, Pay, and Job Satisfaction: Test of a Model Using Data Collected in the U. S. and Japan," *Journal of International Business Studies*, 1998. Summarized in *Harvard Business Review*, Editor's Briefing Section, September-October 1997, pp. 9–10.

## Case 4–8 Alan AeroSpace

One response to this question is to stay tough. If the Japanese side doesn't relent, then perhaps the business should be foregone. If Alan AeroSpace does decide to withdraw from the talks it should be done with very complete explanations and in a manner that might serve to recover some of the good personal relations established with Suzuki so long ago. This is probably the response most Americans would advocate.

However, a second viable approach is to replace the entire American team as Suzuki requests and begin taking a more cooperative, creative approach with the Japanese customer. That means making some concessions. If the relationship with Sakano Corporation is handled with care and in ways appropriate in Japan, then Sakano can be depended upon to not take advantage of Alan AeroSpace in the long run.

This latter scenario is exactly what played out in the actual events after which this case is modeled. The American side (Ford AeroSpace) replaced the entire team and the satellite was sold to the Japanese company (Mitsubishi Electric). When Ford ran into problems later and was forced to postpone delivery, the Japanese side moved the delivery date and kept the early delivery bonus in place. The Japanese customer took care of the American seller because the Ford team had good explanations and they had behaved with cross-cultural acumen. Few, very few, American companies would allow a supplier to take the early delivery premium in such circumstances.

The key lesson here is that buyer-seller relationships in Japan are paternalistic and work very differently than the more adversarial buyer-seller relationships common in the U.S. If you're selling $200 million satellites in Japan your representatives need a clear understanding of these differences.

See Chapter 9, pages 127–132 in John L. Graham and Yoshihiro Sano's *Smart Bargaining, Doing Business with the Japanese*, New York: Harper-Collins, 1989 for details regarding the Ford story.

## Case 4–9 AIDS and Condoms

This may be a difficult topic for some in class discussions. However, we feel that we should not let a disease "hide" behind cultural norms about appropriate topics for class. Indeed, assuming you have foreign students in your class, an interesting associated topic is how sex/health education is handled in schools in foreign countries. Where do people in foreign countries first hear about AIDS?

When it comes to the global AIDS problem we really don't have very good answers. Perhaps your students can suggest some. The key points to be made through this case are two-fold: First, any actions to market condoms and associated changes in social behavior will require the most careful research in each country and in each market segment within the countries. Second, cooperative efforts between governments, health institutions, and for-profit companies like LIG/Durex will achieve the best results.

Answers to questions:

1. The Brazilian approach of distributing 10 million condoms during Carnival in Rio de Janeiro seems quite simple-minded. Trying to get "euphoric drunks" to behave rationally and responsibly seems like a major waste of precious Health Ministry resources. The attitudes and behaviors related to safe sex are quite complex and the marketing/social change problem for health officials is akin to other difficult public health issues like birth control, smoking (see Case 4–15), alcoholism, and the HIV/infant formula conundrum (discussed in Case 1–3). Alternatively, the Indian approach of using barbers to dispense condoms and health advice seems quite well considered. One wonders if such an approach might be worth trying in Brazil?

2. The AIDS problem in the United States is relatively more under control. Education levels and growing success with medical treatment has slowed its advance here. However, prevention in the United States can certainly be improved through creative thinking and research regarding the encouragement of safe sex, particularly among young people.

3. It's hard to imagine distributing condoms during Mardi Gras in New Orleans or at the latest rock concert. It's also hard to imagine a barber engaging a customer in a conversation about safe sex here in America. But the key with this question is to promote a creative discussion among your students on these issues. During class you might ask, "If these approaches won't work in the U.S., what might work?" You might also ask how research should be conducted on these issues. Certainly the methods most appropriate will be in-depth interviews and other qualitative approaches. Evaluation of pilot programs/test marketing will also be important.

4. The key is for LIG/Durex to work with local health officials in developing education and condom distribution programs. The key will be work at the local level to modify successful approaches used elsewhere and to develop new approaches to marketing the condoms and the associated social change. This kind of work will be the best example of marketers as cultural change agents.

Useful associated articles:

David Lamb, "Vietnam Seeks to Modernize Its Methods of Birth Control," *Los Angeles Times*, April 11, 1998, page A2. Condoms are being smuggled in from China.

Marilyn K. Nations and Maria Auxiliadora de Souza, "*Umbanda* Healers as Effective AIDS Educators: Case-control Study in Brazilian Urban Slums (*Favelas*)," *Tropical Doctor*, Supplement 1, 1997, pp. 60–66. This article provides an in-depth discussion of the problem of AIDS in Brazil and the successful testing of research-based, locally produced education programs.

Teresa Poole, "China Starts Chain of Condom Shops," *San Francisco Examiner*, March 29, 1998, page E7. LIG/Durex is investing $3 million to build a plant in China.

Gary A. Richwald and Jane Baeumler, "Condoms Can Dramatically Reduce the Risk of Infection," *Los Angeles Times*, April 6, 1998, pp. S1 and S10. Provides latest information about problem in U.S.

## Case 4–10 Making Social Responsibly and Ethical Marketing Decisions: Selling Tobacco to Third-World Countries

This case is designed to provide the student with real world situations that require corporate strategic solutions. The case is presented in an international context so students can experience the complexity and importance of ethical decision-making in a global environment.

Initially, the instructor may sense some discomfort with the level of uncertainty that is inherent in such analyses, but the instructor is advised to let the case speak for itself in analysis.

Business decisions and strategies are always made into the future, into uncertainty. Business decisions rarely have the precision of a Balance Sheet or a P/L statement; they reflect decisions about what is strategically *appropriate* for the firm as it currently assesses its options. Strategic decisions have AN ETHICS COMPONENT because they reflect the *basic assumptions* and *ground rules* the firm holds to be important. The options the firm sees in any given situation reflect its assumptions about its mission and what is an appropriate course of action for the present, or for the future. The common component of both strategic and ethical decisions is that they both constitute *judgments about what 'should' be done next.*

Questions may come up about the differences in ethical beliefs between differing cultures or differences between countries approaches to doing business. There is a trap here that leads to the logical extension of cultural RELATIVISM—"When in Rome, do as the Romans do." This argument is circular and feeds on itself. Clearly, throughout history, peoples of differing cultures have honored and given credence to fundamentally human and rational characteristics—such as the value of honesty or trustworthiness, the basic need to be believable and not be deceitful—basically to be authentic, not to lie, to do what one says or promises. Even cultures that authorize bribery or coercion lay down ground rules or parameters within which these actions are to take place. To maintain integrity, remain "legal," cultures set ground rules by which business is to be conducted—if such rules are known by the players, then the issues of ethics become a matter of knowing how the game is to be played.

For the United States, the ground rules by which business is to be conducted are set by the institutions this society has developed and which are currently emerging. In the USA, governmental entities as a representation of society set these rules—legislative statutes, agency regulations, and court rulings. These constitute the corpus of what this society requires of its citizens and its business activities. One may point to the Foreign Corrupt Practices Act as a case in point: this society has asked its business leaders not to succumb to the seduction of bribery or kickbacks that may go on in international competition, but to conduct business without resorting to payoffs. There is a price to be paid for this societal mandate, whether in losses of business opportunities, in allegations of naiveté, or losses to competitors. But this is the standard set and required of American business standard of honesty (with a known price to be paid for integrity) that is known to the entire world. The USA has mandated that businesses will engage in free market competition freely and honestly—and not by the exigencies of *expediency.* U.S. society has mandated business not to "...do as the Romans do."

What about international companies that transact business with firms in the USA? This issue is more complex. Essentially, these firms are asked to respect and abide by the rules. In similar fashion, U.S. firms should be sensitive to and respect foreign customs, traditions and legal actions—without compromise of U.S. principles and precedents. This is not an easy world. The situation reflects this complexity.

The case involves the exportation of cigarettes to Third World countries or LDCs. This is an ethical as well as economic issue. The case depicts how the more developed and enlightened countries are CUTTING BACK on cigarette consumption—and finding that there are CLEARLY DOCUMENTED HEALTH RISKS associated with this consumption. However, manufacturers are beginning to feel these cutbacks in demand as losses in revenue and profitability. This is causing these manufacturers to expand their search for new markets anywhere they can find them in the world. LDCs provide an excellent new growth market for these manufacturers. The tradeoff is economics vs. ethics. Is it morally permissible to take competitive advantage of an LDC who lacks the sophistication and understanding of the hazards of smoking to be able to make an informed choice as to risks? Is it morally acceptable to *generate demand* in LDCs by heavy and sophisticated advertising that has already been banned in this country by societal mandate?

Market trends and conflicting objectives of governments and multinational companies make this one of the most complex situations confronting those involved. Tobacco consumption in major markets of the Western developed world has been declining in the last decade. Negative public opinion about smoking coupled with aggressive anti-smoking campaigns have finally stemmed the rate of growth. At the same time, Eastern Europe, Russia, China, India, and Latin America are huge markets with less strict regulations against smoking and advertising that offer new opportunities for tobacco companies. For example, Poland has an annual cigarette market of almost 100 billion cigarettes; Ukraine, 81 billion; 32 billion; the Commonwealth of Independent States as a whole, about 456 billion. World sales of cigarettes are currently estimated to be $225 billion a year and rising. Brazil exported $1 billion worth of tobacco in 1994, double the level of five years earlier.

To capitalize on the opening of markets in Eastern Europe, China, and the potential growth elsewhere, multinational tobacco companies are investing heavily in the developing world. For example, Philip Morris has signed an agreement with Russia to help modernize its cigarette industry—$100 million in a new factory near St. Petersburg with an annual output of 10 billion cigarettes. The company has bought a factory in Hungary and has licensing deals with state producers in Poland and Bulgaria. In the Czech Republic, the company has acquired the entire state industry—five factories, 56% of the market and valued at $400 million. RJ. Reynolds is building a $33 million plant in Warsaw. Similar investments are being made in China and elsewhere by the major tobacco companies. To fully capitalize on the potential and to establish major market share in these markets, heavy investments in promotions, sampling, and advertising are being made. In China, for example, commercials by Philip Morris and British American Tobacco alone account for about 25% of television advertising.

The government's role in many countries seems to be in conflict in one hand, governments enter agreements with tobacco companies to build manufacturing plants and collect taxes on cigarette sales. At the same time, laws limiting cigarette advertising are being passed. In Brazil, a ban on advertising cigarettes from sporting and cultural events and on television have been passed. In addition, prime-time shows and television news programs will also be forbidden from showing people smoking and advertisements will not be able to suggest that smokers are socially, professionally or sexually successful. China has also passed a ban on tobacco advertising. Its Law of Advertisement bans advertising in the media and public places, such as theaters and at sporting events.

So, if you are a tobacco company, how do you react to declining sales in the major markets, growth in demand and opportunity for investment in the developing world, and restrictions on advertising in the Western developed world and in many countries in the developing world? Is it ethical and socially responsible for tobacco companies to expand their reach throughout the world? There is no simple answer.

The situation presents the students with opportunities to exercise moral judgment—in the same way they will have to in business, to identify and understand the ethical components of business decisions, to familiarize them with the experience of "thinking through" complex strategic choices, and finally to come to *conclusions* with an understanding of the moral implications or consequences of their decisions. The purpose of the exercise is to ASK STUDENTS TO ARTICULATE WHY THEY HAVE DECIDED AS THEY HAVE—TO ARTICULATE THE ASSUMPTIONS AND GROUND RULES BEHIND THEIR STRATEGIC CHOICES.

To assist both instructor and students, the authors have devised a DECISION TREE approach to identifying the ethical components of the decision. By overlaying the three key questions in the tree on any strategic decision being contemplated, the ethical dimensions of the choice options will become apparent. The Decision Tree allows the student to work his/her way through the case situations highlighting and identifying ethical considerations.

What remains is the need for the student to COME TO SOME CONCLUSIONS ABOUT THE SITUATION AND ARTICULATE THE WHY (GROUND RULES) BY WHICH THEY HAVE ARRIVED AT THEIR DECISIONS. These can then be discussed in class, or handled on an individual basis (e.g. have student take a position on the situation and advise the instructor by memorandum of this conclusion and give recommendations for alleviating the situation). The key to making this a successful learning experience for the students is for the instructor to forego a modicum of control for a simplistic or single answer, and to allow some freedom to assert differences of opinion within the class. At the same time, the instructor must not condone sloppy thinking or levity and be rigorous in the requirement that the student ARTICULATE RATIONALES FOR HIS/HER CHOICES.

The professor may want students to read the following in preparation for discussion of this case.

Jana Guyon, "Tobacco Companies Race for Advantage in Eastern Europe While Critics Fume," *The Wall Street Journal*, January 18, 1992, p. B–1

"The Big Cigarette Scramble," *World Press Review*, April 1993, p. 38.

James Brooke, "Brazil Comes Down Hard on Cigarette Ads," the *New York Times*, January 15, 1995, p. 6.

Marcus W. Brauchli, "Ad Ban In China Makes Tobacco Tricky Business," *The Wall Street Journal*, December 28, 1994, p. B–1.

Below are excerpts from recent (1998) articles that will provide some background in Europe. You may want students to read these articles before preparing the case.

**The Wall Street Journal Europe:**

Europe is saying au revoir to Joe Camel and adios to the Marlboro Man. In another major setback for the beleaguered tobacco industry, the European Parliament approved a virtually total ban on tobacco advertising despite frenzied last-minute lobbying by cigarette companies, the advertising industry and media interests. Although the restrictions will be imposed gradually over an eight-year period, they will be all-encompassing—prohibiting tobacco ads on billboards, in newspapers and magazines, and even preventing tobacco companies from using direct-mail marketing and putting logos on non-tobacco products, such as clothing. Sponsorship of sporting and cultural events also is outlawed.

The new law, adopted after a recommendation by European health ministers in December, affects tobacco advertising in 15 countries in Western Europe, where tobacco companies now spend an estimated $1 billion a year on marketing. And anti- tobacco groups expressed hope that the legislation will have a ripple effect, leading to similar curbs elsewhere. "This sends a strong signal that Europe is united against the tobacco industry, and that other countries can also stand up to them," said Amanda Sandford, spokeswoman for a British antismoking group, Action on Smoking and Health, in London.

Under European Union rules, the legislation must be formally adopted by EU ministers and will take effect three years from its publication in the EU's Official Journal, which is expected in the next few months. But the law allows further delays of one year for the ban on ads in the press—or until about 2001 or 2002 – and two years for the prohibition of tobacco sponsorship. Moreover, international events, such as Formula One racing, won't be affected until October 2006. Critics of the ban—led by tobacco companies, but including advertising-industry associations and publishing companies—contend that the ban raises serious issues about the right to advertise, press freedom and alleged EU interference in national affairs of member countries.

What is more, some say the restrictions might drive tobacco companies to market their products in new, unregulated areas, such as the Internet, which is a gray area for trans-national legislation. "There's no magic way to get out of this difficult bind, but we won't give up," said Michael Prideaux, spokesman for B.A.T Industries PLC, the world's second-largest tobacco company, which owns Brown & Williamson Co., in the U.S. "The battle goes on." He added that the industry will appeal the decision to the European Court of Justice, and possibly in the courts of member states.

The ban is indeed severe, compared to current voluntary agreements in many European countries to restrict tobacco advertising. (Complete bans in EU countries are already in place in France, Italy, Sweden, Finland and Portugal.) The EU ban broadly matches one proposed in the U.S., as part of the $368.5 million tobacco-liability settlement. This would prohibit sports promotions and billboard ads, as well as the appearance of people or cartoon characters in advertising.

Under the EU directive, any "commercial communication," direct or indirect, that promotes tobacco would be illegal. The only exceptions would be so-called point-of-sale displays in places where tobacco products are sold; publications brought into the EU; and tobacco-trade publications. Publishing companies are likely to feel the pinch first, as print ads are in the first phase of implementation within four years. Almost half of all tobacco-advertising revenue goes to newspapers, magazines and outdoor billboards. Magazines—especially national weeklies aimed at an adult audience—could suffer. "This will hurt, and hurt very badly for some titles," said Julius Waller, director of the European Magazine Publishers Federation in Brussels. Further, publishers say the ban is chipping away at press freedom, because reduced ad revenue could lead many publications to fold. Ad agencies, some of which already refuse to handle tobacco accounts, also will lose out. However, what the industry fears most is that the ban might spread to other products deemed "unhealthy" by different interest groups. "It's scary to think that constitutional means can be used to ban" the advertising for certain products, said Stig Carlson, director of the European Association of Advertising Agencies. Instead, the association says voluntary agreements and self-regulation are the best way to reach the EU's health objectives of reducing tobacco consumption. In the U.K., for example, ads aren't allowed to feature attractive models, be humorous or show cheerful scenes or landscapes that imply fresh air. A spokeswoman for the EU's social-affairs commissioner, Padraig Flynn, rejected suggestions that the measure would have a domino effect and lead to advertising curbs on other products.

"Mr. Flynn certainly doesn't believe that alcohol is in the same category as tobacco. Indeed, there's evidence that moderate consumption of alcohol can be beneficial to health," said the spokeswoman, Barbara Nolan. "That is a scare tactic by the tobacco industry."

The commission said Mr. Flynn would now press countries applying to join the EU—including those in Eastern Europe, where cigarette consumption levels are among the world's highest—to control tobacco advertising and sponsorship.

The EU also defended the legislation, saying it is necessary to prevent varying national rules that are springing up and disrupting efforts to establish Europe's unified market. On Wednesday, Mr. Flynn said, "the way is now clear for a better-functioning internal market in the area of tobacco advertising and sponsorship." But the use of internal-market laws, which aren't subject to unanimity by EU ministers, has always been controversial. For its part, the tobacco industry contends that advertising is used to maintain or increase brand market share—not to lure new smokers—and that ads are aimed at adult smokers only. There is evidence to support the claim that advertising's impact is mixed. In Britain, smoking levels have fallen continuously over the past 20 years, although advertising has been restricted, not banned. In Norway, though, a total ban has been in effect for 25 years, and consumption among certain population groups has increased.

Tobacco-industry insiders say that snuffing out public advertising could lead to a price war as a mechanism to stimulate market demand, and prompt tobacco companies to look for ways around the law to peddle their products. "By banning, you lose control," explained Mr. Waller, of the publishers federation. "Cigarette companies are flush with cash, and they will find a way to spend their money."

**Abstracted from Expansion in Spanish, Source: World Reporter**

Tabacalera, the Spanish tobacco group, and its main competitors (Philip Morris, Reynolds and BAT) have their sights set on Asia. According to Cesar Alierta, the chairman of Tabacalera, Asia is a market with great potential and represents unfinished business for the sector. However, in the short and medium term Tabacalera will concentrate its efforts on Russia, Eastern Europe and North Africa with its brands Fortuna and Ducados through its strategic alliance with the French company Seita. Alierta added that one objective for the company is to bid for the privatisation of the Moroccan state tobacco company. Regarding the EC rule which will ban all tobacco advertising and which come into force in Spain within five years, Alierta has said that the company thus has five years to consolidate its position. Tabacalera has an ample capacity for borrowing, with a ratio of thirty per cent for debts over equity. This will allow the company to spend Pta 100 billion on financial investments. According to Alierta this will be spent on developing its distribution network, adding that the company does not intend to increase its stakes in Aldeasa, Midesa and Inmobiliaria Zabalburu. He also ruled out a future takeover bid for Zabalburu.

**Facts About the Global Tobacco Business**

SMOKING IN AMERICA

Percentage of American adults who smoke: 25.5%

Men: 28.2%
Women: 23.1%

1996 consumer spending on tobacco products: $46.6 billion

Federal, state and local excise taxes collected from cigarettes in 1996: $13.1 billion

Average number of Americans who die each day from smoking-related illnesses: 1,145

Health-care costs of smoking-related illnesses: $50 billion

Largest tobacco-producing state: North Carolina: $943 million

Average price per pack nationwide: $1.91

THE GLOBAL MARKET

World-wide sales of cigarettes in 1996: $295.8 billion

Total number of cigarettes sold last year: 5,505 billion

Average number of cigarettes sold per second: 174,562

Top five cigarette markets in 1996, in billions of cigarettes:

China: 1,791
U.S.: 488
Japan: 335
Russia: 180
Indonesia: 173

World market share of five largest tobacco companies:

Philip Morris: 16.2%
B.A.T: 12.8%
R.J. Reynolds: 5.9%
Japan Tobacco: 5.1%
Rothmans: 4.2%

Biggest cigarette brands and world market share:

Marlboro (Philip Morris): 8.4%
Mild Seven (Japan Tobacco): 2.3%
L&M (Philip Morris/Liggett): 1.8%
Winston (R.J. Reynolds): 1.6%
Camel (R.J. Reynolds): 1.2%

Highest annual per capita spending on tobacco: Denmark: $407.80

U.S. annual per capita spending on tobacco products: $185.30

Countries with the heaviest smokers (annual per capita smoking rate):

1. Greece: 2,774 cigarettes, 139 packs
2. Japan: 2,669 cigarettes, 133 packs
3. Poland: 2,365 cigarettes, 118 packs
11. U.S.: 1,831 cigarettes, 92 packs

ADVERTISING AND HOLLYWOOD

Spending on advertising and promotion in the U.S. by cigarette companies in 1994: $4.83 billion

Number of Marlboro men who have died from smoking-related illnesses in the past five years: Three

Percentage of 133 top-grossing movies in 1994 and 1995 showing tobacco use: 77%

Smokiest U.S. television network: Fox: with 2.67 smoking scenes an hour

SMOKING AND KIDS

Percentage of U.S. high school kids in 1995 who said they had smoked in the past month:

34.8% (27.5% in 1991)

Number of kids who become "regular" smokers each day: 3,000

Average age kids start smoking: 13

Number of U.S. children under age 18 today who are expected to die from smoking-related illnesses: 5 million

TRYING TO QUIT

Percentage of smokers who say they want to quit: 70%

Annual U.S. spending on products to help people quit smoking: $417.7 million

Average weight gained when a smoker quits: Three to five pounds

OTHER TOBACCO PRODUCTS

Fastest-growing tobacco product in the U.S. in 1996: Cigars (+18%)

Value of Cuban cigars seized by U.S. customs in 1996: $1 million ($140,000 in 1994)

Sources: World Tobacco Market report from Chicago-based Euromonitor; Centers for Disease Control; U.S. government data (Department of Agriculture, Commerce Department, Federal Trade Commission, Food and Drug Administration); American Lung Association; Center for Tobacco Free Kids; Tobacco Institute; Information Resources Inc.

**The Wall Street Journal**

SANTA CRUZ DO SUL, Brazil—The tobacco industry may be reeling from an antismoking backlash in the U.S., but you wouldn't know it here. This quaint Germanic city on the rolling southern frontier of Brazil has become one of the key staging areas for Big Tobacco's push into the developing world. Only a few blocks from the leafy beer gardens and cobbled walkways favored by tourists, multinational tobacco companies are investing hundreds of millions of dollars to expand what is already the continent's largest tobacco-leaf export center.

In January, B.A.T Industries PLC's Souza Cruz unit opened an $80 million processing plant with an annual capacity of 120,000 tons, greater than that of any other facility in the world, the company says. Just down the road, Philip Morris Cos. is working on its own $220 million expansion. And Universal Leaf Tobacco Co. is gearing up a $30 million investment program. Big increases in per-capita tobacco consumption – up more than 20% in the developing world over the past decade—and enthusiastic political support have made nonindustrial countries a key element in the tobacco industry's growth strategy. "When the antitobacco movement attacks in an exaggerated way in one area, the industry naturally tends to expand someplace else," says Helio Fensterseifer, president of the local tobacco industry association. "Certain mutations are created."

If Santa Cruz's tobacco industry is growing disproportionately because of the U.S. public health wars, no one here is complaining. Thanks to tobacco, the city's 100,000 people boast per-capita income that's three times the national average. City fathers had few problems collecting funds for the restoration of the town's Gothic-style cathedral. And there's enough disposable income left over in Santa Cruz to support a professional basketball team that draws 7,000 fans a game. "Seventy percent of the economy is tobacco, and there is tremendous loyalty to the industry for having elevated us, in a sense, out of the developing world," says Fernando Kothe, the city's industrial-development director. Santa Cruz is the hub of a thriving three-state tobacco belt, and throughout the area, quality-of-life indicators are superior to national norms in virtually every category but one: Lung cancer rates among men are extraordinarily high, says Mara Brognoli, a public health official in the neighboring state of Santa Catarina. And there's the rub. "It is very hard for people in a poor country to refuse a bargain like that offered by rich tobacco companies, even though it is a bargain that might kill them," says Vera Luisa Costa e Silva, the coordinator of primary cancer prevention for Brazil's National Cancer Institute. Brazil desperately needs the tax revenue, export income and jobs provided by the tobacco companies. Kathryn Mulvey, executive director of Infact, a Boston-based activist group, adds that "there is a clear challenge to put in place strong public-health regulations in countries like Brazil" where the industry has a big economic impact.

Santa Cruz reveals in microcosm how far tobacco's reach extends. The industry serves as banker and agrarian extension agent for 160,000 small farmers in the southern region, providing them with seed, fertilizer and technical assistance on credit. But tobacco's role only begins on the farm. When local government was working on the cleanup of a polluted river, the industry was tapped for its technical expertise. When the local university library needed to buy some new bibliographical files, the industry picked up the tab. Most significantly, B.A.T's Souza Cruz, which controls 83% of Brazil's cigarette market, has teamed up with state education authorities and a local newspaper to operate ambitious programs promoting gardening and reforestation in grade schools. By providing teaching materials and vegetable and tree seeds to schools, the company is practicing good corporate citizenship and doing its part to replace the large amounts of wood consumed in tobacco curing ovens, says Souza Cruz executive Roberto Eisenberger. Company officials don't deal directly with students, and tobacco isn't mentioned in the curriculum, he adds. "To kids, Souza Cruz means the 'Arbor Club,' not tobacco," agrees Jane Ellvvanger, the assistant principal of a local elementary school. Critics say the distinctions aren't so neat. "The company talks about reforestation and healthy living, but the educational literature includes the Souza Cruz symbol: a tobacco leaf," says Ms. Brognoli, the health official. People here have been living side by side with tobacco ever since a wave of small farmers from Northern Europe started emigrating here back in the 1850s. Unlike the vast tobacco farms of the Carolinas, Brazilian tobacco plots tend to average only four or five acres. At the office of the local growers association, pride in ethnicity and in tobacco are evident in a placard featuring a smoldering cigarette and the German legend: "Mein Vergnugen, Meine Wahl." ("My Pleasure, My Choice.") "Thanks to the immigrant culture, you see agriculture conducted on an almost artisanal level," says Guido Knies, export operations manager for Souza Cruz. But with plenty of help from the companies, small planters like Selvino Mueller have become cogs in the global export economy. The income that Mr. Mueller and his six children earn farming about 15 acres of tobacco has provided him with the start-up capital to develop a sideline trucking business. "In other parts of Brazil, you see people being forced to abandon the land for the city," says Mr. Mueller, inspecting a row of tobacco seedlings covered with plastic to protect them from the cold. "Never in Santa Cruz."

# PART III
# TEACHING OBJECTIVES, COMMENTS AND SUGGESTIONS, LECTURE OUTLINES, ANSWERS FOR END-OF-CHAPTER QUESTIONS

**Introduction**

This section offers teaching objectives, suggestions and comments, lecture outlines and end-of-chapter questions for each chapter. How these suggestions are used will depend on a professor's individual teaching style. To allow for personal adjustment, several suggestions and tips for lectures and classroom activity are offered instead of a structured lecture format. Here are some suggestions, however, that are applicable throughout the course.

**Student Reading Assignment**. The author has found that the one activity that adds to classroom discussions and results in students reading international topics beyond the text is the reading assignment described above in Part I, E-1, Current Readings and Class Reports and illustrated in Part I, B, Sample Syllabus (for 15 weeks).

An important objective of teaching an international course is to introduce and to encourage students to read current business periodicals and journals. Their interest increases when they read current articles which relate to class material. Using this as an assignment throughout the semester provides several advantages: 1) there is always a segment of the class ready with current, relevant topics for class discussion; 2) it provides the professor with an abundance of interesting and current examples to use as a "jumping off point" for discussion of the topic for the day; 3) it has a hidden benefit. The author's experience is that students read or at least scan many more articles that the six or so required. In the author's opinion, this is one of the most successful projects he has used in conjunction with in-class discussions and lectures.

**Transparency Masters**. Be sure to look at the transparency masters (published separately) as you prepare your lectures. Many of the exhibits in the text are reproduced there as well as exhibits that do not appear in the text. In the following discussion, reference will be made to some but not all the available transparency masters. It is a good idea to check the transparency master manual to see if there are others that you would prefer using.

**Map Transparencies**. Besides the exhibits, transparency masters of all the maps in the text plus some others are provided.

**PowerPoint® Presentation**. Many other exhibits and maps are available for PowerPoint®. Please contact your Irwin/McGraw-Hill representative for a copy of the PowerPoint® Presentation material.

## Chapter 1 – The Scope And Challenge Of International Marketing

### Teaching Objectives

As an introductory chapter, the broad goal is to provide a view of international marketing that sets the boundaries and scope of the course. The teaching objectives are to:

1. Provide students with a broad picture of the global environment within which business operates today and into the future.

2. Give students an appreciation of how the globalization of world markets and the internationalization of U.S. business and U.S. markets influence all functions of business including marketing.

3. Show how the internationalization or globalization of markets affects their professional futures regardless of where they work in business. In short, just as domestic or international business cannot escape the internationalization of business and U.S. markets, neither can students escape the influences of these international trends on their professional careers.

4. Illustrate the scope of the international marketing task.

5. Show the importance of one's self-reference criterion in assessing international issues.

6. Illustrate the stages of becoming international and the international marketing concepts used in international marketing management.

7. Impress students with the importance of becoming globally aware.

### Comments and Suggestions

1. TM 1–1 and 1–2 can help in illustrating the globalization of business and markets. Key points to make are: a) An increasingly larger share of corporate profits are generated by international operations; b) Until recently competition for U.S. markets was only among U.S. businesses with the same relative cost of money, labor, and product but now it includes competitors from the world over; c) U.S. multinationals face competition for lucrative markets from new rivals from developed as well as developing countries; and d) The growth of new markets created by changes in Latin America, Asia, Eastern Europe and the former members of USSR, India etc.

2. Exhibit 1–3 (TM 1–3, The International Marketing Task) serves as a guide when discussing the international marketing managers task. With this illustration, points about the environment of business, uncontrollables and controllables can be made.

3. As an assignment for class discussion, Case 1–1, AOL in Latin America, can be used to have students think about the marketing mix and the effects of uncontrollables and controllables both in the domestic and foreign environments. Have students read and answer the questions in the case before class. During class, have the students illustrate the various controllables and uncontrollables in Using Exhibit 1–3, The International Marketing Task, with examples from the case. Students can be challenged by asking how they would have done things differently to overcome some of the problems illustrated in the case.

4. A key point to make when discussing the self-reference criterion is that a person from one culture is often not aware that a reaction is influenced by one's cultural background and that those from another culture may have a different perspective. It often uses Hall's idea of the silent language of space (see

Edward T. Hall, "The Silent Language in Overseas Business," Harvard Business Review, May–June 1960, pp. 87–96 or Edward T. Hall, The Silent Language (New York: Doubleday & Co., 1959) to make this point. In this first chapter and throughout the course it is important to stress the nature of the SRC, that is, whenever confronted by some aspect of another culture one's reaction and evaluation is routinely clouded by one's own cultural experiences.

5. When exploring the different orientations, Domestic Market Expansion Concept, Multi-Domestic Market Concept and Global Marketing Concept, it is important that students understand that the differences between global markets and global products. Further, they need to understand that a global marketing orientation does not necessarily mean standardization across all markets. Instead it may mean operating as if all the country markets in a company's scope of operations (including the domestic market) are approached as a single global market that may have multiple market segments extending across country borders and that the company is seeking commonalties across country markets in order to standardize the marketing mix where culturally feasible and cost effective.

**Lecture Outline**

I. The Internationalization of U.S. Business

II. International Marketing Defined

III. The International Marketing Task
   - A. Marketing Controllables
   - B. Domestic Uncontrollables
   - C. Foreign Uncontrollables

IV. Self-Reference Criterion: An Obstacle

V. Becoming International
   - A. Phases of International Marketing Involvement
   - B. International Marketing Concepts
     1. Domestic Market Expansion Concept
     2. Multi-Domestic Market Concept
     3. Global Marketing Concept
   - C. Global Markets and Global Marketing

VI. Developing A Global Awareness

**Discussion Questions**

1. Define:

| | |
|---|---|
| International marketing | Foreign uncontrollables |
| Controllable elements | Marketing relativism |
| Uncontrollable elements | Self-reference criterion (SRC) |
| Domestic uncontrollables | Global awareness |

2. ". . . the marketer's task is the same whether applied in Dime Box, Texas, or Dar es Salaam, Tanzania."

   Discuss. The only difference between domestic marketing and international marketing is that the activities take place in more than one country. Therefore, the marketing task is the same throughout the world.

3. How can the increased interest in international marketing on the part of the U.S. firms be explained?

   Increased interest has been brought about because of changing competitive structures, coupled with shifts in demand characteristics throughout the world. The U.S. market has reached saturation levels for many products, and increasing numbers of firms are faced with surpluses which must be sold. Also, many firms find that return on investment may be higher in foreign markets than in domestic markets. Finally, more and more firms realize that tomorrow's markets will be world markets and it is imperative that they establish world market positions early.

4. Discuss the four phases of international marketing involvement.

   The first phase includes those domestic firms which have no foreign business activity except those sales made to foreign customers who come directly to the firm. The second phase includes domestic firms which have temporary surpluses which are sold abroad. Therefore, sales are made on an availability basis with little or no intention for continuing market representation. The third phase includes the domestic firms that have permanent productive capacity which is utilized to produce goods which are sold on a continuing basis in foreign markets. The fourth phase includes the international company that produces a product for the world market.

5. Discuss the conditions that have led to the development of global markets.

   According to the Professor Levitt and others who suggest that there is a global market for goods, this phenomenon has resulted from new communications technology, travel and other factors which have led to the markets of the world being more aware of different products and processes. As a result of this awareness, there are segments in each market who have had similar experiences and thus have common needs. These common needs are described as a demand for high quality, reasonably priced, standardized products. There is a strong feeling that within each country's market there is a growing segment that has been exposed to ideas from around the world and thus have had their tastes and perceived needs affected. There is a strong feeling that world markets are being driven toward a converging commonality of taste and needs leading toward global markets.

6. Differentiate between a global company and a multinational company.

   The main distinction between a global and a multinational company is that a global company assumes there are segments across countries which have the same needs and wants and designs a standardized, high quality, reasonably priced product for those segments and markets it as if there are no differences among the country markets. On the other hand, a multinational company operates in a number of countries and adjusts its products and marketing practices for each market. The multinational company has a specific marketing plan and adapts products for each country market. The philosophy for the multinational company is that there are cultural differences among countries that require specific adaptations for those markets. This is contrasted with the global company which sees the entire world, or major regions of it, as a single entity requiring no specialized adjustments. This distinction may be more myth than fact and reflects Professor Levitt's opinion.

7. Differentiate among the three international marketing concepts.

   Companies can be described by one of three orientations to international marketing management:

   1. Domestic Market Expansion Concept
   2. Multi-Domestic Market Concept
   3. Global Marketing Concept

It is expected that differences in the complexity and sophistication of a company's marketing activity depend on which of these orientations guides its operations.

The Domestic Market Extension Concept. This orientation to international marketing is illustrated by the domestic company that seeks sales extension of its domestic products into foreign markets. It views its international operations as secondary to and an extension of its domestic operations. The primary motive is to dispose of excess domestic production. Domestic business is its priority and foreign sales are seen as a profitable extension of domestic operations. While foreign markets may be vigorously pursued, the orientation remains basically domestic. Its attitude toward international sales is typified by the belief that if it sells in Peoria it will sell anywhere else in the world. Minimal, if any, efforts are made to adapt the marketing mix to foreign markets. The firm's orientation is to market to foreign customers in the same manner the company markets to domestic customers. It seeks markets where demand is similar to the home market and its domestic product will be acceptable. This Domestic Market Expansion Strategy can be very profitable. Large and small exporting companies approach international marketing from this perspective.

Multi-Domestic Market Concept. Once a company recognizes the importance of differences in overseas markets and the importance of offshore business to their organization, its orientation toward international business may shift to a Multi-Domestic Market Strategy. A company guided by this concept has a strong sense that country markets are vastly different (and they may be, depending on the product) and that market success requires an almost independent program for each country. Firms with this orientation market on a country-by-country basis with separate marketing strategies for each country. Subsidiaries operate independently of one another in establishing marketing objectives and plans. The domestic market and each of the country markets have separate marketing mixes with little interaction among them. Products are adapted for each market with minimum coordination with other country markets, advertising campaigns are localized as are the pricing and distribution decisions. A company with this concept does not look for similarity among elements of the marketing mix that might respond to standardization. Rather, it aims for adaptation to local country markets. Control is typically decentralized to reflect the belief that the uniqueness of each market requires local marketing input and control.

Global Marketing Concept. A company guided by this new orientation or philosophy is generally referred to as a global company, its marketing activity is global marketing, and its market coverage is the world. A company employing a Global Marketing Strategy strives for efficiencies of scale by developing a standardized product, of dependable quality, to be sold at a reasonable price to a global market (that is, the same country market set throughout the world). Important to the Global Marketing Concept is the premise that world markets are being "driven toward a converging commonalty" that seek much the same ways to satisfy their needs and desires and thus, constitute significant market segments with similar demands for the same product the world over. With this orientation a company attempts to standardize as much of the company effort as is practical on a world-wide basis. Some decisions are viewed as applicable worldwide, while others require consideration of local influences. The world as a whole is viewed as the market and the firm develops a global marketing strategy.

8. Relate the three international marketing concepts to the EPRG schema.

   Companies can be described by one of three orientations to international marketing management:

   1. Domestic Market Expansion Concept: Firms with this marketing approach are classified as ethnocentric in the EPRG schema.
   2. Multi-Domestic Market Concept: Firms with this orientation would be classified in the EPRG schema as polycentric.
   3. Global Marketing Concept: The global marketing company would fit the regioncentric or geocentric classifications of the EPRG schema.

It is to be expected that differences in the complexity and sophistication of a company's marketing activity depends on which of these orientations guides its operations. The ideas expressed in each of these concepts reflect the philosophical orientation that also can be associated with successive stages in the evolution of the international operations in a company. Among the many approaches that describe the different orientations that evolve in a company as it moves through different phases of international marketing involvement from casual exporting to global marketing is the often quoted EPRG schema. The authors of this schema suggest that firms can be classified as having an Ethnocentric, Polycentric, Regioncentric or Geocentric orientation (EPRG) depending on the international commitment of the firm. Further, the authors state that, "a key assumption underlying the EPRG framework is that the degree of internationalization to which management is committed or willing to move towards affects the specific international strategies and decision rules of the firm." The EPRG schema is incorporated into the three concepts listed above in that the philosophical orientations described by the EPRG help explain management's view when it is guided by one of the concepts.

9. Prepare your lifelong plan to be globally aware.

   Student exercise. A minimum would be a reading list plus some commitment to study different countries.

10. Discuss the three factors necessary to achieve global awareness.

    The three factors necessary to achieve global awareness are: 1) objectivity; objective in assessing opportunities, evaluating potential, and responding to problems. Too often mistakes are made because companies are swept away with generalities and make investments only later to find out that their commitment or abilities were not sufficient to succeed, 2) tolerance toward cultural differences; tolerance is understanding cultural differences and accepting and working with others whose behavior may be different from yours, 3) knowledgeable; knowledgeable about cultures, history, world market potentials, and global economy and social trends is critical for a person to be culturally aware. To be successfully in international business and globally aware, a person needs to keep abreast of the enormous changes occurring throughout the world. The 21st century will usher in great change and opportunities. The knowledgeable marketer will identify those opportunities long before it becomes evident to others.

11. Define and discuss the idea of global orientation.

    A global orientation means operating as if all the country markets in a company's scope of operations (including domestic market) are approachable as a single global market and to standardize the marketing mix where *culturally feasible* and *cost effective* or to adapt the marketing mix where culturally required and cost effective. A global orientation does not mean to follow a single strategy of standardization without regard for cultural differences nor does it imply that the marketing effort must be adapted to every cultural difference. Instead, it means looking for market segments with similar demands that can be satisfied with the same product, standardizing the components of the marketing mix that can be standardized, and, where there are significant cultural differences that require parts of the marketing mix to be culturally adapted, adapting.

12. Visit the Bureau of Economic Analysis homepage (www.bea.doc.gov). Select the section, International articles, and find the most recent information on Foreign Direct Investments in the United States. Which country has the highest dollar amount of investment in the United States? Second highest?

This exercise is designed to familiarize the student with the Internet and the data available from the BEA. At the time this was written (1998), the following was found at the address above.

**U.S. Direct Investment Abroad**

Direct Investment Positions for 1996 Country and Industry Detail By Sylvia E. Bargas

The U.S. direct investment position abroad valued at historical cost—the book value of U.S. direct investors' equity in, and net outstanding loans to, their foreign affiliates—was $796.5 billion at yearend 1996. The largest positions by far remained those in the United Kingdom ($142.6 billion, or 18 percent of the total) and in Canada ($91.6 billion, or 11 percent of the total).

## Chapter 2 — Global Business Environment

### Teaching Objectives

This chapter has a short history of international trade. Included is a history of GATT and the role of multinationals from the end of World War II through the decade of the nineties and beyond.

The aim of this chapter is to provide a brief overview of the international trade issues that constitute the environment of global business. Issues reflecting the political and economic trade policies that affect how international business is conducted. The teaching objectives are to:

1. Provide some insight into the balance of payments and the relationship of a country's current account and balance of trade.

2. Show the U.S. government's role in helping to ease restrictions on trade through the Omnibus Trade and Competitiveness Act.

3. Explore the provisions and effects of protectionism on world trade and to show that no country, including the United States, has "clean hands" when it comes to protecting home markets.

4. Illustrate the types of trade barriers that may confront a business.

5. Explore how GATT and the new World Trade Organization are designed to eliminate trade restrictions and provide a means for countries to settle trade disputes.

6. The importance of the Internet to global business.

### Comments and Suggestions

1. The discussion on the evolution of the multinational company during the 20th Century and the decade of the nineties may be used as an extension of the discussion of Chapter One since it illustrates the changing role of the U.S. multinational. The focus in this section is how the relative importance of U.S. MNCs after WW II changed from one of dominating world markets to a more competitive world market where U.S. multinationals compete with strong multinationals from Japan, Western Europe, Asia and many developing countries. This competitive environment is forcing MNCs to examine new ways to remain competitive. Some of these changes will be discussed as the course evolves.

2. Besides the discussion of the concept of protectionism and different trade barriers, a class discussion on how markets are protected can be interesting. On the one hand the United States alleges to be for free trade, yet it ignores the WTO in its trade dispute with Japan over opening its markets for U.S. automobile parts (see, for example, "Your Move, Japan," Business Week, May 22, 1995, pp. 38–40). The U.S. also has trade barriers. See, for example, Crossing Borders 2–1.

3. The cost of protectionism is born by the consumer and in many cases, the cost for jobs protected far exceeds any reasonable justification (See Exhibit 2–6, TM 2–5, The Price of Protectionism). A recent study by Japanese economists revealed that trade barriers cost Japanese consumers somewhere between $75 billion and $110 billion in 1989 or between 3% and 4% of Japan's GNP. On the whole, it was reported that Japanese consumers effectively paid upwards of $600,000 for each job protected by barriers. ("Japan's Price of Protection," Fortune, March 6, 1995, p. 48) It is difficult to justify such costs.

4. A review of GATT and the new WTO should be provided since the WTO will be an important agency in the future event if the first reaction of the United States seems somewhat timid. See TM 2–7, What WTO Will Mean to Different Industries.

**Lecture Outline**

GLOBAL BUSINESS ENVIRONMENT

I. The Twentieth Century
   A. World Trade and U.S. Multinationals
   B. The Decade of the Nineties and Beyond
II. Balance of Payments
   A. Current Account
   B. Balance of Trade
III. The Omnibus Trade and Competitiveness Act
IV. Protectionism
   A. Protection Logic and Illogic
   B. Trade Barriers
      1. Tariffs
      2. Quotas
      3. Voluntary Export Restraints
      4. Boycott
      5. Monetary Barriers
      6. Standards
V. Easing Trade Restrictions
   A. General Agreement on Tariffs and Trade (GATT)
   B. World Trade Organization
   C. International Monetary Fund
VI. The Internet and Global Business

**Discussion QUESTIONS**

1. Define:

| | |
|---|---|
| GATT | Protectionism |
| Balance of payments | IMF |
| Balance of trade | Nontariff barriers |
| Current Account | Voluntary export restraint (VER) |
| Tariff | WTO |

2. Discuss the globalization of the U.S. economy.

America's involvement in the global economy has passed through two distinct periods: a development era during which the United States sought industrial self-sufficiency in the eighteenth and nineteenth centuries, and a free-trade in the early and middle twentieth century during which open trade was linked with prosperity. Now America has entered a third, more dangerous era—an age of global economic interdependence.

With surprising swiftness, the United States has shifted from relative economic self-sufficiency to global interdependence. In 1960, trade accounted for only 10 percent of the country's GNP; by the mid-1980s, that figure had more than doubled. American farmers now sell 30 percent of their grain production overseas; 40 percent of U.S. farmland is devoted to crops for export. In fact, more U.S. farmland is used to feed the Japanese than there is Japanese farmland. American industry exports more than 20 percent of its manufacturing output, and one out of every six manufacturing jobs in the U.S. depends on foreign sales. More than 70 percent of American industry now faces stiff foreign competition within the U.S. market.

3. Differentiate among the current account, balance of trade, and balance of payments.

**BALANCE OF PAYMENTS**

When countries trade, financial transactions among businesses/consumers of different nations occur. Products and services are exported and imported, monetary gifts are exchanged, investments are made, cash payments are made and cash receipts received, and vacation and foreign travel occurs. In short, over a period of time, there is a constant flow of money into and out of a country. The system of accounts that records a nation's international financial transactions is called its balance of payments.

A balance-of-payments statement includes three accounts: the current account, a record of all merchandise exports, imports, and services plus unilateral transfers of funds, the capital account, a record of direct investment, portfolio investment, and short-term capital movements to and from countries; and the official reserves account, records of exports and imports of gold, increases or decreases in foreign exchange, and increases or decreases in liabilities to foreign central banks. Of the three, the current account is of primary interest to international business.

**CURRENT ACCOUNT**

The current account is important because it includes all international trade and service accounts, i.e., accounts for the value of all merchandise and services imported and exported and all receipts and payment from investments. The balance of trade reflected in the current account is the single most important factor in the U.S. economy for the 1990s.

**Balance of Trade**

The relationship between merchandise imports and exports is referred to as the balance of merchandise trade or trade balance. If a country exports more goods than it imports, it is said to have a favorable balance of trade; if it imports more goods than it exports, as did the United States in 1988, it is said to have an unfavorable balance of trade. Usually a country that has a negative balance of trade also has a negative balance of payments. Both the balance of trade and the balance of payments do not have to be negative; at times a country may have a favorable balance of trade and a negative balance of payments or vice versa. This was the case for the United States during the Korean and Vietnam Wars when there was a favorable balance of trade but a negative balance of payments. The imbalance was caused by heavy foreign aid assistance by the United States to other countries and the high cost of conducting the Korean and Vietnam Wars.

In only three years since 1970 has the United States had a favorable balance of trade. This means that for each year there was an unfavorable balance, the United States imported goods with a higher dollar value than the goods it exported. These imbalances resulted primarily from heavy U.S. demand for foreign petroleum, foreign cars, industrial machinery, and other merchandise. Such imbalances have drastic effects on balance of trade, balance of payments, and therefore, the value of local currency in the world marketplace.

4. Explain the role of price as a free market regulator.

   As a free market regulator, price serves as a primary variable in regulating supply and demand and aids in resource allocation. Prices that are too low deplete product supply, and prices that are too high stop consumer purchases.

5. "Theoretically, the market is an automatic, competitive, self-regulating mechanism which provides for the maximum consumer welfare and which best regulates the use of the factors of production." Explain.

   Productivity and market demand are the determinants of the standard of living differentials throughout the world as determined by the market if (theoretically) free competition exists. However, many variables pollute this "best of all possible worlds" model. Government interference, cartels and other monopolistic practices, and market barriers all corrupt this market (free) system.

6. Interview several local businessmen to determine their attitudes toward world trade. Further, learn if they buy or sell goods produced in foreign countries. Correlate the attitudes and report on your findings.

**Independent project.**

7. What is the role of profit in international trade? Does profit replace or complement the regulatory function of pricing? Discuss.

   Profit in international trade provides the specific motivation for the traders. It is the catalyst of international trade. Profit complements the regulatory function of pricing in international trade. Out of the differential between cost and price comes profit.

8. Why does the balance of payments always balance even though the balance of trade does not?

   The balance of payments must always balance because the record is maintained on a double-entry bookkeeping system. In the balance of payments, debits must off-set the credits. The balance of trade doesn't have to be in balance. Exports can exceed imports or vice versa or they can be in balance.

9. Enumerate the ways in which a nation can overcome an unfavorable balance of trade.

   A country can overcome an unfavorable balance of trade by increasing exports or decreasing imports. Temporary aid may also result from infusions of capital, loans, or foreign aid.

10. Support or refute each of the various arguments commonly used in support of tariffs.

    Many arguments are commonly used in support of tariffs:

    (1) **Infant industry** – theoretically this argument has a considerable degree of validity. However, practically, the argument is carried too far. How do you determine which particular potential industries would develop a comparative advantage and be able to withstand foreign competition? When protection is a mistake, it is difficult to remove the protection. Unless there is a definite timetable, the incentive to develop increasing efficiency is weakened. This argument for tariffs has validity if it is used very carefully and controlled closely.

    (2) **Protection of the home market** – this argument asserts that low costs of production in other countries pauperizes American labor, and foreign goods would flood the American markets. For example, American producers would be forced to lower wage rates approximating foreign wage rates. This argument is invalid because low money wages do not necessarily mean low wage costs per unit of output. The latter is a function of two elements–money wage rates and the productivity of labor. Therefore, since free trade raised productivity rather than lower it, the above argument is *invalid.*

    (3) **Keep money at home** – this fallacious reasoning is based on the mercantilist identity of money and wealth. A higher volume of money makes no direct contribution to the real income and wealth of a country. If a country is experiencing monetary problems, central bank and fiscal policies are much more potent weapons of monetary control than is manipulation of trade balance. Therefore, this argument is *invalid.*

    (4) **Capital accumulation** – a country indeed does increase capital accumulation by imposing tariffs, but this gain is at the expense of other countries and retaliation soon follows which in the end leaves everybody losing, including the original tariff imposer. Therefore, this argument is *invalid.*

    (5) **Standard of living and real wage** – this argument is parallel to number (4), except that the imposition of tariffs eventually leads to a lower national income and wage level due to retaliation. This argument is self-defeating and *invalid.*

    (6) **Conservation of natural resources** – tariffs tend to cause extreme dependence on national resources and, therefore, our economy actually depletes its resources more quickly than if free trade existed and other countries bought our resources. Instead of conservation, there is depletion of natural resources; therefore, this argument is *invalid.*

    (7) **Industrialization of low wage nation** – quite pertinent to underdeveloped countries. However, many times the foreign competition isn't the problem, but the paucity of capital and technical knowledge are problems. The danger of tariffs for this argument lies in the fact that the wrong kind of industries will be created. The types of industries which the underdeveloped areas can economically create and maintain are generally those which don't require protection on any large scale because they are based on natural advantages. Again, this argument is valid if it is used very carefully and closely controlled.

    (8) **Maintain employment and reduce unemployment** – this argument becomes useless upon retaliation of other countries. The problem compounds itself. Also, if countries don't retaliate, there is still a gross inefficient allocation of resources in the tariff-setting country. Alternative policies are available which would relieve unemployment at home while encouraging greater

employment abroad and a larger volume of international trade. Therefore, this argument is *invalid.*

(9) **National defense** – in particular instances there may be merit to this argument, but it becomes *invalid* if applied indiscriminately. We must trade to get the proper resources and conserve ours. (See #6). If the economy weakens, the military strength weakens. "National Security depends upon many factors, not the least of which is a community of economically healthy nations devoted to living in harmony and tied together by mutually beneficial trade."[1]

(10) **Increase business size** – with fully employed resources, aggregate domestic production can't be expanded by protective tariffs; expansion in one area of the economy must be at the expense of reduced output in other fields. Tariffs tend to draw resources away from previous employments into protected industries; hence, an inefficient allocation of resources. Also some of these reallocated resources are likely to be drawn away from production of export goods. Domestic expansion would be at the expense of the export market. Therefore, this argument is *invalid.*

(11) **Retaliation and bargaining** – retaliation doesn't recover the losses that are suffered due to foreign tariffs. Retaliation further reduces the volume of trade. Bargaining as a reciprocal tool; i.e., tariffs are raised and then offered to be lowered if the other countries will lower theirs. If the reciprocal agreement isn't reached, then the tariffs usually remain. These arguments are sometimes a front for other reasons for erecting tariffs. Therefore, most of the time, this argument is *invalid.*

11. France exports about 18 percent of its GDP, neighboring Belgium exports 46 percent. What areas of economic policy are likely to be affected by such variations in exports?

12. Does widespread unemployment change the economic logic of protectionism?

    Increased validity is being granted to the argument that it is better to have workers employed even if the consumer must pay more. Many economic trade models assume full employment but the "real world" does not necessarily reflect the theory.

13. Review the economic effects of major trade imbalances such as those caused by petroleum imports.

    Trade imbalances cause shifting balance of payments patterns, unstable monetary exchange rates, wage and employment levels. Eventually a nation's economic base is significantly modified. As money value is depreciated, imports become more expensive and exports less expensive so an automatic adjustment process is set into motion.

14. Discuss the main provisions of the Omnibus Trade and competitiveness Act of 1988.

    Just as its name implies, the Omnibus Trade and Competitiveness Act is many faceted, focusing on assisting businesses to be more competitive in world markets as well as correcting perceived injustices in trade practices. Congressional concern centered around the issue that the United States, the world's largest economy, was open to Japan, Western Europe and the newly industrializing countries of Asia but was closed out in parts of their markets. Some see the trade bill as a protectionist measure, but the government sees it as a means of providing stronger tools to open foreign markets and to help U.S. exporters be more competitive. The bill covers three areas considered critical in improving the U.S. trade position: improving access to foreign markets, assisting U.S. exporters to be more competitive, and providing relief to U.S. businesses affected by unfair trade activities.

---

[1] U.S. Senate, "Foreign Economic Police: Report No. 2629 (84$^{th}$ Cong. 2nd session), 1956, p.28

**Market Access** There has been growing concern that U.S. business does not have the same access to foreign markets that foreign business has to U.S. markets. There are many barriers restricting or prohibiting goods from entering a foreign market: unnecessarily restrictive technical standards, compulsory distribution systems, customs barriers, tariffs, quotas, and restrictive licensing requirements are just a few. The Act gives the President authority to deal with countries where specific barriers unfairly keep U.S. products from entering those countries' markets. If a country violates a trade agreement, the President can retaliate by restricting the country's products in U.S. markets.

Two other issues addressed under the market access section of the law are government procurement procedures and market access to telecommunications markets. Foreign government procurement procedures must not discriminate against U.S. firms; if they do, the President has the authority to impose a ban on U.S. Government procurement of goods and services from that country.

Deregulation and the divestiture of American Telephone and Telegraph assured foreign telecommunications suppliers full access to the American market. By contrast, U.S. companies enjoy limited access to the major foreign telecommunications markets, most notably in Europe. The 1988 Act clearly indicates that the United States regards telecommunications market access a top priority of U.S. trade policy and, when negotiation fails to open foreign markets, the government will take retaliatory action.

**Export Expansion** In addition to making foreign markets more accessible to U.S. goods, the 1988 Act reflects on awareness that some problems with U.S. export competitiveness stemmed from impediments on trade imposed by U.S. regulations and export disincentives. Export controls, the Foreign Corrupt Practices Act (FCPA), and export promotion were specifically addressed. The new regulations make it easier and speed up the process for obtaining export licenses for products on the export control list. Much of the ambiguity in the FCPA was removed by clarifying the legality of most types of payments. In addition, the act reaffirmed the government's role in the promotion of export trade in general, agricultural trade in particular, and the continued financial assistance to small businesses engaged in exporting.

**Import Relief** Export trade is a two way street; that is, we must be prepared to compete with imports in the home market if we force foreign markets to open to U.S. exports. The Act provides a menu of remedies for U.S. businesses adversely affected by imports; it recognizes that foreign penetration of U.S. markets can cause serious competitive pressure, loss of market share and, occasionally, severe injury. Measures dealing with antidumping, countervailing duty, and intellectual property protection laws are designed to redress competitive advantages obtained by foreign companies through unfair trade practices. The Act also provides temporary relief from competition to firms injured by fairly traded imports.

15. The Tokyo Round of GATT has emphasized the reduction of nontariff barriers. How does the Uruguay Round differ?

Nontariff barriers are all the restrictions imposed on the importation of goods by a host government with the exception of tariffs. Such things as standards, quotas, import licenses, countervailing duties, border taxes can be classified as nontariff barriers. The Tokyo Round considered nontariff barriers as having become one of the major deterrents to international trade. Earlier rounds of negotiations by GATT members had been successful in reducing tariffs but nontariff barriers are considered to be insidious protectionist devices and the Tokyo Round focused on the reduction of nontariff barriers.

The Tokyo Round made a good start at addressing a number of nontariff barriers that have become more serious in recent years. Despite the success of these past rounds, high tariffs have not disappeared entirely and nontariff barriers are still widely used. There are also areas that, until now, GATT has not addressed such as services, intellectual property rights, and investment. Specifically, GATT negotiations in this round are to address key areas of importance in international trade which are not now under the scope of GATT rules. For example, GATT rules do not apply to the international trade of services which represent an increasing percentage of international trade flows. Similarly, GATT rules have little influence over government investment policies affecting international trade or on policies concerning the protection of intellectual property rights such as patents, trademarks, and copyrights. Agricultural trade is another area where GATT rules either do not apply or are not effective. Finally, the dispute settlement mechanism is seen to be increasingly ineffective at resolving conflicts among GATT members.

16. Discuss the impact of GATS, TRIMS, AND TRIPS on global trade.

An important objective of the United States in the Uruguay Round was to reduce or eliminate barriers to international trade in services. While there is still much progress to be made before free trade in services will exist throughout the world, the General Agreement on Trade in Services (GATS) is the first multilateral, legally enforceable agreement covering trade and investment in services sector. It provides a legal basis for future negotiations aimed at eliminating barriers that discriminate against foreign services trade and deny them market access. For the first time, comprehensive multilateral disciplines and procedures covering trade and investment in services have been established. Specific market-opening concessions from a wide range of individual countries were achieved and provision was made for continued negotiations to further liberalize telecommunications and financial services.

Equally significant were the results of negotiations in the investment sector. Trade-Related Investment Measures (TRIMs), established the basic principle that investment restrictions can be major trade barriers and therefore are included, for the first time, under GATT procedures. An initial set of specific practices were prohibited including: local content requirements specifying that some amount of the value of the investor's production must be purchased from local sources or produced locally; trade balancing requirements specifying that an investor must export an amount equivalent to some proportion of imports or condition the amount of imports permitted on export levels; and, foreign exchange balancing requirements limiting the importation of products used in local production by restricting its access to foreign exchange to an amount related to its exchange inflow. As a result of TRIMs, restrictions in Indonesia which prohibit foreign firms from opening their own wholesale or retail distribution channels can be challenged. And so can investment restrictions in Brazil that require foreign-owned manufacturers to buy most of their components from high-cost local suppliers and that affiliates of foreign multinationals maintain a trade surplus in Brazil's favor by exporting more than they sell within.

Another objective of the United States from the Uruguay Round was achieved by an agreement on Trade-Related Aspects of Intellectual Property Rights (TRIPs). The TRIPs agreement establishes substantially higher standards of protection for a full range of intellectual property rights (patents, copyrights, trademarks, trade secrets, industrial designs, and semiconductor chip mask works) than are embodied in current international agreements and it provides for the effective enforcement of those standards both internally and at the border.

17. Discuss the evolution of world trade that has led to the formulation of the WTO.

Since the inception of GATT, there have been eight "rounds" of intergovernmental tariff negotiations. The most recently completed was the Uruguay round which built on the success of the Tokyo Round, the most comprehensive and far-reaching round undertaken by GATT up to that time. The Tokyo Round resulted in tariff cuts and set new international rules for subsidies and countervailing measures, anti-dumping, government procurement, technical barriers to trade (standards), customs valuation, and import licensing. While the Tokyo Round addressed non-tariff barriers, there were some areas not covered by that round which continued to impede free trade. In addition to market access, there were issues of trade in services, agriculture, and textiles; intellectual property rights; and investment and capital flows.

The Uruguay Round was begun in 1986 in Punta del Este, Uruguay and finally concluded in 1994. By 1995, 80 GATT members including the United States, the European Union (and it member states) Japan, and Canada had accepted the agreement. Perhaps the most notable achievement of the Uruguay Round was the creation of a new institution as a successor to the GATT, the World Trade Organization (WTO). At the signing of the Uruguay Round trade agreement, U.S. representatives pushed for an enormous expansion of the definition of trade issues. The result was the creation of the World Trade Organization that encompasses the current GATT structure and extends it to new areas not adequately covered in the past. The WTO is an institution—not an agreement as was GATT. It will set the rules governing trade between its 117 members, provide a panel of experts to hear and rule on trade disputes between members and, unlike GATT, issue binding decisions. It will require for the first time, the full participation of all members in all aspects of the current GATT and the Uruguay Round agreements and, through its enhanced stature and scope, provide a permanent, comprehensive forum to address the trade issues of the 21st century global market. Trade disputes will be heard by a panel of experts. A panel of experts, selected by the WTO, will hear both sides and issue a decision; the winning side will be authorized to retaliate with trade sanctions if the losing country does not change its practices. While the WTO has no actual means of enforcement, international pressure to comply with WTO decisions from other member countries is expected to force compliance. The WTO ensures that member countries agree to the obligations of all the agreements, countries, including developing countries (the fastest growing markets of the world) will undertake obligations to open their markets and to be bound by the rules of the multilateral trading system.

18. Visit http://www.usitc.gov/taffairs.htm (U.S. Customs tariff schedule) and look up the import duties on leather footwear. You will find a difference in the duties on shoes of different value, material composition, and quantity. Using what you have learned in this chapter, explain the reasoning behind these differences. Do the same for frozen and/or concentrated orange juice.

    This exercise is designed to familiarize the student with the Internet and the information available from the U.S. Customs tariff schedule. There are various reasons why there will be different import duties on leather footwear and orange juice. The student should rclate some of the issues discussed in the text as reasons for the different tariffs.

19. The GATT has had a long and eventful history. Visit http://www.wto.org/wto/about/about.htm and write a short report on the various Rounds of GATT. What were the key issues addressed in each round?

    This exercise is designed to familiarize the student with the Internet and issues GATT as well as the WTO. In addition to the various Rounds of GATT, this site is a complete discussion of WTO. The discussion of this question could include a broader discussion of WTO.

## GATT trade rounds

| Year | Place/name | Subjects covered | Countries |
|---|---|---|---|
| 1947 | **Geneva** | Tariffs | 23 |
| 1949 | **Annecy** | Tariffs | 13 |
| 1951 | **Torquay** | Tariffs | 38 |
| 1956 | **Geneva** | Tariffs | 26 |
| 1960–1961 | **Geneva (Dillon Round)** | Tariffs | 26 |
| 1964–1967 | **Geneva (Kennedy Round)** | Tariffs and anti-dumping measures | 62 |
| 1973–1979 | **Geneva (Tokyo Round)** | Tariffs, non-tariff measures, "framework" agreements | 102 |
| 1986–1994 | **Geneva (Uruguay Round)** | Tariffs, non-tariff measures, rules, services, intellectual property, dispute settlement, textiles, agriculture, creation of WTO, etc | 123 |

## Chapter 3 – Geography and History – The Foundation of Cultural Understanding

### Teaching Objectives

Understanding the geography and history of a country can help a marketer have a better appreciation for many of the characteristics of its culture. A culture of a people evolves in response to the environment which it confronts. The geography of a country, its topography, climate, physical position relative to other countries affect a culture's evolution including its marketing and distribution systems. While is impractical for a marketer to be an expert on the geography of every country in the world, it is important for a marketer to understand that geography plays an important role in the economy of a country and its marketing system. One objective of this chapter is to sensitize students to the importance of geography as one of the explanations of a country's market and economy.

The history of a country is also important in understanding many aspects of a culture. In the author's opinion, it is imperative that an international marketer making a long-term commitment in a country have some knowledge of a its history.

One cannot fully understand how businesspeople negotiate, how they conduct business, their attitudes toward foreign investment, the legal system, and other aspects of the market/business system without a historical perspective. A historical perspective helps prepare an international marketer for many of the cultural differences that often cause misunderstandings and in many cases, mistakes. While a marketer may not be able to change a person's attitude or behavior, if you have an historical perspective of why they react as they do, you can gain insights that can possibly make it easier to adapt your strategies for a successful outcome. Today with the importance of NAFTA and its possible expansion throughout Latin America, a knowledge of geography of the region and an appreciation for the history of the region, especially U.S./Latin American relations, is a must in order to be culturally aware. The teaching objectives of this chapter are to:

1. Help students understand the importance of geography and history in understanding a country's economy and markets.
2. Appreciate the effect that topography and climate have on products, population centers, transportation, and economic growth.
3. Be sensitive to the growing problem of environmental damage and its effect on business and the social and moral responsibility of each citizen to protect the environment.
4. Understand the effect of the history of each culture on international marketing.

### Comments and Suggestions

1. To illustrate some of the geographic differences among countries, I have had students study the folio of color maps of the text, and prepare a comparative analysis. Divide the class into three or four groups, assign different sets of countries to each group and then have each student within a group do a comparative analysis of the set of countries (select countries that will be very different, for example, the United States, China, and Mexico). During class, have the students contribute what they have learned to illustrate the geographic diversity that exists among the countries analyzed. The professor's discussion can build on this example and illustrate the vast differences in population, resources, transportation networks, economic activity and their effect upon markets. For an interesting article on which industries will benefit from current population and world growth, see Patricia M. Carey, "Population and World Growth: Which Industries Benefit," International Business, October 1994, pp. 50–58.

2. The ability to physically move goods to markets is a major problem in much of the developing world. These are the markets where the greatest growth is expected in the next few decades. Some of the potential demand in these markets will be building infrastructure necessary to overcome geographical barriers. To illustrate these two points and to stress the importance of understanding geography, I use transportation, that is, highway systems, railroads, seaports, and airports as a basis for my lecture. Any number of countries can be used. I use Mexico and China. The need for more highways, better railroads, and the connection of seaports with major markets are necessary in both countries but the problems to achieve a better transportation infrastructure are substantially different. Both countries offer enormous market opportunity as they invest in infrastructure.

3. The importance of NAFTA and Latin America to the United States makes it imperative that we have a better understanding of the history between the U.S. and these countries. Our political and economic relations are affected by the legacy of our long history of intervention and meddling in the affairs of these countries. While all of this is history and, for the most part the United States does not behave as it did during much of the late 1800s and early 1900s, it is still very much a part of the attitudes citizens of these countries have towards the United States and U.S. business. I use Global Perspective—Birth of a Nation—Panama in 67 Hours (TM 3–5 to 3–8) to begin a discussion of the U.S. role in Latin America. After a brief discussion, I ask the students to give other examples of U.S. intervention in Latin America which then can lead to a lively discussion of this history. I make a special point of discussing the Mexican revolution and the U.S. role in Mexico to help students understand some of the attitudes held by Mexicans. Two sources that serve as an excellent source for a quick picture of Mexican history and U.S. relations are: John C. Condon, Good Neighbors (Yarmouth, Maine: Intercultural Press, Inc., 1985) and Alan Riding, Distant Neighbors: A Portrait of the Mexicans (New York: First Vantage Books, 1986).

4. For an excellent article that illustrates why the long-simmering resentment toward the United States by many Mexicans bubbled to the surface with the $52 billion bailout package to help save Mexico from a financial crash, see Dianne Solis "Americans Grow Ugly in Mexicans' Eyes," The Wall Street Journal, March 21, 1995, p. A–10. This article offers an excellent example of how the legacy of our history with Mexico affects Mexican attitudes and creates suspicion about U.S. motives in what is considered by most in the United States as an attempt to help Mexico.

5. Throughout the discussion of history I stress that history is subjective and that an international marketer must strive to understand history from the other country's perspective.

**Lecture Outline**

GEOGRAPHY AND HISTORY – The Foundation of Cultural Understanding

I. History and Geography: The Foundations of Cultural Understanding Global Perspective—Birth of a Nation—Panama in 67 Hours.

II. Geography and Global Markets

III. Climate and Topography

IV. Geography, Nature, and Economic Growth

V. Social Responsibility and Environmental Growth

VI. Resources

VII. World Population Trends

  A. Controlling Population

  B. Growth

  C. Rural/Urban Migration

  D. Population Decline and Aging

E. Worker Shortage and Immigration

VIII. World Trade Routes

IX. Historical Perspective in Global Business

X. History and Contemporary Behavior

XI. History is Subjective

XII. Summary

## DISCUSSION QUESTIONS

1. Define:

| | |
|---|---|
| Manifest Destiny | Sustainable development |
| Roosevelt Corollary | Monroe Doctrine |

2. Why study geography in international marketing? Discuss.

Geography is a study of the physical characteristics of a particular region of the earth. Involved in this study are climate, topography, and population. The interaction of the physical characteristics is one of the principal determinants of a country's customs, products, industries, needs, and methods of satisfying those needs.

Marketing is concerned with satisfying the needs of people. International marketing seeks out the whole world as its marketplace. Therefore, for an international marketer to know how to satisfy the needs of the international market, he must be familiar enough with geography to know what the various causal factors of the people's needs are. He must know that various climates and topographies do exist and that they are vital in shaping the marketing plans that an international marketer must make. As an example, a producer selling machinery in the tropics would have to realize that special protection is needed to keep a machine running properly in hot and humid climates.

3. Pick a country and show how employment and topography affect marketing within the country.

Library project.

4. Discuss the bases of world trade. Give examples illustrating the different bases.

The basis for world trade is the differences between countries. One of these differences is the difference between people. Different heritages have resulted in the development of certain unique skills in the people of a country. An example would be the watchmaking skill developed by the Swiss. Thus, they have a unique skill on which to base trade. Another difference is the one of differing stages of economic development existing in the world today. Some countries are highly developed and industrialized. These nations, such as the United States and France, might be trading in luxuries, whereas an underdeveloped nation, such as Kenya, might be forced to trade only in essential capital goods. A third difference in countries serving as a basis for world trade is the availability of natural resources. Great Britain, poor in mineral resources, imports petroleum, where West Germany, rich in mineral resources but not food, imports large amounts of fruits and vegetables. Thus, trade is created by these differences: (1) Differences in skills – other countries seek the products of skills, (2) differences in economies – countries seek products they don't produce but need, and (3) differences in national resources – countries buy and sell resources which they do not have or have an abundance of.

5. The marketer "should also examine the more complex effect of geography upon general market characteristics, distribution systems, and the state of the economy." Comment.

There can be no doubt that geography has had a "complex effect upon general market characteristics, distribution systems, and the state of the economy." Therefore, the world marketer should be careful not to look just at how his product must be changed to fit into a foreign market. That is, he must not just fit his electric motors, say, with high-temperature operating characteristics and stop there.

There's more to it than that. Consider the diverse nature of South America, for example. The channels of distribution that a domestic marketer has been accustomed to using might not even exist because of natural barriers. These same natural barriers also cause quite varied levels of economic development within the same country. Cities and rural areas might not even be on the same economic plane. Finally, as a result of these barriers and thus physical isolation of various population centers, areas of the same economic development might have entirely different cultures. Therefore, the general market characteristics of these areas would also differ greatly and have a direct effect upon the success of marketing plans.

6. The world population pattern trend is shifting from rural to urban areas. Discuss the marketing ramifications.

   There are many marketing ramifications to the world rural-urban population shift. One of the obvious ones is that the world market is becoming more unified in location. Thus, it is becoming easier to reach a larger segment of the market by just marketing in the urban population centers. The types of products marketed will also change with this population shift. For example, food might become a more important product in international marketing with few people raising their own. Similarly, these shifts will result in greater industrialization in countries with presently low levels of industrialization. This again implies marketing changes that might affect the world marketer, increased sales of capital goods, for example. In summary, people living in cities have different needs than those living in the country. Thus, the shift from country to city means that the world marketer has a different market to serve with different characteristics.

7. Select a country with a stable population and one with a rapidly growing population. Contrast the marketing implications of these two situations.

   Library project.

8. "The basis of world trade can be simply stated as the result of equalizing an imbalance in the needs and wants of society on one side and the supply and demand of goods on the other." Explain.

   The basis for world trade is the same as that for intracountry trade. That is, within a country someone has a need for a certain product but another person has this product which he is willing to give up in trade for something that he wants. Thus, there is trade. On a world level, it works the same except that the parties are in different countries. Thus, in one country there is an excess of demand for a product and in another country there is an excess supply. Generally, the roles for supplier and consumer are reversed for another product. Therefore, there is world trade. In summary, the needs and wants of a people for products are not in balance with the supply and demand of the products. World trade attempts to equalize this imbalance by creating trade between countries with such imbalances.

9. How do differences in people constitute a basis for trade?

   The primary way that differences in people constitute a basis for world trade is that various people, through cultural heritages, have developed unique skills and talents in demand throughout the world. The Swiss are an example as watchmakers. Another example would be that of the Japanese as camera makers. Thus, the way that this might serve as a basis for world trade is that a Swiss might buy a Japanese camera and a Japanese might buy a Swiss watch. A trade between Switzerland and Japan has thus resulted from a difference in people; and further, all other countries whose people do not possess these talents but desire the products will be engaged in trade.

10. ". . . world trade routes bind the world together . . ." Discuss.

    World trade routes bind the world together. This statement means that the world trade routes serve as avenues of minimizing differences between countries. Without these routes, countries would stand alone – each different from the rest in resources, economy, and people. The trade routes allow both people and products to flow, making more of a unified, balanced world. The physical imbalances overcome, also smooth, cultural and economic differences through the exchange of ideas as well as products.

11. Some say the global environment is a global issue rather than a national one. What does this mean? Discuss.

    Many view the problem as a global issue rather than a national one. One report on the global environment stressed . . . "it is quite clear that a number of critical problems—the threat to the ozone layer, the greenhouse effect, the loss of biodiversity, and ocean pollution—cannot be addressed by nations in isolation."

    Companies looking to build manufacturing plants in countries with more liberal pollution regulations than they have at home are finding that regulations everywhere are becoming stricter. Many Asian governments are drafting new regulations and strictly enforcing existing ones. A strong motivator for Asia and the rest of the world is the realization that pollution is on the verge of getting completely out of control.

    Neither Western Europe nor the rest of the industrialized world are free of environmental damage; rivers are polluted and the atmosphere in many major urban areas is far from clean. The very process of controlling industrial wastes leads to another and perhaps equally critical issue: the disposal of hazardous waste, a by-product of pollution control. Estimates of hazardous wastes collected annually exceed 300 million tons; the critical question is disposal that does not move the problem elsewhere.

    The business community is responding positively to the notion that the focus must be on the global environment rather than "the quality of the air, land, and water in our own backyards." An International Chamber of Commerce Industry Forum on the environment reflected a shift in company attitudes toward environmental issues away from a reactive and largely defensive stance to a proactive and constructive approach. Some skeptics may dismiss such statements as "window dressing" and they could be, but the beginning of change is awareness. Responsibility for cleaning up the environment does not rest solely with governments, businesses, or activist groups. Each citizen has social and moral responsibility to include environmental protection among his/her highest goals.

12. How does an understanding of history help an international marketer?

    To understand, explain, and appreciate a people's image of itself and the fundamental attitudes and unconscious fears that are often reflected in its view of foreign cultures, it is necessary to study the culture as it is now as well as to understand culture as it was, that is, a country's history. An awareness of the history of a country is particularly effective for understanding attitudes about the role of government and business, the relations between managers and the managed, the sources of management authority, and attitudes toward foreign MNC's. History is what helps define a nation's "mission," how it perceives its neighbors, and how it sees its place in the world. To understand a country's attitudes, prejudices, and fears it is necessary to look beyond the surface or current events to the inner subtleties of the country's entire past for clues.

13. Why is there a love/hate relationship between Mexico and the United States? Discuss.

    A crucial element in understanding any nation's business and political culture is the subjective perception of its history. To a Mexican, the United States is seen as a threat to their political, economic, and cultural independence. To most citizens in the United States, the causes for such feelings are a mystery. After all, the U.S. has always been Mexico's "good neighbor." Most would agree with President Kennedy's proclamation during a visit to Mexico, "Geography has made us neighbors, tradition has made us friends." North Americans may be surprised to learn that most

Mexicans felt it more accurate to say, "Geography has made us closer, tradition has made us far apart."

North Americans feel they have been good neighbors. They see the Monroe Doctrine as protection for Latin America from European colonization and the intervention of Europe in the governments of the Western Hemisphere. Latin Americans tend to see the Monroe Doctrine as an offensive expression of U.S. influence in Latin America. Or to put it another way, "Europe keep your hands off, Latin American is only for the United States."

United States Marines sing with pride of their exploits "form the Halls of Montezuma to the shores of Tripoli." To the Mexican, the "Halls of Montezuma" is remembered as U.S. troops marching all the way to the center of Mexico City and extracting as tribute 890,000 square miles that included Texas, New Mexico, Arizona and California. Most U.S. citizens probably do not know of the boy heroes of Chaptultepec Park but every Mexican can recount the heroism of "Los Ninos Heroes," and the loss of Mexican territory to the United States.

14. Discuss how an American's interpretation of Manifest Destiny and the Monroe Doctrine might differ from a Latin American's.

    Manifest Destiny and the Monroe Doctrine were accepted basis for U.S. foreign policy during much of the 19th and 20th centuries. Manifest Destiny, in its broadest interpretation, meant that Americans were a chosen people ordained by God to create a model society. More specifically, it referred to the desires of American expansionists in the 1840s to extend the U.S. boundaries from the Atlantic to the Pacific; the idea of "Manifest Destiny" was used to justify U.S. annexation of Texas, Oregon, New Mexico, and California; and later, U.S. involvement in Cuba, Alaska, Hawaii and the Philippines.

    The Monroe Doctrine, a cornerstone of U.S. foreign policy, was enunciated by President James Monroe in a public statement proclaiming three basic dicta: no further European colonization in the New World, abstention of the U.S. from European political affairs, and nonintervention of European governments in the governments of the Western Hemisphere.

    After 1870, interpretation of the Monroe Doctrine became increasingly broad. In 1881, its principles were evoked in discussing the development of an interoceanic canal across the Isthmus of Panama. The Monroe Doctrine was further applied by Theodore Roosevelt with what became known as the Roosevelt Corollary to the Monroe Doctrine. The corollary stated that not only would the U.S. prohibit non-American intervention in Latin American affairs but it would police the area and guarantee that Latin American nations met their international obligations. The corollary sanctioning American intervention was applied in 1905 when Roosevelt forced the Dominican Republic to accept the appointment of an American economic advisor who quickly became the financial director of the small state; it was used in the acquisition of the Panama Canal Zone from Colombia and the formation of a provisional government in Cuba in 1906.

    According to U.S. history, these Latin American adventures were a justifiable part of our foreign policy; to Latin Americans, they were unwelcome intrusions in Latin American affairs. The way historical events are recorded and interpreted in one culture can differ substantially from those same events recorded and interpreted in another. A comparison of histories goes a long way in explaining the differences in outlooks and behavior of people on both sides of the border. Many Mexicans believe that their "good neighbor" to the North is not reluctant to throw its weight around when it wants something. There are suspicions that self-interest is the primary motivation in good relations with Mexico, whether it be fear of Fidel Castro 25 years ago or eagerness for Mexican oil today.

15. The telegraph, telephone, television, satellites, computer, and the Internet have all had an effect on how international business operates. Discuss how each of these communications innovations affects international business management.

An underpinning of all commerce is effective communications, knowledge of where goods and services exist and where they are needed and the ability to communicate instantaneously across vast distances. Facilitating the expansion of trade have been continuous improvements in electronic communications. First came the telegraph, then the telephone, television, satellites, the computer and the Internet. Each revolution in electronic technology has had a profound effect on human conditions, economic growth and the manner in which commerce functions. As each "new" communications technology has had its impact, new business models have been spawned and some existing businesses re-invented to adapt to the new technology while other businesses have failed to respond and thus ceased to exist. The Internet revolution will be no different; it too affects human conditions, economic growth, and the manner in which commerce operates. As we will discuss in subsequent chapters, the Internet has already begun to shape how international business is managed. However, as the Internet permeates the fabric of the world's cultures, the biggest changes are yet to come!

# Chapter 4 – Cultural Dynamics in Assessing Global Markets

## Teaching Objectives

Culture in this text is defined in an anthropological sense in that culture refers to the entire social heritage of a group of people. Thus, culture includes a country's economy, society, behavior, etc. It is imperative for international marketers to learn to appreciate the intricacies of cultures different from their own. A vast majority of the mistakes make by international businesses can be attributed to a lack of understanding some aspect of the culture of a country. The teaching objectives of this chapter are to:

1) Set the tone for the entire course, which is the importance of culture to an international marketer.
2) Create a strong sensitivity in students to the cultural differences that exist among countries and the effect of cultural elements on the total fabric of doing business in another country.
3) Re-emphasize the idea of the Self-Reference Criterion (SRC) and its influence on doing business in another culture. The insidious nature of the SRC – that is, you are often unaware of how your SRC is affecting your reaction to an event, your evaluation of a market opportunity or the evaluation of a situation or event, etc. – is especially important to stress in this chapter and throughout the course. Many marketing mistakes and misfires can be explained by someone's SRC interfering with a proper interpretation of a marketing action. Because cultures are different, often what is obvious and important in your home culture is not so obvious and important in another or vice versa.
4) Explore the strategy of planned change. By understanding how cultures change, companies can overcome resistance to change and accelerate rates of acceptance. This idea is more fully developed in Chapter 12 but the concept can be introduced here.
5) Stress that in many cultures, an international marketer is a change agent in that their activities cause cultural change. Sometimes the consequences of change can be very beneficial but in other cases, change can be harmful – the marketer has the responsibility to guard against causing harmful change.

## Comments and Suggestions

1. There are several ways to achieve the teaching objectives of this chapter. If you like case there are several that will serve as a basis for illustrating the important points of the chapter. By asking students to identify the cultural aspects of Case 2–1 The Not So Wonderful World of EuroDisney (in a broader scope, this case can also be used in conjunction with Chapter 11) various cultural differences between Disney in the U.S. and EuroDisney can be explored.
2. I often begin a lecture on culture by reading the quote in the section on "Cultural Borrowing." (". . . begins breakfast with an orange from the eastern Mediterranean . . .") and using it to help illustrate several aspects of cultures, for example, that cultures borrow, that they change, but that they also resist change and that once they accept a "new way" it is their own regardless of how they acquired the new way. This idea is important to stress since it will be important later in the course when the students are exposed to the idea of products being innovations to which there may be cultural resistance to acceptance.
3. I think it is important to discuss briefly the various elements of culture to set the stage for the next several chapters which explore some of the elements in depth. Using transparency, Elements of Culture, as a visual guide, I briefly comment on each, giving appropriate examples.

Case 1–3, Nestle – The Infant Formula Incident, is a good case to discuss since many will have heard of the case and it can be used to illustrate several aspects of culture discussed in the chapter. It also serves as a good example of a marketer causing harmful cultural change. A key question to explore is how Nestle could have avoided the problems in the case and still marketed their product.

**Lecture Outline**

I. Culture and Its Elements
   A. Elements of Culture
      1. *Material*
      2. *Social Institutions*
      3. *Humans and Universe*
      4. *Aesthetics*
      5. *Language*
   B. Analysis of Elements
II. Cultural Knowledge
   A. Factual vs. Interpretive Knowledge
   B. Cultural Sensitivity and Tolerance
III. Cultural Values
   A. Individualism/Collective Index
   B. Power Distance Index
   C. Uncertainty Avoidance Index
IV. Linguistic Distance
V. Cultural Change
   A. Cultural Borrowing
   B. Similarities: An Illusion
   C. Resistance to Change
VI. Planned Cultural Change
VII. Consequences of an Innovation

## DISCUSSION QUESTIONS

1. Define:

| | |
|---|---|
| Cultural sensitivity | Factual knowledge |
| Culture | Interpretive knowledge |
| Ethnocentrism | Cultural values |
| Strategy of cultural congruence | Cultural borrowing |
| Linguistic distance | Material culture |
| Strategy of unplanned change | Aesthetics |
| Social institutions | Strategy of planned change |

2. Which role does the marketer play as a change agent?

   Whether or not the marketer is aware of it, he assumes the role of a change agent when he introduces into another culture new ideas or new products requiring some form of change in behavior for acceptance and use of the new idea or product. The international marketer must concern himself with the impact of his actions upon the new culture.

3. Discuss the three cultural change strategies a foreign marketer can pursue. There are three strategies. (a) Culturally congruent strategy, (b) Strategy of unplanned change, (c) Strategy of planned change. The culturally congruent strategy involves marketing products similar to ones already on the market in a manner as congruent as possible with existing cultural norms, thereby minimizing resistance. A strategy of planned change means deliberately setting out to change those aspects of a culture most likely to offer resistance to predetermined marketing goals. The strategy of unplanned change consists of introducing an innovation and then waiting for an eventful cultural change that will permit the culture to accept the innovation. The essence of unplanned change lies in the fact that the marketer does nothing to accelerate or help to bring about the necessary change where the marketer deliberately sets about to overcome resistance and to cause change that will accelerate the rate of adoption of his product or innovation.

4. "Culture is pervasive in all marketing activities." Discuss.

   Marketers are constantly in the process of adjusting their efforts to the demands of the culture of their markets. Although in the long run they may affect their market's culture as a result of their efforts, most current activity involves reconciling marketing activity to the immediate culture.

5. What is the importance of "cultural empathy" to the foreign marketer? How does he or she acquire "cultural empathy?"

   The importance of "cultural empathy" to the foreign marketer is that being culturally sensitive allows him or her to objectively see, evaluate, and appreciate another culture. A marketer can obtain cultural empathy by studying the culture and living with it. The latter is not always possible, and it may be expedient to hire natives who speak your tongue and their own. This procedure will often give you the intuition which is necessary for success.

6. Why should a foreign marketer be concerned with the study of culture?

   A foreign marketer should study culture in order to avoid making blunders which would not be made if he or she had cultural knowledge. Culture should be studied because it affects the consumer's desire and ability to buy.

7. What is the popular definition of culture? What is the viewpoint of cultural anthropologists? What is the importance of the difference?

   The popular definition of culture is that a person is either "cultured" or "uncultured" according to his or her ability in certain specialized fields of knowledge. The cultural anthropologist defines culture as "all the knowledge, beliefs, and skills he or she acquires as a member of society." The importance to the marketer of the differences between these two definitions is the fact that the anthropologist's definition includes all parts of life, and all of these parts affect a consumer's desire and ability to pay for a product.

8. It is stated that members of a society borrow from other cultures to solve problems that they face in common. What does this mean? What is the significance to marketing?

   Cultural borrowing entails using the *best* solutions to a problem that different cultures face. This best solution, borrowed by one culture from another, is incorporated into the borrowing culture's system, and becomes part of their cultural heritage. This fact is significant to the marketer because although the solutions to the problems are similar they are put together in a unique manner which is strictly American, Chinese, French, etc. In realizing the "similar but different" aspect of culture, the marketer is aided in gaining cultural empathy.

9. "For the inexperienced marketer, the "similar but different" feature of culture creates an illusion of similarity which usually does not always exist." Discuss and give examples.

   Although some cultures seem similar, they most likely are not. For example, two different countries speaking the same language may use words or phrases which are acceptable to one, but totally unacceptable to the other. Some cultures may have subcultures in which the "similar but different" principle applies.

10. Outline the elements of culture as seen by an anthropologist. How can a marketer use this "cultural scheme?"

    a. Material Culture
        1. Technology
        2. Economics
    b. Social Institutions
        1. Social organizations
        2. Education
        3. Political structures
    c. Man and the Universe
        1. Belief systems
    d. Aesthetics
        1. Graphic and plastic arts
        2. Folklore
        3. Music, drama, and the dance
    e. Language

    The foreign marketer may use the above outline of cultural elements (1) to provide a meaningful framework to use in evaluating a marketing plan or in studying the potential of a foreign market, (2) to point out those things which must be learned about the culture of the people since most of these elements are reacted to automatically in a cultural system, (3) as factors with which the market interacts and which are basic in the understanding of the character of the marketing system of any society.

11. What is material culture? What are its implications for marketing? Give examples.

    Material culture consists of technology and economics. Technology is the techniques used to make material goods; it is the "know-how" possessed by the people of a society. Economics is the manner in which people employ their capabilities and the resulting benefits. Economics includes the production of goods and services, their distribution, consumption, means of exchange, and the income derived from the creation of utilities. The marketer must remember that material culture affects the level of demand, the quality and type of products demanded, their functional features, and the means of production and distribution of these goods. Examples of material culture would be the availability and cost of gasoline in regulating demand for and size of automobiles. The availability of electricity can regulate demand for any electrical product.

12. Social institutions affect marketing in a variety of ways. Discuss, give examples.

    Social institutions affect marketing because they regulate the consumer's behavior and attitudes by organizing his activities and teaching him acceptable behavior. Examples of social institutions affecting marketing are the literacy rate as a function of education, the strength of the family unit, and political acceptance or hindrance of marketing activities.

13. "Markets are the result of the triune interaction of a marketer's efforts, economic conditions, and all other elements of the culture." Comment.

    This statement emphasizes the point that markets evolve out of the interrelationship of three major factors. They are a marketer's efforts, economic conditions and all the other elements of the culture. Marketers are constantly in the process of adjusting their efforts to cultural demands of the market, but they are also agents of change whenever the product or idea being marketed is innovative. Whatever the degree of acceptance and whatever level of culture, the use of something new is the beginning of cultural change and the marketer becomes a change agent. This statement is important because it emphasizes the fact that the marketer is not a passive influence in a culture and that, while the marketer attempts to react to cultural demands, in so doing the marketer also influences cultural change.

14. What are some particularly troublesome problems caused by language in foreign marketing? Discuss.

    Language poses some difficult problems in foreign marketing not merely because of the obvious differences in tongues, but because the idiomatic interpretations mean something different than what the marketer had intended. Examples of this are "Body by Fisher" which translates to "Corpse by Fisher" and "Let Hertz Put You in the Drivers Seat" which translates to "Let Hertz Make You a Chauffeur."

15. Suppose you were requested to prepare a cultural analysis for a potential market, what would you do? Outline the steps and comment briefly on each.

    The best procedure for making a cultural analysis for a potential market is to go through each of the elements of culture and evaluate each on the basis of how it could possibly affect a proposed marketing program.

    a. Material Culture
        1. Technology – the techniques and "know-how" of producing material goods.
        2. Economics – the employment of capabilities and the results.
    b. Social Institutions
        1. Social organizations – family life, status, age.
        2. Education – literacy and intelligence and how informed the public is.
        3. Political structures – control over business.
    c. Man and the Universe
        1. Belief systems – how do these affect product and promotional acceptance?
    d. Aesthetics
        1. Graphic and plastic arts – degree of modernization.
        2. Folklore – superstition, tradition, etc.
        3. Music, drama, and the dance – promotional possibilities.

16. Cultures are dynamic. How do they change? Are there cases where change is not resisted but actually preferred? Explain. What is the relevance to marketing?

    Cultures change gradually with resistance to changes. The resistance varies inversely with the interest a society has in the change. Culture doesn't resist change if the product is a status-valued imported item, a fashion item, or is given the advantage of inferior feelings about local products. Marketers can expect resistance to their products, with greater resistance to those products with the greatest deviation from the cultural norm or status quo.

17. How can resistance to cultural change influence product introduction. Are there any similarities in domestic marketing? Explain, giving examples.
    Resistance to cultural change will affect new product introduction in the respect that the greatest resistance will confront products which are farthest from the status quo, but this resistance can be lowered by gaining public interest. Lowering resistance in this situation means shortening the duration of the resistance. Domestic marketing is subject to the same resistance to change. Examples of this resistance in the domestic market are the introduction of contact lenses and using motorcycles as an acceptable means of recreation.

18. Innovations are described as being either functional or dysfunctional. Explain and give examples of each.

    The consequences of diffusion of an innovation may be functional or dysfunctional depending on whether the effects of the social system are desirable. A dysfunctional innovation is one where the effects within the social system are undesirable. In most instances, the marketer's concern is with perceived functional consequences, i.e., the positive benefits of product use. For many products, such as the cake mix described in the chapter, there would be no dysfunctional consequences. However, it cannot always be assumed that an innovative product's consequences will be functional. An example mentioned in the text was the introduction of condensed milk to the diet of babies in underdeveloped countries where protein deficiency is a health problem. On the surface it would appear that the consequences of the addition of condensed milk to the diet would result in better nutrition and health, stronger and faster growth, etc. However, evidence tends to indicate that in at least one situation there were dysfunctional consequences of the innovation. Instead of health benefits, a substantial increase in dysentery, diarrhea, and a high infant mortality rate resulted.

19. Defend the proposition that a MNC has no responsibility for the consequences of an innovation beyond the direct effects of the innovations such as the product's safety, performance, and so forth.

    It would be difficult to defend this proposition since the dysfunctional consequences of an innovation may not only have negative consequences on the social system but may ultimately impact on the success of the multinational concern. While most multinational companies have not concerned themselves with the consequences of an innovation beyond product safety, it appears that in the future there will be greater concern on the part of host countries in holding companies responsible for the consequences of their marketing activities. It would seem that from an enlightened self-interest viewpoint, companies should attempt to determine the consequences of their innovations, and should they prove to be dysfunctional, include in their marketing strategies attempts to eliminate the negative aspects of the acceptance of diffusion of their product.

20. Find a product whose introduction into a foreign culture may cause dysfunctional consequences and describe how the consequences might be eliminated and the product still profitably introduced.

    Library project.

## Chapter 5 – Business Customs and Practices in Global Marketing

### Teaching Objective

Business customs within a country are an extension of the country's culture. There are many similarities in how business is conducted from country to country but the differences, if not properly adjusted for, often cause enormous problems.

It is not necessary for a business person to forsake their ways and to change to conform to local customs but, rather, to be aware of differences and willing to accommodate those differences that can cause misunderstandings. Just as is the case with all cultural differences, a person's SRC can cause problems when trying to operate under different business customs. The literature is full of examples of misunderstandings between business persons from different cultures when each responds to the other from his/her own SRC without an appreciation of the SRC at work. The classic example is time. In some Latin cultures, there is a different urgency placed on time. The punctuality of someone from the United States can appear "pushy, too much in a hurry to make a decision, and so on" while the lackadaisical response to time by a Latin can be erroneously interpreted as being lazy or indifferent. Or, in the United States, calling someone by their first name when first introduced implies friendliness but appears as rude or boorish to a Frenchman or German. The teaching objectives of this chapter are to:

1) Acquaint the student with some of the more frequently encountered differences in business customs.
2) Emphasize the importance of adaptation or accommodation to differences in behavior patterns.
3) Discuss those business customs that are important to adapt to since many differences that exist within a culture do not require adaptation.
4) Become aware of the disparate standards for business ethics that exist and to test one's own ethical values.
5) Explore a guide to help you make ethical and socially responsible decisions.

### Comments and Suggestions

1. I begin the discussion of this chapter by stressing the importance of tolerance when dealing with cultural differences and a need to gain insight into "where the other person is coming from." The key is to remain "yourself" but be aware of local customs and be willing to accommodate those differences that can cause misunderstanding. First you must be aware of your own culture. You need to understand the other person's cultural differences so those differences do not cause you to be anxious, frustrated or misunderstand the host's intentions.

   Equally important is for you to understand your host's customs so you will not unintentionally offend. A recent study by Prudential Relocation Intercultural Services found that 35% of the personnel managers of multinational companies considered the best trait for overseas success was cultural adaptability including patience, flexibility, and tolerance for others' beliefs. Some of the horror stories they uncovered in their research included the company that sent an evangelical Christian to Saudi Arabia. He offended locals by setting up a Bible group and got booted out of the country. A U.S. oil company executive sent to Peru told jokes deriding the natives' industriousness and excluded them from his parties. His employees complained to the government and the company's oil concession was canceled. (Reported in "Working Overseas: Rule No. 1: Don't Diss the Locals," Business Week, May 15, 1995, p. 8.) The first example is probably a misunderstanding of how Saudi Arabians relate to Christianity but the last example is just insensitively and poor manners. You cannot always know all the customs in a culture but when in doubt, "good manners" and a little sensitivity will go a long way in helping you over the rough spots. Sources that may be helpful are:

For a comprehensive discussion of business culture, see Bjorn Bjerk, *Business Leadership and Culture: National Management Styles in the Global Economy* (Northampton, MA: Edward Elgar Publishing, 2000)

For an excellent discussion of cultural differences and etiquette, see: Dean Allen Forster, *The Global Etiquette Guide to Asia* (New York: John Wiley & Sons, 2000). Carol Hymowitz, "Companies Go Global, But Many Managers Just Don't Travel Well," *The Wall Street Journal*, August 5, 2000, B1.

Oliver F. Williams, Editor, *Global Codes of Conduct: An Idea Whose Time Has Come* (Notre Dame, IN: University of Notre Dame Press, 2000)

2. To those less experienced with cultural diversity, the number of differences can be overwhelming. Which ones of the many cultural differences are important? To bring some order out of the chaos of cultural diversity, I suggest that business customs can be classified into three groups: those that one must accommodate (imperatives); those that only a person of the culture can participate in (exclusives); and, those that are optional, i.e., one can participate in or not. The only requirement is proper, courteous manners (adiaphora). After I briefly explain the idea and define each of the groupings, I ask students to examine their own culture and to identify some "imperatives" to which a foreigner must conform. If there are students in class from countries other than the U.S., I ask them to answer the question from both their country perspective and as a foreigner in the United States. I repeat the process for "exclusives" and "adiaphora." What becomes apparent is that there are not a large number of imperatives or exclusives and that many of the suggestions they make are adiaphora. The point is that there are not a large number of customs that must be adapted to but those that require adaptation are critical for ultimate success in business relations.

3. I use the discussion on m-time and p-time to introduce the discussion on modes of doing business. Again, I try to involve the students in the discussion by asking them to help with examples. TM 5–2, Contextual Background of Various Countries, is helpful in this discussion.

4. Gender bias is an important issue in business customs discussion. The main point I want to make is that while there are cultural biases against women, there are also many myths that need to be exposed. Nevertheless, there are some cultures where the decision to send a woman must be carefully evaluated.

5. The other topic that needs special attention is the issue of ethical behavior. Because there is no easy answer to the question of ethical and socially responsible behavior it is important to discuss all the many and sometimes conflicting issues that arise. Case 2–3, Starnes-Brenner Machine Tool Company – To Bribe or Not to Bribe is helpful in exploring many of these issues. The different variations of bribery and U.S. law vs. other countries, and U.S. business response can all be explored by using this case. One point I think important to stress is that abiding by the letter of the law is not the only criterion for ethical behavior – you must abide by the law but ethical behavior requires more than just being "legal."

6. Exploring the various issues of acting socially responsible when making decisions can be addressed using Exhibit 5–2, Transparency International 1999 Corruption Perception Index as a guide. I create a hypothetical situation and ask the students to go through each of the steps in the decision tree. Case 4–10, Making Socially Responsible and Ethical Marketing Decisions: Selling Tobacco to Third-World Countries is also helpful in exploring these issues. While a consensus is rarely reached, both of these exercises provide an excellent opportunity for each student to examine his/her own values.

**Lecture Outline**

BUSINESS CUSTOMS AND PRACTICES IN GLOBAL MARKETING

I. Required Adaptation
   A. Degree of Adaptation
   B. Imperative, Adiaphora, and Exclusives
II. Modes of Doing Business
   A. Sources and Level of Authority
   B. Management Objectives and Aspirations
      1. Personal Goals
      2. Security and Mobility
      3. Personal Life
      4. Social Acceptance
      5. Power
   C Communications Emphasis
   D. Formality and Tempo
   E. P-Time vs. M-Time
   E. Negotiations Emphasis
   F. Gender Bias in International Business
III. Business Ethics
   A Bribery – Variations on a Theme
   B. Ethical and Socially Responsible Decisions
IV. Business Customs and the Internet

## DISCUSSION QUESTIONS

1. Define:

| | |
|---|---|
| Cultural imperative | M-time |
| Cultural adiaphora | Subornation |
| Cultural exclusive | Principle of utilitarian ethics |
| FCPA | Principle of justice or fairness |
| P-time | Silent language |

2. "More than a toleration of an alien culture is required . . . there is a need for affirmative acceptance as different but equal." Elaborate.

   Adaptation is one of the key concepts for success in international marketing. Through this "affirmative acceptance as different but equal," adaptation becomes easier. One gains an appreciation of the outlook of those with whom one is dealing.

3. "We should also bear in mind that in today's business-oriented world economy, the cultures themselves are being significantly affected by business activities and business practices." Comment.

   The business activities and the culture of a nation are intermixed. A change in one results in a change in another. When a foreign culture encounters the domestic culture, there is a mixing of cultures. When a foreign business encounters another, the result is the same because business and culture are inextricably intertwined.

4. "In dealing with foreign businesses, the marketer must be particularly aware of the varying objectives and aspirations of management." Explain.

   The marketer cannot judge what he feels that the objectives of management of a foreign firm are by what they are in a similar firms of his own country. With every firm in our country, the objectives and aspirations of management are different. Therefore, it is quite likely that they are quite different in foreign countries. The marketer must deal with a company in a way to correspond with the objectives of the company, or it is possible that he might lose his dealings with that company.

5. Suggest ways in which persons might prepare themselves to handle unique business customs that may be encountered in a trip abroad.

   The businessman should:

   a. Learn all he can about foreign cultures by reading, visiting with foreigners and those who have traveled or lived in the countries he will visit.

   b. Condition and sensitize himself by projecting himself into possible situations and analyzing his learned belief patterns.

   c. Seek advice from consultants, ambassadors, and others who can provide professional guidance.

6. Business customs and national customs are closely interrelated. In what way would one expect the two areas to coincide and in what ways would they show differences? How could such areas of similarity and difference be identified?

**Coincide**

a. Language used
b. Methods of carrying on business must coincide with local customs
c. Religious effect
d. Political effect
   1. Laws
   2. Taxes

**Differ**

a. Subject matter
b. Degree of technicalities involved
c. Business customs are continually changing—national customs do not
d. Business customs cause some change in national customs

   One would have to examine each possible difference and similarity to determine whether or not they exist.

7. Identify both local and foreign examples of cultural imperatives, adiaphora, and exclusives. Be prepared to explain why each example fits into the category you have selected.

   Domestic examples:

   a. Cultural imperatives: It is imperative that one pay income tax, license one's car, or wear a coat and tie to a fine restaurant, not belch in public, etc.

   b. Cultural adiaphora: One may or may not attend church, one may eat local foods, but doesn't have to.

   c. Cultural exclusives: An African wouldn't join the KKK. A foreigner couldn't sell firearms for the purpose of overthrowing the government.

   Foreign examples:

   a. Cultural imperatives: Not wearing shorts in Mazatlan, Mexico; not doing business on Saturday in Israel.

b. Cultural adiaphora: An American businessperson in Mexico may or may not drink tequila or eat burritos.

c. Cultural exclusives: It would be inappropriate for an American to go to Vietnam and act like a Moslem.

8. Contrast the authority roles of top management in different societies. How will the differing views of authority affect marketing activities?

There are three main different types of authority patterns: (1) top management decision making, (2) decentralized decision making, and (3) committee decision making. In Europe, top management makes most of the major decisions. One of the reasons for this is their belief that subordinates are generally inadequate people. In the United States, the subordinates are given more responsibility and top management doesn't have complete responsibility of decision making. This is what can be called more decentralized decision making. In the Far Eastern countries, group decision making predominates because of their culture.

The marketing approach to each of these different situations is quite varied. The problem is to determine what system is being used, and who is in authority.

9. Do the same for aspirational patterns.

In the United States, management tends to emphasize profit or high wages. In foreign countries, managers are more likely to emphasize security, good personal life, acceptance status, advancement, or power. Individual goals vary from country to country and from manager to manager. By knowing the goals of management, a marketing man can aim the marketing of his product toward these different goals.

10. What effects on business customs might be anticipated from the recent rapid increases in the level of international business activity?

Business customs are bound to be altered in all countries. It is axiomatic in anthropology that when two cultures meet, there is a blending rather than an elimination of one or the other. We would therefore expect business practices to become more standard because of the necessity of dealing in the same ways. This would take much time.

11. Interview some foreign students to determine the types of cultural shock they encountered when they first came to your country.

Individual project.

12. Differentiate between:

Private ownership and family ownership.

Decentralized and committee decision making.

"Private ownership" means ownership by private investors and not government ownership. "Family ownership" refers to a business dynasty controlled by one or a few families.

"Decentralized decision making" means subordinates have the authority to make certain decisions, with top management making the most important decisions.

"Committee decision making" means emphasis is placed on group participation, with endorsement of a decision by a group.

13. In which ways does the size of a customer's business affect his business behavior?

The large organizations of the different countries have a professionalized management which is much the same from country to country. In medium-sized businesses, the management is likely to be in direct contact with the workers and customer. The management of the smaller firms is likely to be closely tied to the customs and attitudes of the country. Management is directly responsible for the supervision of employees and comes into direct contact with the customers.

14. Identify and explain four main patterns of business ownerships.

    a. Private ownership is the ownership of a business by first- or second-generation businesspeople or is owned by private investors who have purchased stock and have vested management in professional managers.

    b. Government ownership is when the government plays a large and perhaps a dominant role in the business ownership in many countries.

    c. Family ownership is the ownership of a company or perhaps a complete industry by a family. These holdings are a result of residuals from a feudal age or generations of expansion.

    d. Cooperative ownership is a general ownership by many people which contributes to development of the utilization of professional managers.

15. Compare three decision-making authority patterns in international business.

    The top management decision making is the centralized decision making whereby only the people at the top make the decisions. The reason for this is management's distrust of the ability of the subordinates.

    The decentralized decision making is the system whereby executives at various levels of the business hierarchy are given rather complete decision making authority over their own functions.

    The committee decision making places great emphasis on group participation, group harmony, and group decision making.

16. Explore the various ways in which business customs can affect the structure of competition.

    The customs would affect the structure of competition mainly by determining whether or not there is competition in that country. If the industries are government controlled, then there is obviously no competition. There may be different policies on how competition may occur in different countries. Some countries might have a rigid competition requirement, whereas another could have a quite loose competition requirement.

17. Why is it important that the business executive be alert to the significance of business customs?

    The business executive must be very sensitive to the cultural variations; he must be alert and prepared to adapt when necessary; he must realize that he is not a native and will always be treated as an outsider. If he does not follow these points, he will be excluded from doing business or will lose out in doing business in different countries.

18. Suggest some cautions that an individual from a high-context culture should take when dealing with someone from a low-context culture. Do the same for low- to high-context situations.

    An individual from a high-context culture operating in a low-context culture should be careful about:

    a. assuming that he has communicated when he has not.

    b. leaving out major elements of communication.

    c. depending too much on the spoken word and not enough on writing.

    d. becoming frustrated by lack of feedback in interpersonal communication.

    An individual from a low-context culture operating in a high-context culture should be careful about:

    a. communicating messages he did not intend.

b. becoming frustrated from the imprecision of his counterpart's communication.

c. expending too much on reports and letters.

d. missing important communication cues.

19. Political payoffs are a problem; how would you react if you faced the prospect of paying a bribe? If you knew that by not paying you would not be able to complete a $10 million contract?

    The response to this question is obviously, one deals with an individual's own code of ethics. In discussing the question, it should be stressed that paying the bribe or any other illegal act is not permissible by most company rules. Further, to do so would violate U.S. law as well as a law in many host countries.

20. Differentiate among the following:

    Subornation

    Lubrication

    Extortion

    Bribery

    **Subornation** generally involves large sums of money, frequently not properly accounted for, which are designed to entice an official to commit an illegal act of magnitude on behalf of the one paying the bribe.

    **Lubrication,** on the other hand, involves a relatively small sum of cash, gift, or service made to a low-ranking official in a country where such offerings are not prohibited by law; the purpose of such a gift being to facilitate or expedite a normal, lawful performance of a duty by an official.

    **Extortion** is payment extracted under duress by someone in authority from a person seeking only what one is lawfully entitled to.

    **Bribery** is money voluntarily offered by someone seeking unlawful advantage.
    Lubrication payments are a request for a person to do a job more rapidly or more efficiently, whereas subornation is a request for officials to turn their heads, not do their job, or to break the law. An example of extortion would be a Finance Minister of a country demanding heavy payments under the threat that millions of dollars of investment would be confiscated.

21. Distinguish between P-time and M-time.

    Edward Hall defines two kinds of time systems in the world – monochronic and polychronic time. M-time (monochronic) typifies most North Americans, Swiss, Germans, and Scandinavians. In these Western cultures, they tend to concentrate on one thing at a time. They divide time into small units and are concerned with promptness. M-time is used in a linear way and it is experienced as being almost tangible in that we save time, waste time, bide time, spend time and lose time. Most low context cultures operate on M-time.

    P-time is more dominant in high context cultures where the completion of a human transaction is emphasized more than holding to schedules. P-time is characterized by the simultaneous occurrence of many things and by "a great involvement with people." P-time allows for relationships to build and context to be absorbed that are a part of high-context cultures. In Japan there is a mix between P-time and M-time. For appointments, Japan is very M-time but for all other interaction, they are more P-time.

    The American desire to "get straight to the point," to "get down to business" and other indications of directness are all manifestations of M-time cultures. While the P-time system gives rise to looser time schedules, deeper involvement with individuals and a "wait and see what develops" attitude. For example, two Latins conversing would likely opt to be late for their next appointments rather than abruptly terminate the conversation before it came to a natural conclusion.

22. Discuss how a P-time person reacts differently from an M-time person in keeping an appointment.

    When business people from M-time and P-time meet, adjustments on both sides need to be made for a harmonious relationship. P-time is characterized by a much "looser" notion of what is "on time" or "late." Interruptions are routine, delays to be expected. It is not so much putting things off until "manana" but the concept that human activities are not expected to proceed like clockwork.

    One study comparing perceptions of punctuality in the U.S. and Brazil found that Brazilian timepieces were less reliable and public clocks less available than it was in the United States. Researchers also found that Brazilians more often described themselves as late arrivers, allowed greater flexibility in defining early and late, were less concerned about being late, and were more likely to blame external factors for their lateness than were Americans.

    Often clarity can be gained by specifying tactfully, for example, whether a meeting is to be on "Mexican time" or "American time." An American who has been working successfully with the Saudis for many years says he has learned to take plenty of things to do when he travels. Others schedule appointments in their offices so they can work until their P-time friend arrives.

23. What is meant by "laws are the markers of past behavior that society has deemed unethical or socially irresponsible?"

    It means that to be ethical does not mean just abiding by the law. Most laws reflect societies' concern that some type of behavior is not proper and that people do not voluntarily refrain from the offensive behavior, thus, laws are passed. In many countries, the law may help define the borders of minimum ethical or social responsibility, but the law is only the floor above which one's social and personal morality is tested. Ethical business conduct should normally exist at a level well above the minimum required by law.

24. What are the three ethical principles that provide a framework to help distinguish between right and wrong?

    Explain.

    There are three ethical principles that provide a framework to help the marketer distinguish between right and wrong, determine what ought to be done, and properly justify his or her actions. They are:

    Utilitarian ethics, i.e., does the action optimize the common good or benefits of all constituencies?

    Rights of the parties, i.e., does the action respect the rights of the individuals involved?

    Justice or fairness, i.e., does the action respect the canons of justice or fairness to all parties involved?

    Answers to these questions can help the marketer ascertain the degree to which decisions are beneficial or harmful, right or wrong, or whether the consequences of actions are ethical or socially responsible.

25. Visit Transparency International Web page and check to see how the CPI Index for countries listed in Exhibit 5–2 has changed. Searching TI's databank, explain why the changes have occurred. The site is found at: http://www.transparency.de .

## Exhibit 5–2 Transparency International 1999 Corruption Perception Index*

**(Selected Countries 1999)**

| Country* | CPI 1999 | Country | CPI 1999 |
| --- | --- | --- | --- |
| Denmark (1) | 10.0 | Brazil (45) | 4.1 |
| Finland (2) | 9.8 | S. Korea (50) | 3.8 |
| Singapore (7) | 9.1 | China (58) | 3.4 |
| Norway (9) | 8.9 | Mexico (58) | 3.4 |
| Switzerland (9) | 8.9 | India (72) | 2.9 |
| U.S.A. (18) | 7.3 | Russia (82) | 2.4 |
| France (22) | 6.6 | Nigeria (98) | 1.6 |
| Czech Rep. (39) | 4.6 | | |

The ranking for 1999 is based on 99 countries studied.

* () number is rank for 1999

**The maximum score is 10.00; the minimum score is 0. A perfect score of 10.00 would be a totally corrupt free country.

---

Source: *The 1999 Transparency International Corruption Perceptions Index* (CPI), www.transparency.org/documents/cpi/index.html, March 2000.

26. Discuss the pros and cons of "there is no controlling legal authority," as a basis for ethical behavior.

In many countries, the law may help define the borders of minimum ethical or social responsibility, but the law is only the floor above which one's social and personal morality is tested. The statement that "there is no controlling legal authority" may mean that the behavior is not illegal but it does not mean that the behavior is morally correct or ethical. "Ethical business conduct should normally exist at a level well above the minimum required by law" or "controlling legal authority." In fact, laws are the markers of past behavior that society has deemed unethical or socially irresponsible.

One researcher suggests that regardless of how corrupt a society might be, there are core human values that serve as the underpinning of life, no matter where a person lives. Participants in 43 countries and more than 50 faiths were given 17 values and asked to rate each as a core value. Five values—compassion, fairness, honesty, responsibility, and respect for others—were the most often selected regardless of culture.[1] The researcher suggests that an action should only be taken if the answer is no to the question, "Is the action a violation of a core human value?" When people are clear about their own values and can identify the principles and core values that make up ethical behavior, they have the tools for looking at potential decisions and deciding whether or not a decision is ethical.

27. "The **company.com** page is a company's front door and that doorway should be global in scope." Discuss. Visit several Web pages of major multinational companies and evaluate their "front door" to the global world.

The **company.com** page is a company's front door and that doorway should be global in scope. Not only can you select and purchase goods through a company's Web page, but support services, training programs, additional product literature, even career information, are all being moved to the home page. Thus, the precept, "think globally, act locally, applies not only to global marketing strategies but to the World Wide Web as well."

The message on a Web site is an extension of the company and should be as sensitive to business customs as any other company representative would be. Once a message is posted, it can be anywhere at any time. As a consequence, the opportunity to convey an unintended message is always present. Nothing about the Web will change the extent to which people identify with their own languages and cultures, thus, language should be at the top of list when examining the viability of a company's Web site.

The solution to the problem is to have country specific Web sites such as IBM, Microsoft and others have. Dell Computer, for example, makes its Premier Pages Web sites, built for its business clients, available in 12 languages. There are a host of companies that specialize in Web site translations and, in addition, there are software programs to translate the company message into another language. However, cultural and linguistic correctness can be a problem with machine translation. If not properly done, there is the likelihood that English phrases will be translated in a way that will embarrass or even damage a company. One way to avoid this is to prepare the original source material in easy-to-translate English devoid of complicated phrases, idioms or slang. Unfortunately, no machine translation is available to manage all the nuances of language or syntaxes.

In addition to being language friendly, a Web site should be examined for any symbols, icons, and other non-verbal impressions that could convey an unwanted message. Icons that are frequently used on a Web site can be misunderstood. For example, an icon such as a hand making a high-five sign will be offensive in Greece; an image of a thumb-to-index finger, the A-OK gesture, will infuriate visitors in Brazil, a two-fingered peace sign when turned around has a very crude meaning to the British and AOL's "You've Got Mail" looks a lot like a loaf of bread to a European. Colors can also pose a problem; green is a sacred color in some Middle Eastern cultures and should not be used for something frivolous like a Web background.

---

[1] Patricia Digh, "Shades of Gray in the Global Marketplace," HRMagazine, April 1997, p. 90.

Besides being language and icon friendly, is the site customer friendly? A European could not understand why his on-line order from an American company was repeatedly rejected. It took him some time to determine that since he couldn't fill out the "state" section, the order form was incomplete and thus, rejected. He sent the company an e-mail describing his trouble but it didn't respond. The company probably doesn't realize its address information is preventing it from getting as much business as it could.

28. Visit the Web sites of Shell and Nike at: http://www.shell.com/royal-en/directory/0,5029,25413,00.html for Shell and http://www.nikebiz.com/social/index.shtml for Nike and compare their statements on corporate values. What are the major issues each address? Do you think their statements are useful as guides to ethical and socially responsible decision-making?

    The following is an excerpt are from the Shell Web site as of May 2001

    **Our values – an introduction**

    Having unshakable moral values and sound business principles means we take pride in what we do. It gives us clarity when making decisions, unifies and motivates staff, and it allows society to measure our performance beyond the generation of wealth.

    Since our earliest days, we have been guided by a passionate commitment to honesty, integrity and respect for people. We believe in the promotion of trust, openness, teamwork and professionalism.

    But in the last few years we've had to tackle some particularly difficult issues, and we realize we have not always taken enough care to show how they were resolved in line with our core values. So this section looks at each of our General Business Principles, and how they apply to a series of topical issues and dilemmas.

    This section is also about dialogue. We want you to know more about how we work and how we strive to live up to our principles. We also want to know your views on the many difficult issues and dilemmas we are all faced with as we enter a new millennium. You can join in the debate by entering the various forums that are attached to each subject or by sending us your view by email. We promise to listen.

**Our General Business Principles**

1. **Objectives**

   The objectives of Shell companies are to engage efficiently, responsibly and profitably in the oil, gas, chemicals and other selected businesses and to participate in the search for and development of other sources of energy. Shell companies seek a high standard of performance and aim to maintain a long-term position in their respective competitive environments.

2. **Responsibilities**

   Shell companies recognize five areas of responsibility:

   a. To shareholders

      To protect shareholders' investment, and provide an acceptable return.

   b. To customers

      To win and maintain customers by developing and providing products and services which offer value in terms of price, quality, safety and environmental impact, and which are supported by the requisite technological, environmental and commercial expertise.

   c. To employees

To respect the human rights of their employees, to provide their employees with good and safe conditions of work, and good and competitive terms and conditions of service, to promote the development and best use of human talent and equal opportunity employment, and to encourage the involvement of employees in the planning and direction of their work, and in the application of these principles within their company. It is recognized that commercial success depends on the full commitment of all employees.

d. To those with whom they do business

To seek mutually beneficial relationships with contractors, suppliers and in joint ventures and to promote the application of these principles in so doing. The ability to promote these principles effectively will be an important factor in the decision to enter into or remain in such relationships.

e. To society

To conduct business as responsible, corporate members of society, to observe the laws of the countries in which they operate, to express support for fundamental human rights in line with the legitimate role of business and to give proper regard to health, safety and the environment consistent with their commitment to contribute to sustainable development.

These five areas of responsibility are seen as inseparable. Therefore, it is the duty of management continuously to assess the priorities and discharge its responsibilities as best it can on the basis of that assessment.

**Principle 3: Economic principles**

Profitability is essential to discharging these responsibilities and staying in business. It is a measure both of efficiency and of the value that customers place on Shell products and services. It is essential to the allocation of the necessary corporate resources and to support the continuing investment required to develop and produce future energy supplies to meet consumer needs. Without profits and a strong financial foundation, it would not be possible to fulfill the responsibilities outlined in this section.

Shell companies work in a wide variety of changing social, political and economic environments, but, in general, they believe that the interests of the community can be served most efficiently by a market economy.

Criteria for investment decisions are not exclusively economic in nature but also take into account social and environmental considerations and an appraisal of the security of the investment.

**Principle 4: Business integrity**

Shell companies insist on honesty, integrity and fairness in all aspects of their business and expect the same in their relationships with all those with whom they do business. The direct or indirect offer, payment, soliciting and acceptance of bribes in any form are unacceptable practices. Employees must avoid conflicts of interest between their private financial activities and their part in the conduct of company business. All business transactions on behalf of a Shell company must be reflected accurately and fairly in the accounts of the company in accordance with established procedures and be subject to audit.

**Principle 5: Political activities**

a. Of companies

Shell companies act in a socially responsible manner within the laws of the countries in which they operate in pursuit of their legitimate commercial objectives.

Shell companies do not make payments to political parties, organizations or their representatives or take any part in party politics. However, when dealing with governments, Shell companies have the right and the responsibility to make their position known on any matter which affects themselves, their employees, their customers, or their shareholders. They also have the right to make their position known on matters affecting the community, where they have a contribution to make.

b. Of employees

Where individuals wish to engage in activities in the community, including standing for election to public office, they will be given the opportunity to do so where this is appropriate in the light of local circumstances.

Some of the issues in this Principle are hard to measure, and little quantified evidence is available. We are trying to develop suitable measures so that we can track and publish our future performance. If you have any suggestions on the sort of evidence you would like to see, please send us an e-mail or participate in the relevant forum.

**Principle 6: Health, safety and the environment**

Consistent with their commitment to contribute to sustainable development, Shell companies have a systematic approach to health, safety and environmental management in order to achieve continuous performance improvement.

To this end, Shell companies manage these matters as any other critical business activity, set targets for improvement, and measure, appraise and report on performance.

**Principle 7: The community**

The most important contribution that companies can make to the social and material progress of the countries in which they operate is in performing their basic activities as effectively as possible. In addition, Shell companies take a constructive interest in societal matters which may not be directly related to the business. Opportunities for involvement—for example, through community, educational or donations programs will vary depending upon the size of the company concerned, the nature of the local society, and the scope for useful private initiatives.

**Principle 8: Competition**

Shell companies support free enterprise. They seek to compete fairly and ethically and within the framework of applicable competition laws; they will not prevent others from competing freely with them.

**Principle 9: Communication**

Shell companies recognize that, in view of the importance of the activities in which we they engaged and their impact on national economies and individuals, open communication is essential. To this end,

Shell companies have comprehensive corporate information programs and provide full relevant information about their activities to legitimately interested parties, subject to any overriding considerations of business confidentiality and cost.

Note:

For excerpt from Nike Web site see question 29 below.

29. Go to your favorite Web reference source and access some recent news articles on Nike and alleged human rights violations. Access the Nike statement on corporate values at http://www.nikebiz.coi-n/social/index.shtml and write a brief statement on the alleged violations and Nike's statement of corporate values.

The following is an excerpt from the Nike Web site as of May 2001.

NIKE Inc. was founded on a handshake.

Implicit in that act was the determination that we would build our business with all of our partners based on trust, teamwork, honesty and mutual respect. We expect all of our business partners to operate on the same principles.

At the core of the Nike corporate ethic is the belief that we are a company comprised of many different kinds of people, appreciating individual diversity, and dedicated to equal opportunity for each individual.

Nike designs, manufactures and markets products for sports and fitness consumers. At every step in that process, we are driven to achieve not only what is required, but also what is expected of a leader. We expect our business partners to do the same. Specifically, Nike seeks partners that share our commitment to the promotion of best practices and continuous improvement in:

1. Occupational safety and health, compensation, hours of work and benefits standards
2. Minimizing our impact on the environment.
3. Management practices that recognize the dignity of the individual, the rights of free association and collective bargaining, and the right to a work place free of harassment, abuse or corporal punishment.
4. The principle that decisions on hiring, salary, benefits, advancement, termination or retirement are based solely on the ability of an individual to do the job. There shall be no discrimination based on race, creed, gender, marital or maternity status, religious or political beliefs, age or sexual orientation.

Wherever Nike operates around the globe, we are guided by this Code of Conduct. We bind our manufacturing partners to these principles. Our manufacturing partners must post this Code in all major workspaces, translated into the language of the worker, and must endeavor to train workers on their rights and obligations as defined by this Code and applicable labor laws.

While these principles establish the spirit of our partnerships, we also bind these partners to specific standards of conduct. These standards are set forth below.

1. Forced Labor: The manufacturer does not use forced labor in any form—prison, indentured, bonded or otherwise.
2. Child labor: The manufacturer does not employ any person below the age of 18 to produce footwear. The manufacturer does not employ any person below the age of 16 to produce apparel, accessories or equipment. Where local standards are higher, no person under the legal minimum age will be employed.

3. Compensation: The manufacturer provides each employee at least the minimum wage, or the prevailing industry wage, whichever is higher; provides each employee a clear, written accounting for every pay period; and does not deduct from worker pay for disciplinary infractions, in accordance with the Nike Manufacturing Leadership Standard on financial penalties.
4. Benefits: The manufacturer provides each employee all legally mandated benefits. Benefits vary by country, but may include meals or meal subsidies; transportation or transportation subsidies; other cash allowances; health care; child care; emergency, pregnancy or sick leave; vacation, religious, bereavement or holiday leave; and contributions for social security and other insurance, including life, health and worker's compensation.
5. Hours of Work/Overtime: The manufacturer complies with legally mandated work hours; uses overtime only when each employee is fully compensated according to local law; informs each employee at the time of hiring if mandatory overtime is a condition of employment; and, on a regularly scheduled basis, provides one day off in seven, and requires no more than 60 hours of work per week, or complies with local limits if they are lower.
6. Management of Environment, Safety and Health (MESH): The manufacturer has written health and safety guidelines, including those applying to employee residential facilities, where applicable; has a factory safety committee; complies with Nike's environmental, safety and health standards; limits organic vapor concentrations at or below the Permissible Exposure Limits mandated by the U. S Occupational Safety and Health Administration (OSHA); provides Personal Protective Equipment (PPE) free of charge, and mandates its use; and complies with all applicable local environmental, safety and health regulations.
7. Documentation and Inspection: The manufacturer maintains on file all documentation needed to demonstrate compliance with this Code of Conduct; agrees to make these documents available for Nike or its designated auditor to inspect upon request; and agrees to submit to labor practices audits or inspections with or without prior notice.

Minimum Age Requirements

"Nike has zero tolerance for under-age labor." Nike CEO Phil Knight. In May 1998, Nike increased the minimum age of footwear factory workers to 18 years old, and the minimum age for all other light-manufacturing workers (apparel, accessories, and equipment) to 16 years old. These new minimum age requirements in footwear factories are equal or in some cases higher than those in the United States because these jobs require heavier machinery and more complex manufacturing processes.

"At 18," says Knight, "workers are generally more mature, have more work experience, are easier to train in health and safety issues, and are therefore better suited to work in a footwear factory than a younger person."

In many regions of the world where our products are made, Nike's age standards exceed those mandated by the local government. In some rare cases, local standards are more strict. Our contract manufacturers must adopt the strictest standard—either the local minimum age, or the Nike minimum age standard.

To ensure these standards are being met on a continuous basis, Nike production and labor staff are trained to look for younger-age workers, and to report that possibility to the labor management staff In addition, all factories making Nike products around the world are subject to labor practices monitoring visits and audits by teams of independent inspectors. Those inspectors verify all workers meet the Nike age standards through documented records and interviews with workers.

Adults should work. Children should study and play. We do everything we can to ensure this happens. Setting the highest age standards in the industry, and requiring independent certification that factories meet those standards, is our best practice to make it so.

## Chapter 6 – The Political Environment: A Critical Issue

### Teaching Objectives

All the cultural elements are important in international marketing but the political element is by far the most pervasive and must always be examined from both domestic and foreign country perspectives. Regardless of where a company does business, the political element is always a partner and further, often an unpredictable one. Governments both encourage and control business and the goal of an MNC is to take steps to lower its political vulnerability.

While confiscation and expropriation have rarely been imposed in the last decade, they are the most severe political risk and can always be imposed. Today, most governments encourage foreign investment but this does not mean that there are no political risks. The teaching objectives of this chapter are to:

1) Stress that government polices and their stability are influenced by political parties and nationalism.
2) Make the point that the U.S. government is just as important in creating political risks for U.S. business as are foreign governments.
3) Examine the various types of political risks from the most severe, confiscation, to the less severe.
4) Discuss the various ways governments encourage foreign investment.
5) Explore the means companies have to reduce political vulnerability and protect their foreign investment.

### Comments and Suggestions

1. Even though expropriation and forced domestication that existed in the 1960s and 1970s no longer loom as major political risks, I still like to discuss these issues in some depth. My purpose is threefold; first, it is important for students to be aware of the power that a government can have over a foreign business and a foreign company's relative inability to change government decrees once they are made; second, while, not perfect, there are ways companies can operate to lessen vulnerability; and, third, many of the investment decisions and the manner in which business operate routinely today stem from their experiences during the period when expropriation was more prevalent. Most foreign investments include local partners rather than trying "to go it alone," and efforts to operate in such a way that they add to the country's economic and social development beyond their individual investments albeit much is mandated by the host government. TM 6–1, Political Risks, lists the types of political risks confronting a firm.

2. One of the types of risks that seem to be on the increase are terrorists acts. Sometimes these acts of violence are directed against an specific MNC for some alleged "crime," in other cases the MNC is the victim but the violent act is designed to embarrass the government. Airlines have often been the victim when it is the government the terrorist is targeting. TM 6–2, International Terrorist Incidents, 1993 By Region and TM 6–3, International Terrorist Incidents, 1993 by Type of Facility illustrate the severity of this problem.

   For the most recent data on terrorist incidents and other information on the extent of international terrorist activities visit the State Department Web site http://www.state.gov/index.cfm, "Patterns of Global Terrorism: 2000" is an interesting exhibit that can be downloaded to be displayed in class.

**Lecture Outline**

The Political Environment: A Critical Concern

Global Perspective—Chiquita Bananas and Prosciutto di Parma, Louis Vitton Handbags, Scented Bath Oils and Soaps, and Batteries—Strange Bedfellows from the World of Politics.

I. The Sovereignty of Nations

II. Stability of Government Policies
   - A. Political Parties
   - B. Nationalism

III. Political Risks of Global Business
   - A. Confiscation, Expropriation, and Domestication
   - B. Economic Risks
     1. Exchange Controls
     2. Local-Content Laws
     3. Import Restrictions
     4. Tax Controls
     5. Price Controls
     6. Political Sanctions
   - C. Political and Social Activists
     1. Violence and Terrorism
     2. Cyber Terrorism

IV. Assessing Political Vulnerability
   - A. Politically Sensitive Products and Issues
   - B. Forecasting Political Risk

V. Reducing Political Vulnerability
   - A. Good Corporate Citizenship
   - B. Managing External Affairs
   - C. Strategies to Lessen Political Risk
     1. Joint Ventures
     2. Expanding the Investment Base
     3. Marketing and Distribution
     4. Licensing
     5. Planned Domestication
   - D. Political Payoffs

VI. Government Encourage of Global Business
   - A. Foreign Government Encouragement
   - B. U.S. Government Encouragement

VII. Summary

## DISCUSSION QUESTIONS

1. Define:

| | |
|---|---|
| Sovereignty | Confiscation |
| Nationalism | Domestication |
| Expropriation | Planned domestication |
| PSAs | |

2. Why would a country rather domesticate than expropriate?
Expropriation creates problems with other governments and can cause potential investors to shy away from investments in their country. Further, if a country domesticates, they are able to achieve almost all, if not all, the advantages of expropriation without the negative aspects associated with such a drastic move.

3. How can government-initiated domestication be the same as confiscation?

Government-initiated domestication can be as disastrous as confiscation from the viewpoint of the domesticated company. For example, in the process of domestication, if a host country requires the multinational to sell stock or ownership within a given time, the market value of the investment will go down because the potential buyer will wait for the deadline. Thus, the selling price can be confiscatory in nature. In addition to outright loss of investment, lack of control because of forced hiring of nationals and regulations requiring increased purchases of local supplies, government-initiated domestication can slow down or halt growth, limit markets or market expansion, decrease profits, and disrupt overall global marketing planning for the multinational company. These effects may be the same as that which would occur with expropriation.

4. Discuss planned domestication as an alternative investment plan.

Planned domestication is in essence, a gradual, planned process of participating with nationals in all phases of company operation. Initial investment planning should include steps to: sell equity to nationals at fair prices over a number of years; prepare nationals for top decision-making positions; integrate local companies (where feasible) into worldwide marketing programs; develop local companies as sources of supply; and, build on a sound economic base or make unnecessary any government concessions initially needed for successful investment. Since legal questions also establish insurmountable road blocks, the wisest course for the international marketer is to have reference to a council well versed in the intricacies of the international legal environment planning should contain provisions for eventual sale of a significant interest (perhaps even controlling interest) to nationals and incorporation of national economic needs and national managerial talent into the business as quickly as possible. Such a policy would more likely result in reasonable control remaining with the parent company even though nationals would have an important position in management and ownership. If company plans include training and developing nationals to hold major positions in the investment, they would have the opportunity to insure that those who reached top positions would be qualified and in harmony with total corporate objectives. Such company-trained nationals would be more likely to have a strong corporate point of view instead of just a country (national) point of view.

If initial development provided for the use of local supplies it would eliminate sudden short-term crash programs to provide supplies. Local suppliers developed over a period of time ultimately could handle a significant portion of total needs, thus meeting government demands for encouraging local business and industry. Further, a sound, sensible plan to sell ownership over a number of years could insure a fair and equitable return on investment, in addition to encouraging ownership throughout the populace and discouraging attempts by a few to exert undue corporate control. Finally, if government concessions and incentives essential in early stages of investment were rendered economically feasible or unnecessary, the company's political vulnerability would be lessened considerably.

5. "A crucial fact when doing business in a foreign country is that permission to conduct business is controlled by the government of the host country." Comment.

   It is extremely critical for a company to examine, evaluate, and comprehend the present and future policies of the government in a foreign country. To do this, the type of government and the types of political parties and their basic philosophies toward foreign business must be studied in depth. The level of economic development and the accompanying political policies are directly correlated with the attitude of the government toward foreign business. This attitude may or may not change with changes in government, political parties, economic conditions, etc. Also, the importance of products to the country is a deciding factor in restricting or encouraging foreign business.

6. What are the main factors to consider in assessing the dominant political climate within a country?

   a. Current form of government.

   b. Current political party systems.

   c. Stability and permanency of government policy.

   d. Risks or encouragements of foreign business resulting from political activity.

7. Why is working knowledge of party philosophy so important in a political assessment of a market? Discuss.

   A working knowledge of party philosophies is necessary if there is a possibility that a change in government policy toward foreign business could result from a change in government or political parties.

8. What are the most common causes of instability in governments? Discuss.

   The most common causes of instability in governments are:

   a. a change in the form of government – this is the most drastic cause because a "reform" government is often replacing a government which encouraged foreign business,

   b. a shift in political parties – the policy of various parties quite often differs concerning restrictions or encouragements of foreign business,

   c. a rise in feelings of nationalism – the people may pressure the government or party in control to negatively influence the extent of trade with foreign countries (i.e., "Buy American").

9. Discuss how governmental instability can affect marketing.

   Government instability affects marketing because of the risks which are inherent in foreign marketing. Much can be lost if a company invests money in a plant or operation within a foreign country and is later subjected to restrictions, controls, or expropriation by the present or new government.

10. What are the most frequently encountered political risks in foreign business? Discuss.

    a. Expropriation – the acquisition of a company's property by the host country. The companies may or may not be compensated.

    b. Exchange Controls – used to conserve the supply of foreign exchange. Controls may be levied against foreign companies or types of products.

    c. Import Restrictions – restrictions on the imports of raw material, parts, etc., are employed to induce the foreign industry to purchase its supplies locally.

    d. Taxes – they are sometimes increased despite prior agreements calling for a specific tax rate.

    e. Price Controls – generally applied during inflationary periods to essential products.

f. Labor Problems – unions may have strong government support which allows special labor concessions from the foreign business. Companies may be forced to abide by rules set up by labor unions through the government.

11. Expropriation is considered a major risk of foreign business. Discuss ways in which this particular type of risk has been minimized somewhat as a result of company activities. Explain how these risks have been minimized by the activities of the U.S. government.
The risk of expropriation has been minimized by:

    a. a change in attitude of foreign governments toward expropriating an industry or company.

    b. application of strict economic pressures by the country of the expropriated firm.

    c. encouraging the people of the host country to invest in the business venture and work in the enterprise.

    d. The U.S. government also offers support in minimizing political risks by establishing agencies (such as export-import Bank) to underwrite the investment activities of American companies. The U.S. government also supplies pressure to countries which expropriate U.S. firms by cutting off foreign aid via the Hickenlooper amendment.

12. How do exchange controls impede foreign business? Discuss.

    Exchange controls are established by a country in order to maintain a specific level of foreign exchange. They are used especially during periods when the country faces shortages of foreign currency. This control keeps the company from exchanging its earnings into the currency of its own country. Also, demand for imported goods may exist, but exchange controls may limit currency and thus render the demand ineffective.

13. How do foreign governments encourage investment? Discuss.

    Foreign governments encourage foreign investment by offering tax exemptions, protection against competing imports, and unimpeded movement of capital and profits.

14. How does the U.S. government encourage foreign investment? Spell out the implications in foreign marketing.

    The U.S. government encourages foreign investment by attempting to create favorable climates in foreign countries for investment and by assisting in current operations of the foreign-located firm. The United States does this by minimizing investment risks. These encouragements by the United States set the stage for foreign investment. However, it is basically up to the company to combine its self-interest with that of the host country. By doing so, the U.S. government will probably not be called upon to apply political or economic pressures.

15. Discuss some measures a company might take to lessen its political vulnerability.

    Companies investing in foreign countries can minimize the political and economic risks by:

    a. establishing a management of Americans and nationals,

    b. employing nationals,

    c. selling stock in the company to nationals,

    d. sharing the profits and earnings in a fair manner,

    e. understanding the traditions of the people in the host country,

    f. having the national work with you, not for you.

16. Select a country and analyze it politically from a marketing viewpoint.

    A library project.

17. The text suggests that violence is a politically motivated risk of international business. Comment.

    Although violence is not generally government initiated, it is a risk that multinational companies must consider in assessing the political vulnerability of their activities. Violence against government, as well as against multinational firms, has been on a steady increase during the 1970s. Violence against multinational companies may have governmental-political overtones since it is frequently directed toward a multinational in order to embarrass a government. Much of the violence is designed to disrupt the relationship between a government and a multinational firm forcing the government to expropriate or force a multinational to leave the country. A recent example would be the experience of Owens-Illinois Company in Venezuela. The government admitted that their decision to expropriate Owens-Illinois was directly related to the violence that leftist groups caused against that company.

18. There is evidence that expropriation and confiscation are less frequently encountered today than just a few years ago. Why? What other types of political risks have replaced expropriation and confiscation importance?

    Risks of confiscation and expropriation have lessened over the last decade because experience has shown that few of the desired benefits materialized after government takeover. Rather than a quick answer to economic development, expropriation and nationalization often lead to nationalized businesses that were inefficient, technologically weak, and noncompetitive in world markets. As the world became more economically interdependent and it became obvious that much of the economic success of countries like South Korea, Singapore, and Taiwan could be tied to foreign investments, countries began to view foreign investment as a means of economic growth. Even in Mexico, MNCs that were heavily restricted until only a few years ago, are now courted for direct investment as well as a source of much needed capital and technology. Additionally, Mexico has begun to privatize many nationally owned companies. A national airline was sold to private investors and the nationalized telephone company was sold to a consortium of investors from Mexico, U.S. and France. The benefits realized by Mexico of privatizing the national telephone company were almost immediate because the government received hundreds of millions of dollars of much needed capital from the sale. In addition, Mexico's antiquated telephone system will be replaced by the latest technology, something the financially strapped government could not do. A similar scenario is being played out in Brazil, Argentina, India, and many Eastern European countries.

    Although expropriation and confiscation are waning in importance as a risk of doing business abroad, more frequently international companies are confronted with a variety of economic restraints that are often imposed with little warning. These economic risks may be imposed under the banner of national security, protection of infant industry, protection of scarce foreign exchange, or as taxes to raise revenue. They include such things as exchange controls, local content laws, import restrictions, tax controls, price controls, and labor problems.

19. You are an executive in a large domestic company with only minor interests in international markets; however, corporate plans call for major global expansion. Visit the homepage of Control Risks Group www.crg.com. After thoroughly familiarizing yourself with the services offered by CRG, write a brief report to management describing how its services could possibly help with your global expansion.

    Although CRG is a "for profit company" and will charge for complete reports, they do provide summaries of the reports which contain a synopsis of the report. Visiting this site will illustrate the types of information available to MNCs seeking information on political conditions in countries and regions. At the time this was written (2001) the following report was available;

    > RiskMap 2001 provides a critical assessment of global and regional political, security and business practice issues that will challenge and energize business leaders in 2001 and beyond.

RiskMap 2001 global essays cover issues as diverse as:

- the growing threat to business from AIDS;
- the powerful politics of hydro-electric construction projects; and
- the short- and medium-term effects arising from price changes and technological developments in the oil sector.

The regional sections include articles on key countries as well as political and security risk ratings for all countries. A new feature is a map illustrating these risks, suitable for wall display.

**Key predictions for 2001**

*Sub-Saharan Africa*

Despite containing most of the world's Extreme-rated areas, the prospects for subSaharan Africa as a whole provide some reason for optimism. Gradual political and economic reform is likely, albeit accompanied by phases of political instability and renewed conflict. Countries such as Tanzania, Mozambique and Zambia will achieve new successes, while old favorites such as Ghana and Ethiopia could again hit the spotlight. Areas of concern include Liberia, the Central African Republic, Chad, Kenya, Zimbabwe, Guinea-Conakry and Equatorial Guinea.

*Americas*

The situation in the Americas is increasingly stable, with star-performing countries like Argentina, Brazil and Mexico maintaining their commitment to fiscal austerity and attracting the bulk of inward investment into Latin America. On the negative side, however, Brazil and Mexico will experience serious crime problems and some of the smaller economies, especially in the Andean region, could experience continued political volatility and this could undermine investor confidence in the region.

*Asia and the Pacific*

Both perennial hazards and new areas of uncertainty confront foreign investors in Asia and the Pacific in 2001. The main areas of concern will remain Pakistan, Indonesia and the Philippines, with potential for more unrest in the South Pacific countries of Fiji and the Solomon Islands. Basic political stability in the continent's giants, India and China, will not be in question.

*Europe and the FSU*

In Europe and the Former Soviet Union, new risks, from cybercrime to physical direct action campaigns, will come to the fore. Although overt gangsterism is declining in most of Eastern Europe, criminal groups are becoming more sophisticated, engaging in complex economic fraud, cybertheft and money-laundering. Western Europe, in particular, will witness further episodes of direct action, while terrorism will remain a specter in countries such as Spain and Greece.

*Middle East and North Africa*

The Middle East and North Africa will see continued political stability combined with moderate growth. Israel's fragmented parliament will result in weak governing coalitions and further clashes are likely in the West Bank and Gaza. The power struggle between reformists and conservatives in Iran will continue to open to foreign investment. An increasingly nationalist political atmosphere in Turkey may heighten political risk to foreign business.

The successor to Control Risks' Outlook series. RiskMap 2001 is an important annual milestone in the political and security risk assessment process that is now a required part of good corporate governance.

20. Visit the homepage of Agora www.politicalresources.net and select *political comer*. Select the *Political Site of the Week* and write a brief political analysis highlighting potential problem areas for a company interested in investing in that country.

    Individual research. Instructor may want to visit the Web site and assign countries for students to study.

21. Search the Web for topics on activities of PSAs outside the United States and write a briefing paper for international management on potential problems.

    Individual research. Most of the large periodical search sources will result in numerous articles about PSA activities.

22. Discuss ways the companies discussed in the Global Perspective could have minimized their losses in the Banana Wars. Discuss any ethical and socially responsible issues that may be implied in the Global Perspective.

    Opinion. This question can be used for a debate or discussion in class.

## Chapter 7 – The International Legal Environment

### Teaching Objectives

This chapter deals with two broad issues involving the legal environment. The first issue is concerned with the problems that arise with international commercial contracts and settling disputes when they arise. Since there is no international commercial law or international commercial courts, disputes must be settled under the laws of one of the countries where the parties of the contract reside or, if an arbitration clause is included in the contract, by arbitration. Although there is no international commercial law per se, the agreement to enforce arbitration decisions that exists among a large number of countries does create a system that approaches international commercial court. The second issue concerns the common law bases for the U.S. legal system which creates problems for U.S. companies when interpreting the laws in countries whose legal systems are based either on code, socialist, or Islamic law. A review of the different legal systems is important for students to appreciate the problems that arise in protecting such things as intellectual property rights, etc. I continue to discuss socialist law even though most formerly socialist countries are moving toward a different system. My reasoning is that the legacy of a socialist legal system continues to influence how businesspeople think about legal matters. The teaching objectives of this chapter are to:

1) Help students understand the four legal systems of the world's countries.
2) Appreciate the critical nature of jurisdiction when legal disputes arise and thus, the need for solutions other than litigation.
3) Understand the difficulty of protecting intellectual property rights and how those rights can easily be lost if the company depends on its rights as defined in a common law country to protect it in a code law country.
4) Know that in addition to the commercial laws within in a country, a U.S. company must abide by certain U.S. laws as well.

### Comments and Suggestions

1. I use Case 2-4, When International Buyers and Sellers Disagree, to open the discussion on this chapter. I have the students read the case in class (it's short) and then ask them to use facts in the case to illustrate the various points made in the chapter. This case illustrates the importance of jurisdiction—whose law applies, the influence of different attitudes toward pig livers if the case were brought in front of a German court or a U.S. court, the importance of precision in descriptions in a contract, i.e., "customary merchandisable quality," and how the SRC can have influence at all levels. This is a case where both parties were correct from their individual perspective and yet were not pleased with the outcome. It also illustrates the importance of arbitration in international legal disputes.
2. Cultural differences in interpreting similar legal concepts, for example, patent law, is illustrated in the comparison of patent law illustrated in Crossing Borders 7-1, Patent Law: The United States Versus Japan. TM 7-6, Invoice for Shipment of 10 Buses from Brazil to Kuwait, is a good example of the statement made on shipments that comply with the Arab League boycott of Israel.
3. In the discussion of intellectual property rights there are two points to make: 1) gaining legal protection for patents, trademarks, processes, copyrights, etc. under the legal system of a country and, 2) the problems of counterfeiting and/or piracy of intellectual property rights. While a company may have the legal protection of a patent or trademark that law abiding companies honor, there is the ever-growing problems of piracy and counterfeiting.

I differentiate between piracy and counterfeiting. Although most discussions do not differentiate between the two, they are two separate problems. When piracy occurs, the pirated product is of the same quality as an original, for example, a company duplicates a piece of software or copies a video tape. In counterfeiting, the product is make to look like an original but is not of the quality as the original. Books, audio and video tapes, movies, and software are often pirated. In such cases, the product is of the same quality as the original but, of course, the company does not get any revenue from the sale. It is estimated that over $40 billion is lost annually to piracy.

With a counterfeit product, not only does the company not receive revenue from the sale of the counterfeit product, but if the quality is poor, as is often the situation, damage is also done to the product image and the use of counterfeit products can cause accidents and product failure. I have seen counterfeit Levis that look like the real thing but after two or three washings, the poor quality of the fabric is apparent. Auto and air craft accidents have been attributed to counterfeit parts sold in the United States. The only protection companies have against piracy and counterfeiting is through the cooperation of host countries and efforts by the U.S. government. Articles that explores these issues are: Dave Savona, "Waging War on Pirates," International Business, January 1995, pp. 42-46 and "Modern Day Pirates A Threat Worldwide," Advertising Age, March 20, 1995, p. I-3.

This article has some interesting data on losses by product category and country. For example, in 1994, motion picture companies lost $145 million in the Russian Federation and $321 million in Italy while software losses in Japan amount to $1.1 billion.

**Lecture Outline**

I. The International Legal Environment: Playing by the Rules

II. Global Perspective—The Pajama Caper

III. Bases for Legal Systems

  A. Common and Code Law

  B. Islamic Law

  C. Marxist-Socialist Tenets

IV. Jurisdiction in International Legal Disputes

V. International Dispute Resolution

  A. Conciliation

  B. Arbitration

  C. Litigation

VI. Protection of Intellectual Property Rights—A Special Problem

  A. Inadequate Protection

  B. Prior Use versus Registration

  C. International Conventions

VII. Commercial Law within Countries

  A. Marketing Laws

  B. Green Marketing Legislation

  C. Antitrust

VIII. U.S. Laws Apply in Host Countries

  A. Foreign Corrupt Practices Act

  B. National Security Laws

  C. Antitrust Laws

D. Antiboycott Laws

D. Extraterritorially of U.S. Laws

IX. Cyber Law—Unresolved Issues

A. Domain Names

B. Taxes

C. Jurisdiction of Disputes and Contracts

X. Summary

**DISCUSSION QUESTIONS**

1. Define:

| | |
|---|---|
| Common Law | Code Law |
| Islamic Law | Marxist-Socialist tenets |
| Prior use vs. registration | Conciliation |
| Arbitration | Litigation |

2. How does the international marketer determine what legal system will have jurisdiction when legal disputes arise? Since there is no judicial body to deal with legal problems arising between citizens of different countries, the foreign marketer must look to the legal systems of all the countries involved; that is, the laws of his own country and the laws of the country in which he is conducting business. In general, a U.S. citizen is subject to the laws of the United States as well as to those of any foreign country in which he lives or works. In the case of a conflict, and unless the government of the citizen takes up the citizen's case in an international court, jurisdiction is generally determined (1) on the basis of jurisdictional clauses included in the contract, (2) on the basis of where a contract was entered into, or (3) on the basis of where the provisions of the contract were performed. The jurisdictional clause is the most clear-cut and is usually honored. If there is no such clause or if it is ineffective, either of the other two methods is used.

3. Discuss the state of international commercial law.

   Commercial law, as seen in Question 1, varies in meaning between common law (where commercial disputes are subject either to civil or commercial law) and code law (where a codified inclusive commercial law exists). Consequently, there is no such thing as an "international" commercial law, and the question of jurisdiction is handled as described in Question 2. In general, the marketer must deal with *national* commercial laws and must vary his operations from country to country with regard to its individual laws. Progress toward unification is being taken with greatest success in the EEC countries, which eventually aim toward a unified commercial legal system as well as unification in all other areas, especially political.

4. Discuss the limitations of jurisdictional clauses in contracts.

   In general, jurisdictional clauses, when present in a contract, are honored by the courts. For example, it is not unusual for a court to use the law of another country for its decisions. However, if the contractual events are not in effect, entered into or executed within the state indicated, courts have been known to disregard the jurisdictional clause and apply different rules in determining what law governs. Since there is no obligation for the courts to uphold jurisdictional clauses, the parties must be reasonable when adding such clauses, or they are liable to have very limited actual value.

5. What is the "objective theory of jurisdiction?" How does it apply to a firm doing business within a foreign country?

   The question of U.S. sovereignty over its citizens abroad has been dealt with by the "objective theory of jurisdiction" which states that "even if an act is committed abroad, that is outside the territorial jurisdiction of the courts, those courts can nevertheless have jurisdiction over it if this act produces consequences or effects within the United States." Broadly interpreted, this means that an American is always a citizen of the United States and is subject to its laws as interpreted by the U.S. courts. Commonly interpreted, however, only those violations of U.S. laws which "affect our foreign or domestic trade" are considered subject to the U.S. legal system when operations are outside the legal jurisdiction of U.S. courts. Since an American working, traveling, or living in a foreign country is subject to the laws of that country and must obey them, he will not be punished by an American court if he is at the same time violating a domestic U.S. law. It is obvious, however, that a firm (U.S.) in a foreign country must consider at least two sets of laws, and perhaps more. This is especially important in antitrust cases, or with laws governing loyalty and U.S. citizenship (i.e., trading with enemy, political office in foreign countries, offices in political parties, etc.).

6. Discuss some of the reasons why it is probably best to seek an out-of-court settlement in international commercial legal disputes rather than sue.

   The most important reasons for avoiding court settlements of international legal disputes is that they are time consuming, frustrating, and costly. In addition, court cases are often publicized and may create a poor image of the company; the courts may not be well versed in the problem and thus hand down an unfair decision; and a more fair, less time consuming and less expensive decision can often be reached through arbitration. As a result of the high costs of litigation, the philosophy of most companies is to first "placate," second to "arbitrate," and to "litigate" as a last resort.

7. Illustrate the procedure generally followed in international commercial disputes when settled under the auspices of a formal arbitration tribunal.

   Arbitration obviously depends upon the willingness of both parties to accept the arbitrator's rulings; it has been most successful when provision for this method of settlement is included in the contract. However, there is some question of the legality of enforcing arbitration agreements which have been made prior to a dispute. While the theory of arbitration is that each of the parties involved in the dispute selects or agrees upon a referee or judge of the case, in actual practice most arbitration is submitted to one of the established arbitration boards and to established rules and procedures. The general procedure followed by an established arbitration tribunal is that of immediately attempting a conciliation between the parties. If not successful, each party selects an arbitrator to defend its case, the court appoints a third member (from a list of arbitrators it maintains), hearings of both sides take place, a decision and an award is made. Such decisions have had a great deal of success, i.e., they are upheld by the parties.

8. What are intellectual property rights? Why should a company in international marketing take special steps to protect them?

   Industrial property rights are rights to the exclusive or limited use of products, processes, designs, formulas, brand names, and trademarks which provide a company with advantages over competitors; i.e., patents, trademarks, and copyrights. Such industrial properties are among the most important assets of a company because they symbolize quality, entice consumers, and have a psychological or intangible quality which is invaluable. Because of this fact and the fact that millions of dollars are spent developing such qualities, the international marketer should take special steps to govern these properties since the rules governing them vary from country to country. (See next question.)

9. In many code law countries, ownership of intellectual property rights is established by registration rather than prior use. Comment.

   Most countries of the world follow a code law principle concerning property rights. That is, rights are established by registration, and the first to register a product is its legal owner. In the United States, the common law principle is observed: prior use established ownership. That is, whoever can establish first use is considered the owner and has legal rights. Obviously, an oversight in understanding these differences may result in much pirating and the loss of property rights, or at least in the loss of a great deal of time, effort, and/or money. Obviously, uniform laws would help since the international marketer must necessarily consider the world as his or her market and should have a means of obtaining worldwide intellectual property rights.

10. Discuss the advantages to the international marketer arising from the existence of the various international conventions on trademarks, patents, and copyrights.

    The obvious advantage to international marketers arising from the existence of the various international conventions on trademarks, patents, and copyrights is that their product, their sales, their profits are more easily protected, i.e., the marketer may register the product at the same time in many countries, thus avoiding piracy, eliminating time-consuming patent procedures and bureaucracy. in addition, such conventions make an attempt at establishing uniform requirements. Obviously, the situation is difficult when different countries have different attitudes toward the rights of individuals. In most countries, the individual may not obtain exclusive monopoly of a product without manufacturing and selling that product (as an individual may in the United States) but must share the product with the citizens of the country. The patent will revert to public domain if the product isn't manufactured within a specified time. Thus, conventions aid the businessperson by enabling him or her to more easily patent the product, to jog his or her memory that laws are not uniform and that he or she needs a worldwide basis of protection, and to eliminate much time. In addition, conventions serve as the machinery for obtaining these rights and as a possible means of establishing uniform worldwide industrial property rights laws.

11. "The legal environment of the foreign marketer takes on an added dimension of importance since there is no single uniform international commercial law which governs foreign business transactions." Comment.

    As discussed in Question 10, the lack of uniform commercial laws results in the expenditure of much time, energy, and money on the part of the marketer. In addition, a lack of understanding of foreign laws or customs may have serious consequences for the unwary businessperson. Furthermore, information concerning these customs and laws might be hard to obtain. Since any mistakes are liable to have legal consequences, they thus represent some sort of loss to the company. Since customs, politics, geography and innumerable other factors vary greatly, affect, and are affected by the legal environment, it is imperative that the businessperson be acquainted with all aspects. Since legal questions also establish insurmountable road blocks, the wisest course for the international marketer is to have reference to a council well versed in the intricacies of the international legal environment.

12. What is the "credulous person standard" in advertising and what is its importance in international marketing?

    The "credulous person standard" reflects the increasing concern on the part of governments toward advertising. Canadian Courts have been directed by Canadian law to take into account when determining whether an advertising representative is false or misleading, the "general impression" conveyed by the representation as well as its literal meaning. In essence, the courts are expected to apply the "credulous—person standard" which means that if any reasonable person could possibly misunderstand the representation, the representation is misleading. In essence, "puffery," an acceptable practice in the United States, could be interpreted in Canada as false and misleading advertising. Thus, statements such as "the strongest driveshaft in Canada" would be judged misleading in Canada unless there was absolute evidence that the driveshaft was stronger than any other driveshaft for sale in Canada.

13. Why is conciliation a better way to resolve a commercial dispute than arbitration?

    Although arbitration is generally regarded as the best means of settling international disputes, a preliminary effort at conciliation is the best method for resolving disputes with a Chinese business partner. In fact, some Chinese companies may avoid doing business with companies that go first to arbitration when differences arise. Conciliation is considered by the Chinese to be far friendlier than arbitration or litigation in settling disputes. The Chinese believe that when a dispute occurs, friendly negotiation should be used first to solve the problem; if that fails, then conciliation should be tried. The Chinese are less threatened with conciliation but, unfortunately, neither side is bound to a conciliation settlement as would be the case under arbitration.

14. Differentiate between conciliation and arbitration.

    The main difference between conciliation and arbitration is that neither side is bound to a conciliation settlement as would be the case under arbitration. Conciliation can be either formal or informal. Informal conciliation can be established by both sides agreeing on a third party to mediate. In China, formal conciliation is conducted under the auspices of the Beijing Conciliation Center that assigns one or two conciliators to mediate. If agreement is reached, a conciliation statement based on the signed agreement is recorded. Although conciliation may be the friendly route to resolving disputes in China, it is not legally binding so an arbitration clause should be included in all conciliation agreements. Experience has shown that having an arbitration clause in the conciliation agreement makes it easier to move to arbitration if necessary. For companies doing business in China, settlement of disputes should follow four steps; first informal negotiation; if this does not work, conciliate, arbitrate; and finally, litigate.

15. Assume you are a vice-president in charge of a new business-to-business e-commerce division of a well-known major international auto parts manufacturer. A) A cyber squatter has registered the company name as a domain Web name. What are your options to secure the domain name for your company? B) Discuss the steps you should take to ensure worldwide protection of your domain name.

    Existing law is vague or does not exist for such issues as the protection of domain names, taxes, jurisdiction in cross-border transactions and contractual issues. Countries are beginning to draft legislation to deal with myriad legal questions not clearly addressed by current law.

    Companies need to ensure their domain names are protected in all countries where they intend to maintain country specific Web sites. Unless a domain name is registered in a specific country, a company faces a costly battle to regain its use if another party has registered it. If a cyber squatter has registered a domain name a company wants, the only alternative is to buy it back or sue if it infringes on the company's intellectual property or some how damages a company's reputation. Toymaker Hasbro recently brought a successful action against an adult entertainment Web site, "candyland.com." Hasbro markets a game for children called Candy Land, although not directly infringing on its trademark, the courts deemed it to be damaging the reputation of Hasbro and its children's game. The Web address now takes you directly to a Hasbro site.

    If a business has taken steps to properly defend its brand names, trade names or product names and properly registers them, it greatly enhances its ability to defend against improper use of the name by a third party. Steps can be taken to secure trade names and trademarks through an international program of trademark registration that would be tied into registration of domain names. Countries that recognize intellectual property will generally refer to those laws to resolve disputes. In Germany, for example, regional and local courts have held that reserving and using an internet domain that infringes third party rights (e.g., the party's duly registered trademark) is prohibited and that the courts have jurisdiction over any such infringement if the domain name can be duly accessed in Germany.

    The U.S. has taken a giant step to develop laws for dealing with domain name pirates by passing the Anticybersquatting Consumer Protection Act, a formal policy for protection of trademark owners. It facilitates action against domain name squatters if the domain name infringes on a trademark or personal name.[1] Julia Roberts, the movie actor, was one of the first to sue under this law to regain the use of "juliaroberts.com" registered by a cyber squatter.

Nevertheless, laws covering domain names remains uncertain and the rush to register domain names by third parties will continue. Registering a domain name offers the best protection in countries like Singapore where the law stipulates that the first person to register a domain name, whether the rightful owner or not, will be given exclusive right to its use. If there is any dispute, the parties will have to seek resolution in a Singapore court. Companies must protect against the use of domain names that infringe on its intellectual property, threaten its reputation or confuse the public. They should be mindful that if they do not register their desired domain name first, the only recourse is to purchase the right or go to court.

[1] John Musgreave and Graham Porter, "Domain Name Pirates Whip Up Web Havoc," *The London Free Press*, May 22, 2000.

## Chapter 8 – Researching Global Markets

### Teaching Objectives

The availability and accuracy of secondary data and the challenge of collecting primary data are the main themes of this chapter. The need for good market data is becoming more important in today's global markets as companies are seeking market segments across country markets. While more and better quality secondary data are becoming available, sources of secondary data in most countries is substantially less than U.S. companies are accustomed to at home. The collection of primary data is also affected by the availability of good quality secondary data. All in all, international marketing "market entry" decisions to "continuous operations" decisions creates a need for different types of information and data. What assistance does an MMIS provide?

1) Make students aware of the breadth and scope of international marketing research and the steps of the research process.
2) Explore the issues of availability of secondary data and the need to validate data.
3) Examine qualitative and quantitative research and the problems of gathering primary data.

### Comments and Suggestions

1. While the quality of secondary data are improving, there are major problems with data from some countries including many developing markets. Most countries are aware of the need to improve the quality of data collected and are taking steps to correct accidental as well as deliberate errors. An article in The Wall Street Journal (August 26, 1994, p. A-6) reported that the National Statistics Enforcement Office in China said it uncovered about 60,000 instances of false statistical reports since it began a crackdown. Most bogus reports involved industrial output. Seeking advantage or hiding failures, local officials, factory managers, rural enterprises and other have filed fake numbers on everything from production levels to birth rates. Such inaccurate reporting is not unusual throughout the developing world although conditions are improving. It is important to stress the need to validate secondary data. The transparency, Validating Secondary Data, lists several questions to help in validating secondary data.

2. If a major research project such as the one described in Part I-F, The Country Notebook—A guide for Developing a Marketing Plan or a similar research project, is used, it is important to stress the issues discussed about secondary data since the students will confront most of these problems when doing the research for their projects. Also, the appendix on sources of secondary data should also be brought to their attention. If students have access to the NTDB CD-ROM, an in-class demonstration of the use of the CD-ROM is helpful. You may also want to share with your students the data sources presented in this Instructor's Manual including I-H, Strengthening the Quality of an In-Class Export Feasibility Project (this project suggestion includes data sources for each step of the project) and Flashfacts (data sources by FAX from different country desks of the Department of Commerce).

3. Several other cases are pertinent to Marketing Research issues and questions. Decision making in cases 1-3 (infant formula) and 4-14 (AIDS and condoms) are completely dependent on the best kinds of qualitative research. Secondary data collection will be important aspects of decisions regarding cases 2-1 (Disneyland Paris) and 3-4 (Olympics pricing and the Scottish Claymores).

#### Lecture Outline

I. Breadth and Scope of International Marketing Research

II. The Research Process

A. Defining the Problem and Establishing Research Objectives

III. Problems of the Availability and Use of Secondary Data
  A. Availability of data
  B. Reliability of data
  C. Comparability of data
  D. Validating secondary data

IV. Gathering Primary Data—Quantitative and Qualitative Research

V. Problems of Gathering Primary Data
  A. Ability to Communicate Opinions
  B. Willingness to Respond
  C. Sampling in Field Surveys
  D. Language and Comprehension
    1. Back Translation
    2. Parallel Translation
    3. Decentering

VI. Multicultural Research—A Special Problem

VII. Research on the Internet—A New Opportunity

VIII. Problems in Analyzing and Interpreting Research Information

IX. Responsibility for Conducting Marketing Research

X. Estimating Market Demand
  A. Expert Opinion
  B. Analogy
  C. Income Elasticity

XI. Communicating with Decision Makers

**DISCUSSION QUESTIONS**

1. Define:

Marketing research
International marketing research
Research process
Secondary data
Primary data
Expert opinion
Multicultural research
Back translation
Analogy
Parallel translation
Decentering

2. Discuss how the shift from making "market entry" decisions to "continuous operations" decisions creates need for different types of information and data. What assistance does an MMIS provide?

   The fundamental difference hinges on the type of information necessary for the two different decisions. Market entry decisions require information that may be, for all practical purposes, important only in the original decision to enter or not to enter a market. Those kinds of information that help the marketer make a decision on short-term as well as long-term demand for his product or the profitability of his product after entry are the types necessary to decide market entry. Once a decision to enter a market has been made and a beachhead established, then the marketer needs the constant monitoring of his relative position in the new market, as well as his market share, to continue his operations within that country. This kind of information requires a constant or continuous monitoring of one's market position. Thus, some continuous system designed to generate, store, catalog, and analyze information from sources within the firm and external to the firm are necessary for decision making. MMIS is designed specifically to provide this kind of continuous flow of information.

3. Discuss the breadth and scope of international marketing research. Why is international marketing research generally broader in scope than domestic marketing research?

   The information requirements of foreign market research can be divided into at least three different types. These three types are: (1) general information about the country, area, and/or market, (2) the study of specific information used to solve such problems as advertising, pricing, distribution, and product development in a marketing of specific products, and (3) forecasting future marketing requirements by anticipating social, economic and consumer trends in specific markets or countries.

   A researcher's activities are frequently much broader than those of a domestic marketer and can involve all types of information essential to conducting business abroad. It would not be unusual to expect a foreign marketer to provide all the information relevant to the question of a firm entering a new market, political stability of a country, cultural attributes, geographical characteristics, and market characteristics as well as projections of potential economic growth. In addition, a foreign research department might be expected to be a source of information necessary to compensate for the possible lack of empathy within a strange environment. Research should provide assistance for adequate foreign market information. This would include foreign factors which can vary from country to country or quite frequently from area to area within a country.

   International marketing research is generally broader in scope than domestic marketing research because the foreign marketer must make up for a lack of knowledge which the domestic marketer has gained from years of business experience within a single market. For the foreign marketer, each market is a completely new market, and thus kinds of information which a domestic marketer would be expected to know from his general experience and from having lived within a country must be attained for every new market the foreign marketer enters.

4. "The measure of a competent researcher is his ability to utilize the most sophisticated and adequate techniques and methods available within the limits" (of time, cost, and the present state of the arts). Comment.

   The main theme of the comment on this question should center around the awareness that marketing research is not as sophisticated or as capable of providing information as most would like to believe. In each market research case, the researcher is faced oftentimes with severe limitations imposed by the foreign environment and by his lack of complete understanding of the problems imposed by the environment. In spite of these limitations, he must provide the best information possible. Limitations to research are extremely important in international marketing research since they may be greater than in domestic situations. In any case, while the limitations in foreign marketing research may be severe, the real test is the ability of the researcher to provide adequate information in spite of these limitations. An important point is that there are no special "foreign marketing research techniques" to be applied. A foreign marketing researcher must be able to apply his regular techniques as deftly as possible.

5. What is the task of the international market researcher? How is it complicated by the foreign environment?

   The task of the international market researcher is to answer questions with current, valid information that a marketer can use to design and implement successful marketing programs. This task is complicated by the foreign environment in the case of secondary data by a lack of collected data or data which have been poorly collected and the reliability of the secondary data available. In many countries, national pride comes before statistical accuracy, and frequently secondary data are opinions rather than fact. Another difficulty with secondary data involves the comparability and currency of available data. Oftentimes, data are not comparable from period to period, nor are they current or collected on a predictable basis.

6. Discuss the stages of the research process in relation to the problems encountered. Give examples.

   The research program should include the following steps:

   a. Define the research problem and establish research objectives.

   b. Determine the sources of information to fulfill the research objectives.

   c. Gather the relevant data from secondary and/or primary sources.

   d. Analyze, interpret, and present the results.

   The task of the research is to execute each of these steps with maximum objectivity and accuracy within the limits of cost and time. The major difficulty in defining the problem and establishing research objectives is translating the business problem into a research problem with a set of specific research objectives. This first stage frequently goes astray because of improper problem definition. The problem may be more acute in foreign marketing research than in domestic marketing research, since unfamiliarity with the foreign environment tends to cloud problem definition, thereby complicating the process. Most difficulty arises when the researcher fails to anticipate the influence of the local culture upon the problem. A second difficulty in foreign research stems from the failure to establish sufficiently broad problem limits, which include all the relevant variables. This problem arises mainly because of the researcher's failure to appreciate the kinds of information that the decision maker lacks. In domestic marketing research, much of these kinds of information are taken as "given" and thus is not included in the typical market research project. However, foreign marketing research is much broader in scope; that is, it must include more information than is ordinarily included in domestic research, and thus in defining the problem, the inexperienced researcher may fail to define the problem as broadly as it should be defined.

   The second step in the research process is to determine the sources of information to fulfill the research objectives. The major problem here is being aware of the availability of secondary data and its reliability. The researcher is faced with the problem of making a decision between using secondary data, which may not be as reliable as he wishes, versus collecting primary data. Cost is a major factor in this decision; that is, the cost of collecting the data from primary sources versus using what may be poor or secondary data.

   The third step concerns the problems of gathering the relevant data from either secondary and/or primary sources. There is a general lack in most cases of extensive secondary data as are available in the United States. For those data which are available, there are some very real problems with their reliability. These problems are listed as: (1) the availability of detailed data on specific areas. While broad data covering an entire country may be available, data for subregions within the country are surprisingly unavailable. (2) The reliability of the secondary data which are available. These data may, in some cases, be too optimistic, either on purpose or as a result of not being collected properly. They may tend to understate conditions because of improper collection procedures. (3) Comparability and currency of the data which are available. Data may be many years out of date, they may have been collected on an infrequent and unpredictable schedule, there may be no historical series with which to compare the current information, and the data which are collected may be in categories which are much too broad to be of specific value.

The problems of gathering primary data are also important. The major problem facing the foreign market researcher in gathering primary data is one of getting the unwilling respondent to provide current and truthful information. Cultural variations also hamper the foreign researcher in locating knowledgeable sources of information as well as influencing the general willingness to respond. In some cultures, to discuss personal or family matters is taboo. Private matters are just not discussed with strangers. There is also the problem of taxes when a researcher must ask questions which may cause the respondent to feel that there is some possibility of divulging income. The respondent may be reluctant for fear that the researcher is collecting tax information. Tax evasion is an accepted practice if it can be successfully accomplished. In fact, it can even be a point of pride for the more adept tax evaders. In many countries, this philosophy is not considered immoral or unethical as it would be in the United States. As a consequence, the art of income tax evasion may interfere with the researcher's ability to gather information which may be remotely related to taxes. Another problem is the inability of the respondent to articulate the desired response. It is difficult for a person to clearly articulate his feelings or to provide reasonable information about purchase intentions, likes or dislikes, when he has little understanding of the product or has never used the product.

Another major problem in the collection of primary data is concerned with sampling procedures. An important problem stems from the lack of adequate detail on universal characteristics and lists from which to draw meaningful samples. Current and reliable lists are frequently not available. Telephone directories, census tract and block data and detailed social and economic characteristics of the universe are not available, if at all. Thus, sampling becomes much more complex and frequently less reliable than if these kinds of lists were available. Besides the inadequacy of details on universal characteristics, the effectiveness of the various methods of communication (mail, telephone, and personal interview) in surveys is also limited. In many countries, for example, telephone ownership is extremely low, making telephone interviews virtually worthless. Adequate mailing lists and poor postal service also pose problems for the market researcher who wants to use the mail to conduct research. And last, inadequate lists and inadequate details of the population may make personal interviewing virtually impossible or very difficult.

A final problem with sample surveying is the language. The difference in idioms and the difficulty of exact translations create problems in obtaining the desired information and the interpretation of the respondent's answers. Coupled with this language difficulty is illiteracy. In many countries with low literacy rates, written questionnaires are completely useless. The problem of dialects in different languages can make a national questionnaire survey impractical. In addition, some respondents with a minimum of education may have difficulty in comprehending the meaning of questions asked. Although answers may be given, they may not be the answers of the questions the researcher has in mind, but rather answers to the respondent's misinterpretation.

The last step in the research process is analyzing the problem and interpreting research information. Once the data have been collected, the final and perhaps most critical step is the analysis and interpretation of the findings in light of the stated marketing problem. Final analysis must take into consideration the limitations mentioned above, and in spite of the limitations, produce meaningful guides for management. The meaning of words, the consumer's attitude toward a product, the interviewer's attitude or the interview situation can all distort research findings. Just as culture and tradition can influence the willingness to give information, it can also influence the type of information given. In foreign market research, accepting information at face value can be a dangerous practice. Newspaper circulation figures, readership of the census studies, retail figures, and sales volume can all be distorted through local business practices.

The market on which he is doing research. In order to analyze and in some cases to compensate for research findings, he must determine the customs, viewpoints, semantics, current attitudes, and business customs of a society, or a subsegment of a society. Second, the researcher must possess a creative talent in adapting research findings. Ingenuity and resourcefulness, patience and a sense of humor, and a willingness to be guided by original research finding even when they conflict with popular opinion or prior assumptions are all necessary aspects in the interpretation of foreign market research. Third, the researcher should be skeptical in handling both primary and secondary data. He or she is frequently the only individual in a business firm capable of making an accurate judgment on the reliability and validity of primary and secondary data sources.

7. Why is the formulation of the research problem difficult in foreign market research?

   The formulation of the research problem is difficult in foreign market research because of the cultural variation from country to country and because of the vast amount of information which should be known but often is not available to the decision maker. The situation is oftentimes acute in foreign market research since unfamiliarity with the foreign environment tends to cloud problem definition. In most cases, this is the result of the researcher failing to anticipate the influence of the local culture upon the problem. Other difficulties in foreign research stem from failure to establish sufficiently broad problem limits to include all the relevant variables. Such limits must include a far greater range of factors than necessary for domestic research in order to offset a totally unfamiliar background on the part of the researcher. Much of the information which a domestic market researcher has acquired through a lifetime of living in a country is not available to the foreign market researcher. Therefore, this tends to cloud or to limit his ability in defining a problem since he or she is not in a position to bring to bear all of the possible variations upon the problem formulation. As a consequence, there is a tendency not to define the problem clearly or to define the problem much too narrowly.

8. Discuss the problems of gathering secondary data in foreign markets.

   The problems of gathering secondary data are:

   a. The availability of detailed data on specific market areas. There often is a lack of detailed data on such items as numbers of wholesalers, retailers, manufacturers, and facilitating services. Surprisingly, enough data on population and income are often unavailable as well.

   b. Reliability of the secondary data which are available. When there is an abundance of data, it must be screened carefully. The data can be overstated, understated, or riddled with holes.

   c. Comparability and currency of available data. In many countries, especially the lesser developed, data can be many years out of date as well as having been collected on an infrequent and unpredictable schedule. Furthermore, there are often very little historical data available with which to compare the current information. Data from a secondary source from any country, including the United States, should always be checked very carefully. As a practical matter, the following questions should be asked in order to judge the reliability of data sources: Who collected the data? Would there be any purpose for misrepresenting the facts? For what purpose were the data collected? How were they collected? Are the data generally consistent and logical in light of known data sources or market factors?

9. "In many cultures, personal information is inviolably *private* and absolutely not to be discussed with strangers." Discuss.

   This, of course, is a major problem in the collection of primary data. This factor leads to some very difficult and challenging problems in the collection of primary data, and it is one of the primary reasons why respondents are unwilling to answer or participate in market research surveys. In many cultures, the housewife's role is such that she is not available to any stranger, let alone to a stranger asking personal or private questions. In other cultures, for example, the French Canadians, people tend to be simply reticent about family affairs and do not answer questions as a result. In other cultures, the male would not under any circumstances answer questions about his personal behavior. These and other factors certainly test the creative abilities of the foreign market researcher. He must be able to get around or over these kinds of difficulties in order to get certain types of information.

10. What are some of the problems created by language and the ability to comprehend in collecting primary data? How can a foreign market researcher overcome these difficulties?

    The problems created by language are many. The obvious, of course, is the ability of the individual to understand or the ability of the researcher to translate accurately a question into the language of the respondent. Dictionary translation is seldom adequate. The key is the ability to translate the question into the proper idiom of the respondent. A questionnaire is difficult to construct even in one's own tongue. When one has to translate the questionnaire from his own tongue into an unfamiliar tongue, the difficulties can be great. The most important one, of course, is being certain that the question being asked is the same when translated. These problems can be overcome by the researcher by the use on nationals. A warning, however, is that one must be certain that the national does understand the language of the researcher and can translate it correctly.

11. Discuss how "decentering" is used to get an accurate translation of a questionnaire.

    A hybrid of back translation, is called "decentering." A successive iteration process of translation and retranslation of a questionnaire, each time by a different translator. The two English versions are compared and where there are differences, the original English version is modified and the process is repeated. If there are differences between the two English versions, the original English version of the second iteration is modified and the process of translation and back translation is repeated. The process continues to be repeated until an English version can be translated into French and back translated, by a different translator, into the same English. In this process, wording of the original instrument undergoes a change and the version that is finally used and "its translation have equally comprehensive and equivalent terminologies in both languages."

12. Discuss when qualitative research may be more effective than quantitative e research.

    Qualitative research is more effective than quantitative research when: 1) the researcher seeks open-ended, in-depth and unstructured responses that reflect the person's thoughts and feelings on a subject. Qualitative research interprets what the " . . . people in the sample are like, their outlooks, their feelings, the dynamic interplay of their feelings and ideas, their attitudes and opinions, and their resulting actions," 2) the researcher wants to formulate and define a problem more clearly and to determine relevant questions to be examine in subsequent research. It can also be used where interest is centered on gaining an understanding of a market, rather than quantifying relevant aspects; 3) the researcher seeks an understanding of the impact of sociocultural factors on behavior patterns and wants to develop research hypothesis that can be tested in subsequent studies designed to quantify the concepts and relevant relationships uncovered in qualitative data collection. Research conducted by Procter & Gamble in Egypt is an example of how qualitative research leads to specific points that can be measured by using survey or quantitative research; and, 4) the respondent has no immediate experience with the product or concept under study and a small sample of carefully selected consumers is sufficient. For example, it is often difficult for respondents to know whether a product, flavor, concept or some other new idea is appealing if they have no experience with the issue being studied. To simply ask in a direct way may result in no response or worse, a response that does not reflect how respondents would react if they had more experience.

13. Sampling offers some major problems in market research. Discuss.

    There are several difficulties encountered in the process of taking samples and conducting field surveys. The greatest problem stems from the lack of adequate detail of universal characteristics and lists from which to draw meaningful samples. If current and reliable lists are not available, sampling becomes much more complex and generally less reliable. In many countries, telephone directories, cross-index street directories, census tract and block data, and detailed social and economic characteristics of the universe are not available on a current basis, if at all. The researcher then has to estimate characteristics and population parameters, sometimes with little basic data on which to build an accurate estimate. To add to the confusion, in some cities in South America, Mexico, and Asia, street maps are unavailable; and in some large metropolitan areas of the Near East and Asia, streets are not identified and houses are not numbered.

    A lack of detailed social and economic information also can hamper the effectiveness of sampling techniques. Without an age breakdown of the universe, for example, the researcher can never be certain he or she has a representative sample on an age criterion since there is no basis or comparison with the age breakdown in the sample. Although a lack of detailed information does not prevent the use of sampling in obtaining reliable market information, it does make it more difficult. In place of the probability techniques, many researchers who have found themselves faced with such situations have had to rely upon conveniences, samples in marketplaces and other public gathering places.

    Besides the inadequacy of details on universal characteristics, the effectiveness of the various methods of communications (mail, telephone, and personal interview) in surveys is also limited. In many countries, for example, telephone ownership is extremely low, making telephone surveys virtually worthless unless the survey is intended to cover only the wealthy.

    In addition to potentially poor service within countries, there is also the major problem of the time required for delivery and returns when a mail survey is to be conducted from another country. Surface delivery can require three weeks or longer between some points on the globe, and although airmail reduces this time drastically, it also increases costs considerably.

    Although adequate lists and adequate detail on the population may be critically short in some countries, this is not universally true. In those countries where every adult is required to register with various government agencies, there are extremely adequate lists of people, along with ample socio-economic detail. In many European countries, as well as in Japan, voter lists, police registration lists, and tax records are available to researchers. In those areas where there is a paucity of adequate lists, other research tools must be relied upon. Mainly the various convenience sample methods are used.

14. Select a country. From secondary sources compile the following information for at least a 10-year period prior to the present data.

    Principal imports

    Principal exports

    Gross national product

    Chief of state

    Major cities and population

    Principal agricultural crop

    Library Project.

15. "The foreign market researcher must possess three essential capabilities in order to generate meaningful marketing information." Discuss.

The foreign market researcher must possess three essential capabilities in order to generate meaningful marketing information. First, he must possess a high degree of cultural understanding of the market on which he is doing research. In order to analyze, and in some cases, to compensate for research findings, he must understand the customs, viewpoint, semantics, current attitudes, and business customs of a society or a subsegment of a society. Second, the researcher must possess a creative talent in adapting research findings. Unfortunately, the researcher in foreign markets often finds himself "flying by the seat of his pants," and he or she is sometimes called upon to produce results under the most difficult of circumstances. Third, the researcher should be skeptical in handling both primary and secondary data. He might find it necessary to have a newspaper press run checks over a period of time to get accurate circulation figures, or he or she might find it necessary to deflate or inflate reported consumer income in some areas by 25 to 50 percent on the basis of observable socioeconomic characteristics. Frequently, he is the only individual in a business firm capable of making an accurate judgment on the reliability and validity of primary and secondary data sources.

These essential capabilities suggest that the foreign market researcher should be either a foreign national or should be advised by someone who can accurately appraise the data collected in light of the local environment, thereby helping to validate secondary as well as primary data.

# Chapter 9 – Emerging Markets and Market Behavior

## Teaching Objectives

Barring a major political and economic shift in the developing world, evidence is strong that through the first decade of the 21st century emerging markets will be where the majority of world's total trade growth will occur. Growth will occur on a variety of fronts: development of infrastructure, opportunities of foreign investors, and a spectacular growth of the consumer market. The events taking place in emerging markets make international business exciting and will create opportunities and challenges for multinational firms.

The impact of trends that are sweeping the developing countries—transition from socialist to market-driven economies, the liberalization of trade and investment policies in developing countries, the transfer of public-sector enterprise to the private sector, and the rapid development of regional market alliances—should be the emphasis of this chapter. The emerging markets, especially the BEMs—those identified by the Department of Commerce as big emerging markets—will be the centerpiece of global economic growth. The teaching objectives of this chapter are to:

1) Stress the importance of the political and economic changes affecting global marketing.
2) Illustrate the connection between the economic level of a country and the opportunities created as economic growth occurs.
3) Explore the various developing markets in the Americas, Eastern Europe and the Baltic States, and Asia.
4) Examine the idea of the Department of Commerce's Big Emerging Markets.
5) Discuss the growth of new market segments and the emerging middle class in the BEMs and other emerging markets.

## Comments and Suggestions

1. There are an abundance of data to illustrate the growth of a middle-class and new market segments that are evolving. Two articles that provide relevant data are: "The Emerging Middle Class," Business Week/21st. Century Capitalism, (Special Issue) 1994, pp. 176–194, "Global Growth Is on a Tear," Fortune, March 20, 1995, pp. 108–114, and "The Big Emerging Markets," Business America, March 1994 and subsequent issues which have articles on individual countries.

   The growing importance of new market segments is reflected in the number of studies on consumers that are being conducted. A recent Roper Starch Worldwide global study of 40,000 consumers in 40 countries identified four major styles of shopping. Deal Makers (29%), who love the process of buying; Price Seekers (27%), who place primary value on the product they are buying; Brand Loyalists (23%), who purchase name brands and remain true to them; and Luxury Innovators (21%), those who seek the new, prestigious brands.

The following is a breakdown by country.

| | Brand Loyalists | Price Seekers | Luxury Innovators | Deal Makers |
|---|---|---|---|---|
| U.S. | 11.3%, | 35.5%, | 16.6% | 36.6% |
| Mexico | 19.1 | 23.4, | 19.9 | 35.0 |
| China | 27.9 | 23.4 | 22.8 | 25.7 |
| India | 34.6 | 7.4 | 35.8 | 22.2 |
| Japan | 23.5 | 41.0 | 7.9 | 27.1 |
| Saudi Arabia | 14.8 | 8.9 | 34.4 | 40.3 |
| France | 19.5 | 45.5 | 8.5 | 26.6 |
| Germany | 16.9 | 43.7 | 15.7 | 21.9 |
| Spain | 27.0 | 34.4 | 18.1 | 19.6 |
| U.K. | 28.7 | 27.2 | 17.5 | 25.5 |
| Czech Republic | 23.9 | 26.9 | 25.7 | 22.6[1] |

2. Besides demand created by an emerging middle-class, the need for heavy infrastructure investments will add to total global demand. The World Bank estimates that in Asia alone between $1 trillion and $1.9 trillion will be spent on infrastructure projects by the year 2000 including projects such as roads, railroads, power plants, telecommunications, gas and oil pipelines, dams and airports. An article that explores investments in infrastructures and provides some interesting data is Dave Savona, "Remaking the Globe," International Business, March 1995, pp. 30–36.

3. Case 3–1, Asian Yuppies, Having It All, can be used as the starting point for a discussion of the emerging middle class and the creation of viable marketing segments. It also serves as a good illustration of how levels of income and purchasing patterns in many developing countries do not match those patterns found in more prosperous economies. Demand for many classes of goods may be higher in emerging markets than one would expect if estimates are based on mature markets. On the other hand, TM 9–11, Average Monthly Expenditures for Chinese Households National and Urban Areas – 1994, presents a realistic picture of average monthly expenditures of Chinese households nationally and in urban areas.

4. The Big Emerging Markets, BEMs, is where the growth of international trade in the future will be. TM 9–2, Common Traits of Big Emerging Markets, lists the characteristics of these markets and TM 9–3, Big Emerging Markets details some of the economic characteristics of these markets.

**Lecture Outline**

I. Global Perspective—Wal-Mart, Tide, and Three-Snake Wine

II. Marketing and Economic Development

   A. Stages of Economic Development

   B. NIC Growth Factors

   C. Information Technology, the Internet and Economic Development

   D. Objectives of Developing Countries

   E. Infrastructure and Development

   F. Marketing's Contributions

---

[1] Source: "How the World Shops," *Advertising Age*, June 5, 1995, p.3

III. Marketing in a Developing Country
   A. Level of Market Development
   B. Demand in A Developing Country
IV. Developing Countries and Emerging Markets
   A. The Americas
   B. Eastern Europe and the Baltics
   C. Asia
      1. Asian Pacific Rim
      2. China
      3. Hong Kong
      4. Taiwan
      5. India
      6. Newest Emerging Markets
V. Strategic Implications for Marketing
VI. Summary

**DISCUSSION QUESTIONS**

1. Define:

| | |
|---|---|
| Underdeveloped | BEM |
| Economic development | Infrastructure |
| NICs | Economic dualism |

2. "It is possible for an economy to experience growth as measured by total GNP without a commensurate rise of the standard of living." Discuss fully.

   A country's "gross national product" is the total of its economic output and assets. However, the GNP figure in no way indicates the manner in which this wealth is distributed. One percent of the population may control 80 percent of the wealth, which is the case in many so-called "underdeveloped" countries. Thus, though the economy may expand and the GNP increase greatly, the largest percentage of the population may not experience a commensurate rise in their standard of living. There is also the problem of population growth. Though total national income may greatly increase, the average per capita GNP will decline if population growth is extremely high.

3. Why do technical assistance programs of more affluent nations typically ignore the distribution problem or relegate it to a minor role in development planning? Explain.

   If an underdeveloped country cannot produce a certain product, it does not have to worry about distributing that product. The first aim of a technical assistance program is to see that the country has the capacity to turn out the desired product. But sometimes production is so overemphasized that the marketing end is almost completely ignored. There is also the problem of transferability of marketing skills and techniques. It is easier to teach the production of a product than the marketing of the same product. Cultural and traditional bias against the concept of marketing in many foreign countries often makes the more affluent nation rather reluctant to press its ideas on marketing upon the underdeveloped nation it is aiding.

4. Discuss each of the stages of evolution of the marketing process. Illustrate each stage with a particular country.

The marketing institutions which develop as a country passes from one stage to another are as follows:

A brief study of Exhibit 9–3 will reveal roughly the state of marketing at each stage of economic development. As a generalization, a nation develops and industry grows with marketing institutions evolving to fulfill the distribution needs created at each new level. The more developed an economy, the greater the variety of marketing functions demanded, and the more sophisticated and specialized the institutions become to perform marketing functions. Also developed are the myriad facilitating agencies required to support a growing economy. Advertising agencies, facilities for marketing research, repair services, specialized consumer financing agencies, and storage and warehouse facilities are created to service the particular needs of expanded markets and economies. It is important to remember that these institutions do not automatically come about nor do the necessary marketing institutions simply appear.

**EXHIBIT 9–3**

**EVOLUTION OF THE MARKETING PROCESS**

| **Stage** | **Substage** | **Marketing Functions** |
|---|---|---|
| Agricultural and raw materials (MK. (f) = Prod.)[2] | Self-sufficient | None |
| | Surplus Commodity producer | Small-Scale Merchants, Traders, Fairs |
| Manufacturing (Mk. = Prod.) | Small-Scale | Merchants, Wholesalers, Export-Import |
| | Mass Production | Merchants, Wholesalers, Traders, and Specialized Institutions |
| Marketing (Prod. (f) = Mk.) | Commercial–Transition | Large-Scale and Chain Retailers Increase in Specialized Middlemen |
| | Mass Distribution | Integrated Channels of Distribution Increase Specialized Middlemen |

5. As a country progresses from one economic stage to another, what in general are the marketing effects?

   As a general rule, the more complex a nation's economy becomes, the more complex its marketing system becomes. The marketing function matures and becomes more specialized. It must expand to meet the increased problems of planning, distribution, and transportation. The text indicates the need for such agencies in a more mature economy as "advertising agencies, facilities for marketing research, repair services, specialized consumer financing agencies, and storage and warehouse facilities." Not only do these functions arise from economic expansion, but they are also necessary if the economy is to continue an increased growth pattern.

6. Locate a country in the agricultural and raw material stage of economic development and discuss what changes will occur in marketing when it passes to a manufacturing stage.

   A country with little industry will not find it necessary to carry on extensive marketing. Most of the agricultural products will be used for local consumption and the various facets of marketing will not be overly important. However, when these raw materials are put into the manufacturing process, marketing has a function. Marketers will be necessary to plan how much and what kinds of goods will

[2] Mk (f) = Prod: Marketing is a function of production.

be manufactured. Without this plan, it would be much more difficult to determine the amount of raw materials needed since there would be no indicator of demand. The range of the market would change. No longer would products be used mostly for local consumption. Now, distribution over a wide area would be necessary–perhaps even outside the country's boundaries. The goods manufactured must be sold, so advertisement is necessary to increase the market demand. There is always a fairly set demand for agricultural products, but the demand for manufactured products may vary greatly. Demand can be increased considerably by the skillful marketer.

7. What are the consequences of each stage of marketing development on the potential for industrial goods within a country? For consumer goods?

   Demand for industrial goods is affected by economic change, and is tied to the economy's stage of industrialization. As a country progresses toward economic maturity, demand for industrial goods changes in character with the degree of industrialization. When there is no industrial base, demand is for the equipment to build manufacturing plants, highways, power plants, and other basic products. Once the next stage is achieved, demand shifts emphasis upon the parts and supplies to maintain plants. As a country develops, industrial demand then shifts to those items other countries can produce more competitively than the home country.

   Demand for consumer goods is influenced by the level of economic achievement since the market must have sufficient purchasing power to acquire goods and services. As an economy develops, levels of income and its distribution among the people change, and the effect upon market demand is felt in a variety of ways. The demand for different kinds of goods changes as a smaller proportion of income is needed to maintain a bare subsistence. Sometimes these changes are very drastic and occur in a very short period of time. In addition to increases in the demand for particular kinds of goods, consumption patterns often change as basic needs are fulfilled, and the result is a more discretionary income.

8. Discuss the significance of economic development to international marketing. Why is the knowledge of economic development of importance in assessing the world marketing environment? Discuss.

   Economic development is significant in international marketing because (1) the stage of economic development has tremendous influence upon the demand for both consumer and industrial goods, and (2) the level of economic development also has an effect upon the acceptance of a foreign marketer within the country. The political environment within which the marketer must operate is influenced in part by the stage of economic development of the particular country. Economic development is also significant in international marketing because of marketing's important role in the economic development of a particular country. While marketing's contribution may not be accepted, nevertheless its contribution can be important and thus should be recognized by the international marketer. Furthermore, economic development is important to international marketing in terms of long range forecasting of market potential. While the market in a particular country may not be of significance today, if it is a developing country, market potential may be such that the marketer will want to become established in the developing country. Finally, the stage of economic development is important to international marketing because a developing country is a dynamic one, and the marketer must prepare to adjust to dramatic shifts in the economy.

   An international marketer must be capable of adjusting to a foreign economic environment. He must be able to answer such questions as: (1) What are the objectives of the developing nations? (2) What role is marketing assigning, if any, in economic growth plans? and (3) What contribution must marketing make whether overtly planned or not in order for a country to grow successfully? The answers to these questions are significant in assessing a particular country's attitude toward marketing because they will affect the attitude and behavior of a particular country toward marketing. Most countries want to be free to determine the economic, political, and cultural future and thus will view a foreign marketer as an outsider and possibly as one which may limit the achievement of their particular growth objectives. This frequently leads to political and governmental harassment and sometimes consumer boycott of goods.

Often there is a widespread fear and resentment of foreign control of the economy and policies and actions are sometimes adopted which may retard economic progress and do restrict a foreign marketer's operations. Without this knowledge of the possible reaction of a developing country toward a foreign marketer, the marketer would not be able to properly assess his risks nor the potential of a new market.

9. The Internet accelerates the process of economic growth. Discuss.

In addition to growth factors discussed above, a country's investment in information technology (IT) is also an important key to economic growth. The cellular phone, the Internet and other advances in IT open opportunities for emerging economies to catch up with richer ones. New, innovative electronic technologies can be the key to a sustainable future for developed and developing nations alike.

For example:

It is argued that because the Internet cuts transaction costs and reduces economies of scale from vertical integration, it reduces the economically optimal size for firms. Lower transaction costs makes it possible for small firms in Asia or Latin America to work together to develop a global reach.[3] Smaller firms in emerging economies can now sell into a global market. It is now easier, for instance, for a tailor in Shanghai to make a suit by hand for a lawyer in Boston, or a software designer in India to write a program for a firm in California. One of the big advantages rich economies have is their closeness to wealthy consumers that will be eroded as transaction costs fall.

The Internet accelerates the process of economic growth by speeding up the diffusion of new technologies to emerging economies. Unlike the decades it took before many developing countries benefited from railways, telephones or electricity, the Internet is spreading rapidly throughout Asia, Latin America and Eastern Europe. IT can jump-start national economies and allow them to leapfrog from high levels of illiteracy to computer literacy.

The Internet facilitates education, a fundamental underpinning for economic development. The African Virtual University links 24 African under-funded and ill equipped campuses to classrooms and libraries worldwide, and will soon grant degrees in computer science, computer engineering and electrical engineering. South Africa's School Net program links 1,035 schools to the Net while the government's Distance Education program brings multimedia teaching to rural schools.

Mobile phones and other wireless technologies greatly reducc the need to lay down a costly telecom infrastructure to bring telephone service to areas not now served. In Caracas, Venezuela, for example, where half of the city's 5 million population lives in non-wired slums, cell phones with pay-as-you-go cards have provided service to many residents for the first time.

The Grameen Bank, a private commercial enterprise in Bangladesh, has a program to supply phones to 300 villages. There are only three phones for every 1,000 people in Bangladesh, one of the lowest phone-penetration rates in the world. The new network will be nationwide, putting every villager within two kilometers of a cellular phone.

Cyber post offices in Ghana offer e-mail service for the price of a letter. Telecenters in five African countries provide public telephone, fax, computer and Internet services where students read online books and local entrepreneurs seek potential business partners.

Medical specialists from Belgium help train local doctors and surgeons in Senegal via video linkups between classrooms and operating centers and provide them with Internet access to medical journals and databases. It would be prohibitively expensive if they had to travel there to teach; via Internet technology it costs practically nothing.

---

[3] Thomas Sancton, "A Great Leap Developing Countries Are finding Way to Leverage Advances in Information Technology and Help Narrow the North-South Divide," *Time International*, January 31, 2000, p. 42.

10. Discuss the impact of the IT revolution on the poorest countries

    Substantial investments in the infrastructure to create easy access to the Internet and other aspects of IT are being made by governments and entrepreneurs. Hong Kong is investing in a $1.7 billion cyber port to house high-tech companies. If successful, it will create a new information economy and thousands of new jobs. Singapore's broadband network brings fast digital transmission capacity to homes and offices, allowing delivery of advanced multimedia services. Vietnam has entered the first stage of e-commerce development with the opening of a software "zone" in Hanoi and plans to spend $32.4 million to develop an information technology park.

11. Select one country in each of the five stages of economic development. For each country, outline the basic existing marketing institutions and show how their stages of development differ. Explain why.

    Library project.

12. Why should a foreign marketer study economic development? Discuss.

    Economic development should be studied by a foreign marketer in order to (1) assess present demand within a country, (2) to assess potential and future demand within a country, (3) become aware of the probable consequences of his actions within a developing country, i.e., that is political reaction to his involvement, and (4) determine what contributions as a marketer he can and should make to the development of a particular country.

13. The infrastructure is important to the economic development of an economy. Comment.

    One indicator of economic development is the extent of social overhead capital or infrastructure within the economy. The quality of infrastructure directly affects a country's economic growth potential and the ability of an enterprise to engage effectively in business. When an infrastructure does not develop with an expanding population and economy, countries begin to lose economic development ground. A country can produce commodities for export but cannot sell them because of inadequacies of the infrastructure. For example, in Zimbabwe there was excess agricultural product for sale but only about a third available could be moved to ports because of weaknesses in the railroads. The infrastructure is also a crucial component of the uncontrollable elements for the marketer. Without adequate transportation facilities a marketer's distribution costs can increase substantially and the ability to reach certain segments of the market may be impaired. The market's full potential may never be realized because of an inadequate existing infrastructure.

14. What are the objectives of economically developing countries? How do these objectives relate to marketing? Comment.

    Industrialization is the fundamental objective of most developing countries; although for an appreciation of its impact upon a nation's people, economic growth must be viewed as a means to an end rather than as the end itself. Certainly, most countries see in "economic growth" the achievement of social as well as economic goals. Satisfaction of nonmaterial as well as material needs must be achieved in order to fulfill the desires and aspirations of most underdeveloped nations. This would include better education for all, better and more effective government, and the elimination of social inequities as well as improvements in moral and ethical responsibilities of both the public and private sectors of the economy. A knowledge of these objectives can help explain the attitude and behavior toward marketing which often exists within an underdeveloped country in the growth stage. The fact that most countries wish to be free to determine their economic, political, and cultural future goes far in explaining the potential vulnerability of a foreign marketer in these countries. Because foreign marketers are outsiders, it is often assumed that their presence is limiting the achievement of these objectives. Frequently, this feeling results in political and governmental harassment and sometimes consumer boycott of goods. The widespread fear and resentment of foreign control of the economy commonly leads to the adoption of policies and actions which at times retard rather than facilitate economic progress.

15. Using the list of NIC growth factors, evaluate India and China as to their prospects for rapid growth. Which factors will be problems for India? For China?

    Students should be encouraged to search current information about these two countries since many of the factors are influenced by ongoing conditions. At the time this was written, both seemed to be on a path of nuclear expansion, a costly venture, that will drain much need capital from economic growth. This exercise is the basis for a discussion of these two important nations. The correctness of responses is a matter of debate.

    The factors that existed to some extent during the economic growth of NICs were:

    - Political stability in policies affecting its development
    - Economic, political and legal reforms
    - Entrepreneurship. In all of these nations, free enterprise in the hands of the self-employed was the seed of the new economic growth.
    - Planning. A central plan with observable and measurable development goals linked to specific policies.
    - Outward orientation. Production for the domestic market and export markets with increases in efficiencies and continually differentiating exports from competition.
    - Factors of production. If deficient in the factors of production – land (raw materials), labor, capital, management and, technology – an environment where these factors could easily come from outside the country and be directed to development objectives.
    - Industries targeted for growth. Strategically directed industrial and international trade policy to identify those sectors where opportunity existed. Key industries encouraged to achieve better positions in world markets by directing resources into promising target sectors.
    - Incentives. Incentives to force a high domestic rate of savings and to direct capital to update the infrastructure, transportation, housing, education and training.
    - Privatization. Privatized SOEs that placed a drain on national budgets. Privatization released immediate capital to invest in strategic areas and gave relief from a continuing drain on future national resources. Often when industries are privatized, new investors modernize thus creating new economic growth.

    The final factors that must be present are large, accessible markets with low tariffs. During the early growth of many of the NICs, the first large open market was the United States later joined by Europe and now, as the fundamental principles of the World Trade Organization (WTO) are put into place, much of the rest of the world.

16. What is marketing's role in economic development? Discuss marketing's contributions to economic development.

    Marketing is critical to economic development. Marketing is an economy's arbiter between productivity, capacity, and consumer demand. The marketing process is a critical element in effectively utilizing the production resulting from economic growth to provide a higher standard of living. Effective marketing helps to improve the life-style and well being of the people in a specific economy, but it has more far-reaching effects by upgrading world markets.

    Essential to the growth of any economy is a developed marketing system that provides effective distribution for whatever a country produces. What generally exists in an underdeveloped country is an inefficient, "outrageously" high-cost market structure where most of those engaged in marketing are barely managing to survive. Marketing can help to eliminate some of the inefficiencies which sap the economies of underdeveloped countries.

Marketing also helps to increase the size of existing markets. Although marketing cannot create purchasing power, it can uncover and direct that which already exists and thereby increase the level of economic activity.

Effective and efficient marketing leads to increasing market size which leads to further improvements in marketing and production efficiency, and so on.

Another important contribution of marketing to very underdeveloped economies is the growth or spreading of a money economy. Until an economy has established monetary systems, growth is stunted at a very low level. Since marketing requires a money system in order to flourish effectively, it helps to spread the use of money throughout the economy.

The growth and stimulation which result from increased desire for material possessions frequently lead to the development of much needed managers and entrepreneurs. For accelerated economic growth, a country must have a ready supply of entrepreneurs who "can see and seize the opportunities for joining the available capital with the available resources in new combinations."

Effective marketing leads to the higher levels of economic opportunity which can spawn local entrepreneurs by creating the opportunities for small business and the stimulus for development of professional management.

Finally, marketing contributes to the development of standards for economic behavior, integrity, and product and service reliability. In many underdeveloped countries, there is a painful lack of standards of morality in business and personal relationships.

17. Discuss the economic and trade importance of the big emerging markets.

    The Department of Commerce estimates that over 75 percent of the expected growth in the world trade over the next two decades will come from the more than 130 developing and newly industrialized countries (NICs). There is a small core of these that will account for over half of that growth. They predict that the countries identified as Big Emerging Markets (BEMs) alone will be a bigger import market by the end of this decade than the European Union and by the year 2010, will be importing more than the EU and Japan combined.

    The BEMs differ from other developing countries because they import more than smaller markets an more than economies of similar size. As they embark on economic development, demand for capital goods to build their manufacturing base and develop infrastructure increases. Increased economic activity means more jobs and more income to spend on products not yet produced locally. Thus, as their economies expand, there is an accelerated growth in demand for goods and services, much of which must be imported. BEM merchandise imports are expected to be nearly one trillion dollars higher than they were in 1990; if services are added, the amount jumps beyond one trillion dollars.

18. What are the traits of those countries considered to be big emerging markets? Discuss

    Those BEMs, as the Department of Commerce refers to them, share a number of important traits: They are all physically large; have significant populations; represent considerable markets for a wide range of products; all have strong rates of growth or the potential for significant growth have all undertaken significant problems of economic reforms; are all of major political importance within their regions; are "regional economic drivers;" will engender further expansion in neighboring markets as they grow.

    While these criteria are general ion nature and each country does not meet all the criteria, the Department of Commerce has identified the following BEMs. In **Asia**: *China, Indonesia, India, and*

*South Korea*. In **Latin America:** *Mexico, Argentina, and Brazil*. In **Africa**: *South Africa*. In **Central Europe**: *Poland*. In **Southern Europe**: *Turkey*. Vietnam, Thailand, Venezuela, and Columbia may warrant inclusion in the near future. The list is fluid in that some countries will drop off while others will be added as economic conditions change. The message is clear, the Department of Commerce is focusing on countries that demonstrate the greatest potential for growth.

19. Discuss how the economic growth of BEMs is analogous to the situation after World War II when tremendous demand was created during the reconstruction of Europe. As Europe rebuilt its infrastructure and industrial base, demand for capital goods exploded and, as more money was infused into its economies, consumer demand also increased rapidly. For more than a decade, Europe could not supply its increasing demand for industrial and consumer goods. During that period, the U.S. was the principal supplier since most of the rest of the world was rebuilding or had underdeveloped economies. Meeting this demand produced one of the largest economic booms the United States had ever experienced. Now Japan, Europe and NICs will become fierce rivals in emerging markets.

20. Discuss the problems a marketer might encounter when considering the socialist countries as a market.

    Contrasting political systems and economic philosophies account for the major differences in the trade characteristics of Eastern and Western countries. For example: Within a nonsocialist economy, supply and demand are the most important determinants of price. However, in socialist countries national goals for economic development are more critical determinants for pricing policies than are demand characteristics of the market. In addition, because of centralized planning, most, if not all, trade is conducted by state trading organizations rather than by individual profit-oriented end users as is the situation in most Western economies. As a consequence, suppliers very rarely are able to negotiate directly with the final user of a product. Arrangements for sales require contact with the trading companies or national buying agencies. Thus purchase patterns and demand estimations are different; promotion and advertising must be approached differently; and methods of payments and a demand for certain class of goods may be different than in Western countries. The three items with the greatest difference found are: (1) in estimating market demand, especially future demand, (2) the process of communicating with end users and decision makers, and (3) negotiating a trade.

21. One of the ramifications of emerging markets is the creation of a middle class. Discuss.

    One of the ramifications of emerging markets is the creation of a middle class household that generates new markets for everything from disposable diapers to automobiles. Middle-class in emerging markets differs from that in the United States. Whey they do not have two automobiles and suburban homes, they have discretionary income that is income not needed for food, clothing and shelter. It is income that can be spent on goods such as washing machines, TVs radios, better clothing, and special treats. Examining how income is spent in households between developing and developed countries reveals that more household money goes for food in emerging markets than in developed markets. Second to food, the next category of high expenditure for emerging and developed alike is appliances and other durables; Iran and India are the exceptions.

    When incomes rise, so do consumer appetites for everything from soap to automobiles despite low per capita incomes. How can those who earn $100 a month be a lucrative consumer market? Officially, per capita income in China is under $400 a year. But nearly every independent study by academics and multi-lateral agencies put income, adjusted for black market activity and purchasing power parity, at three or four times that level. Further, large households can translate into higher disposable incomes. Young working people in Asia and Latin America usually live at home until they marry. With no rent to pay, they have more discretionary income and can contribute to household purchasing power. Low per capita incomes are potential markets for a variety of goods; consumers show remarkable resourcefulness in finding ways to buy what really matters to them. In the United States, the first satellite dishes sprang up in the poorest parts of Appalachia. Similarly, the poorest slums of Calcutta are home to 70,000 VCRs and in Mexico, homes with color televisions outnumber those with running water.

A London securities firm says a person earning $250 annually in developing countries can afford Gillette razors, and at $1,000 he can become a Sony television owner. A Nissan or Volkswagen could be possible with a $10,000 income. Whirlpool estimates that in Eastern Europe a family with an annual income of $1,000 can afford a refrigerator and with $2,000 they can buy an automatic washer as well.

22. The needs and wants of a market and the ability to satisfy them are the result of the triune interaction of the economy, culture, and marketing efforts of business.

    The statement recognizes the point that markets are not static, but are constantly changing, and that change can be influenced by changes in the economy, changes in the culture, and, certainly, changes brought about by businesses. For example, the very fact that a business offers a product for sale in a market can and frequently does have an affect on the way that market perceives its needs and wants. The important part of this statement is the recognition of the dynamic nature of markets and the interaction of all the efforts of business, the economy, and all the culture.

23. Discuss changing market behavior and the idea that "markets are not, they become."

    There is an ever-expanding and changing demand for goods and services the world over. Markets are dynamic, developing entities reflecting the changing lifestyles of a culture–they become different, larger, and more demanding as they mature. When economies grow and markets evolve beyond subsistence levels, the range of tastes, preferences, and variations of products sought by the consumer proliferate; they demand more, better, and/or different products. As countries prosper and their people are exposed to new ideas and behavior patterns via global communications networks, old stereotypes, traditions, and habits are cast aside or tempered, and new patterns of consumer behavior emerge. Instant tortilla meal is consumed in Guatemala, hot dogs and hamburgers in France and traditional market vendors and specialty stores give way to supermarkets and 24-hour convenience stores. With these changes come opportunity and the need for sophisticated marketing strategies.

    Markets evolve from a three-way interaction of the economy, the culture, and the marketing efforts of companies. *Markets are not, they become*, that is, they are not static but are constantly changing as they affect and are affected by changes in incomes, awareness of different life styles, exposure to new products and exposure to new ideas. Changing incomes raise expectations and the ability to buy more and different goods. The accessibility of global communications, TV, radio, and print media means that people in one part of the world are aware of lifestyles in another. Global companies span the globe with new ideas on consumer behavior and new products to try. With the prosperity that results from economic growth, markets grow and distinct segments begin to emerge.

24. Discuss the strategic implications for marketing in India.

    The IT revolution is not limited to broad, long range economic goals but, as Exhibit 9–2 illustrates, it can have almost immediate impact upon the poorest in an emerging country.

    The eleventh largest industrial economy in the world, India has a population of approximately one billion, of which 200 to 250 million are considered middle class. The modern sector demands products and services similar to those available in any industrialized country; the remaining 750 million in the traditional sector, however, demand items more indigenous and basic to subsistence. As one authority on India's market observed, "A rural Indian can live a sound life without many products. Toothpaste, sugar, coffee, washing soap, bathing soap, kerosene are all bare necessities of life to those who live in semi-urban and urban areas."

    India not only stands firmly at the center of many success stories in Silicon Valley (Indian engineers provide some 30 percent of the workforce for California's Silicon Valley) but is seeing Internet enthusiasm build to frenzy on its own shores. Indian entrepreneurs and capital are creating an Indian Silicon Valley of their own. Dubbed "Cyberabad," exports are growing 50 percent annually and each worker adds $27,000 of value per year, an extraordinary figure in a country where per capita GDP is below $500. After a little more than a decade of growth, the Indian industry has an estimated 280,000 software engineers in about 1,000 companies.

Similar investments are being made in Latin America and Eastern Europe as countries see the technology revolution as a means to leapfrog their economic and social development. As one economist commented, "Traditional economic reforms in the 1980s and 1990s managed to stop hyper-inflation and currency crises, but further change will not produce significant new growth needed to combat poverty. Governments must work to provide public access to the Internet and other information technologies."

25. Too much emphasis is usually laid by Chinese policymakers as well as by foreign businessmen on China's strength as an export machine. China is so big that its economic potential might more usefully be compared with continental America's. Discuss fully.

In the long run the economic strength of China will not be as an exporting machine but as a vast market. The economic strength of the United States comes from its resources, productivity and vast internal market that drive its economy. China's future potential might better be compared with America's economy driven by domestic demand rather than Japan's driven by exports. China is neither an economic paradise nor an economic wasteland, but a relatively poor nation going through a painfully awkward transformation from a socialist market system to a hybrid socialist/free-market system, not yet complete and with the rules of the game still being written.

# Chapter 10 – Multinational Market Regions and Market Groups

## Teaching Objectives

The two most important trends in international marketing today are the emerging markets discussed in Chapter 9 and the creation and growing importance of the multinational regional market alliances. The EU has continued to evolve despite serious wrangling among its members but more far reaching for the next decades are the creation of NAFTA and its probable expansion, the serious discussion occurring among Pacific Rim countries to create APEC, Asia-Pacific Economic Cooperation and almost, overnight, discussions by both EU officials and the United States on creating a North Atlantic Free Trade Area (see, for example, Lionel Barber, "Does America Need A Contract with Europe?" Europe, pp. 6–16.) The overall objectives of this chapter are to explore the various patterns of multinational cooperation and the strategic marketing implications of economic cooperation for marketing. The teaching objectives are to:

1) Explore the patterns of multinational economic cooperation in different regions of the world – the Americas, Europe, Asia, Africa, and Middle East.
2) Review the history and current status of European cooperation from the early days of the European Common Market to the EU and its expansion beyond Western Europe to include Eastern Europe.
3) Review the evolution of NAFTA and its implications for Latin America.
4) Review economic cooperation in Asia from ASEAN to AFTA and on the APEC.

## Comments and Suggestions

1. As a basis for a general discussion of economic cooperation I use the factors discussed in the section "La Rasion d'Etre" in the text. I ask students to prepare questions 21 and 22 and then have them contribute their evaluations to the class discussion. The important point in this exercise is that not all the factors are positive but any major weakness in any one factor must be offset by overwhelming strength in the others. Many of the disagreements among members of the EU can be attributed to differences in one factor or another between members. TM 10–1, Successful Economic Union Requirements, lists the factors discussed in the text.
2. I suggest ending the chapter on multinational market regions and market groups with a discussion of future multinational market groups. This will provide an opportunity to challenge the students to ponder several questions about free trade in a world that is divided into regional trade groups: What will become of those countries not part of a regional trade group?; What will Japan's role be in Asia?; What are the implications if the U.S. enters into an agreement with the EU and also enters an agreement with APEC? (See, for example, Clinton Shiells, "Regional Trade Blocs: Trade Creating or Diverting?", Finance & Development, March 1995, pp. 30–32 for an interesting review of the impact of regional trade blocs). The questions are endless but relevant to trade over the coming decades. This is a good way to end this part of the course before moving to the last section on developing marketing strategies.

## Lecture Outline

Multinational Market Regions and Market Groups

I. Global Perspective—Free Trade Means Losing Jobs—or Does It?

II. La Raison d'être

   A. Economic Factors

   B. Political Factors

C. Geographic Proximity
D. Cultural Factors

III. Patterns of Multinational Cooperation
  A. Regional Cooperation Groups
  B. Free-Trade Area
  C. Custom Union
  D. Common Market
  E. Political Union

IV. Global Markets and Multinational Market Groups

V. Europe
  A. European Community
    1. The Single European Act
    2. EC Institutions
    3. European Free-Trade Area (EFTA) and European Economic Area (EEA)
  B. European Union and Maastricht Treaty
    1. Economic and Monetary Union (EMU)
  C. The Treaty of Amsderdam
  D. EU Expansion
  E. Strategic Implications for Marketing in Europe
    1. Opportunities
    2. Market Barriers
    3. Reciprocity
    4. Marketing Mix Implications
    5. The Commonwealth of Independent States (CIS)
    6. Central European Free-Trade Agreement (CEFTA)

VI. The Americas
  A. The North American Free Trade Area (NAFTA)
  B. NAFTA: A Progress Report
  C. Southern Cone Free Trade Area (MERCOSUR)
  D. Latin American Economic Cooperation
    1. Latin American Integration Association (LAIA)
    2. The Andean Common Market (ANCOM)
    3. Caribbean Community and Common Market (CARICOM)
  E. NAFTA to FTAA or SAFTA?

VII. Asian Pacific Rim
  A. Association of Southeast Asian Nations (ASEAN)
  B. Asia-Pacific Economic Cooperation

VIII. Africa

IX. Middle East

X. Regional Trading Groups and Emerging Markets

XI. Summary

## DISCUSSION QUESTIONS

1. Define:

| | |
|---|---|
| United States–Canada Free Trade Agreement | Free-trade area |
| EMU | Customs union |
| Single European Act | Common market |
| NAFTA | Political union |
| AFTA | Maastricht treaty |
| Mercosur | Treaty of Amsterdam |
| APEC | ASEAN+3 |

2. Elaborate on the problems and benefits for international marketers from multinational market groups.

   A multinational market group has both problems and benefits for an international marketer, although the benefits far exceed the disadvantages. A multinational market group (comprised of a number of individual countries) has two important goals. The first of these is to limit and eventually eliminate tariffs between member countries. The second is to agree to common external tariffs on all imports from nonmember countries. The first goal or policy of the participating countries increases internal commerce. Each member may specialize in the area in which that country has a relative advantage. The policy of having no internal trade barriers is expected to be self-sufficient as a result of the increase in trade within the market, hence hampering imports from international markets outside the multination group. The second policy, of a uniform external tariff on all imports entering the group, and uniform export rates on all goods leaving the group, will usually increase exports for the international marketer for the following reasons:

   a. The uniform external tariff will usually be much lower than for any individual country, because such a common market also believes in the benefits of world trade.

   b. It is easier for the international marketer to deal with a greater and more uniform market, rather than being troubled by all kinds of peculiar tariffs and restrictions of smaller markets (i.e., nations).

   c. A multinational market group, by specialization and keener cooperation, gains a higher economic base. Thus a higher standard of living is established. The inhabitants will then have more purchasing power, creating a demand for more goods; therefore, a market for outside imports will be created.

   This means benefits both to the multinational market group, as well as the international marketer.

3. Explain the political role of multinational market groups.

   The political role of a multinational market group is of importance if such a market is to be economically successful. This is a touchy subject because any nation has created throughout history a sensitive image called national sovereignty, i.e., feelings, rights, and often imaginary national power. A nation is not likely to give up these things easily, but some have realized that they must, to gain the benefits a multinational market group can yield.

   The United States is fortunate in having such a relatively young history. There is no ancient tradition in this country as there definitely still is in European nations. This is a major reason why it has taken such a long time to establish a common economic market in Europe. Finally, after two worldwide conflicts that both started in the historical trouble zone, Europe, eventually six European nations gave up some of their national sovereignty and united in a beneficial undertaking, the European Common Market in 1957.

There is a long route in establishing a common market containing all of Western Europe. Because of tradition and national feelings, the "outer 7" countries found the Treaty of Rome to interfere with the individual nation's rights, in a political way. They, instead, formed a looser type of multinational market, the European Free Trade Association (a title somewhat misleading), the EFTA.

The more closely politically tied EC has been far more successful than the looser collaboration of EFTA. EFTA members currently have become very eager to accept the Treaty of Rome and thus join the EC. In the future, there is hope of making all Western Europe economically strong, creating a powerful third bloc to act as a balancing power between the two powers of today. The political role of a multinational market group is important, even universally. In judging the political success or failure of a multinational group, it is possible to refer to the EC and the EFTA. Although EFTA is not a failure, it has had a limited success compared with the more politically bound EC. A better example may be LAFTA (now LAIA), in which Latin American countries have shown great political controversies. The group might be characterized as a failure.

4. Identify the factors on which one may judge the potential success or failure of a multinational market group.

   The political factors necessary for a successful common market are: (1) similar political base, views, and objectives, and (2) willingness to give up some national sovereignty to cooperate for the total benefit of all.

5. Explain the marketing implications of the factors contributing to the successful development of a multinational marketing group.

   There are at least four basic types of factors that must be favorable and which must fit smoothly together for any form of multinational market group to be successful: (1) economic, (2) political, (3) social, and (4) geographic. Of these factors, the economic factor is primary. The foremost goal of any market group is to become economically strong, but the other factors must also be present and in too weak a form to provide sufficient strength to build up the market. To expand such a market, increased trade is important, both within the market boundaries as well as outside these boundaries.

   Marketing is the feat of distributing commodities. In this manner, marketing introduces trade, which in turn introduces economic growth. In the developing of a multinational market group, marketing methods practiced to increase trade have pointed the way to create strong economic entities.

   Such marketing forms, to be implemented after World War II, include the establishment of lower trade barriers, long-term development loans, and liquid short-term funds, all of which cause world trade to grow. GATT, IMF, IBRD, and the U.S. Marshall Plan for the reconstruction of war-torn Europe; all can be viewed as marketing implements used by the United States to reestablish a bankrupt area and help it become a valuable source for international trade.

   By the formation of OEEC in 1948, the United States, by channeling 12 1/2 billion dollars to its members, gave a tangible demonstration of the benefits of economic cooperation, which soon led to the founding of multinational market groups. First was the establishment of the European Coal and Steel Community in 1951, which was the forerunner of the EEC.

6. Imagine that the United States was composed of many separate countries with individual trade barriers. What marketing effects might one visualize?

   The greatest asset the United States has is being the world's largest common market. If this were to be destroyed by interstate regulations of tariff boundaries and trade barriers, this would be a disaster for the U.S. economy. The marketing difficulties would be enormous when trading between states. Import-export restrictions, quotas, tariffs might exist. Although the basic marketing principles would be the same, their applications would vary from state to state. The international marketer meets the same sort of differentiation's when dealing with different individual nations abroad.

This separation of states would result in a decrease of trade between the states with the consequence of each individual state being self-sufficient rather than specializing, and marketing practices would become more limited and specialized and probably more dishonest and less ethical.

7. Discuss the possible types of arrangements for regional economic integration.

   There is usually considered to be four types of regional economic integration arrangements:

   I. Free Trade Associations

   II. Custom Unions

   III. Common Markets

   IV. Political Unions

   I. Free Trade Associations are the weakest forms of regional economic integration. Their key function is to facilitate easier trading within their area. Each individual membercountry keeps its own external barriers against nonmembers, and there is no provision for free flow of labor and capital within the group. Although limited, their members' cooperative ventures have important trade benefits to the international marketer who, to a certain degree, can view such an area as one unit. At least he knows what each member-country stands for economically and politically, and why they have agreed to form a free trade association. Also, such an attitude is important for facilitating world commerce.

   II. A Custom Union is a logical stage in the development of multinational market groups, standing between a free trade association and a common market, although no free custom union is in existence today. In addition to the internal trade liberations of a free trade association, a custom union would establish a common external tariff for imports from outside the union. The Be-Ne-Lux nations were the best example of a custom union that is known. They were in existence before they joined the European Common Market.

   III. A Common Market adds further elements to facilitate international trade that in effect makes it become a common marketplace, not only for goods, but also for services (labor), and for capital. It is to a far extent a unified economy lacking only political unity to become one state. The objectives of a common market are: (1) the elimination of tariffs within the market, (2) a common external tariff, (3) a common antitrust law, and (4) removal of restrictions on movement of capital and manpower, and tax harmonization.

   IV. A Political Union of commercial matters is either voluntary or enforced. Typical of the voluntary type is the British Commonwealth. Its very loose form of cooperation provides easier trading terms among its members and provides that the commodities of necessity (i.e., what the United Kingdom needs the most from its former colonies) should primarily be traded within the Commonwealth. COMECON is the typical example of the enforced type. It was made up of the U.S.S.R. and its East European satellites. Its existence was mainly as a counterforce to the establishment of NATO and EEC. It was a failure, politically and economically, and with the dissolution of the USSR and independence of Eastern Europe, COMECON was disbanded.

8. Differentiate between a free trade area and a common market. Explain the marketing implication of the differences.

   A free trade area and a common market have at least one common objective: to eliminate tariffs within their respective boundaries. In addition, a common market has the far more fetching goals of a common external tariff, a common antitrust law, and the removal of restrictions on movement of capital and manpower, and tax harmonization.

   A common external tariff, that usually will be lower than the individual external tariffs of any free trade nation-member, makes it easier for the international marketer to enter and operate in a common market, a large area of individual, but economically and politically cooperating nations. (That is also what EEC intended, but for the time being to a somewhat limited degree because of "les grand Charles.")

Common antitrust laws advocate that nay foreign investor or marketer should be able to compete on the same level as native firms. Cartels should not exist.

Abolition of capital movement restrictions makes it easier for any foreign marketer's currency to be accepted, and free flow of manpower makes such a market even more united. Tax harmonization makes it easier for the international marketer to enter any of the member-nations as the base for his marketing ventures, instead of having small plants in each separate nation, as the case might still be in a free trade association. Now, one large plant in one of the common market member-countries can supply the rest of the members from this base source more economically.

All these additional trade facilitating arrangements in a common market make it easier and more lucrative for the international marketer to operate effectively and with more profits and opportunity in a larger, closer-tied unity.

9. It seems indeed obvious that the founders of the European Community intended it to be a true common market; so much so that economic integration must obviously be supplemented by political integration in order to accomplish these objectives completely. Discuss.

   The Treaty of Rome signed by the EC members in 1957 spells out their obligations. This document also touches the political role of a fully economically integrated market. It directly refers to the nations' sovereign rights, the rights which so many other European nations at that time could not give up, and instead formed EFTA (The outer 7), which does not have any political clauses.

   Today, nearly a decade later, although some misfortunes have occurred, the more tightly politically knit EC has shown to be far more effective than EFTA. Hence, for a trade union to be effective and most prosperous, political as well as economic integration is necessary.

10. The European Commission, the Council of Ministers, and the Court of Justice of the EC have gained power in the last decade. Comment.

   As the European Community has become more economically interdependent, the Community's institutions, the Commission, the Council of Ministers, and the Court of Justice, have gained in their influence over business dealings among member countries. For example, the European Commission has recently won the right to take part in consultations on European Community foreign policy. This is a significant step in enhancing its importance among the governments of the ten member countries. Also, the European Commission has been active in exercising its powers of investigation over unfair trading practices by member countries. In addition, the Court of Justice has become very important in enforcing Community laws and regulations. Other examples of the influence of these three branches of the European Community are the attempts by the Commission to harmonize trademark law among its members and establish an EC trademark versus trademarks in each member country; there is also a move under way to allow lawyers to practice law as EC attorneys, and most antitrust enforcement is now handled by the European Commission. The only question that remains is when the European Commission would reach the point where it controls more of the economic activity among its members than individual member countries do. The European Community is moving rapidly toward that.

11. Select any three countries which might have some logical basis for establishing a multinational market organization (such as Canada, United States, and Mexico). Identify the various problems which would be encountered in forming multinational market groups of such countries.

   Individual research (sample below).

Assumptions: Canada, United States, and Mexico establishing a common market. Problems that will arise are:

a. Difference in economic as well as political base (especially Mexico) will indeed hinder the validity and possibly the duration of such a market.

b. The relative advantages of the United States and Canada in nearly all industrial products will force Mexico to give up most of its industry and instead try to specialize in whatever it may have comparative advantage, and that is not comparable with the United States and Canada. There may be some semitropical agricultural consumer products.

c. There would be an invasion of Mexican labor especially to the United States to seek higher wages, but few, if any North American laborers would go "south of the border" with little opportunity of good wages. The result would be an increase in unemployment.

d. Mexico would become a recreation resort for North Americans and would perhaps specialize in that area, making a decent income as the result of the free flow of capital from the North in such investments.

e. Not relevant to an arbitrary example as this; in reality Canada asa member of the British Commonwealth, could not engage in any such collaboration as this one with the United States and Mexico without losing her privileges in the United Kingdom.

12. U. S. exports to the European Community are expected to decline in future years. What marketing actions may a company take to counteract such changes?

An economic unity such as the EC is primarily concerned with increases of trade within its member-countries because they want to raise their own production and gain through economic growth that their specialized members can supply. It may be said that the EC wants to decrease their trade with nonmember nations. One study has shown some proportional declines already.

What the U.S. marketer should do to counteract such actions is to, as rapidly as possible, expand exports to this market. More important, the marketers should build new and expand EC-located, U.S.-owned industries and marketing facilities to strengthen their position before it becomes too late. EC members are now busy building new plants and establishing their outlets and markets. From the U.S. foreign marketer's point of view, there is no time to waste, otherwise they will lose some of the grip they have established in Europe.

Also, keeping in mind that many other Western European countries are again interested in joining EC. The typical argument: "It will be too expensive to stay outside." A sound policy for American companies wanting or dependent upon marketing in the European market might increase their potential in EFTA.

13. "Because they are dynamic and because they have great growth possibilities, the multinational markets are likely to be especially rough-and-tumble for the external business." Discuss.

The attractive growth and profit opportunities in multinational markets tend to draw the more aggressive marketers into competition. Whereas, a company may have virtually no competition in its home market, it may be competing with three or four major firms in the multinational market. National interest gives preferential treatment of various types to firms from member nations and intensifies the normal market competition.

14. Differentiate between a full customs union and a political union.

A full customs union would reduce or eliminate internal duties and establish a common external tariff. A political union, either voluntary or enforced, has no such clauses. A political union (especially a voluntary one such as the British Commonwealth) is the loosest form to be classified as an economic integration, and must depend on political logic for success, more than the strict objectives of the full customs union.

15. Why have African nations had such difficulty in forming effective economic unions?

African common market activities are affected by the following factors:

1. Most national governments are not strong in Africa.
2. Government turnover.
3. Poor communications between countries.
4. Many rivalries exist between countries and within national subgroups.
5. All are extremely poor and jealous of giving up sovereignty.
6. Many are new to the roles of self-government and cooperation.
7. Many have similar economies and economic base.

16. Discuss the implications of the European Union's decision to admit Eastern European nations to the group.

The admission of Eastern European nations into the EU will create an ever larger and more economically important than the present EU. The globalization of markets, the restructuring of Eastern Europe into independent market-driven economies, the dissolution of the Soviet Union into independent states, the worldwide trend toward economic cooperation, and enhanced global competition make it important that market potential be viewed in the context of regions of the world rather than country by country. Formal economic cooperation agreements such as the EC are the most notable examples of multinational market groups but many new coalitions are forming, old ones are being re-energized, and the possibility of many new cooperative arrangements is on the horizon.

17. Discuss the consequences to the United States of not being a part of the SAFTA.

Not to be an active participant in the FTAA and not to be able to influence the final architecture of the FTAA could be a blow to the U.S. economy and trade. As a market for U.S. goods, the Western Hemisphere is nearly twice as large as the European Union and nearly 50 percent larger than Asia. Moreover, between 1960 and 1996 U.S. goods exports globally increased 57 percent but U.S. exports to Latin America (excluding Mexico) increased by 110 percent. If these trends were to continue, Latin America alone could exceed Japan and Western Europe combined as an export market for U.S. goods by 2010

With or without U.S. influence, FTAA continues to evolve but it may evolve into a South American Free Trade Area (SAFTA) with Mercosur at the center providing the necessary drive. Mercosur's negotiations with Canada are going smoothly since Canadian business supports the FTAA and the Canadian government is a strong champion of liberalized trade. Negotiations underway with Europe and the rest of South America also seem positive. Other countries are also getting involved with their own negotiations. A meeting with the Pacific Economic Cooperation Council (PECC) was organized by Chile to discuss establishing a partnership between Pacific Asia and Latin America. Chile was praised as performing a most laudable role as the gateway for Pacific Asia (East Asia and Australia, New Zealand) into Latin America.

18. Discuss the strategic marketing implications of the Canada-United States-Mexico Free Trade Agreement.

NAFTA affects a variety of strategic issues, the most important of which are:

**Market Access.** Within 10 years of implementation, all tariffs will be eliminated on North American industrial products traded between Canada, Mexico, and the United States. All trade between Canada and the U.S. not already duty free will be duty free by 1998 as provided for in CFTA. Mexico will immediately eliminate tariffs on nearly 50 percent of all industrial goods imported from the U.S., and remaining tariffs will be phased out entirely within 15 years.

**Nontariff Barriers.** In addition to elimination of tariffs, Mexico will eliminate nontariff barriers and other trade-distorting restrictions. U.S. exporters will benefit immediately from the removal of most import licenses that have acted as quotas essentially limiting the importation of products into the Mexican market. NAFTA also eliminates a host of other Mexican barriers such as local content, local production, and export performance requirements that have limited U.S. exports.

**Rules of Origin.** NAFTA reduces tariffs only for goods made in North America. Tough rules of origin will determine whether goods qualify for preferential tariff treatment under NAFTA. Rules of origin are designed to prevent "free riders" from benefiting through minor processing or transshipment of non-NAFTA goods. For example, Japan could not assemble autos in Mexico and avoid U.S. or Canadian tariffs and quotas unless the auto had a specific percentage of Mexican (i.e., North American) content. For goods to be traded duty free, they must contain substantial (62.5 percent) North American content. Since NAFTA rules of origin have been strengthened, clarified, and simplified over those contained in the U.S.-Canada Free Trade Agreement, they supersede the CFTA rules.

**Customs Administration.** Under NAFTA, Canada, Mexico, and the U.S. have agreed to implement uniform customs procedures and regulations. Uniform procedures ensure that exporters who market their products in more than one NAFTA country will not have to adapt to multiple customs procedures. Most procedures governing rules of origin documentation record keeping, and origin verification will be the same for all three NAFTA countries. In addition, the three will issue advanced rulings, on request, on whether or not a product qualifies for tariff preference under the NAFTA rules of origin.

**Investment.** NAFTA will eliminate investment conditions that restrict the trade of goods and service to Mexico. Among conditions eliminated are the requirements that foreign investors export a given level or percentage of goods or services, use domestic goods or services, transfer technology to competitors, or limit imports to a certain percentage of exports.

**Services.** NAFTA establishes the first comprehensive set of principles governing services trade. U.S. and Canadian financial institutions are permitted to open wholly owned subsidiaries in Mexico, and all restrictions on the services they offer will be lifted by the year 2000. U.S. and Canadian trucking companies are able to carry international cargo into Mexican border states and, by 1999, they will be able to truck throughout Mexico.

**Intellectual Property.** NAFTA will provide the highest standards of protection of intellectual property available in any bilateral or international agreement. The agreement covers patents, trademarks, copyrights, and trade secrets, semiconductor integrated circuits, copyrights for North American movies, computer software, and records.

**Government Procurement.** NAFTA guarantees businesses fair and open competition for procurement in North America through transparent and predictable procurement procedures. In Mexico, Pemex (national oil company), CFE (national electric company), and other government-owned enterprises will be open to U.S. and Canadian suppliers.

**Standards.** NAFTA prohibits the use of standards and technical regulations used as obstacles to trade. However, NAFTA provisions do not require the United States or Canada to lower existing health, environmental, or safety regulations, nor does NAFTA require the importation of products that fail to meet each country's health and safety standards.

19. How is the concept of reciprocity linked to protectionism?

Reciprocity is an important part to the trade policy of Europe 1992. If a country does not open its markets to an E.C. firm, it cannot expect to have access to the E.C. market. Europeans see reciprocity as a fair and equitable way of allowing foreign companies to participate in the European Market without erecting trade barriers while at the same time giving Europeans equal access to foreign markets. There are strong feelings that the Japanese market is not equally accessible to foreign firms and reciprocity addresses such inequities. The community will not grant trade concessions to Japan if Japan fails to reciprocate for European exporters. Reciprocity is to be directed to all outsiders. A French government-sponsored advertisement on TV captured the European attitude. As the advertisement opens, "a skinny French boxer is squaring off to battle a giant American football player and a menacing Japanese sumo wrestler. Suddenly 11 buddies–the rest of the E.C. of course–rush to his side, and the aggressors turn away."

While the U.S.-Canada FTA does not have a reciprocity clause, it contains safeguards to prevent products of third countries from being shipped through one of the FTA parties to avoid tariffs. The agreement contains rules of origin to prevent such products from profiting from the benefits of FTA tariff elimination. A crucial decision for MN's will be whether or not to invest within market groups in order to secure access to other member countries. However, investment within the EC is not a guarantee of access to the entire market unless the home country of the MNC is willing to offer European companies the same privileges.

20. Visit the Web pages for NAFTA (www.mac.doc) (www.gov/nafta/nafta2.htm) and Mercosur (http://mercosur.com or www.mercosur.org/english/) and locate each group's rules of origin. Which group has the most liberal rules of origin? Why the difference?

Students will have to do some intensive searching to determine the rules of origin. However, the purpose behind this exercise is to get students familiar with NAFTA in some detail. The rules of origin for NAFTA, in short, only goods which qualify under the NAFTA rules of origin can obtain NAFTA tariff preference, i.e., reduced or eliminated tariffs. The NAFTA rules of origin take into account where goods are produced and what materials are used to produce them. The purpose is to ensure that North American goods traded among the three NAFTA partner countries receive preferential tariff treatment. Products of other countries merely being transhipped through or undergoing only minor operations in North America are not eligible for NAFTA benefits.

The NAFTA sets out four "origin criteria," meaning that there are four ways in which goods generally meet the NAFTA rule of origin, and therefore qualify for NAFTA tariff preference.

A. Goods "wholly produced or obtained" in the NAFTA region, i.e., they contain no non-NAFTA material.

B. Goods containing non-originating inputs, but meeting the Annex 401 origin rules.

C. Goods produced in the NAFTA region wholly from originating materials, i.e. produced from materials which may contain non-NAFTA materials, but meet the NAFTA rule of origin.

D. Unassembled goods and goods classified in same (HS) Harmonized System category as their parts, which do not meet the Annex 401 rule of origin, but contain sufficient North American regional value content. (Goods qualify in this category only in very limited circumstances.)

The mercosur.com site above is in Spanish and at the time this was written (1998) the second Mercosur site was still under construction. If the site is not complete, students will have to search other sources for information. One other possibility is to substitute the rules of origin for APEC countries which can be found at http://apecsun.apecsec.org.sg . The rules of origin are:

## Rules of Origin

Rules of origin (ROO) are the basis on which the country of origin of goods is determined for international trade purposes. They are used to determine the country in which goods have been produced or manufactured in cases where the production or manufacture took place in more than one country. These rules are necessary to ensure that provisions applying selectively on the basis of origin are not avoided by minimal processing, trade diversion and similar circumvention methods.

There are two types of ROO:

### Non-preferential Rules of Origin

Non-preferential rules of origin are important for a number of reasons, including the application of tariffs, quotas, dumping and marketing of goods.

### Preferential rules of origin

Preferential rules of origin are used to determine goods which may enter a country under preferential treatment. That is, they are used to establish whether the goods are eligible for special treatment under a trading arrangement between two or more economies. Preferential (or reduced) rates of duty are applied to goods which are found to be the products or manufacture of a country defined as a preference country. The principal objective of preferential rules of origin is to ensure that benefits are restricted to those goods which originate and are traded within the particular preference area.

## Substantial Transformation

Annex D1 of the International Kyoto Convention provided the international basis for signatories to determine the origin of goods produced in more than one country. Without being definitive about the process, it indicated that the origin of goods should be determined by the last/final country in which "substantial transformation" of the goods took place. It indicated that "substantial transformation" could be determined by applying one of three different methods:

- percentage of value added;
- change in tariff heading; or
- specified process of manufacture.

Within APEC, some economies use the "value-added" method, others use the "change in tariff heading" method, and some use a combination, as a means of determining substantial transformation and thereby the origin of products.

## Value-added

Under this method, a minimum percentage of the value of a good must have been added within the country or preferential area for which origin is being claimed. There are a range of minimum percentages applied under different trade agreements described in this compendium. There may also be other requirements which need to be satisfied.

## Change in Tariff Heading

Under this method, "substantial transformation" is said to have occurred if a good is classified to a different tariff heading than that of its component materials after production

In some specific instances, change of tariff heading alone will not necessarily confer origin. In such instances, supplementary criteria must be used to determine whether the change in tariff heading confers origin.

**Specified Process of Manufacture**

Under this method, the origin is based on the country in which a specified manufacturing or processing operation for a specific product is undertaken.

**Generalized System of Preferences**

The Generalized System of Preferences (GSP) is a system subscribed to by many countries, which gives preferential treatment to developing countries on certain types of goods. The GSP will not be discussed in this compendium, but a comprehensive account of it may be found in the United Nations Conference on Trade and Development (UNCTAD) volume entitled *Digest of Rules of Origin: Generalized System of Preferences*. In this compendium, some APEC members have chosen to list GSP-based preferential tariff treatments among their trade initiatives. However, this should not be taken as a comprehensive list of APEC members which subscribe to the GSP. For information on which countries subscribe to the GSP, please refer to the above-mentioned volume.

21. Using the factors that serve as the basis for success of an economic union (political, social, and geographic), evaluate the potential success of the EC, NAFTA, AFTA, and Mercosur.

    This question is designed to engender a discussion of the factors for success of an economic union. Individual student responses will offer but they should all reflect the understanding that even if there isn't communality on the factors among members countries, strengths in one or two can override weaknesses in the others. Also that outside factors may be strong enough to bring a group of countries together with a commitment to overcome differences. The fear of communism was an important reason for former enemies in Europe to put their differences aside for economic union. Nevertheless, economic difference and social/cultural differences continue to be a problem for the EC.

    NAFTA members are economically and socially different but the concern for the strength of the EU and the desire for the three countries to bind more closely economically were important reasons for the creation of NAFTA. Yet, cultural, social, political and economic differences will cause problems and the long-term success of NAFTA will depend on how strong is the desire for economic integration and the concern for other regional trading groups.

    Of all the four, MERCOSUR members may have the most in common on all the factors except perhaps the economic dimension.

22. For each regional trade group—EC, NAFTA, AFTA, ASEAN+3 and Mercosur—cite which of the factors for success are the strongest and which are the weakest. Discuss each factor.

    Students will have different responses to this question. The important point is if they realize the importance of the different factors on the ultimate success of any regional trade group. In most cases, there are cultural, social, economic, political and ever, geographical differences among country members. The critical point is if their commitment to economic integration is sufficiently strong to allow them to deal with the differences that will arise as a result. Each response to this question will be different. For what it is worth, the author would rank them as follows:

| | POLITICAL | ECONOMIC | SOCIAL | GEOGRAPHIC |
|---|---|---|---|---|
| EC | S | S to W | S | S |
| NAFTA | W to S | W to S | S to W | S |
| AFTA | S, | S | W to S | W to S |
| MERCOSUR | S to W | W to S | S | S |

23. What is the motive behind ASEAN+3 and what are the probable implications for global trade?

One result of the Asian financial crisis of 1997–98 was the creation of ASEAN+3 (ASEAN plus China, Japan and South Korea), to deal with trade and monetary issues facing Asia. Most East Asia felt that they were both let down and put upon by the West who they felt created much of the crisis by pulling out in the midst of the crisis. It was felt that the leading financial powers either declined to take part in the rescue operations, as the US did in Thailand, or that they proposed unattainable solutions. The result was the creation of ASEAN+3,[1] consisting of the foreign and finance ministers of each country, which meets annually after ASEAN meetings. Their first meeting was devoted to devising a system whereby they share foreign exchange reserves to defend their currencies against future attack. While still only tentative, there was also discussion among the members of ASEAN+3 of creating a common market and even a single currency or, perhaps, a new Asian entity encompassing both Northeast and Southeast Asia.[2] Closer links between Southeast Asia and Northeast Asia is seen as a step towards strengthening Asia's role in the global economy and the creation of a global three-block configuration.[3]

24. NAFTA has been in existence for several years, how has it done? Read the section in the text "North American Free-Trade Area (NAFTA)" that discusses the initial provisions of the agreement, and, using the Internet, evaluate how well the provisions have been met.

NAFTA is a comprehensive trade agreement that addresses, and in most cases improves, all aspects of doing business within North America. The elimination of trade and investment barriers among Canada, Mexico, and the United States creates one of the largest and richest markets in the world.

NAFTA has its detractors and it is safe to say that there has been constant turmoil since its inception-namely, Mexico had a serious financial crisis that led to the devaluation of the peso and the expansion of NAFTA became a political hot potato in the United States when it was severely politicized during the 1996 presidential election. Unfortunately, all the candidates presented a distorted picture. Opponents painted a picture of economic doom. One candidate claimed that NAFTA would produce a "giant sucking sound" of jobs running from the US to Mexico. Proponents created an equally distorted picture of economic bliss. Neither side presented a factual picture; first, it was much too early to estimate accurately the effect of NAFTA and second, during the short run, it was expected that jobs would be lost and companies displaced. Misinformation prevailed and the general public turned sour on NAFTA. With public opinion turning against the expansion to Chile, the next stage in the NAFTA agreement, it became obvious that a request for fast-track authorization was in jeopardy and the Clinton administration lost interest and NAFTA progress languished.[4] While none of its members advocated disbanding NAFTA, it did appear that the United States administration directed its attention elsewhere and did not follow through to the second stage-expansion beyond Mexico.

Depending on the source, NAFTA has been a "wash," a costly creator of deep U.S. trade deficits and job losses, or a success. A survey taken three years after its beginning revealed that 67 percent of the Mexicans surveyed believed that Mexico had had little or no success with NAFTA. In another study, 5 7 percent of U.S. citizens said they are against any new trade pacts with Latin American countries.

Regardless of such sentiments, a complete evaluation of the success or failure of NAFTA cannot be made until after 2008 when all the provisions are in place. Further, those companies and industries that are adversely affected by lowering tariffs and opening the U.S. market to Mexican and Canadian goods have not had time to adjust to the new trading environment.

---

[1] "Towards a Tripartite World," *The Economist*, July 13, 2000.
[2] Eric Teo, "ASEAN Needs East Asian Regionalism," *Jakarta Post*, August 30, 2000.
[3] Julius Ceasar Parrenas, "Step by Step, Asians Are Finally Getting Together," *International Herald Tribune*, May 2, 2000.
[4] Fast-track authority allows the President to negotiate trade agreements with the assurance that Congress will vote to either accept or reject the agreement without amendments or changes. Without fast track, countries are reluctant to negotiate seriously since the President cannot assure that agreements will survive Congressional approval intact.

Nevertheless, there have been some measurable positive results. The NAFTA Commission's most recent report indicates that trade among the countries has grown by about 75% since the Agreement came into force. From less than US$289 billion in 1993, trilateral trade reached US$507 billion in 1998.[5] Investment among the three has also significantly increased, with more than US$189 billion invested in each other's economies in 1997. Meanwhile, total foreign direct investment into the NAF has reached US$864 billion. Most importantly, job creation has surged in all three NAFTA countries with employment levels now at record highs. Since the NAFTA was implemented, employment in Canada has grown by 10. 1 percent (1.3 million jobs), by 22 percent (2.2 million jobs) in Mexico and by over 7 percent (12.8 million jobs) in the United States.

One of the major criticisms was that NAFTA would result in many manufacturing companies moving to Mexico thereby reducing the number of US manufacturing jobs. While some companies did move to Mexico, US manufacturing output is higher than at any other time in the nation's history and data does not show a major change in the number of jobs. Since 1991, the total number of men and women on the payrolls of U.S. manufacturing companies has hovered around 18.5 million. Further, manufacturing output contributed a staggering $1.43 trillion to GDP in 1998. From 1992 to 1999 durable-goods production-which includes such things as computer equipment and motor vehicles, was up by 73 percent.

Even though manufacturing jobs have gone up since NAFTA, a nagging question about jobs that have been lost specifically because of NAFTA. The answer depends on whom you ask. One economist estimates 440,000 net jobs have been lost in the U.S. since NAFTA went into effect in 1994. Another, representing the U.S. Library of Congress, says more than twice as many jobs have been created as lost in the wake of NAFTA-73 5,000 jobs have been gained and 277,700 have been lost.

A Commerce Department rule of thumb is that for every $1 billion of US exports 14,000 jobs are created; this translates into more than I million US jobs having been generated from exports to Canada and Mexico since 1993.

Another complaint of organized labor against NAFTA stemmed from the fear that new investments would be made south of the border instead of in U.S. In fact, American direct investment in Mexico has averaged less than $3 billion a year since 1994. That is less than 0.5 percent of American firms' total spending on plant and equipment. it is true that there has been an investment boom in Mexico but not all of it has come from the United States. U.S. and foreign investors with apparel and footwear factories in Asia have been encouraged to relocate their production operations to Mexico. For example, Victoria's Secret lingerie chain opened a new manufacturing plant near Mexico City. The company previously used contractors in Asia for its lingerie line but now, because of NAFTA, it produced in Mexico. Even with wages in Mexico three times the monthly wages in Sri Lanka, the company will still come out ahead because it is cheaper and faster to move goods from Mexico City to the U.S. than from Colombo – the time it takes to make a sample can be cut from weeks to days. Further, there are no tariffs on Mexican goods, while Sri Lanka goods carry a 19 percent duty.

Mexico's apparel exports to the U.S. have tripled to $3.3 billion since NAFTA began. Last year Mexico surpassed Hong Kong and China to become the U. S.' top source of imported apparel. This is a great boon for U.S. fabric and yarn makers. In years past they have supplied only minuscule amounts of fabric to the vertically integrated Asian apparel markets, now they supply 70 percent of the raw material going to Mexican sewing shops.

Total foreign direct investment in Mexico has averaged $11 billion a year since 1995 as companies from all over the world poured money into auto and electronics plants, telecommunications,

---

[5] For a comprehensive review of NAFTA, see: Ambassador Thomas E. McNamara, President and CEO, Council of the Americas, "Lessons of NAFTA for U.S. Relations with the America." *Testimony Before the Subcommittee on Western Hemisphere, Peace Corps, Narcotics and Terrorism, Senate Foreign Relations Committee,* April 27, 2000, www.counciloftheamericas.org.

petrochemicals, and a host of other areas. A large chunk of investment is earmarked for factories that will use Mexico as an export platform for the rest of North America, and increasingly the rest of Latin America.

The investment boom in Mexico has been a major source of new demand for U.S. manufacturers of capital goods. The largest post-NAFTA gains in U.S. exports to Mexico have been in such high technology manufacturing sectors as industrial machinery, transportation and electronic equipment, plastics, rubber, fabricated metal products, and chemicals.

Job losses have not been as drastic as once feared, in part because companies like Lucent Technologies have established maquiladora plants in anticipation of the benefits from NAFTA. The plants have been buying more components from U.S. suppliers, while cutting back on Asian sources. Miles Press, a $2 million maker of directory cards, saw orders from Lucent grow 20 percent in just a few months. Berg Electronics, a $700 million component maker, expects to triple sales to Lucent's Guadalajara plant next year. This ripple effect has generated U.S. service-sector jobs as well. Fisher Price Inc. shifted toy production for the U.S. market from Hong Kong to a plant in Monterey. Celadon Trucking Services Inc., which moves goods produced for Fisher Price from Mexico to the U.S., has added 800 new U.S. drivers to the payroll.

For Valley Drive Systems, manufacturer of automobile front-wheel-drive assemblies, NAFTA has been a success. Because Canadian tariffs on its products were lowered, Valley Drive products are now competitive with Taiwan. The company made its first-ever exports in 1996 and now exports 17 percent of its products.

NAFTA is a work in progress. It is too early to pass judgment; after all, the EU has been in existence for more than 40 years and has had its ups and downs. NAFTA is a mere babe in arms by comparison. What is happening is that economic relationship among the three countries is becoming more intense each day, mostly quietly and profitably. In short, it will take at least 10 to 15 years for an objective evaluation of NAFTA.

## Chapter 11 – Developing Global Marketing Strategies: Planning Organization

### Teaching Objectives

An issue facing many multinationals today is how to compete in an increasingly competitive global market. Whether a small company or one of the giants, staying competitive means constantly re-accessing marketing strategies. How product, promotion, distribution, and pricing strategies evolve in international marketing is dependent on the approach to internationalization the company takes. Of the three operating concepts that characterize a company's international orientation, Domestic Market Extension Concept, Multidomestic Market Concept, or Global Market Concept, the main focus of this chapter and the text is on the Global Market Concept. I believe that regardless of the size of a company or in how many countries it operates, it should have a global orientation. The teaching objectives of this chapter are to:

1) Present the operating concepts an international company may have and explore the idea of global marketing management.
2) Discuss the benefits of global orientation.
3) Stress the importance of quality and cost containment in global marketing competition.
4) Examine the different types of collaborative relationships and show how these alliances are being embraced by international companies.
5) Focus on relationship marketing and strategic international alliances as two important types of collaborative relationships for the global marketer.
6) Stress the need for strategic planning to achieve company goals.

### Comments and Suggestions

1. It is important to stress the changing competitive structure of international marketing and show how firms have to reexamine the way they operate to remain competitive. An analysis of multinational versus global companies and the benefits of global orientation serve as basis of a good discussion. Exhibit 11–1 is a good illustration of how the two approaches differ. A point that needs to be stressed is that having a global orientation is more a philosophy of how to approach international markets than how large you are, whether or not you have a "global" product, or in how many countries you market your products. For some good examples of small companies that are moving into global markets see, "It's A Small (Business) World," Special Report, Business Week, April 17, 1995, pp. 96–101.

2. The subject of collaborative relationships and the subsequent discussion of relationship marketing and strategic international alliances are important ideas to focus on in this chapter. Changes in technology, the shortening product life cycle, competition, the rapid growth of emerging markets and the need for cost containment as major trends in global marketing means that many firms must engage in collaborative relationships to remain competitive. There are several good examples in the text that illustrate how these relationships have been used. Also, Michael Schrage, "Notes on Collaboration," The Wall Street Journal, June 19, 1995, p. A–10, has three good examples of important collaborations by IBM, Microsoft, and Boeing. As Schrage states, "... 'winning' in tomorrow's global markets isn't going to be a matter of scoring points but of creating value with customers, clients, suppliers and colleagues in innovative ways." These relationships span the complete range of contacts a company has from customers through suppliers to other companies.

   It is important to stress that relationships are not necessarily permanent but exist to achieve mutually beneficial goals and when those goals are achieved or change, then the relationships are dissolved. This may be the case in the alliance between Ford and VW in Brazil. (See Rik Turner, "Why Ford, VW's Latin Marriage Succumbed to 7-Year Itch," Advertising Age, March 20, 1995, p. I-22.).

3. Exhibit 11–1, International Planning Process, gives students a comprehensive overview of the planning process. If a country project similar to the one described in Part VI, of the text, developing a marketing plan, is used, Exhibit 11–1 is helpful in giving students an overall view of the steps in the project. A brief review of this exhibit elicits many questions students have about the project and affords the professor the opportunity give them a guided tour through the project.

4. Not to be overlooked in this chapter are the various alternative market entry strategies. It is important to stress that there are a variety of ways to enter international markets and a company may use only one or a combination depending on the goals of the company and target market characteristics.

**Lecture Outline**

I. Global Marketing Management
   A. Global versus International Marketing Management
   B. Benefits of a Global Orientation

II. Planning for Global Markets
   A. Company Objectives and Resources
   B. International Commitment
   C. The Planning Process

III. Alternative Market-Entry Strategies
   A. Exporting
   B. The Internet
   C. Contractual Agreements
      1. Licensing
      2. Franchising
      3. Joint Ventures
      4. Consortia
   D. Direct Foreign Investment
   E. Strategic International Alliances (SIA)

IV. Organizing for Global Competition
   A. Locus of Decision
   B. Centralized versus Decentralized Organizations

## DISCUSSION QUESTIONS

1. Define:

| | |
|---|---|
| Global marketing management | Licensing |
| Corporate planning | Franchising |
| Direct exporting | Joint Venture |
| Strategic planning | Global market concept |
| Indirect exporting | SIA |
| Tactical planning | |

2. Define strategic planning. How is strategic planning different for international marketing than domestic marketing?

Strategic planning is a systemized way of relating to the future. It is an attempt to manage the effects of external uncontrollable factors on the firm's strengths, weaknesses, objectives, and goals to attain a desired end. Further, it is a commitment of resources to a country market to achieve specific goals.

The principles of planning are not in themselves different between international and domestic marketing, but the intricacies of the operating environments of the MNC (host country, home, and corporate environments), its organizational structure, and the task of controlling a multicountry operation create differences in the complexity and processes of international planning. Strategic planning on an international level allows for rapid growth of the international function, changing markets, increasing competition, and the ever-varying challenges of different national markets. The plan blends the changing parameters of external country environments with corporate objectives and capabilities to develop a sound, workable marketing program.

3. Discuss the benefits to an MNC of accepting the global market concept. Explain the three points that define a global approach to international marketing.

Economies of scale in production and marketing are the most frequently cited benefits. Black & Decker Manufacturing Company (electrical hand tools, appliances, and other consumer products) realized significant production cost savings when they adopted a global strategy. They were able to reduce not only the number of motor sizes for the European market from 260 to 8 but also 15 different models to 8.

The savings in the standardization of advertising can be substantial. PepsiCo has saved an estimated $10 million per year by using the same film for TV ads in individual national markets.

Transfer of experience and know-how across countries through improved coordination and integration of marketing activities is also cited as a benefit of globalization. Unilever, N.V., successfully introduced two global brands originally developed by two subsidiaries. Their South African subsidiary developed Impulse body spray and a European branch developed a detergent that cleaned effectively in European hard water.

Another benefit derived from globalization is a uniform global image. Global recognition of brand names and/or corporate logos accelerates new product introductions and increases the efficiency and effectiveness of advertising. Uniform global images are increasingly important as satellite communications spread throughout the world.

Establishing a brand image in emerging markets is an important strategy as these markets evolve. In many of the emerging markets, assurance of product quality is difficult for the consumer to attain. Without institutions such as Underwriters Laboratory, FDA (Food and Drug Administration), and Good Housekeeping seals or merchandise return policies to use as proxy variables for quality, safety or protection against faulty products the consumer must depend on the reputation of the merchant and the brand name.

Control and coordination of operations is another often-mentioned benefit of globalization. It is easy to imagine the difference in controlling one or two worldwide advertising projects in 40 countries versus 40 different country-specific advertisements. The same quality standards, promotional campaigns, product inventories, and spare parts inventories are easier to control and manage with a global strategy than with a multidomestic strategy.

As discussed in an earlier chapter, there is still debate about the extent of global markets today. A reasonable question concerns whether a global marketing strategy is possible only when a completely standardized marketing mix can be achieved. Global marketing strategy and the globalization of markets are two separate although interrelated ideas. One has to do with efficiency of operations, competitiveness, and orientation, the other with the homogeneity of demand across cultures. A global marketing strategy can be cost effective and competitively advantageous without absolute homogeneity in global market demand when standardization across markets is sought. There are at least three points that help define a global approach to international marketing: 1) the world is viewed as the market (that is, sets of country markets); 2) homogeneous market segments are sought across country market sets; and, 3) standardization of the marketing mix is sought wherever possible but adapted whenever culturally necessary.

4. Discuss the effect of shorter product life cycles on a company's planning process.

   Global competition is placing new emphasis on some basic tenets of business. It is reducing time frames and focusing on the importance of quality, competitive prices, and innovative products. Time is becoming a precious commodity for business, and expanding technology is shortening product life cycles and creating greater opportunities for innovative products. A company no longer can introduce a new product with the expectation of dominating the market for years while the idea spreads slowly through world markets. In any given year, for example, two thirds of Hewlett-Packard's revenue comes from product introduced in the prior three years. Shorter product life cycles mean that a company must maximize sales rapidly to recover development costs and generate a profit by offering its products globally. Along with technological advances have come enhanced market expectation for innovative products at competitive prices. Today, strategic planning must include emphasis on quality, technology, and cost containment. To achieve the flexibility and speed required under such conditions, many firms are entering collaborative relationships to shore up their weaknesses whether in distribution, technology or manufacturing that will enable them to respond to the problems created by shorter life cycles.

5. What is the importance of collaborative relationships to competition?

   The competitive environment of international business is changing rapidly. To be competitive in global markets a company must meet or exceed new standards for quality and new levels of technology. There is an increasing change of pace for product development and profitability. Cost efficient, technologically advanced products are being offered by competitors and demanded in established markets as well as in markets rising from formerly Marxist-socialist economies. Opportunities abound the world over, but to benefit, firms must be current in new technology, have the ability to keep abreast of technological change, have distribution systems to capitalize on global demand, have cost-effective manufacturing, and have capital to build new systems as necessary.

   The accelerating rate of technological progress, market demand created by global industrialization, and the creation of new middle classes will result in tremendous potential in global markets. But, along with this surge in global demand comes an increase in competition as technology and management capabilities spread beyond global companies to new competitors from Asia, Europe, and Latin America. Although global markets offer tremendous potential, companies seeking to function effectively in a fragmented global market of five billion people are being forced to stretch production, design\engineering, and marketing resources and capabilities because of the intensity of competition and the increasing pace of technology. Improvements in quality and staying on the cutting edge of technology are critical and basic for survival but often are not enough. Restructuring, reorganizing and downsizing are all avenues being taken by firms to strengthen their competitive positions. Additionally, many multinational companies are realizing they must develop long term, mutually beneficial relationships throughout the company and beyond to competitors, suppliers, governments, and customers. In short, multinational companies are developing orientations that focus on building collaborative relationships to promote long-term alliances and they are seeking continuous, mutually beneficial exchanges.

   The environment facing multinational companies demands flexibility, quality, cost containment, cutting edge manufacturing skills, and a rapid response to market changes to sustain a competitive advantage. The strengths and capabilities a company must have to be a major player are enormous and few companies can cover all the bases all of the time. To shore up weaknesses, companies are entering relationships with others to share what each does best whether in marketing, research or manufacturing. Collaborative relationships are becoming a common way to meet the demands of global competition and a successful collaboration means that each achieves more together than either can accomplish alone.

6. In phases one and two of the international planning process, countries may be dropped from further consideration as potential markets. Discuss some of the conditions in each phase that may exist in a country that would lead a marketer to exclude a country.

   In phase one of the planning process, there are a host of reasons why a country would no longer be considered. On balance, those countries that do not offer sufficient potential for further consideration will be eliminated. Some of the reasons why this may occur are that product acceptance within the country could not be achieved without extensive investment and new product development, and the firm does not have sufficient resources to make that investment; the legal structure may be such that it would be impossible for the company to function within that country. Competition in the country is such that, based on the company's objectives, resources, etc., it is felt that it would not be a profitable venture. In other words, any problem that would lead to minimum market potential, minimum profit, minimum return on investment, unacceptable competitive levels, unacceptable political stability, unacceptable legal requirements, etc., may all lead to the dropping of a country.

   While the major reasons for dropping a country in phase one center around general environmental constraints, the reasons that a country may be dropped in phase two center around the more specific questions of what cultural environmental adaptations are necessary for successful acceptance of the company's marketing mix, and will adaptation costs allow for profitable market entry. In phase two, the marketing mix is the focal point of analysis. Still, the final determination of whether or not a country is dropped depends upon the anticipated profitability of the market after necessary adaptations are made.

7. Assume that you are the director of international marketing for a company producing refrigerators. Select one country in Latin America and one in Europe and develop screening criteria to use in evaluating the two countries. Make any additional assumptions about your company that are necessary.

   This is a library-type project. Whatever the details of the screening criteria, the major points that should be considered are: (1) company objectives and goals, (2) product-use characteristics, (3) country environmental characteristics.

8. "The dichotomy typically drawn between export marketing and overseas marketing is partly fictional; from a marketing standpoint, they are but alternative methods ofcapitalizing on foreign market opportunities." Discuss.

   The dichotomy drawn between export marketing and overseas marketing is very misleading, for in fact they are but alternative methods of approaching the foreign markets. Yet, on the other hand, these approaches are often interrelated in the complete marketing structure. Both exporting and overseas marketing can be successfully interchanged to reach various heterogeneous markets. Depending on market structure, competition, and company policies, the organizational structure can be so devised so as to use exporting, overseas marketing, or a combination of both to successfully reach a wide assortment of foreign markets. In one country, due to high tariff rates, overseas production and marketing might be advised; on the other hand, poor communications or resources might necessitate exporting.

9. How will entry into a developed foreign market differ from entry into a relatively untapped market?

   The differences between entering a fully developed market and an untapped foreign market are many and extremely varied. Some of these differences are channels of distribution which may or may not be developed. Governmental attitudes toward business, foreigners, and industry may be very liberal in a growing economy, while an established market may be very restrictive. Communication and transportation may be highly limited in untapped markets and highly developed in successful countries. The amount of capital, banks, and exchange-rate systems will vary according to the market's development. Finally, the degree and amount of competition will vary accordingly. To this list, endless factors could be added such as cost of entering the market, social customs, laws, etc.

10. Why do companies change their organizations when they go from being an international to a global company?

    An international marketing plan should optimize the resources committed to stated company objectives. The organizational plan includes the type of organizational arrangements to be used, and the scope and location of responsibility. Many ambitious multinational plans meet with less than full success because of confused lines of authority, poor communications, and lack of cooperation between headquarters and subsidiary organizations.

    Companies are usually structured around one of three alternatives: global product divisions responsible for product sales throughout the world; geographical divisions responsible for all products and functions within a given geographical area; and a matrix organization consisting of either of these arrangements with centralized sales and marketing run by a centralized functional staff, or a combination of area operations and global product management.

    Market-oriented firms are finding greater competitiveness in world markets makes it essential to assume a global perspective in planning and organizational structure. Global competition also requires quality products designed to meet ever-changing customer needs in the face of rapidly growing competition from every corner of the world. Cost containment, escalating technology, customer satisfaction and a greater number of players mean that every opportunity to refine international business practices must be examined in light of company goals. Strategic international alliances, strategic planning and alternative market entry strategies are important avenues to global marketing that must be implemented in the planning and organization of global marketing management.

11. Formulate a general rule for deciding where international business decisions shoud be made.

    International business decisions should reflect the culture of the country in which they will be implemented. Thus the decision should be as close to the country where it is to be implemented as possible.

12. Explain the popularity of joint ventures.

    Joint ventures have become popular for a number of reasons. One important marketing reason is to gain access to markets. Nearly all of the developing countries, and many developed countries, require some degree of local participation for operating in their country. Mergers with distributor companies or companies which already have well-established local distribution may provide rapid market access and distribution to foreign companies entering a country. Sometimes companies join forces in order to broaden the line of merchandise that they have available, thereby gaining marketing efficiency and better public image. Another market reason for joining ventures is that local firms possess market information and the marketing know-how which would take years for a foreign company to acquire. Such participation minimizes the risk of market failure and speeds the marketing effort. Joint ventures may also arise for financial and manpower reasons. Financially it is sometimes desirable to merge with foreign companies because the merger provides access to local capital markets and combines the resources and fund raising capabilities the companies have. It may also give access to a higher quality and more capable managerial manpower.

13. Compare the organizational implications of joint ventures versus licensing.

Joint ventures involve the partners in a new venture and usually require significant inputs of both capital and management. In licensing, the companies retain separate identity. Usually the licensor is little affected by his licensing actions.

14. Visit the homepages of Maytag Corporation (http://www.maytag.com/) and the Whirlpool Corporation (http://www.whirlpool.com/), both appliance manufacturers in the United States. Each has some international involvement. Search their Web sites and compare their international involvement. How would you classify each, as exporter, international, or global?

The following excerpts from the homepages of these two companies reveals rather forcefully that these two giants in the U.S. market are far apart when it comes to international marketing. Maytag is an exporter with some desire to become international while Whirlpool is an international company with global sales.

**Maytag**

**Maytag's** heritage is more than a hundred years old and synonymous with a single product: washing machines. Today, Maytag Corporation is a $3.4 billion home *and* commercial appliance company focused in North America and targeted international markets.

**Maytag** International is responsible for finished goods export sales, licensing of the corporation's appliance and floor care brands, and joint ventures worldwide.

Investing for profitable growth is a key corporate objective. That was underscored in September 1996 when Maytag announced a joint venture with Hefei Rongshida, the leading washing machine company in the People's Republic of China.

Maytag invested $35 million for an ownership position in the China joint venture and both parties will each invest $35 million over approximately two years to expand the joint venture into the Chinese refrigerator market. Maytag's interests in the joint venture are managed by Maytag International, the division responsible for appliance exports, licensing and international ventures. China is a huge appliance market with tremendous growth potential. For example, Chinese consumers buy more than 8 million refrigerators a year, which is comparable to the U.S. market. However, fewer than one out of four households in China has a refrigerator.

Maytag's China joint venture involves a well-established, profitable business with high-quality washers, a widely recognized brand name, RSD, and an effective nationwide sales and distribution network. Their annual revenues more than doubled from 1993 to 1995, and operating margins are strong. Maytag will receive a full-year benefit from its China joint venture in 1997, and significant growth opportunities exist in the years ahead. The China joint venture is part of Maytag's strategy to grow profitably by making selective investments domestically and abroad.

**Whirlpool**

**Whirlpool** Appliances are manufactured in 13 countries and marketed in approximately 140 countries around the world. Whirlpool Corporation is the world's leading manufacturer and marketer of major home appliances. Its growth, from primarily a U.S. manufacturer to "world leader," is the result of strategic direction set in the mid 1980s and reaffirmed through an exhaustive and integrated strategic planning process in 1992.

In the 1980s, four manufacturers accounted for almost all major home appliance sales in the United States, a market where approximately 40 million appliances are sold annually. Each was a tough, seasoned competitor fighting for greater sales in a market predicted to grow little in the decade ahead. Whirlpool was one of those companies. Unable to find growth potential in the U.S. appliance market and unwilling to accept the status quo, the company began a systematic evaluation of opportunities—both inside and outside the appliance industry—worldwide.

At the same time, Whirlpool established parameters within which decisions about the company's future would be made. New ventures would provide opportunity for growth, build on existing company strengths, and be market driven. Leadership opportunities, too, would be a consideration.

With growth parameters established and study data in, the decision was made to remain focused on major home appliances but to expand into markets not already served by Whirlpool. The goal was world leadership in a rapidly globalizing major appliance industry in which approximately 190 million appliances are sold each year. A major acquisition in Europe, joint ventures with companies in Mexico and India and increased ownership in companies in Canada and Brazil swiftly followed.

Throughout the early 1990s, the company continued its expansion in Latin America and Europe and a manufacturing and marketing presence was established in Eastern Europe. And, to manage its small appliance business on a global basis, including the KitchenAid stand and hand mixers, a Small Appliance Business Unit was formed.

In the past four years, Whirlpool has aggressively pursued its Asian strategy. A headquarters office and four regional offices were established in 1993. Two years later, five majority-owned joint ventures were announced in India and China to expand the company's Asian manufacturing base.

In Asia, Latin America, North America, Europe, and in all the countries where it has a presence, Whirlpool seeks to set the standards against which the global major domestic appliance industry is measured. To that end, the company vigorously pursues the goals of its Worldwide Excellence System (WES). Initiated in 1991, WES incorporates the best of all Whirlpool quality programs, worldwide, with Malcolm Baldrige Award and International Standards Organization criteria to establish a common approach to quality, one that dedicates the company to the pursuit of excellence and total customer satisfaction.

15. Using the sources in question above i.e., (http://www.maytag.com/) and (http://www.whirlpool.com/), list the different alternative entry modes each uses.

Both use foreign direct investment although Whirlpool is the most advanced. Maytag exports from the United States.

16. Visit the Nestlé Corporation homepage http://www.nestle.com and Unilever N.V. (http://www.unilever.com/) and compare their strategies towards international markets. In what ways to they differ (besides product categories) do they differ in their international marketing?

This exercise can lead to a good class discussion of multinational and/or global companies and strategies. These two global giants probably are among the first real global companies. From their beginning they viewed the world as their market and still follow that direction. The excerpts below from their home pages gives a brief look at their philosophies.

**Nestlé**

In a world of endless diversity, there is one activity that almost everyone shares. No matter where you go, you'll find people of all ages, from every social class, and representing every religion and ethnic group enjoying some Nestlé food or drink product. Our products (more than 8,500 in all) are sold in more than 100 countries, and they bring pleasure to millions of people. Whether it's ready-to-eat meals, instant coffee, chocolate bars or mineral water, Nestlé products are enjoyed around the world.

Meeting the needs and desires of a diverse and ever-changing world requires respect for and knowledge of local values and desires. To achieve that, Nestlé has made decentralization a basic principle. We have offices, factories and research centers throughout the world. It is our policy to adapt as much as possible to local customs and circumstances while allowing decisions about products, marketing and personnel to be made at the local level.

Nestlé is The World's Largest Food Company. Only two percent of sales are generated in Switzerland, our country of origin, and our management and staff reflect a truly international outlook. As a Company, we do not believe in mission statements, because one would either be so general as to become meaningless, or so specific that it wouldn't be applicable or relevant everywhere—we would like to offer a set of principles that will provide insight into the Company's attitudes and culture.

At Nestlé, we try to take the mentality and customs of individual countries into account, but there are some general guidelines that we apply everywhere. Those include:

- A positive attitude toward work
- A pragmatic, realistic approach to doing business
- An open-minded approach to the world
- A minimal number of systems and written guidelines
- A personal style of management
- An atmosphere of mutual trust
- An avoidance of showing off, windy rhetoric and hypocritical remarks
- An emphasis on practical experience and on the setting of good examples.

Employees, people and products are more important at Nestlé than systems. Systems and methods, while necessary and valuable in running a complex organization, should remain managerial and operational aids but should not become ends in themselves. It is a question of priorities. A strong orientation toward human beings, employees and executives is a decisive, if not *the* decisive, component of long-term success.

Our focus is on products. The ultimate justification for a company is its ability to offer products that are appealing because of their quality, convenience, variety and price—products that can stand their ground even in the face of fierce competition.

Nestlé makes clear a distinction between strategy and tactics. It gives priority to the long-range view. Long-term thinking defuses many of the conflicts and contentions among groups—this applies to employment conditions and relations with employees as well as to the conflicts and opposing interests of the trade and the industry. Of course, our ability to focus on long-term considerations is only possible if the company is successful in the struggle for short-term survival. This is why Nestlé strives to maintain a satisfactory level of profits every year.

Switzerland is home to Nestlé's Swiss subsidiary, its international headquarters and the registered office of Nestlé's holding company, but Nestlé does not regard its Swiss headquarters as the center of the universe. Decentralization is a basic principle of Nestlé. Our policy is to adapt as much as possible to regional circumstances, mentalities and situations. By decentralizing operational responsibility, we create strength and flexibility and are able to make decisions that are better attuned to specific situations in a given country. Policies and decisions concerning personnel, marketing and products are largely determined locally. This policy creates stronger motivation for Nestlé's executives and employees and a greater sense of identification with Nestlé's business. It is not Nestlé's policy to generate most of its sales in Switzerland, supplemented by a few satellite subsidiaries abroad. Nestlé strives to be an "insider" in every country in which it operates, not an "outsider."

A very important concern at Nestlé has to do with uniformity: how consistent Nestlé's principles, policies, rules of conduct and strategies should be, and to what extent they should differ depending on the country, subsidiary, region, branch or group of products. In general, Nestlé tries to limit the uniformity of its policy to a requisite minimum. This minimum is then systematically enforced, unless there are compelling reasons in a given market that justify deviation from policy.

Nestlé does not want to become either a conglomerate or a portfolio manager. Nestlé wants to operate only those businesses about which it has some special knowledge and expertise. Nestlé is a global company, not a conglomerate hodgepodge. We regard acquisitions and efforts at diversification as logical ways to supplement our business, but only in the context of a carefully considered corporate marketing policy.

The public's sense of the power and size of a corporation is often inaccurate, for a company's power is limited by a host of factors including legislation, competition, regulatory bodies and publicity. From a business point of view, it is desirable for a firm to achieve the size best suited to a specific industry or mode of production. To be competitive internationally and make significant investments in research and technology, a larger company has an advantage. From a strictly organizational point of view, flexible, simple structures work best and excessively large units should be avoided whenever possible. In both respects Nestlé has a natural advantage: Although it is a big company, it is spread out over many countries and each of Nestlé's factories has its own management and responsibility.

Nestlé is probably unique in the food industry in having an integrated research and development program that engages in applied and basic research in the fields of human physiology, health, nutrition and raw materials. Our research and development program gives us the capacity to create new types of products that we cannot even imagine today, especially in the critical area where preventive medicine and food products overlap. In addition, as concern for the environment grows, research will play an important role in overcoming environmental problems. For Nestlé, this is particularly important in packaging. Concern for the effects of packaging on the environment is forcing us to look for new solutions and to consider their interaction with our biological product—food.

At present, the world faces daunting questions about its ability to provide enough wholesome food for everyone. Malnutrition and poor eating habits are still serious problems in many developing countries. By 2100, the world's population will double. Will it be possible to feed a world with so many inhabitants? At Nestlé, the big picture is all about feeding the world and providing food and nutrition for an ever-growing population. Our response to this situation is to intensify research, strive for innovations and improve quality.

## Chapter 12 – Products and Services for Consumers

### Teaching Objectives

Products and services, the first part of the marketing mix to be discussed, is covered here with consumer products and the next chapter on industrial products and services. An overall point that needs to be made with these two chapters is that companies face two different problems in developing products for international markets – they either have an existing product that needs to be evaluated for possible adaptation or they are developing a product for global markets from scratch. The two situations require different approaches to product development. The decisions as to whether to standardize or adapt, to develop global products and global brands need to be addressed at the beginning of the chapter since the direction taken will influence later discussions. The teaching objectives are to:

1) Familiarize students with the debate between standardization and adaptation and global products and brands.
2) Stress the importance of offering products and services suitable to the intended market. That the issue is not whether to adapt or standardize, but how much adaptation is necessary and to what point a product can be standardized.
3) Make them aware of the country of origin effect on how products are perceived.
4) Explore the relationship between consumer perceptions of products and culture. Special emphasis on the product as an innovation and the possibility of resistance to an innovation if it is too new or disruptive of the norm.
5) Present two methods for screening products and services for adaptation; the analysis of characteristics of innovation and analysis of product components model.

### Comments and Suggestions

1. Coverage of this chapter can be divided into three parts. First, a broad discussion of how cultural factors and the country of origin affect the acceptance of a product, how a product is received if it is perceived as an innovation and the issues of global products and standardization versus adaptation. Second, there are physical and mandatory requirements that require adaptation, and third, screening products for adaptation. This third point recognizes the fact that most companies have existing products that require evaluation for adaptation, whether mandatory or cultural, before being introduced in another country.
2. Exhibit 13–1, Product Component Model (TM 13–3) is helpful in focusing on the different components of a product that may require adaptation. Using this model also helps me discuss the issue of the core component and product platform–the most costly part of a product to adapt yet possibly the most easily standardized. An interesting article on the problems four companies encountered in their attempts to develop a global product is Gregory L. Miles, "Tailoring a Global Product," International Business, March 1995, pp. 50–52.
3. If the students are asked to do a research project similar to the one described Part I-F, above, The Country Notebook – A Guide for Developing a Marketing Plan, many of the points in the chapter can be brought out in class. I bring a product to class and ask students to respond on how they think the product will need to be adapted or could be standardized in the country they are studying.

**Lecture Outline**

I. Quality Products
   A. Quality Defined
   B. Maintaining Quality
II. Products and Culture
   A. Innovate Products and Adaptation
   B. Diffusion of Innovations
   C. Degree of Newness
   D. Analysis of Characteristics of Innovations
III. Physical or Mandatory Requirements and Adaptation
IV. Screening Products For Adaptation
V. Consumer Services
VI. Green Marketing and Product Development
VII. Marketing Consumer Services Globally
VIII. Global Markets and Product/Service Development
   A. Global Brands
      1. National Brands
   B. Country of Origin Effect and Global Brands
   C. Private Brands

## DISCUSSION QUESTIONS

1. Define the following terms and show their significance to international marketing:

| | |
|---|---|
| Product diffusion | Innovation |
| Product Component Model | Green marketing |
| Quality | Homologation |
| Global brands | |

2. Debate the issue of global versus adapted products for the international market.

A recurring debate exists relative to product planning and focuses on the question of standardized products marketed worldwide versus differentiated products adapted or even redesigned for each culturally unique market. Those with a strong production and unit cost orientation advocate standardization and others, perhaps more culturally sensitive, propose the policy of a different product for each market. The issue cannot be resolved with a simple either/or decision. Cost revenue analyses need to be done and decisions made in the hard, cold lights of profitability. There is no question that significant cost savings can be realized from having standardized products, packages, brand names, and promotional messages but this makes sense only if there is adequate demand for the standardized products: costs must be balanced with demand. On the other hand, if the cost of an individualized product when evaluated against price/demand characteristics within a market exceeds potential profit, then it is ridiculous not to consider other alternatives including not marketing the product at all.

To differentiate for the sake of differentiation is no solution, and realistic business practice requires a company to strive for uniformity in its marketing mix whenever and wherever possible. Economies of production, better planning, more effective control, and better use of creative managerial personnel are all advantages of standardization.

3. Define the country-of-origin effect and give examples.

   Country of Origin Effect (COE) can be defined as any influence that country-of-manufacturer has on a consumer's positive or negative perception of a product. Today a company competing in global markets will manufacture products worldwide and, when the customer is aware of the country of origin, there is the possibility that the place of manufacture will affect product/brand image. Some examples are French wines, German beer, Swiss watches, Cuban cigars, and Irish woolens are some positive COEs. A negative COE is an automobile from Yugoslavia (the Yugo).

4. The text discusses stereotypes, ethnocentrism, degree of economic development, and fads as the basis for generalizations about country-of-origin effect on product perception. Explain each and give an example.

   The country, the type of product, and the image of the company and its brands all influence whether or not the country of origin will engender a positive or negative reaction. There are a variety of generalizations that can be made about country of origin effects on products and brands. Consumers tend to have stereotypes about products and countries that have been formed by experience, hearsay, and myth. Following are some of the more frequently cited generalizations.

   Consumers have broad but somewhat vague stereotypes about specific countries and specific product categories that they judge "best": English tea, French perfume, Chinese silk, Italian leather, Japanese electronics, Jamaican rum, and, so on. Stereotyping of this nature is typically product specific and may not extend to other categories of products from these countries.

   Ethnocentrism can also have country of origin effect; feelings of national pride, the "buy American" effect among members, for example, can influence attitudes toward foreign products. Honda, which manufactures one of their models almost entirely in the United States, recognizes this phenomenon and points out how many component parts are made in America in some of their advertisements. On the other hand, others have a stereotype of Japan as producing the "best" automobiles. A recent study found that U.S. automobile producers may suffer comparatively tarnished in-country images regardless of whether they actually produce superior products.

   Countries are also stereotyped on the basis of whether they are industrialized, in the process of industrializing or less-developed. These stereotypes are less country-product specific; they are more a perception of the quality of goods in general produced within the country. Industrialized countries have the highest quality image, and there is generally a bias against products from developing countries. Within groups of countries grouped by economic development there are variations of image. For example, one study of COE between Mexico and Taiwan found that a microwave oven manufactured in Mexico was perceived as significantly more risky than an oven made in Taiwan. However, for jeans there was no difference in perception between the two countries. One might generalize that the more technical the product, the less positive is the perception of one manufactured in a less-developed or newly industrializing country. There is also the tendency to favor foreign made products over domestic made in less developed countries. Not all foreign products fare equally well since consumers in developing countries have stereotypes about the quality of foreign made products even from industrialized countries. A survey of consumers in the Czech Republic found that 72 percent of Japanese products were considered to be of the highest quality, German goods followed with 51%, Swiss goods with 48%, Czech goods with 32% and, last, the United States with 29%.

   One final generalization about COE involves fads that often surround products from particular countries or regions in the world. These fads are more often product specific and generally involve goods that are themselves faddish in nature. European consumers are apparently enamored with a host of American made products ranging from Jeep Cherokees, Budweiser beer, and Jim Beam bourbon, to Boise sound systems. In the 1970s and 80s there was a backlash against anything American, but, in the 1990s, American is in. In China, anything Western seems to be the fad. If it is Western it is in demand even at prices three and four times higher than domestic products. In most cases such fads wane after a few years as some new fad takes over.

5. Discuss product alternatives and the three marketing strategies: domestic market extension, multidomestic market, and global market strategies.

   The marketer has at least three viable alternatives when entering a new market: (1) sell the same product presently sold in the home market (Domestic Market Extension Strategy); (2) adapt existing products to the tastes and specific needs in each new country market (Multi-Domestic Market Strategy); or (3) develop a standardized product for all markets (Global Market Strategy.)

   An important issue in choosing which alternative to use is whether or not a company is starting from scratch (i.e., no existing products to market abroad), or whether it has products already established in various country markets. For a company starting fresh, the prudent alternative is to develop a global product. If the company has several products that have evolved over time in various foreign markets, then the task is one of repositioning the existing products into a global product.

6. Discuss the different promotional/product strategies available to an international marketer.

   The marketer has at least three viable alternatives when entering a new market: he can (1) sell the same product he presently sells elsewhere, (2) individualize existing products to the tastes and specific needs of the new country, or (3) develop a totally new product. These three basic alternatives, when combined with promotional effort, can be developed into five different product strategies available to the international marketer. First, a company can sell the same product using the same promotional message worldwide as Pepsi-Cola and the Coca-Cola company do. A second version is to sell the same product but with promotions featuring different use patterns, for example, garden power equipment designed for United States home use but sold as agricultural equipment in underdeveloped countries. A third strategy involves altering the basic physical features of the product to meet local environmental needs but promoting the product to fill the same use patterns as are prevalent in the domestic market. Detergents redesigned to function in cold water but still promoted to get clothes clean is an example of this strategy. The fourth strategy requires both a change in the product to meet different use patterns and a change in the promotional message accompanying it. For example, the fifth strategy is one of investing or developing a totally new product rather than adapting an existing one. This is less frequently done, but as companies move into less developed markets and seek greater economic penetration into these markets it becomes more prevalent. As examples, the Coca-Cola company has developed Saci, a protein fortified beverage to sell in foreign countries as a diet supplement; and Ford and General Motors are experimenting with a "bare bones" Model T-type truck to sell in developing countries. The success of any of these strategies depends upon the product and the fundamental need it fulfills, its characteristics and their perception within the culture, and finally, the associated costs of each program.

7. Assume you are deciding to "go international" and outline the steps you would take to help you decide on a product line.

   Library research project.

8. Products can be adapted physically and culturally for foreign markets. Discuss.

   Products can be adapted to a new culture in a variety of ways ranging from simple package changes to total redesign in the physical product. Some need for change becomes obvious with relatively little analysis. For example, a cursory analysis of a country will uncover the need to require electrical goods if it uses a different voltage system, or to indicate product simplification when the local level of technologies is not high, or the need for a color change if the present color violates local taboos, etc. Most such superficial changes can be spotted by looking at product use patterns, the economy, and other related culture elements. One international scholar has categorized these changes into thirteen environmental factors listed below. Each is quickly detected and requires only basic changes to bring the product in line with a culture.

| Environmental Factor | Design Change |
|---|---|
| Level of technical skills | Product simplification |
| Level of labor cost | Automation or manualization of product |
| Level of literacy | Remarking and simplification of product |
| Level of income | Quality and price change |
| Level of interest rates | Quality and price change (investment in high quality might not be financially desirable |
| Level of maintenance | Change in tolerances |
| Climatic differences | Product adaptation |
| Isolation (heavy repair difficult and expensive) | Product simplification and reliability improvement |
| Differences in standards | Recalibration of product and resizing |

The suggested changes are primarily concerned with the price and physical or mechanical properties of a product. Such product characteristics certainly can impede effective use of a product within another culture, but more subtle differences within a culture require other kinds of changes that must be resolved before a product gains acceptance.

Internal cultural variations may require product adaptation that hinges more on the product's conflict with norms, values, and behavior patterns than on its physical or mechanical aspects. For example, introduction of a new product into a culture that does not perceive a need for such an item can conflict with established norms, locally accepted values can be upset by trying to introduce personal care items into a culture that prefers body functions remain very private and assuming too high a level of sophistication in product usage may overlook local behavior patterns.

9. What are the three major components of a product? Discuss their importance to product adaptation.
The three major components of a product are: (1) its core, the physical product and all its functional features; (2) the packaging component that includes the physical package in which the product is presented, as well as the brand name, trademark, styling and design features, price and quality levels; (3) the support services component, which completes the product buyers receive and from which the bundle of satisfactions received are derived. This support services component includes repair and maintenance services, installation, delivery, warranty, spare parts, training and instructions, credit, and any other services related to the use and purchase of the product. The importance of each component, as well as the perceived component attributes are functions of culture. What may be desirable in one culture may be unimportant in another. A product is, in a large part, a cultural phenomenon; that is, culture determines the individual's perception of what a product is and what satisfaction that product provides. Therefore, in developing products for international markets, adaptation of that bundle of utilities or satisfaction received may be necessary to bring the product in line with the culture's needs. Such adaptation may require changes of any one or all of the product components as defined above.

10. How can the knowledge of the diffusion of innovations help a product manager plan his international investments?
Knowledge of the diffusion of innovation provides the international marketer with several important pieces of information; for example, a knowledge of the concept may provide the marketer with an estimate of the time it will take before his innovation would be accepted by a culture, and therefore help him decide whether or not to make the necessary investment. It can also give him insights into how to accelerate the rate of acceptance of his product and the steps that he as a marketer can take to

eliminate some of the "newness" thereby gaining more rapid acceptance of his product. In preparing a characteristics of innovations study of the new product, he or she might determine a product profile which could be extremely useful as a model for planning product strategy. By analyzing the product in terms of those attributes which contribute to its newness (or innovativeness) the marketer's attention is focused on those factors which give rise to resistance; thus, the marketer can estimate the possible rate of adoption and perhaps effect the rate of adoption of an innovation by changing its characteristics through physical modifications, advertising, and/or sales promotion efforts.

11. Old products (that is, old to the U.S. market) may be innovations in a foreign market. Discuss fully. It is important for the marketer to appreciate that a product which has gained acceptance and is now at the top or perhaps even in the declining stage of the product life cycle, may be perceived in another culture as a new and, in fact, very innovative product. The marketer must guard against assuming that an "old hat" in one market which has achieved acceptance after many years of exposure and learning and adaptation on the part of the culture toward the product can be transferred to another culture with its learned acceptance intact. In fact, the "old hat" may be so outside the experience of the new market that the marketer will have to start at the beginning of the assimilation process.

12. ". . . If the product sells in Dallas, it will sell in Tokyo or Berlin." Comment.

    Basically, the needs and hence the demand for a product are the same in all markets. Similarities in wants are universal and, as income increases, practically everyone desires the "good life." The important aspect to consider is that in crossing one culture to another, separate characteristics of nationality and stages of economic and industrial development determine consumer behavior to a great extent. Hence, each group's interpretation of the "good life" as reflected in consumer behavior relates heavily to cultural heritage. Thus, the statement can be very wrong and represents an attitude which has frequently led to international market failures.

13. How can a country with a per capita GNP of $100 be a potential market for consumer goods? What kinds of goods would probably be in demand? Discuss.

    A country with a low GNP can have a large demand for consumer goods because of the need that exists for certain products and because there are no production facilities or very limited ones within the country. India, for example, has a per capita income of $58/year, yet its imports were about $2.4 billion in 1963. The type of goods that likely are in demand are the more basic type of consumer goods, such as clothing or basic housing needs.

14. Discuss the four types of innovations. Give examples of the products which would be considered by the U.S. market as one type of innovation but a different type in another market. Support your choice.

    There are four types of innovations: (1) Congruent innovation, (2) continuous innovation, (3) dynamically continuous innovation, and (4) discontinuous innovation. A congruent innovation is actually no innovation at all because it causes absolutely no disruption of established consumption patterns. Some products do fit this category; the best example would be an exact duplicate of an already existing product. A continuous innovation has the next least disruptive influence on established consumption patterns. Alternative of a product is almost always involved, rather than the creation of a new product. An example may be fluoride toothpaste and menthol cigarettes, etc. A dynamically continuous innovation has more disruptive effects than a continuous innovation, although it still does not generally involve new consumption patterns. It may mean the creation of a new product or considerable alternation of an existing one.

    Examples would include such items as electric toothbrushes, electric haircurlers, and the Mustang automobile. A discontinuous innovation involves the establishment of a new consumption pattern and the creation of previously unknown products. Examples might include such items as a television, the computer, and the automobile. In any one of these situations a single product may range from being a congruent innovation to a discontinuous innovation. For example, in the United States another small car would either be considered a continuous or a congruent innovation, whereas the same automobile in a very underdeveloped country that has no automobiles would be a discontinuous innovation.

15. Discuss the characteristics of an innovation which can account for differential diffusion rates.

    The characteristics of an innovation which can account for differential diffusion rates are: (1) relative advantage, (2) compatibility, (3) complexity, (4) trialability, and (5) observability. Relative advantage is the degree to which an innovation is better than the products it replaces or with which it competes. Compatibility is concerned with how consistent a product is with existing value and behavior patterns. Complexity refers to how difficult it is to understand and use the new product. Trialability is the degree to which a product may be tried, on a limited basis, without complete commitment to the product. And, observability refers to the ease with which the results of an innovation may be communicated to others.

16. Discuss "environmentally friendly" products and product development.

    Germany has a strict Eco-labeling program to identify, for the concerned consumer, products that have a lesser negative impact on the environment than similar products. Under German law, a manufacturer is permitted to display a logo, called the "Blue Angel," on all products that comply with certain criteria that make it environmentally friendly. More than 3,200 products in 58 product categories have been examined and given the Blue Angel logo. While it is difficult to judge the commercial value of a Blue Angel designation, manufacturers are seeking the eco-label for their products in response to growing consumer demand for environmentally friendly products. Similar national labels are under discussion in France, Denmark, the Netherlands and the United Kingdom. The EC Commission issued guidelines for eco-labeling that became operational in October 1992. Under the EC directive, a product is evaluated on all significant environmental effects throughout its life cycle, from manufacturing to disposal, a cradle-to-grave approach. Companies will be encouraged to continuously update their environmental technology because eco-labels will be granted for only a limited period. As more environmentally friendly products come onto the market, the standards will become tougher, and products that have not been improved will lose their eco-label.

    The "Blue Angel" and similar eco-labels are awarded on the basis of a product's environmental friendliness, that is, how "friendly" when used and when its residue is released into the environment. A detergent formulated to be bio-degradable and not pollute would be judged more friendly than a detergent whose formulation would be harmful when discharged. Aerosol propellants that do not deplete the ozone layer are another example of environmentally friendly products. No country's laws yet require products to carry an "eco-label" to be sold. The designation that a product is "environmentally friendly" is voluntary and its environmental success depends on the consumer selecting the "eco-friendly" product. However, laws that mandate systems to control solid waste management, while voluntary in one sense, do carry penalties in that consumers may not select their products.

# Chapter 13 – Products and Services for Businesses

## Teaching Objectives

The overall objective of this chapter is to illustrate how the differences in the motives between buyers of consumer products and industrial goods and services place different emphasis on the marketing of these products. It is important to stress that much of what has been discussed in Chapter 13 is relevant for industrial goods and services but that emphasis is affected by the inherent nature of industrial goods. The teaching objectives are to:

1) Emphasize a fundamental difference in consumer demand vis-à-vis industrial demand—the inherent volatility of the latter.
2) Explore the relationship between a country's stage of economic development and demand for industrial goods.
3) Stress the growing importance of technology and quality in successful product development.
4) Illustrate the important role of relationship marketing in maintaining competitiveness in industrial goods marketing.
5) Examine industrial trade shows as an important means of promotion.
6) Present the major issues in marketing business services globally and the affect of the fundamental characteristics of business services on marketing.

## Comments and Suggestions

1. Perhaps the most important point to make regarding the marketing and development of industrial products is the inherent volatility of derived demand. Demand for capital equipment is particularly susceptible to huge fluctuations in demand. This is the central issue of case 4–10 (Boeing).
2. The growing importance of technology and quality in successful industrial goods marketing cannot be overstressed. The level of technology reflected in the product, compliance with standards that reflect customer needs, support services and follow through, and the price relative to competitive products are all part of a customer's evaluation and perception of quality.
3. Business services are a major growth export industry for the United States. Its importance as a positive contributor to the balance of trade is only now being fully recognized. As is the case for industrial goods, the unique characteristics associated with business services affects the manner in which they are marketed. There are a number of cases which well illustrate international services marketing issues: 2–1 (Disneyland Paris), 3–4 (Olympics and the Scottish Claymores), 4–8 (Rallysport), and 4–9 (Architectural Services).

## Lecture Outline

I. The Volatility of Derived Demand

II. The Industrial Product Market

- A. Stages of Economic Development
- B. Technology and Market Demand
- C. Attributes of Product Quality
- D. Quality is Defined by the Customer
- E. Service and Replacement Parts
- G. Universal Standards

H. ISO 9000 Certification—An International Standard of Quality

III. Relationship Marketing and Industrial Products

IV. Promoting Industrial Products

A. Industrial Trade Shows

V. Countertrade—A Pricing Tool

VI. Marketing Services Globally

A. Services Opportunities in Global Markets

B. Entering Global Markets

1 Client Followers and Market Seekers

2. Entry Modes

C. Market Environment for Business Services

1. Protectionism

2. Transborder Data Flow

3. Competition

D. Cultural Barriers and Adaptation

## DISCUSSION QUESTIONS

1. Define the following terms and show the significance to international marketing:

| | |
|---|---|
| Derived demand | ISO 9000 |
| Price-quality relationship | Relationship marketing |
| Client followers | |

2. What are the differences between consumer and industrial goods and what are the implications for international marketing? Discuss.

The committee on definitions of the National Association of Marketing Teachers has broken down the differences between consumer and industrial goods by four areas. They are:

a. Nature of the market or buyer – this typically means that consumer goods are used by the end customer in a channel of distribution and are consumed by this customer in its finished stage. The industrial goods are typically those goods which are used for the further production of other goods and are not used for the personal benefit of the customer. There are, however, many overlapping categories within this description.

b. Organization or operational setup.

c. Characteristics of the product – as was mentioned, industrial goods are typically used for the production of other goods while consumer goods are consumed by the final customer.

d. Miscellaneous differences – including such points as the need for a sales force (highly skilled or not), speed and dependability of delivery, and the like.

e. We must of course add the volatility of derived demand, which if noticed, has huge implications for the marketing of industrial products.

These differences are the same in international marketing, and they are further complicated by the foreign environment.

3. Discuss how the various stages of economic development affect the demand for industrial goods.

Perhaps the most significant environmental factor affecting the market for industrial products is the degree of industrialization. Although generalizing about countries is a dangerous practice, the stage of economic development of a country can be used as a rough gauge of market characteristics for industrial goods. Regardless of the stage, demand for industrial goods exists, but different levels of development typically result in changes in the demand and the kinds and quality of the industrial goods sought. According to the text in the first stage, that is preindustrial or commercial stage, there is little or no manufacturing, and the economy is almost wholly based upon the exploitation of raw materials and agricultural products. There is, however, a demand for industrial products even though it is limited to those items used in the simple production of the country's resources; that is, the industrial machinery, equipment, and goods required in the production of the country's natural resources. Also in this stage, a transportation system typically develops and this creates a market for highly specialized and expensive construction equipment that must be imported from other countries.

The second stage generally reflects the development of primary manufacturing industry concerned with the partial processing of raw materials and resources. At this level, there is a demand for the machinery and other industrial goods necessary for the processing of the raw materials prior to exportation.

The third stage of development is characterized by the growth of manufacturing facilities for nondurable and semidurable consumer goods. Generally, industry consists of small local manufacturers of consumer goods which have relatively large mass field. The demand for industrial products extends to entire factories and the supplies necessary to support manufacturing. Such a degree of industrialization requires machinery and equipment to build and supply the factories and the supplies to keep them operating.

A country at stage four is really a fairly well-industrialized economy. This stage reflects the production of capital goods as well as consumer goods including such products as automobiles, refrigerators, and machinery. Even though industrial goods are in production, there is still the need for the importation for other goods which the country does not produce. Demand is generally for more specialized and heavy capital equipment to supply the domestic industry.

A country in stage five has reached the point of complete industrialization which generally denotes world leadership in the production of a large variety of goods. Even though these countries have achieved the highest level of industrialization, there is still a market for industrial products because a country at this stage typically does not produce all of the goods it needs but specializes in the production of certain goods and imports those highly specialized items which it cannot profitably produce but still needs. Although each stage of economic development appears to be clear cut, most countries are actually in a stage of economic and industrial flux, striving for greater and more rapid economic growth. Thus, a country may be in more than one stage at any one time, which again has an effect on the industrial demand within that country.

4. "Industrialization is typically a national issue, and industrial goods are the fodder for industrial growth." Comment.

The main points in the solution of this problem center around the desire of the underdeveloped countries to industrialize. This industrialization is not a haphazard, natural growth, but a planned growth, and as a consequence the sale or purchase of industrial goods both to help industrialize a nation as well as the purchase of those industrial goods which a country cannot produce become virtually a national issue rather than just a private venture between a buyer and a seller. The reason is very obvious since industrial goods are part of industrialization in the sense that industrial goods must be purchased to build plants and to supply raw materials for plants. In those cases when plants have not been built, industrial goods are still in need in the country but are always subject to evaluation in terms of should the country build the plant; that is, further industrialize, and thereby not have to import the goods, or should it continue to import the goods. Industrialization is a national issue which adds another ingredient to the environment that the foreign marketer must face. There are political overtones to the statement in that a country may have support for its industrialization from a second country, and this support may take the form of industrial products at very low prices or extra-liberal credit terms. All of this, of course, adds still another dimension to the competitive situation for industrial goods in the industrializing country.

5. "... The adequacy of a product must be considered in relation to the general environment within which it will be operated rather than solely on the basis of technical efficiency." Discuss the implications of this statement.

   The statement really refers to a major problem faced by many U.S. marketers in that the industrial goods they intend to sell abroad are the same ones which have a market in the United States. The United States, being a highly industrialized nation, obviously has need for equipment of the highest technical standards and technical efficiency. For example, highly technical automotive equipment that can operate within extremely close tolerances. The demand for as fine a piece of equipment as is produced in the United States and consumed in the United States may not exist in countries which are less developed and have different labor cost structures, or it may not exist in the sense or in relationship to the price that must be charged for the equipment. Besides the price, there is the capability of the labor force to utilize the equipment in terms of maintenance and in terms of being able to effectively make use of some of the refinements that may exist. Thus, a product should be considered in relation to how it is going to be used, the purpose for which it is going to be used, the environment within which it is going to operate in measuring its efficiency rather than on the basis of it being technically sound from an engineering viewpoint or from the viewpoint of a highly industrialized country as the United States.

6. Why hasn't the United States been more helpful in setting universal standards for industrial equipment? Do you feel that the argument is economically sound? Discuss.

   It seems that the main reason why the United States has not been more helpful in setting universal standards is that a rather large demand still exists for products or replacement parts which are based on the inch-pound system of measurement. This demand exists in the United States and foreign countries as well. Another reason for the lack of help is that the expenses involved in such a change are considerable, and no one particular firm is willing to incur such an expense when none of its competitors or other companies are willing to either lead or follow the example. This argument may be economically sound when one considers a short-run period but not sound over a longer period of time. Over a short period of time, the domestic sales lost and the foreign sales gained would probably not be enough to offset each other nor adequate enough to cover the expenses incurred in such a change. However, when one considers the impact of such a change over a long-run period, the foreign sales gained would probably be substantial enough to cover both the domestic sales lost and the expenses incurred from such a change. What is presently being done is that companies are sitting back and waiting for the "other fellow" to make the first move and seeing what effect this has on the profitability of the company and its accompanying aspects.

7. What role do service, replacement parts, and standards play in competition in foreign marketing? Illustrate.

   Service, replacement parts, and standards are an important aspect of competition in foreign marketing. These aspects all rate high with the foreign customer; and the company which can meet these demands, and several others, is the company which will profit and will be more competitive. It should also be noted that the lack of any one of these factors may mean the loss of business for a foreign or a domestic based firm. Take, for example, the factor of delivery time on spare parts. If two companies are equal in all other factors, the company which can deliver the goods the fastest and most economically will be the company which will get the business. This is true for many of the other aspects as well as for those mentioned above.

8. Discuss the part industrial trade fairs and trade centers play in international marketing of industrial goods. What is the difference between industrial trade fairs and trade centers?

   A trade center is a permanent, year round display location in which the products of a particular country are displayed, demonstrated, and sold. These centers are located in countries other than the "guest" countries which display the products. Thus, an American-based company may be able to utilize the display facilities in such centers as London, Frankfurt, Milan, Bangkok, or other such cities. These centers provide a place where foreign-based companies can exhibit their goods and stimulate sales for these goods.

   A trade fair is a government-sponsored attempt to facilitate foreign trade with the "host" country. Foreign-based companies are invited to exhibit their goods within the "host" country at a particular location. Trade fairs are scheduled periodically and any interested manufacturer can reserve space to exhibit his goods.

9. Describe the reasons an MNC might seek an ISO 9000 certification.

   One research report examining the purchase decision variables of importer managers found that product quality, including dependability of suppliers and timely delivery, were the most important variables influencing purchase decisions.

   With quality becoming the cornerstone of global competition, companies are requiring assurance of standard conformance from suppliers just as their customers are requiring the same from them. Outside of regulated product areas, the importance of ISO 9000 registration as a competitive market tool in the EC varies from sector to sector. In some sectors, European companies may require suppliers to attest that they have an approved quality system in place as a condition for purchase. ISO 9000 may be used to serve as a means of differentiating different "classes" of suppliers (particularly in high-tech areas) where high product reliability is crucial. In other words, if two suppliers are competing for the same contract, the one with ISO 9000 registration may have a competitive edge.

   If a company practices Total Quality Management (TQM), the system probably meets ISO 9000 standards but it would have to be audited and certified as such.

10. What ISO 9000 legal requirements are imposed on products sold in the EC? Discuss.

    ISO 9000 is not a legal requirement for access to the EC market but ISO 9000 certification is required under EC law for product certification on a few highly regulated, high-risk products such as medical devices, telecommunications terminal equipment, gas appliances, and personal protective equipment. Although ISO 9000 is voluntary, except for regulated products, the EC Product Liability Directive puts pressure on all companies to become certified. The directive holds that a manufacturer, including an exporter, will be liable, regardless of fault or negligence, if a person is harmed on an object that has been damaged by a faulty product. Thus, customers in the EC need to be assured that the components of their products are free of defects or deficiencies. A manufacturer with a well-documented quality system will be better able to prove that products are defect-free and thus minimize liability claims.

11. Discuss the competitive consequences of being ISO 9000 certified.

    A strong level of interest in ISO 9000 is being driven more by "marketplace" requirements than by government regulations and ISO 9000 is becoming an important competitive marketing tool in Europe. As the market demands quality and more and more companies adopt some form of TQM (total quality management), manufacturers are increasingly requiring ISO 9000 registration of their suppliers. Although a legal requirement in only a small number of directives, ISO 9000 is becoming increasingly important commercially for gaining access to EC markets. As of 1991, 42 countries had adopted the ISO 9000 standards as national standards.

12. Discuss how the characteristics that define the uniqueness of industrial products lead naturally to relationship marketing. Give some examples.

    Two basic factors account for greater market similarities among industrial goods customers than consumer goods customers. First is the inherent nature of the product: industrial goods are goods and services used in the process of creating other goods and services. Consumer goods are in their final form and are consumed by individuals. And second, the motive or intent of the user differs: industrial consumers are seeking profit whereas the ultimate consumer is seeking satisfaction. These factors are manifest in specific buying patterns, demand characteristics, and a special emphasis on relationship marketing as a competitive tool.

    The characteristics that define the uniqueness of industrial products discussed above lead naturally to relationship marketing. The long-term relationship with customers which is at the core of relationship marketing fits the characteristics inherent in industrial products and is a viable strategy for industrial goods marketing. The first and foremost characteristic of industrial goods markets is the motive of the buyer—to make a profit. Industrial products fit into a business or manufacturing process and its contributions will be judged on how well it contributes to that process. In order for an industrial marketer to fulfill the needs of its customer, the marketer must understand those needs as they exist today and how they will change as the buyer strives to compete in global markets that call for long-term relationships.

    Relationship marketing ranges all the way from gathering information on customer needs to designing products and services, channeling products to customers in a timely and convenient manner, and following up to make sure the customer is satisfied.

    The industrial customer's needs in global markets are continuously changing and suppliers' offerings must also continue to change. The need for the latest technology means that it is not a matter of selling the right product the first time but one of continuously changing the product to keep it right over time. The objective of relationship marketing is to make the relationship an important attribute of the transaction thus differentiating oneself from competitors. It shifts the focus away from price to service and long-term benefits. The reward is loyal customers that translate into substantial profits.

    Relationship marketing can often give a company the competitive edge when a customer's ultimate success depends on more than technical expertise.

13. Discuss some of the more pertinent problems in pricing industrial goods.

    Pricing industrial goods in a foreign market is a problem which domestic manufacturers find to be shaded oftentimes with political overtones. That is, political rather than economic reasons may often be the backbone of a country's pricing policy with respect to certain goods. Such is the case in many of the underdeveloped, yet industrializing, nations. Russia is able to undercut American prices by as much as 50 percent because of the degree of government control over industry and the desire to build goodwill in these countries.

    Another area where pricing policies led to a problem is that many American manufacturers insist on payment in cash. Credit terms are often lacking for other countries, especially the underdeveloped ones. Thus, those manufacturers in competition with American manufacturers oftentimes have a competitive advantage when they extend more liberal credit terms to various countries.

14. What is the price-quality relationship? How does this affect a U.S. firm's comparative position in world markets?

The price-quality relationship is a factor related to standards of various products a country will produce. Typically, the higher the quality of a product, the higher the ensuing price. This relationship oftentimes has an adverse effect on the marketability of American products in their competitive stand against products of another country. That is, the standards for American products are too often domestic standards and are not commensurate with the needs of a foreign country whose standards are not as high as ours. Hence, our high-quality products are more costly and less needed than lower-quality, lower-priced products.

15. Select several countries each at a different stage of economic development and illustrate how the stage affects demand for industrial goods.

Library project.

16. England has started the process of shifting from the inch-pound system to the metric system. What effect do you think this will have on the traditional U.S. reluctance to such a change? Discuss the economic implications of such a move.

With England's recent indication of changing from the inch-pound system to the metric system, the American reluctance to such a change will probably be softened to a certain extent. That is, with pressures from competing countries and the search for new markets for U.S. products, the inch-pound system is slowly but surely being pushed out of competition with the metric system. England realized that the demands for products measured by the metric system in foreign countries is greater than demands for inch-pound measured products. America, to a large extent, is not following the basic marketing concept; we insist on making a product and then looking for the market instead of the reverse. Even though such a change is one of a large scale, American industry will probably have to make it eventually if it expects to grow by marketing industrial products to foreign countries, especially since England's move will leave the United States virtually alone with the inch-pound system. This should put added force behind those in the United States who have advocated that the United States shift to the metric system. If the decision is made to adopt a metric system, the period of changeover will be at least a decade, and the cost will be very high. In the long run, the United States cannot afford not to convert.

17. Discuss the importance of international business services to total U.S. export trade. How do most U.S. service companies become international?

International trade in services is becoming more important in the economies of both the United States and other countries. It is the fastest growing sector of international trade. It is estimated that services account for about 1/4 of the value of all international trade. Currently international trade and services are estimated to be 650 billion dollars compared to $1,870 billion in global merchandise exports. The United States portion of services and merchandise export is 35–40 percent of overall trade. These figures, however, may be underestimated since such services as advertising, accounting, management, consulting, legal services, most insurance, and most of the new computer and communications services are omitted from the balance of payments figures from which the service portion of trade is determined.

Most U.S. service companies' initial entry into the international market is to follow their American customers to overseas markets. However, as they became established in these countries, they began to expand their services to local companies. Many firms established branches and acquired local affiliations to serve both U.S. as well as local clients.

18. Discuss the international market environment for international business services.

Service firms face most of the same environmental constraints and problems confronting merchandise traders. Protectionism, controls on transborder data flows, competition, and the protection trademarks processes and patents are probably the most important problems confronting multinationals in today's international service market. Protectionism looms because U.S. business service firms are threatening local companies. Many local companies have developed as a result of foreign service companies operating in their countries and are now seeking direct and indirect trade barriers to restrict foreign companies from domestic business service markets. A study of U.S. service firms reported that ownership restrictions or prepaid royalties, discriminatory tax policies, and barriers to transborder data flow were the most frequently encountered barriers to trade.

Restrictions, however, are not generated only by foreign firms. The U.S. government also creates problems for service firms. The biggest domestic headache is U.S. export controls. Getting a U.S. export license is the greatest domestic barrier foreign selling services abroad face. Not only is it time consuming but it is frequently not clear which of the many U.S. agencies are involved in approving the request. A last issue of importance facing the business services is protection of property rights. Since most business services can be duplicated with ease, there is a major problem in protecting services from piracy. In many cases, laws are not clear and as a result, it is difficult to enforce laws to protect processes, trademarks, etc.

## Chapter 14 – International Marketing Channels

### Teaching Objectives

In some markets the distribution system may be the single biggest impediment to successful marketing. An inadequate distribution system may make the cost of reaching some consumers so high that it puts the price of the product out of reach of the market. In China, for example, the market for a product that exists in areas outside the major urban centers is often inaccessible because of a lack of a viable distribution system. In others, the distribution system may be so structured and difficult to enter that is serves as a major non-tariff barrier. Although beginning to show signs of weakening, the hold that wholesalers and manufacturers have over many small retailers and laws that protect the system make the distribution network almost inaccessible to an outsider. The broad focus of this chapter is to present an overview of a range of distribution systems that confront an international marketer. The teaching objectives are to:

1) Present the variety of distribution channel structures and show how they affect cost and efficiency in marketing.
2) Examine the Japanese distribution system as it exists today, changes that are rapidly occurring, and speculate on the eventual changes that will come about there.
3) Detail both the home country and foreign country middleman alternatives available to an international marketer.
4) Discuss the factors affecting the choice of a channel.
5) Review the methods of locating, selecting, and motivating channel members.

### Comments and Suggestions

1. To illustrate the extreme channel structures that can confront an international marketer, I like to begin the discussion of this chapter with a comparison of a channel structure with a minimum number of middlemen (import-oriented distribution structure), the channel structure found in the United States, and the Japanese distribution system. This discussion provides students with a comprehensive view of some of the types of channel structures confronting the international marketer. TM 15–5, Comparison of Distribution Channels between the Untied States and Japan, serves as a good illustration of the fundamental differences between the two. Transparency masters 15–1 through 15–9 are useful in helping to focus on the issues under discussion.
2. Following the discussion above, I present a brief overview of the international channel of distribution alternatives, Exhibit 14–4 followed by a discussion of the six Cs of channel strategy.
3. Catalog sales and mail order are growing in importance as an effective way to enter some markets. There have been a number of large U.S. catalog retailers, L.L. Bean, Lands' End, and Eddie Bauer for example, that are experiencing some success in Japan. Such companies have a good "quality" image in Japan and, furthermore, U.S. goods are cheaper than comparable Japanese goods. The strength of the yen helps U.S. companies to be price competitive but the biggest benefit may come from the personal exemption on import tariffs a Japanese consumer receives when ordering from the U.S., up to 10,000 yen (approximately $115) per order. With express shipping, a U.S. company can deliver in 72 hours. For more details on this topic see, "Japan Is Dialing 1–800 Buyamerica," *Business Week*, June 12, 1995, pp. 81–82.
4. Locating and the management of middlemen conclude the discussion on this chapter.

5. There are several cases that illustrate the point made in this chapter. Case 3–5, Konark Television India is a comprehensive case dealing with channel strategy in India. This is an excellent case to have the students prepare for discussion in class. Case 4–6, Selling White Dove Shampoo in the Philippines, is also a good case for in-class discussion. Although this case includes other parts of the marketing mix, distribution is an important issue.

**Lecture Outline**

I Global Perspective—400 Million Sticks of Doublemint Today—A Billion Tomorrow

II. Channel of Distribution Structures

- A. Import Oriented Distribution Structure
- B. Japanese Distribution Structure
  1. High Density of Middlemen
  2. Channel Control
  3. Business Philosophy
  4. Large-Scale Retail Store Law
- C. Trends – From Traditional to Modern Channel Structure

III. Distribution Patterns

- A. General Patterns
  1 Middlemen Services
  2. Line Breadth
  3. Costs and Margins
  4. Channel Length
  5. Nonexistent Channels
  6. Eastern Europe Presents a Special Problem
  7. Blocked Channels
  8. Stocking
  9. Power and Competition
- B. Retail Patterns
  1 Size Patterns
  2. Direct Marketing
  3. Resistance to Change

IV. Alternative Middleman Choices

- A. Home Country Middlemen
  1. Global Retailers
  2. Export Management Companies
  2. Trading Companies
  3. U. S. Export Trading Companies
  4. Complementary Marketers
  5. Manufacturer's Export Agent
  6. Home Country Brokers
  7. Buying Offices

8. Selling Groups
    a. Webb-Pomerene Export Associations (WPEA)
    b. Foreign Sales Corporation (FSC)
9. Export Merchant
10. Export Jobbers

B. Foreign Country Middlemen
1 Manufacturer's Representatives
2. Distributors
3. Foreign Country Brokers
4. Managing Agents and Compradors
5. Dealers
6. Import Jobber, Wholesalers, and Retailers

C. Government-Affiliated Middlemen

V. Factors Affecting Choice of Channels
A. Cost
B. Capital Requirement
C. Control
D. Coverage
E. Character
F. Continuity

VI. Locating, Selecting, and Motivating Channel Members
A. Locating Middlemen
B. Selecting Middlemen
1. Screening
2. The Agreement
C. Motivating Middlemen
D. Terminating Middlemen
C. Controlling Middlemen

VII. World Wide Web

VIII. The Internet and Traditional Channels

IX. Summary

## DISCUSSION QUESTIONS

1. Define:

| | | | |
|---|---|---|---|
| Distribution process | Export Trading Company Act (ETC) | Norazi agent | Large-Scale Retail Store Law |
| Distribution structure | Export management company (EMC) | Manufacturer's agents | Government-affiliated middlemen |
| Distribution channel | Webb-Pomerene Export Association (WPEA) | Foreign distributor | E-commerce |
| Facilitating agency | Manufacturer's export agent (MEA) | Foreign-country broker | Complementary marketing |
| Agent middlemen | | Managing agent | |
| Merchant middlemen | | Foreign sales corporation (FSC) | |
| Home country middlemen | | Structural Impediments Initiative (SII) | |
| Dealer | | | |
| Import jobber | | | |

2. Discuss the distinguishing features of the Japanese distribution system.

Distribution in Japan has long been considered the most effective non-tariff barrier to the Japanese market. The distribution system is different enough from its United States or European counterparts that it should be carefully studied by anyone contemplating entry. The Japanese system has four distinguishing features: 1) a structure dominated by many small wholesalers dealing with many small retailers; 2) channel control by manufacturers; 3) a business philosophy shaped by a unique culture; and 4) laws that protect the foundation of the system, the small retailer.

**High Density of Middlemen.** There is a density of middlemen, retailers and wholesalers in the Japanese market unparalleled in any Western industrialized country. The traditional structure serves consumers who make small, frequent purchases, at small conveniently located stores. The high density of small stores with small inventories is supported by an equal density of wholesalers. It is not unusual for consumer goods to go through three or four intermediaries before reaching the consumer—producer to primary, secondary, regional, and local wholesaler, and finally to retailer to consumer.

**Channel Control.** Manufacturers depend on wholesalers for a multitude of services to other members of the distribution network. Financing, physical distribution, warehousing, inventory, promotion and payment collection are provided to other channel members by wholesalers. The system works because wholesalers and all other middlemen downstream are tied to manufacturers by a set of practices and incentives designed to ensure strong marketing support for their products and to exclude rival competitors from the channel.

**Business Philosophy.** Coupled with the close economic ties and dependency created by trade customs and the long structure of Japanese distribution channels is a unique business philosophy that emphasizes loyalty, harmony, and friendship. The value system supports long-term dealer/supplier relationships that are difficult to change as long as each party perceives economic advantage. The traditional partner, the insider, generally has the advantage.

**Large-Scale Retail Store Law.** Competition from large retail stores has been almost totally controlled by *Daitenho*–the Large-Scale Retail Store Law. Designed to protect small retailers from large intruders into their markets, the law requires that any store larger than 5,382 square feet (500 square meters) must have approval from the prefectural government to be "built, expanded, stay open later in the evening, or change the days of the month they must remain closed." All proposals for new "large" stores are first judged by MITI (Ministry of International Trade and Industry). Then, if local retailers unanimously agree to the plan, it is swiftly approved. However, without approval at the prefecture level (all small retailers in the area must agree), the plan is returned for clarification and modification that may take several years (ten years is not unheard of) for approval. Besides the large-scale retail store law, there are myriad licensing rules. One investigation of the regulations that governed the opening of a retail store revealed 39 different licenses, each with a separate law, needed to open a full-service store.

3. Discuss the ways Japanese manufacturers control the distribution process from manufacturer to retailer.

   Manufacturers depend on wholesalers for a multitude of services to other members of the distribution network. Financing, physical distribution, warehousing, inventory, promotion and payment collection are provided to other channel members by wholesalers. The system works because wholesalers and all other middlemen downstream are tied to manufacturers by a set of practices and incentives designed to ensure strong marketing support for their products and to exclude rival competitors from the channel.

   Wholesalers typically act as agent middlemen and extend the manufacturer's control through the channel to the retail level. Control is maintained by: 1) inventory financing, sales made on consignment with credits extending for several months; 2) cumulative rebates, rebates given annually for any number of reasons including quantity purchases, early payments, achieving sales targets, performing services, maintaining specific inventory levels, participating in sales promotions, loyalty to suppliers, maintaining manufacturer's price policies, cooperation, and contribution to overall success; 3) merchandise returns, all unsold merchandise may be returned to the manufacturer; and, 4) promotional support, intermediaries receive a host of displays, advertising layouts, management education programs, in-store demonstrations, and other dealer aids which strengthen the relationship among middlemen and the manufacturer.

4. Describe the large-scale retail store law found in Japan and show how the Structural Impediments Initiative (SII) is bringing about change in Japanese retailing.

   Competition from large retail stores has been almost totally controlled by *Daitenbo,* the Large-Scale Retail Store Law. Designed to protect small retailers from large intruders into their markets, the law requires that any store larger than 5,382 square feet (500 square meters) must have approval from the prefectural government to be built, expanded, stay open later in the evening or change the days of the month they must remain closed. All proposals for new large stores are first judged by MITI (Ministry of International Trade and Industry). Then, if local retailers unanimously agree to the plan, it is swiftly approved. However, without approval at the prefecture level (all small retailers in the area must agree), the plan is returned for clarification and modification that may take several years (10 years is not unheard of) for approval.

   Designed to protect small retailers against competition from large stores, the law has been imposed against both domestic and foreign companies. It took ten years for one of Japan's largest supermarket chains to get clearance for a new site. Toys 'R' Us fought rules and regulations for over three years before it gained approval for a store. Besides the "large-scale retail store" law, there are myriad licensing rules. One investigation of the regulations governing the opening of retal stores uncovered 39 different laws, each with a separate license, that had to be met to open a full-service store.

   Agreements between the United States and Japan under the Structural Impediments Initiative (SII) have had a profound impact on the Japanese distribution system by leading to deregulation of retailing and strengthening rules on monopoly business practices. The retailing law has been relaxed to permit new outlets as large as 1,000 square meters without prior permission and limits on store hours and business days per year have also been lifted. Officially relaxing laws and regulations on retailing is but one of the important changes signaling the beginning of profound changes in how the Japanese shop.

The SII negotiations to pry open new markets for American companies is producing strong evidence of cracks in the system. Japanese businesspeople are challenging the traditional system and Japanese consumers are undergoing a change in attitude toward shopping and traditional retailing by responding favorably to bargain prices.

SII and deregulation will undoubtedly have a part in changing Japanese distribution practices but those merchants willing to challenge traditional ways and give the consumer quality products at competitive, fair prices will bring about the demise of the way department stores and small shops wedded to the traditional distribution system operate. Specialty discounters are sprouting up everywhere and entrepreneurs are slashing prices by buying direct and avoiding the distribution system altogether. Japanese consumers, described as brand loyal and more interested in services and quality than price, seem to be willing accomplices to the changes taking place and understandably so. The Japanese consumer has traditionally paid the highest prices in the world for the goods they buy. Before Toys `R' Us changed the price levels, toys in Japan cost four times as much as toys in any other country. Japanese-made products imported to the United States can be purchased in the U.S. for less than they cost in Japan. Such inequities did not seem to matter to the Japanese consumer when they had no other alternatives. But, more often now, the Japanese consumer has a choice of prices for everything from appliances to beer.

The "new" retailers are relatively small and account for no more than three percent of retail sales, compared with 14 percent for all specialty discounters in the U.S. But their impact extends beyond their share of market because they are forcing the system to change. Traditional retailers are modifying marketing and sales strategies in response to the new competition as well as to take advantage of changing Japanese lifestyles. There are also indications that some wholesalers are modernizing and consolidating operations as retailers demand to buy direct from the manufacturer or from the largest wholesalers. The process is slow because the characteristics of the distribution system are deeply rooted in the cultural history of Japan.

5. "Japanese retailing may be going through a change similar to that which occurred in the United States after World War II." Discuss and give examples.

Japanese retailing may be going through a change similar to that which occurred in the United States after World War II. At that time the U.S. retailing structure was made up of many small retailers served by a multilayered wholesaling system and full service department stores and specialty stores offering all the needs of the shopper from soup to nuts including a long list of "services." Resale price maintenance laws (also referred to as fair trade laws) allowed national manufacturers to dictate high retail prices necessary to support an inefficient distribution system and amenities, i.e., "services," which, when offered the opportunity, the consumer was willing to give up for lower prices. High margins were an attraction to the discounter who offered few, if any services and priced items well below manufactured suggested prices. Department stores and other "traditional retailers" fought back with attempts to enforce fair trade laws. When that failed, they also began to discount items but found they could not continue to operate in the old way with discounted prices. At that point, retailing in the United States began to change. Some traditional stores went out of business, others down-sized and dropped entire lines, others reinvented themselves into different operations and many of the small "mom and pop" stores went out of business. Thus began a retailing revolution that ultimately spawned new types of retailers like Wal-Mart, Kmart, Target, Price/Costco, Levitz Furniture, Best, Toys `R' Us, and a whole host of other retail store types that did not exist a few decades earlier. If retailing follows a similar pattern in Japan, as it appears to be doing, Japanese retailing will not be recognizable in a decade or two. What seemed to be an impenetrable retailing system just a few years ago now appears to be on the verge of opening up and creating opportunities for U.S. marketers.

6. Discuss how the globalization of markets, especially Europe 1992, will affect retail distribution.

   There are some important trends in distribution systems that will lead to their eventual globalization. That is, there is greater commonalty than disparity among middlemen in different countries. U.S. based Southland Corporation's 7-Eleven Stores are replacing many of the traditional "Mom and Pop" stores that have dominated a significant part of Japan's retail food distribution. In Spain, 7-Eleven and Campsa, the Spanish gasoline monopoly, opened 200 7-Eleven minimarkets at Campsa service stations. Hypermarkets, a retailing innovation developed in France, have expanded beyond French borders to other European countries and to the United States. Discount, home repair, self-service, and supermarkets are all mass merchandising concepts gradually spreading all over the world. In anticipation of Europe 1992, national and international retailing networks are developing throughout the world. European integration, global brands, globalized media communications, consumers that expect rational and predictable product assortments, and global companies anxious for their products to be distributed in the most efficient manner are factors driving a growing number of traditional distribution channel members to greater efficiencies and competitiveness. Many are developing into transnational, if not global, operations. Global products require integrated, efficient distribution systems to achieve maximum effectiveness.

7. To what extent, and in what ways, do the functions of domestic middlemen differ from their foreign counterparts?

   The functions of the domestic and foreign middlemen are quite similar in many areas, but there are certain differences. First, the domestic agent usually takes possession of the goods, whereas the foreign agent does not. In the area of setting prices, the domestic agent has the authority to do so, while his foreign counterpart does not. Both types of domestic middlemen arrange for the shipping of goods, but the foreign middlemen do not. Two other differences exist between foreign and domestic agents. The domestic agent does some promotion and selling, and occasionally extends credit. On the other hand, foreign agents usually do not participate in these activities.

8. Why is the EMC sometimes called an independent export department?

   The EMC is sometimes called an international marketing department. There are several reasons for this title. First, many of the firms it represents are small and cannot afford extensive overseas marketing themselves. They must rely on the EMS. The EMC does business in the name of the manufacturer. This includes not only normal selling activities, but also active promotion, provision of credit information, physical handling, and even financing. In this light the EMC appears to be an independent marketing arm of the manufacturer.

9. Discuss how physical distribution relates to channel policy and how they affect one another.

   Two extremely different channel policies exist in various areas which affect physical distribution. For example, in Turkey the buyer must seek out the seller with very little service offered by the latter. This is an example of the marketing channel working backwards. The normal policy is for the seller to seek out the buyer, excluding the retail market, and for the seller to offer a whole range of services. In some areas, middlemen are characterized by specialization. This practice tends to make the distribution process overly complex. Another channel policy found in many countries is the existence of huge middlemen and tiny middlemen with no one in between these two. The large ones tend to be very efficient in distribution, while the other is not. In most countries other than the United States and U.S.S.R., channel length is very long. This slows up the physical distribution of goods. Often, distribution of goods is slowed up because of low inventories caused by the high cost of money. It is unprofitable to maintain a large stock of goods.

10. Explain how and why distribution channels are affected as they are when the stage of development of an economy improves.

As an economy advances, the distribution system begins to take the form of distribution in the U.S. The apparent reason for this change in structure is due to the decentralization of the total marketing function. As an economy becomes more sophisticated it places increasingly complicated and sophisticated demands upon the marketing function. This results in modification of the existing system to be able to meet the increased demand placed upon it by the emerging economy. Consumer segments become much larger and diversified and each in turn places new demands on the distribution system which causes modification in order to administer to the requirements of that segment.

11. In what circumstances is the use of a EMC logical?

The export management company is the logical choice of middlemen for firms with relatively small international volume or for those that do not want to involve their own personnel in the international function.

12. In what circumstances are trading companies likely to be used?

Trading companies are likely to be employed when adequate coverage of a market, market access, or political acceptability is not possible by one firm. This would be the case in trade between developed and underdeveloped countries as well as between Western nations and the former Communist bloc countries.

13. How is the distribution channel structure affected by increasing emphasis on the government as a customer and by the existence of state trading agencies?

The growth of government both as a user and as a middleman has placed new emphasis on marketing to monopsonies. Government is especially important in dealing with industrial goods and commodities. Facilitating middlemen are often used to gain advantage from their strong government contacts and ability to cut red tape. In general government dealings call for short channels with direct contact or one local middleman at most.

14. Review the key variables that affect the marketer's choice of distribution channels.

The four main variables which affect the marketer's choice of distribution channels are (1) the availability of middlemen, (2) the cost of their services, (3) the functions performed (and the effectiveness with which each is performed) and (4) the extent of control which the manufacturers can exert over the middlemen's activities.

15. Account, as best you can, for the differences in channel patterns which might be encountered in a highly developed country and an underdeveloped country.

The attitude toward the middlemen in underdeveloped countries is generally negative, whereas his or her place in developed countries is accepted. This feeling in underdeveloped areas exists because the people emphasize production and consider the middleman unproductive. The result is often that this function is done on the side or secretly, which makes distribution overly difficult. Also, distribution is done on a small scale, whereas developed countries are often characterized by the extremely large middlemen. The poor nations live on a subsistence level. They are not so dependent on trade as developed countries are. Therefore, the importance of distributors is low. Distribution is slow and inefficient in underdeveloped countries because the population is widely scattered, inventories are low (high cost of capital), the middleman is very small, and margins are high. The developed nations are generally of opposite character.

16. "One of the first things companies discover about international channel of distribution patterns is that in most countries it is nearly impossible to gain adequate market coverage through a simple channel of distribution plan." Discuss.

    A single channel of distribution is often unavailable in foreign countries. One reason is that the channels used may be very unfamiliar to the producer and only seem to be complicated. More realistic reasons may be true in financial arrangements or the unavailability of middlemen. In many countries, middlemen may be specialists in either product or market area or both. If this is the case, several different middlemen are needed to distribute a single product in a country or to distribute several products within a single contiguous area.

17. Discuss the various methods of overcoming blocked channels.

    Buying equity in the middlemen and thereby gaining entrance to the channel. Buying distribution through wide margins, contract bonuses, and other forms of cash settlements will unblock the channel.

    Seeking alternative channels or new channels can get around the dilemma. The most expensive means is for the company to build its own channel.

18. What strategy might be employed to distribute goods effectively in the dichotomous small-large middleman pattern which characterizes merchant middlemen in most countries?

    The strategy in this situation is no different than it would be in the United States in that selection of wholesaler middlemen should be based on at least two criteria. One, to whom the wholesaler sells or distributes, i.e., selects a wholesaler to reach a specific target market and the cost efficiency of a particular wholesaler middleman. In most countries if complete distribution of your goods is to be achieved, both small and large middlemen must be utilized to effectively reach all segments of the market. However, the smaller middlemen may be sufficiently inefficient to increase the cost of distribution thereby increasing the cost of the product to a point that it is no longer priced competitively.

19. Discuss the economic implications of charging termination penalties or restricting the termination of middlemen. Do you foresee such restrictions in the United States?

    Termination penalties restrict the freedom of marketers to adjust to changing needs of the market and therefore reduce market efficiency. Such restrictions may stultify company growth and restrict its flexibility. Risk taking and experimentation are minimized because the marketer has a difficult time terminating experimental channels that fail.

    There are indicators and a few legal precedents restricting manufacturer's middleman termination in the United States but growth of such restriction has been slow and cautious.

20. Discuss why Japanese distribution channels can be the epitome of blocked channels.

    Distribution in Japan has long been considered the most effective non-tariff barrier to the Japanese market. The distribution system is different enough from U.S. or European countertrades to give an advantage to domestic competitors. The Japanese system has three layers (1) a structure dominated by small wholesalers dealing with small retailers, (2) unique trade customs, and, (3) a philosophy shaped by unique culture. It is not unusual for consumer goods to go through three or four intermediaries before reaching the consumer producer—the primary, secondary, regional and local wholesaler, and finally to retailers and consumers. The high degree of fragmentation and specialization makes it difficult to go direct and thus forces a manufacturer to rely on middlemen with an elaborate set of trade customs. Traditions unknown to the U.S. marketer make these channels the epitome of blocked channels.

21. What are the two most important provisions of the Export Trading Act of 1982?

The two most important provisions of the Export Trading Act of 1982 are that companies are exempt from Sherman Antitrust violations for their activities as an export trading company for sales of products outside the United States. This exemption is given by the Department of Commerce as a certificate which enables the export trading company to have the added assurance that the export program in which they are engaging will not be challenged by the courts. The second provisions of the Export Trading Act is that financial institutions, i.e., banks, can be owners of export trading companies. Prior to the ETC act, banks were not permitted to own commercial enterprises.

22. Why are WPEAs considered more risky from an anti-trust perspective than are ETCs?

WPEAs are considered more risky because of potential anti-trust violation. There is no way members of the WPEA can know for certain in advance of the activities that their business will not be challenged by the Justice Department for antitrust violation. An Export Trading Company (ETC) can apply for a certificate of review which permits specific anti-trust exemption to be issued prior to the formulation of an ETC. Thus, participating members of ETCs have a greater assurance of protection from anti-trust violations.

23. Eddie Bauer, a U.S. retailer, has a Web site in the U.S. at http://www.eddiebauer.com and is also included in the German Web Mall, http://www.shopping24.de. Visit both stores, the one in the U.S. and the one in Germany. Find the same article for sale in each store and compare price. The German store will list the product in German marks but you can convert to U.S. dollars by visiting the Universal Currency Converter at http://www.xe.net/currency. Is the article you selected higher in Germany or the United States. What would be the delivered price to your hometown from both stores? Would it be to the advantage of the German to buy the article in the United States? For you to buy in Germany?

The response to this question will vary depending on the article of clothing selected. At the time this was written (1998), the same shirt, Polo-Pullover, was accessed at both sites. The price in Germany was DM79 or U.S.44.76 and the price in the United States was U.S. $48 or DM84.72. For this article it would seem that the best for the German is to buy in Germany although taxes in Germany may be higher than in the U.S.—but taxes have to be paid regardless. It is interesting to collect the prices and compare a variety of garments.

24. What are the benefits for a small retail company that wants to get international sales to engage in e commerce? What are some of the problems that might be encountered? Suggest ways the problems can be overcome.

E-commerce is a fast and relatively easy to acquire international sales. In fact, many who have e-commerce Web pages for domestic sales get international orders. However if a company wants to target foreign customers then there are important steps to be taken if sales from international markets are to be maximized.

An important advantage of selling direct is that total costs can be lowered so the final price overseas is considerably less than it would have been through a distributor. However, doing business in other countries has always required someone who can translate prospective customer inquiries and orders into English, and reply in their language. Often a local distributor in each country, who stocks and provides the local interface between vendor and client, provides these services. Intermediaries can be eliminated but someone, either the seller or the buyer, must assume the functions they perform. Consequently, an e-vendor must be concerned with the following issues.

- **Translation**. Ideally, a Web site should be translated into the languages of the target markets. This may not be financially feasible but at least the most important pages of the site should be translated. A reasonable solution is to use automatic translator software such as that offered by

Globalink http://www.globalink.com. The resulting text is not perfect, but you can understand what is being asked, and you can respond easily.

- **Local contact.** Many companies are creating "virtual offices" abroad, whereby a company has a phone number in important cities that doubles as a voicemail/fax contact point. Companies fully committed to foreign markets buy server space and create "mirror sites" in key markets. The feeling is that foreign customers are more likely to visit sites in their own country and in the local language.
- **Payment**. For all amounts over $10, a credit card number – either by e-mail (from a secure page on your Web site), by fax, or over the phone can be made. A company not set up to accept credit cards can use companies like First Virtual (http://www.fv.com) that provide this service at a reasonable charge.
- **Delivery.** For companies operating in the United States, surface postal delivery of small parcels is the most cost effective but takes the longest time. For more rapid, although expensive, deliveries Federal Express, United Parcel Service, and others provide delivery worldwide. For example, Tom Clancy's bestseller "Executive Orders" shipped express to Paris from Seattle-based Amazon.com, would cost a reader $55.52. The same book delivered in four to 10 weeks via surface mail costs $25.52, substantial savings over the cost of the book in a Paris bookstore where it sells for $35.
- **Promotion**. Although the WWW is a means of promotion, if you are engaging in e-commerce you need also to advertise your presence and the products or services offered. The old adage, "build a better mouse trap and the world will beat a path to your door" does not work for e-commerce just as it does not work with other products unless you tell your target market about the availability of the "better mouse trap." How do you attract visitors from other countries to your site? The same way you would at home except in the local language. Index registration, press releases, local newsgroups and forums, mutual links and banner advertising are the traditional way. However, it is the authors' opinion that one of the weakest links in e-commerce is the promotion of Web sites. It is still a hit and miss proposition for a prospective customer to be exposed to one of the traditional ways that Internet sites are promoted. There is so much clutter on the Web, and its increasing as the Web grows, that an e-vendor needs to attract attention. One method is to advertise via other media to the target market. Some companies do this indirectly by listing their Web address somewhere in an advertisement—generally as a tag line. A more effective way would be to advertise directly to the target market using other media.

25. Assume you owned a small manufacturing company that produced widgets. How could you go about finding buyers for your widgets using the Internet? How could commercial Internet companies help you in expanding your business overseas using the Internet?

    As the Internet matures it is becoming a viable venue for finding buyers and other middlemen to represent companies as well as direct sales. Internet based services such as Unibex, a global business center. http://www.unibex.com provides a plethora of information and services available to the international marketer, some free and some fee-based. Here is a brief overview of two.

    **Unibex** (http://www.unibex.com). Unibex Corporation is a Web-based import-export support service, which offers one-stop on-line shopping for the full range of trade services, from market research to settlement. Subscribers can create offers, negotiate deals, and close business—all on line. The Global Business Center has three internal sites: The Global Exhibit Center has over 16 million records for companies; The Global Exchange Center has specific business opportunities presented as offers from Unibex Exchange subscribers; and, The Global Resource Center provides access to information from over 600 professional sources including company profiles, credit reports, market research and other data.

Companies like Dun & Bradstreet (country market reports, identify prospects, commercial risk management), Deloitte & Touche – (verification services as to trading partner's credit line, product quality, and business references), and The Chase Manhattan Corporation – (credit card and fund transfer services) are among the companies to be found on Unibex.

**Trade Compass** (http://www.tradecompass.com). Trade Compass is organized into four categories: World Infodesk provides a variety of information sources, U.S. laws and regulations, over 10,000 market reports, and country guides: International Business Center provides insurance, finance and travel: Strategic Analysis provides market intelligence, and trade consulting: and Trade Leads provides sources for projects and prospects, export offer services, and links to potential agents, distributors, joint venture partners and licensing opportunities.

Visit these sites for more detailed information. Both are fee based but each does provide a free visit.

## Chapter 15 – Exporting and Logistics: Special Issues for the Small Business

### Teaching Objectives

When engaging in international marketing a company cannot escape the mechanics of exporting—moving goods from one country into another involves rules and regulations that control the movement of these goods. Further, goods must be physically moved across borders. These mechanics add to the cost of international marketing and while they cannot be completely avoided, their effects can be minimized. Although mechanical in nature, the importance of exporting should not be minimizedas it is an uncontrollable element faced by all companies, large or small. The teaching objectives of this chapter are to:

1) Illustrate the exporting process and provide students with an overall view of the steps of moving goods from one country to another.
2) Examine U.S. export regulations and import regulations that face an exporter.
3) Review the types of customs privileged facilities and how companies utilize them to lessen the effects of export and import regulations.
4) Look at the interdependence of physical distribution activities and the benefits of physical distribution systems.
5) Highlight the foreign-freight forwarder as an important agent that can assist companies in dealing with the mechanics of exporting.

### Comments and Suggestions

1. Exhibit 15–1, The Exporting Process (The Exporting Process), is useful in presenting an overall picture of export mechanics. A list of export documents including an example from the Commerce Control List for viruses and software, and western red cedar, illustrate some of the different bases on which the exports of products are controlled. Crossing Borders 15–3, Underwear, Outerwear, and Pointed Ears—What Do They Have in Common, and Crossing Borders 15–5, When Is a Car a Truck or a Truck a Car? illustrate just how convoluted some of the regulations can be.
2. The discussion of the exporting process leads nicely into a discussion of Customs Privileged Facilities, e.g, foreign trade zones. It is important to cover the details of foreign trade zones and the various tariff and non-tariff barriers in this chapter since both of these issues are important in the discussion on price escalation and its control in the pricing chapter, Chapter 18.
3. Who's Responsible for Costs Under Various Terms? (Exhibit 15–5), is an illustration of the various terms of sale and when responsibility for certain costs shift from the seller to the buyer. It is reasonable to stress the importance of this information since a company's profit can be wiped out if these costs are not included when quoting the terms of sale.
4. Transportation and the related costs of moving goods from one country to another constitute a major marketing cost. Exhibit 15–8 in the text is a good illustration of how transportation costs differ between types of commodities as well as differences in costs between conventional versus containerized cargo handling. Firms have found that when they adopt a total systems approach to the management of the physical distribution process costs can be reduced substantially. Exhibit 15–7 of the text (Real Physical Distribution Costs Between Air and Ocean Freight – Singapore to the United States) is a graphic illustration of how the various components of physical distribution impacts on total cost. The foreign-freight forwarder is an agent that can help even the smallest firm in lowering physical distribution costs.

**Lecture Outline**

I. Export and Logistics: Special Issues for Business

II. Global Perspective—An Export Sale: From Trade Show to Installation

III. Export Restrictions

  A. Determining License Requirements

  B. ELAIN, STELA, ERIC, and SNAP

IV. Import Restrictions

  A. Tariffs

  B. Exchange Permits

  C. Quotas

  D. Import Licenses

  E. Boycott

  F. Standards

  G. Voluntary Agreements

  H. Other Restrictions

V. Terms of Sale

VI. Getting Paid: Foreign Commercial Payments

  A. Letters of Credit

  B. Bills of Exchange

  C. Cash in Advance

  D. Open Accounts

  E. Forfaiting

VII. Export Documents

VIII. Packing and Marking

IX. Customs-Privileged Facilities

  A. Foreign-Trade Zones

  B. Offshore Assembly (Maquiladoras)

X. Logistics

  A. Interdependence of Physical Distribution Activities

  B. Benefits of Physical Distribution Systems

  C. Export Shipping and Warehousing

XI. The Foreign-Freight Forwarder

XII. Summary

## DISCUSSION QUESTIONS

1. Define the following terms and show the significance to international marketing.

| | | |
|---|---|---|
| Commerce Control List (CCL) | Commercial invoice | Forfaiting |
| Commerce Country Chart (CCC) | Customs-privileged facilities | Export declaration |
| Export regulations | Foreign-trade zone | Consular invoice |
| Import regulations | Maquiladora | Logistics management |
| Export Administrative Regulations (EAR) | Export Classification Control Number (ECCN) | Physical distribution system |
| Terms of sale | Open account | ELAIN |
| Bill of lading | Letter of credit | STELA |
| | Bill of exchange | ERIC |
| | | SNAP |

2. Explain the reasoning behind the various regulations and restrictions imposed on the exportation and importation of goods.

   The reasons for many regulations and restrictions on the exportation of certain products are mainly protective. The government wants to control the excessive exportation of scarce products, and it also wants to control to which countries certain products are exported. The reason for this is that certain products are of a strategic nature and could be used in actions against the United States. Many import regulations are also protective. Besides the protection offered to domestic industries and markets, they are a source of revenue, as in the case of tariffs. Import restrictions can also serve to prevent the excessive flow of money of scarce foreign currencies out of the country.

3. What determines the type of license needed for exportation? Discuss.

   The following five types of facts determine an exporter's obligations and the licensing requirements for an item.

   (1) What is it? What an item is, for export control purposes, depends on its classification on the Commerce Control List.

   (2) Where is it going? The country of ultimate destination for an export or re-export also determines licensing requirements.

   (3) Who will receive it? The ultimate end-user of an item cannot be an unapproved end-user.

   (4) What will be done with it? The ultimate end-user of the item cannot be an unapproved end-user. The need for such export licenses enables the U.S. government to adapt rapidly to changing international political relations.

4. Discuss the most frequently encountered trade restrictions.

   The most frequently encountered trade restrictions are: tariffs, exchange permits, quotas, and import licenses.

5. What is the purpose of an import license? Discuss.

   Import licenses can control exchanges, quotas, and tariffs; or they can be used to limit the import. The use of such licenses is effective in obtaining exact data concerning importation. The import license is a much more flexible way of protecting the domestic industry or maintaining a certain stock of foreign currencies than quotas. The reason is that quotas are generally set for a certain period of time, but import licenses can limit quantities on an individual, day-to-day basis.

6. Explain free-trade zones and illustrate how they may be used by an exporter. By an importer. How do free-trade zones differ from bonded warehouses?

   In a free-trade zone, goods can be imported and warehoused or processed without having any import duties paid on them until they leave the zone. This system enables suppliers to transport in large quantities in which lower costs are involved. Since no investments have to be made in the payment of duties or tariffs, the goods can be distributed from the zone area to another part of the country in smaller quantities whenever there is a favorable demand. Thus, the owner of the goods does not have to rush the transportation because of duties. Another advantage of this system is that after processing the goods, they can be re-exported from the zone without paying any extra duties for importation into the United States. This means that the importer has the advantage of shipping goods in large quantities, whereas the exporter forgoes the actual payment of import duties until the goods are shipped into a duty area. The difference between free-trade zones and bonded warehouses is that bonded warehouses are used mainly for storage purposes and are smaller areas than free-trade zones. Free-trade zones are larger areas in which processing can also take place.

7. How do "in-bond" areas differ from foreign-trade zones? How would an international marketer use an in-bond area?

   In-bond areas are the result of a special agreement between the Mexican and U.S. governments which creates a favorable opportunity for U.S. companies to utilize abundant low-cost labor. The Mexican government allows U.S. firms to process, package, assemble, or repair goods in in-bond areas. The U.S. firm may import the necessary parts, process materials without paying import taxes, providing the finished products are re-exported to the United States or to another foreign country. In turn, the U.S. government permits the re-importation of the packaged, processed, assembled, or repaired goods back to the United States with a reasonably low import tariff that is only applied to the value added to the goods while in Mexico. There are more than 400 U.S. companies in electronics, health care, automotive, furniture, clothing and toy manufacturing participating in the in-bond program.

8. Explain each of the following export documents:

| | |
|---|---|
| Bill of lading | Commercial invoice |
| Consumer invoice or of origin | Insurance certificate |

9. What are the differences between "straight bill of lading" and "order bill of lading"? What are the differences between "clean bill of lading" and "foul bill of lading"?

   A straight bill of lading is not negotiable, whereas an order bill of lading is. A bill of lading is called "clean" when the shipment is undamaged and properly packed when presented to the shipper. When the shipment is damaged or improperly packed when presented to the shipper, it is called "foul."

10. Why would an exporter use the services of a foreign freight forwarder? Discuss.

   When a company cannot afford an in-house specialist to handle the type of work and other export trade mechanics a foreign freight forwarder is typically used. Even in large companies with active export departments capable of handling documentation, a forwarder is useful as a shipment coordinator at the port or at the destination. The full service foreign freight forwarder provides information and advice on routing, scheduling, rates and related changes, consular and licensing requirements, labeling requirements, and export restrictions. Both large and small shippers find the freight forwarders' wide range of services useful and well worth the fees normally charged.

11. Besides cost advantages, what are the other benefits of a physical distribution system?

   The other benefits of a physical distribution system besides cost advantage are being able to maintain optimal inventory levels and, in multiplant operations, optimal production capacity. Both of these result in better use of working capital. A physical distribution system may also result in better (more dependable) delivery service to the market and when products are produced at different locations they are able to quickly determine the most economical source for a particular customer. Finally, a physical distribution system can render the natural obstructions created by geography less economically critical for the multinational marketer.

12. Discuss customs-privileged facilities. How are they used?

    Customs-privileged facilities are designed to facilitate export trade. Countries designate areas within their borders as customs-privileged areas i.e., areas where goods can be imported for storage or processing with tariffs postponed until the products leave the designated area. Foreign-trade zones, free ports and in-bond arrangements are all varieties of customs-privileged facilities. Customs-privileged facilities can be used for storage, for light processing, or in the case of Maquiladoras, (that is, in-bond companies), for off shore assembly. In all cases, the idea of customs-privileged facilities is to enable a foreigner to store and process goods and perhaps avail itself of cheap labor without having to pay import taxes while the goods are being processed within the facilities. This enables cost cutting and a variety of other savings.

13. Why would a company engage the services of an intermodal transportation service instead of performing activities in house?

    Intermodal services, a transportation system that unites various modes of transportation into one seamless movement of goods from factory to the customer's port of entry, have become more efficient as deregulation has allowed the coupling of various modes of transportation. In addition, intermodal marketing companies (IMC) have evolved to broker transportation services so an exporter can make one transaction with an IMC that entails the movement of goods from factory to customer, rivaling the simplicity of single-mode freight transportation. The IMC stitches together each of the transportation modes involved in the intermodal freight movements which may involve as many as four separate transportation modes. All of this can be done within guaranteed time frames, with 98 percent on-time performance schedules more the norm than the exception.

14. You are the manager of a small company that manufacturers and sells various types of personal restraints, for example, handcuffs, leg irons, that you sell to law enforcement agencies, private security companies, and novelty stores. You receive a larger order from an importer in Madrid. You have never done business with this importer although you have previously sold your product in Spain. Do you need a special export license? Outline the steps you would take to ensure that your transaction is legal. (Note: The solution to this problem cannot be completely answered from information in the text. Information will have to be obtained from sources on the Internet.)

    Students should consult the text for examples of how a license is determined. Then, using the Internet, the answer to this question can be determined.

    The exporter is responsible for determining if a license for export is required by the EAR. The first step in that process is to determine the proper ECCN (Export Control Classification Number) for the commodity to be exported. Every product has an export control classification number within the Commerce Control List (CCL). Each ECCN consists of five characters that identify the category, product group, type of control, and country group level.

    Once the proper ECCN number is obtained, the next step is to locate the number in the Commodity Control List

    The next step is to consult the Commerce Country Chart (CCC) which helps you to determine, based on the reason(s) for control associated with your item, if you need a license to export or reexport your item to a particular destination. The Commerce Country Chart contains licensing requirements based on destination and reason for control. In combination with the CCL, the Commerce Country Chart allows you to determine whether a license is required for items on the CCL to any country in the world.

The only instances where the chart cannot be used for this purpose are items controlled for short supply reasons and the catch all clause, unique entries where no license exceptions apply and all the items are controlled for the specific countries.

An exporter must establish that the end-user is not listed in the Table of Denial Orders which lists orders that currently deny export privileges; in other words, no shipments to any person or company on the denial orders list.

In addition to checking the denial list, the exporter needs to make a general check to be sure there are no indications that the end user's intentions will lead to an unauthorized use of the product.

15. You are the sales manager of a small company with sales in the United States. About 30 percent of your business is mail order and the remainder from your two retail stores. You have recently created an e-store on the Web and a few days later received an order from a potential customer from a city near Paris, France. The shipping charges listed on the Web are all for locations in the United States. You don't want to lose this $350 order. You know you can use the postal service but the customer indicated she wanted the item in about a week. Air Express seems logical but how much will it cost? Consult both the FedEx homepage (http://www.fedex.com) and the UPS homepage (http://www.ups.com) and get some estimates on shipping costs. Here are some details you will need: Value $350, total weight of the package, 2.5 pounds, package dimensions, height: 4 inches, and length: 6 inches width: 4.5 inches. U.S. zip code: 97035 and French zip code: 91400. (Note: It's not fair to call UPS or FedEx – use the Internet)

    Fedex charge for delivery of the package is $56.70 and UPS is $53.30. These calculations can easily be made by consulting the Web pages of each of the companies.

16. Based on the information collected in Question 15, how practical would it be to encourage foreign sales? Your average order ranges from about $250 to $800. All prices are quoted plus shipping and handling. You handle a fairly exclusive line of Southwestern Indian jewelry that sells for about 15 to 20 percent higher in Europe than in the United States. The products are light weight and high in value.

    Using the data above, it would seem that for $250 dollar items a French customer would about breakeven from buying via e-commerce versus buying in France. However, for a higher value item, assuming that the weight would not increase substantially, the French customer would benefit buying from e-commerce.

## Chapter 16 — Integrated Marketing Communications and International Advertising

### Teaching Objectives

The debate on the merits of standardization compared to modification of international advertising has always seemed to be a fallacious issue—it seems obvious that it is best to standardize any marketing activity whenever possible but, on the other hand, if there is any activity in marketing that is culture specific, it is advertising. After all, advertising is communications and to be understood and to communicate effectively you must express yourself in the cultural language of your audience. So, how can the idea of global advertising ever be anything other than standardize when feasible and adapt where culturally necessary. In any case, since this issue continues to be debated and because there is often confusion about global advertising, these topics need to be discussed. In most cases, actual practice is to standardize parts of the message and to localize other parts. The teaching objectives are to:

1) Present a complete coverage of the issue of global advertising covering specifically global advertising, world brands, pattern advertising and the relationship of global market segmentation an promotional strategy.
2) Detail the creative challenges confronting the international advertiser.
3) Examine the effects of pan-European advertising.
4) Review the communications process as a way of better understanding the diversity that exists in developing an international promotional program.

### Suggestions and Comments

1. The international communications process, Exhibit 16–1, is useful in bringing the discussion of international advertising together. It is a good way to illustrate the many ways a promotional campaign can go awry. Examples of misfires are legion and there are many to chose from for examples. The transparency, Misfires in Advertising, offers a few more. Some recent reports of problems are: A highly successful ad campaign which had boosted sales in the U.S., Canada, Europe and Australia for a brand of toothpaste for children was not well-received in Bangkok. "Too American" and the French and U.K. versions were rejected as well. The problem had to do with the "pat on the head" mnemonic device which was at the center of all the executions. That scene, which closed all commercials in the campaign, was designed to express the parent's appreciation for the good brushing the child had done with the toothpaste. But one does not touch the head of another person in many Asian countries. Other examples are given in Jacques R. Chevron, "Global Branding: Married to the World," Advertising Age, May 15, 1995, p. 23. Of a little different bent is the example of advertising bottled water. South Korea's Environment Ministry proposed halting all TV spots for saengsu, or bottled water, because ". . . TV commercials of bottled water are apt to arouse public mistrust of tap water and create discord among those who can afford to buy it and those who cannot . . ." Yoo-Lim Lee, "So. Korea Threatens to Pull Plug on Water Ads," *Advertising Age*, April 17, 1995, p. I–6.
2. I like to approach the problems created by differences in laws, language, culture, etc. as creative challenges in that it takes real creativity to overcome some of these road blocs and still present an effective promotional program. There are several examples in the text that can be used as illustrations. For additional examples see, Peter Waldman, "Please Don't Show your Lingerie in Iran, Even if It's For Sale," *The Wall Street Journal*, June 21, 1995, p. A-1. Among the many discussed in this article, the one that struck me as being the most challenging had to do with advertising lingerie. There are a variety of laws and prohibitions and as the article explains, ". . . things not specifically prohibited are usually not allowed." A case in point is that product information other than the name cannot be given

in advertisements. To get through the censors, one billboard for an Iranian brand of women's lingerie displayed no women, no lingerie and no mention of the unmentionable product at all. The ad's sole image was of the underwear's plain green box with the words "soft and delicate" written alongside. "No one had a clue what it meant."

**Lecture Outline**

I. Sales Promotions and Public Relations

II. Global Advertising

- A. Pattern Advertising—Plan Globally, Act Locally
- B. Global Advertising and World Brands
- C. Pan-European Advertising
- D. Global Market Segmentation and Promotional Strategy

III. Creative Challenges

- A. Legal Considerations
- B. Language Limitations
- C. Cultural Diversity
- D. Media Limitations
- E. Productions and Cost Limitations

IV. Media Planning And Analysis

- A. Tactical Considerations
- B. Specific Media Information

V. The Internet—A Media Mix Alternative

VI. Global Advertising and the Communications Process

VII. The Advertising Agency

VIII. International Control of Advertising

## DISCUSSION QUESTIONS

1. Define:

| | |
|---|---|
| Noise | Advertising |
| Market segment | Public relations and sales promotion |
| Integrated marketing communications | |

2. "Perhaps advertising is the side of international marketing with the greatest similarities from country to country throughout the world. Paradoxically, despite its many similarities, it may also be credited with the greatest number of unique problems in international marketing." Discuss.

   The paradox lies in the fact that advertising methodology is similar from country to country but that the unique problems of company policy limitations, legal aspects, linguistics, media limitations, all pose a distinct problem to the international advertiser. Advertising must be related to the basic and existing motivation patterns. The unique problem is to find this motivation and orient your campaign to the stimuli which must make the majority of the people buy the product. But these problems are generally mechanical and can be easily overcome by long-range research.

3. Someone once commented that advertising is America's greatest export. Discuss.

   This comment portrays the fact that America was first to realize that advertising is a crucial element in the integrated marketing plan. Since the American "philosophy" of advertising has penetrated the foreign market, it is said to have been "exported." Many of America's largest advertising agencies successfully operate in the foreign market. World advertising is generally patterned after the American advertising approach and system.

4. With satellite TV able to reach many countries, discuss how a company can use satellite TV and deal effectively with different languages, different cultures, and different legal systems.

   The reality of satellite TV provides the means to have truly global advertising. This raises the question of the effectiveness of standardized advertising versus locally produced ads. Problems of different languages and laws raise doubts about the effectiveness of pan-European ads. In European satellite broadcasting, English is the preferred language for programming since the satellites must cover a territory with 12 languages and 17 national borders. A study done on Sky Channel viewers indicated that the English language programs are unacceptable for many. Germans watch the English language programs for about a minute before deciding they have the wrong station. European programming is developing, but slowly. One of the reasons for using U.S. made programming is that producing quality programs for each country is too costly. One approach to language differences and the production costs of programming is a six-part series called "Eurocops." It is a police series in which each country produces one episode based in the country with their own police, in their own style and with their own problems. Each broadcaster provides the episode produced in his country to the other five. The five are then dubbed into the local language and broadcast locally. The idea is to produce European programming but at a much lower cost per country than if each country had to produce all six shows. There is no question that cable, satellites, privatization and the advent of Europe 1992 will revolutionize broadcasting and create greater demand for global advertising.

5. Outline some of the major problems confronting an international advertiser.

   Of all the elements of the marketing mix, decisions involving advertising are the ones most often affected by cultural differences among country markets. Consumers reflect their culture, its style, feelings, value systems, attitudes, beliefs, and perceptions. Since advertising's function is to "interpret or translate the need/want satisfying qualities of product and services in terms of consumer needs, wants, desires, and aspirations," the emotional appeals, symbols, persuasive approaches and other characteristics of an advertisement must coincide with cultural norms to be effective.

   Reconciling international advertising and sales promotion effort with cultural uniqueness of markets is the challenge confronting the international or global marketer. The global advertiser is confronted with legal and tax considerations, language limitations, media limitation and production and cost limitations. These limitations must all be dealt with effectively if a company is to have an effective advertisement.

6. Defend either side of the proposition that advertising can be standardized for all countries.

   Yes, the basic theme, objectives, and philosophy of international advertising can be standardized; but the vast mechanical problems most certainly cannot be solved through international standardization. The ad man can adapt his basic skills to all countries. If buying motives and company objectives are the same for various countries, then the advertising approach may be the same. If they vary, then customizing your approach to each country is a must.

7. Review the basic areas of advertising regulation. Are such regulations purely foreign phenomena?

   a. The basic areas of advertising regulation are (1) the legal type such as Germany's Comparative Terminology and Direct Comparison Laws, and (2) taxation on advertising, prevalent in Britain, France, and Austria.

   b. No, these regulations are not purely foreign. Here in the United States there are certain advertising codes and standards that one must follow. These are generally enforced by the advertising industry itself—but the FCC also imposes strict standards of "truth in advertising."

8. How can advertisers overcome the problems of low literacy in their market?

   They can overcome low literacy by making use of ads that are self-explanatory, and extensive use of radio which doesn't have written words.

9. What special media problems confront the international advertiser?

   Special problems in media—availability, cost, and coverage—confront the international advertiser. Local variations and lack of market data are also great headaches.

   Availability of media varies from country to country due to government restrictions. Countries have either too many or too few media to adequately cover the majority of the population. As far as price goes, the United States ad man must be prepared to haggle greatly over costs. Most media costs are subject to negotiation. Agency discounts are often split with the client to bring costs down. Coverage problems generally arise when trying to reach certain sections of the population. There are many uneconomical media divisions which do not permit enough regionality. Underlying all these problems is the lack of market information which hampers a good communication mix in foreign markets and causes much waste in ad campaigns.

10. After reading the section in this chapter on direct mail, develop guidelines to be used by a company when developing a direct mail program.

    Guideline for direct mail should be the same as for any advertising program, i.e., identify the target market, select a medium that reaches the target market, develop a message that communicates how the attributes of your product fit the needs of the target market. On this last point is the issue of translation. You want to avoid the mistake a catalog producer, R.R. Donnelley, made when a collection of a dozen American catalogs sent to Japanese consumers received only modest responses and orders. Failure to receive sufficient response may have reflected more on the*American Showcase* package than on the success of direct mail in the Japanese market. Even though the covering letter and brochure describing the catalogs were in Japanese, the catalogs were all in English. This error was further amplified by the fact that the mailing list id not target English-speaking Japanese. In addition to these general issues, special attention needs to give to characteristics of mail. Are mailing lists that include your target market without excessive coverage of non-target market recipients? Does the mailing system impose some additional burden on the recipient? For example, the situation in Chile where the person receiving mail must pay a portion of the postage.

11. Will the ability to broadcast advertisements over TV satellites increase or decrease the need for standardization of advertisements? What are the problems associated with satellite broadcasting? Comment.

    The ability to broadcast advertising over TV satellites will increase the need for standardization of advertisements. The problems associated with satellite broadcasting will focus on creating an advertisement that will be culturally acceptable in all the countries receiving the BC satellite broadcast and created in such a manner that language differences that may exist within the countries will not affect the message sent. There are those, however, who feel that such an advertisement would be so bland that it would be relatively ineffective.

12. In many of the world's marketplaces, a broad variety of media must be utilized to reach the majority of the market. Explain.

    Due to the uneconomical division of media coverage, a large amount of media must be engaged to cover a majority of the market. If an advertiser wants to reach his total market, the expenditure he will have to incur in using a broad variety of media is great. The media competitors have segmented the market so that one must employ most of them in a successful campaign.

13. Cinema advertising is unimportant in the United States but a major media in such countries as Austria. Why?

Austria has 20 percent of all advertising in cinema as a solution to its huge taxes against the other media; and the effectiveness of this type of advertising is reflected by its dollar expenditure in this medium—11 percent of the total ad expenditure in the country per year.

14. "Foreign newspapers obviously cannot be considered as homogeneous advertising entities." Explain.

Literacy rates vary, and this results in coverage not being constant (selective rather than intensive). Many countries have too many papers to run an effective campaign because one must utilize all of them if one desires to cover large geographic areas. Even then, it is not known if effective readership exists. Political position of the newspaper in which you decide to run an ad may have a bad effect on the reputation of the product.

15. Borrow a foreign magazine from the library. Compare the foreign advertising to that in an American magazine.

Library project.

16. What is sales promotion and how is it used in international marketing?

Sales promotions include all marketing activities other than advertising, personal selling, and publicity that stimulate consumer purchases and improve retailer or middleman effectiveness and cooperation. Sales promotions include such items as cents-off, in store demonstrations, samples, coupons, product tie-ins, contests, sweepstakes, sponsorship of special events, and point-of-purchase displays. Sales promotions are used as short-term efforts directed at consumer and/or retailer to achieve such specific objectives as (1) consumer product trial and/or immediate purchase, (2) consumer introduction to the store, (3) gaining retail point-of-purchase displays, (4) encouraging stores to stock a product, and (5) supporting and augmenting the advertising, personal sales efforts.

17. Show how the communications process can help an international marketer avoid problems in international advertising.

Since promotional activities are basically communications processes, all the attendant problems in developing an effective promotional strategy is domestic marketing plus all the cultural problems discussed in the chapter must be overcome to have a successful international promotional program. A major consideration for a foreign marketer is to ascertain that cultural diversity, media limitations, legal problems and constraints, or control of the message can be communicated properly. International advertising and promotional communications fail for a variety of reasons: (1) the message may not get through because of media inadequacy, (2) the message may be received by the intended audience but not be understood because of different cultural interpretations, and (3) the message may be received by the intended audience and be understood but have no effect because the marketer did not correctly assess the needs and wants of the target market. Because of the many different influences that may jeopardize the success of a promotional strategy, those international executives who understand the communications process will probably be better equipped to manage that diversity since the communications process forces the international advertiser to examine all of those areas where problems in promotion may surface.

18. Take each of the steps in the communications process and give an example of how culture differences can affect the final message received.

The *information source* may create a problem because the marketer does not truly understand the needs and wants of the target market. This is especially important if the marketer relies on the self-reference criterion and makes the naive assumption that "if it sells in one country it would sell in another." An example would be bicycles designed and sold in the United States to consumers fulfilling recreational, exercise needs which cannot be successfully sold for the same reasons in a market where the primary use of the bicycle is transportation. The *encoding step* of the communications process can also cause problems because such factors as colors, values, beliefs, tastes and other symbols utilized by the international marketer do not correctly symbolize the message intended. For example, "Body by Fisher" which decoded meant "Corpse by Fisher" was not General Motors' intended message. The *message channel* may create problems because of the difficulty of effectively reaching target markets in many countries. Problems, such as illiteracy, the availability and types of media, create problems at this level. Decoding problems are generally created by improper encoding. The decoding process is one in which the receiver interprets the message in terms of one's own culture, thereby receiving an incorrect message. For example, Pepsi's "Come Alive" was decoded by many as "Come Out Of The Grave." Sometimes decoding can create problems even when the encoder purposely attempted to develop a message with no symbolism. An example was the toothpaste CUE which was decoded as a pornographic word. Finally, the feedback step can create problems in the sense that companies do not use feedback to effectively measure their communications efforts and attempt to correct any problems that may have been created by the other steps.

19. Discuss the problems created because the communications process is initiated in one cultural context and ends in another.

    The major problem here is that the encoder is in one culture using one's own SRC and the message is decoded in another culture where the decoders are using their own SRC. The challenge is that the encoder needs to be certain that the message is being encoded in such a manner that it will be decoded in the other culture in a manner in which it is intended. Thus, cultural decoding misinterpretations can be avoided.

20. What is the importance of feedback in the communications process? Of noise?

    The importance of feedback is to provide the marketers who are generally in one cultural context with an immediate interpretation of the message sent so that any problems created by errors in the communications process or errors created by the different cultural contexts can be adjusted before significant harm occurs. The importance of noise in the system is that such things as competitive activity and other types of confusion can detract from the communications process and affect any or all of the six steps. The most important factor about noise is that it is generally uncontrollable and unpredictable, yet it can influence the outcome. Noise is also a significant reason why feedback in any communications process is so very important.

# Chapter 17 – Personal Selling and Personnel Management

## Teaching Objectives

The problems of managing marketing and sales personnel in global markets is the focus of this chapter. The unique qualities of American management thinking are contrasted with the variety of cultural contexts in which American executives must operate around the world. The teaching objectives are:

1) Understanding the crucial role of interpersonal selling in international marketing.
2) Accounting for cultural and other differences in designing an international salesforce.
3) Understanding the nuances of recruiting, selecting, evaluating, and motivating international sales representatives.
4) How to design training programs and compensation systems for international employees.
5) How to prepare Americans for assignments abroad.
6) The important characteristics of the global manager of the $21^{st}$ century.

## Comments and Suggestions

1. One of the key themes of this chapter is well represented in Exhibit 17–2, that is, Japan is the toughest market for American firms. More adjustments have to me made in sales force management there than in any other single country. Case 4–7 (National Office Machines) works quite well to make the differences between the American and Japanese business systems quite clear.
2. A useful homework assignment is asking students to interview a local foreign executive asking questions about his/her foreign company prepared them for the overseas assignment.
3. A class discussion might be organized around students from other countries (or American students who have lived in other countries) talking about what aspects of cultural adjustment were most difficult when coming to the States.

## Lecture Outline

I. Designing the Sales Force

II. Recruiting Sales and Marketing Personnel
  - A. Expatriates
  - B. Local Nationals
  - C. Third-Country Nationals
  - D. Host Country Restrictions

III. Selection of Sales and Marketing Personnel

IV. Impact of Cultural Values on Managing

V. Training for International Marketers

VI. Motivating Sales Personnel

VII. Designing Compensations Systems
  - A. For Expatriates
  - B. For A Global Sales Force

VIII. Evaluating and Controlling Sales Representatives

IX. Preparing U.S. Personnel for Foreign Assignments
  - A. Overcoming Reluctance to Accept a Foreign Assignment

B. Reducing the Rate of Early Returns

C. Successful Expatriate Repatriation

X. Developing Cultural Awareness

XI. The Changing Profile of the Global Manager

XII. Foreign Language Skills

## DISCUSSION QUESTIONS

1. Define:

| | |
|---|---|
| Relationship marketing | TCN |
| Expatriate | "Master of destiny" philosophy |
| Local nationals | Separation allowance |

2. Why may it be difficult to adhere to set job criteria in selecting foreign personnel? What compensating actions might be necessary?

   It may be difficult to adhere to set job criteria in selecting foreign salesmen because there may be several different levels of job criteria and the company must move down these levels after having trouble hiring individuals who conform to the established criteria. Compensating actions which may be necessary include sales commissions, as this motivates the better personnel and eliminates the receiving of equal wages by both the better and poorer salesmen.

3. Why does the global sales force cause special compensation problems? Suggest some alternate solutions.

   The global sales force causes special compensation problems because an imbalance is created, as the expatriate salesman would normally receive more than would the foreign salesman, and the foreign salesman will feel aggrieved and mistreated. Motivational devices are valuable in providing solution but perhaps a foreign sales force managed by expatriate salesmen is best.

4. Under what circumstances should expatriate salesmen be utilized?

   Expatriate salesmen should be used when a more technical approach is necessary, when communication with the parent company is vital, when legal barriers dictate the use of expatriate salesmen, or when the markets will not support full-time salesmen.

5. Discuss the problems which might be encountered in having an expatriate sales manager supervising foreign salesmen.

   Problems encountered would include the following: legal barriers, a lack of communication between the expatriate sales manager and the foreign sales force, and the expatriate's inability to adapt to the foreign environment.

6. "To some extent, the exigencies of the manpower situation will dictate the approach to overseas sales organization." Discuss.

   Sales organization approach will vary for a number of reasons which are: inadequately trained foreign personnel (so expatriate personnel are required), foreign personnel must be employed for legal reasons, expatriate salesmen are unwilling or unavailable to enter the market, and foreign personnel are unwilling or unavailable to enter the market.

7. How do legal factors affect international sales management?

   Legal factors may affect international sales management because some countries require that the sales force be composed all or partly of natives. In other cases (such as in Argentina), severe regulations regarding the firing or discharging of personnel force companies to hire expatriates or be stuck with incompetent or noncooperative nationals who cannot be discharged without a legal struggle.

8. How does the sales force relate to company organization? To channels of distribution?

The sales force may be domestic salesmen working from the parent company, expatriate salesmen and/or foreign salesmen. Home office management or decentralization of the above vary with the type of sales force. If a market is small, chances are that it will not be serviced by a resident expatriate salesman or foreign salesmen but by a domestic salesman from the parent company.

9. "It is costly to maintain an international sales force." Comment.

It is certainly more expensive to maintain an international sales force than a domestic sales force because travel, living expenses, interpreters, training and establishing a sales force, etc., all contribute to higher expenses. However, the increasing number of companies going overseas indicates it is well worth it.

10. Adaptability and maturity are traits needed by all salesmen. Why should they be singled out as especially important for international salesmen?

These two traits are singled out as especially important for international salesmen because the foreign market is extremely different from the domestic market and calls for different policies and more independent decisions and commitments. The traits are credited with being two of the prime causes for failure of international salesmen.

11. Can a person develop good cultural skills?

Yes. Good cultural skills just as good social skills can be developed. Cultural skills provide the individual with the ability to relate to a different culture, even when the individual is unfamiliar with the details of that particular culture. Anyone being sent to another culture should receive training to develop cultural skills. In addition, they should receive specific schooling on the customs, values, and the social and political institutions of the host country. There are a variety of organizations that provide intercultural training.

12. Describe the six attributes of a person with good cultural skills.

Someone with cultural skills can: (1) communicate respect and convey verbally and nonverbally a positive regard and sincere interest in people and their culture; (2) tolerate ambiguity and cope with cultural differences and the frustration that frequently develops when things are different and circumstances change; (3) display empathy by understanding other people's needs and differences from their viewpoint rather than from the individual's own viewpoint; (4) be nonjudgmental, avoid judging the behavior of others on their own value standards; (5) recognize and control the SRC, that is, recognize their own cultural values as an influence on their perceptions, evaluations, and judgment in a situation; and (6) laugh things off, a good sense of humor helps when frustration levels rise and things do not work out as planned.

13. Interview a local company which has a foreign sales operation. Draw an organization chart for the sales function and explain why that particular structure was used by that company.

Individual project.

14. Evaluate the three major sources of multinational manpower.

Expatriates—declining in importance as foreign nationals are found to fill marketing positions. The cost of an expatriate is often much greater than a foreign national. The advantages of the expatriate are more adequate technical training, better knowledge of the firm and its product, and often better communication with the parent company. The weakness is that the expatriate often suffers from the cultural differences existing in the host company.

Cosmopolitan personnel—type of expatriate who is not a national of the parent company's country. Reflects the growing nature of international business. Used nearly exclusively at the top level of management.

Foreign national—an increase in the mobility of foreign nationals is making them more useful to the firm. At the sales level, the foreign national is at an advantage. Salary levels are lower for them as well as their selling expenses, because they are able to transcend legal and cultural barriers. However, they sometimes are too close to the culture which impedes their effectiveness. They sometimes are too close to the culture which impedes their effectiveness. They are most effective in situations which do not require great technical training.

15. Which factors complicate the task of motivating the foreign sales force?

    The biggest factor is the cultural differences that occur, which cause motivation and behavior to vary from the domestic salesmen. The cultural differences reviewed in Chapters 4 and 7 affect the motivational pattern of the foreign sales force.

16. Discuss how the "Master of Destiny" viewpoint would affect attitudes of an American and a Mexican toward promotion. Give an example.

    The "Master of Destiny" viewpoint is a belief that people can substantially influence the future and that they are in control of their own destinies. This viewpoint also reflects the attitude that while luck may have some influence on one's future, persistence, hard work, and a commitment to fulfill expectations and an effective use of time will ultimately give people control over their destinies. Other cultures including many Latin Americans have a fatalistic approach to life, i.e., a belief that one's destiny is determined by a higher order and whatever happens cannot really be controlled. Thus, a U.S. citizen who believes in the "Master of Destiny" philosophy would work diligently with the expectation that effort would be ultimately rewarded by promotion, while someone who possessed the fatalistic approach to life would perhaps be less concerned with present behavior in terms of its effects on future promotions.

17. Discuss the basic ideas on which U.S. management practices are based.

    The basic ideas are (1) "Master of Destiny" viewpoint, (2) independent enterprise—the instrument of social action, (3) personnel selection on merit, (4) decisions based on objective analysis, (5) wide sharing in decision making and (6) never-ending quest for improvement. These are the views on which U.S. management practices are based.

18. Why do companies include an evaluation of their employees' families among selection criteria?

    An evaluation of employees' families is becoming more important for overseas assignments since it is recognized that the family's ability to adjust to a foreign environment may be the most important factor determining whether or not an employee will stay in a foreign assignment for the length of time the company desires.

19. Concern for career and family is the most frequently mentioned reason for managers to refuse a foreign assignment. Why?

    The most important career-related reservation is that a two- or three-year absence will adversely affect opportunities for advancement. This "out of sight, out of mind" fear is closely linked to the problems of repatriation. Without evidence of forward planning to protect career development, the better qualified and ambitious personnel may decline the offer to go abroad. Concern for one's family may also interfere with many accepting an assignment abroad. Initially, most potential candidates are concerned with the problems of uprooting a family and taking them into a strange environment. Such questions as the education of the children, isolation from relatives and friends, proper medical and health care, and, in some countries, the potential for violence reflect the misgivings the family may have about relocating in another country.

20. Discuss and give examples why returning U.S. expatriates are dissatisfied. How can these problems be overcome?

Low morale among returning U.S. expatriates and a growing amount of attrition among returnees have many reasons. Some of the complaints and problems are family related, while others are career related. The family-related problems generally deal with financial and lifestyle readjustments. For example, some expatriates find that in spite of the higher compensation program received, their net worth has not increased. Many have found, on returning home, that with inflation of intervening years they are not able to buy a home comparable to the one they sold on leaving. The hardship compensation program used to induce the executive to go abroad creates readjustment problems on the return home. Such compensation benefits permitted the family to live at a much higher level abroad than at home. Since most compensation benefits are withdrawn when the employee returns to the home country, the standard of living decreases and the family must readjust. Another objection to returning to the United States is the location of the new assignment; frequently, the new location is not considered as desirable as the location before the foreign tour. While family dissatisfaction may cause stress within the family on returning home, the problem is not as severe as career-related complaints.

A returning expatriate's dissatisfaction with the perceived future is usually the reason many resign their positions after returning to the United States. The most frequently heard complaint involves the lack of a defined plan for the expatriate's career when returning home. New home-country assignments are frequently mundane and do not reflect the experience gained or the challenges met during the foreign assignment. Some feel that their time out of the "mainstream" of corporate affairs has made them technically obsolete and thus ineffective in competing immediately on their return. Finally, there is some loss of status that requires ego adjustment when an executive returns home. The expatriate executive enjoyed a certain degree of autonomy, independence, and power with all the prerequisites of office not generally afforded in a comparable position domestically. On returning home, many find it difficult to adjust to being just another middle manager. Companies with the least amount of returnee attrition differ from those with the highest attrition in one significant way—personal career planning for the expatriate. Expatriate career planning begins with the initial decision to send the person abroad. The initial transfer abroad should be made in a context of a long-term company plan. Under these circumstances, the individual knows not only the importance of the foreign assignment but when to expect to return and at what level. The critical aspect of the returning process is to keep the executive completely informed; propose return time, a new assignment, and future prospects. If it is understood that foreign corporate experience is a necessary prerequisite for growth and promotion within the company, then many of the problems faced today with foreign assignments will be eliminated.

21. If "the language of international business is English," why is it important to develop a skill in a foreign language? Discuss.

Proponents of language skills argue that learning a language improves cultural understanding and business relationships. Others point out that to be taken seriously in the business community, the expatriate must be at least conversational in the host language. Some recruiters want candidates who speak at least one foreign language even if the language will not be needed in a particular job. Having learned a second language is a strong signal to the recruiter that the candidate is willing to get involved in someone else's culture.

Though most companies offer short, intensive language training courses for managers being sent abroad, many are making stronger efforts to recruit people who are bi- or multilingual. According to the director of human resources at Coca-Cola, when his department searches its data base for people to fill overseas posts, the first choice is often someone who speaks more than one language.

The author feels strongly that language skills are of great importance; if you want to be a major player in international business in the future, learn to speak other languages or you might not make it—your competition will speak more than one language.

22. The global manager of the year 2010 will have to meet many new challenges. Draw up a sample resume for someone who could be considered for a top-level executive position in a global firm.

    A resume for the global manager of the year 2010 should reflect the experiences and skills in the description below. Experience in domestic operations as well as foreign experience in at least two or three foreign assignments, fluent in at least two languages and conversant in others (reflecting his/her foreign assignments), and management experience in marketing, operations and/or finance would all appear on the resume of someone destined for a top-level executive position in a global firm.

    The executive of the year 2010 will be a completely different person. His or her education will include an undergraduate degree in French literature as well as a joint MBA/engineering degree. Starting in research, this executive for the 21st century will quickly move to marketing and then on to finance. Along the way there will be international assignments that will take him or her to Brazil where turning around a failing joint venture will be the first real test of ability that leads to the top. This executive of the year 2010 will speak Portuguese and French and will be on a first-name basis with commerce ministers in half a dozen countries.

    As the 40-year postwar period of growing markets and domestic-only competition fades, so too is the narrow one-company, one-industry chief executive. By the turn of the century, companies' choices of leaders will be governed by increasing international competition, the globalization of companies, technology, demographic shifts, and the speed of overall change.

    While this description of tomorrow's business leaders is speculative, there is mounting evidence that the route to the top for tomorrow's executives will be different from today's. A Whirlpool Corporation executive was quoted as saying that the CEO in the 21st century "must have a multi-environment, multicountry, multifunctional, and maybe even multi-company, multi-industry experience."

    Until recently the road to the top was well marked. A 1987 survey of chief executives reported that more than three quarters of them had either finance, manufacturing or marketing backgrounds. In the future, it will be very difficult for a single-discipline individual to reach the top.

    The executive recently picked to head Procter and Gamble's U.S. operations is a good example of the effect globalization is having on businesses and the importance of experience, whether in Japan, Europe or elsewhere. The head of all P&G's U.S. business was born in the Netherlands, received an MBA from Rotterdam's Eramus University, then rose through P&G's marketing ranks in Holland, the U.S., and Austria. After proving his mettle in Japan, he moved to Cincinnati to direct P&G's push into East Asia and then to his new position. Speculation is that if he succeeds in the U.S., as he did in Japan, he will be a major contender for the top position at P&G.

# Chapter 18 – Pricing for International Markets

## Teaching Objectives

Basic pricing policy questions that arise from the special cost, market, and competitive factors in foreign markets are the focus of this chapter. The additional costs of international marketing that lead to price escalation and ways to minimize these costs and countertrades as a special pricing problem should all be stressed. The teaching objectives are to:

1) Review pricing policies as they are affected by the differences in international marketing and especially parallel imports.
2) Explore fully the problem of price escalation and ways to lessen price escalation.
3) Examine foreign trade zones as an important means of controlling and possibly lessening some of the costs associated with price escalation.
4) Discuss countertrades as an important tool in international pricing and the importance of taking a proactive countertrade strategy.

## Comments and Suggestions

1. With the continuing unification of the European Community, fluctuating exchange rates and the general globalization of markets, parallel imports is a growing problem. A discussion of this topic can be built around Crossing Borders 18–1.
2. When products are moved across borders, additional costs are incurred. Some can be attributed to the extra cost of the physical movement of goods and others to tariffs and non-tariff barriers. Until that time when there is truly free trade, international marketers will always be confronted with price escalation. Greater profit and the ability to be more price competitive can be gained by the company that controls, if not eliminate, many of the costs associated with price escalation. Exhibit 18–2, Sample Causes and Effects of Price Escalation, is a hypothetical illustration of three different situations of price escalation. As a side note, there have been many comments by business people on this illustration and the unanimous response is that it is too conservative, i.e., the problem of price escalation is often worse than illustrated. TM 18–4, 18–5 and 18–6, Cosmetics and Haircare Products Imported into South Africa: Effect of Import Duties on Costs, is a "real life" example of the effect of taxes on price escalation. See "An Uphill Journey to Japan," The New York Times, May 16, 1995, p. C1 for a comprehensive report on the price of a Jeep Cherokee with the steering wheel on the right as it leaves the Toledo plant at $19,100 ($20,698 is the sticker price for a comparably equipped model in the U.S.) and finally sold in Japan for a retail price of $31,372. The challenge facing the international marketer is controlling or eliminating such costs.
3. Of the three ways of lessening price escalation, lowering tariffs either through reclassification or, better yet, the elimination of a tariff often has the greatest impact. Also, lowering manufacturing costs and distribution costs can be very effective if a company has had a tendency to overlook these costs. TM 18–9, Lessening Price Escalation, is a list of the different approaches that a company may use in lessening prices escalation. A side note on marginal-cost pricing—a dumping charge is always lurking in the background when using marginal cost pricing.
4. Foreign trade zones can be very useful in helping a company lessen the costs of exporting and importing. Achieving the benefits of the steps for lessening price escalation listed in TM 18–9 can be aided by effectively using a FTZ. FTZs are not always available in all countries but in those where they are, their use should be evaluated carefully.
5. Countertrading continues to be important in many of the growth markets today. It is important to stress that companies need to include countertrading as one of its pricing tools and to be proactive

rather than reactive. Cash is always preferred but those companies that plan ahead for the possibility of being asked to accept some form of countertrade in order to consummate a sale have the most success with this pricing issue.

**Lecture Outline**

I. Global Perspective—The Price War

II. Pricing Policy
   - A. Pricing Objectives
   - B. Parallel Imports

III. Approaches to International Pricing
   - A. Full-Cost versus Variable-Cost Pricing
   - B. Skimming versus Penetration Pricing

IV. Price Escalation
   - A. Costs of Exporting
     1. Taxes
     2. Tariffs and Administrative Costs
     3. Inflation
     4. Exchange-Rate Fluctuations
     5. Varying Currency Values
     6. Middleman and Transportation Costs
   - B. Sample Effects of Price Escalation
   - C. Approaches to Lessening Price Escalation
     1. Lower Cost of Goods
     2. Lower Tariffs
     3. Lower Distribution Costs
   - D. Using Foreign-Trade Zones to Lessen Price Escalation
   - E. Dumping
     1. Dumping and Countervailing Duty

V. Leasing in International Markets

VI. Countertrade as a Pricing Tool
   - A. Types of Countertrade
   - B. Problems of Countertrading
   - C. The Internet and Countertrade
   - D. Proactive Countertrade Strategy

VII. Transfer Pricing Strategy

VIII. Price Quotations

IX. Administered Pricing
   - A. Cartels
   - B. Government Influenced Pricing

X. Summary

## DISCUSSION QUESTIONS

1. Define:

| | | |
|---|---|---|
| Dumping | Compensation deal | Skimming |
| Parallel imports | Subsidy | Price Escalation |
| Exclusive distribution | Cartel | Barter |
| Buy-back agreement | Countertrade | Counterpurchase |
| Administered pricing | Variable-cost pricing | Transfer pricing |
| Countervailing duty | Full-cost pricing | Advanced Pricing Agreement (APA) |

2. Discuss the causes and solutions of parallel imports and their effect on price.

Parallel imports develop when importers buy products from distributors in one country and sell them in another to distributors who are not part of the manufacturer's regular distribution system. This practice is lucrative when wide margins exist between prices for the same products in different countries. There are a variety of conditions that can create the profitable opportunity for a parallel market.

Variations in the value of currencies between countries frequently lead to conditions that make parallel imports profitable. When the dollar was high relative to the West German mark, Cabbage Patch dolls were purchased from German distributors at what amounted to a discount and resold in the United States.

Purposefully restricting the supply of a product in a market is another practice that can cause abnormally high prices and thus make a parallel market lucrative. Such was the case with the Mercedes-Benz automobile whose supply was limited in the U.S. Americans could buy a Mercedes-Benz automobile which was partially supplied by Americans returning to the United States with cars they could sell for double the price they paid in Germany. This situation persisted until the relative value of the dollar to the mark weakened and the price differential created by limited distribution evaporated.

Pricing policies that permit large price differentials between country markets is another condition conducive to the creation of parallel markets. Japanese merchants have long maintained vary high prices for consumer products sold within the Japanese market. As a result, prices for Japanese products sold in other countries are often lower than they are in Japan. For example, Japanese can buy Cannon Cameras from New York catalogue retailers and have them shipped to Japan for a price below that of the camera purchased in Japan. In addition to the higher prices for products at home, the rising value of the yen makes these price differentials even wider. For example, the New York price for Panasonic cordless telephones is $59.95 versus $152 in Tokyo and the Sony Walkman is $89.00 versus $165.23.

Foreign companies doing business in Japan generally follow the same pattern of high prices for the products they sell in Japan, thus creating an opportunity for parallel markets in their products also. Eastman Kodak prices its film higher in Japan than in other parts of Asia. Enterprising merchants buy Kodak film in South Korea for a discount and resell it in Japan at 25% less than the authorized Japanese Kodak dealers. For the same reasons, Coca-Cola syrup imported from Los Angeles is cheaper than that purchased through normal channels in Japan.

The possibility of parallel market occurs whenever price differences are greater than the cost of transportation between two markets. In Europe, because of differing taxes and competitive price structures, prices for the same product vary between countries. When this occurs, it is not unusual for companies to find themselves competing in one country with their own products imported from a lower priced country.

Perfume and designer brands like Gucci and Cartier are especially prone to gray markets. To maintain the image of quality and exclusivity, prices for such products traditionally include high profit margins at each level of distribution, differential prices among markets, limited quantities, and distribution that is restricted to upscale retailers. In the U.S., wholesale prices for exclusive brands of fragrances are often 25% more than wholesale prices in other countries. These are the ideal conditions for a lucrative gray market for unauthorized dealers in other countries who buy more than they need at wholesale prices lower than U.S. wholesalers pay. They then sell the excess at a profit to unauthorized U.S. retailers, but at a lower price than the retailer would have to pay to an authorized U.S. distributor.

To prevent parallel markets from developing when such marketing and pricing strategies are used, companies must maintain strong control systems. These control systems are difficult to maintain and there remains the suspicion that some companies are less concerned with controlling gray markets than they claim.

3. Why is it so difficult to control consumer prices when selling overseas?

   There are many variables which must be considered when attempting to control consumer prices overseas. Among these are: tariffs on imports, "dumping" tariffs, sales taxes, distributive channel costs, added middlemen costs, and shipping costs. It is very difficult to control consumer prices when selling overseas. Price escalation is one of the main reasons, as prices escalate differently. Some profiteering is also found in some countries, thus upsetting any consumer price control. Dumping, being defined differently, is treated differently under various laws making for more varied prices. Firms operating overseas have less ways to protect themselves from price variations and fluctuating exchange rates also tend to increase price fluctuations. In addition, many retailers overseas don't like price competition and avoid it if possible by raising or lowering their prices.

4. Explain the concept of "price escalation" and tell why it can mislead an international marketer.

   Price escalation is price increases due to added costs produced by such things as tariffs, taxes, longer lines of distribution, etc. It can mislead many international marketers into thinking that exorbitant prices that are charged in foreign countries for goods that are relatively reasonable in the domestic market can increase profits in the foreign market. This is just the opposite of the real case in many situations where the effects for price escalation, not added profit, account for the high prices.

5. What are the causes of price escalation? Do they differ for exports and goods produced and sold in a foreign country?

   Some of the causes of price escalation are:

   a. profiteering

   b. shipping costs

   c. longer channels of distribution

   d. larger middlemen margins

   e. special taxes

   Exports may be subject to all of the above, but many times goods produced and sold in a foreign country may have reduced shipping costs, lower tariffs, and are subject to fewer special taxes.

6. Why is it seldom feasible for a company to absorb the high cost of international transportation and reduce the net price received?

   A company can seldom reduce their price to an overseas market (by absorbing transportation costs, for example) because if the prices are lower than competition in the country of origin or lower than normal export prices, "dumping tariffs will just raise the price back up by inducing a new cost on the manufacturer."

7. Price escalation is a major pricing problem for the international marketer. How can this problem be counteracted? Discuss.

   The key to counteracting the problem of price escalation centers on any method that will reduce the price of the product, tariffs, or any other cost in marketing the product. Some of the more frequently used methods are: (1) offsetting tariffs and transportation charges by the net price for goods sold in foreign markets. A problem which may arise here however is the possibility that the importing country will consider this move as dumping. (2) Modify the product in a way that tariffs are reduced. For example, assemble in the foreign country which may lower the tariff and transportation costs. The foreign trade zone is especially useful in this process. (3) Manufacture within the country thereby eliminating tariffs and perhaps also benefiting from lower labor costs. (4) Shorten the channels of distribution especially in those countries that have value added taxes or turnover taxes. (5) Eliminate costly functional features on the product thereby reducing the overall cost and price. For U.S. products this is a reasonable alternative since for many markets U.S. products have unwanted or unnecessary functional features. In addition, depending on market needs, the overall quality of the product may also be lessened in order to lower the cost of goods.

   In all of these situations the main thrust is to lower entry cost of the product thereby lowering the tariffs and the transportation cost which are the two major contributors to price escalation.

8. Changing currency values have an impact on export strategies. Discuss.

   In addition to the risks from exchange rate variations other risks result from changing values of a country's currency relative to other currencies. A strong dollar produces price resistance since it takes a large quantity of local currency to buy a U.S. dollar. Conversely, when the U.S. dollar is weak, demand for U.S. goods increases since fewer units of foreign currency are needed to buy a U.S. dollar. Each additional market in which a company operates adds to the problem. Currency- exchange rate swings are considered by many global companies to be a major trade barrier. For a company whose long range plans call for continued operation in foreign markets and who wants to remain price competitive, price strategies need to reflect variations in currency values. When the value of the dollar is weak relative to the buyer's currency (i.e., it takes fewer units of the foreign currency to buy a dollar), companies generally employ cost plus pricing. To remain price competitive when the dollar is strong (i.e., when it takes more units of the foreign currency to buy a dollar), companies must find ways to offset the higher price caused by currency values.

9. "Regardless of the strategic factors involved and the company's orientation to market pricing, every price must be set with cost considerations in mind." Discuss.

   This statement is true, as all products must be priced with cost considerations in mind. However, most firms overplay this aspect of pricing and don't rely enough on pricing to the market. The latter is usually a higher price; therefore, manufacturers lose by not taking advantage of market pricing.

10. "Price fixing by business is not generally viewed as an acceptable procedure (at least in the domestic market); but when governments enter the field of price administration, they presume to do it for the general welfare to lessen the effects of 'destructive' competition." Discuss.

    This statement typifies the general viewpoint of the public (unknowledgeable public), but the statement's implications are invalid. The statement implies that price setting is good if done by the government and bad otherwise. This is not always the case. Companies are forever entering into some form of price setting which affects the economy either positively or negatively. Governmental price setting can also be either good or bad. However, government knowledge and research usually results in better forms of action.

11. Do value added taxes discriminate against imported goods?

Typically, value added taxes are applied within the country to all products. As a consequence these taxes do not directly discriminate against imported goods. However, imported goods frequently have a higher cost due to tariffs and additional transportation costs and thus may have to pay higher value added taxes. When compared with the lower amount charged to locally produced and nonimported goods, the value added tax may increase the price to the point that the market will not buy the product. However, relatively speaking, value added taxes do not discriminate against imported goods.

12. Explain specific tariffs, ad valorem tariffs, and combination tariffs.

Specific tariffs are fees charged at a flat rate per physical unit imported. Ad valorem tariffs are duties levied as a percentage of the value of the goods. Combination tariffs include both of the above.

13. Suggest an approach a marketer may follow in adjusting prices to accommodate exchange-rate fluctuations.

Prices may be quoted in the currency of the home country or in terms of some stable monetary unit, such as the U.S. dollar.

Hedging (the process of selling or buying foreign currencies in such a manner as to offset exchange fluctuations) may be employed.

14. Explain the effects of indirect competition and how it may be overcome.

Indirect competition is competition from goods which are substitutes for a certain product but which are not exactly the same. For example, indirect competition for coffee might come not only from other coffee manufacturers but also from tea manufacturers. This type of competition may be overcome by the same processes that overcome any type of competition: good advertising, fair prices, good services rendered, and achieving a strategic position in the market.

15. Why has dumping become such an issue in recent years?

The growing importance of world trade to individual companies has combined with saturated domestic markets, overproduction and increased competition to encourage dumping in many product areas. Procedures are looking to the marginal revenue contribution which can be gained when products are sold above direct cost into markets not normally sold. In recent years the number of dumping complaints in the United States has exploded and interest in antidumping enforcement and legislation has grown apace.

16. Cartels seem to rise phoenix-like after they have been destroyed. Why are they so appealing to business?

Cartels are appealing to business because they allow participating companies greater power by taking over the selling function (pricing, types of goods produced, licensing agreements.) Cartels put industry in a position to promote rationalization and specialization; consequently, technical progress results. Cartels are similar to monopolies in that they benefit at the expense of consumers. Thus, wherever it is politically acceptable, cartels tend to spring up.

17. Develop a cartel policy for the United States.

Individual project.

18. Discuss the various ways in which governments set prices. Why do they engage in such activities?

Governments set prices in various ways:

a. By requiring middlemen to mark up their goods by a governmentally dictated *margin*. Some manufacturers may have margins governmentally controlled.

b. *Setting price limits* (floor and ceiling) on actual prices.

c. *Restrict price changes*—government allows no deviation from original price settings unless officially requested.

d. Governments may compete in the market to control prices.

e. Governments grant subsidies to companies if they lower their prices.

f. Government monopolies and monopsonies.

g. Governments are now forming international agreements in relation to pricing.

Governments engaged in such activities to better control the economic standards of their countries. They can combat inflation or deflation to some extent through price setting and can also control monopolizing situations or economically unhealthy ones.

19. Discuss the alternative objectives possible in setting prices for intracompany sales.

Maximizing profits for the corporation as a whole. Facilitating parent-company control. Offering management at all levels, both in the product divisions and in the international divisions, an adequate basis for maintaining, developing, and receiving credit for their own profitability.

The problem of pricing is complex and awareness of the variations in local conditions should be taken into account when determining a strategy. Maintaining market initiative of the international divisions is a prerequisite of the pricing strategy.

20. Why do governments so carefully scrutinize intracompany pricing arrangements?

The tax and financial manipulation possibilities of transfer pricing have not been overlooked by governmental authorities. As multinational firms gain increasing prominence in the world marketing scene, national governments are becoming increasingly restrictive and paying special attention to transfer pricing in tax audits.

21. Why are costs so difficult to assess in marketing internationally?

Elements complicating international cost assessment:

a. Taxes and tariffs

b. Middleman costs

c. Transportation costs

d. Financing and risk costs

These elements vary greatly in the international marketplace and due to the additional problem of currency conversion are complicating the cost assessment of the international firm.

22. Discuss why countertrading is on the increase.

There has been a significant increase in countertrading transactions during the late 1960's and 1970's. This is primarily the result of shortages of hard currency available to industrializing nations. For Communist countries, purchase from non-Communist suppliers must be made with monies earned from Western nations; in less developed countries (LDCs), inflation ridden or weak currencies are reserved for top priority purchases while an increasing dollar volume of goods of less importance are being purchased through some form of countertrading.

23. Discuss the major problems facing a company that is countertrading.

The critical problems confronting the seller in a countertrade negotiation is having the expertise to determine the value and the potential demand of the goods offered. Frequently, there is inadequate time to conduct a market analysis. In fact, it is not unusual to have sales negotiations almost completed before countertrade is introduced as a requirement. Barter houses, specialized in trading goods acquired through barter arrangement, are the primary outside source of aid for companies beset by the uncertainty of a countertrade. Barter houses, most of which are found in Europe, can find a market for bartered goods, but the time it may take can put a financial strain on a company which has to have its capital tied up for a longer period than normal. In the long run, if companies are going to be involved in countertrades, they should establish personnel who can effectively evaluate the products to be traded.

24. If a country you are trading with has a shortage of hard currency, how should you prepare to negotiate price?

    If a customer you are trading with is in a country with a shortage of hard currency an astute marketer should have an understanding of countertrade methods. The request for countertrade is increasing in both developing and developed countries. Every international marketer should include in his/her pricing skills some knowledge of countertrade. This is especially important if there is any indication that countertrades are a part to trade with customers in that country. One of the difficulties firms have in countertrade is not being prepared when a countertrade offer is made. If a country's trade practices are studied, you can determine what products typically are offered for countertrade. Then you can determine the market price of the products offered and also get some idea of how the products can be disposed of. Such information will enable the marketer to reach a more profitable countertrade agreement should it arise.

25. Of the four types of countertrade discussed in the text, which is the most beneficial to the seller? Explain.

    Of the four types, the buyback may be the most beneficial since the seller receives products that can be sold in the seller's regular marketing program. In a buyback arrangement, the seller agrees to take back the goods produced by the process as total or partial payment. However, a problem arises if the goods in the buyback arrangement are in competition with the marketer's own produced merchandise. Of the other three, the counterpurchase is probably the most beneficial to the seller. The advantage of the counterpurchase is that the seller gets payment up front but then agrees to offset or counterpurchase other goods from the country over a period. Generally, there is a list of goods the seller can select from. The seller has time to seek markets for the goods on the list. The seller is then in a better position to effectively plan for the disposition of goods received in a counterpurchase.

26. Why should a "knowledge of countertrades" be part of an international marketers pricing tool kit? Discuss.

    This is important because countertrades are a growing part of international business and if the marketer does not have any knowledge of countertrade and is confronted with a countertrade proposal, he/she may be dissuaded from consummating the deal or make costly mistakes. The biggest problems in a countertrade transaction are knowing how to place value on the goods received and successful disposition of the goods received. Without knowledge of countertrades, these two decisions are difficult to make during a price negotiation that includes countertrade.

27. Discuss the various reasons purchasers impose countertrade obligations on buyers.

    There are a variety of reasons purchasers impose countertrade obligations on the seller. The most important being a shortage of hard currencies. This is the most prevalent, however, when a country produces a product in large quantities in which there is a low market demand, the country may offer products in counterpurchases as a means of getting rid of excess supply. Generally speaking, goods are offered for countertrade when there is a low or minimal market for the goods. Another reason that products may be offered in countertrade is because the country does not have an established international market in which to dispose of the goods. There may be a world market for the goods but the country does not have the ability or access to the market and thus may force products in countertrade.

28. Discuss how FTZ's can be used to help reduce price escalation.

A common use for foreign trade zone or free trade zone is to reduce price escalation. A foreign trade zone allows a marketer to store products in quantity for later distribution and forgo import taxes while goods are within the FTZ. This obviously allows the marketer to save part of the cost of financing the import taxes that would be required if the goods had to be kept in storage and taxes paid while in storage. Another more common use of the FTZ to help reduce price escalation is to import unassembled goods for assembly in the foreign trade zone using lower cost labor. This can result in lower tariffs as well since unassembled goods frequently are subject to lower tariffs than are assembled goods. The result is that import tariffs are reduced and the final cost of the product is also reduced by using the foreign trade zone. In addition, there may be savings that are derived from shipping costs since typically it is more costly to ship fully assembled goods than unassembled goods since shipping rates are determined on weight plus volume. This too may enable the marketer to reduce the cost basis for the product and thereby reduce price escalation.

29. Why is a proactive countertrade policy good business in some countries?

A proactive countertrade strategy probably will be most effective for global companies that market to exchange poor countries. Economic development plans in Eastern European countries, the Commonwealth of Independent States (CIS), and much of Latin America will put unusual stress on their ability to generate sufficient capital to finance their growth. To be competitive, companies must be willing to include some countertraded goods in their market planning. Companies with a proactive strategy make a commitment to use countertrade aggressively as a marketing and pricing tool. They see countertrades as an opportunity to expand markets rather than as an inconvenient reaction to market demands.

Capital poor countries striving to industrialize will account for much of the future demand for goods companies not prepared to seek this business with a proactive countertrade strategy will miss important market opportunities.

30. Differentiate between a proactive and reactive countertrade policy.

A company that waits until a customer suggests a countertrade has a reactive countertrade policy. Whereas, the company that enters the marketplace with countertrading as part of its pricing toolbox and has planned to make a countertrading offer as part of the price is practicing a proactive countertrade policy.

31. One free trade zone is ZFM of Montevideo. Visit http://www.zfm.com and discuss how it might be used to help solve the price escalation problem of a product being exported from the United States to one of the Mercosur countries.

The following was excerpted from the ZFM Web site in 2001.

The many advantages offered by ZFM, its **infrastructure**, services, or its advanced technology, make it an exclusive promotional tool, born to become an ideal **Distribution Center**.

Its strategic **location** in the very heart of the **Mercosur** makes it even more attractive. After the World's latest historical changes, the present trend to group regional economies has obtained favorable results, to the point that today, the most important multinational corporations are looking at these markets with great interest.

In order to understand the attraction of the Mercosur for these companies, we only need to remember that it groups over 200 million consumers.

ZFM's particular **location** in a country such as Uruguay, with its natural attributes and its stability - known internationally and historically—add even more incentives for the great investors. On its path to political and economic consolidation, Uruguay has conquered many achievements, and it is today a very interesting financial market due to its advantages.

Among these advantages, we must mention the following:

- its natural port with exceptional characteristics, and efficient services offered by private companies.
- its modern and agile banking system, permanently updated according to the trends in the main financial centers.
- deregulation of insurance monopolies, and free competition among international companies.
- its tradition of respect and fulfillment of local and international commitments.

The country's legislation on free trade zones is another pillar on which ZFM bases its many benefits. As an example, let us mention the following:

- 100% tax and Customs exemption
- deregulation of state monopolies
- exemption of social security payments for foreign personnel for companies with 25% or less foreign personnel.

32. Select, "What are FTZs" and "What are benefits of FTZs" from the Web page of the national Association of Foreign Trade Zones www.naftz.org and visit the home page of a FTZ in McAllen Texas www.medc.org on the border between the United States and Mexico. How does the description of this FTZ differ from the discussion in the text? Discuss how an exporter from the United States could use this FTZ, to lower distribution costs.

**What is MEDC?**

MEDC stands for the *McAllen Economic Development Corporation.*

It is a not-for-profit corporation under contract with the City of McAllen to create jobs for McAllen by attracting new industry and helping existing companies to expand. It is also the grantee and operator of the McAllen Foreign Trade Zone.

**How is MEDC managed?**

As a corporation, the MEDC consists of its Board of Directors and its Officers. The Board of Directors is made up of leading business leaders such as manufacturers, bankers, attorneys, business executives, owners of small businesses and city officials who oversee the activities of the MEDC. The Officers are Senior Staff Members responsible for the day-to-day operations of the MEDC.

**Who works for MEDC?**

Currently, MEDC has a staff of 27, MEDC's President, Mike Allen, is responsible for the coordination and supervision of all the activities of the organization. Other professional staff works with prospective industrial clients, handles marketing and public affairs, and provides corporate support to existing manufacturing and supplier companies.

**Who are Industrial Clients?**

These clients are people who represent companies or industries looking for a site to expand or relocate their plant or service operation. They include the full realm from suppliers to manufacturers.

**Does MEDC promote business location in Mexico?**

Labor availability and cost, strategic location for distribution, turn-key operations and land availability have promoted companies around the world to view Mexico as an attractive alternative in their relocation decision-making. Many of the companies that have moved to Reynosa, Mexico have also established offices in McAllen; and, almost all of them have key employees who live on the U.S. side of the U.S./Mexico border. This location decision creates a win-win situation for both Reynosa and McAllen. MEDC offers information and assistance for industrial relocations to Reynosa, Mexico. There is no charge for the services provided by the McAllen Economic Development Corporation.

**What is a Foreign-Trade Zone?**

A foreign-trade zone is a "free port" that is regulated by U.S. Customs. Raw materials and/or finished goods may be brought into the Zone from another country duty-free and then may be stored, assembled, repackaged, graded, manufactured, or re-exported without payment of U.S. Customs duties.

**Where is the McAllen Foreign-Trade Zone?**

The McAllen Foreign-Trade Zone is a 783-acre industrial district on the southwest side of McAllen, located on West Military Highway (FM 1016) between South 23rd Street and South Ware Road. Approximately $1.2 billion of products move in and out of the Zone annually. This volume of business is due primarily to the companies relocating in nearby Reynosa as a part of the **Maquiladora** program. McAllen Foreign-Trade Zone # 12 includes Sharyland Business Park, which is owned and operated by Hunt/Woodbine Development. Sharyland Business Park is a 900-acre, manufacturing, distribution and other business use sites in McAllen and Mission, Texas. This development is part of the larger development area known as the McAllen CrossPort, which includes an international airport, McAllen Foreign-Trade Zone # 12, two international bridges, rail and freight outlets, countless land and building options, the Center for Advanced and Applied Technologies facility to assist in product design and development, and much more. McAllen Foreign-Trade Zone #12 also has an air-cargo facility for in-bound merchandise located at McAllen-Miller International Airport.

Additional information can also be found at www.naftz.org

33. Visit Global Trading, Inc. (a division of Minnesota Mining and Manufacturing Company) at www.mmm.com/globaltrading/edge.html and select "the competitive edge" and "who are we," and write a short report on how Global Trading, Inc. could assist a small company that anticipates having merchandise from a countertrade.

The following was excerpted from the 3M Web site on May 5, 2001.

The competitive Edge:

Companies of every size are looking for ways to capitalize on opportunities in international trade and expand their business across borders.

If these are your company's objectives, then 3M Global Trading offers the solutions to your needs. As an international trading company backed by 3M's financial strength and worldwide business expertise, we offer importers a broad range of sourcing and financial services. For companies interested in purchasing products from developing countries, we also provide an attractive alternative to traditional banks and trading companies by offering flexible programs that are custom-designed to meet your specific requirements.

3M Global Trading offers the following advantages to meet your company's business needs and sharpen your competitive edge.

We offer you:

<u>Global Strength and Expertise: A Full Range of Services</u>

If you're looking for a reliable business partner with extensive international expertise who can offer a broad range of services, look to 3M Global Trading.

**Services**

As an international trading company backed by 3M's financial strength and worldwide business expertise, 3M Global Trading, Inc. offers importers a broad range of sourcing and financial services. Our programs are flexible and custom-designed to meet your specific requirements. We offer the following services:

- Credit Services
- Customs Clearance
- Financing for Buyers
- Financing for Suppliers
- Sales and Marketing Services
- Sourcing
- State-of-the-Art Communications Network
- Transportation and Competitive Freight Rates

**Credit Services**

Using the services of 3M's credit professionals, we can provide you with additional sources of credit information and analysis on your potential customers.

**Customs Clearance**

We can provide customs clearance as needed to save you time and money.

**Financing for Buyers**

We will work with you to develop the best financing program for your company. For creditworthy buyers, we offer payment terms of 30 days up to 120 days.

If you have a relatively new or smaller company that is selling to major accounts, it may be possible to base our credit decisions on bona fide orders from these major accounts. We can also issue Letters of Credit to suppliers on your behalf or make other forms of payment to suppliers as required.

By eliminating the need for you to open Letters of Credit, your banking costs will be reduced and bank credit lines will be freed up for other purposes. Import costs, including the cost of the product, freight, and duty, can be financed, allowing you to purchase on a "landed, duty paid" basis.

**Financing for Suppliers**

Our involvement in the import transaction also benefits your suppliers. It may be possible to arrange for financing to qualified suppliers through one of 3m's local subsidiaries at terms that are competitive with their local banks. In some instances, preshipment payments can be made to suppliers to allow them to purchase needed raw materials and components for your order.

## Chapter 19 – Negotiating with Intentional Customers, Partners, and Regulators

### Teaching Objectives

The main thrust of this last chapter is the recognition that all international marketing strategies and plans are implemented via negotiations with managers, partners, and customers from foreign countries. Cross-cultural negotiation skills are a key attribute of the successful international executive. The teaching objectives are:

1) To clearly describe the dangers of stereotyping foreign managers.
2) To illustrate the pervasive influence of culture on negotiations styles.
3) To list the most common problems that arise in cross-cultural negotiations.
4) To understand how negotiation processes differ across cultures.
5) To outline the most important considerations in selecting negotiators and preparing for negotiations in foreign countries.
6) To make clear the greater importance of follow-up communications and procedures in foreign countries.

### Comments and suggestions

1. The material in this chapter is perhaps best presented "surrounded" by the two negotiation simulations included in the cases. Before the lecture material and the Chapter 19 reading assignment it is recommended that the students participate in the case 3-4 Olympics negotiations. This will give them some idea of what their "natural" negotiation behaviors are like. Indeed, case 3–4 (questions 1 and 2) can be used as an interesting Pricing case related to Chapter 18. Then deliver the material in 19 and close with a second experiential negotiation – case 4–5. The students then will see the effects of training and knowledge. They can be asked how their behavior changed from the first simulation to the last. Another approach is to start the entire course with a bang, that is, case 3-4.
2. Video material will be quite important in demonstrating how culture influences negotiation behavior. Several excellent sources are represented in an earlier section of the Instructors' Manual.
3. A useful assignment would be for each student to pick a country and write a 5-page memo to their "boss" advising her/him on how to negotiate in that country. Ample literature is available on many countries and each student should interview an executive from the chosen country. The interview will help verify and amplify the lessons from the literature.

### Lecture Outline

I. The Dangers of Stereotypes

II. The Pervasive Impact of Culture on Negotiation Behavior
   - A. A Hierarchy of Problems
   - B. Problems at the Level of Language
   - C. Differences in Nonverbal Behaviors
   - D. Summary Descriptions Based on Videotaped Negotiations
   - E. Differences in Values
     1. Objectivity
     2. Competitiveness and Equality
     3. Time

F. Thinking and Decision-Making Processes

III. Implications for Managers and Negotiators

A. Selecting Negotiation Teams

B. Negotiation Preliminaries

C. At the Negotiation Table

1. Non-task Sounding
2. Task-related Information Exchange
3. Persuasion
4. Concessions and Agreement

D. After Negotiations

IV. Conclusions

**DISCUSSION QUESTIONS**

1. Define:

BATNA | Task-related information exchange
Non-task sounding

2. Why can cultural stereotypes be dangerous? Give some examples.

Cultural stereotypes are quite common—the aggressive American, the quite Japanese, the pushy Brazilian. Often there is some truth to them, but quite often they are incorrect. Culture does have a pervasive impact on negotiation behavior, but so do personality and experience. In face-to-face negotiations you are communication with and trying to persuade another PERSON, not a company or culture. People must be treated as individuals, but understanding their culture can help you understand them.

We know of one Japanese-American cross-cultural negotiation that didn't work out because both participants held stereotypes and acted on them. The Japanese explained the failure of the negotiation by explaining that since Americans don't pad prices much, my first offer left me little room to negotiate. His American partner explained that Asians always pad their prices and he was surprised when his Japanese counterpart wouldn't make concessions.

3. List three ways that culture influences negotiation behavior.

Actually this list is infinitely long. The three aspects of American culture which seem to most often cause problems are impatience (related to values for time), poor listening skills (a part of our unconscious conversational style), and obstinacy (related to ethnocentricity).

4. Describe the kinds of problems that usually come up during international business negotiations.

Four kinds of problems usually come up in international business negotiations. (1) The most obvious are language problems. Fluency in a foreign language helps of course, but even the best speakers of a second language have substantial problems. (2) Nonverbal behaviors are another important kind of problem, particularly so because negotiators tend to be unaware of problems at this level. When Brazilians interrupt Americans, the latter attributes it to rudeness. Cultural differences in conversational styles are most likely the best explanation. (3) Differences in values is another important problem area. Americans value frankness while Chinese value saving face. (4) The sensible order of discussions varies across cultures. Westerners tend to break up a complex negotiation task into smaller parts (e.g., price, delivery, quantity, warranty) and settle each issue sequentially building up an agreement. Asian negotiators tend to discuss issues in a more holistic not settling any one issue until the end when all issues are agreed to.

5. Why are foreign language skills important for international negotiators?

   Even a low level of language skills demonstrates some interest in the partner's culture and can help in social occasions.

   However, the most important task of an international negotiator is gathering information that leads to the most creative negotiation agreements. Language skills will be crucial in gathering information from foreign counterparts.

6. Describe three cultural differences in nonverbal behaviors and explain how they might cause problems in international business negotiations.

   Interruptions, silence, and touching all vary across cultures. When Spaniards interrupt Americans, Americans often respond with anger. When Japanese go silent, Americans often respond with talk. So information tends to flow in only one direction, to the Japanese. When Americans don't touch Brazilians or Mexicans they seem "cold" and unfriendly.

7. Why is time an important consideration in international business negotiations?

   As anthropologist Edward Hall so eloquently points out Americans are in a hurry. Most foreigners know this and a common negotiation tactic is to "just make the Americans wait—they always concede." Time constraints must be manipulated to one's advantage or consequences will be dire.

8. What might be different about how a Japanese manager might address a complex negotiation compared to an American negotiator?

   The Japanese will tend to take a holistic approach vis-à-vis the American's sequential approach. This causes two main problems for the Americans: (1) the talks seem unorganized and Americans become easily exasperated; and (2) progress can't be measured by the number of issues settled. In the latter case Americans are often heading to the airport when their Japanese partners are getting ready to agree on everything.

9. What are the most important considerations in selecting a negotiation team? Give examples.

   Language skills and influence at headquarters are the two most important negotiator characteristics as discovered in our research at Ford and AT&T. Given that the negotiator's job is to communicate with both clients and headquarters, these two selection criteria make perfect sense. Another important consideration is the make up of the foreign negotiation team. Particularly, in high-context cultures where status is a crucial issue, American negotiation teams must "match up" well with the group on the other side of the negotiation table. When Disney first began developing EuroDisney Michael Eisner began taking French. He knew he would be meeting with key French government and industry leaders and he invested some of his most valuable time preparing in that way. Peter Ueberroth attributes much of his success negotiating television contracts with the Japanese for the 1984 Olympics to his Japanese language skills.

10. What kinds of training would be most useful for international business negotiators?

    Living and working in foreign countries is really the best training, particularly when language learning is part of the experience. Short of that ideal some experiential training is quite useful. The Managing Negotiations: Japan Program at Ford is the best example of these kinds of training wherein executives rehearse future actual negotiations using videotape analyses. The Japanese approach to international negotiations training can also be useful—they take junior people along on negotiations and give them listening and note taking responsibilities. Young Japanese learn by direct observation and role modeling. Japanese managers see the extra expense of bringing along a junior person as a good investment in people.

11. Name three aspects of negotiation situations which might be manipulated before talks begin? Suggest how this might be done.

Time, location, and the number of parties are all situational factors that should be manipulated before negotiations begin. It will be most important for negotiators to argue at headquarters for longer time periods than would be appropriate in domestic negotiations. Hotels and flight reservations should be made somewhat indefinite so your foreign partners don't use time pressures against you. Ideally, your customers and clients will call on you at your home offices. Next best is a neutral location where both parties are traveling. If you must travel to their offices you can still invite them to work at your hotel—rent a meeting room—that gets them off their turf. Finally, the typical American approach is to bring all concerned parties together to "hammer out a solution." A better idea, even in the United States, is to lobby. That is, it's better to talk to the customer, her trading company, and bankers separately. Then once they agree with your views hold a general meeting.

12. Explain why Americans spend so little time on non-task sound and Brazilians so much.

Americans depend on the legal system and a tightly written contract to settle future disputes. Brazilians cannot and do not depend on their legal system. Instead they depend on strong personal relationships, invested in ahead of time. Brazilians will not do business with some one they do not trust based on long acquaintance.

13. Why is it difficult to get negative feedback from counterparts in many foreign countries? Give examples.

In high-context cultures maintaining positive personal relationships is more important that accurate information, particularly when it involves saying "no." In both Mexico and Japan it is difficult to get a direct "no" from a business partner, particularly in formal settings. Particularly important points should be aired out in less formal settings or through third parties where tougher questions can be answer more forthrightly.

14. Why won't getting mad work in Mexico or Japan?

Chester Karrass suggests in his books that getting mad in the States can work—it demonstrates commitment, that this is an important issue. In high-context cultures like Mexico and Japan getting mad can ruin positive personal and business relationships. Aggressively negative messages must be delivered in other informal contexts, not at the formal negotiation table.

15. Why are questions the most useful persuasive tactic?

The primary task in a negotiation is gathering information. Presumably you know what your side wants. Once you have a good understanding of what the other side wants then creative solutions can best be explored. That means keeping your mouth shut. Your questions keep the other side talking and the information flowing in your direction. Questions can also be used as persuasive tactics. When the other side makes an unreasonable request most often the best response is a question, not anger. Ask them WHY they need it delivered so quickly or HOW they came up with that price. If their answers are good perhaps you will need to concede on that issue. When their answers are weak, then they will be obligated to concede the point. When you cannot think of anything else to say, ask a question.

# PART IV

# TEST BANK

# Chapter 1 The Scope and Challenge of International Marketing

## True/False Questions

1. Only large firms having facilities in foreign countries can participate in international business.

   Answer: False Difficulty: Easy Page: 4

2. Firms like Boeing Aerospace are leading the way to an "interplanetary marketing concept."

   Answer: True Difficulty: Easy Page: 4

3. The financial and market power enjoyed by large American corporations allows these firms to ignore global business and political trends.

   Answer: False Difficulty: Medium Page: 5

4. The America-First Corporation is determined to confine its activities to domestic enterprises. The firm will continue its operations in the United States, hire only American workers and ensure that it always "buys and sells American". The policies adopted by America-First will ensure that it will be unaffected by international concerns and competition.

   Answer: False Difficulty: Hard Page: 5

5. Ford Motor Company has evolved from a 100% American firm to a truly global enterprise to emerge from the merger of its U.S. and European organizations in the year 2000.

   Answer: True Difficulty: Medium Page: 6

6. The United Kingdom is the largest single foreign investor in American companies.

   Answer: True Difficulty: Easy Page: 6

7. The internationalization of American business has been primarily driven by the need to secure outlets for surplus productive capacity and maintain customary rates of growth.

   Answer: True Difficulty: Medium Page: 5-6

8. RCA is the only American-owned company that still manufactures television sets and VCR units.

   Answer: False Difficulty: Easy Page: 6

9. For many domestic firms, foreign sales are more profitable than U.S. sales and foreign returns on assets are better than in the United States.

   Answer: True Difficulty: Easy Page: 7

10. Of all U.S. multinationals, Coca-Cola derives the largest percentage of both total revenues and total profits from foreign sources.

    Answer: False Difficulty: Medium Page: 7

11. Conceptually, international marketing differs from domestic marketing only by virtue of the fact that the marketer must operate in more than one nation.

    Answer: True Difficulty: Easy Page: 7-8

12. The America-First Corporation was among one of the first domestic corporations to successfully compete in the Japanese market. The firm should be able to employ the same programs and techniques it developed in this market to ensure its successful entry into the Chinese market.

    Answer: False Difficulty: Hard Page: 8

13. The fact that the marketer must change the "controllable" elements of the marketing mix to adapt to the unique demands of foreign consumers and environments means that he or she does not have final control over even this portion of the marketing task.

    Answer: True Difficulty: Medium Page: 8

14. The successful international marketer must adapt the controllable elements of the marketing mix to the uncontrollable elements of each of the unique foreign environments in which he or she must compete.

    Answer: True Difficulty: Medium Page: 9

15. Amanda Archer has been recruited to help the American-First Corporation overcome the problems the previous marketing manager encountered during the firm's entry into international marketing. She should probably begin by carefully analyzing the unique characteristics of each of the firm's foreign markets.

    Answer: True Difficulty: Hard Page: 9-10

16. The uncontrollable elements of an international firm's home-country have little, or no, impact upon its success in the international environment.

    Answer: False Difficulty: Medium Page: 10

17. Foreign nationals typically view American firms, and their representatives, as "aliens" who are seeking to exploit consumers in a culture they do not understand or appreciate.

    Answer: True Difficulty: Medium Page: 11

18. The single most challenging and important task facing the international marketer is that of adjusting to unfamiliar cultures.

    Answer: True   Difficulty: Easy   Page: 14

19. The America-First Corporation is preparing to market its line of sterile gauze bandages, and over-the-counter medications in Asia. While the firm must carefully monitor the creation of commercial messages appropriate to the language and tradition of the area, it will be able to maintain the traditional white packaging that projects an image of purity the world over.

    Answer: False   Difficulty: Hard   Page: 14

20. The America-First Corporation routinely requires its potential marketing managers to spend a year in those foreign countries for which they may be later responsible. The firm is attempting to overcome the subtle, but potentially devastating, problem of assuming that foreign customers are similar to the American culture.

    Answer: True   Difficulty: Hard   Page: 14

21. The key to successful international marketing is adaptation to the environmental differences from one market to another.

    Answer: True   Difficulty: Easy   Page: 14

22. The primary obstacle to success in international marketing is a person's self-reference criterion (SRC) in making decisions.

    Answer: True   Difficulty: Easy   Page: 15

23. In order to be globally aware, the marketer must cultivate the traits of objectivity and tolerance—and apply those traits in a context of global knowledge and target market trends.

    Answer: True   Difficulty: Medium   Page: 18

24. The America-First Corporation has only recently entered the international arena. The firm should prepare for this event by planning a logical, step-by-step progression through the five linear stages of international marketing involvement.

    Answer: False   Difficulty: Hard   Page: 20

25. The America-First Corporation utilizes subsidiaries to establish marketing objectives and plans for its domestic market and each of its foreign markets. Each market is served by a marketing mix that has been specifically developed for it. The firm would be <u>BEST</u> described as following the domestic market extension concept.

    Answer: False   Difficulty: Hard   Page: 23

# Chapter 1 The Scope and Challenge of International Marketing

26. A truly global orientation requires that the marketer apply the marketing practices, procedures, and philosophy used in its domestic operations to treat the entire world as its market.

    Answer: True Difficulty: Medium Page: 23

**Multiple Choice Questions**

27. America's largest exporter is:
    A) General Motors.
    B) The Boeing Company.
    C) Coca-Cola.
    D) Wal-Mart.

    Answer: B Difficulty: Easy Page: 3

28. All of the following trends are MAJOR forces in influencing the future shape of international business EXCEPT the:
    A) rapid growth of the World Trade Organization.
    B) impact of the Internet.
    C) rapid growth of regional free trade areas.
    D) recent resurgence of nationalism.

    Answer: D Difficulty: Medium Page: 4

29. The internalization of American business is:
    A) increasingly necessary for survival.
    B) a luxury that can be afforded only by the largest of domestic firms.
    C) a threat to the profitability of domestic firms.
    D) a major force in the dilution of stockholder equity.

    Answer: A Difficulty: Medium Page: 4-5

30. The America-First Corporation is preparing to enter the French and German markets. This firm's strategy will be affected by the policy and regulatory environment created by:
    A) EC.
    B) AFTA.
    C) NAFTA.
    D) GERFRA.

    Answer: A Difficulty: Hard Page: 4-5

# Chapter 1 The Scope and Challenge of International Marketing

31. 7-Eleven, the convenience store chain, is owned by a firm based in:
    A) Japan.
    B) Korea.
    C) Mexico.
    D) Taiwan.

    Answer: A Difficulty: Medium Page: 6

32. Which of the following nations owns Zenith, the television manufacturer?
    A) the United States.
    B) Japan.
    C) Great Britain.
    D) South Korea.

    Answer: D Difficulty: Medium Page: 6

33. The single greatest amount of foreign investment in U.S. firms comes from investors in:
    A) Japan.
    B) Germany.
    C) the United Kingdom.
    D) the Netherlands.

    Answer: C Difficulty: Medium Page: 6

34. Multinational firms:
    A) expanded manufacturing employment much faster than their domestic rivals.
    B) grew sales twice as fast as U.S. domestic firms.
    C) earned significantly lower returns on assets than domestic firms.
    D) earned significantly lower returns on equity than domestic firms.

    Answer: B Difficulty: Medium Page: 7

35. Which of the following firms earned the LARGEST percentage of their total profits from foreign sources?
    A) Coca-Cola.
    B) Colgate-Palmolive.
    C) McDonald's.
    D) Compaq Computer.

    Answer: D Difficulty: Medium Page: 7

# Chapter 1 The Scope and Challenge of International Marketing

36. The America-First Corporation defines its mission as "planning, pricing, promoting and distributing the firm's goods and services to consumers in more than one nation for a profit." The firm's statement indicates that it is engaged in:
    A) international marketing.
    B) foreign exchange.
    C) global investment.
    D) multinational barter.

    Answer: A Difficulty: Hard Page: 7

37. Which of the following is the MOST important factor in an international marketer's success?
    A) creation of a new marketing concept.
    B) the ability to adapt to different marketing environments.
    C) development of new marketing processes.
    D) the evolution of unique marketing principles.

    Answer: B Difficulty: Medium Page: 8

38. The controllable elements of the marketer's task includes all of the following EXCEPT:
    A) promotion.
    B) product.
    C) competition.
    D) distribution.

    Answer: C Difficulty: Medium Page: 8

39. The international marketer who fails to meet his or her objectives is MOST likely to be a victim of:
    A) unfamiliar marketing environments.
    B) an inability to adapt products.
    C) an inability to adapt commercial messages.
    D) weak pricing skills.

    Answer: A Difficulty: Medium Page: 8

40. All of the following are elements in the uncontrollable environment faced by the international marketer EXCEPT:
    A) competition.
    B) politics.
    C) the level of technology.
    D) promotion.

    Answer: D Difficulty: Medium Page: 8

# Chapter 1 The Scope and Challenge of International Marketing

41. James Wells is preparing to direct the America-First Corporation's entry into the Asian market. His success will depend upon the skill with which he:
A) masters a foreign language.
B) adapts the marketing mix to the uncontrollable factors unique to the area.
C) selects media.
D) translates domestic prices into foreign currency.

Answer: B Difficulty: Hard Page: 8

42. International marketing success depends upon the skill with which the marketer balances the subtle, complex interactions which exist in the:
A) domestic uncontrollable environment.
B) controllable environment.
C) foreign uncontrollable environment(s).
D) all of the above.

Answer: D Difficulty: Medium Page: 8

43. Recently, the Japanese economy has been battered by a variety of factors that have precipitated a fall in the value of the yen vis-à-vis the dollar. The stronger dollar has adversely affected the export business of the America-First Corporation. The firm's experience is an example of how foreign ventures can be affected by domestic:
A) legal structure.
B) economic conditions.
C) political forces.
D) technological developments.

Answer: B Difficulty: Hard Page: 10

44. In recent years, the federal government has moved to "normalize" relations with China by, among other moves, awarding and maintaining most favored nation status. This action has opened a vast potential market and source of "cheap" labor to American firms. The government's action is an example of how foreign ventures can be affected by domestic:
A) political policy.
B) legal policy.
C) technological policy.
D) currency policy.

Answer: A Difficulty: Hard Page: 9-10

45. During the recent economic surge enjoyed by America, the America-First Corporation attracted significant amounts of capital which it, in turn, invested in foreign operations. The firm's fortunes are an example of positive impacts that may be derived from the home nation's:
A) legal policy.
B) technological policy.
C) economic policy.
D) political policy.

Answer: C Difficulty: Hard Page: 9-10

46. For years, General Motors reigned supreme in the domestic automobile industry. Secure from serious domestic and foreign competition, the firm could afford to pursue a leisurely strategy in all of its markets. This all changed with the arrival of high-quality, inexpensive foreign imports which posed a direct threat to the firm's domestic market share and an indirect threat to the firm's domestic market share and an indirect threat by galvanizing its domestic rivals. GM's experience demonstrates the impact of:
A) political policy.
B) the competitive environment.
C) economic policy.
D) legal policy.

Answer: B Difficulty: Hard Page: 9-10

47. To protect the "international property" of American film and recording studios, the government has vigorously sought the assistance of the Chinese government in the enforcement of copyright and patents aimed at the prevention of the practice of film and recording piracy. American producers could recoup significant foreign revenues as a result of a successful implementation of domestic:
A) political policy.
B) technological policy.
C) competitive policy.
D) economic policy.

Answer: A Difficulty: Hard Page: 9-10

48. Many domestic firms feel that the extension of American statutes to apply to their foreign activities places American firms in an unfair competitive position vis-à-vis foreign rivals. This is an example of a negative impact associated with domestic:
A) political policy.
B) economic policy.
C) legal policy.
D) technological policy.

Answer: C Difficulty: Medium Page: 9-10

# Chapter 1 The Scope and Challenge of International Marketing

49. The process of evaluating the uncontrollable elements in an international marketing program is frequently attended by:
A) cultural shock.
B) political shock.
C) economic shock.
D) all of the above.

Answer: D Difficulty: Easy Page: 10

50. The America-First Corporation is contemplating an entry into several attractive Middle-East markets. The firm is concerned, however, about strong anti-American factions that frequently conflict with generally pro-American governments in the area. America-First's entry choices will be strongly affected by its evaluation of each nation's:
A) economic climate.
B) political stability.
C) technological climate.
D) cultural climate.

Answer: B Difficulty: Hard Page: 10-11

51. Many American firms have experienced frustration resulting from expensive breakdowns and malfunctions in the sophisticated equipment installed in foreign installations. Often, the cause of the problem is the failure of foreign nationals in these plants to provide the maintenance required by the equipment. American firms typically fail to appreciate critical differences in its foreign market's:
A) political market.
B) competitive market.
C) technological climate.
D) economic climate.

Answer: C Difficulty: Hard Page: 11

52. The "alien status" of a foreign firm is <u>MOST</u> likely to impact that firm in its efforts to understand and successfully deal with its host country's:
A) political environment.
B) economic environment.
C) cultural environment.
D) technological environment.

Answer: A Difficulty: Medium Page: 11

53. In the broadest sense, the "culture" of international marketing is composed of:
A) the uncontrollable elements of the foreign market.
B) the controllable elements of the foreign market.
C) the uncontrollable elements of the domestic market.
D) the controllable elements of the domestic market.

Answer: A Difficulty: Easy Page: 11-12

54. The America-First Corporation is preparing to engage in international marketing for the first time in the long and successful history of the firm. Ironically, the firm's domestic success is likely to make it more difficult for the firm to adjust to foreign:
A) economic systems.
B) technologies.
C) cultures.
D) political systems.

Answer: C Difficulty: Hard Page: 13

55. The natural tendency for international marketers to base their judgements and marketing strategies in foreign markets upon their experiences in their "home" culture is BEST described as the:
A) domestic marketing concept.
B) self-reference criterion.
C) principle of comparative advantage.
D) international marketing concept.

Answer: B Difficulty: Easy Page: 15

56. Prior to allowing new international marketers to assume control of a foreign program, the America-First Corporation insists that the candidate, and his or her family, take a year to "immerse" themselves in the host country's culture. The firm's program is designed to minimize the impact of:
A) comparative economics.
B) technology shock.
C) alien seclusion.
D) self-referencing and ethnocentrism.

Answer: D Difficulty: Hard Page: 15

57. Self-referencing is a subtle, and unintended, result of:
A) formal education.
B) cross-cultural experience.
C) cultural conditioning.
D) international experience.

Answer: C Difficulty: Easy Page: 15

58. The conscious attempt to anticipate the influences of foreign and domestic uncontrollable influences upon a proposed marketing mix in order to minimize those impacts is the goal of:
A) adaptation.
B) acculturation.
C) adjustment.
D) assimilation.

Answer: A Difficulty: Easy Page: 15-16

59. The international marketer's ability to assess foreign cultures in an objective, unbiased manner is often inhibited by unconscious reliance upon his or her:
A) ethnocentric education.
B) self-reference criterion.
C) repetitive action syndrome.
D) cross-cultural criterion.

Answer: B Difficulty: Medium Page: 15-16

60. An American automobile manufacturer dubbed one of its vehicles the "Matador" to project an image of fun and adventure. The firm discovered, to its horror, that the name translated as "killer" in many Spanish speaking markets. Mistakes such as these result PRIMARILY from the marketer's unconscious reliance upon his or her:
A) ethnocentric education.
B) cross-cultural criterion.
C) repetitive-action syndrome.
D) self-reference criterion.

Answer: D Difficulty: Hard Page: 15-16

61. In order to minimize the likelihood and/or impact of making inappropriate decisions based upon the self-reliance criteria of domestic executives, international executives should subject such decisions to:
A) cross-cultural analysis.
B) ethnocentric analysis.
C) decision-tree analysis.
D) computer simulation analysis.

Answer: A Difficulty: Medium Page: 17-18

62. Which of the following elements of cross-cultural analysis derives its impact and pervasive influence PRIMARILY from its subconscious nature?
A) linguistics.
B) the self-reference criterion.
C) cross-cultural analysis.
D) ethnocentric simulation.

Answer: B Difficulty: Medium Page: 17-18

63. The globally aware marketer must possess:
A) objectivity.
B) tolerance.
C) Knowledge of cultures, history, world market potential, and global economic, social, and political trends.
D) all of the above.

Answer: D Difficulty: Medium Page: 18

64. Which of the following is MOST important to the identification of future world markets?
    A) the self-reference criterion.
    B) a knowledge of global economic, social, and political trends.
    C) a knowledge of world culture and history.
    D) objectivity and tolerance.

    Answer: B Difficulty: Medium Page: 19

65. The America-First Corporation has recently sought to augment its traditional domestic marketing program by establishing a presence on the Internet. The firm has been surprised by the large and increasing volume of foreign orders this move spawned. At this stage, America-First's international role would be BEST described as:
    A) global marketing.
    B) international marketing.
    C) no direct foreign marketing.
    D) regular foreign marketing.

    Answer: C Difficulty: Hard Page: 20

66. Firms that have decided to domestically produce products specifically designed and intended for foreign export would be BEST described as being engaged in:
    A) regular foreign marketing.
    B) international marketing.
    C) no direct foreign marketing.
    D) global marketing.

    Answer: A Difficulty: Medium Page: 20

67. The America-First Corporation has established a group of foreign-based facilities to produce and market products for a variety of carefully selected foreign markets. The firm would be BEST described as engaging in:
    A) global marketing.
    B) no direct foreign marketing.
    C) regular foreign marketing.
    D) international marketing.

    Answer: D Difficulty: Hard Page: 21

68. In which of the following phases of international marketing involvement is characterized by the firm treating the entire world, including the home country, as a single market?
    A) international marketing.
    B) global marketing.
    C) ethnocentric marketing.
    D) cross-cultural marketing.

    Answer: B Difficulty: Medium Page: 21

69. In which of the following phases of international marketing involvement is worldwide standardization of business activities MOST likely to be used to achieve advantages whenever and wherever it is cost effective and culturally feasible?
A) international marketing.
B) regular foreign marketing.
C) cross-cultural marketing.
D) global marketing.

Answer: D Difficulty: Medium Page: 21

70. All of the following are elements of the EPRG framework for evaluating the degree of internationalism a firm's management is committed to EXCEPT:
A) ethnocentric orientation.
B) geocentric orientation.
C) raceocentric orientation.
D) polycentric orientation.

Answer: C Difficulty: Easy Page: 22

71. While the America-First Corporation focuses primary attention upon its domestic market, it has begun to seek profitable foreign markets for its domestically produced products. The firm would be BEST described as following a:
A) domestic market extension concept.
B) multidomestic market concept.
C) international market concept.
D) global market concept.

Answer: A Difficulty: Hard Page: 23

72. Firms that market on a country-by-country basis, which typically entails development of essentially independent programs for each unique market, are following a:
A) domestic market extension concept.
B) multidomestic market concept.
C) international market concept.
D) global market concept.

Answer: B Difficulty: Medium Page: 23

73. Where would a firm following a global marketing concept BEST fit in the EPRG schema?
A) the ethnocentric/polycentric classification.
B) the polycentric/regiocentric classification.
C) the geocentric/ethnocentric classification.
D) the regiocentric/geocentric classification.

Answer: D Difficulty: Medium Page: 23

74. The America-First Corporation expects that the trend toward internationalization of the competitive environment will continue and intensify. In accordance with this belief, the firm is MOST likely to embrace the:
A) polydomestic market concept.
B) domestic market extension concept.
C) global market concept.
D) multidomestic market concept.

Answer: C Difficulty: Hard Page: 23-25

75. Global "homogenization" is PRIMARILY the result of:
A) the influence of mass media and communications.
B) the work of the United Nations.
C) the fall of the Soviet Union.
D) the emergence of the European Economic Community.

Answer: A Difficulty: Easy Page: 23-25

76. Global marketing has been made possible by:
A) the dissolution of national borders.
B) the emergence of similar segments having similar demands in an increasing number of different countries.
C) the triumph of American culture and democracy the world over.
D) the creation of a "new world order" by the United Nations.

Answer: B Difficulty: Medium Page: 23-25

**Fill in the Blank Questions**

77. Increasingly, the business of American business is ______________ business.

Answer: international Difficulty: Easy Page: 4

78. ______________ is the performance of business activities designed to plan, price, promote, and direct the flow of a company's goods and services to consumers or users in more than one nation for a profit.

Answer: International marketing Difficulty: Easy Page: 7

79. Uncontrollable forces in the foreign environment include ______________ forces, ______________ forces, ______________ forces, the level of ________________, the structure of ________________, ______________, and ________________, and ______________ forces.

Answer: political/legal; economic; competitive; technology; distribution; geography and infrastructure; cultural Difficulty: Medium Page: 9

# Chapter 1 The Scope and Challenge of International Marketing

80. The most difficult task facing the international marketer is frequently that of cultural ______________.

    Answer: adjustment  Difficulty: Medium  Page: 13

81. Cultural conditioning affects the international marketer through the process of ______________ and ______________.

    Answer: self-referencing; ethnocentrism  Difficulty: Medium  Page: 15

82. In order to become globally aware, an international marketer must develop the traits of ______________, ______________, of cultural differences, and ______________ of cultures, history, world market potential, and global trends affecting business.

    Answer: objectivity, tolerance, knowledge  Difficulty: Medium  Page: 18

83. An unsolicited order from a foreign buyer is often the stimulus that moves a firm from a policy of ______________ to a more active role in the international arena.

    Answer: no direct foreign marketing  Difficulty: Easy  Page: 20

84. On occasion, the America-First Corporation seeks to dispose of production overruns and unsold "perishable" inventories by exporting those surpluses to any foreign market that might take them. The firm would be BEST described as engaging in ______________.

    Answer: infrequent foreign marketing  Difficulty: Hard  Page: 20

85. After several years of exporting surplus inventory to foreign markets, the America-First Corporation has decided to produce products specifically for selected foreign markets through foreign subsidiaries. The firm would be BEST described as engaging in ______________.

    Answer: regular foreign marketing  Difficulty: Hard  Page: 20

86. Firms that are fully committed to, and involved in, marketing activities in countries throughout the world are said to be in ______________.

    Answer: international marketing  Difficulty: Easy  Page: 21

87. ______________ marketers are distinguished by their ability to see, and treat, the world, including their "home" country, as one market.

    Answer: Global  Difficulty: Easy  Page: 21

88. Global marketers seek to maximize returns through global ______________ of business activities—whenever it is cost effective and culturally feasible.

    Answer: standardization  Difficulty: Easy  Page: 21-22

89. Under the EPRG schema, firms are classified as having a(n) ______________, ______________, ______________, or ______________ orientation.

Answer: ethnocentric, polycentric, regiocentric, geocentric Difficulty: Medium Page: 22

90. While the America-First Corporation primarily focuses upon its domestic market, the firm does sell excess inventory in foreign markets as a means of enhancing its profitability. The firm would be BEST described as following a(n) ______________ concept.

Answer: domestic market extension Difficulty: Hard Page: 23

91. The America-First Corporation utilizes a series of foreign subsidiaries to establish independent marketing objectives and plans to be implemented and achieved through unique marketing mixes developed for each country. The firm apparently follows the ______________ concept.

Answer: multidomestic market Difficulty: Hard Page: 23

92. The development of a standardized product, of uniform quality, to be sold at a reasonable price throughout the world is at the core of the ______________ concept.

Answer: global marketing Difficulty: Medium Page: 23

93. As the competitive environment facing U.S. businesses becomes more internationalized, the most effective orientation for many firms involved in marketing in another country will be a(n) ______________.

Answer: global orientation Difficulty: Medium Page: 25

94. According to Levitt, a global market now exits in the sense that ______________ exist in many different countries that have similar values, needs, and behavioral patterns.

Answer: segments Difficulty: Easy Page: 25

95. It is generally agreed that advances in ______________ have played a major role in the homogenization of the nations of the world.

Answer: mass communications Difficulty: Medium Page: 25

96. The successful international marketer must strike a fine balance between ______________ whenever feasible and ______________ whenever necessary.

Answer: standardization; adaptation Difficulty: Medium Page: 25

# Chapter 1 The Scope and Challenge of International Marketing

## Essay Questions

97. What relationship, if any, exists between the worldwide growth in mass production that has occurred over the past twenty years and the current emphasis on international marketing?

    Answer:
    The rapid acceleration in the productive capacity of many nations of the world has resulted in a growing number of firms in those countries whose capability to produce has outgrown domestic demand. In an attempt to sustain growth and profitability, these firms have increasingly sought foreign markets—in many cases with the active participation of governments who see foreign trade as a means of promoting national growth.

    Difficulty: Hard Page: 5-7

98. Does the marketer REALLY control the elements of the marketing mix (product, promotion, price and distribution)? Defend your position.

    Answer:
    No. In fact, the consumer is the final "controller" of all marketing efforts. The marketer seeks to understand consumer desires—and, acting as the consumer's agent, seeks to translate that knowledge into market offerings that will satisfy the customer's demands within the constraints imposed by non-market uncontrollables. Those marketers who perform their agent role well, succeed—those who do not, fail.

    Difficulty: Hard Page: 8-15

99. How can educational and business institutions assist the marketer in overcoming the problems posed by the unconscious use of the self-reference criterion?

    Answer:
    Educational institutions can warn future marketers of the potential problems that often accompany the unconscious application of cultural conditioning. Business curricula could be modified to include electives in the language and culture of major foreign markets. International marketing tracks should require such courses—with a choice of specific countries for study. Business should routinely "sensitize" marketing managers assigned to specific foreign nations to the basics of its cultures.

    Difficulty: Hard Page: 15-19

# Chapter 1 The Scope and Challenge of International Marketing

100. Briefly discuss the interrelationships between the primary prerequisites for global awareness.

Answer:
A globally aware marketer must be OBJECTIVE in his/her evaluation of foreign marketing opportunities. This objectivity must be based on a KNOWLEDGE of the target nation's history, culture, and institutions and must be characterized by a TOLERANCE for cultural behaviors and solutions that differ from our own. Finally, the marketer must understand that change is the one universal commonality—trends must be tracked over time and adjustments made as necessary.

Difficulty: Hard Page: 18-19

101. What relationship, if any, exists between the growth of international communications and the trend toward global marketing?

Answer:
Global communications technology has literally "wired the world"—allowing the nations of the world to witness events that transcend our differences and emphasize our similarities. As nations learn to understand and appreciate the cultures of other countries, an ever-growing range of alternative solutions to common problems are presented to a world of potential customers.

Difficulty: Hard Page: 21-25

# Chapter 2 The Dynamic Environment of Global Business

## True/False Questions

1. An increase in international competition tends to lead to an increase in protectionism.

   Answer: True   Difficulty: Easy   Page: 30

2. As late as 1968, J. J. Servan-Schreiber wrote that American industry in Europe would rank third in world industrial power behind the United States and Russia.

   Answer: True   Difficulty: Easy   Page: 32

3. U.S. dominance, as measured by the nationality of the world's largest industrial corporations, has steadily increased over the last 30 years.

   Answer: False   Difficulty: Medium   Page: 33

4. In the 1990s, the United States must deal with many of the same challenges, doubts and fears that faced Europe 20 years ago.

   Answer: True   Difficulty: Medium   Page: 34

5. By the year 2020, there will be a shift in economic power and influence away from the United States, Japan, and other industrialized nations to countries in Latin America, Eastern Europe, Asia, and Africa.

   Answer: True   Difficulty: Medium   Page: 35

6. The growing interdependence of world economies is reflected in the reaction of the American stock market to events in Asia, Latin America, Europe, Africa, and the Middle East.

   Answer: True   Difficulty: Medium   Page: 35

7. A nation's balance-of-payments statement records all transactions between its residents and those of the rest of the world during a given period of time—usually a year.

   Answer: True   Difficulty: Easy   Page: 36

8. In spite of the designation "balance-of-payments", no nation's statement ever balances.

   Answer: False   Difficulty: Medium   Page: 36

9. Of the three components of the balance-of-payments statement, international business is MOST interested in the current account.

   Answer: True   Difficulty: Medium   Page: 36

10. If a nation has a favorable balance of trade, it must also have a favorable balance of payments.

    Answer: False Difficulty: Medium Page: 37

11. In order to improve the U.S. balance-of-trade vis-à-vis Japan, the Clinton administration was determined to adopt a policy that would enhance U.S. exports while discouraging Japanese imports. To this end, the dollar was allowed to decline in value against the yen.

    Answer: True Difficulty: Hard Page: 37

12. The World Trade Organization has ruled that Japan's complex distribution structure is a deliberate barrier to trade and is, therefore, a form of illegal protectionism.

    Answer: False Difficulty: Medium Page: 37

13. Economists do not recognize any governmental attempt to restrain trade in order to protect domestic industry as valid.

    Answer: False Difficulty: Medium Page: 39

14. While protectionism may raise the cost of some goods to consumers in those nations that employ such practices, that cost is more than outweighed by beneficial impacts on domestic wages and employment.

    Answer: False Difficulty: Medium Page: 39

15. The America-First Corporation is leading the efforts of its industry to persuade Congress to impose limits upon the number of units foreign rivals may sell in the United States. The firm, and its industry are seeking protection through the imposition of quotas.

    Answer: True Difficulty: Hard Page: 40

16. Unlike tariffs, which are a direct tax on imported goods, quotas do not result in higher prices for foreign goods.

    Answer: False Difficulty: Medium Page: 40

17. Under pressure from American automobile producers, Japanese automakers agreed to restrict their exports to the U.S. to levels acceptable to both parties. The use of such voluntary export restraints is a model for future trade management efforts that involve no political pressure and have no adverse impacts upon any party to the agreement.

    Answer: False Difficulty: Hard Page: 40-41

18. The U.S. boycott of Iraq has demonstrated that politically motivated trade restraints can effectively "punish" dictatorial regimes without harming consumers in either of the nations involved in the dispute.

    Answer: False Difficulty: Hard Page: 41

19. When a differential exchange rate is used to control importation, the exporter of "undesirable goods" is forced to pay higher amounts of domestic currency for foreign exchange units that must be used to purchase products in undesirable categories.

    Answer: False Difficulty: Medium Page: 42

20. Japan is a major user of standards—non-tariff barriers designed to protect the health and safety of its citizens and/or ensure product quality.

    Answer: True Difficulty: Medium Page: 42

21. The market access provisions of The Omnibus Trade and Competitiveness Act of 1988 are designed to "force" our trading partners to open their markets to American goods.

    Answer: True Difficulty: Medium Page: 43

22. The America-First Corporation has recently lost domestic market share to Japanese producers who have been able to sell a superior product at a lower price. While the firm struggles to regain its competitive edge, it may petition the government for relief provisions of The Omnibus Trade and Competitiveness Act of 1988.

    Answer: True Difficulty: Hard Page: 43

23. The General Agreement on Tariffs and Trade (GATT) was the first effective worldwide tariff agreement.

    Answer: True Difficulty: Easy Page: 45

24. The America-First Corporation has become increasingly concerned with the problems created by foreign producers placing its brand names and symbols on poor quality "rip-off" goods. The firm may seek protection under the Trade Related Aspects of Intellectual property Rights (TRIPs) provision of GATT.

    Answer: True Difficulty: Hard Page: 46-47

25. The America-First Corporation is concerned that several of the nations in which it produces, requires the firm to purchase significant components from high-cost local producers. The firm may petition for relief from such practices under the Trade Related Investment Measures (TRIMs) provision of GATT.

    Answer: True Difficulty: Hard Page: 46

26. The World Trade Organization (WTO) provides a forum in which trade disputes may be discussed and non-binding rulings issued to resolve differences and redress injuries.

    Answer: False Difficulty: Medium Page: 47-48

27. The America-First Corporation is preparing a presentation for the World Trade Organization in order to stop foreign rivals from selling products in its domestic market for less than the cost of their production. The firm is seeking relief from the practice of dumping.

    Answer: True Difficulty: Hard Page: 49

28. The use of countervailing duties to offset advantages associated with governmental subsidies has been outlawed by the World Trade Organization.

    Answer: False Difficulty: Medium Page: 49

29. Special drawing rights are allowed by the World Bank as an incentive for member nations to abandon the use of universally floating exchange rates.

    Answer: False Difficulty: Medium Page: 50

30. The America-First Corporation is preparing to join with several other domestic and foreign firms to form a global web-based system designed to cut purchasing costs and enhance sales through cooperation and information sharing. The World Trade Organization is likely to rule this venture illegal.

    Answer: True Difficulty: Hard Page: 52-53

**Multiple Choice Questions**

31. The last half of the $20^{th}$ century is unique as a result of:
    A) increasing economic interdependence among the nations of the world.
    B) increasing opportunities for international trade.
    C) increasing potential global demand.
    D) all of the above.

    Answer: D Difficulty: Medium Page: 30

32. The post World War II boom enjoyed by the United States and Europe was largely the legacy of:
    A) the Manhattan Project.
    B) the Marshall Plan.
    C) the World Bank.
    D) the International Monetary Fund.

    Answer: B Difficulty: Medium Page: 30

# Chapter 2 The Dynamic Environment of Global Business

33. The agreements reached under the umbrella of GATT sought to reverse the trend toward higher tariffs, which followed passage of the:
    A) Smoot-Hawley Law.
    B) World Trade Organization Act.
    C) Marshall Plan.
    D) Robinson-Patman Act.

    Answer: A Difficulty: Medium Page: 31

34. Servan-Schreiber's prediction that American MNCs would dominate the world primarily failed to come to pass because:
    A) America could not maintain its wartime rate of growth in peacetime.
    B) World War II drained away vital human and material resources America could not replace.
    C) after World War II, America was confronted by a worldwide resurgence in competition.
    D) the World Trade Organization took bold steps to regulate U.S. monopolies.

    Answer: C Difficulty: Medium Page: 31

35. Since 1963:
    A) America's position as home to the majority of the world's largest industrial corporations has been take by Japan.
    B) America's share of world GNP has steadily risen.
    C) America's share of world manufacturing output has nearly doubled.
    D) South Korea has recorded the most dramatic growth in terms of its standing with regard to the number of the world's largest industrial corporations it hosts.

    Answer: D Difficulty: Medium Page: 33

36. The United States enjoyed a favorable world balance of trade:
    A) until 1971.
    B) until 1991.
    C) until 1985.
    D) until 1995.

    Answer: A Difficulty: Medium Page: 33

37. From 1983 to 1987, the great majority of the growth in the U.S. trade deficit resulted from a continual deterioration in America's competitive position with regard to:
    A) oil and other petroleum products.
    B) capital goods and automobiles.
    C) electronic devices and computers.
    D) agricultural products.

    Answer: B Difficulty: Medium Page: 33

38. The America-First Corporation had long been a major producer of television sets and other electronic devices sold throughout the world. The firm began losing foreign, and domestic, market share to foreign manufacturers as the 20th century has drawn to a close. Ironically, the plight of America-First, and other domestic corporations was largely the result of the success of the:
A) Smoot-Hawley Plan.
B) Robinson-Patman Act.
C) Pan-American Trade Pact.
D) Marshall Plan.

Answer: D Difficulty: Hard Page: 33

39. The return to world competitiveness enjoyed by U.S. business beginning in the mid-1990s has been largely fueled by American expertise in:
A) advanced technology products and equipment.
B) agricultural production.
C) automotive production.
D) textile equipment and machinery.

Answer: A Difficulty: Medium Page: 33

40. Exports predict that world trade leadership will, after the year 2000, increasingly shift to:
A) the United States.
B) Western Europe.
C) Asia.
D) Japan

Answer: C Difficulty: Medium Page: 34

41. After 2020, economic power and influence is expected to shift to all of the following areas EXCEPT:
A) Latin America.
B) Africa.
C) The European Union.
D) Asia.

Answer: C Difficulty: Medium Page: 34-35

42. The American economy of present and future is BEST characterized by which of the following descriptions?
A) economic self-sufficiency.
B) global interdependency.
C) global self-sufficiency.
D) global dependency.

Answer: B Difficulty: Medium Page: 34-35

43. According to World Bank estimates for the year 2010, the world's largest economy will be in:
    A) China.
    B) Japan.
    C) the United States.
    D) the European Community.

    Answer: A Difficulty: Medium Page: 34-35

44. The America-First Corporation is preparing to produce a compact, fuel-efficient automobile designed for export to the densely populated urban centers of affluent emerging markets. According to World Bank estimates, the firm's MOST attractive markets are likely to be in:
    A) Japan.
    B) the European Community.
    C) Latin America.
    D) Asia.

    Answer: D Difficulty: Hard Page: 35

45. The system of accounts that records a nation's international financial transactions is called its:
    A) Balance of Trade.
    B) balance of payments.
    C) global account balance.
    D) international balance of accounts.

    Answer: B Difficulty: Easy Page: 36

46. The balance-of-payments statement:
    A) employs single-entry accounting conventions.
    B) typically reflects the global financial dealings for a particular period, usually a year.
    C) can be, and often is, out of balance.
    D) is primarily a political, rather than economic, document.

    Answer: B Difficulty: Medium Page: 36

47. All of the following statements about the balance-of-payments statement are true EXCEPT:
    A) A nation's balance-of-payments presents an overall view of its international economic position.
    B) Export sales made by the U.S. would appear on the plus side of its balance-of-payments statement.
    C) A nation's balance-of-payments records both payments received from and payments made to other countries.
    D) A nation is in a strong economic position as long as its balance of payments statement remains balanced.

    Answer: D Difficulty: Medium Page: 36

48. The America-First Corporation has enjoyed a favorable position vis-à-vis the foreign companies and countries with which it deals. The exports made by this domestically-owned firm would appear on America's balance-of-payments statement as:
A) an offset reducing foreign tax liability.
B) a component of domestic exports displayed on the positive side of the U.S. balance-of-payments statement.
C) a major item among the factors that negatively impact America's balance-of-payments.
D) a neutral factor that has no impact upon the nation's balance-of-payments.

Answer: B Difficulty: Hard Page: 36

49. All of the following items would appear on the positive side of a nation's balance-of-payments statement EXCEPT:
A) spending by tourists overseas.
B) export sales.
C) dividends and/or interest from foreign investments.
D) new foreign investments in the United States.

Answer: A Difficulty: Medium Page: 36

50. In order to produce finished items for export, the America-First Corporation imports a significant volume of parts and material from foreign suppliers. The goods imported by the firm would appear on:
A) the plus side of the U.S. balance-of-payments schedule.
B) production offset schedule of the World Bank.
C) the minus side of the U.S. balance-of-payments schedule.
D) the tariff schedule section of the U.S. balance-of-payments statement.

Answer: C Difficulty: Hard Page: 36

51. All of the following are a component of a balance-of-payments statement EXCEPT the:
A) current account.
B) capital account.
C) official reserves account.
D) balance of tariff account.

Answer: D Difficulty: Medium Page: 36

52. The America-First Corporation has become increasingly involved in international trade. With which of the following components of the U.S. balance-of-payments statement would the firm be MOST concerned?
A) the official reserves account.
B) the current account.
C) the capital account.
D) the foreign exchange account.

Answer: B Difficulty: Hard Page: 36

53. It is very likely the U.S. exports are underrepresented by a significant amount as a result of:
   A) the falling value of U.S. currency.
   B) a method of recording trade transactions that tends to understate the actual value of high-tech devices and equipment.
   C) the difficulties inherent in identifying and reporting many of the services that comprise a major, and increasing, portion of American exports
   D) biases built into the system by the World Trade Organization.

   Answer: C Difficulty: Medium Page: 36

54. Imports are generally thought to be more accurately reported than exports because:
   A) imports represent a major source of revenue for the importing country.
   B) tariffs are typically collected on imports.
   C) countries tend to underreport any activity which, as exports, represent a payment of funds to other nations.
   D) imports are restricted specifically to only large tangible items that are easy to identify and evaluate.

   Answer: B Difficulty: Medium Page: 36

55. The America-First Corporation is a major exporter of computer software encrypted on CD-ROMs. The fact that custom officials often value such exports according to the commodity value of the media upon which they are stored:
   A) would contribute to significant under-valuation of the worth of such exports.
   B) ensure proper valuation of such exports.
   C) would have no impact upon the valuation of such exports.
   D) would contribute to significant overstatement of the value of such exports.

   Answer: A Difficulty: Hard Page: 36-37

56. U.S. Customs is scheduled to implement an Automated Export System in 1998 that will hopefully correct much of the underreporting that probably contributes to the nation's deficits with regard to which of the following?
   A) the current account.
   B) the balance of trade.
   C) the capital account.
   D) the foreign exchange account.

   Answer: A Difficulty: Hard Page: 36-37

57. The relationship between merchandise imports and exports is called the:
   A) export/import index.
   B) trade ratio.
   C) global economic index.
   D) trade balance.

   Answer: D Difficulty: Easy Page: 37

58. A nation that continuously imports more than it exports will probably eventually face:
    A) an increase in the value of its currency.
    B) trade arbitration before an assembly of the World Court.
    C) currency devaluation.
    D) currency resizing.

    Answer: C Difficulty: Hard Page: 37

59. When the value of the U.S. dollar declines relative to foreign currencies,:
    A) U.S. imports tend to increase.
    B) U.S. exports tend to increase.
    C) the demand for foreign-made goods is enhanced.
    D) the World Bank will automatically place tariffs on foreign goods to protect U.S. imports.

    Answer: B Difficulty: Hard Page: 37

60. Which of the following argument for protectionism is LEAST favored by economists?
    A) the infant industry argument.
    B) the national defense argument.
    C) the underdeveloped nation industrialization argument.
    D) the reduction of unemployment argument.

    Answer: D Difficulty: Easy Page: 39

61. Ultimately, the costs of tariffs are borne by:
    A) the consumer.
    B) foreign export firms.
    C) the World Bank.
    D) foreign importing firms.

    Answer: A Difficulty: Easy Page: 39

62. On average, the per year cost of "saving" one U.S. job through the use of protectionist measures is approximately:
    A) $100,000.
    B) $83,000.
    C) $170,000.
    D) $45,000.

    Answer: C Difficulty: Medium Page: 39

63. The America-First Corporation often lobbies in support of the imposition of taxes on the goods of foreign competitors. The firm is seeking protection from the government through the use of:
A) quotas.
B) tariffs.
C) voluntary trade restraints.
D) voluntary export restraints.

Answer: B Difficulty: Hard Page: 40

64. An absolute governmental restriction against the purchase and importation of specified goods from particular countries is called a:
A) tariff.
B) quota.
C) voluntary trade restraint.
D) boycott.

Answer: D Difficulty: Easy Page: 41

65. An importer is required to pay varying amounts of domestic currency for foreign currency used to pay for foreign products according to their relative "desirability" as defined by the government under a system of:
A) boycotts.
B) quotas.
C) differential exchange rates.
D) embargoes.

Answer: C Difficulty: Medium Page: 42

66. Japan has been particularly successful in its attempts to restrict imports through the adroit use of:
A) standards.
B) quotas.
C) boycotts.
D) embargoes.

Answer: A Difficulty: Medium Page: 42

67. The United States and Japan have had ongoing disagreements regarding the relative ease with which each can sell in the other's country. On several occasions, the U.S. has threatened to impose trade sanctions if Japan did not loosen or remove some of the "artificial" barriers to entry that were deemed unfair to American firms. Such action might be taken under which of the following provisions of the Omnibus Trade and Competitors Act of 1988?
A) export expansion.
B) market access.
C) import relief.
D) trade equalization.

Answer: B Difficulty: Hard Page: 43

68. American firms hampered by domestic export controls may gain relief under which of the following sections of the Omnibus Trade and Competitiveness Act of 1988?
A) market access.
B) trade equalization.
C) import relief.
D) export expansion.

Answer: D Difficulty: Medium Page: 44

69. The America-First Corporation has been seriously impacted by fairly traded imports of products for which the firm admits it has lost its competitive edge. The firm may petition for temporary relief to allow it to adjust to competition under which of the following provisions of the Omnibus Trade and Competitiveness Act of 1988?
A) market access.
B) import relief.
C) export expansion.
D) export relief.

Answer: B Difficulty: Hard Page: 44

70. The America-First Corporation has long felt the imposition of high local-content requirements adversely impacting its ability to compete in foreign markets. Which of the following provisions of the Uruguay Round of GATT can be used to address the firm's concerns?
A) TRIMS.
B) GATS.
C) ITS.
D) TRIPS.

Answer: A Difficulty: Hard Page: 46

# Chapter 2 The Dynamic Environment of Global Business

71. The American motion picture and recording industries have long been concerned about the piracy and sale of their products by unlicensed distributors in foreign countries. The Uruguay Round of CATT may provide relief through its:
A) RIMS agreement.
B) GATS agreement.
C) ITS agreement.
D) TRIPS agreement.

Answer: D Difficulty: Hard Page: 46-47

72. For its 132 members, binding decisions regarding disputes under GATT and other trade agreements will be issued by the recently established:
A) World Court.
B) Import/Export Bank.
C) World Trade Organization.
D) United Nations Trade Council.

Answer: C Difficulty: Medium Page: 47

73. The practice of selling at a lower price in a foreign market than in other markets or selling below average total costs is defined by the WTO as:
A) a boycott.
B) dumping.
C) predatory marketing.
D) an illegal boycott.

Answer: B Difficulty: Easy Page: 49

74. The America-First Corporation has requested vigorous protection against the practice of dumping foreign goods in its domestic market. The firm has asked the Department of Commerce and the ITC to investigate each claimed incident and, if appropriate, to take action, including the imposition of a duty equal to the amount by which the estimated foreign market value of the offending goods exceeds the U.S. price. The firm is requesting the imposition of:
A) countervailing duties.
B) punishment taxes.
C) boycott duties.
D) foreign exchange duties.

Answer: A Difficulty: Hard Page: 49

75. The America-First Corporation often employs special drawing rights (SDRs) in its international transactions. The firm's use of such "paper gold" was made possible by the:
A) World Court.
B) International Monetary Fund.
C) Import/Export Bank.
D) World Trade Organization.

Answer: B Difficulty: Hard Page: 50

76. Those nations that attempt to systematically manipulate the value of their currency vis-à-vis the value of other nations' currencies are said to utilize:
A) SDR float.
B) clean float.
C) dirty float.
D) variable float.

Answer: C Difficulty: Easy Page: 50

77. Traditionally, the U.S. has avoided the temptation to manipulate the value of its currency in the international market. Amerca's approach is BEST described as:
A) natural float.
B) no float.
C) dirty float.
D) clean float.

Answer: D Difficulty: Hard Page: 50

78. The institutions which comprise the World Bank provide funds to governments and/or investors for all of the following purposes EXCEPT:
A) replacement of losses due to careless investments.
B) assist developing nations in financing education, health, and/or infrastructure projects.
C) direct loans to strengthen the private sector in developing nations.
D) providing investors with guarantees against "noncommercial" risks.

Answer: A Difficulty: Medium Page: 50

79. The WTO and IMF have been criticized for all of the following "unintended consequences" EXCEPT:
A) environmental damage.
B) worker exploitation.
C) lower oil prices.
D) diminished national sovereignty.

Answer: C Difficulty: Medium Page: 51

80. The America-First Corporation has recently completed plans to employ Womex Online as part of its international marketing strategy. This decision indicates that the firm is attempting to take advantage of the:
A) World Trade Organization.
B) World Bank.
C) SDR services of the International Monetary Fund.
D) Internet.

Answer: D Difficulty: Hard Page: 52

# Chapter 2 The Dynamic Environment of Global Business

## Fill in the Blank Questions

81. Throughout the history of the world, the growth of international trade and competition has been accompanied by an increase in _______________ as individual nations seek to assure their own positions.

    Answer: Protectionism   Difficulty: Medium   Page: 30

82. The _______________, designed to rebuild Europe and Japan after World War II, was intended to avoid the disastrous consequences of international protectionist legislation modeled after the _______________ passed by the U.S. after World War II.

    Answer: Marshall Plan; Smoot-Hawley Law   Difficulty: Medium   Page: 30-31

83. Most exports predict a shift of economic power away from the established industrial powers to countries in _______________, _______________, _______________, _______________ and _______________ by the year 2020.

    Answer: Latin America; Eastern Europe; Asia; Africa   Difficulty: Medium   Page: 35

84. The system of accounts that records a nation's international financial transactions is called its _______________.

    Answer: balance of payments   Difficulty: Easy   Page: 36

85. The balance-of-payments statement is composed of three accounts: the _______________; the _______________; and the _______________.

    Answer: current account; capital account; official reserves account   Difficulty: Medium   Page: 36

86. The America-First Corporation is a major provider of international services. The value of its exports would be reported in the _______________ section of the balance-of-payments statement.

    Answer: current account   Difficulty: Hard   Page: 36

87. The relationship between merchandise imports and exports is referred to as the _______________.

    Answer: balance of trade   Difficulty: Easy   Page: 37

88. Regardless of the form of protectionism employed, the ultimate cost is borne by the _______________.

    Answer: consumer   Difficulty: Medium   Page: 39

# Chapter 2 The Dynamic Environment of Global Business

89. Basically, a(n) _______________ is a tax imposed by a government on goods entering at its borders.

    Answer: tariff Difficulty: Easy Page: 40

90. Non-tariff barriers to trade include quality, sanitary and health _______________, _______________, _______________, ________, and _______________ penalties.

    Answer: standards; quotas; embargoes; boycotts; anti-dumping Difficulty: Medium Page: 40

91. Reeling from the success of Japanese imports in its domestic market, the American automobile industry successfully petitioned the government for pressure to limit those imports. The Japanese finally accepted a system of _______________.

    Answer: voluntary export restraints Difficulty: Hard Page: 40

92. The purchase and importation of certain goods may be prohibited under a government _______________.

    Answer: boycott Difficulty: Easy Page: 41

93. Governments may manipulate the volume of favored and unfavored foreign goods imported by controlling the price of importing such goods through use of a(n) _______________.

    Answer: differential exchange rate Difficulty: Hard Page: 42

94. The Japanese have been quite successful in keeping foreign goods out of their domestic market by claiming that such goods did not meet their _______________.

    Answer: standards Difficulty: Medium Page: 42

95. The Omnibus Trade and Competitiveness Act of 1988 covered the three critical areas of _______________, _______________, and _______________.

    Answer: market access; export expansion; import relief Difficulty: Medium Page: 43

96. The America-First Corporation feels that the Foreign Corrupt Practices Act places unfair restrictions upon them in many nations in which bribery is an accepted practice. The firm may seek relief under the _______________ section of the Omnibus Trade and Competitiveness Act of 1988.

    Answer: export expansion Difficulty: Hard Page: 44

97. Of all the new provisions of the Uruguay Round of GATT, IBM and Microsoft would be MOST interested in the _______________ agreement.

    Answer: TRIPs Difficulty: Hard Page: 46-47

98. The America-First Corporation feels that the local content requirements utilized by some foreign nations unfairly impacts its ability to compete. The firm may seek relief under the _______________ provisions of GATT.

Answer: TRIMs Difficulty: Hard Page: 46

99. The _______________ is a globally focused institution that will hear and issue binding decisions regarding trade disputes among its 132 members.

Answer: World Trade Organization Difficulty: Easy Page: 47

100. Foreign firms accused of dumping products may be assessed a(n) _______________ duty to offset any advantage they may have gained.

Answer: countervailing Difficulty: Medium Page: 49

**Essay Questions**

101. How did the post-World War II Marshall Plan and the Agency for International Development prove to be a "two-edged" sword for the United States?

Difficulty: Hard Page: 30-31
Answer:
These, and other post-World War II plans, helped make it possible for Japan, Germany, and other "defeated" nations to acquire funds to rebuild their economies. Initially, the tremendous growth in purchases abroad benefited U.S. manufacturers. As employment and income rose in these nations, their citizens were able to purchase still more American goods. However, with continued growth of domestic industry, Germany and Japan became capable of satisfying more of their domestic demand <u>and</u> began to increasingly cut into the American market. Today, the U.S. is concerned with its ability to compete.

102. Where is the <u>GREATEST</u> rate of growth likely to occur through the decade of the 1990s? What problems do such trends present for the U.S.?

Answer:
As Japan matures and its growth slows, the growth "spotlight" will shift to the Pacific Rim and the emerging nations of Latin America China will emerge as the largest market in the world by the year 2010. Japan may have some advantages with regard to China and other Pacific Rim countries by virtue of greater cultural similarities. U.S. firms must step up their attempts to understand oriental culture. Conversely, the U.S. may have a slight advantage in Latin American markets. All emerging nations tend to be politically volatile--and subject to erratic economic swings.

Difficulty: Hard Page: 34-35

# Chapter 2 The Dynamic Environment of Global Business

103. Evaluate the use of a "weak dollar" policy and the pressure for protectionism as possible remedies for U.S. balance-of-payments problem.

Answer:
In the short run, a cheap dollar policy may stimulate U.S. exports and discourage imports--helping to reduce the trade deficit. Long term, however, the policy denies the consumer the ability to purchase foreign goods, artificially supports higher domestic prices and may destroy confidence in the dollar. Protectionism, in the form of tariffs, quotas, and other means of restricting trade, tends to breed retaliation and result in higher prices with less choice. As always, the consumer ultimately pays. The best long term solution is to take action to improve American competitiveness in a global free market.

Difficulty: Hard Page: 36-39

104. Why has it been difficult to "open' Japanese markets? Will the World Trade Organization be effective in opening Japanese markets/

Answer:
Japan has primarily relied upon a complex system of standards that supposedly protect the health and safety of Japanese consumers and protect product quality--instead of utilizing tariffs, quotas or boycotts. The World Trade Organization was designed to deal with the impact of direct trade restraints as a non-tariff restraint; standards are essentially beyond the scope of the World Trade Organization. The World Trade Organization will likely have less success in opening Japanese markets than in sanctioning other nations that retaliate by imposing traditional trade restraints.

Difficulty: Hard Page: 42-49

105. What are the objectives of the IMF? What role is played by SDRs and why are SDRs the preferred "monetary denomination" for international trade contracts?

Answer:
The International Monetary Fund (IMF) attempts to overcome the problems associated with inadequate monetary reserves and unstable currencies. Special Drawing Rights (SDRs) represent an average base of value derived from the value of a group of major currencies. SDRs are preferred since they are less susceptible to exchange-rate fluctuations and/or attempts to manipulate rates.

Difficulty: Hard Page: 49-50

# Chapter 3 History and Geography: The Foundations of Cultural Understanding

## True/False Questions

1. The importance of culture is rooted in the fact that the development and maintenance of a culture is essential to the survival of every nation.

   Answer: True Difficulty: Medium Page: 58

2. The America-First Corporation, a major producer of washers and dryers for the domestic market, is preparing to enter the African market. Although its target markets differ greatly in terms of altitude, humidity and temperature extremes, the firm will be able to sell its domestic products in these markets without modification.

   Answer: False Difficulty: Hard Page: 58

3. While climate variations between countries are often extreme enough to require product modifications, climatic variations within a country are rarely significant enough to require such adjustments.

   Answer: False Difficulty: Medium Page: 59

4. The rugged geographic features of South America have been a major factor in that continent's slow pace of national growth, trade, and communication.

   Answer: True Difficulty: Medium Page: 59-60

5. National unity and an equal degree of economic development are nearly impossible when inadequate roads and poor communication often separate major cities from each other.

   Answer: True Difficulty: Medium Page: 60

6. The isolation created and perpetuated by physical terrain features is often a major factor inhibiting the development of a homogeneous language, culture, or market within a continent or country.

   Answer: True Difficulty: Medium Page: 60

7. The America-First Corporation is preparing to enter the Russian and Chinese markets. The geographic and climatic challenges the firm will face in serving these markets may require the use of higher safety stock levels and reorder points to ensure adequate inventories.

   Answer: True Difficulty: Hard Page: 60

8. The historical importance of geography is easily seen in the universal dominance of trade enjoyed by coastal cities and cities located on navigable waterways.

   Answer: True Difficulty: Easy Page: 60

9. Globalization has generally resulted in nations seeking to maintain physical barriers and erect artificial barriers to protect their isolation and national identity.

   Answer: False Difficulty: Medium Page: 61

10. The quest for economic development is frequently the impetus behind a nation's attempts to overcome natural barriers by constructing tunnels, bridges, and roads.

    Answer: True Difficulty: Easy Page: 62

11. The global rush toward industrialization and economic growth has often served to highlight the importance of environmental issues.

    Answer: True Difficulty: Easy Page: 62-63

12. The nations of Eastern Europe and Asia, whose environments had remained pristine during the decades of communistic rule, have faced serious pollution problems since the emergence of more capitalistic regimes.

    Answer: False Difficulty: Medium Page: 63

13. As pollution became a more pressing problem for industrialized nations, many began to export their waste materials to less developed nations.

    Answer: True Difficulty: Medium Page: 64

14. Sustainable development is, at its core, an economic philosophy that seeks to neutralize the efforts of environmentalists.

    Answer: False Difficulty: Easy Page: 65

15. The United Nations' conference on Environment and Development resulted in the first set of environmental principles enforceable under international law by the World Court.

    Answer: False Difficulty: Medium Page: 65-66

16. Since World War II, the increasing reliance of industrialized nations upon energy resources provided by the less stable developing nations has injected a new source of economic uncertainty into the global business environment.

    Answer: True Difficulty: Medium Page: 67

17. As the global demand for resources intensifies and prices rise, resources will continue to increase in importance among the uncontrollable elements of the international marketer's decisions.

    Answer: True Difficulty: Medium Page: 68

# Chapter 3 History and Geography: The Foundations of Cultural Understanding

18. During the coming century, a major problem is expected to emerge from the imbalance between the growth of jobs in industrialized nations and the tremendous population increases expected in under-developed nations.

    Answer: True Difficulty: Medium Page: 68

19. In recent years, population shifts from rural to urban locals have occurred on a worldwide basis.

    Answer: True Difficulty: Medium Page: 70

20. By 2025, more than 60 percent of the world's population is expected to reside in urban areas.

    Answer: True Difficulty: Easy Page: 70

21. Given current growth trends, India's population will exceed that of China by 2050.

    Answer: True Difficulty: Easy Page: 69-70

22. Experience has shown that strict governmental measures are the most effective, if not the only, means of controlling population growth.

    Answer: False Difficulty: Medium Page: 69-70

23. During the coming century, Europe, Japan, and the United States will face difficult problems associated with the rising percentage of elderly citizens which must be supported by a declining number of skilled workers.

    Answer: True Difficulty: Easy Page: 72

24. Trade routes represent the attempts of countries to overcome economic and social imbalances created in part by the influence of geography.

    Answer: True Difficulty: Easy Page: 75

25. The United States leads the nations of the world in both exports and imports.

    Answer: True Difficulty: Easy Page: 76

26. The America-First Corporation is preparing to enter markets in several undeveloped areas of the world. In spite of its cost, the firm will probably have to rely heavily on the use of air freight.

    Answer: True Difficulty: Hard Page: 76

## Chapter 3 History and Geography: The Foundations of Cultural Understanding

27. Of all the factors influencing a nation's current actions in the global economy, its history is, by far, the least important.

    Answer: False Difficulty: Medium Page: 77

28. In order to understand any nation's business and political culture, one must understand the subjective perception of its history.

    Answer: True Difficulty: Easy Page: 78

29. The doctrine of Manifest Destiny laid the groundwork for America's long-standing and deep friendship with Mexico and the whole of South America.

    Answer: False Difficulty: Medium Page: 79

30. The Roosevelt Corollary to the Monroe Doctrine basically held that whatever is good for the United States is justifiable.

    Answer: True Difficulty: Medium Page: 80-81

**Multiple Choice Questions**

31. A nation's "program for survival" is <u>BEST</u> explained by its:
    A) history.
    B) economic system.
    C) geography.
    D) culture.

    Answer: D Difficulty: Medium Page: 58

32. The accepted basis for responding to external and internal events is provided by a nation's:
    A) history.
    B) culture.
    C) geography.
    D) economic system.

    Answer: B Difficulty: Medium Page: 58

33. The study of the earth's surface, climate, continents, countries, peoples, industries, and resources is, by definition, the study of:
    A) geography.
    B) history.
    C) culture.
    D) topography.

    Answer: A Difficulty: Easy Page: 58

# Chapter 3 History and Geography: The Foundations of Cultural Understanding

34. The America-First Corporation, a major producer of heavy construction equipment, has recently won a contract to provide machinery to be used in an ambitious program to bring water to the Sahara Desert by constructing a network of canals. The firm:
   A) will be able to fill this order from standing inventory.
   B) must build new plants in the Sahara area in order to fill this order.
   C) must make extensive modifications to existing equipment to cope with this hostile environment.
   D) should refuse this contract as unworkable.

   Answer: C Difficulty: Hard Page: 58

35. The America-First Corporation is preparing to produce washing machines for the European market. After checking the climatic differences between nations, the firm was able to determine the minimum spin cycle speeds required for machines to be delivered to each country. Which of the following countries is likely to require the LOWEST spin cycle speed?
   A) Germany
   B) Italy
   C) Scandinavia
   D) England

   Answer: B Difficulty: Hard Page: 59

36. In South America, forests and jungles account for:
   A) more than 60% of the total land area.
   B) almost 90% of the total land area.
   C) approximately 48% of the total land area.
   D) less than 25% of the total land area.

   Answer: C Difficulty: Easy Page: 59-60

37. The major factor contributing to the traditional division of South America into secluded, isolated communities has been:
   A) long-standing tribal feuds.
   B) the influence of European colonial cultures.
   C) the intrusion of communistic philosophy.
   D) a harsh geography that divides the continent.

   Answer: D Difficulty: Medium Page: 60

38. The world's greatest rain forest is found in:
   A) South America.
   B) Africa.
   C) Russia.
   D) Europe.

   Answer: A Difficulty: Medium Page: 60

# Chapter 3 History and Geography: The Foundations of Cultural Understanding

39. All of the following nations are characterized by extremes in topographic and climatic variations that impact marketing efforts EXCEPT:
    A) Canada.
    B) Japan.
    C) Russia.
    D) India.

    Answer: B Difficulty: Medium Page: 60

40. The America-First Corporation does business in both the United States and Canada. In order to assure distribution in Canada's hostile environment, the firm must increase:
    A) advertising volumes.
    B) prices.
    C) reorder points and safety stock levels.
    D) None of the above.

    Answer: C Difficulty: Hard Page: 60

41. The impact of globalization on traditional isolationist attitudes is exemplified by:
    A) the Eurotunnel.
    B) the Oresund Link.
    C) the Colonia Bridge.
    D) All of the above.

    Answer: D Difficulty: Medium Page: 60

42. The Eurotunnel carries over ______________ percent of London to Paris passenger traffic.
    A) 50
    B) 75
    C) 30
    D) 90

    Answer: A Difficulty: Easy Page: 60

43. The regional commitment to economic cooperation nurtured for fifty years by _____ finally resulted in the construction of the Colonia Bridge connecting Argentina and Uruguay.
    A) GATT.
    B) The European Community.
    C) Mercosur.
    D) Amazonia.

    Answer: C Difficulty: Medium Page: 63

# Chapter 3 History and Geography: The Foundations of Cultural Understanding

44. China's pursuit of economic progress will displace 1.2 million Chinese when the _______________ is completed.
    A) Chin-Wu Dam
    B) Three Gorges Dam
    C) Xi-Ming Dam
    D) Four Dragons

    Answer: B Difficulty: Easy Page: 62

45. The global rush toward industrialization and economic growth has spawned:
    A) disrupted ecosystems.
    B) inadequate hazardous waste management.
    C) industrial pollution.
    D) All of the above.

    Answer: D Difficulty: Medium Page: 62

46. The decade of the 1990s has been appropriately called the:
    A) Decade of globalization.
    B) Decade of the Environment.
    C) Decade of the Woman.
    D) Decade of Decadence.

    Answer: B Difficulty: Easy Page: 62-63

47. According to the most recent reports, the world's most polluted cities are in:
    A) the United States.
    B) Russia.
    C) Asia.
    D) Western Europe.

    Answer: C Difficulty: Easy Page: 63

48. Which of the following areas has been described as the world's greatest polluter?
    A) Eastern Europe.
    B) Japan.
    C) the United States.
    D) Scandinavia.

    Answer: A Difficulty: Easy Page: 63

## Chapter 3 History and Geography: The Foundations of Cultural Understanding

49. The amount of hazardous waste annually collected exceeds:
    A) 1 billion tons.
    B) 500 million tons.
    C) 300 million tons.
    D) 750 million tons.

    Answer: C Difficulty: Easy Page: 63-64

50. Which of the following countries was the last to take steps to control or ban the use of their nation as a dumping ground for the hazardous waste of more advanced countries?
    A) China
    B) Japan
    C) Brazil
    D) Peru

    Answer: A Difficulty: Medium Page: 64

51. The dumping of hazardous waste by industrialized nations was first regulated, and then banned, by the:
    A) Basel Convention.
    B) GATT Agreement.
    C) One-World Convention.
    D) U.N. Hazardous Waste Accord.

    Answer: A Difficulty: Easy Page: 64

52. The task of achieving economic development while ensuring the safety of the global environment is the challenge of:
    A) the Global Ecosystem Consortium.
    B) continuous development.
    C) sustainable development.
    D) constructive development.

    Answer: C Difficulty: Medium Page: 65

53. In 1992, the United Nations produced a set of principles to guide environmentally responsible global economic development as part of its:
    A) Global Summit.
    B) Earth Summit.
    C) Developmental Convention.
    D) World Energy Summit.

    Answer: B Difficulty: Easy Page: 65-66

# Chapter 3 History and Geography: The Foundations of Cultural Understanding

54. The America-First Corporation is widely recognized as among the most advanced of the world's high-technology firms. As it scans the globe for future production sites, the firm must increasingly consider the availability of:
    A) natural means of transportation.
    B) favorable climatic conditions.
    C) plentiful, cheap labor.
    D) raw materials and energy resources.

    Answer: D Difficulty: Hard Page: 66

55. Which of the following "resources" is inexhaustible?
    A) technology
    B) petroleum
    C) iron ore
    D) natural gas

    Answer: A Difficulty: Medium Page: 66

56. By the early 2000s, the United States is likely to be dependent upon OPEC for ____ percent of its petroleum needs.
    A) 36
    B) 70
    C) 50
    D) 60

    Answer: B Difficulty: Medium Page: 67

57. At present, the world's population is in excess of:
    A) 7.5 billion.
    B) 6 billion.
    C) 8.8 billion.
    D) 9.1 billion.

    Answer: B Difficulty: Easy Page: 68

58. By 2025, it is estimated that more than __________ percent of the world's population will live in urban areas.
    A) 20
    B) 40
    C) 50
    D) 60

    Answer: D Difficulty: Easy Page: 70

# Chapter 3 History and Geography: The Foundations of Cultural Understanding

59. Which of the following is the largest city in the world?
    A) Tokyo
    B) Mexico City
    C) New York City
    D) London

    Answer: A Difficulty: Easy Page: 70

60. All of the following play a critical role in attitudes about family size EXCEPT:
    A) politics.
    B) religion.
    C) inefficient distribution.
    D) education.

    Answer: C Difficulty: Medium Page: 68

61. The United Nations has long sought to encourage smaller family sizes in developing countries. The single MOST important factor that the UN must seek to change is probably:
    A) income levels.
    B) basic cultural beliefs.
    C) improved hygiene.
    D) education for women.

    Answer: B Difficulty: Hard Page: 69

62. By 2050, _____ is projected to have the largest population in the world.
    A) Russia
    B) China
    C) India
    D) the United States

    Answer: C Difficulty: Medium Page: 69

63. The decline in birth rates in Europe and the United States was the result of:
    A) improved social status for women.
    B) urbanization.
    C) growing industrialization.
    D) All of the above.

    Answer: D Difficulty: Medium Page: 69

# Chapter 3 History and Geography: The Foundations of Cultural Understanding

64. The extension of true globalization to the world's lesser-developed countries was <u>PRIMARILY</u> made possible by the expansion of:
    A) air freight.
    B) ocean freight.
    C) rail freight.
    D) truck freight.

    Answer: A Difficulty: Medium Page: 76

65. The key to understanding the culture of a country is found in the study of its:
    A) history.
    B) political structures.
    C) economic institutions.
    D) religious institutions.

    Answer: A Difficulty: Medium Page: 77

66. Perhaps the most basic premise of Japanese ideology is the emphasis placed upon:
    A) individualism.
    B) short-term results.
    C) democracy.
    D) cooperation for the public good.

    Answer: D Difficulty: Medium Page: 77

67. By its very nature, history is:
    A) objective.
    B) subjective.
    C) altruistic.
    D) realistic.

    Answer: B Difficulty: Medium Page: 78

68. The history of a nation, as recorded by its historians, is:
    A) a totally factual record of events.
    B) an objective record of the life of the country.
    C) filtered through the cultural biases of the historian.
    D) filtered through the biases of other nations.

    Answer: C Difficulty: Medium Page: 78

# Chapter 3 History and Geography: The Foundations of Cultural Understanding

69. The desire of American expansionists to extend U.S. boundaries from the Atlantic to the Pacific was at the core of the:
A) concept of Manifest Destiny.
B) Monroe Doctrine.
C) American Manifesto.
D) American Bill of Rights.

Answer: A Difficulty: Medium Page: 80

70. In its broadest interpretation, the idea that Americans were a chosen people ordained by God to create a model society was at the root of the:
A) American Manifesto.
B) concept of Manifest Destiny.
C) Monroe Doctrine.
D) Constitution.

Answer: B Difficulty: Medium Page: 80

71. The creation of Texas, Oregon, New Mexico, and California from land taken from Mexico was justified by the:
A) American Manifesto.
B) Monroe Doctrine.
C) Constitution.
D) concept of Manifest Destiny.

Answer: D Difficulty: Easy Page: 79-80

72. The United States prohibited non-American intervention in Latin America, pledged to police the area, and guaranteed that Latin America would meet its obligations under the terms of the:
A) American Manifesto.
B) concept of Manifest Destiny.
C) Roosevelt Corollary to the Monroe Doctrine.
D) Latin American Doctrine.

Answer: C Difficulty: Medium Page: 81

73. Land for the Panama Canal was acquired under the sanctions of the:
A) American Manifesto.
B) concept of Manifest Destiny.
C) Latin American Doctrine.
D) Roosevelt Corollary to the Monroe Doctrine.

Answer: D Difficulty: Medium Page: 81

# Chapter 3 History and Geography: The Foundations of Cultural Understanding

74. The Roosevelt Corollary to the Monroe Doctrine basically held that:
    A) the Monroe Doctrine had gone "too far."
    B) whatever is good for the United States is justifiable.
    C) the business of business is business.
    D) government should not intervene in business.

    Answer: B Difficulty: Medium Page: 81

75. In 1994, President Clinton sent U.S. troops to Haiti to "return" democracy to that country. The president's actions would seem to be a current application of the:
    A) Monroe Doctrine.
    B) Roosevelt Corollary to the Monroe Doctrine.
    C) Democratic Imperative.
    D) Prime Directive.

    Answer: B Difficulty: Hard Page: 81

76. The history shared by the United States and _____ is at the root of the uneasy "friendship" between these "Good Neighbors."
    A) England
    B) Canada
    C) Hawaii
    D) Mexico

    Answer: D Difficulty: Medium Page: 82

77. The expropriation of American oil wells and drilling equipment by Middle Eastern states can be <u>BEST</u> understood when viewed in the context of the region's:
    A) religion.
    B) economic structure.
    C) history.
    D) socialist leanings.

    Answer: C Difficulty: Hard Page: 81-82

### Fill in the Blank Questions

78. ______________ is, essentially, a society's program for survival.

    Answer: Culture Difficulty: Easy Page: 58

79. In order to fully understand why culture operates as it does, the marketer should also study the _____________ and ______________ of that country.

    Answer: geography, history Difficulty: Medium Page: 58

## Chapter 3 History and Geography: The Foundations of Cultural Understanding

80. The ______________ of a nation is, perhaps, the principal and broadest determinant of both the characteristics of a society and the means by which that society undertakes to supply its needs.

    Answer: physical character  Difficulty: Medium  Page: 58

81. The major considerations associated with a country's geography are its ______________ and ______________.

    Answer: climate; topography  Difficulty: Medium  Page: 58

82. In Canada, Latin America and many other countries, the nation is often divided into discrete markets by the location of ______________.

    Answer: physical barriers  Difficulty: Medium  Page: 60

83. Increasing ______________ is leading many nations to "tame" the natural barriers that had traditionally been valued as protection against aggression.

    Answer: globalization  Difficulty: Medium  Page: 60

84. Industrialized nations have overcome many problems related to geography and climate--but, success has come at the cost of the "industrial ills" of ______________ and ______________ disposal.

    Answer: pollution, hazardous waste management  Difficulty: Medium  Page: 63

85. As mankind's vision becomes more international in scope, pollution is increasingly viewed as a(n) ______________ problem.

    Answer: global  Difficulty: Medium  Page: 64-65

86. Some nations, such as Mexico and Guyana, offer to accept and dispose of the hazardous waste of industrialized countries for a price. Such actions, though legal, still generate ______________ concerns.

    Answer: ethical  Difficulty: Hard  Page: 64-65

87. The America-First Corporation has decided to enter the energy field. Given usage trends, the firm should probably focus its short-run attention upon the ______________ market.

    Answer: petroleum  Difficulty: Hard  Page: 66

88. Intense urban growth, in the absence of economic opportunity, creates ______________ that breed disease, despair, and social unrest.

    Answer: slums  Difficulty: Medium  Page: 70

## Chapter 3 History and Geography: The Foundations of Cultural Understanding

89. While the experience of _____ has demonstrated the problems associated with forced population control, that of _____ has highlighted the impact of improved medical care.

    Answer: China; India Difficulty: Medium Page: 69

90. Generally, a birthrate of 2.1 births per female is the "magic number" required to meet the goal of _____________ population growth-exact maintenance.

    Answer: zero Difficulty: Medium Page: 71

91. As older, wealthier nations "age," _____ will become an increasingly important source of labor.

    Answer: immigration Difficulty: Medium Page: 72

92. ____________ represent the attempts of countries to overcome economic and social imbalances created in part by the influence of geography.

    Answer: Trade routes Difficulty: Medium Page: 75

93. While _____________ freight is most closely associated with industrialized nations, it is also important in countries in which navigable waterways, roads or rail routes are not available.

    Answer: air Difficulty: Medium Page: 76

94. A nation's history helps to define its _____________--its view of its neighbors and its place in the world.

    Answer: mission Difficulty: Easy Page: 77

95. By its very nature, history is _____________.

    Answer: subjective Difficulty: Easy Page: 78

96. According to the concept of _____________, Americans are a chosen people ordained by God to create a model society.

    Answer: Manifest Destiny Difficulty: Easy Page: 80

97. The _____________ proclaimed that there would be no further European colonization in the New World, abstention of the United States from European political affairs, and nonintervention of European governments in the governments of the Western Hemisphere.

    Answer: Monroe Doctrine Difficulty: Medium Page: 80

# Chapter 3 History and Geography: The Foundations of Cultural Understanding

## Essay Questions

98. Briefly discuss the impact of a nation's geography upon its trade history.

    Answer:
    The natural barriers of a nation's geography have a major impact upon the development of internal and external trade routes. Physical barriers are a prime factor in encouraging/discouraging isolation--and, therefore, trade. Conversely, favorable topographical features facilitate a nation's interaction with other countries--and tend to facilitate the development of a richer, more urbane culture. Climate affects both the ease with which trade may be conducted and the type/characteristics of the goods traded for.

    Difficulty: Hard Page: 58-62

99. Pollution, waste management, and resource scarcity would seem to be a problem primarily affecting industrialized nations. Why should these problems be treated as global concerns?

    Answer:
    The air and water pollution of "advanced" nations affects global climate and the air and water that advanced and underdeveloped nations must share. In some cases, underdeveloped nations become the willing, or unwilling, "dumping grounds" for the hazardous wastes of industrialized countries. In other cases, the natural resources of underdeveloped nations are "sacrificed" as exports to developed countries for short-term gain rather than serving the development needs of their country of origin.

    Difficulty: Hard Page: 62-66

100. What dangers attend the depletion of natural resources within the borders of the powerful, industrialized nations of the world?

    Answer:
    The continuous availability of raw materials is vital to the growth/survival of the industrialized nations of the world. As domestic supplies diminish, these nations are likely to seek to secure sources in other, less-developed nations. Such efforts can lead to a "new colonialism," policies that work against the best interests of resource-rich less-developed nations, and/or conflicts between industrialized nations spawned by competition for the resources of such countries.

    Difficulty: Hard Page: 66-68

# Chapter 3 History and Geography: The Foundations of Cultural Understanding

101. Why must the world control its population? Why is the age/distribution of population at least AS important as the sheer number of people?

Answer:
Obviously, total world population must be kept within the limits of the capacity of the planet to support life. Unfortunately, population growth tends to be greatest in those nations least able to support such growth. If continued, this trend can lead to serious confrontation between the "have" and "have not" nations of the world. Further, as the population of industrialized nations continues to age, there will be fewer productive workers to support the needs of people of all ages throughout the world.

Difficulty: Hard Page: 68-73

102. Why is it important for the international marketer to understand the history of potential foreign market countries?

Answer:
The nature and sequence of the events that affected a nation have a major impact upon its perception of itself, its mission, and its role vis-a-vis other nations and the world. These events shape the nation's culture as it attempts to survive in, and make sense of, its environment. From this background emerges the institutions, philosophies, and behaviors the marketer faces in his/her efforts to successfully trade in other nations.

Difficulty: Hard Page: 77-82

# Chapter 4 Cultural Dynamics in Assessing Global Markets

## True/False Questions

1. Culture is the only portion of the human environment that is "man-made."

   Answer: True Difficulty: Medium Page: 98

2. Markets, and market behavior, are part of a nation's culture.

   Answer: True Difficulty: Easy Page: 98

3. In cultural terms, the marketer is a "change agent".

   Answer: True Difficulty: Medium Page: 98

4. The America-First Corporation routinely "briefs" executives assigned to foreign countries in the subtle nuances that attend the characteristic traits and patterns of their new "host nation. While this practice may enhance the enjoyment the executive derives from his or her stay abroad, it is not likely to contribute significantly to the firm's business success.

   Answer: False Difficulty: Hard Page: 99

5. The America-First Corporation has had difficulty in getting foreign nationals to perform preventative maintenance on the equipment in many of its foreign plants. This problem is MOST closely associated with the way in which different cultures perceive aesthetics.

   Answer: False Difficulty: Hard Page: 101

6. The traditional components of the marketing mix are most directly affected by the elements of material culture.

   Answer: True Difficulty: Medium Page: 101

7. Marketers seeking to understand the impact of social roles and status positions would be MOST concerned with the social institutions segment of a nation's culture.

   Answer: True Difficulty: Medium Page: 102

8. While religion is important to many types of behavior in a culture, it has little significance for those behaviors of interest to the marketer.

   Answer: False Difficulty: Medium Page: 102

9. The United States is, perhaps, the only country in the world in which marketing behavior is not affected by superstition.

   Answer: False Difficulty: Medium Page: 103

10. Product styling, packaging, logos, and advertising are heavily impacted by the aesthetic standards of a culture.

    Answer: True Difficulty: Medium Page: 105

11. Advertising copywriters should be concerned less with obvious differences between languages and more with the idiomatic meanings expressed.

    Answer: True Difficulty: Medium Page: 106

12. While language may be one of the most difficult cultural elements to master, it is probably the most important key to an effort to acquire some degree of empathy.

    Answer: True Difficulty: Medium Page: 106

13. The America-First Corporation routinely utilizes a "cultural translator" to facilitate its entry into foreign cultures. The firm should limit the activities of this person to the important task of teaching foreign languages to those executives to be assigned abroad.

    Answer: False Difficulty: Hard Page: 107

14. The America-First Corporation confines its international marketing efforts to England. The firm knows that the cultural similarities between America and England guarantee that products that are successful in its domestic market will also be successful in England.

    Answer: False Difficulty: Hard Page: 107

15. While culture is composed of many individual elements, its impact is synergistic in nature.

    Answer: True Difficulty: Medium Page: 107

16. By definition, cultural facts are immutable truths that are not affected by the context in which they occur.

    Answer: False Difficulty: Medium Page: 108

17. Interpretative knowledge of a culture requires a degree of insight that may be BEST described as a feeling for that culture that is often derived from a sensitivity to, and experience with, the culture.

    Answer: True Difficulty: Medium Page: 108

18. Prior to sending executives to a new host country, the America-First Corporationtypically arranges for them to spend time with bilingual nationals who have a marketing background. The firm is seeking to assist its executives in the development of an improved interpretative knowledge of their new host country.

    Answer: True Difficulty: Hard Page: 108

19. Cultural sensitivity is BEST developed by applying one's self-reference criterion to the nuances of the foreign culture.

    Answer: False Difficulty: Medium Page: 109

20. One of the factors underlying the difficulties experienced by American executives attempting to understand and relate to the Japanese culture is rooted in the significant differences between the two cultures with regard to the individualism/collective index.

    Answer: True Difficulty: Hard Page: 109

21. The United States and Great Britain rank near the top of the Uncertainty Avoidance Index (UAI).

    Answer: False Difficulty: Medium Page: 110

22. The First-American Corporation has never received complaints or grievances from employees in any of its Mexican plants. The firm can rightly conclude that its Mexican operation is "trouble free".

    Answer: False Difficulty: Hard Page: 112

23. While one of the major roles of culture is to provide a stable frame of reference for society, a culture's survival ultimately depends upon its willingness and ability to adapt to change.

    Answer: True Difficulty: Medium Page: 113-114

24. Once a culture "borrows" thoughts or behaviors from another culture and adapts it to its own particular needs, it will pass those elements along as part of its own "unique" cultural heritage.

    Answer: True Difficulty: Medium Page: 114

25. Unlike many determinants of human behavior, culture is learned.

    Answer: True Difficulty: Medium Page: 114

26. The success of the Common Market in Europe has produced a vast market that is economically and culturally homogeneous.

    Answer: False Difficulty: Medium Page: 116-117

27. If a nation is politically unified, the marketer may safely assume that it is culturally unified as well.

    Answer: False Difficulty: Medium Page: 117

# Chapter 4 Cultural Dynamics in Assessing Global Markets

28. Ethnocentrism refers to the tendency to assume that one's own culture is superior to foreign cultures.

    Answer: True Difficulty: Easy Page: 117-118

29. The America-First Corporation is preparing to introduce its fast-food restaurants in several South American countries that value leisurely prepared and consumed home-cooked meals. The firm must function as a change agent if it is to be successful.

    Answer: True Difficulty: Hard Page: 118-119

30. The marketer's ethical responsibility for any dysfunctional effects of its marketing activity is limited to only those effects that were intentionally sought.

    Answer: False Difficulty: Medium Page: 119-120

## Multiple Choice Questions

31. Marketers are PRIMARILY concerned with providing satisfaction for:
    A) physical necessities.
    B) economic needs.
    C) economic wants.
    D) physiological requirements

    Answer: C Difficulty: Medium Page: 98

32. Which of the following is BEST described as the "human-made portion of the human environment"?
    A) topography
    B) climate
    C) geography
    D) culture

    Answer: D Difficulty: Easy Page: 98

33. Markets are a result of:
    A) the marketer's efforts.
    B) economic conditions.
    C) general cultural influences.
    D) all of the above.

    Answer: D Difficulty: Medium Page: 98

# Chapter 4 Cultural Dynamics in Assessing Global Markets

34. As a major source of cultural innovation, marketers function as:
    A) change agents.
    B) cultural defenders.
    C) cultural destroyers.
    D) agent middlemen.

    Answer: A Difficulty: Medium Page: 98

35. The marketer would be well-advised to approach the study of foreign marketing from the viewpoint of the:
    A) linguist.
    B) economist.
    C) psychiatrist.
    D) anthropologist.

    Answer: D Difficulty: Medium Page: 99

36. The entire social heritage of the human race forms the basis of:
    A) linguistics.
    B) economics.
    C) culture.
    D) religion.

    Answer: C Difficulty: Easy Page: 99

37. Technology and economics are the prime components of:
    A) social institutions.
    B) material culture.
    C) aesthetics.
    D) social organization.

    Answer: B Difficulty: Easy Page: 100

38. The practice of preventative maintenance is MOST closely associated wit which of the following elements of culture?
    A) material culture.
    B) Aesthetics.
    C) social institutions.
    D) social organizations.

    Answer: A Difficulty: Medium Page: 101

39. The America-First Corporation has encountered difficulty in training Chinese peasants to properly use and maintain the farm equipment it is introducing to some of China's most remote areas. This problem is MOST closely related to which of the following elements of culture?
A) aesthetics.
B) social institutions.
C) social organizations.
D) material culture.

Answer: D Difficulty: Hard Page: 101

40. Manufacturing and marketing activities in a culture are MOST closely related to which of the following elements of culture?
A) aesthetics.
B) linguistics.
C) economics.
D) technology.

Answer: C Difficulty: Medium Page: 101

41. The educational and political structures of a culture are MOST closely associated with which of the following elements of culture?
A) aesthetics.
B) material culture.
C) social institutions.
D) religion.

Answer: C Difficulty: Medium Page: 101

42. Which of the following cultural elements are MOST closely associated with the task of "passing" culturally acceptable behaviors from one generation to the next?
A) linguistics.
B) aesthetics.
C) material culture.
D) social institutions.

Answer: D Difficulty: Medium Page: 102

43. The America-First Corporation is especially interested in gender roles and status positions in the markets that it serves. The firm can BEST understand the evolution of trends in such behavior by studying.
A) material culture.
B) social institutions.
C) aesthetics.
D) linguistics.

Answer: B Difficulty: Hard Page: 102

44. The religious beliefs and superstitions of a culture are part of which of the following cultural elements?
    A) humans and the universe.
    B) material culture.
    C) aesthetics.
    D) linguistics.

    Answer: A Difficulty: Easy Page: 102

45. The America-First Corporation has decided to develop a line of kosher foods for domestic sales and export to other nations having a large Jewish population. The success of this effort will be PRIMARILY affected by the firm's understanding of which of the following elements of culture?
    A) material culture.
    B) aesthetics.
    C) humans and the universe.
    D) linguistics.

    Answer: C Difficulty: Hard Page: 102

46. American multinational corporations seeking acceptance in the Middle East areMOST likely to encounter problems stemming from a lack of understanding of which of the following religions?
    A) Catholicism.
    B) Judaism.
    C) Islam.
    D) Protestantism.

    Answer: C Difficulty: Medium Page: 103

47. A nation's art, folklore, music, drama and dance are part of which of the following elements of its culture?
    A) material culture.
    B) linguistics.
    C) social institutions.
    D) aesthetics.

    Answer: D Difficulty: Medium Page: 105

48. The America-First Corporation is preparing special product designs, packaging, and promotional campaigns for a new line of goods to be sold in the Middle East. Which of the following elements of the region's culture will MOST directly affect the firm's efforts?
    A) aesthetics.
    B) material culture.
    C) social institutions.
    D) linguistics.

    Answer: A Difficulty: Hard Page: 105

# Chapter 4 Cultural Dynamics in Assessing Global Markets

49. With which of the following elements of culture must an advertising copywriter be MOST concerned?
   A) material culture.
   B) linguistics.
   C) social institutions.
   D) economics and technology.

   Answer: B Difficulty: Medium Page: 106

50. With which of the following types of "meanings" must an advertising copywriter preparing messages for a foreign market be MOST concerned?
   A) object-tied meanings.
   B) idiomatic meanings.
   C) "dictionary" meanings.
   D) personal meanings.

   Answer: B Difficulty: Medium Page: 106

51. Although it is one of the most difficult elements of culture to master, a marketer seeking cultural empathy should strive to develop a thorough understanding of a host company's:
   A) social institutions.
   B) language.
   C) aesthetics.
   D) superstitions.

   Answer: B Difficulty: Medium Page: 106

52. In which of the following situations is a study of a foreign nation's total culture MOST crucial?
   A) marketing an existing product in an already developed market.
   B) marketing a new product in an already developed market.
   C) marketing an existing product in a new, but similar, market.
   D) marketing a new product in a new market.

   Answer: D Difficulty: Medium Page: 107

53. The relationship that exists between the various elements that compose a nation's culture is BEST described as:
   A) hierarchical.
   B) isolated.
   C) synergistic.
   D) systematic.

   Answer: C Difficulty: Medium Page: 107

54. Prior to designing packaging for its Asian markets, the America-First Corporation required its advertising staff to study the meaning of colors and shapes in those countries. The firm was attempting to avoid potential problems by employing:
A) cultural interpretation.
B) factual cultural knowledge.
C) ethnocentric knowledge.
D) cultural dynamics.

Answer: B Difficulty: Hard Page: 107

55. The ability to understand and appreciate fully the nuances of different cultural traits and patterns results from:
A) interpretative knowledge of the culture.
B) factual knowledge of the culture.
C) ethnocentric knowledge of the culture.
D) dynamic knowledge of the culture.

Answer: A Difficulty: Medium Page: 108

56. To have maximum usefulness, factual knowledge about a country:
A) should be accepted without question.
B) should be interpreted according to one's own SRC.
C) should be interpreted within the context of the culture.
D) must be discounted as ethnocentric exaggeration.

Answer: C Difficulty: Medium Page: 108

57. Which of the following types of cultural knowledge is MOST akin to a "feeling"?
A) factual.
B) interpretative.
C) iterative.
D) experiential.

Answer: B Difficulty: Easy Page: 108

58. Past experience is MOST likely to be applied in the use of which of the following types of cultural knowledge?
A) factual.
B) iterative.
C) interpretative.
D) sensitive.

Answer: C Difficulty: Medium Page: 108

59. Interpretative knowledge about a culture is MOST likely to be misunderstood when:
 A) the marketer has too few facts to analyze.
 B) the marketer has too many facts to analyze.
 C) the assistance of "locals" is sought.
 D) the marketer relies on his/her own cultural frame of reference.

 Answer: D Difficulty: Medium Page: 109

60. The ability to become attuned to the nuances of a culture, to view it objectively, evaluate it fairly, and to appreciate the differences it presents is the goal of:
 A) cultural sensitization.
 B) ethnocentric evaluation.
 C) SRC analysis.
 D) factual investigation.

 Answer: A Difficulty: Medium Page: 108-109

61. Which of the following adjectives is MOST appropriate to apply to foreign cultures?
 A) correct.
 B) inferior.
 C) different.
 D) unintelligible.

 Answer: C Difficulty: Medium Page: 109

62. The America-First Corporation would like to reduce conflict, improve communications and enhance collaborative relationships between its American managers and the staffs they must work with in foreign countries. This can BEST be accomplished by:
 A) sensitizing the American to the cultures of the host countries.
 B) introducing team management.
 C) sensitizing foreign employees to American culture.
 D) minimizing misunderstandings by ignoring them.

 Answer: A Difficulty: Hard Page: 109

63. Mistakes in interpreting the cultural behaviors of foreigners are USUALLY the result of:
 A) conscious bias against the foreign culture.
 B) the unconscious reliance on a self-reference criterion based on one's "home" culture.
 C) efforts to deceive American managers.
 D) language difficulties.

 Answer: B Difficulty: Medium Page: 109

64. A nation's tolerance of social inequality is BEST measured by the:
   A) Individualism/collective Index. (IDV).
   B) Uncertainty Avoidance Index. (UAI).
   C) Masculinity/Femininity index (MAS).
   D) Power Distance Index (PDI).

   Answer: D  Difficulty: Easy  Page: 109

65. The America-First Corporation is frequently frustrated by the fact that many of the foreign nationals that manage its operations in France and Germany seem obsessed" with reports and paperwork. The source of this phenomenon is BEST explained by the:
   A) Power Distance Index (PDI).
   B) Uncertainty Avoidance Index (UAI).
   C) Masculinity/Femininity Index (MAS)
   D) Individualism/Collective Index (IDV).

   Answer: B  Difficulty: Hard  Page: 110

66. The desire for achievement and entrepreneurial tendencies is BEST measured by:
   A) Power Distance Index (PDI).
   B) Uncertainty Avoidance Index (UAI).
   C) Masculinity/Femininity Index (MAS).
   D) Individualism/Collective Index (IDU).

   Answer: A  Difficulty: Medium  Page: 109

67. The America-First Corporation often employs social class and status-based appeals in its domestic advertising. This form of promotion will BEST translate to other nations that score high on the:
   A) Power Distance Index (PDI).
   B) Uncertainty Avoidance Index (UAI).
   C) Masculinity/Femininity Index (MAS).
   D) Individualism/Collective Index (IDU).

   Answer: A  Difficulty: Hard  Page: 100

68. By its nature, culture is:
   A) dynamic.
   B) isolationist.
   C) ethnocentric.
   D) static.

   Answer: A  Difficulty: Easy  Page: 109

# Chapter 4 Cultural Dynamics in Assessing Global Markets

69. With regard to international marketing, the marketer is BEST described as a(n):
    A) businessperson.
    B) capitalist.
    C) interventionist.
    D) change agent.

    Answer: D Difficulty: Medium Page: 113

70. Cultures seek solutions to problems shared with other cultures through a process of:
    A) cultural theft.
    B) cultural borrowing.
    C) cultural homogenization.
    D) cultural amalgamation.

    Answer: B Difficulty: Medium Page: 114

71. Once a culture adopts, and adapts, behaviors borrowed from another culture, those behaviors are:
    A) "lost" to the original culture.
    B) part of a secondary, inferior culture.
    C) passed on as part of the adopting nation's cultural heritage.
    D) typically rejected as "foreign."

    Answer: C Difficulty: Medium Page: 114

72. Culture can be described as:
    A) a learned behavior.
    B) a distinguishing characteristic of human society.
    C) composed of a group of synergistic elements.
    D) all of the above are correct.

    Answer: D Difficulty: Medium Page: 114

73. Which of the following would be BEST described as a homogeneous market?
    A) the North American market.
    B) the European Common market.
    C) the Asian market.
    D) None of the above are homogeneous entities.

    Answer: D Difficulty: Medium Page: 114

# Chapter 4 Cultural Dynamics in Assessing Global Markets

74. The tendency of each nation to perceive its own culture as superior to that of other nations is BEST described by the term:
    A) ethnocentrism.
    B) material culture.
    C) centrality.
    D) provincialism.

    Answer: A Difficulty: Easy Page: 117

75. The America-First Corporation is preparing to introduce its new line of microcomputers to the Orient. The firm feels that people in this market have a strongcuriosity about its products, but it sees the long tradition of reliance upon the abacus as an obstacle. America-First appears to be MOST concerned about:
    A) the degree of interest in the product.
    B) the degree of disruption associated with the product.
    C) the price of the product.
    D) the appearance of the product.

    Answer: B Difficulty: Hard Page: 118

76. The first step in effecting a planned change in a society is to:
    A) identify the cultural obstacles to change.
    B) create massive advertising campaigns.
    C) produce a limited number of prototypes.
    D) provide cultural "counseling" sessions.

    Answer: A Difficulty: Medium Page: 118

77. The America-First Corporation attempts to minimize resistance to its products in foreign markets by marketing products similar to those already on the market in a manner as consistent as possible with existing cultural norms. The firm is following a:
    A) strategy of unplanned change.
    B) strategy of planned change.
    C) strategy of ethnocentrism.
    D) culturally congruent strategy.

    Answer: D Difficulty: Hard Page: 119

78. Under which of the following strategies does a firm simply introduce a product and "hope for the best?"
    A) a strategy of unplanned change
    B) a strategy of planned change
    C) a strategy of ethnocentrism
    D) a culturally congruent strategy

    Answer: A Difficulty: Easy Page: 119

79. A "change agent" is a vital element in implementing:
    A) a strategy of planned change.
    B) a strategy of unplanned change.
    C) an ethnocentric strategy.
    D) a culturally congruent strategy.

    Answer: A Difficulty: Medium Page: 119

80. Negative effects associated with innovations are said to be:
    A) culturally material.
    B) ethnocentrically valid.
    C) dysfunctional.
    D) functional.

    Answer: C Difficulty: Easy Page: 119

**Fill in the Blank Questions**

81. In order to effectively provide consumer satisfactions and earn a profit for the firm, the international marketer must study the ______________ of its foreign markets.

    Answer: culture Difficulty: Medium Page: 98

82. The student of foreign marketing should approach an understanding of culture from the viewpoint of the ______________.

    Answer: Anthropologist Difficulty: Easy Page: 99

83. The factor of material culture is composed of ______________ and ______________.

    Answer: Technology; economics Difficulty: Medium Page: 100

84. The America-First Corporation has had difficulty in convincing its foreign employees to provide preventative maintenance. Such problems typically stem from differences in the host country's ______________ culture.

    Answer: material Difficulty: Hard Page: 101

85. ______________ is the manner in which people employ their capabilities—and the benefits that result.

    Answer: Economics Difficulty: Easy Page: 101

86. A prime role for the ______________ of a nation is to pass the culture of the nation from one generation to the next.

    Answer: social institutions Difficulty: Medium Page: 101

87. The cultural factor termed "humans and the universe" contains the elements of _______________ and _______________ and their related power structures.

    Answer: religion; superstition  Difficulty: Medium  Page: 102

88. The America-First Corporation is currently attempting to overcome the adverse effects of its most recent advertising campaign in Saudi Arabia. The ad, which featured Saudi women modeling the firm's new line of "skimpy" beachwear, was found to be offensive. America-First must become most sensitive to the precepts of the Islamic _______________ to avoid such problems in the future.

    Answer: religion  Difficulty: Hard  Page: 102

89. _______________ refers to the arts, folklore, music, drama and dance of a culture.

    Answer: Aesthetics  Difficulty: Easy  Page: 105

90. The America-First Corporation is preparing the logo and packaging for a new line of products to be sold in Japan. The firm wants to be sure that it avoids any problems related to cultural misunderstandings. America-First should become as familiar as possible with the _______________ element of Japanese culture.

    Answer: aesthetics  Difficulty: Hard  Page: 105

91. Advertising copywriters should take special care to understand the _______________ meanings associated with the language of a foreign country.

    Answer: idiomatic  Difficulty: Medium  Page: 106

92. _______________ knowledge provides the ability to understand and appreciate fully the nuances of different cultural traits and patterns.

    Answer: Interpretive  Difficulty: Easy  Page: 107

93. Executives of the America-First Corporation have often experienced difficulty in interpreting the culture of the foreign nations in which they work. This is probably due to their reliance upon their home country's _______________.

    Answer: frame of reference  Difficulty: Hard  Page: 109

94. In order to view a new culture objectively, evaluate it fairly and appreciate it fully, the marketer must develop cultural _______________ or _______________.

    Answer: sensitivity; empathy  Difficulty: Medium  Page: 109

# Chapter 4 Cultural Dynamics in Assessing Global Markets

95. The degree of preference for behavior that promotes one's own self-interest is BEST measured by the _______________ index.

    Answer: Individualism/Collective   Difficulty: Medium   Page: 109

96. Cultural _______________ refers to the effort to find solutions to the cultural problems of one culture through adapting the solutions to similar problems practices by other cultures.

    Answer: borrowing   Difficulty: Easy   Page: 114

97. Cultural similarity is often an illusion. Even within the United States, _______________ defy complete homogenization.

    Answer: subcultures   Difficulty: Medium   Page: 117

98. The America-First Corporation has traditionally simply introduced a new product into a foreign market and "hoped for success." The firm is following a "strategy of _______________."

    Answer: unplanned change   Difficulty: Hard   Page: 119

99. Under a(n) _______________ strategy, a firm attempts to market products similar to those already in a foreign market in a manner as compatible as possible with the host culture's norms in order to minimize resistance.

    Answer: culturally congruent   Difficulty: Medium   Page: 119

100. Ethically, if not legally, a firm is responsible for any _______________ consequences of its activities as a change agent.

    Answer: dysfunctional   Difficulty: Easy   Page: 120

## Essay Questions

101. Your text details a number of cultural "elements" of interest to the marketer. How can these elements be BEST used by the marketer to facilitate success in international marketing efforts?

    Answer:
    The division of a culture into its components is a useful tool to ensure that the marketer does not overlook an important facet of a foreign culture. BUT, culture is a totality of influences that interact to form a coherent whole. The synergistic relationships between cultural elements form the fabric that the marketer must understand, appreciate, and work within to ensure success.

    Difficulty: Hard   Page: 99-104

# Chapter 4 Cultural Dynamics in Assessing Global Markets

102. Briefly describe the two types of cultural knowledge of use to the marketer. Which is MOST likely to cause cultural misunderstandings? How can such misunderstandings be minimized?

Answer:
Factual knowledge refers to the more "obvious" ways in which cultures differ--language, customs, the meaning of colors and tastes. The marketer may study and absorb such information comparatively easily. Interpretative knowledge--the ability to understand and fully appreciate the nuances of different cultural traits and patterns--is more difficult to master and more likely to cause problems for the marketer. The challenges presented by interpretive culture can be best approached by attempting to develop cultural sensitivity and empathy.

Difficulty: Hard Page: 107-109

103. Culture has been described as BOTH static AND dynamic. How can culture fulfill both roles?

Answer:
Culture provides stability by developing and passing from one generation to another, a cultural heritage and a set of approved solutions to social problems. At the some time, culture must assist society in its adaptation to changing conditions and new challenges. The culture of a society actually is an important tool that allows society to "manage change"--to select those new ideas that are acceptable and to introduce them in an acceptable way at an acceptable pace.

Difficulty: Hard Page: 113-117

104. What is "ethnocentrism"? What problems would such an attitude cause the marketer?

Answer:
Ethnocentrism refers to the tendency to view foreign cultures as wrong and/or inferior. Marketers who approach other cultures in this fashion are likely to fail to understand their foreign customers--and often offend them through their condescending or insensitive behavior or comments.

Difficulty: Hard Page: 117-118

105. Why is the marketer appropriately described as a "change agent"? What ethical responsibilities attend this role?

Answer:
The marketer is usually trying to introduce some form of change--a new form of behavior or a new alternative for addressing a social need or problem. To accomplish this goal, the marketer employs persuasion--and provides favorable outcomes. As a result, the marketer should also be prepared to accept responsibility for any dysfunctional consequences that may attend the acceptance of their persuasive efforts.

Difficulty: Hard Page: 118-121

# Chapter 5 Business Customs in Global Marketing

## True/False Questions

1. Because other countries seek to emulate American culture and business practices, the study of foreign cultures, languages and customs is not useful to international marketers.

   Answer: False Difficulty: Easy Page: 126

2. Many of the business and trade problems troubling Japan and the United States would be more easily resolved if each country better understood the other's culture.

   Answer: True Difficulty: Easy Page: 126

3. The America-First Corporation routinely attempts to market any product that succeeds in the American market in all of the foreign countries it serves. The firm's unwillingness to alter its products and/or marketing plans to adjust for cultural differences is likely to increase its failure rates in foreign markets.

   Answer: True Difficulty: Hard Page: 126

4. A successful international marketer must possess the qualities characteristic of all good executives PLUS the quality of adaptability.

   Answer: True Difficulty: Medium Page: 127

5. "Open tolerance" requires the marketer to accept other cultures as "different but equal."

   Answer: True Difficulty: Easy Page: 127

6. Knowledge of foreign cultures is critical to the avoidance of misunderstandings that may otherwise result from the tendency to interpret the actions of foreign businesspeople through use of the "self-reference criterion."

   Answer: True Difficulty: Medium Page: 127

7. In order to achieve success in international marketing, American executives must completely divest themselves of all American traits and behaviors and take on those of their foreign host.

   Answer: False Difficulty: Medium Page: 127

8. The America-First Corporation has decided to provide cultural training courses for its executives prior to their assignment to foreign markets. The firm should place primary emphasis upon preparing its executives to participate in the cultural exclusives of their assigned country.

   Answer: False Difficulty: Hard Page: 128

9. The cultivation and maintenance of friendship is a cultural imperative for business success in Asia and Latin America.

   Answer: True Difficulty: Medium Page: 128

10. The majority of customs are best described as cultural adiaphora, which do not necessitate conformity on the part of the foreign executive.

    Answer: True Difficulty: Medium Page: 129

11. While cultural adiaphora do not require conformity, the executive who is willing to take the time required to do so may benefit from his/her apparent appreciation of and sensitivity to the finer points of the host culture.

    Answer: True Difficulty: Medium Page: 129

12. Although there are comparatively few cultural imperatives, or exclusives, their violation accounts for the majority of serious cultural misunderstandings.

    Answer: True Difficulty: Medium Page: 130

13. A business card should be presented at the close of a business meeting in Japan to allow the Japanese host to more easily remember the names and titles of their American guests.

    Answer: False Difficulty: Medium Page: 130

14. The America-First Corporation is preparing to enter the Middle East market. In accordance with custom, the firm should be sure that all contacts made with potential customer firms be handled by representatives who have been empowered to make decisions for the firm.

    Answer: True Difficulty: Hard Page: 132

15. Under a decentralized, decision-making approach, managers are allowed authority over their own functional areas.

    Answer: True Difficulty: Easy Page: 132

16. Asian cultures and religions tend to promote consensus and group decision-making within their business communities.

    Answer: True Difficulty: Medium Page: 132

17. Despite other cultural differences, both American and Kuwati managers are equally likely to make business decisions that are consistent with their personal goals.

    Answer: False Difficulty: Easy Page: 133

# Chapter 5 Business Customs in Global Marketing

18. Cultural influences affect management attitudes toward innovation and new products as well as the way business is conducted.

    Answer: True Difficulty: Medium Page: 133

19. The concept of "security" is, perhaps, the only managerial goal that is consistent and uniform in meaning across all cultures.

    Answer: False Difficulty: Medium Page: 133

20. In Japan, the company life IS the personal life of the worker and/or manager.

    Answer: True Difficulty: Easy Page: 134

21. The inherent vague nature of their language has led Japanese businessmen to prefer English-language contracts.

    Answer: True Difficulty: Hard Page: 134

22. Generally, managers representing two different countries are more likely to communicate successfully if both nations are low-context cultures.

    Answer: True Difficulty: Medium Page: 136

23. True communications mastery requires a mastery of culture and customs as well as language.

    Answer: True Difficulty: Easy Page: 137

24. The America-First Corporation is preparing a group of its managers for delicate negotiations with important Arab executives. The firm should stress the fact that Arabs are notoriously impatient negotiators who hate to waste time and insist on making decisions quickly.

    Answer: False Difficulty: Hard Page: 137

25. The United States is a highly time-conscious society that tends to measure time precisely as a means of assuring that lineal schedules are promptly met. These traits indicate that America is a high-context culture that operates on P-Time.

    Answer: False Difficulty: Hard Page: 138

26. As global markets expand, more businesspeople from P-Time cultures are adapting to M-Time.

    Answer: True Difficulty: Easy Page: 139

27. Generally, women have found it much easier to attain executive positions in Asian,Arab, and Latin American cultures than in the United States.

Answer: False Difficulty: Medium Page: 140

28. American firms are sometimes placed at a disadvantage by SEC regulations that extend the anti-bribery laws of this nation to the international dealings of domestic firms.

Answer: True Difficulty: Medium Page: 141-142

29. The America-First Corporation routinely employs agents to represent the firm in its international transactions. If bribes are expected in some of these countries, the firm can protect itself from prosecution under the Foreign Corrupt Practices Act by employing such agents to pay the bribes.

Answer: False Difficulty: Hard Page: 144

30. Acceptable legal, ethical, and environmental practices have recently been codified under United Nations' Resolution #747 to ensure uniform standards in international marketing.

Answer: False Difficulty: Hard Page: 145-146

**Multiple Choice Questions**

31. The criteria for day-to-day business behavior and general patterns of attitude and motivation are established by a nation's:
A) Supreme Court.
B) culture.
C) legislature.
D) religious institutions.

Answer: B Difficulty: Easy Page: 126

32. Which of the following terms <u>BEST</u> describes the Japanese culture?
A) individualism
B) elitist
C) status-driven
D) consensus-oriented

Answer: D Difficulty: Easy Page: 126

# Chapter 5 Business Customs in Global Marketing

33. Which of the following is the MOST critical factor for success in international marketing?
    A) adaptation.
    B) economic superiority.
    C) a strong legal system.
    D) military strength.

    Answer: A Difficulty: Easy Page: 127

34. Which of the following terms BEST describes the concept of "different but equal" as applied to cultures?
    A) humility.
    B) open tolerance.
    C) curiosity/interest.
    D) flexibility.

    Answer: B Difficulty: Easy Page: 127

35. Janet Thompson is being considered for an international assignment in her firm. Which of the following characteristics would be MOST directly associated with success in this position?
    A) intelligence
    B) ambition
    C) adaptability
    D) curiosity

    Answer: C Difficulty: Hard Page: 127

36. The tendency to evaluate the behavior of a person from another culture in terms of what is acceptable to us is BEST described by the:
    A) self-reference criterion.
    B) adaptability criterion.
    C) criterion of flexibility.
    D) valuative criterion.

    Answer: A Difficulty: Easy Page: 127

37. The self-reference criterion is MOST significant in the area of:
    A) business law.
    B) constitutional law.
    C) business customs.
    D) international law.

    Answer: C Difficulty: Medium Page: 127

38. Those customs that <u>MUST</u> be met and conformed to if relationships are to be successful are called:
A) adiaphora.
B) imperatives.
C) exclusives.
D) excessives.

Answer: B Difficulty: Easy Page: 128

39. The America-First Corporation routinely sends its key negotiating team to meet their counterparts in potential client countries located in Asian nations well in advance of any business talks. This practice recognized that the establishment of friendship and trust is a cultural:
A) adiaphora.
B) exclusive.
C) mandate.
D) imperative.

Answer: D Difficulty: Hard Page: 128

40. In Asian and Latin American countries, the establishment of "Guan-Xi, Ningen Kankei, or Compadre" is a cultural:
A) adiaphora.
B) imperative.
C) mandate.
D) exclusive.

Answer: B Difficulty: Medium Page: 128

41. Those areas of behavior or customs that cultural aliens may want to conform to or participate in, although such conformity or participation is not necessary, are called cultural:
A) adiaphora.
B) imperatives.
C) mandates.
D) exclusives.

Answer: A Difficulty: Easy Page: 129

42. After many years in Asia, Brent Spinner of the America-First Corporation has become a knowledgeable patron of traditional Japanese music and theater. Brent's patronage would be <u>BEST</u> described as a cultural:
A) imperative.
B) mandate.
C) adiaphora.
D) exclusive.

Answer: C Difficulty: Hard Page: 129

# Chapter 5 Business Customs in Global Marketing

43. Which of the following is BEST described as an indication of cultural sensitivity and appreciation that may be acknowledged as a gesture of goodwill?
    A) cultural imperatives.
    B) cultural mandates.
    C) cultural exclusives.
    D) cultural adiaphora.

    Answer: D Difficulty: Medium Page: 129

44. In dealing with Arab businesspeople, it is imperative to:
    A) make strong eye contact.
    B) bow when the host enters.
    C) greet the host with a kiss.
    D) accept the offer of traditional, strong alcoholic beverages.

    Answer: A Difficulty: Medium Page: 129

45. The majority of customs fall into the category of:
    A) cultural imperatives.
    B) cultural exclusives.
    C) cultural mandates.
    D) cultural adiaphora.

    Answer: D Difficulty: Easy Page: 129

46. Those customs or behavior patterns that are reserved solely for the local members of a culture are called:
    A) cultural imperatives.
    B) cultural exclusives.
    C) cultural mandates.
    D) cultural adiaphora.

    Answer: B Difficulty: Easy Page: 130

47. The America-First Corporation trains its managers to avoid criticism of their host culture's politics and/or religion. The firm is attempting to preclude the violation of cultural:
    A) imperatives.
    B) mandates.
    C) exclusives.
    D) adiaphora.

    Answer: C Difficulty: Hard Page: 130

48. The majority of offensive behavior on the part of foreign businesspeople results from the violation of cultural:
    A) mandates and imperatives.
    B) imperatives and exclusives.
    C) adiaphora and imperatives.
    D) mandates and adiaphora.

    Answer: B Difficulty: Medium Page: 130

49. In Japan, one's business card should be presented:
    A) exactly halfway through the conversation.
    B) during the earliest stages of introduction.
    C) by mail, in advance of the actual meeting.
    D) at the close of the conversation.

    Answer: B Difficulty: Medium Page: 130

50. Presentation of a "Meishi" is, to the Japanese, a cultural:
    A) imperative.
    B) mandate.
    C) exclusive.
    D) adiaphora.

    Answer: A Difficulty: Medium Page: 130

51. McDonald's use of an eagle on place mats used in some of its Mexican restaurants was interpreted by locals as a violation of a:
    A) cultural mandate.
    B) cultural imperative.
    C) cultural adiaphora.
    D) cultural exclusive.

    Answer: D Difficulty: Hard Page: 132

52. In emerging nations characterized by a semi-feudal, land-equals-power heritage, decision making tends to be:
    A) highly centralized.
    B) a committee responsibility.
    C) concentrated among top management or owners.
    D) consensus-oriented.

    Answer: C Difficulty: Medium Page: 132

# Chapter 5 Business Customs in Global Marketing

53. In Middle Eastern countries, the top executive makes all decisions and prefers to deal ONLY with:
    A) female middle managers.
    B) other executives with decision making powers.
    C) decision teams composed of functional experts.
    D) male middle managers.

    Answer: B Difficulty: Hard Page: 132

54. Managers are granted functional authority over their individual areas under a system of:
    A) decentralized decision making.
    B) committee decision making.
    C) consensus decision making.
    D) centralized decision making.

    Answer: A Difficulty: Easy Page: 132

55. BritLand, Inc., a large English corporation is MOST comfortable when dealing with other firms who share its preference for decentralized decision making. The firm is MOST likely to encounter this organizational approach among firms located in:
    A) Japan.
    B) Latin America.
    C) Russia.
    D) the United States.

    Answer: D Difficulty: Hard Page: 132

56. Japanese firms tend to favor:
    A) highly centralized decision making by the top executive.
    B) group decision making at the top management level.
    C) highly decentralized decision making.
    D) function-oriented decision making.

    Answer: B Difficulty: Medium Page: 132

57. Which of the following decision-making approaches would pose the GREATEST challenge to the international marketer's social and/or cultural skills?
    A) the authoritative approach.
    B) the delegated approach.
    C) the committee approach.
    D) all of the above require the same amount of knowledge, diversity,and application skills.

    Answer: C Difficulty: Hard Page: 132

58. Accurate generalizations about the specific concerns of managers in any particular country are MOST difficult to make with regard to:
A) security and mobility.
B) formality and tempo.
C) social acceptance.
D) personal goals.

Answer: D Difficulty: Medium Page: 133

59. One's personal life and company life are perceived as being synonymous in:
A) Japan.
B) England.
C) the United States.
D) Latin America.

Answer: A Difficulty: Easy Page: 134

60. Generally, personal power is a greater motivating force for managers in:
A) the United States.
B) Latin America.
C) France.
D) Japan.

Answer: B Difficulty: Easy Page: 134

61. Mohammed Yasin closely studies the eyes of his counterpart in every business transaction. When Mohammed notices the first sign of pupil dilation, he immediately increases his efforts to close the deal. To Mohammed, pupil dilation signals:
A) interest.
B) anger.
C) boredom.
D) frustration.

Answer: A Difficulty: Hard Page: 135

62. Generally, managers probably function best at a(n):
A) average-context level.
B) high-context level.
C) low-context level.
D) high-slang level.

Answer: C Difficulty: Easy Page: 136

# Chapter 5 Business Customs in Global Marketing

63. Communication mastery requires mastery of:
    A) language.
    B) customs.
    C) culture.
    D) all of the above.

    Answer: D Difficulty: Easy Page: 137

64. The America-First Corporation has begun to provide executive training programs in the interpretation of expressions and body language. The firm is hoping to improve its performance in:
    A) low-context cultures.
    B) high-context cultures.
    C) average-context cultures.
    D) formalized cultures.

    Answer: B Difficulty: Hard Page: 137

65. The apparent informality and haste of American business relationships would be BEST described as an:
    A) American imperative.
    B) American adiaphora.
    C) American exclusive.
    D) attempt to Americanize other cultures.

    Answer: C Difficulty: Hard Page: 137

66. Which of the following cultures is the MOST time conscious?
    A) Latin American
    B) Japanese
    C) Middle Eastern
    D) North American

    Answer: D Difficulty: Medium Page: 138

67. M-Time is MOST consistent with a(n):
    A) low-context culture.
    B) high-context culture.
    C) older culture.
    D) emerging culture.

    Answer: A Difficulty: Easy Page: 138

68. The America-First Corporation attempts to prepare its executives to function effectively in cultures that are less time-driven than our own. The firm is seeking to train its people to deal with:
A) M-Time.
B) P-Time.
C) Q-Time.
D) L-Time.

Answer: B Difficulty: Hard Page: 138

69. Which of the following tends to place the greatest emphasis on involvement with other people?
A) P-Time
B) M-Time
C) Q-Time
D) L-Time

Answer: A Difficulty: Medium Page: 138

70. The expansion of global markets and the growing importance of business-oriented behavior has resulted in more businesspeople adapting to:
A) P-Time.
B) Q-Time.
C) L-Time.
D) M-Time.

Answer: D Difficulty: Medium Page: 139

71. Differences in business customs and culture are MOST critical in:
A) negotiations.
B) social encounters.
C) travel.
D) obtaining meals and lodging.

Answer: A Difficulty: Medium Page: 139

72. In which of the following cultures are female executives MOST common?
A) Asian
B) American
C) Latin American
D) Arab

Answer: B Difficulty: Medium Page: 140

73. Voluntarily offered payments by someone seeking an unlawful advantage is BEST described as:
    A) bribery.
    B) extortion.
    C) an agent's fee.
    D) a finder's fee.

    Answer: A Difficulty: Easy Page: 143

74. Yasif Araza, the oil minister of a small Middle Eastern sheikdom, has threatened to nationalize the drilling assets of any foreign-owned firm that does not pay the agreed-upon price for his country's oil in a prompt manner. The minister's threat would be BEST described as:
    A) bribery.
    B) lubrication.
    C) extortion.
    D) subornation.

    Answer: C Difficulty: Hard Page: 143

75. Attempts to provide payments in order to persuade officials to ignore improprieties, not do their jobs, or break the law are BEST described as:
    A) lubrication.
    B) subornation.
    C) extortion.
    D) an agent's fee.

    Answer: B Difficulty: Easy Page: 143

76. When entering a new foreign market, the America-First Corporation often hires a local familiar with that country's rules and regulations as its representative. The firm's action is BEST described as:
    A) payment of an agent's fee.
    B) extortion.
    C) bribery.
    D) lubrication.

    Answer: A Difficulty: Hard Page: 144

77. The America-First Corporation has been charged with hiring agents in foreign markets to facilitate, and conceal, the firm's use of bribery. This action, if true, would be illegal under the:
    A) Federal Trade Commission Act.
    B) Sherman Anti-Trust Act.
    C) Robinson-Patman Act.
    D) Foreign Corrupt Practices Act.

    Answer: D Difficulty: Hard Page: 144

78. Small payments that are merely intended to facilitate or expedite the normal, lawful performance of a duty regularly performed by a foreign official is BEST described as:
   A) extortion.
   B) an agent's fee.
   C) lubrication.
   D) subornation.

   Answer: C Difficulty: Easy Page: 143

79. Ethical business conduct should normally exist:
   A) at a level well above the minimum required by law.
   B) at a level required by law.
   C) at a uniform level set by the United Nations.
   D) at a level somewhat below the legal minimum.

   Answer: A Difficulty: Easy Page: 145

80. Business actions should optimize the "common good" or benefits of all constituencies according to the concept of:
   A) justice or fairness.
   B) rights of the parties.
   C) utilitarian ethics.
   D) functional ethics.

   Answer: C Difficulty: Easy Page: 145

**Fill in the Blank Questions**

81. An open tolerance of foreign cultures as being "different but equal" is at the core of the critical attitude of ______________ acceptance necessary for success in international marketing.

   Answer: Affirmative Difficulty: Easy Page: 127

82. Frequently, misunderstandings in international marketing result from the natural tendency to interpret the behavior of foreign nationals within the context of one's own culture. The tendency to apply this ______________ is especially operative with regard to business customs.

   Answer: self-reference criterion Difficulty: Hard Page: 127

83. ______________ are customs that MUST be recognized and accommodated.

   Answer: Imperatives Difficulty: Easy Page: 128

# Chapter 5 Business Customs in Global Marketing

84. The great majority of business customs fall into the category of cultural ______________ to which conformity is optional.

    Answer: adiaphora  Difficulty: Medium  Page: 129

85. While visiting the Middle East, Janet Ison insisted upon visiting and worshiping in a mosque. Her Arab hosts did not approve of this violation of a cultural ______________.

    Answer: exclusive  Difficulty: Hard  Page: 130

86. In a(n) _________ approach to management decision making, functional executives exercise authority over their own areas of responsibility.

    Answer: decentralized  Difficulty: Medium  Page: 132

87. Japanese firms tend to employ ______________ decision making at the top management level to achieve consensus.

    Answer: group  Difficulty: Medium  Page: 132

88. To the Japanese, ______________ life and company life are one and the same.

    Answer: personal  Difficulty: Medium  Page: 134

89. Maukmoud Aramine always wears dark glasses when he engages in negotiation. This behavior is in conformity with the Arab tradition of observing the emotional reactions of their adversaries as revealed by the involuntary behavior of their ______________ while seeking to hide their own.

    Answer: pupils  Difficulty: Hard  Page: 134

90. Mastery of the nuances of body language, gesticulation and eye contact are MOST important in ______________ cultures.

    Answer: high-context  Difficulty: Medium  Page: 135

91. Business negotiations are more likely to begin more quickly and proceed more smoothly in a(n) ______________ culture.

    Answer: low-context  Difficulty: Medium  Page: 136

92. Low-context cultures are more likely to operate on ______________ Time.

    Answer: M- (monochronic)  Difficulty: Hard  Page: 138

93. High-context cultures are more likely to operate on ______________-Time.

    Answer: P- (polychronic)  Difficulty: Medium  Page: 138

## Chapter 5 Business Customs in Global Marketing

94. As high-context cultures increasingly enter international trade, their business people are increasingly adapting to ______________-Time.

Answer: M- (monochronic) Difficulty: Medium Page: 139

95. The growth of international business has contributed to a reduction in the ______________ bias that has been a traditional feature of many cultures.

Answer: gender Difficulty: Medium Page: 140

96. The term ______________ describes voluntarily offered payments by someone seeking an unlawful advantage.

Answer: bribery Difficulty: Easy Page: 143

97. ______________ refers to the practice of using duress to attain an outcome or result to which an individual is lawfully entitled.

Answer: Extortion Difficulty: Easy Page: 143

98. The practice of ______________ typically involves the use of large sums of "hidden" monies intended to entice an official to commit an illegal act on behalf of the person making the payment.

Answer: subornation Difficulty: Easy Page: 143

99. The America-First Corporation has been charged with hiring agents for the purpose of offering, and hiding, illegal bribes to foreign officials in return for favorable treatment. The firm's actions would, if true, be a violation of the ______________ Act.

Answer: Foreign Corrupt Practices Difficulty: Hard Page: 144

100. The goal of ______________ ethics is to optimize the "common good" as defined by the benefits that would accrue to all constituencies involved.

Answer: utilitarian Difficulty: Medium Page: 145

# Chapter 5 Business Customs in Global Marketing

## Essay Questions

101. Why is the capacity to adapt critical to success in international marketing? How does the self-reference criterion affect the marketer's adaptation efforts?

Answer:
International marketing executives must be able to view the various cultures in which they operate as different, but equal in order to avoid misunderstandings and tensions. This requires the executive to resist the temptation to judge the actions of foreign businessmen according to the familiar context of their self-reference criterion which, of course, reflects the customs and behaviors of their own culture. The successful international marketer approaches other cultures with a willingness to expend the effort required to understand and accommodate the cultural backgrounds of their foreign customers and/or partners.

Difficulty: Hard Page: 127-128

102. Briefly differentiate between cultural imperatives, adiaphora and exclusives. Why are such distinctions important?

Answer:
Cultural imperatives refer to business customs and expectations that must be recognized and accommodated. Adiaphora are customs to which adaptation is optional. Cultural exclusives refer to those customs in which an outsider must not participate. The marketer must identify and respond appropriately to the comparatively small number of cultural imperatives and exclusives that account for most serious cultural misunderstandings. Those behaviors in the adiaphora category should be approached carefully. While optional behaviors may signify acceptance and/or approval of a foreign culture, even those behaviors may cause problems if performed poorly or inappropriately.

Difficulty: Hard Page: 128-130

103. Based on your understanding of the problems that attend international marketing, what changes or additions to university business programs would you recommend to improve the student's preparation for this important field?

Answer:
Given the importance of cultural context to successful international marketing, students in such programs would benefit from courses in the history, language and customs of those nations in which they may like to work. Such courses may be used as electives in the student's business program--and may be taken outside the college of business. Courses in non-verbal communication would also be a useful addition to the preparation of future international marketers.

Difficulty: Hard Page: 131-135

104. Briefly describe the differences that tend to exist between high- and low- context cultures. In which of the two would an American executive tend to be MOST comfortable? Why?

Answer:
Low-context cultures tend to rely heavily upon explicit, verbally expressed communications while high-context cultures depend heavily upon the context or nonverbal aspects of communication. Furthermore, low-context cultures tend to emphasize M- (monochronic) time with its emphasis on promptness, linear scheduling, and the literal value of time while high-context cultures tend to feature P-(polychronic) time with its emphasis on looser schedules, greater personal involvement, and a wait-and-see approach to decision making. The American executive is most comfortable in low-context M-Time cultures that resemble his or her own.

Difficulty: Hard Page: 135-141

105. American businesspeople often complain that U.S. laws place them at a disadvantage in international dealings. Do you agree? Support your position. How might this problem be resolved?

Answer:
The argument is generally true. Generally, the U.S. (as a good low-context culture) has many more laws that set specific standards for a variety of practices that are treated much more loosely in other cultures. Often, our laws prohibit American firms from engaging in practices that are legal and/or expected in other cultures. Perhaps the most promising solution is to seek international agreements specifying acceptable international business practices. Of course, ethical standards should always exceed the minimum requirements set by law.

Difficulty: Hard Page: 141-146

# Chapter 6 The Political Environment: A Critical Concern

## True/False Questions

1. Following the advice of Adam Smith's Laissez-Faire policy, modern governments exert little influence upon the conduct of business.

   Answer: False Difficulty: Easy Page: 152

2. The political environment of nations is a critical concern for the international marketer.

   Answer: True Difficulty: Easy Page: 152

3. A sovereign state is, essentially, a creation of international law.

   Answer: True Difficulty: Medium Page: 152

4. The United States has played a leading role in persuading other nations to accept the North American Free Trade Agreement (NAFTA), the North Atlantic Treaty Organization, and many other such pacts. In so doing, America has encouraged other nations to voluntarily abridge their sovereign rights.

   Answer: True Difficulty: Hard Page: 152

5. Of all the factors considered by international marketers, the stability or instability of prevailing government policies is of greatest concern.

   Answer: True Difficulty: Medium Page: 153

6. The concern of international marketers for the stability of potential foreign markets transcends the nature of the political party or faction in power to focus on the consistency and predictability of the policies followed by its government.

   Answer: True Difficulty: Hard Page: 153

7. At present, the questions concerning long-term stability, trade policy, and a host of other issues make central Africa, the most politically unstable foreign market on the globe.

   Answer: True Difficulty: Medium Page: 155

8. PepsiCo's Russian experience proved that a multinational corporation based in a capitalistic country cannot be profitable in a communistic nation.

   Answer: False Difficulty: Medium Page: 155

9. The America-First Corporation is considering entry into the Mexican market. The recent victory of that country's PAN party means that the firm will only have to concern itself with its policies.

   Answer: False Difficulty: Hard Page: 155

10. Nationalism is best described as an intense feeling of national pride and unity.

    Answer: True Difficulty: Easy Page: 156

11. Economic nationalism often leads a country to adopt restrictions on imports, restrictive tariffs, and other barriers to trade.

    Answer: True Difficulty: Easy Page: 156

12. Unlike emerging states, industrialized countries such as the United States, Great Britain, and Japan are immune to the "disease" of economic nationalism.

    Answer: False Difficulty: Medium Page: 156-157

13. Confiscation, the seizure of a foreign nation's assets without payment, is the most serious political risk faced by a multinational firm.

    Answer: True Difficulty: Medium Page: 158

14. The America-First Corporation has just been informed that governments that have promised to pay the firm at least a portion of their value have seized some of its foreign assets. The firm has become a victim of confiscation.

    Answer: False Difficulty: Hard Page: 159

15. Under a policy of domestication, host countries take steps to transfer foreign investments to national control and ownership through a series of government decrees.

    Answer: True Difficulty: Easy Page: 159

16. The ultimate goal of domestication is to force foreign investors to share more of the ownership and management with nationals.

    Answer: True Difficulty: Medium Page: 159

17. With the increasing trend toward globalization, a more positive attitude toward MNC's, and a growing desire for foreign investment, political risk is no longer a concern for multinational firms.

    Answer: False Difficulty: Medium Page: 160

18. The America-First Corporation is currently doing business in several foreign nations experiencing foreign exchange shortages. The firm may encounter the use of multiple exchange rates as these countries seek to allocate this scarce commodity among competing foreign goods sold in a political environment.

    Answer: True  Difficulty: Hard  Page: 160

19. The North American Free Trade Agreement (NAFTA) effectively eliminated international local-contract laws.

    Answer: False  Difficulty: Medium  Page: 161

20. The America-First Corporation's investments in several poor, developing nations has produced a number of profitable businesses. The firm's success may place it at risk for unreasonable tax controls.

    Answer: True  Difficulty: Hard  Page: 161

21. Boycotts may be imposed to ban all trade between specific nations—or sanctions may be issued to restrict the trade of specific products.

    Answer: True  Difficulty: Medium  Page: 162

22. Generally, products perceived to have an effect on the environment, exchange rates, national and/or economic security, and the welfare of people are more likely to be politically sensitive. This sensitivity is greatly enhanced if the product is also highly visible.

    Answer: True  Difficulty: Medium  Page: 166

23. Products deemed nonessential by a foreign government face greater political risks than those judged to be essential to the achievement of national goals.

    Answer: True  Difficulty: Medium  Page: 166

24. The America-First Corporation has just begun to use political risk assessment as a tool in selection of potential foreign markets. Through the use of this procedure the firm can eliminate the risks associated with hostile acts of foreign governments.

    Answer: False  Difficulty: Hard  Page: 167

25. Whenever possible, the America-First Corporation seeks to employ a joint-venture with a local firm when entering a foreign country. This approach provides vital knowledge about the host country and a measure of protection against hostile government action.

    Answer: True  Difficulty: Hard  Page: 170

26. Whenever possible, the America-First Corporation seeks to enlist the financial assistance of banks that have made loans to the governments of domestic firms of countries it is planning to enter. This strategy may prove useful should the host country threaten expropriation or other types of takeovers.

    Answer: True Difficulty: Hard Page: 171

27. Licensing is an especially effective technique for minimizing political risk when the technology to be employed is unique and the risk is high.

    Answer: True Difficulty: Medium Page: 171

28. In those cases in which political risks are extremely high, a multinational corporation may employ a strategy of planned domestication to protect profitability as long as possible.

    Answer: True Difficulty: Medium Page: 171

29. While U.S. firms are prohibited from the use of bribery, it is legal for American firms to provide money to foreign governments in return for political favors <u>IF</u> such actions are legal under the host nation's laws.

    Answer: False Difficulty: Medium Page: 172

30. The Department of Commerce is the primary U.S. government agency charged with assisting American multinational corporations in the global marketplace.

    Answer: True Difficulty: Easy Page: 173

### Multiple Choice Questions

31. A sovereign state:
    A) is independent and free from external control.
    B) enjoys full legal equality with other states.
    C) has the power to enter into agreements with other nations.
    D) enjoys all of the above powers.

    Answer: D Difficulty: Medium Page: 152

32. The powers exercised by a state in relation to other countries and the supreme powers exercised over its citizens is described by the term:
    A) sovereignty.
    B) independence.
    C) isolation.
    D) democracy.

    Answer: A Difficulty: Easy Page: 152

# Chapter 6 The Political Environment: A Critical Concern

33. Most of the conflict situations arising in international business occur when a country:
    A) declares war on its neighbors.
    B) withdraws from the United Nations.
    C) seeks to extend its national laws beyond its borders.
    D) exercises its powers within its borders.

    Answer: C Difficulty: Medium Page: 152

34. The acceptance of the terms of the NAFTA agreement:
    A) was enforced upon signatory nations by the United States.
    B) represented a voluntary abridgement of the sovereign rights of signatory states.
    C) was forced upon Japan and Germany following World War II.
    D) signifies the weakness of signatory states.

    Answer: B Difficulty: Medium Page: 152

35. A multinational corporation (MNC) is affected by the:
    A) laws of multiple nation-states.
    B) laws of the host countries.
    C) laws of its home country.
    D) all of the above.

    Answer: D Difficulty: Medium Page: 153

36. The America-First Corporation is considering entry into one or more potential host countries. The firm's choice for entry will be <u>MOST</u> affected by:
    A) the current exchange rates in each country.
    B) the potential size of host country markets.
    C) the favorability and stability of the political environment.
    D) the size of the domestic army.

    Answer: C Difficulty: Hard Page: 153

37. Which of the following areas is beset with the greatest number of questions concerning long-term stability, trade policy, and many other issues?
    A) central Africa.
    B) Japan.
    C) Russia.
    D) Afghanistan.

    Answer: A Difficulty: Medium Page: 155

38. The ability of multinational corporations to survive and profit, even under the most extreme of governments, as long as there is at least some long-run productability and stability is best exemplified by:
A) GM in Germany.
B) PepsiCo in Russia.
C) McDonald's in China.
D) IBM in Cuba.

Answer: B Difficulty: Medium Page: 155

39. Which of the following British political parties has traditionally been MOST restrictive of trade?
A) the Conservative Party
B) the PAN Party.
C) the PRI Party.
D) the Labour Party.

Answer: D Difficulty: Medium Page: 155

40. The America-First Corporation is preparing to enter the Mexican market. After its political advances in 1997, the firm will have to gain as much knowledge as possible about the:
A) Liberal Party.
B) PRI Party.
C) PAN Party.
D) Conservative Party.

Answer: C Difficulty: Hard Page: 155

41. The intense pride the people hold for their country is best described as:
A) sovereignty.
B) nationalism.
C) isolationism.
D) colonialism.

Answer: B Difficulty: Easy Page: 156

42. National interests and security take precedence over international considerations according to the doctrine of:
A) patriotism.
B) isolationism.
C) economic nationalism.
D) sovereignty.

Answer: C Difficulty: Medium Page: 156

# Chapter 6 The Political Environment: A Critical Concern

43. Feelings of economic nationalism may be expressed in:
    A) tariffs.
    B) import restrictions.
    C) exhortations to buy only domestic products.
    D) all of the above.

    Answer: D Difficulty: Medium Page: 156

44. The era of militant nationalism began to subside after:
    A) 1980.
    B) 1960.
    C) 1970.
    D) 1950.

    Answer: A Difficulty: Easy Page: 157

45. In recent years, strong, nationalistic feelings have hindered trade relations between the United States and:
    A) Great Britain.
    B) Japan.
    C) Italy.
    D) Russia.

    Answer: B Difficulty: Medium Page: 157

46. Which of the following represents the <u>MOST</u> severe form of political risk?
    A) import restrictions.
    B) price controls.
    C) exchange controls.
    D) forced equity transfers.

    Answer: D Difficulty: Medium Page: 158

47. Which of the following is the <u>MOST</u> severe political risk?
    A) confiscation.
    B) expropriation.
    C) nationalism.
    D) domestication.

    Answer: A Difficulty: Medium Page: 158

48. The seizing of a company's assets without payment is called:
    A) domestication.
    B) expropriation.
    C) confiscation.
    D) nationalism.

    Answer: C Difficulty: Easy Page: 158

49. Over the years, the America-First Corporation has had significant amounts of its foreign assets taken, without compensation, by the governments of countries in which the firm did business. America-First has been victimized by:
A) expropriation.
B) confiscation.
C) domestication.
D) nationalism.

Answer: B Difficulty: Hard Page: 158

50. Which of the following describes the act of a foreign government seizing the assets of a multinational corporation with only a partial reimbursement of their value?
A) confiscation.
B) nationalism.
C) domestication.
D) expropriation.

Answer: D Difficulty: Easy Page: 159

51. The America-First Corporation has recently received partial reimbursement for assets seized by governments in some of the foreign countries in which it operates. America-First has been subjected to:
A) expropriation.
B) Nationalism.
C) confiscation.
D) domestication.

Answer: A Difficulty: Hard Page: 159

52. The transfer of foreign investments to national control and ownership through a series of government decrees is called:
A) expropriation.
B) nationalism.
C) domestication.
D) confiscation.

Answer: C Difficulty: Easy Page: 159

53. Governments may seek to domesticate foreign-held assets by mandating:
A) a transfer of ownership in part or whole to nationals.
B) greater decision-making power for nationals.
C) a greater number of locally-produced component products.
D) all of the above.

Answer: D Difficulty: Medium Page: 159

54. The ultimate goal of domestication is to:
A) sell off foreign-owned assets at a profit.
B) punish foreign firms for violation of domestic laws.
C) to share more ownership and management with nationals.
D) pirate foreign technology.

Answer: C Difficulty: Medium Page: 159

55. The America-First Corporation is currently in negotiations with several host nations who are demanding a greater share of the firm's assets and a stronger voice in their management the firm's host countries are attempting to engage in:
A) confiscation.
B) domestication.
C) expropriation.
D) nationalism.

Answer: B Difficulty: Hard Page: 159

56. Which of the following has become the most common threat to foreign-owned assets in recent years?
A) expropriation.
B) confiscation.
C) domestication.
D) all of the above are equally likely.

Answer: C Difficulty: Medium Page: 159

57. Which of the following forms of political risk are LEAST likely to occur in the future?
A) expropriation.
B) currency conversion restrictions.
C) unresponsive bureaucrats.
D) political and economic uncertainty.

Answer: A Difficulty: Medium Page: 160

58. The shortage of funds available for foreign trade is at the root of:
A) expropriation.
B) exchange controls.
C) confiscation.
D) domestication.

Answer: B Difficulty: Easy Page: 160

59. The America-First Corporation markets a variety of luxury goods throughout the world. In those countries in which funds for foreign exchange are limited, the importation of the firm's products may be hindered by:
A) confiscation.
B) expropriation.
C) domestication.
D) exchange controls.

Answer: D Difficulty: Hard Page: 160

60. Some nations require any product sold within the country to contain domestic components under:
A) tax controls.
B) local-content laws.
C) price controls.
D) import restrictions.

Answer: B Difficulty: Easy Page: 161

61. The America-First Corporation runs several "screwdriver operations" in foreign countries that are part of the NAFTA pact. The firm is likely to be subject to:
A) local-content laws.
B) expropriation.
C) confiscation.
D) domestication.

Answer: A Difficulty: Hard Page: 161

62. Host governments may enforce local-content requirements by enforcing:
A) tax controls.
B) price controls.
C) import restrictions.
D) nationalistic labor programs.

Answer: C Difficulty: Hard Page: 161

63. The America-First Corporation has been able to operate profitably in several nations that face constant fund shortages. In today's world, the firm's profits are MOST at risk through the imposition of:
A) price controls.
B) import restrictions.
C) nationalistic labor controls.
D) tax controls.

Answer: D Difficulty: Hard Page: 161

64. Host countries may seek to control the cost of living during inflationary times and/or force foreign companies to sell equity to local interests through the imposition of:
A) tax controls.
B) price controls.
C) import restrictions.
D) local-content laws.

Answer: B Difficulty: Medium Page: 161

65. One nation may "punish" another by stopping all trade with it by imposing:
A) price controls.
B) local-content laws.
C) import restrictions.
D) boycotts.

Answer: D Difficulty: Medium Page: 162

66. Products are more apt to be politically sensitive if they have a perceived or real effect upon:
A) the environment.
B) exchange rates.
C) national and economic security.
D) all of the above.

Answer: D Difficulty: Medium Page: 166

67. Products are MOST likely to receive negative political attention if they:
A) are perceived to be essential items.
B) are perceived to be nonessential items.
C) are perceived to have favorable economic impact.
D) are perceived to have favorable environmental impact.

Answer: B Difficulty: Medium Page: 166

68. The America-First Corporation is considering entry into several Latin American and Middle Eastern countries. As part of its decision-making activity, the firm should:
A) conduct a political risk assessment.
B) petition the U.N. for political immunity.
C) bribe governmental officials to ensure favorable treatment.
D) establish only "screwdriver operations".

Answer: A Difficulty: Hard Page: 167

69. Good corporate citizenship requires that American firms do all of the following EXCEPT:
    A) act as a "good guest" in the host company.
    B) share the benefits of the enterprise with the host country.
    C) attempt to Americanize the host company.
    D) provide cultural training for its executives.

    Answer: C Difficulty: Medium Page: 169

70. Government-MNC relations are generally positive if the investment:
    A) creates jobs.
    B) transfers capital, technology, and/or skills.
    C) uses locally produced resources.
    D) all of the above.

    Answer: D Difficulty: Medium Page: 170

71. An MNC may reduce its financial and political risk in a host country by sharing those risks with a domestic company through the use of:
    A) import controls.
    B) a joint venture.
    C) local-content laws.
    D) loss insurance.

    Answer: B Difficulty: Hard Page: 170

72. The America-First Corporation has made contact with several banks that have had prior investments in countries under consideration for entry by the firm. America-First is attempting to reduce political and financial risk by:
    A) expanding the investment base.
    B) controlling distribution.
    C) licensing.
    D) planned domestication.

    Answer: A Difficulty: Hard Page: 171

73. The America-First Corporation is concerned that some of the miens it owns in Third World nations may be subject to expropriation. The firm may lessen the risk and impact of such an occurrence if it maintains DOMESTIC control of:
    A) advertising.
    B) marketing and distribution.
    C) accounting.
    D) production.

    Answer: B Difficulty: Hard Page: 171

74. Which of the following eliminates almost all forms of political risk?
    A) licensing.
    B) joint ventures.
    C) expanding the investment base.
    D) domestic control of marketing and distribution.

    Answer: A Difficulty: Medium Page: 171

75. The America-First Corporation routinely employs its unique technology in a number of foreign markets subject to high political risks. The firm may minimize most of the risk it faces by:
    A) domestic control of marketing and distribution.
    B) using joint ventures.
    C) expanding the investment base.
    D) the use of licensing.

    Answer: D Difficulty: Hard Page: 171

76. If an MNC is, or will be, subjected to the nationalization of foreign assets, it is probably best advised to employ:
    A) licensing.
    B) joint ventures.
    C) planned domestication.
    D) expanded investment bases.

    Answer: C Difficulty: Medium Page: 171

77. The America-First Corporation conducts business in several politically hostile nations. Given the high risk of loss of assets, the firm is MOST likely to prefer:
    A) expropriation.
    B) confiscation.
    C) planned domestication.
    D) nationalization.

    Answer: C Difficulty: Hard Page: 171

78. Which of the following methods of dealing with political risk is LEAST feasible for American MNCs?
    A) joint ventures.
    B) political payoffs.
    C) expanding the investment base.
    D) planned domestication.

    Answer: B Difficulty: Medium Page: 172

79. Which of the following U.S. government agencies is MOST directly charged with assisting American firms overseas?
A) the United Nations.
B) the Agriculture Department.
C) the Department of the Treasury.
D) the Department of Commerce.

Answer: D Difficulty: Medium Page: 173

80. An American firm facing political risk in foreign lands may obtain insurance against loss through the:
A) Eximbank.
B) Agency for International Development.
C) Overseas Private Investment Corporation.
D) Any, or all, of the above.

Answer: D Difficulty: Medium Page: 173

**Fill in the Blank Questions**

81. A(n) _______________ state exercises powers with regard to other countries and its own citizens.

Answer: Sovereign Difficulty: Easy Page: 152

82. An MNC is affected by the laws of multiple _______________, the laws of _______________ countries, and the laws of its _______________ country.

Answer: nation-states; host; home Difficulty: Medium Page: 153

83. The MOST important of the political conditions that concern foreign businesses is the _______________ of prevailing government policies.

Answer: stability Difficulty: Medium Page: 155-156

84. _______________ is best described as an intense feeling of national pride and unity.

Answer: Nationalism Difficulty: Easy Page: 156

85. The America-First Corporation fears that some of the host nations in which it operates may seize its assets without payment. The firm is expressing a fear of _______________.

Answer: confiscation Difficulty: Hard Page: 158

86. Under ______________, a host nation will make at least some reimbursement for government-seized investments.

Answer: expropriation   Difficulty: Medium   Page: 159

87. ______________ occurs when host countries take steps to transfer foreign investments to national control and ownership through a series of government decrees.

Answer: Domestication   Difficulty: Easy   Page: 159

88. ______________ stem from shortages of foreign exchange hard in a country.

Answer: Exchange controls   Difficulty: Medium   Page: 160

89. The America-First Corporation has decided to assemble some of the automobiles it produces in Mexico under the terms established by NAFTA, the firm will have to incorporate up to 62 percent ______________ in the cars it produces.

Answer: local content   Difficulty: Hard   Page: 161

90. Host countries sometimes employ ______________ to force MNCs to purchase more supplies in the host country.

Answer: import restrictions   Difficulty: Medium   Page: 161

91. Occasionally, a host company will use ______________ controls to squeeze revenue from the profits of foreign MNCs and/or ______________ controls to force foreign companies to sell equity to local interests.

Answer: tax; price   Difficulty: Medium   Page: 161

92. The America-First Corporation operates fast-food restaurants in several foreign host nations. The ______________ of this activity, and the possible impact upon the ______________ of the public make the firm's efforts politically sensitive.

Answer: visibility; Health   Difficulty: Hard   Page: 166

93. The attempt to forecast political instability in order to better assess potential foreign investments is at the root of ______________.

Answer: political risk assessment   Difficulty: Medium   Page: 167

94. Whenever possible, the America-First Corporation seeks to form alliances with firms native to potential host countries. The firm is attempting to minimize political risk through the use of ______________.

Answer: joint ventures   Difficulty: Hard   Page: 170

# Chapter 6 The Political Environment: A Critical Concern

95. The recruitment of several investors and banks to assist in financing an investment in a host nation and/or to reduce political risk is at the core of the strategy of ______________.

    Answer: expanding the investment base  Difficulty: Medium  Page: 171

96. The America-First Corporation has significant investments in several unstable host nations. The firm may reduce political risk by maintaining domestic control of ______________ and ______________.

    Answer: marketing; distribution  Difficulty: Hard  Page: 171

97. Of all the techniques for reducing political risk, perhaps ______________ is the most effective for firms possessing unique technologies.

    Answer: licensing  Difficulty: Medium  Page: 171

98. If a foreign investment is, or will be, nationalized, the best course for an MNC may be the policy of ______________.

    Answer: planned domestication  Difficulty: Medium  Page: 171

99. On occasion, an MNC may utilize ______________, or political payoffs, to preclude intervention into its affairs.

    Answer: Bribery  Difficulty: Medium  Page: 171

100. The primary governmental agency that supports American MNCs overseas is the ______________.

    Answer: Department of Commerce  Difficulty: Easy  Page: 173

**Essay Questions**

101. Why should the factor of political stability be at the very top of the list of criteria used to evaluate the attractiveness of potential foreign investments?

    Answer:
    Multinational firms can typically enjoy profitable investments in almost any political environment--as long as the rules of the game are known and consistent. Investments chosen to fit a specific set of circumstances can, however, quickly become unprofitable should the anticipated circumstances change. Multinationals can minimize political risk by fully understanding the philosophies of rival political parties--and assessing the likelihood of their ascendancy. Such firms may also seek protection from a variety of public and private organizations that provide some insurance against political risk.

    Difficulty: Hard  Page: 153-158

102. Briefly compare the severity of the risks associated with confiscation, expropriation, and domestication.

Answer:
Confiscation, seizing a foreign firm's assets without compensation, is the most severe risk faced by a multinational. Expropriation involves the seizure of assets with at least some compensation. Both of these risks are associated with a sudden loss of profits and assets. Foreign firms would be well advised to avoid such risks where possible, to utilize insurance where feasible, and to employ a wide range of strategies designed to minimize these risks. Domestication, in contrast, is an attempt to transfer ownership and control to foreign nationals over time. The firm should seek to minimize the risk through good corporate citizenship and plan revenue streams to cover investments and return profits as quickly as possible.

Difficulty: Hard Page: 158-160

103. Local-content laws are especially popular in developing and underdeveloped countries. Why?

Answer:
Developing and underdeveloped nations frequently have a large, relatively unskilled labor force willing to work for relatively low wages. As a result, such countries tend to attract "screwdriver assembly shops" which exploit the labor force but do little to support small, local producers who tend to be unable to compete effectively on price. Local content laws require foreign manufacturers to support the growth of local suppliers as the price for access to a cheap labor supply.

Difficulty: Hard Page: 161

104. Briefly describe the major alternatives available to an MNC in ITS attempts to minimize political risks.

Answer:
An MNC may seek to reduce political risk by seeking joint ventures with either locals or other third-country MNCs. Another strategy seeks to include several investors and banks to expand the investment base—and perhaps bring political pressure on foreign governments. An MNC may reduce the impact of political action, and may preclude it, by maintaining domestic control over vital marketing and distribution activities. Licensing unique technologies for a fee may offer the best answer for high-risk situations. If nationalization is almost a certainty, or has begun, an MNC may seek to at least participate in a gradual transfer of assets through a strategy of planned domestication.

Difficulty: Hard Page: 170-171

105. Briefly describe the basic domestic alternatives available to U.S. firms seeking to obtain "insurance" against the political risks involved in entering a foreign market.

Answer:
The Export-Import Bank, through the Foreign Credit Insurance Association, will insure an exporter against nonpayment of a buyer's obligations when it is due to political reasons. The Agency for International Development provides protection against basic political risks when incurred during the provision of "essential" projects or products in "approved" countries. In addition to these government agencies, the Overseas Private Investment Corporation is also a provider of political-risk insurance.

Difficulty: Hard Page: 171-173

# Chapter 7 The International Legal Environment: Playing by the Rules

## True/False Questions

1. The recent creation of Uniform International Commercial law under the auspices of the United Nations has greatly simplified the conduct of international trade.

   Answer: False Difficulty: Medium Page: 178

2. The four common heritages shared by the majority of legal systems of the world are Islamic law, socialist law, civil law, and the Judeo-Christian ethic.

   Answer: False Difficulty: Medium Page: 178

3. The basis for common law derives from the habits and customs that the people of a nation have generally, or commonly, held as appropriate through their history.

   Answer: False Difficulty: Medium Page: 178

4. Code law is based on an all-inclusive system of written rules of law.

   Answer: True Difficulty: Easy Page: 179

5. Common law achieves the status of "complete inclusivity" by encompassing the commercial, civil, and criminal codes.

   Answer: False Difficulty: Medium Page: 179

6. The America-First Corporation recently failed to complete a contract as a result of earthquake damage to its primary production site. This "Act of God" would automatically excuse the firm from non-compliance under BOTH common and code law.

   Answer: True Difficulty: Hard Page: 180

7. The basis for the Shari'ah is interpretation of the Koran.

   Answer: True Difficulty: Easy Page: 181

8. Islamic nations are the only nations in the world in which interest is not charged or paid.

   Answer: True Difficulty: Medium Page: 181

9. Russian law regarding copyright violations is the most clear and severe in the world.

   Answer: False Difficulty: Medium Page: 182

10. The World Court is primarily concerned with resolving legal disputes between multinational corporations under the precepts of International Commercial Law developed by the United States.

    Answer: False  Difficulty: Hard  Page: 184

11. The America-First Corporation routinely includes a jurisdictional clause in all contracts between the firm and other multinational firms. This practice will generally ensure that any disputes between parties will be settled under terms of the law in effect in the location cited in the contract.

    Answer: True  Difficulty: Hard  Page: 184

12. Conciliation is a nonbinding agreement between parties to resolve disputes by asking a third party to mediate differences.

    Answer: True  Difficulty: Easy  Page: 184

13. Generally, contract and other legal documents cannot abridge the right of the parties to a contract to sue by specifying the use of arbitration to settle disputes.

    Answer: False  Difficulty: Medium  Page: 186

14. Despite the attention given to conciliation and arbitration, litigation is still the preferred means of settling international disputes.

    Answer: False  Difficulty: Medium  Page: 186

15. Advances in technology have unfortunately increased the problems associated with the detection and punishment of piracy or counterfeiting.

    Answer: True  Difficulty: Medium  Page: 188

16. The America-First Corporation is a major developer and marketer of computer software. The firm can BEST protect its intellectual property by registering its trademarks in every country in which it plans to sell its goods.

    Answer: True  Difficulty: Hard  Page: 190

17. The Paris Convention, the Inter-American Convention, and the Madrid Agreement provide intellectual property protection in all member states for any member who registers such property in any member state.

    Answer: True  Difficulty: Medium  Page: 191

18. The United States is one of the few countries in the world in which an individual may hold a patent throughout the duration of the patent period without ever producing or selling the protected item.

Answer: True Difficulty: Medium Page: 192

19. The America-First Corporation has registered its trademarks in every country in which it does business. The firm can be confident that the governments of these states will vigorously police and aggressively prosecute trademark violations for the firm.

Answer: False Difficulty: Hard Page: 192

20. The America-First Corporation is a major use of comparable advertising in the United States.

Answer: False Difficulty: Hard Page: 194

21. Green marketing laws are a uniquely American business obstacle that is largely ignored in Europe.

Answer: False Difficulty: Medium Page: 195

22. With the exception of the United States, antitrust laws have been either nonexistent or unenforced in most of the world's countries for the better part of the $20^{th}$ century.

Answer: True Difficulty: Medium Page: 196

23. As the America-First Corporation enters more foreign nations, it will have to contend with a confusing maze of laws affecting its actions. Luckily, the firm will not have to comply with U.S. law during its operations in those host countries.

Answer: False Difficulty: Hard Page: 197

24. The Foreign Corrupt Practices Act makes it illegal for companies to pay bribes to foreign officials, candidates, or political parties.

Answer: True Difficulty: Easy Page: 197

25. With the end of the Cold War, the U.S. government repealed the Trading With the Enemy Act.

Answer: False Difficulty: Medium Page: 198

26. The basis for determining the jurisdiction and application of U.S. antitrust laws is ultimately Sections I and II of the Sherman Act.

Answer: True Difficulty: Medium Page: 199

27. Under the Antiboycott Law of 1977, U.S. firms are forbidden to participate in any foreign boycott.

    Answer: False Difficulty: Medium Page: 200

28. The tertiary provision of the Arab League's boycott of Israel is limited to prohibiting Arab governments from direct trade with Israel.

    Answer: False Difficulty: Medium Page: 200

29. During the height of tensions between the Arab League and Israel, the America-First Corporation refrained from direct trade with Israel, but did continue to trade with some nations that did so. America-First may be subjected to the secondary boycott of the Arab League.

    Answer: True Difficulty: Hard Page: 200

30. Host governments welcome the extraterritorial application of U.S. laws and foreign policy as a major force restraining the power and influence of American MNCs.

    Answer: False Difficulty: Medium Page: 200

**Multiple Choice Questions**

31. All of the following serve as a basic foundation of the world's legal system EXCEPT:
    A) Islamic law.
    B) the Judeo-Christian ethic.
    C) socialist law.
    D) common law.

    Answer: B Difficulty: Medium Page: 178

32. Islamic law is derived from the teachings of:
    A) Buddha.
    B) the Old Testament.
    C) Christ.
    D) the Koran.

    Answer: D Difficulty: Medium Page: 178

33. England, the United States, and Canada operate under:
    A) the common law.
    B) Islamic law.
    C) socialist law.
    D) civil law.

    Answer: A Difficulty: Medium Page: 178

34. Japanese citizens and businesses operate under:
    A) the common law.
    B) Islamic law.
    C) civil law.
    D) socialist law.

    Answer: C Difficulty: Medium Page: 178

35. The America-First Corporation is preparing to enter China. The firm should be prepared to conduct its affairs in its new host country according to:
    A) socialist law.
    B) civil law.
    C) Islamic law.
    D) the common law.

    Answer: A Difficulty: Hard Page: 178

36. The legal environment of the United States is primarily shaped by:
    A) civil and secular law.
    B) democratic and socialist law.
    C) common and code law.
    D) English and Napoleonic Law.

    Answer: C Difficulty: Medium Page: 179

37. The basis for common law is:
    A) tradition.
    B) past practices.
    C) legal precedents.
    D) all of the above.

    Answer: D Difficulty: Medium Page: 178

38. Court interpretations and precedents amassed over time are most significant to the development of:
    A) socialist law.
    B) common law.
    C) code law.
    D) Islamic law.

    Answer: B Difficulty: Medium Page: 179

39. Which of the following is considered to be the MOST "inclusive" of the major forms of law?
A) code law.
B) Islamic law.
C) common law.
D) civil law.

Answer: A Difficulty: Medium Page: 179

40. All of the following are components of code law EXCEPT:
A) a commercial code.
B) a criminal code.
C) a Judicial code.
D) a civil code.

Answer: C Difficulty: Medium Page: 179

41. The "completeness" of code law is generally attributed to:
A) the large number of nations that employ it.
B) the diligence of the judges in such systems.
C) the experience of the court reporters in its courts.
D) the use of "catch all" provisions.

Answer: D Difficulty: Medium Page: 179

42. The America-First Corporation bases its actions on the merging precepts of commercial law. The firm's lawyers should be familiar with the underlying foundations of this body of law derived from:
A) Islamic law.
B) socialist law.
C) common law.
D) civil law.

Answer: C Difficulty: Hard Page: 179

43. The MOST striking difference between common law and code law systems is found in those laws that govern:
A) contract rights and duties.
B) intellectual property rights.
C) the payment of interest.
D) the sale of land.

Answer: B Difficulty: Medium Page: 179

# Chapter 7 The International Legal Environment: Playing by the Rules

44. Under common law, the ownership of intellectual property is established by:
    A) title.
    B) possession.
    C) use.
    D) registration.

    Answer: C Difficulty: Medium Page: 179

45. Under code law, the ownership of intellectual property is established by:
    A) title.
    B) possession.
    C) use.
    D) registration.

    Answer: D Difficulty: Medium Page: 179

46. The America-First Corporation has just registered its latest trademark as required by the Lanham Act. This provision of U.S. law is MOST consistent with:
    A) socialist law.
    B) code law.
    C) Islamic law.
    D) common law.

    Answer: B Difficulty: Hard Page: 179

47. Under common law in the United States, all of the following would be considered to be "Acts of God" EXCEPT:
    A) floods.
    B) lightning.
    C) earthquakes.
    D) labor strikes.

    Answer: D Difficulty: Medium Page: 180

48. The America-First Corporation has occasionally been unable to fulfill a contract due to "Acts of God." Under which of the following legal systems would the firm enjoy the BROADEST interpretation of this defense against failure to perform?
    A) code law.
    B) Islamic law.
    C) common law.
    D) socialist law.

    Answer: A Difficulty: Hard Page: 181

49. Islamic law is based on an interpretation of the:
 A) Torah.
 B) Koran.
 C) Apocrapha.
 D) Bible.

 Answer: B Difficulty: Medium Page: 181

50. The America-First Corporation is preparing to enter a number of Muslim countries. The firm must understand that in these nations, the PRIMARY concern of law is:
 A) religious freedom.
 B) economic profit.
 C) contract creation.
 D) social justice.

 Answer: D Difficulty: Hard Page: 181

51. Islamic law is unique in its prohibition against the:
 A) payment of interest.
 B) use of contracts.
 C) use of arbitration.
 D) leasing.

 Answer: A Difficulty: Medium Page: 181

52. The America-First Corporation routinely applies interest to the credit plans it offers its customers. The firm is MOST likely to have its practices questioned in countries that operate under:
 A) civil law.
 B) code law.
 C) Islamic law.
 D) socialist law.

 Answer: C Difficulty: Hard Page: 181

53. The America-First Corporation is concerned about the prohibition against the use of interest under Islamic law. The firm may avoid this problem by negotiating a mutually acceptable margin to be included in:
 A) trades with markups.
 B) cost-plus sales.
 C) leasing arrangements.
 D) any, or all, of the above.

 Answer: D Difficulty: Hard Page: 181

# Chapter 7 The International Legal Environment: Playing by the Rules

54. In its original form, which of the following is MOST "foreign" to the basic precepts of U.S. laws?
    A) socialist law.
    B) Islamic law.
    C) commercial law.
    D) code law.

    Answer: A Difficulty: Medium Page: 182

55. Socialist law was primarily based on:
    A) religious dicta.
    B) the sanctity of private property.
    C) political/economic philosophy.
    D) profit maximization.

    Answer: C Difficulty: Medium Page: 182

56. All of the following are forms of law that may affect international business EXCEPT:
    A) Islamic law.
    B) common law.
    C) international commercial law.
    D) code law.

    Answer: C Difficulty: Medium Page: 182

57. The World Court handles legal disputes:
    A) between governments.
    B) between a company and a government.
    C) between two companies.
    D) between private citizens and a company.

    Answer: A Difficulty: Medium Page: 182

58. Jurisdiction in the event of legal dispute is MOST easily determined when:
    A) the contract was entered into under socialist law.
    B) the contract contains a jurisdictional clause.
    C) the contract was performed under civil law.
    D) the World Court intervenes.

    Answer: B Difficulty: Medium Page: 184

59. A nonbinding agreement between parties to resolve disputes by asking a third party to mediate differences is the basis of:
A) litigation.
B) adjudication.
C) conciliation.
D) arbitration.

Answer: C Difficulty: Easy Page: 184

60. The America-First Corporation has just begun doing business in China. In the event of a dispute with one of its host suppliers or customers, which of the following should be the FIRST step taken to seek resolution of the problem?
A) conciliation.
B) informal negotiation.
C) arbitration.
D) litigation.

Answer: B Difficulty: Hard Page: 184

61. Which of the following is the LEAST preferred means of settling an international commercial dispute?
A) arbitration.
B) conciliation.
C) negotiation.
D) litigation.

Answer: D Difficulty: Medium Page: 184

62. The America-First Corporation has encountered problems with some of its Chinese business partners. Which of the following is MOST likely to be successful in dealing with this problem?
A) arbitration.
B) litigation.
C) forced contractual compliance.
D) conciliation.

Answer: D Difficulty: Hard Page: 184

63. The America-First Corporation believes that arbitration is the best way to settle trade disputes. The firm can BEST ensure that arbitration will be used in the event of a dispute by:
A) incorporating an arbitration clause into all of its contracts.
B) refusing to negotiate.
C) avoiding litigation at any cost.
D) becoming a member of the International Chamber of Commerce.

Answer: A Difficulty: Hard Page: 185

64. Which of the following requires signatory countries to automatically uphold foreign arbitral awards issued in member countries?
A) the International Chamber of Commerce
B) the World Court
C) the New York Convention
D) the International Arbitral Association

Answer: C Difficulty: Medium Page: 186

65. Even if a firm "wins" an international lawsuit, many experts believe that it still lost because of the:
A) costs incurred.
B) frustrating delays involved.
C) extended aggravation.
D) combined impact of all of the considerations above.

Answer: D Difficulty: Medium Page: 186

66. Which of the following "costs" of litigation is MOST likely to be overlooked?
A) damage to the firm's image or public relations efforts.
B) difficulty in collecting any judgement.
C) fear of unfair treatment in foreign courts.
D) the high cost of litigation.

Answer: A Difficulty: Medium Page: 186

67. America-First is having problems with several of its foreign "partners." Which of the following approaches would the firm probably be advised to try FIRST?
A) conciliation.
B) arbitration.
C) placation.
D) litigation.

Answer: C Difficulty: Hard Page: 187

68. The processes, formulas, and designs owned by a firm are considered to be:
A) its product.
B) intellectual property.
C) a logo.
D) common law goods.

Answer: B Difficulty: Medium Page: 187

# Chapter 7 The International Legal Environment: Playing by the Rules

69. The America-First Corporation is preparing to enter Jordan. The firm can best protect its trademarks in that country by:
    A) registering all trademarks in Jordan immediately.
    B) notifying Jordanian officials of the firm's prior usage.
    C) preparing to "buy back" its trademarks.
    D) creating all-new Jordanian trademarks.

    Answer: A Difficulty: Hard Page: 190

70. All of the following are major international conventions concerned with the recognition and protection of intellectual property rights EXCEPT:
    A) the Paris Convention for the Protection of Industrial Property.
    B) the Inter-American Convention.
    C) the Madrid Arrangement.
    D) the Registration Cooperation Treaty.

    Answer: D Difficulty: Medium Page: 191

71. Unlike the United States, Japanese patent law:
    A) protects individual inventors.
    B) maintains secrecy for patent applications.
    C) grants a patent within 24 months.
    D) promotes technology sharing.

    Answer: D Difficulty: Medium Page: 192

72. In many countries, a patent holder forfeits protection if the patent is not used within an AVERAGE of:
    A) five years.
    B) ten years.
    C) one year.
    D) three years.

    Answer: D Difficulty: Medium Page: 192

73. In which of the following countries is the government MOST willing to assist a patent or trademark owner in his or her efforts to police and prosecute cases of piracy or infringement?
    A) China.
    B) United States.
    C) Japan.
    D) Korea.

    Answer: B Difficulty: Medium Page: 192

# Chapter 7 The International Legal Environment: Playing by the Rules

74. Which of the following is typically the MOST difficult to overcome for the marketer who would like to use a standardized marketing plan in all the foreign countries in which it operates?
    A) language differences.
    B) legal differences.
    C) customs differences.
    D) habit differences.

    Answer: B Difficulty: Medium Page: 193

75. The America-First Corporation boasts that its headache remedy offers "the fastest relief known to man." In its Canadian market, this statement may violate the:
    A) credulous person standard.
    B) comparative advertising standard.
    C) anti-puffery proviso.
    D) Code of Good Advertising Practice.

    Answer: A Difficulty: Hard Page: 194

76. The America-First Corporation has noted that many nations are passing laws that regulate the management and recycling of packaging waste. The firm will face the MOST stringent of such laws in:
    A) China.
    B) Korea.
    C) Japan.
    D) Germany.

    Answer: D Difficulty: Hard Page: 195

77. A U.S. firm that violates U.S. law in a foreign country:
    A) is outside the jurisdiction of U.S. courts.
    B) is subject only to the mandates of the World Court.
    C) is subject to U.S. law under the "objective" theory of jurisdiction.
    D) will lose its membership in the International Chamber of Commerce.

    Answer: C Difficulty: Medium Page: 197

78. Which of the following makes it illegal for companies to pay bribes to foreign officials, candidates, or political parties?
    A) the Sherman Anti-trust Act
    B) the Robinson-Patman Act
    C) the Smoot-Hawley Act
    D) the Foreign Corrupt Practices Act

    Answer: D Difficulty: Easy Page: 197

79. Questions of jurisdiction and application regulating U.S. antitrust laws are ultimately based on interpretation of:
A) the Robinson-Patman Act.
B) the Sherman Anti-trust Act.
C) the Clayton Anti-trust Act.
D) the Smoot-Hawley Trust Act.

Answer: B Difficulty: Medium Page: 199

80. The America-First Corporation has exported pesticides that failed to meet U.S. standards to foreign countries whose standards are less stringent. The firm may be subject to trade restrictions designed to protect U.S. consumers from:
A) tertiary boycotts.
B) exchange manipulations.
C) a "circle of poison."
D) misleading advertising

Answer: C Difficulty: Hard Page: 199

**Fill in the Blank Questions**

81. The basis for the majority of the world's legal systems are derived from ______________ law, derived from English law; ______________ or ______________ law, derived from Roman law; and ______________ law, derived from the Koran.

Answer: common; civil or code; Islamic Difficulty: Medium Page: 178

82. ______________ law seeks to apply interpretation based on past higher court decisions and customary principles of law to similar current cases in dispute.

Answer: Common Difficulty: Medium Page: 178

83. Code law is based on ______________, ______________, and ______________ codes composed on an "all-inclusive" system of written rules.

Answer: commercial; civil; criminal Difficulty: Medium Page: 179

84. Under common law, the ownership of intellectual property is established by ______________; under code-law, ownership is determined by ______________.

Answer: use; registration Difficulty: Medium Page: 179

85. The America-First Corporation has failed to perform on a contract when its shipments to England were lost at sea in a major unexpected typhoon. The firm's attempts to avoid liability for non-performance will probably be based on a claim that the loss results from a(n) _______________.

Answer: "Act of God" Difficulty: Hard Page: 180

86. Religious duties and obligations as well as the secular aspect of law regulating human acts is at the basis of _______________ law.

Answer: Islamic Difficulty: Medium Page: 181

87. The America-First Corporation is seeking to avoid the prohibition against interest or usury under Islamic law. This may be accomplished by employing trades with mutually acceptable _______________, using _______________ sales, or emphasizing _______________ arrangements.

Answer: markups; cost-plus; leasing Difficulty: Hard Page: 181

88. International legal disputes can arise _______________; _______________; and, _______________.

Answer: between governments; between a company and a government; between two companies Difficulty: Medium Page: 182

89. Jurisdiction is usually determined on the basis of jurisdictional clauses contained in the _______________, on where the contract was _______________, and where the provisions of the contract were _______________.

Answer: contract; entered into; performed Difficulty: Medium Page: 184

90. If informal settlement of a dispute is not possible, _______________ is usually recommended as the next best step.

Answer: conciliation Difficulty: Medium Page: 184

91. The America-First Corporation has not been able to settle a dispute with one of its foreign partners through informal discussions or conciliation. The firm should probably attempt _______________ next.

Answer: arbitration Difficulty: Hard Page: 185

92. A(n) _______________ clause is recommended by the International Chamber of Commerce to ensure that disputes are effectively dealt with.

Answer: arbitration Difficulty: Medium Page: 186

# Chapter 7 The International Legal Environment: Playing by the Rules

93. _______________ should be the last step a firm takes in its attempts to settle a dispute.

    Answer: litigation  Difficulty: Medium  Page: 186

94. In recent years, MNCs have had to deal with losses that result from the _______________ or _______________ of goods that cause increasing losses.

    Answer: counterfeiting; piracy  Difficulty: Medium  Page: 187

95. Generally, the ownership of intellectual property rights is established by _______________ in a common law country, and by _______________ in many code-law nations.

    Answer: prior use; registration  Difficulty: Medium  Page: 190

96. The America-First Corporation is currently operating in the European Union. Under the _______________ of the EU, the firm will have intellectual property protection throughout all member states.

    Answer: European Patent Convention  Difficulty: Hard  Page: 192

97. As interpreted in Canada, "the credulous person standard" may threaten advertising messages dismissed as harmless _______________ in the U.S.

    Answer: puffery  Difficulty: Medium  Page: 194

98. The America First Corporation is preparing to launch a "World Wide Web presence." To protect its global sites, the firm should register its _____ names in each nation in which it operates.

    Answer: domain  Difficulty: Hard  Page: 201

99. In the rush to collect sales taxes from global websites, it has been proposed that _____ be considered as "virtual permanent establishments."

    Answer: Servers  Difficulty: Medium  Page: 202-203

100. The greatest difficulty in creating a uniform cyberlaw is being faced by the ______.

    Answer: European Union  Difficulty: Medium  Page: 201

# Chapter 7 The International Legal Environment: Playing by the Rules

## Essay Questions

101. Briefly identify the four bases for modern law. Why is it important for the international marketer to understand the basic precepts of, and differences between, these legal systems?

Answer:
The world's legal systems are based on Islamic, socialist, common, or code law. The various systems exhibit significant differences that are important to the international marketer. Islamic law does not allow the imposition of interest. Socialist law employs unique, fluid applications of basic legal concepts based on economic conditions. Common law is founded on a heritage of precedents and interpretations. Code law consists of a system of inclusive rules. The international marketer must be familiar with the basics of the systems under which they operate and appreciate the impact of the unique features of each.

Difficulty: Hard Page: 178-182

102. It is important to know what the law says—but it is MORE important to understand the trend of thinking in the courts and regulatory agencies. Do you agree? Why? Under which legal system(s) would this be MOST true?

Answer:
Generally, this is true. The law is a dynamic entity that may be, and is, interpreted to fit the times. The "meaning" or "spirit" of the law is constantly being redefined by those charged with administering it. For this reason, the trend of thinking in the courts and regulatory agencies is of greater importance than the mere words found in a statute. While the statement is generally true, it is even more important in those nations that employ a system of common law.

Difficulty: Hard Page: 178-182

103. How does arbitration differ from conciliation? Why are both of these approaches to dispute resolution preferable to litigation?

Difficulty: Hard Page: 184-187
Answer:
Conciliation, formal or informal, is nonbinding by its nature--its successdepends upon the goodwill of the parties involved. The decisions reached in formal arbitration, by contrast, are enforceable under the law. The process can be greatly strengthened through the inclusion of an arbitration clause in the original contract. The use of litigation is extensive and time consuming--and tends to generate ill will between the litigants as well as a poor public image.

# Chapter 7 The International Legal Environment: Playing by the Rules

104. Why has the theft, or piracy, of intellectual property become a greater problem in recent years? How can this problem be addressed?

Answer:
As the service economy has grown worldwide, so has the opportunity for piracy. Movies, recordings, computer programs and video games are expensive to create, but highly profitable. The fact that such products can be easily, and cheaply, copied has made them prime targets for piracy. The problem requires a greater standardization of international law and-- more importantly--a broader agreement among nations to police violations and prosecute violators.

Difficulty: Hard Page: 187-193

105. How has the growing concern with environmental issues affected the international marketer? What opportunities do the problems resulting from such concerns offer for the international marketer?

Answer:
Worldwide environmental concern has expanded beyond traditional manufacturing/pollution problems to focus on the impact of packaging. A ready-made market exists for packaging materials that provide better product protection with less volume and/or waste and that are easier and less expensive to recycle. The creation of such materials would allow the marketer to reduce costs while garnering a favorable public reaction.

Difficulty: Hard Page: 195-196

# Chapter 8 Developing a Global Vision through Market Research

## True/False Questions

1. Marketing research is the systematic gathering, recording, and analyzing of data to provide information useful in marketing decision making.

   Answer: True Difficulty: Easy Page: 208

2. While international marketing research is fundamentally similar to domestic marketing research efforts, it is subject to different environmental and communication challenges.

   Answer: True Difficulty: Medium Page: 208

3. A marketing research study is ALWAYS a compromise dictated by limits of time, cost, and the present state of the art.

   Answer: True Difficulty: Medium Page: 208

4. While domestic marketing research rarely produces data regarding political stability, cultural attributes, or geographic characteristics, such information is often a critical first step in international marketing research.

   Answer: True Difficulty: Medium Page: 209

5. The America-First Corporation is preparing a marketing research study to guide its initial entry into a new foreign market. The firm should understand that the first stage of the research process, problem definition and the establishment of research objectives, will be crucial to the success of the project.

   Answer: True Difficulty: Hard Page: 210

6. The availability, reliability, comparability, and validity of secondary data in foreign markets is similar to that the marketer is accustomed to enjoying in the United States.

   Answer: False Difficulty: Medium Page: 211

7. Less-developed nations are especially susceptible to data reliability problems stemming from overly optimistic estimates and/or distortions related to tax evasion attempts.

   Answer: True Difficulty: Medium Page: 212

8. The lack of uniform definitions for products, processes, and types of stores/transactions are a major source of comparability problems in the secondary data available to international marketers.

   Answer: True Difficulty: Medium Page: 213

9. Generally, the availability and accuracy of recorded secondary data increases as the level of economic development increases.

   Answer: True Difficulty: Easy Page: 213

10. Prior to introducing its latest new product, the America-First Corporation conducted a massive survey of consumer opinion in each of its foreign markets. The firm was collecting primary data to guide its marketing efforts.

    Answer: True Difficulty: Hard Page: 214

11. Quantitative research is used to generate information to aid in more clearly formulating a problem for later, more qualitative study.

    Answer: False Difficulty: Medium Page: 214

12. The focus group is probably the most widely used form of quantitative research employed to gather primary data.

    Answer: False Difficulty: Medium Page: 215

13. Most problems encountered in collecting primary data in international marketing stem from economic differences among countries.

    Answer: False Difficulty: Easy Page: 216

14. Due to their speed and low cost, telephone surveys are the most efficient and widely used method of collecting international marketing research data.

    Answer: False Difficulty: Medium Page: 218

15. The lack of detailed socio-economic data in many foreign countries may force the international marketer to use convenience, instead of the more accurate probability, sampling.

    Answer: True Difficulty: Medium Page: 218

16. The most universal survey sampling problem in foreign countries is the literacy barrier.

    Answer: False Difficulty: Easy Page: 218

17. In back translation, the questionnaire is translated from one language to another, then a second party translates it back to the original to check for clarity and accuracy.

    Answer: True Difficulty: Easy Page: 220

18. In an attempt to avoid inaccuracies resulting from the varying meanings of idioms commonly used in several languages, the America-First Corporation translates its marketing message into the language of the host country, employs two translators to translate the resulting message back into English, and compares results. The firm is employing parallel translation.

    Answer: True Difficulty: Hard Page: 220

19. Although the process of decentering may produce the most valid instrument for gathering survey data, its comparatively high cost renders its use inappropriate.

    Answer: False Difficulty: Medium Page: 220

20. Decentered research deals with countries that have different languages, economies, social structures, behavior, and attitude patterns.

    Answer: False Difficulty: Easy Page: 220

21. The America-First Corporation is preparing to engage in multicultural marketing research. The firm must ensure that the same data collection method(s) are employed in all of the countries involved or the reliability of the effort will suffer.

    Answer: False Difficulty: Hard Page: 220

22. While the Internet has proven useful for routine transactions with established foreign customers and/or suppliers, cultural and linguistic problems preclude its usefulness in international marketing research.

    Answer: False Difficulty: Medium Page: 222

23. The international market researcher should understand the target country's culture, be capable of adapting research findings as necessary, and exhibit a critical attitude in handling both primary and secondary data.

    Answer: True Difficulty: Easy Page: 223

24. In recent years, there has been a strong trend toward greater decentralization of the research function in order to take full advantage of the cost savings made possible by computerization.

    Answer: True Difficulty: Medium Page: 225

25. The "ideal" approach to multi-country research is to have local researchers in each country, with close coordination between the client company and the local research companies.

    Answer: True Difficulty: Medium Page: 226

26. The America-First Corporation has not been able to locate data necessary to assessing market opportunity and estimating demand for its products in some of its foreign markets. The firm may approximate current trends in market demand by using local production figures plus imports--with adjustments for exports and current inventory levels.

    Answer: True Difficulty: Hard Page: 228

27. Under the expert opinion technique for estimating market demand, the marketer assumes that demand for a product develops in much the same way in all countries as comparable economic development occurs in each country.

    Answer: True Difficulty: Easy Page: 228

28. The use of the analogy approach to demand estimation assumes that demand for a product develops in much the same way in all countries as comparable economic development occurs in each country.

    Answer: True Difficulty: Easy Page: 228

29. Triangulation is an attempt to forecast demand by comparing estimates produced by different sources.

    Answer: True Difficulty: Medium Page: 228

30. The America-First Corporation is developing its first international forecast. Accuracy is likely to be best if the firm can augment macroeconomic data base approaches with interviews conducted with present and potential customers.

    Answer: True Difficulty: Hard Page: 229

**Multiple Choice Questions**

31. The KEY component in developing successful marketing strategies is:
    A) information.
    B) advertising.
    C) packaging.
    D) a low price.

    Answer: A Difficulty: Medium Page: 208

32. All of the following are basic limitations faced by all market researchers EXCEPT:
    A) time.
    B) cost.
    C) government prohibitions.
    D) the current state of the art.

    Answer: C Difficulty: Medium Page: 208

# Chapter 8 Developing a Global Vision through Market Research

33. DOMESTIC marketing research efforts are PRIMARILY focused on which of the following types of information?
    A) general information about the country, area, and/or market.
    B) information required to forecast political trends in the country.
    C) information required to forecast social, economic, or consumer trends in the country.
    D) specific market information used to make marketing mix decisions and develop marketing plans.

    Answer: D Difficulty: Medium Page: 209

34. The America-First Corporation is preparing to enter a new foreign market with which it is completely unfamiliar. The firm's MARKETING research efforts should focus on:
    A) the nation's economic, inflation, and business cycle trends.
    B) the nation's sociological and political climate.
    C) the nation's technological environment.
    D) all of the above are vital.

    Answer: D Difficulty: Hard Page: 209

35. Which of the following factors is the MOST favorable argument in favor of increasing the amount of research carried out in support of international marketing?
    A) the cost of international marketing research.
    B) the time required to carry out international marketing research.
    C) the cost associated with marketing failures.
    D) failure to appreciate the role and impact of international research.

    Answer: C Difficulty: Medium Page: 209

36. A marketing research study is always a compromise dictated by the limits of:
    A) time.
    B) cost.
    C) human elements.
    D) all of the above limit the use of marketing research.

    Answer: D Difficulty: Easy Page: 209

37. The America-First Corporation is preparing to launch a major marketing research effort that will guide its international programs in its prime foreign markets. Which of the following stages of the marketing research process is MOST important to the firm's success?
    A) purchasing appropriate computer equipment.
    B) defining the research problem and establishment of research objectives.
    C) identifying the sources of information to fulfill research objectives.
    D) gathering relevant data from secondary and/or primary sources.

    Answer: B Difficulty: Medium Page: 210

38. The unique difficulties involved in international marketing exert their FIRST, and perhaps GREATEST, impact during which of the following stages of the marketing research process?
A) analyzing, interpreting, and presenting results.
B) defining the research problem and establishing research objectives.
C) determining the sources of information to fulfill research objectives.
D) gathering relevant data from secondary and/or primary sources.

Answer: B Difficulty: Medium Page: 210

39. The self-reference criterion is likely to exert its FIRST, and perhaps most damaging, influence during which of the following stages of the international marketing research process?
A) analyzing, interpreting, and presenting results.
B) determining the sources of information to fulfill research objectives.
C) defining the research problem and establishing research objectives.
D) gathering relevant data from secondary and/or primary sources.

Answer: C Difficulty: Medium Page: 210

40. Pat Dobson is charged with defining the research problem to guide the America-First Corporation's first attempt at international marketing research. Pat's years of experience in domestic marketing research is generally considered to be an asset, but that experience may also lead to a GREATER problem associated with the impact of the:
A) self-reference criterion.
B) foreign-bias phenomenon.
C) repetitive-practice syndrome.
D) iterative-action syndrome.

Answer: A Difficulty: Hard Page: 210

41. After the research problem has been defined, the researcher should next:
A) prepare the final report.
B) immediately begin the collection of primary data.
C) analyze, interpret, and present results.
D) identify and evaluate sources of secondary data.

Answer: D Difficulty: Medium Page: 211

42. Data relevant to a marketing research problem that has been collected, analyzed, and made available by a source or agency other than the researching firm is called:
A) primary data.
B) secondary data.
C) public data.
D) prototypical data.

Answer: B Difficulty: Easy Page: 211

# Chapter 8 Developing a Global Vision through Market Research

43. Which of the following is the largest single source of secondary data in the world?
    A) trade associations.
    B) the United States.
    C) the Organization for Economic Cooperation and Development.
    D) the United States government.

    Answer: D Difficulty: Medium Page: 211

44. Assuming that secondary data is available in a foreign country, a researcher must be concerned with:
    A) the validity of secondary data.
    B) the reliability of secondary data.
    C) the comparability of secondary data.
    D) ALL of the above are critical factors.

    Answer: D Difficulty: Medium Page: 212

45. The America-First Corporation is preparing to enter the Russian market. As the firm begins its efforts to collect secondary data on its new market, the FIRST problem it is likely to encounter will probably relate to the:
    A) limited availability of secondary data.
    B) reliability of secondary data.
    C) comparability of secondary data.
    D) validity of secondary data.

    Answer: A Difficulty: Hard Page: 212

46. Market data produced by foreign countries often reflect political objectives rather than economic reality. This phenomenon will reflect upon the:
    A) availability of secondary data.
    B) reliability of secondary data.
    C) comparability of secondary data.
    D) validity of secondary data.

    Answer: B Difficulty: Easy Page: 212

47. The America-First Corporation is unsure about the reliability of the market statistics available in many of its foreign markets. Which of the following sources is probably the MOST accurate of the sources available to the firm?
    A) the U.S. Census Bureau.
    B) the World Bank Statistical Consortium.
    C) the Organization of Economic Cooperation and Development.
    D) the International Statistical Congress.

    Answer: C Difficulty: Hard Page: 212-213

48. The tendency of many foreign nations to collect socio-economic data on an infrequent and unpredictable schedule creates problems relevant to the:
A) currency of secondary data.
B) validity of secondary data.
C) reliability of secondary data.
D) cost of secondary data.

Answer: A Difficulty: Easy Page: 213

49. The fact that data are reported in different categories in different nations--or in categories that may be too broad to have specific value--has a DIRECT impact upon:
A) the reliability of secondary data.
B) the validity of secondary data.
C) the comparability of secondary data.
D) the availability of secondary data.

Answer: C Difficulty: Easy Page: 213

50. The America-First Corporation sells its products primarily through supermarkets throughout the world. The firm has found that the term "supermarket" HAS a variety of meanings among different nations. This fact DIRECTLY affected the:
A) validity of its secondary data.
B) comparability of its secondary data.
C) reliability of its secondary data.
D) availability of its secondary data.

Answer: B Difficulty: Hard Page: 213

51. Questions related to the entity collecting the data and the purposes for which the data were collected DIRECTLY impact the:
A) reliability of secondary data.
B) comparability of secondary data.
C) availability of secondary data.
D) accessibility of secondary data.

Answer: A Difficulty: Easy Page: 213

52. The America-First Corporation is especially concerned with the methodologies used in the collection of the secondary data it uses in some foreign countries. The firm is PRIMARILY concerned with the:
A) availability of secondary data.
B) accessibility of secondary data.
C) comparability of secondary data.
D) reliability of secondary data.

Answer: D Difficulty: Hard Page: 213

53. Checking the consistency of one set of secondary data against other data of known accuracy is an effective and often used way of judging:
    A) availability of secondary data.
    B) validity of secondary data.
    C) comparability of secondary data.
    D) accessibility of secondary data.

    Answer: B Difficulty: Easy Page: 213

54. In general, the availability and accuracy of recorded secondary data:
    A) increase as the level of economic development increases.
    B) decrease as the level of economic development increases.
    C) increase as the level of economic development decreases.
    D) exhibit no relationship with the level of economic development.

    Answer: A Difficulty: Medium Page: 213

55. Data that is collected for the first time by a decision maker interested in a specific problem is called:
    A) secondary data.
    B) specified data.
    C) primary data.
    D) published data.

    Answer: C Difficulty: Easy Page: 214

56. After exhausting available secondary information, the America-First Corporation still does not feel that it has sufficient information to guide its international marketing efforts. The firm should next:
    A) produce the best marketing plan it can with the data it has.
    B) collect primary data.
    C) hire an outside expert to expand the search for secondary date.
    D) abandon its foreign marketing plans.

    Answer: B Difficulty: Hard Page: 214

57. The use of structured, closed-ended questions is the "hallmark" of:
    A) primary research.
    B) secondary research.
    C) qualitative research.
    D) quantitative research.

    Answer: D Difficulty: Easy Page: 214

# Chapter 8 Developing a Global Vision through Market Research

58. Which of the following types of research is MOST compatible with the use of precise, statistical analysis of results?
    A) quantitative research.
    B) exploratory research.
    C) qualitative research.
    D) focus group research.

    Answer: A Difficulty: Medium Page: 214

59. Survey research is MOST closely associated with:
    A) qualitative research.
    B) focus group research.
    C) quantitative research.
    D) exploratory research.

    Answer: C Difficulty: Medium Page: 214

60. The America-First Corporation has developed a structured, closed-end questionnaire for use in an ambitious survey of consumer demographics in its foreign markets. The firm is preparing to engage in:
    A) qualitative research.
    B) quantitative research.
    C) focus group research.
    D) secondary research.

    Answer: B Difficulty: Hard Page: 200

61. Open-ended, in-depth questions that elicit unstructured responses that reflect the respondent's thoughts and feelings on a subject are at the core of:
    A) primary research.
    B) quantitative research.
    C) secondary research.
    D) qualitative research.

    Answer: D Difficulty: Easy Page: 214

62. The most commonly employed form of qualitative questioning is:
    A) the focus group interview.
    B) primary research.
    C) secondary research.
    D) survey research.

    Answer: A Difficulty: Easy Page: 215

## Chapter 8 Developing a Global Vision through Market Research

63. The America-First Corporation is conducting a series of focus group interviews to gain a better understanding of its foreign markets. The firm is using the most common form of:
    A) survey research.
    B) qualitative research.
    C) quantitative research.
    D) secondary research.

    Answer: B Difficulty: Hard Page: 215

64. Which of the following types of research is <u>MOST</u> likely to be used to assist in the problem-definition stage of the marketing research process?
    A) quantitative research.
    B) survey research.
    C) qualitative research.
    D) statistical research.

    Answer: C Difficulty: Medium Page: 215

65. The America-First Corporation employed a series of focus group interviews to generate a potential brand name for its new product. Prior to making a final choice, the firm would like to gain assurance that the focus group's preference is shared by the larger population. For this purpose, the firm is likely to use:
    A) more, and larger, focus groups.
    B) qualitative research.
    C) secondary research.
    D) survey research.

    Answer: D Difficulty: Hard Page: 215

66. Most problems encountered in collecting primary data for international marketing research stem from:
    A) cultural differences among countries.
    B) the paucity of secondary research.
    C) the diversity of statistical concepts employed.
    D) United Nations' interference.

    Answer: A Difficulty: Medium Page: 216

67. The America-First Corporation is preparing to conduct focus groups in several underdeveloped nations to guide its efforts to introduce its high-tech products in the area. This firm is likely to encounter problems related to respondent's difficulties in formulating needs, attitudes, and opinions about goods:
    A) whose use may not be understood.
    B) that are not in common use in the community.
    C) that have never been available.
    D) all of the above may create problems.

    Answer: D Difficulty: Hard Page: 216

68. The GREATEST problem of sampling stems from:
    A) the difficulty of adequate translation.
    B) the use of different statistical techniques in various countries.
    C) the lack of adequate demographic data and sampling lists.
    D) the lack of trained interviewers.

    Answer: C Difficulty: Medium Page: 217

69. The America-First Corporation is preparing to introduce a new product in Sri Lanka targeted at middle class males. The firm would like to assess its likelihood of success by conducting a consumer survey prior to introduction. Which of the following survey approaches would be LEAST appropriate?
    A) the telephone interview.
    B) the mail interview.
    C) the personal interview.
    D) the focus group interview.

    Answer: A Difficulty: Hard Page: 217

70. The lack of detailed, accurate social and economic information is MOST damaging to the use of:
    A) convenience samples.
    B) probability samples.
    C) focus groups.
    D) qualitative questionnaires.

    Answer: B Difficulty: Medium Page: 218

71. Which of the following creates problems in drawing a random sample?
    A) no officially recognized census of population
    B) incomplete and out-of-date telephone directories
    C) no accurate maps of population centers
    D) ALL of the above are serious problems.

    Answer: D Difficulty: Medium Page: 218

72. The most universal survey sampling problem in foreign countries stems from:
    A) different legal systems.
    B) the language barrier.
    C) the use of different statistical concept.
    D) universal bans against door-to-door interviewing.

    Answer: B Difficulty: Medium Page: 218

73. When developing a questionnaire for use in a foreign country, the America-First Corporation first translates the instrument into the foreign language and then has a second party translate the result back into the original language. The firm is attempting to ensure clarity of meaning through the use of:
A) back translation.
B) parallel translation.
C) decentering.
D) recentering.

Answer: A Difficulty: Hard Page: 220

74. Which of the following employs two translators to translate a questionnaire from its original language to a foreign language and back again to overcome problems that may be introduced by the use of idioms common to both languages?
A) back translation.
B) decentering.
C) parallel translation.
D) recentering.

Answer: C Difficulty: Easy Page: 220

75. The America-First Corporation employs a successive iteration of translations and retranslations of a questionnaire by a series of different translators until a translation is produced that can be perfectly converted into the original English. The firm is utilizing the technique called:
A) back translation.
B) parallel translation.
C) recentering.
D) decentering.

Answer: D Difficulty: Hard Page: 220

76. The cornerstone of a good survey is:
A) probability sampling.
B) full communication.
C) demographic lists.
D) a sophisticated telephone system.

Answer: B Difficulty: Medium Page: 221

77. The America-First Corporation conducts research in a variety of foreign markets that have different languages, economies, social structures, behaviors, and attitude patterns. The firm is using:
A) decentered research.
B) multicultural research.
C) back translation.
D) parallel research.

Answer: B Difficulty: Hard Page: 222

78. The America-First Corporation prides itself on using the very latest research techniques. The firm is likely to be in the forefront with regard to marketing research efforts using:
A) focus groups.
B) the Internet.
C) extrapolation.
D) analogy analysis.

Answer: B Difficulty: Hard Page: 223

79. In order to produce meaningful results, the foreign market researcher must:
A) possess a high degree of cultural understanding.
B) possess a creative talent for adapting research findings.
C) possess a skeptical attitude in handling both primary and secondary data.
D) ALL of the above traits.

Answer: D Difficulty: Medium Page: 225

80. The key to successful use of the export opinion approach to estimating demand is:
A) analogy.
B) extrapolation.
C) triangulation.
D) selection of an appropriate MIS coefficient.

Answer: C Difficulty: Easy Page: 228

## Fill in the Blank Questions

81. Marketing research is traditionally defined as the systematic _______________, _______________, and _____________ of data to provide information useful in marketing decision-making.

Answer: gathering; recording; analyzing Difficulty: Medium Page: 208

# Chapter 8 Developing a Global Vision through Market Research

82. International marketing research is differentiated from marketing research by its emphasis on a country's ______________ stability, ______________ attributes, and ______________ characteristics.

    Answer: political; cultural; geographic  Difficulty: Medium  Page: 209

83. The America-First Corporation is preparing to conduct marketing research in one of its potential foreign markets. The most crucial step in this process will be the clear definition of the research ______________ and the establishment of specific research ______________.

    Answer: problem; objectives  Difficulty: Hard  Page: 210

84. The America-First Corporation has had a history of poor problem definition activities in its international marketing development efforts. This problem is likely the result of its domestic managers defining the problem in the light of their ______________ criterion.

    Answer: self-reference  Difficulty: Hard  Page: 210

85. While international researchers are well-advised to turn to secondary data first to minimize cost, they must be careful to assess the ______________, ______________, ______________, and ______________ of such information.

    Answer: availability; reliability; comparability; validity  Difficulty: Medium  Page: 212

86. The America-First Corporation routinely checks the consistency of one set of secondary data against other data of known accuracy. The firm is attempting to assess the ______________ of potential secondary data.

    Answer: validity  Difficulty: Hard  Page: 213

87. If critical research questions remain after a firm has exhausted secondary data, it must seek to gather ______________ data.

    Answer: primary  Difficulty: Medium  Page: 214

88. Research projects that require a high degree of statistical precision are likely to emphasize the use of ______________ research.

    Answer: quantitative  Difficulty: Medium  Page: 214

89. The America-First Corporation is extremely careful in its efforts to define the problem in its international research as precisely as possible and to identify relevant questions for inquiry. For this purpose, the firm is MOST likely to employ ______________ research.

    Answer: qualitative  Difficulty: Hard  Page: 215

90. The majority of the problems encountered in attempting to gather primary data in foreign countries derive from ______________ differences among nations.

Answer: cultural  Difficulty: Medium  Page: 216

91. The greatest problem of sampling stems from the lack of adequate ______________ data and available lists from which to draw meaningful ______________.

Answer: demographic; samples  Difficulty: Medium  Page: 217

92. Language barriers, compounded by subtle differences in ______________ and the low-level of ______________ existent in many foreign countries are responsible for most universal problems encountered in international marketing research.

Answer: idiom; literacy  Difficulty: Medium  Page: 218-219

93. To avoid language difficulties, the America-First Corporation routinely employs two translators—one to translate from English to the foreign language, and another to translate from the foreign language to English. The firm is attempting to improve communication through the use of ______________.

Answer: back translation  Difficulty: Hard  Page: 220

94. To avoid the problems created by the use of idioms, a firm may utilize ______________ in developing survey instruments.

Answer: parallel translation  Difficulty: Medium  Page: 220

95. The America-First Corporation uses a "pool" of translators to translate and retranslate its survey instruments until a "clean" version is obtained. The firm is employing the process of ______________.

Answer: decentering  Difficulty: Hard  Page: 220

96. Dealing with countries that have different languages, economies, social structures, behavior, and attitude patterns is at the core of ______________.

Answer: multicultural research  Difficulty: Medium  Page: 222

97. In today's climate, the ______________ offers the fastest means of accessing the widest possible range of secondary data.

Answer: Internet  Difficulty: Medium  Page: 223

98. The America-First Corporation tries to have local analysts in each of its foreign markets—and to maintain close coordination between them and domestic headquarters. The firm's approach is MOST consistent with the ______________ philosophy of international research.

    Answer: decentralization Difficulty: Hard Page: 226

99. For new foreign markets, especially those in which secondary data may be scarce, the use of ______________ may be the only way to generate market estimates.

    Answer: expert opinion Difficulty: Medium Page: 228

100. In some cases, a factor that is thought to move in the same way as the item of interests may be used as a(n) ______________ for that good.

    Answer: analogy Difficulty: Medium Page: 228

**Essay Questions**

101. Why is defining the problem and establishing research objectives the MOST critical step in the marketing research process? Why is this step even more crucial in international marketing?

    Answer:
    The problem definition and research objective stage provides the framework for all of the following stages. Based on their initial decision, the researcher will select information sources, determine the appropriate techniques for gathering the required data from those sources, and identify the best techniques to treat the report the data obtained. A mistake made here--an incorrect or incomplete understanding of the problem--dooms the effort to failure. Because the international marketer must operate in an unfamiliar environment that can be easily misunderstood, the care taken in this stage is even more vital to success.

    Difficulty: Hard Page: 210-211

102. Briefly summarize the problems associated with the use of secondary data in international marketing research. Given these problems, why should the international researcher consider its use at all?

    Answer:
    Secondary research is usually not as widely--or easily--available in foreign countries as in the United States. Even when available, the reliability of the data may be suspect. Often, the data may not be current and the way in which it is presented may not be comparable with other data the researcher must employ. However, these concerns are not unique to foreign countries--the questions cited above must always be addressed when using secondary data. If appropriate secondary data exists, it can be collected and used faster, and at less cost, than primary data. Because time and cost considerations are major constraints in any research effort, the attempt to locate and validate secondary data is worthwhile.

    Difficulty: Hard Page: 211-214

# Chapter 8 Developing a Global Vision through Market Research

103. Differentiate between the quantitative and qualitative approaches to gathering primary research data. What barriers often preclude the conduct of primary research? Are qualitative research studies "inferior" to quantitative studies? Defend your position.

Answer:
Quantitative research employs a structured, closed-end instrument to gather specific responses to specific areas of concern. Qualitative research utilizes open-ended questions designed to gather unstructured responses that reflect the respondent's thoughts or feelings about the subject of the study. By definition, quantitative study results can be presented with the precision of statistical analysis--while qualitative results must be evaluated and presented verbally. Quantitative studies appear on their face to be more objective than qualitative studies. Of course, in quantitative studies, the researcher chose the statistical method used and interpreted results--both are subjective actions. Both types of studies may be conducted on a probability (random) or nonprobability basis. Generally, random samples (which assure that all members of the target population have an equal and known chance of sample inclusion) are preferred over nonprobability approaches. Unfortunately, the demographic data and sampling lists taken for granted in the U.S. are not always available in other nations. A qualitative study may be the only form of research possible. Qualitative studies are not automatically inferior-indeed, a well-conceived qualitative study may be better than a poorly conceived quantitative study, even one done on a random basis. And, qualitative studies are better than the alternative of no research.

Difficulty: Hard Page: 214-216

104. What is the most common problem faced by international marketers conducting survey research? How can this problem be minimized?

Answer:
The language barrier is a universal problem facing international marketers. Not only are there basic language differences among nations--but some languages seem to share common idioms that actually carry quite different meanings. The problem can be attacked through back translation--the process of translating a document from the original English to a foreign language and then having a second party translate it back to the original to pinpoint problems for correction. Parallel translation employs more than two translators in the back translation to provide greater sensitivity to the problem of idioms. Decentering employs a successive iteration process of translation and retranslations of a document--each time by a different translator--in an effort to produce final wording that is equally clear in both languages.

Difficulty: Hard Page: 216-221

105. Briefly describe the three major methods that may be used to estimate market demand.

Answer:
For many market estimation efforts, especially in new foreign markets, expert opinion may be the only way to estimate market potential. The analogy approach seeks to measure items of interest by identifying an item that is considered a valid analogy for those goods and using it to predict how these products or factors will behave. If income elasticity coefficients are available or feasible, the researcher may use changes in income in a foreign market to predict product demands.

Difficulty: Hard Page: 227-229

# Chapter 9 Emerging Markets

## True/False Questions

1. During the next decade, the importance of emerging markets to world trade growth is expected to increase significantly.

   Answer: True   Difficulty: Medium   Page: 240

2. Economic development is generally understood to mean an increase in national production that results in an increase in the average per capita GDP—accompanied by a widespread distribution of the increased income.

   Answer: True   Difficulty: Easy   Page: 241

3. The America-First Corporation exports significant amounts of capital equipment and component parts to firms in Korea while purchasing petrochemical and electronic products for its own use. This type of trade flow is typical of the relationship between firms in more-developed countries and those in newly industrialized countries.

   Answer: True   Difficulty: Hard   Page: 242

4. State-owned enterprises (SOEs) have generally retarded rapid economic growth in many of the world's poorest countries.

   Answer: True   Difficulty: Medium   Page: 244

5. Infrastructure is a crucial component of the controllable elements facing marketers.

   Answer: False   Difficulty: Easy   Page: 248

6. An emerging nation must develop a significant capacity to produce before the level of consumption and the development of a distribution system becomes important.

   Answer: False   Difficulty: Medium   Page: 248

7. Economic dualism, the coexistence of communism and socialism sectors within the same economy, is a major factor complicating the estimation of market potential in less-developed countries.

   Answer: False   Difficulty: Easy   Page: 253

8. The America-First Corporation is often the first foreign firm to make significant investments in an emerging market. This is not a good strategy because most of the benefits from the firm's initial investments accrue to the host country and will make it easier for competitors to enter later.

   Answer: False   Difficulty: Hard   Page: 255

# Chapter 9 Emerging Markets

9. By 2010, imports to the Big Emerging Markets (BEMs) will be half as great as those made to nations of the industrialized world.

   Answer: True Difficulty: Medium Page: 255

10. The North American Free Trade Agreement (NAFTA) represents the culmination of a major political and economic revolution that has been going on for decades.

    Answer: True Difficulty: Easy Page: 258

11. Interregional trade alliances such as NAFTA mark the beginning of an era in which all nations of the Americas will eventually join as partners seeking mutual prosperity.

    Answer: True Difficulty: Easy Page: 260

12. The U.S. has deftly used fast-track NAFTA approvals to preclude the growth of Asian influence in Latin America.

    Answer: False Difficulty: Medium Page: 260

13. Because of the current chaos attending the shift from Marxist political/economic systems, Eastern Europe and the Baltic states are expected to rank among the least important emerging markets.

    Answer: False Difficulty: Medium Page: 260

14. The America-First Corporation is preparing to enter Eastern Europe. In selecting the country to enter, the firm has decided to focus on the United States' principal trading partner in the region. America-First is preparing to enter Poland.

    Answer: True Difficulty: Hard Page: 260

15. The Baltic states are ideally positioned geographically, culturally, and historically to serve as a bridge for trade between the west and the former USSR.

    Answer: True Difficulty: Medium Page: 263

16. Eastern Europe and the Baltic states are in the sphere of influence of China—as are most of the states that were formerly part of the USSR.

    Answer: False Difficulty: Medium Page: 263

17. The "Four Dragons" of the Pacific Rim are Singapore, Taiwan, South Korea, and Hong Kong.

    Answer: True Difficulty: Easy Page: 264

18. In recent years, the "Four Tigers" has successfully challenged Japan for Asian economic leadership.

    Answer: True Difficulty: Medium Page: 264

19. According to the International Monetary Fund, China is the world's largest economy.

    Answer: False Difficulty: Easy Page: 265

20. The America-First Corporation is preparing to enter China. The firm will be well advised to think of the country as a group of six regional markets rather than a single homogeneous nation.

    Answer: True Difficulty: Hard Page: 265

21. China's emergence into the front ranks of global economic powers depends to a large degree upon how well it handles the Hong Kong question.

    Answer: True Difficulty: Medium Page: 268

22. As soon as it gained its independence in 1950, India served as a model for economic growth admired and emulated by all other emerging nations of the region.

    Answer: False Difficulty: Medium Page: 269

23. India has the capacity to be one of the more prosperous nations in Asia if allowed to develop and live up to its potential

    Answer: True Difficulty: Medium Page: 270

24. Vietnam may become one of the latest "Asia Tigers" if it continues to follow the same pattern of development as other Southeast Asian companies.

    Answer: True Difficulty: Easy Page: 271

25. The America-First Corporation is considering entry into Vietnam. The firm's plans are doomed by the fact that Vietnam has poor infrastructure and its entry into that country is still prohibited by the Trading With the Enemy Act.

    Answer: False Difficulty: Hard Page: 271

26. Like many American firms, the America-First Corporation left South Africa in protest of its Apartheid policy. As the firm prepares to reenter this market, it must be prepared to face intense competition from foreign firms that took advantage of its absence to bolster their market positions.

    Answer: True Difficulty: Hard Page: 271

# Chapter 9 Emerging Markets

27. The future of Vietnam and South Africa depends primarily on government action and external investment by other governments and multinational firms.

    Answer: True Difficulty: Easy Page: 271

28. Although China has a huge population, the fact that the per capita income for the nation is only $400 means that non-significant market exists for such items as VCRs and television sets.

    Answer: False Difficulty: Medium Page: 271

29. As a country's per capita GNP surpasses the $5,000 level, its consumers become more brand conscious and begins to forego many local brands to seek out foreign brands they recognize.

    Answer: True Difficulty: Medium Page: 273

30. Marketers of "global brands" target consumers earning over $10,000 per year—regardless of their country of origin.

    Answer: True Difficulty: Medium Page: 273

## Multiple Choice Questions

31. The Department of Commerce estimates that, in the next decade, the share of the world's total trade growth held by emerging markets will reach:
    A) 25 percent.
    B) 35 percent.
    C) 75 percent.
    D) 55 percent.

    Answer: C Difficulty: Medium Page: 240

32. The single most important environmental element to which a foreign marketer must adjust is a country's:
    A) economic level.
    B) language.
    C) cultural heritage.
    D) self-reference criterion.

    Answer: A Difficulty: Medium Page: 240

# Chapter 9 Emerging Markets

33. The major market block well into the $21^{st}$ Century will include all of the following areas EXCEPT:
    A) Europe.
    B) Russia.
    C) Asia.
    D) the Americas.

    Answer: B Difficulty: Medium Page: 240

34. An increase in national production that results in an increase in the average per capita gross domestic product (GDP) is at the core of the concept of:
    A) market planning.
    B) environmental dynamics.
    C) economic development.
    D) market growth.

    Answer: C Difficulty: Easy Page: 241

35. Besides a simple increase in per capita GDP, economic development usually implies:
    A) a higher degree of wealth concentration.
    B) a widespread distribution of the increased income.
    C) an increase in the "have-not" class.
    D) political upheaval.

    Answer: B Difficulty: Medium Page: 241

36. Rostow's five stages of economic development are based on all of the following criteria except:
    A) the cost of raw materials.
    B) the cost of labor.
    C) interest rates.
    D) the scale of operations.

    Answer: A Difficulty: Medium Page: 241

37. According to Walt Rostow, all of the following stages are associated with underdeveloped countries except:
    A) the traditional society.
    B) the preconditions for take-off.
    C) the take-off.
    D) the drive to maturity.

    Answer: D Difficulty: Medium Page: 241

38. The America-First Corporation is preparing to enter a number of countries that are characterized by a lack of ability to increase the level of productivity through application of modern science and technology and by low levels of literacy. The firm is preparing to enter nations that are:
    A) developing the preconditions for take-off.
    B) traditional societies.
    C) taking off.
    D) driving to maturity.

    Answer: B Difficulty: Hard Page: 241

39. In which of the following stages of economic development can an economy demonstrate the technological and entrepreneurial skills to produce, of not everything, anything it chooses to produce?
    A) take-off societies.
    B) mass-consumption societies.
    C) societies driving to maturity.
    D) traditional societies.

    Answer: C Difficulty: Medium Page: 241

40. The United States would be best described as a:
    A) mass consumption society.
    B) take-off society.
    C) society driving to maturing.
    D) traditional society.

    Answer: A Difficulty: Easy Page: 241

41. All of the following are part of the United Nations' classification scheme for economic development except:
    A) more-developed countries (MDCs).
    B) newly industrialized countries (NICs).
    C) less-developed countries (LDCs.)
    D) least-developed countries (LLDs).

    Answer: B Difficulty: Medium Page: 241

42. South Korea, Taiwan, and Singapore are best described as:
    A) more-developed countries (MDCs).
    B) less-developed countries (LDCs).
    C) newly industrialized countries (NICs).
    D) least-developed countries (LLDc).

    Answer: C Difficulty: Medium Page: 243

# Chapter 9 Emerging Markets

43. The America-First Corporation is facing increased competition from South Korean electronics manufacturers. Additional competition is also coming from firms in Singapore and Taiwan. The firm's competitors are located in:
A) newly industrialized countries (NICs).
B) less-developed countries (LDCs).
C) least-developed countries (LLDCs).
D) more-developed countries (MDCs).

Answer: A Difficulty: Hard Page: 243

44. The "Four Tigers" of Southeast Asia include all of the following nations except:
A) South Korea.
B) Taiwan.
C) Singapore.
D) Japan.

Answer: D Difficulty: Medium Page: 243

45. The emergence of an NIC requires the availability of large, accessible markets with low tariffs. Which of the following nations was typically the first to meet that need for NICs?
A) America.
B) Japan.
C) China.
D) India.

Answer: A Difficulty: Hard Page: 244

46. The social overhead capital of a nation defines its:
A) environmental status.
B) infrastructure.
C) gross domestic product.
D) cultural heritage.

Answer: B Difficulty: Easy Page: 244

47. The fundamental objective of most developing nations is:
A) a clean environment.
B) efficient government.
C) industrialization.
D) improved education.

Answer: C Difficulty: Medium Page: 247

48. Before entering any foreign country, the America-First Corporation carefully assesses the transportation and communication facilities available. The firm is researching the potential market:
A) infrastructure.
B) environmental status.
C) cultural heritage.
D) gross domestic product.

Answer: A Difficulty: Hard Page: 248

49. Advertising agencies, warehousing storage facilities, credit and banking facilities, marketing research agencies, and quality-level specialized middlemen are part of a nation's:
A) cultural heritage.
B) capital infrastructure.
C) financial and commercial service infrastructure.
D) social overhead infrastructure.

Answer: C Difficulty: Easy Page: 248

50. The continued economic development of Mexico, and many other Latin American countries, is primarily limited by:
A) inadequate infrastructure.
B) inadequate labor supply.
C) inadequate raw materials.
D) high labor costs.

Answer: A Difficulty: Medium Page: 248

51. From the standpoint of the international marketer, a foreign nation's infrastructure is best described as:
A) an elemental factor.
B) an uncontrollable factor.
C) a congruent factor.
D) a controllable factor.

Answer: B Difficulty: Medium Page: 248

52. The capital infrastructure of a country includes all of the following except:
A) railroads.
B) seaport.
C) advertising agencies.
D) communications networks.

Answer: C Difficulty: Medium Page: 248

53. The most effective arbitrator between a nation's productive capacity and consumer demand is:
A) marketing.
B) government.
C) culture.
D) its economy.

Answer: A Difficulty: Medium Page: 251

54. All of the following tend to occur with increasing economic development except:
A) more levels of distribution.
B) less influence for foreign import agents.
C) a larger number of small stores.
D) improved retail margins.

Answer: C Difficulty: Medium Page: 251

55. Demand "creation" first becomes significant during which of the following stages in the evolution of the marketing process?
A) commercial transaction.
B) mass production.
C) mass distribution.
D) small-scale manufacturing.

Answer: B Difficulty: Medium Page: 252

56. Market information first becomes significant during which of the following stages in the evolution of the marketing process?
A) commercial transaction.
B) mass production.
C) mass distribution.
D) small-scale manufacturing.

Answer: A Difficulty: Medium Page: 252

57. Middlemen exercised channel control during which of the following stages in the evolution of the marketing process?
A) agricultural.
B) mass production.
C) commercial transaction.
D) small-scale manufacturing.

Answer: D Difficulty: Medium Page: 252

58. Retailers assumed channel control during which of the following stages in the evolution of the marketing process?
A) mass distribution.
B) small-scale manufacturing.
C) commercial transaction.
D) mass production.

Answer: A Difficulty: Medium Page: 252

59. Marketing became the primary orientation of business during which of the following stages in the evolution of the marketing process?
A) small-scale manufacturing.
B) commercial transaction.
C) mass distribution.
D) mass production.

Answer: C Difficulty: Medium Page: 252

60. Which of the following nations enjoys the highest GDP per capita?
A) America.
B) Japan.
C) Germany.
D) France.

Answer: B Difficulty: Medium Page: 254

61. In many of the foreign markets served by the America-First Corporation, the capital cities are quite modern, but the remainder of the nation relies on traditional institutions andbehaviors. The firm is facing:
A) economic dualism.
B) cultural pluralism.
C) distributed loyalty.
D) legalistic pluralism.

Answer: A Difficulty: Hard Page: 254

62. India and Mexico are characterized by some areas that are modern and affluent and others that are traditional and poor. This phenomenon is best described as:
A) cultural pluralism.
B) economic dualism.
C) distributed loyalty.
D) legalistic pluralism.

Answer: B Difficulty: Hard Page: 254

# Chapter 9 Emerging Markets

63. The America-First Corporation routinely enters emerging markets very early in their development. The firm's strategy is best described as:
   A) economic dualism.
   B) profit skimming.
   C) investment in future growth.
   D) capital piracy.

   Answer: C Difficulty: Hard Page: 254

64. According to the Department of Commerce, over 75% of the growth in world trade that is expected to attend the emergence of 130 developing countries over the next 20 years will be found in so-called:
   A) newly industrialized countries (NICs).
   B) mega-emerging nations (MENs).
   C) emerging super nations (ESNs).
   D) big emerging markets (BEMs).

   Answer: D Difficulty: Medium Page: 255

65. The America-First Corporation is concentrating its attention on China, South Korea, Brazil, South Africa, and Turkey. The firm is apparently focusing on those emerging nations considered to be:
   A) newly industrialized countries (NICs).
   B) big emerging markets (BEMs).
   C) mega-emerging nations (MENs).
   D) emerging super nation (ESNs).

   Answer: B Difficulty: Hard Page: 257

66. Which of the following big emerging markets (BEMs) enjoys the highest per capita GDP?
   A) China.
   B) South Africa.
   C) Argentina.
   D) Brazil.

   Answer: C Difficulty: Medium Page: 257

67. Which of the following big emerging markets boasts the largest amount of total trade?
   A) South Korea.
   B) China.
   C) Mexico.
   D) Brazil.

   Answer: B Difficulty: Medium Page: 257

# Chapter 9 Emerging Markets

68. The privatization of state-owned enterprises (SOEs) signals:
    A) a shift toward greater import substitution.
    B) a shift away from democracy.
    C) a shift toward greater socialism.
    D) a shift away from import substitution and protectionism.

    Answer: D Difficulty: Medium Page: 258

69. Which of the following nations accounted for the largest percentage of both imports and exports in Latin America?
    A) America.
    B) Japan.
    C) Britain.
    D) France.

    Answer: A Difficulty: Medium Page: 260

70. The principal trading partner of the United States in Eastern Europe is:
    A) Poland.
    B) China.
    C) Yugoslavia.
    D) Hungary.

    Answer: A Difficulty: Medium Page: 262

71. The America-First Corporation is seeking entry into an area that may position the firm for trade with the former USSR. The firm is most likely to seek a presence in:
    A) China.
    B) Yugoslavia.
    C) the Baltic states.
    D) Poland.

    Answer: C Difficulty: Hard Page: 263

72. The fastest growing market in the world is found in:
    A) Europe.
    B) Asia.
    C) Latin America.
    D) Canada.

    Answer: B Difficulty: Medium Page: 263

# Chapter 9 Emerging Markets

73. Which of the following is the latest to be recognized as one of the largest emerging markets?
    A) the EU.
    B) NAFTA.
    C) the NIC.
    D) ASEAN.

    Answer: D Difficulty: Medium Page: 264

74. Which of the following Asian markets enjoys the highest GDP?
    A) Japan.
    B) China.
    C) Hong Kong.
    D) Taiwan.

    Answer: A Difficulty: Medium Page: 264

75. All of the following statements about China are true except:
    A) China is still politically unstable at the top.
    B) China is really a group of six regional markets.
    C) China's infrastructure is badly out-of-date.
    D) China has only recently passed a commercial code.

    Answer: D Difficulty: Medium Page: 265-266

76. The America-First Corporation has found that in order to do business in China, it is typically necessary to pay bribes. The firm's ability to compete in China with non-U.S. firms may be harmed by which of the following domestic laws?
    A) the Robinson-Patman Act.
    B) the Foreign Corrupt Practices Act.
    C) the Sherman Act.
    D) the Wheeler-Lea Act.

    Answer: B Difficulty: Hard Page: 266

77. Many marketers feel that the "next Japan or Latin America" will be:
    A) China.
    B) Canada.
    C) Russia.
    D) Alaska.

    Answer: A Difficulty: Medium Page: 267

78. In large measure, the economic future of China is tied to the manner in which it treats:
A) Japan.
B) Taiwan.
C) Hong Kong.
D) Taipei.

Answer: C Difficulty: Medium Page: 268

79. The newest emerging markets are found in:
A) Vietnam and South Africa.
B) Japan and Hong Kong.
C) China and Latin America.
D) the Baltic States and Germany.

Answer: A Difficulty: Medium Page: 270

80. The attempt to identify groups of consumers with similar needs and wants in multiple country markets is at the core of:
A) global distribution.
B) multi-cultural marketing.
C) global segmentation.
D) global marketing.

Answer: C Difficulty: Easy Page: 272-273

**Fill in the Blank Questions**

81. _______________ is generally understood to mean an increase in national production that results in an increase in the average per capita gross domestic product (GDP).

Answer: economic development Difficulty: Easy Page: 241

82. The America-First Corporation is primarily active in Mexico, South Korea, Singapore, and Taiwan. The firm focuses its efforts on _______________.

Answer: newly industrialized markets Difficulty: Hard Page: 242

83. The fundamental objective of most developing countries is _______________.

Answer: industrialization Difficulty: Medium Page: 247

84. Before entering a foreign market, the America-First Corporation carefully assesses the availability and status of roads, railroads, seaports, and communication networks. The firm is focusing on the capital _______________ of its potential markets.

Answer: infrastructure Difficulty: Hard Page: 248

# Chapter 9 Emerging Markets

85. Many developing countries exhibit _______________, the coexistence of modern and traditional sectors within the economy.

    Answer: economic dualism   Difficulty: Easy   Page: 253

86. ASEAN and CEA are two of the newest and largest _______________.

    Answer: Big Emerging Markets   Difficulty: Medium   Page: 258

87. One of the major tasks facing BEMs is the _______________ of traditional SOEs.

    Answer: privatization   Difficulty: Medium   Page: 264

88. In recent years, a nation demonstrating the capacity for rapid, sustained growth has been called "_______________".

    Answer: tigers   Difficulty: Easy   Page: 264

89. Estonia, Latvia, and Lithuania are collectively known as the ________________--the top performing post-communist countries.

    Answer: Baltic Republic   Difficulty: Medium   Page: 263

90. The America-First Corporation would like to eventually enter the former USSR. To that end, the firm has begun operations in several bordering nations that have long had relations with Russia—and who are seen as "bridges" to the area. America-First has entered the _______________.

    Answer: Baltic States   Difficulty: Hard   Page: 263

91. For the past three decades, _______________ has been the fastest growing area in the world.

    Answer: Asia   Difficulty: Easy   Page: 263

92. The "Four Tigers" of the Asian _______________ have recently challenged Japan for area dominance.

    Answer: Pacific Rim   Difficulty: Medium   Page: 264

93. With the sole exception of population, _______________ still leads Asia in every aspect of economic/demographic performance.

    Answer: Japan   Difficulty: Medium   Page: 264

# Chapter 9 Emerging Markets

94. The continued growth of _____________ depends heavily on its ability to deregulate industry, import modern technology, privatize inefficient SOEs, and continue to attract foreign investment.

    Answer: China   Difficulty: Medium   Page: 265

95. The America-First Corporation is very careful to avoid paying bribes to foreign government officials for fear of violating the Foreign Corrupt Practices Act. The firm is likely to face serious problems in _____________.

    Answer: China   Difficulty: Hard   Page: 266

96. China's continued emergence as a global economic power is largely dependent on how it manages the _____________ "problem".

    Answer: Hong Kong   Difficulty: Medium   Page: 268

97. The America-First Corporation believes that political stability is vital to its foreign efforts. Accordingly, the firm is focusing a great deal of its efforts on _____________, the world's largest democracy.

    Answer: India   Difficulty: Hard   Page: 270

98. According to many experts, _____________ has the look and feel of the next China or Latin America.

    Answer: India   Difficulty: Medium   Page: 270

99. The America-First Corporation is intent on being among the first to enter the newest emerging markets. The firm is likely to target _____________ and _____________.

    Answer: Vietnam; South Africa   Difficulty: Hard   Page: 270-271

100. As consumers in a foreign country reach the "$10,000 Club," they become potential customers for _____________ brands.

    Answer: global   Difficulty: Medium   Page: 273

# Chapter 9 Emerging Markets

## Essay Questions

101. What is "infrastructure"? Why is the state of a nation's infrastructure critical to marketing activity and economic development?

Answer:
Traditionally, infrastructure refers to the paved roads, railroads, seaports, communications networks and other capital goods necessary to the support of business activities. A financial and commercial infrastructure--including advertising agencies, warehousing storage facilities, credit and banking facilities, marketing research agencies, and specialized middlemen--is also essential for effective marketing. Without sufficient infrastructure support, production is difficult--and effective marketing/distribution, impossible.

Difficulty: Hard Page: 248-249

102. What contributions can marketing make to a developing country?

Answer:
Production, although important, is not sufficient in and of itself to raise the standard of living of a developing nation. Marketing's job is to educate consumers to the benefits of the newly available goods and to provide the means by which the consumer may attain those benefits. If an efficient method of distribution cannot be developed, the benefits of production cannot reach the people they were created to serve.

Difficulty: Hard Page: 249-251

103. Why does economic dualism tend to exist in developing nations? What problems does this phenomenon pose for the marketer?

Answer:
Economic development tends to occur first in a nation's capital and larger urban areas--those areas that are already relatively advanced in terms of literacy and infrastructure. The more remote areas tend to be more mired in the traditions of the nation--and in possession of little of the social or capital infrastructure of the urban areas. This means that the marketer faces two quite different market segments within the country. These segments require different strategies tailored to the specific problems of each. The marketing task is greatly complicated.

Difficulty: Hard Page: 253-255

# Chapter 9 Emerging Markets

104. What countries constitute the "Four Tigers" of the Pacific Rim? Why are these small nations significant to the international marketer?

Answer:
These four nations were the first in Asia, besides Japan, to move from a status of developing countries to newly industrialized countries. These nations have quickly grown from mere suppliers and/or assemblers for other nations to major competitors of both the United States and Japan in a growing array of products. With economic success has come growing political influence in trade and development in the economies of other countries within their growing spheres of influence. While the Pacific Rim is currently dominated by Japan, one or more of these NICs can be expected to challenge that dominance--or at least gain a strong voice in the area.

Difficulty: Hard Page: 264

105. Why has China received increasing attention from international marketers? What specific problems does trade with China present?

Answer:
China currently boasts the world's third largest economy--and is projected to have the world's largest economy by 2010. The sheer size and growing prosperity of the Chinese population portends profitable trade for those nations and firms able to overcome that nation's unique problems. Politically, China is still unstable. Its sheer size--and cultural traditions--present a collage of six regional markets, each of which is at a different stage of development. Chinese infrastructure is blatantly out-of-date and inefficient. Finally, China has no commercial code nor independent court system to settle disputes.

Difficulty: Hard Page: 264-268

# Chapter 10 Multinational Market Regions and Market Groups

## True/False Questions

1. Multinational market regions, groups of countries that seek mutual economic benefit from reducing intraregional trade and tariff barriers, are becoming less important as multinational firms become larger.

   Answer: False   Difficulty: Medium   Page: 278

2. The America-First Corporation is seeking to establish itself as a major global company. According to Kenichi Ohmae, this can only be accomplished if the firm can develop significant market positions in the European, American, and Asian Triads.

   Answer: True   Difficulty: Hard   Page: 279

3. All that is required for the formation of a successful economic union is common economic goals.

   Answer: False   Difficulty: Medium   Page: 279

4. Common markets, such as the Central American and the Andean Common Markets, represent the highest level of integration possible among multinational market groups.

   Answer: False   Difficulty: Medium   Page: 281

5. The Treaty of Rome, signed in 1987, created the Italian Common Market and established Rome as its hub.

   Answer: False   Difficulty: Medium   Page: 281

6. Harmonization sets forth common standards for the protection of health, safety and the environment and establishes product standards that must be accepted by all members of the European Community.

   Answer: True   Difficulty: Easy   Page: 287

7. The America-First Corporation has successfully introduced its new product in the United Kingdom. Under the EC policy of mutual recognition, the product must be accepted for sale by all member nations of the European community.

   Answer: False   Difficulty: Hard   Page: 287

8. The creation of the single customs document alone reduced distribution costs by half of companies doing cross-border business in the European community.

   Answer: True   Difficulty: Medium   Page: 287

9. The America-First Corporation has encountered German objections to the sale of one of its cosmetic products that, according to the Germans, employs a brand name that may cause confusion with medical treatments. The firm may seek relief by arguing its case before the European court of Justice.

Answer: True Difficulty: Hard Page: 287

10. The final step in the European Community's march to union was ratification of the Maastricht Treaty.

Answer: True Difficulty: Medium Page: 289

11. The Euro is expected to alleviate the problem of parallel imports and facilitate price comparisons within the European Common Market.

Answer: True Difficulty: Medium Page: 297

12. NAFTA seeks to eliminate all tariffs on trade between Canada, the United States, and the Latin-American Trade block.

Answer: False Difficulty: Medium Page: 300

13. The America-First Corporation is a major provider of computer software and services throughout the world. Unfortunately, the marketing of services is not covered by the NAFTA agreement.

Answer: False Difficulty: Hard Page: 300

14. The America-First Corporation is very concerned with the protection of its intellectual property. The firm will enjoy the highest standards of such protection under the North American Free Trade Agreement.

Answer: False Difficulty: Hard Page: 300

15. The Clinton administration's vigorous support of NAFTA has already secured Chile's participation and will soon create an Anglo-Latin Free Trade Zone.

Answer: False Difficulty: Medium Page: 301

16. The United States, through NAFTA, is providing the leadership for creation of the Free Trade Association of the Americas (FTAA).

Answer: False Difficulty: Medium Page: 304

17. At present, FTAA seems likely to evolve into a South American Free Trade Area (SAFTA)—with Mercosur at the center and providing the impetus.

Answer: True Difficulty: Medium Page: 304

18. Given current trends, the United States should continue to dominate world trade well into the 21st century.

Answer: False Difficulty: Medium Page: 307

19. The long-term goal of the Latin-American Integration association (LAIA) is the creation of a Latin American Common Market.

Answer: True Difficulty: Medium Page: 305

20. The America-First Corporation is preparing to enter both Bolivia and Peru. The firm's activities will require it to deal with the Andean Common Market (ANCOM) and the Latin American Integration Association (LAIA).

Answer: True Difficulty: Hard Page: 306

21. The America-First Corporation desired to provide products and services to several resorts located in Jamaica, St. Vincent, and Barbados. The efforts of the firm will be assisted by the existence of the Caribbean Community and Common Market (CARICOM).

Answer: True Difficulty: Hard Page: 306

22. The Third Triad region, consisting of the nations of the Asian Pacific Rim led by Japan, includes many of the world's newly industrialized countries (NICs).

Answer: True Difficulty: Medium Page: 309

23. The growth of Free-Trade areas in Asia's Pacific Rim has led to a sharp decline in the power of Japanese keiretsu networks.

Answer: False Difficulty: Medium Page: 309

24. The primary trade groups in Asia and the Pacific Rim are APEC and ASEAN.

Answer: True Difficulty: Easy Page: 309

25. APEC encompasses the region(s) that constitute America's most important trading partners.

Answer: True Difficulty: Medium Page: 311

26. After a slow start, Africa has made the most dramatic progress of any multinational market development.

    Answer: False Difficulty: Medium Page: 311

27. The America-First Corporation is preparing to enter the emerging African market. The firm will primarily deal with the Economic Community of West African States and the Southern African Development Community.

    Answer: True Difficulty: Hard Page: 311

28. The Arab Common Market has emerged as a model for overcoming internal differences to achieve free internal trade among member states.

    Answer: False Difficulty: Medium Page: 313

29. Many "experts" fear that the growth of the EU, NAFTA, and ASEAN will actually result in more protectionism as industrialized nations discriminate against countries not aligned with a trade group.

    Answer: True Difficulty: Medium Page: 315

30. The America-First Corporation is focusing the great majority of its international efforts on the world's emerging nations. The firm apparently feels that these countries, rather than the mature nations of the world, will offer the greatest opportunities for trade in the future.

    Answer: True Difficulty: Hard Page: 315

**Multiple Choice Questions**

31. Groups of countries that seek mutual economic benefit from reducing intraregional trade and tariff barriers are increasingly likely to form:
    A) multinational market regions.
    B) protectionist unions.
    C) mercantilistic unions.
    D) super-nations.

    Answer: A Difficulty: Easy Page: 278

32. The primary reason for the formation of multinational market regions is:
    A) political.
    B) social.
    C) cultural.
    D) economic.

    Answer: D Difficulty: Easy Page: 278

# Chapter 10 Multinational Market Regions and Market Groups

33. All of the following are "Triads" envisioned by Kenichi Ohmae except:
    A) the Asian Triad.
    B) the Latin-American Triad.
    C) the European Triad.
    D) the American Triad.

    Answer: B Difficulty: Medium Page: 279

34. A successful economic union requires favorable:
    A) economic factors.
    B) political/cultural factors.
    C) geographic factors.
    D) all of the above.

    Answer: D Difficulty: Medium Page: 279

35. Which of the following is the most basic vehicle for economic integration and cooperation—involving only an agreement between governments to participate jointly to develop basic industries beneficial to each country?
    A) the free-trade area.
    B) a customs union.
    C) a regional cooperation group.
    D) a common market.

    Answer: C Difficulty: Easy Page: 281

36. The United States has agreements with both Canada and Mexico under which the parties agree to reduce or eliminate customs duties and nontariff trade barriers between themselves while maintaining individual tariff schedules for external countries. The agreements would be best described as:
    A) a regional cooperation group.
    B) a free-trade area.
    C) a customs union.
    D) a common market.

    Answer: B Difficulty: Hard Page: 281

37. In which of the following forms of multinational trade organization are internal tariffs reduced or eliminated while members impose a common external tariff on goods imported from outside the organization?
    A) a customs union.
    B) a regional cooperation group.
    C) a common market.
    D) a free-trade area.

    Answer: A Difficulty: Easy Page: 281

38. In which of the following forms of multinational trade organizations do members create a unified economy?
A) a regional cooperation group.
B) a customs union.
C) a common market.
D) a free-trade area.

Answer: C Difficulty: Easy Page: 281

39. The European Economic Community (EEC) was established by the:
A) Treaty of Versailles.
B) Maastricht Treaty.
C) One Europe Treaty.
D) Treaty of Rome.

Answer: D Difficulty: Medium Page: 281

40. Which of the following is the most fully integrated form of regional cooperation?
A) a political union.
B) a common market.
C) a customs union.
D) a free-trade area.

Answer: A Difficulty: Easy Page: 282

41. The New commonwealth of Independent States would be best described as a:
A) free-trade area.
B) customs union.
C) political union.
D) common market.

Answer: C Difficulty: Medium Page: 283

42. The America-First Corporation feels that market potential must be viewed in the context of regions of the world rather than country by country. All of the following developments support the firm's view except:
A) the globalization of markets.
B) the rising tide of protectionism.
C) the dissolution of the Soviet Union.
D) enhanced global competition.

Answer: B Difficulty: Hard Page: 283

# Chapter 10 Multinational Market Regions and Market Groups

43. Which of the following serves as the focus of the European region of the First Triad?
    A) the European Union.
    B) the European Community.
    C) the European Economic Area.
    D) the European Free Trade Area.

    Answer: A Difficulty: Medium Page: 283

44. Which of the following is the newest multinational market group to appear in the European region?
    A) the European Union.
    B) the European Community.
    C) the European Free Trade Area.
    D) the Commonwealth of Independent States.

    Answer: D Difficulty: Medium Page: 283

45. Of all the multinational market groups, which is the most secure in its cooperation and economic significance?
    A) the commonwealth of Independent States.
    B) the European Community.
    C) the North American Free Trade Zone.
    D) the Council for Mutual Economic Assistance.

    Answer: B Difficulty: Medium Page: 285

46. Which of the following was designed to eliminate internal border controls within the EC, while strengthening external border controls, unifying technical regulations on product standards, setting up systems to standardize the value-added and excise taxes of member states, and freeing migration of the population?
    A) the single European Act.
    B) the Europe-First Act.
    C) the Hemispheric Unification Act.
    D) the Unified Europe Administration.

    Answer: A Difficulty: Medium Page: 286

47. The most essential requirements for protection of health, safety, the environment, and product standards for EC members are established and enforced under the process of:
    A) unification.
    B) standardization.
    C) harmonization.
    D) averaging.

    Answer: C Difficulty: Easy Page: 287

48. The America-First Corporation has decided to enter the EC. The firm will have to ensure that its products meet the product standards that have been adopted throughout the EC through the process of:
A) unification.
B) averaging.
C) standardization.
D) harmonization.

Answer: D Difficulty: Hard Page: 287

49. Within the EC, each member state is expected to honor each others' national standards for "nonessential" characteristics under the doctrine of:
A) harmonization.
B) homogenization.
C) mutual recognition.
D) unification.

Answer: C Difficulty: Medium Page: 287

50. The America-First Corporation has sought to gain permission to sell the products it has long sold in France throughout the EC under the doctrine of mutual recognition. The firm's petition will be under the jurisdiction of the:
A) Patent Council.
B) European Court of Justice.
C) European Parliament.
D) Council of Ministers.

Answer: B Difficulty: Hard Page: 287

51. The America-First Corporation has successfully introduced its latest product in France. The firm should be able to sell its offering throughout the EC under the doctrine of:
A) mutual recognition.
B) homogenization.
C) harmonization.
D) unification.

Answer: A Difficulty: Hard Page: 287

52. The EC replaced 70 forms once required for transborder shipments to member countries under the terms of the:
A) trans-shipment authorization rule.
B) single customs document.
C) reshipment directive.
D) trans-shipment directive.

Answer: B Difficulty: Medium Page: 287

53. Within the EC, policy is initiated and its observance, once enacted, supervised by the:
    A) Council of Ministers.
    B) European Parliament.
    C) European Court of Justice.
    D) European Commission

    Answer: D Difficulty: Medium Page: 288

54. Which of the following bodies is responsible for passing laws for the EC?
    A) the Council of Ministers.
    B) the European parliament.
    C) the European Court of Justice.
    D) the European Commission.

    Answer: A Difficulty: Medium Page: 288

55. In the EC, the consultative body that passes on most community legislation and exercises budgetary powers is called the:
    A) European Court of Justice.
    B) European Parliament.
    C) European Commission.
    D) Council of Ministers.

    Answer: B Difficulty: Medium Page: 288

56. Challenging any measures incompatible with the Treaty of Rome when they are adopted by the commission, council, or national governments is the first responsibility of the EC's:
    A) European Commission.
    B) European Parliament.
    C) Council of Ministers.
    D) Court of Justice.

    Answer: D Difficulty: Medium Page: 288

57. The final step in the European Community's march to union was ratification of the:
    A) Maastricht Treaty.
    B) European Treaty.
    C) Unification Treaty.
    D) Harmonization Treaty.

    Answer: A Difficulty: Medium Page: 289

# Chapter 10 Multinational Market Regions and Market Groups

58. The world's <u>largest</u> consumer market is the:
    A) North American Free Trade Agreement.
    B) Commonwealth of Independent States.
    C) European Economic Area.
    D) United States-Canada Free Trade Area.

    Answer: C Difficulty: Medium Page: 289

59. The Maastricht Treaty required the creation of a common European currency to be called the:
    A) Yugo.
    B) Euro.
    C) Helo.
    D) Pelo.

    Answer: B Difficulty: Medium Page: 290

60. A nation <u>must</u> open its borders to EC goods if it desires to have access to the EC under the provision of:
    A) reciprocity.
    B) prioritization.
    C) privilege.
    D) accessibility.

    Answer: A Difficulty: Easy Page: 297

61. The America-First Company would like to gain entry to the republics that comprised the former USSR. The firm will have to deal with the:
    A) Commonwealth of Independent States.
    B) Maastricht Union.
    C) Council of Russian Republics.
    D) Ministry of Soviet Republics.

    Answer: A Difficulty: Hard Page: 298

62. The newest free trade area in Europe is the:
    A) Commonwealth of Independent States.
    B) Central European Free-Trade Area.
    C) European Union.
    D) Ministry of Soviet Republics.

    Answer: B Difficulty: Easy Page: 299

63. Prior to NAFTA, the world's largest bilateral trade existed between:
    A) China and Russia.
    B) the United States and Mexico.
    C) Great Britain and France.
    D) the United States and Canada.

    Answer: D Difficulty: Medium Page: 299

64. The America-First Corporation has long complained that the import licenses required by Mexico acted as quotas to restrict the amount the firm could export to that country. The firm's concerns will be addressed by the:
    A) United States-Mexican Trade Accord.
    B) Mexican Anti-Quota Act.
    C) North American Free Trade Agreement.
    D) Western Hemispheric Trade Area.

    Answer: C Difficulty: Hard Page: 300

65. The NAFTA agreement will determine whether a good produced by a nation external to the trade area qualifies for preferential tariff treatment through the use of:
    A) market access rules.
    B) rules of origin.
    C) nontariff rules.
    D) customs agreements.

    Answer: B Difficulty: Medium Page: 300

66. For years, Japanese companies have sought to avoid tariffs by assembling automobiles and other products in Mexico and the United States. Under NAFTA, tariff preference will be based on a requirement that such products contain over 60 percent North American materials and/or parts.
    A) Enforced-Content Rule.
    B) Value-Content Rule.
    C) Made-In-The-Americas Provision.
    D) Tariff-Avoidance Rule.

    Answer: B Difficulty: Hard Page: 301

67. Foreign manufacturers will be able to obtain advanced rulings, on request, as to whether or not specified products will qualify for tariff preference under the NAFTA rules of origin. Which of the following portions of the NAFTA agreement apply most directly to such rulings?
    A) the market access provision.
    B) the non-tariff barriers provision.
    C) the rules of origin provision.
    D) the customs administration provision.

    Answer: D Difficulty: Hard Page: 300

68. The NAFTA agreement established the first set of comprehensive principles governing:
    A) customs administration.
    B) non-tariff barriers.
    C) services trade.
    D) investment.

    Answer: C Difficulty: Medium Page: 300

69. Of all bilateral and/or international agreements, NAFTA provides for the highest standards of protection for:
    A) intellectual property.
    B) non-tariff barriers.
    C) government procurement.
    D) the use of standards and technical requirements to regulate trade.

    Answer: A Difficulty: Medium Page: 300

70. The America-First Corporation is a major producer of entertainment videos, recordings, and video games. The firm would primarily benefit from NAFTA provisions protecting:
    A) government procurement.
    B) local content requirements.
    C) intellectual property.
    D) exchange rates.

    Answer: C Difficulty: Hard Page: 300

71. The America-First Corporation is planning to ship components to Mexico for assembly in order to take advantage of lower wages. The firm is making use of:
    A) maquiladora plants.
    B) margarita plants.
    C) manufactudaro plants.
    D) fabricado plants.

    Answer: A Difficulty: Hard Page: 303

72. The gradual establishment of a Latin American Common Market allowing for the differential treatment of member countries according to their level of economic development is the goal of the:
    A) Latin American Integration Association.
    B) North American Free Trade Area.
    C) Western Hemisphere Free Trade Area.
    D) Pan American Free Trade Area.

    Answer: A Difficulty: Easy Page: 305

# Chapter 10 Multinational Market Regions and Market Groups

73. At present, the primary trade group in the Asia-Pacific Rim is the:
    A) Association of Southeast Asian Nations.
    B) Pan-Asian Free Trade Area.
    C) Pan-Asian Free Trade Area.
    D) Eastern Hemisphere Common Market.

    Answer: A Difficulty: Medium Page: 309

74. A formal structure for the major governments of the Asia-Pacific Rim, the United States, and Canada to discuss mutual interests relevant to open trade and economic collaboration is provided by the:
    A) Pan-Asian Trade Association.
    B) Asia-Pacific Economic Cooperation.
    C) Pacific Rim Economic Council.
    D) Asia-Pacific Rim Ministry of Trade.

    Answer: B Difficulty: Medium Page: 310

75. The most advanced and viable of the African Regional Cooperative Groups is the:
    A) Southern African Development Community.
    B) Greater Africa Common Market.
    C) African Free Trade Council.
    D) Inter-African Trade Ministry.

    Answer: A Difficulty: Medium Page: 313

76. Which of the following African trade organizations is <u>most</u> likely to enjoy major advances?
    A) Southern Free Trade Zone.
    B) North African Community.
    C) Southern African Development Community.
    D) West African Trade Council.

    Answer: C Difficulty: Medium Page: 313

77. Which of the following areas has been the <u>least</u> aggressive in the formation of successful multinational market groups?
    A) North Africa.
    B) Baltic States.
    C) South Africa.
    D) Middle East.

    Answer: D Difficulty: Medium Page: 313

# Chapter 10 Multinational Market Regions and Market Groups

78. In the Middle East, the strongest free-trade organization is likely to be the:
    A) Regional Cooperation for Development.
    B) Economic Cooperation Organization.
    C) Organization of the Islamic Conference.
    D) Arab-Israeli Common Union.

    Answer: C Difficulty: Medium Page: 314

79. Which of the following multinational trade scenarios is most likely to occur?
    A) The Three Trade Triads headed by the U.S., the EC, and Japan will dominate world trade.
    B) International trade will shift radically from the industrialized nations to emerging markets.
    C) Global trade growth will be spurred by formation of trade groups and significant growth in the emerging markets.
    D) None of the above

    Answer: C Difficulty: Hard Page: 315

80. All of the following represent marketing mix adjustments to the emergence of a single European market <u>except</u>:
    A) uniform pricing policies.
    B) significant reductions in the number of brands offered.
    C) the introduction of foreign-owned, large-scale retailing systems.
    D) the introduction of generic products and brands.

    Answer: D Difficulty: Medium Page: 315

**Fill in the Blank Questions**

81. The ________________, a 17-country alliance between the EU and EFTA, is the world's largest single uniform market.

    Answer: European Economic Area Difficulty: Easy Page: 278

82. Several Middle Eastern states have agreed to jointly contribute to the cost of constructing a series of dams and reservoirs to serve their citizen's need for water. The project would be <u>best</u> described as a(n): ________________.

    Answer: Regional Cooperation Group (RCG) Difficulty: Hard Page: 281

83. The Commonwealth of Independent States and the European Union demonstrate that countries having widely different political philosophies can make use of the concept of the ________________.

    Answer: political union Difficulty: Hard Page: 282

84. The ultimate goal of the ______________ was the creation of a United States of Europe.

Answer: Treaty of Rome  Difficulty: Medium  Page: 286

85. The America-First Corporation is at odds with a British firm regarding rights to sell one of its products in the EC. The dispute will probably be settled by the ______________.

Answer: European Court of Justice  Difficulty: Hard  Page: 288

86. The Euro, the proposed common currency of the European Union, was the product of the ______________ Treaty.

Answer: Maastricht  Difficulty: Medium  Page: 289

87. The "final" problems facing the realization of a single market/single currency in Europe was addressed by the Treaty of ______________.

Answer: Amsterdam  Difficulty: Medium  Page: 290

88. The America-First Corporation would like to sell its products to member states of the European Commission. Its success depends on the United States' acceptance of ______________ in its dealings with the EC.

Answer: Reciprocity  Difficulty: Hard  Page: 297

89. The newest free-trade area in Europe is the six-member ______________.

Answer: Central European Free-Trade Area  Difficulty: Medium  Page: 298-299

90. Under NAFTA's ______________ rule, a set percentage of the value of a good must be North American in origin.

Answer: value-contest  Difficulty: Medium  Page: 301

91. The America-First Corporation has experienced problems with trademark, patent, and copyright infringements in many parts of the world. The firm is especially pleased with the ______________ provisions of NAFTA.

Answer: intellectual property  Difficulty: Hard  Page: 300

92. Foreign firms may use Mexican labor to assemble component parts in ______________ plants as a means of cutting labor costs.

Answer: maquiladora  Difficulty: Medium  Page: 303

# Chapter 10 Multinational Market Regions and Market Groups

93. The newest common-market agreement in Latin America is _____________.

    Answer: Mercosur  Difficulty: Easy  Page: 303

94. Initially, NAFTA was to be the foundation for the creation of a U.S.-led _____________ by 2005.

    Answer: Free Trade Area of the Americas  Difficulty: Medium  Page: 306

95. The creation of a Latin American Common Market is the eventual goal of the _______________.

    Answer: Latin American Integration Association  Difficulty: Medium  Page: 305

96. APEC provides a formal structure for the major governments of the region, including the _____ and _____.

    Answer: United States; Canada  Difficulty: Medium  Page: 310

97. The primary multinational trade group in Asia is the _____________.

    Answer: Association of Southeast Asian Nations  Difficulty: Easy  Page: 309

98. The America-First Corporation is preparing to enter South Africa. The firm will be primarily dealing with the members of the _____________.

    Answer: Southern Africa Development Community  Difficulty: Hard  Page: 311

99. While the Middle East has many problems to overcome to form a multinational market group, many experts think that vast national resources, substantial capital, and a cheap labor force give the _____________ an edge.

    Answer: Organization of the Islamic Conference  Difficulty: Medium  Page: 314

100. Most "experts" believe that the primary rivals in future global competition will be _____________, _______________, and the _____________.

    Answer: Japan; Europe; United States  Difficulty: Medium  Page: 315

# Chapter 10 Multinational Market Regions and Market Groups

**Essay Questions**

101. What has been the major reason for the formation of common markets and/or free trade areas? How does this historical trend relate to Kenichi Ohmae's assertion that successful international marketers must have a position within each of the Three Triads he has identified?

Answer:
Historically, nations have entered into trade agreements to gain the advantages of tariff reduction and/or elimination among members--while maintaining tariff barriers against outsiders. The Triads described by Dr. Ohmae are merely larger versions of traditional market arrangements--having the same goals and operating in the same way. Given these assumptions, the international marketer must maintain a presence in each of the Triads in which he or she wishes to deal.

Difficulty: Hard   Page: 278-279

102. Multinational market groups range from regional cooperation groups to political unions in terms of the degree of economic and political integration. Why have successful, VOLUNTARY political unions been so rare? Does such a voluntary political union now exist?

Answer:
A political union requires its member states to adopt a common currency, common laws, a common security system, and a common system of justice. While the members of a market group are willing to adopt SOME unification policies for economic gain, they are less willing to abandon their political/cultural heritage or give up cherished traditions and/or institutions. At present, the European Union is the nearest thing to a voluntary political union. The Maastricht Treaty demonstrates "philosophical acceptance" of the concept of a European Political Union, BUT the treaty has not been fully implemented and faces several years of negotiation before it actually takes effect.

Difficulty: Hard   Page: 281-283

103. What marketing mix adjustments followed the creation of the European Common Market?

Answer:
Differential pricing between nations tends to disappear--the marketer must select a single price that will be acceptable, and profitable, across all nations involved. Product and brand offerings tend to become streamlined as market differences blur and competition forces the marketer to be more cost efficient. Brand reduction also allows the marketer to streamline and better focus their advertising efforts. Finally, the marketer must come to grips with distribution problems that offer both opportunities and challenges. In effect, the marketer is seeking to replace a series of specific, perhaps simpler marketing plans tailored to the needs of individual markets with a single, more sophisticated approach that will satisfy the needs of a much broader group of customers.

Difficulty: Hard   Page: 279-309

# Chapter 10 Multinational Market Regions and Market Groups

104. Briefly review the arguments in favor of the creation of a Japan-United States trade link. What barriers must such an agreement overcome?

Answer:
NAFTA quickly accomplished its primary economic goals--centering, as usual, on the benefits associated with tariff reductions. The provisions relevant to services and intellectual property have served as a model for other agreements. The fears of many critics that American jobs would be lost to cheaper Mexican labor have not, as yet, been justified. The one criticism that has materialized followed the devaluation of the Mexican currency. Devaluation, and the economic disruption that followed, had immediate adverse impacts in the U.S. However, the possible ramifications of economic integration were recognized before the NAFTA agreement was ratified.

Difficulty: Hard Page: 309-311

105. Briefly evaluate the failure of the Middle East to establish a viable common market. Can these problems be overcome?

Answer:
In spite of considerable wealth and natural resources, this region has made little progress when long-term agreement was required on anything. Differences in ideology and long-standing hostilities have proved difficult to overcome. The hostility founded in fervent religious differences is not likely to change. OPEC, a comparatively simple monopoly designed to profit from unified actions against the area's "enemies", has been only partly successful. The area is likely to remain contentious—and fragmented.

Difficulty: Hard Page: 313-314

# Chapter 11 Global Marketing Management: Planning and Organization

## True/False Questions

1. Small firms cannot compete with giant multinationals in the global market.

   Answer: False Difficulty: Medium Page: 320

2. Unlike earlier approaches, the global marketing concept requires the marketer to develop unique marketing mixes tailored specifically to each country in which it operates.

   Answer: False Difficulty: Medium Page: 320

3. The America-First Corporation seeks to identify and target cross-cultural similarities in developing its international marketing strategies. The firm's philosophy of treating the world as one market is MOST consistent with the practice of global marketing management.

   Answer: True Difficulty: Hard Page: 320

4. Global marketing management seeks to standardize the marketing mix wherever possible in order to reap the benefits of economies of scale in production and marketing.

   Answer: True Difficulty: Medium Page: 321

5. Global recognition of brand names and/or corporate logos accelerates new product introductions and increases the efficiency and effectiveness of advertising.

   Answer: True Difficulty: Medium Page: 322

6. The America-First Corporation is currently active in 36 countries throughout the world. If the firm shifts to a global approach to managing its marketing operations, it should realize improved control and coordination of its marketing efforts.

   Answer: True Difficulty: Hard Page: 322-323

7. Generally, the ability to plan successfully for domestic marketing is proof of a manager's ability to successfully plan for international marketing activities.

   Answer: False Difficulty: Medium Page: 324

8. A firm cannot plan effectively unless it has clearly defined objectives.

   Answer: True Difficulty: Medium Page: 324

9. The America-First Corporation is considering entry into the international arena. The firm should first be certain that it is indeed committed to this effort for the long term.

   Answer: True Difficulty: Hard Page: 326

10. During the first phase of the international marketing planning process, a firm should attempt to find a match between the company's needs and the needs of potential markets.

Answer: True Difficulty: Medium Page: 326

11. The America-First Corporation has identified several potential international markets. The firm must now evaluate its marketing mix to identify those components that could be standardized and those that must be adapted to meet unique market needs.

Answer: True Difficulty: Hard Page: 327

12. Once a firm has begun to develop a marketing plan, it is certain that entry into a potential market will, in fact, be successfully accomplished.

Answer: False Difficulty: Medium Page: 329

13. Once a marketing plan has been implemented, the planning process is complete.

Answer: False Difficulty: Medium Page: 329

14. The America-First Corporation sells much of its output to domestic retailers who, in turn, export to foreign customers. The firm is involved in indirect exporting.

Answer: True Difficulty: Hard Page: 331

15. The America-First Corporation would like to engage in direct sales to foreign customers, but desires to minimize the risks associated with direct export. The firm should investigate the use of Internet marketing.

Answer: True Difficulty: Hard Page: 332

16. By definition, contractual agreements involve equity transfers between domestic firms and their foreign representatives.

Answer: False Difficulty: Medium Page: 332

17. The America-First Corporation allows selected foreign companies to use the firm's technology and brand names in return for fees. The firm is engaged in a licensing arrangement.

Answer: True Difficulty: Hard Page: 333

18. Franchising is the fastest-growing market-entry strategy.

Answer: True Difficulty: Easy Page: 334

19. The America-First Corporation has selected a London-based firm as its sole authorized distributor for Britain. The firm has entered into a master franchise arrangement.

    Answer: True   Difficulty: Hard   Page: 335

20. Under a "simple" franchise arrangement, a franchisee is licensed to sell or use the franchiser's property in a specified way, within a specified area, in return for a specified fee.

    Answer: True   Difficulty: Medium   Page: 335

21. Unlike licensing and franchising, a joint venture is a partnership in which two or more firms unite to form a separate legal entity to accomplish a specified goal.

    Answer: True   Difficulty: Easy   Page: 336

22. The America-First Corporation has formed partnerships with several Chinese firms to facilitate entry into the Chinese market. The firm is making use of the joint venture method of market entry.

    Answer: True   Difficulty: Hard   Page: 336

23. A consortia is composed of a foreign firm and a large number of participating "partners" that must all have active domestic dealings within the same country or countries.

    Answer: False   Difficulty: Medium   Page: 337

24. The growth of free-trade areas has encouraged more multinational firms to consider direct foreign investment as a means of market entry.

    Answer: True   Difficulty: Medium   Page: 338

25. A strategic international alliance is a synergistic relationship established to achieve a mutually beneficial common goal.

    Answer: True   Difficulty: Easy   Page: 339

26. Strategic international alliances are feasible only as a means of minimizing political and/or legal risks.

    Answer: False   Difficulty: Medium   Page: 339

27. The America-First Corporation has identified several foreign opportunities, but lacks some of the skills and resources to take advantage of them. The firm may seek to form strategic alliances with foreign firms in order to acquire those assets at minimum cost and risk to itself.

    Answer: True   Difficulty: Hard   Page: 340

28. The matrix organizational structure is the only approach that has proven to be effective in the integration of foreign and domestic marketing activities.

    Answer: False Difficulty: Medium Page: 341

29. If a firm employs a product line organization, it cannot make use of geographical specialization.

    Answer: False Difficulty: Medium Page: 341

30. In spite of the particular organizational approach used, most firms seek to maximize centralization of decision-making.

    Answer: True Difficulty: Medium Page: 342

**Multiple Choice Questions**

31. In global marketing, the greatest advantage enjoyed by small firms results from:
    A) the capital they possess.
    B) flexibility.
    C) governmental subsidies.
    D) their ability to pa "top dollar" for executives.

    Answer: B Difficulty: Hard Page: 320

32. As the America-First Corporation gained experience in international marketing, the firm began to develop a unique marketing mix adapted to the unique cultural characteristics of each country in which it was active. The firm's approach would be best described as a:
    A) Domestic Extension Market Concept.
    B) Modified Market Concept.
    C) Domestic Market Concept.
    D) Global Market Concept.

    Answer: D Difficulty: Hard Page: 320

33. The America-First corporation views the world as its market, and seeks opportunities to develop a standardized marketing mix for entire sets of country markets. The firm is employing a:
    A) Domestic Market Extension Concept.
    B) Multidomestic Market Concept.
    C) Global Market Concept.
    D) Modified Market Concept.

    Answer: C Difficulty: Hard Page: 320

34. Under a global market orientation, market segments:
    A) reflect differences.
    B) identify customized markets.
    C) follow regional/national differences.
    D) reflect cross-cultural similarities.

    Answer: D Difficulty: Medium Page: 321

35. All of the following are characteristics of the global approach to international marketing except:
    A) an emphasis on the heterogeneity of markets.
    B) the world is viewed as the market.
    C) homogeneous markets are sought across country sets.
    D) marketing mix standardization is sought whenever possible.

    Answer: A Difficulty: Medium Page: 321

36. The most frequently cited benefit of globalization and standardization of the marketing mix is:
    A) the creation of a global image.
    B) the transfer of experience and know-how across countries.
    C) economies of scale in production and marketing.
    D) control and coordination of operations.

    Answer: C Difficulty: Medium Page: 322

37. The German subsidiary of the America-First Corporation has developed a new synthetic rubber and tread design that provides better handling, mileage, and tread life on the German autobahns. The firm is finding a strong market for the new offering in the U.S. and other nations with advanced highway systems. America-First's experience demonstrates how a global orientation can:
    A) create economies of scale in production and marketing.
    B) transfer experience and know-how across countries.
    C) create a global image.
    D) improve control and coordination of operations.

    Answer: B Difficulty: Hard Page: 322

38. The America-First Corporation has carefully promoted its brand names and corporate logos across Europe for more than a decade. The firm's strong global image will be invaluable in:
    A) accelerating new product introductions.
    B) improving control of operations.
    C) transferring experience across countries.
    D) improving coordination of operations.

    Answer: A Difficulty: Hard Page: 323

# Chapter 11 Global Marketing Management: Planning and Organization

39. Standardization often results in a reduction in the number of products, brands, and advertising campaigns that allows a firm to:
    A) accelerate new product introductions.
    B) transfer experience and know-how across countries.
    C) create a global image.
    D) improve control and coordination of operations.

    Answer: D Difficulty: Medium Page: 323

40. All of the following factors impede global standardization except:
    A) government and trade restrictions.
    B) differences in the availability of media.
    C) improved global communication.
    D) cultural differences.

    Answer: C Difficulty: Medium Page: 323

41. The firm attempts to manage the effects of external, uncontrollable factors on its strengths, weaknesses, objectives, and goals to attain a desired end through the process of:
    A) global sourcing.
    B) strategic planning.
    C) strategic international alliances.
    D) strategic offsetting.

    Answer: B Difficulty: Easy Page: 324

42. The top management of the America-First Corporation is involved in setting general, long-term goals for the firm's activities in the international market. Management is developing a:
    A) corporate plan.
    B) strategic plan.
    C) tactical plan.
    D) operational plan.

    Answer: A Difficulty: Hard Page: 324

43. Which of the following seeks to relate the firm's products, capital, and research to its long- and short-term goals?
    A) corporate plans.
    B) strategic plans.
    C) tactical plans.
    D) operational plans.

    Answer: B Difficulty: Easy Page: 324

44. Which of the following relates to the specific actions and allocation of resources used to implement the firm's general, long-range goals in specific markets?
A) corporate plans.
B) strategic plans.
C) global plans.
D) tactical plans.

Answer: D Difficulty: Easy Page: 324

45. The first step in international marketing is always:
A) adapting the marketing mix to target markets.
B) developing the marketing plan.
C) evaluation of potential markets.
D) implementation and control.

Answer: C Difficulty: Medium Page: 326

46. The America-First Corporation is beginning the planning process for possible international efforts. Which of the following must be kept in mind in all phases of this process?
A) company location.
B) company objectives and resources.
C) organizational philosophy.
D) form of ownership.

Answer: B Difficulty: Hard Page: 326

47. The need to carefully consider a firm's objectives and resources prior to entering foreign markets has been emphasized by:
A) increasing competition.
B) increased entry costs.
C) more firms having current foreign commitments.
D) all of the above.

Answer: D Difficulty: Medium Page: 326

48. If foreign market opportunities do not match company objectives, it may be necessary to:
A) change the objectives.
B) alter the scale of international plans.
C) abandon international plans.
D) Any of the above.

Answer: D Difficulty: Medium Page: 326

# Chapter 11 Global Marketing Management: Planning and Organization

49. After a firm has reviewed its objectives and resources, it should:
    A) determine the level of commitment it is prepared to support.
    B) develop a marketing plan.
    C) develop advertising copy.
    D) create distribution channels.

    Answer: A Difficulty: Medium Page: 326

50. The America-First Corporation has announced that it is committed to international operations. The firm's announcement means that America-First:
    A) will invest the amounts required.
    B) will hire the necessary personnel.
    C) will enter for the "long-run" payoffs.
    D) all of the above.

    Answer: D Difficulty: Medium Page: 326

51. The first stage of the international marketing planning process is:
    A) evaluation of potential markets.
    B) implementation and control.
    C) marketing mix adaptation.
    D) developing the marketing plan.

    Answer: A Difficulty: Easy Page: 326

52. The America-First Corporation is preparing to evaluate potential foreign markets for entry. During this stage, the firm will primarily rely on:
    A) identifying countries with the largest populations.
    B) identifying nations that speak English.
    C) identifying markets that best fit its objectives and resources.
    D) its competitor's actions.

    Answer: C Difficulty: Hard Page: 326

53. Which of the following activities MOST clearly differentiates international from domestic market planning?
    A) establishment of firm's objectives and resources.
    B) defining the level of commitment to be made.
    C) identifying and understanding uncontrollable elements of the environment.
    D) developing a marketing mix.

    Answer: C Difficulty: Medium Page: 326-327

54. Having completed its initial evaluation of potential foreign markets, the AmericaFirst Corporation is utilizing the data generated to determine the degree of standardization/adaptation of the marketing mix that might be required. A mistake at this stage would lead to:
A) costly mistakes from failure to standardize where possible.
B) products inappropriate for the intended market.
C) costly mistakes in pricing, advertising, and promotion.
D) Any, or all, of the above.

Answer: D Difficulty: Hard Page: 329

55. During which of the following stages of the marketing planning process are budgets and sales and profit expectations developed?
A) preliminary analysis and screening.
B) adapting the marketing mix to target markets.
C) developing the marketing plan.
D) implementation and control.

Answer: C Difficulty: Medium Page: 329

56. The America-First Corporation is preparing to develop a marketing plan for its international efforts. The firm will BEGIN this effort by:
A) conducting a situation analysis.
B) selecting an entry mode.
C) standardizing its advertising.
D) establishing control criteria.

Answer: A Difficulty: Hard Page: 329

57. Which of the following actions mark the END of the marketing planning phase?
A) conducting a situation analysis.
B) selecting an entry mode and action program.
C) standardizing advertising.
D) exercising control.

Answer: B Difficulty: Medium Page: 330

58. Although the America-First Corporation does not actively seek international sales, the firm regularly sells to foreign customers who place orders for its products. The firm is engaged in:
A) joint ventures.
B) licensing.
C) direct exporting.
D) Franchising.

Answer: C Difficulty: Hard Page: 331

# Chapter 11 Global Marketing Management: Planning and Organization

59. Goods-Your-Way is a small, start-up company with little capital or name recognition. Which of the following is the MOST feasible way for the firm to enter the international market?
    A) joint ventures.
    B) direct exporting.
    C) Franchising.
    D) international Internet marketing.

    Answer: D Difficulty: Hard Page: 332

60. Long-term, non-equity associations between a company and another in a foreign market are called:
    A) contractual agreements.
    B) export agreements.
    C) matrix organizations.
    D) vendor's agreements.

    Answer: A Difficulty: Easy Page: 332

61. All of the following are examples of contractual agreements EXCEPT:
    A) consortia.
    B) Internet marketing.
    C) licensing.
    D) franchising.

    Answer: B Difficulty: Medium Page: 332

62. Which of the following MAY be the least profitable, although low risk, means of entering foreign markets?
    A) direct investment.
    B) joint ventures.
    C) licensing.
    D) direct exporting.

    Answer: C Difficulty: Medium Page: 333

63. In which of the following approaches to international marketing does a firm grant a foreign-based company the right to use its intellectual property in return for the payment of royalties or fees?
    A) exporting.
    B) licensing.
    C) joint ventures.
    D) locating manufacturing in foreign nations.

    Answer: B Difficulty: Medium Page: 333

64. In which of the following is a foreign business provided a standard package of products, systems, and management services in return for its market knowledge, capital, and personal involvement in management?
A) joint ventures.
B) wholly owned subsidiaries.
C) consortia.
D) franchising.

Answer: D Difficulty: Medium Page: 333

65. Which of the following is the fastest-growing market-entry strategy?
A) direct export.
B) franchising.
C) licensing.
D) joint ventures.

Answer: B Difficulty: Easy Page: 334

66. The America-First Corporation has granted a single Russian firm the right to sell its products, use its brand and logo, and employ its technology in the greater Moscow area. The firm has negotiated a(n):
A) joint-venture.
B) licensing arrangement.
C) master franchise agreement.
D) consortia.

Answer: C Difficulty: Hard Page: 335

67. Which of the following methods of market entry seeks to minimize political and cultural risks by creating a legal partnership with a foreign firm?
A) joint ventures.
B) direct export.
C) licensing.
D) Internet marketing.

Answer: A Difficulty: Medium Page: 336

68. A joint venture is characterized by which of the following?
A) the partners intent to share in management.
B) the partners are separate legal entities.
C) equity positions are held by all partners.
D) all of the above.

Answer: D Difficulty: Medium Page: 336

69. A joint venture is especially attractive when:
A) it enables the firm to utilize a partner's special skills.
B) allows access to the partner's local distribution system.
C) the target country does not allow wholly-owned activities.
D) any or all of the above.

Answer: D Difficulty: Medium Page: 336

70. The America-First Corporation, on order to gain access to the Japanese market has formed partnerships with several Japanese firms. The legal entity that resulted would be BEST described as a(n):
A) export union.
B) licensing agreement.
C) joint venture.
D) wholly owned subsidiary.

Answer: C Difficulty: Hard Page: 336

71. A form of joint venture that is characterized by a large number of participants and operation in a country or market in which none of the participants is currently active is called a:
A) consortium.
B) joint venture.
C) franchising agreement.
D) wholly owned subsidiary.

Answer: A Difficulty: Easy Page: 337

72. The America-First Corporation is preparing to participate in a major dam construction project in China. The firm is MOST likely to seek partners having the market access and skills it lacks by forming a:
A) joint venture.
B) consortium.
C) licensing agreement.
D) franchising arrangement.

Answer: B Difficulty: Hard Page: 337

73. The growth of free trade areas has made which of the following market entry approaches more feasible and profitable?
A) joint ventures.
B) franchising.
C) direct investment.
D) licensing.

Answer: C Difficulty: Medium Page: 338

74. A business relationship established by two or more companies to cooperate out of mutual need and to share risk in achieving a common objective is called a:
A) mutual venture.
B) strategic offset.
C) strategic international alliance.
D) business partnership.

Answer: C Difficulty: Easy Page: 339

75. The America-First Corporation is seeking a synergistic relationship with other firms to achieve common goals and provide benefits for both parties. The firm should consider the creation of a:
A) strategic international alliance.
B) global sourcing initiative.
C) line reduction policy.
D) global brand image.

Answer: A Difficulty: Hard Page: 339

76. The America-First Corporation is concerned about the possibility of being closed out of the single European market. The firm is seeking to ensure its access to the European market by forging a mutually beneficial relationship with a firm in at least one of the member countries. America-First is contemplating the formation of a:
A) global sourcing initiative.
B) global brand coalition.
C) promotional cartel.
D) strategic international alliance.

Answer: D Difficulty: Hard Page: 339

77. International firms typically organize for their efforts by employing:
A) global product divisions.
B) geographical divisions.
C) a matrix organization.
D) any of the above.

Answer: D Difficulty: Medium Page: 341

78. The America-First Corporation feels that close relationships with its "host" national and local governments are crucial to its success. The firm is MOST likely to use:
A) a geographic organization structure.
B) a matrix organization structure.
C) the global product division approach.
D) none of the above.

Answer: A Difficulty: Hard Page: 341

79. Which of the following is the MOST popular form of organizational structures used by international firms?
A) global product divisions
B) geographic organizations
C) matrix organizations
D) All are equally popular.

Answer: C Difficulty: Medium Page: 341

80. The America-First Corporation seeks the efficiencies of standardization whenever possible, but is sensitive to local preferences that affect its success. Which of the following types of decisions is MOST likely to be made in a centralized fashion:
A) pricing decisions.
B) product decisions.
C) distribution decisions.
D) advertising decisions.

Answer: B Difficulty: Hard Page: 342

**Fill in the Blank Questions**

81. The most important force driving the move toward global marketing is the need to stay _____.

Answer: cost competitive Difficulty: Easy Page: 320

82. The Internet and customized manufacturing may enhance a trend "back" to the strategy of _______.

Answer: localization Difficulty: Easy Page: 320

83. The _______________ concept encourages the standardization of the marketing mix whenever feasible on a cost and culture basis.

Answer: global market Difficulty: Easy Page: 321

84. The benefits of a global orientation include _______________ in production and marketing, the _______________ of experience and knowledge across countries, access to the world's toughest _____, and stability of ______.

Answer: economies of scale; transfer; customers; revenues Difficulty: Medium Page: 322-323

85. The America-First Corporation is preparing to enter the international arena. The firm's planning activities should begin with an evaluation of its ___________ and _______.

Answer: objectives; resources Difficulty: Hard Page: 325

86. The degree of ______________ to an international marketing cause reflects the extent of a company's involvement.

Answer: commitment Difficulty: Medium Page: 326

87. The purpose of preliminary __________ and ______ is to match company and country needs.

Answer: analysis; screening Difficulty: Medium Page: 326

88. During preliminary analysis and screening, the focus is on selection of potential country ______, the identification of _______________ criteria, and an analysis of environmental ______.

Answer: markets; screening; uncontrollables Difficulty: Medium Page: 326

89. The America-First Corporation is engaged in the second phase of the planning process. The firm is attempting to adapt the firm's _______________ to target markets.

Answer: marketing mix Difficulty: Hard Page: 328

90. The marketing plan begins with a(n) _______________ and culminates with the selection of a(n) _______________ and a specific _______________ for the market.

Answer: situation analysis; entry mode; action plan Difficulty: Medium Page: 329

91. No marketing plan is useful until it is ______________ and subjected to _____ and _____.

Answer: implemented; coordination; control Difficulty: Medium Page: 329

92. A firm selling to a buyer in its home country who, in turn, sells abroad is said to engage in _______________ to distinguish such actions from _______________--the sale of goods to customers in other countries.

Answer: indirect exporting; direct exporting Difficulty: Medium Page: 331

93. The America-First Corporation has described its method of entering the international market as high-tech, low cost, and low risk. The firm is probably utilizing _______________ marketing.

Answer: Internet Difficulty: Hard Page: 332

94. Contractual agreements include _______________, _______________, ___________________, and _______________.

Answer: licensing; franchising; joint ventures; consortia Difficulty: Medium Page: 332

# Chapter 11 Global Marketing Management: Planning and Organization

95. The America-First Corporation operates in many diverse cultures characterized by a high degree of political risk. The firm is likely to favor the use of the ______________ in these environments.

    Answer: joint venture   Difficulty: Hard   Page: 336

96. The ______________ is typically composed of a large number of participants working on large projects in a country in which they have not been domestically active.

    Answer: Consortia   Difficulty: Medium   Page: 337

97. The riskiest and most costly method of entering international marketing is through ______________.

    Answer: direct foreign investment   Difficulty: Medium   Page: 338

98. A(n) ______________ is a business relationship established by two or more companies to operate out of mutual need and to share risk in achieving a common objective.

    Answer: strategic international alliance   Difficulty: Easy   Page: 339

99. The ______________ approach is currently the most common form of international business organization.

    Answer: matrix   Difficulty: Easy   Page: 341

100. If a product is culturally sensitive, decisions are more apt to be ______________.

    Answer: decentralized   Difficulty: Medium   Page: 342

## Essay Questions

101. How does global marketing management differ from international marketing management? What benefits are offered by a global orientation?

    Answer:
    Global marketing differs from international marketing in its orientation. Global marketing views the world as its market and is based on identifying and targeting cross-cultural similarities. International marketing is guided by the belief that each foreign market requires its own culturally adapted marketing strategy. The greatest benefit of global marketing lies in the economies of scale in production and marketing it offers. The approach also offers experience and know-how transfers across countries, the ability to build a global image, and improved control and coordination of operations.

    Difficulty: Hard   Page: 320-323

102. Briefly describe the benefits of planning for international marketing efforts. Outline the basic steps in this process.

Answer:
Planning allows the firm to prepare for the future. The firm begins the effort by objectively evaluating its objectives and resources and determining the level of commitment to international marketing the firm is prepared to make. The planning process itself requires the firm to use the knowledge previously developed to match company and country needs, adapt its marketing mix to target markets, finalize the marketing plan, implement the plan, and control results.

Difficulty: Hard Page: 324-330

103. Why is exporting a popular method of entering international marketing? Differentiate between direct and indirect exporting.

Answer:
Traditionally, exporting has allowed domestic firms to sell abroad with minimum cost and risk. Initially, firms saw this as simply a means of expanding the sales of its existing offerings—although expansion of the effort often required modifications later. Under indirect exporting, a domestic firm sells to a buyer in their home market who, in turn, exports to other countries. The marketing costs and problems rest with the exporting firm rather than the producer. Direct exporting places the producing firm in the center of the marketing effort. It must develop marketing and distribution plans for its foreign offerings alone, or in concert with foreign partners.

Difficulty: Hard Page: 331-332

104. Briefly evaluate the problems and potential of the Internet as a tool of international marketing.

Answer:
Like exporting, many firms "happened" onto the Internet almost by accident. The Internet offers global reach at the absolute minimum cost and risk. With experience, communications can be standardized or adaptations instantly provided at the click of a mouse. At present, this approach is "technology limited" and subject to both real and perceived security problems that may preclude use.

Difficulty: Hard Page: 332

105. Briefly describe the major forms of contractual agreements available to the international marketer. How do strategic investment alliances differ from these tools?

Answer:
Contractual agreements (licensing, franchising, joint ventures, and consortia) are long-term, non-equity associations between a company and another in a foreign country. Licensing grants the use of patent rights, trademark rights, and the rights to use technological processes in return for royalties and fees. Franchising, a form of licensing, allows a franchiser to provide a standard package of products, systems, and management services to a franchisee who provides market knowledge, capital, and personal involvement in management. A joint venture is a partnership of two or more participating firms that join to create separate legal entities. A consortium involves a large number of participants that often operates in a country or market in which none of the participants are currently active. A strategic international alliance is a business relationship established by two or more firms to cooperate out of mutual need and to share risk.

Difficulty: Hard Page: 332-338

# Chapter 12 Products and Services for Consumers

## True/False Questions

1. Regardless of the orientation taken by an international firm toward its foreign markets, quality products are a global requirement.

   Answer: True Difficulty: Medium Page: 347

2. In the global economy, quality has become a commodity.

   Answer: True Difficulty: Medium Page: 348

3. In many of its foreign markets, the America First Corporation has had to modify its products to comply with local product and service standards. The firm is a "victim" of product homoginization.

   Answer: False Difficulty: Hard Page: 349

4. The United States is the recognized leader in the global practice of "green marketing."

   Answer: False Difficulty: Easy Page: 349

5. The less economically developed a market is, the greater the degree of change a product may need for acceptance

   Answer: True Difficulty: Medium Page: 349

6. Environmental concerns, which vary in focus and degree around the world, are reshaping the traditional definition of quality.

   Answer: True Difficulty: Medium Page: 349-350

7. Basically, a product consists of all attributes--both tangible and intangible--capable of providing want satisfaction.

   Answer: True Difficulty: Easy Page: 350

8. Advocates of standardization believe that price, quality, and reliability offset any differential advantage of a culturally adapted product.

   Answer: True Difficulty: Medium Page: 350-351

9. In the product area, the real question is not whether to adapt or standardize, but how much adaptation is necessary and to what point a product can be standardized.

   Answer: True Difficulty: Medium Page: 350-351

10. If an international company must adapt its products to meet local cultural preferences, standardization will not be feasible to any degree.

    Answer: False Difficulty: Medium Page: 350-351

11. Product adaptation is limited to changes in the physical attributes of the product.

    Answer: False Difficulty: Medium Page: 352

12. An important first step in adapting a product to a foreign market is to determine the DEGREE of newness that is acceptable in the target market and how the innovation is perceived.

    Answer: True Difficulty: Medium Page: 354

13. Many of the products sold by the America-First Corporation are perceived as innovations in the foreign markets served by the firm. America-First should use its knowledge of the market's willingness to accept change as a guide to its attempt to manage the diffusion process.

    Answer: True Difficulty: Hard Page: 354

14. The America-First Corporation is preparing to introduce several of its successful domestic products into foreign nations. While these products are in the mature stage of their domestic life cycle, the firm must base its foreign marketing programs on the stage of the product life cycle the product will occupy in each foreign market in which it is to be sold.

    Answer: True Difficulty: Hard Page: 354

15. In the final analysis, the consumer determines if a product is "new"--and the "degree of newness" that is involved.

    Answer: True Difficulty: Medium Page: 354

16. In general, the rate of diffusion is positively related to relative advantage, compatibility, trialability, and observability--but negatively related to complexity.

    Answer: True Difficulty: Medium Page: 357

17. The America-First Corporation produces a line of appliances for global distribution. Although variations in cultural preferences exist among its markets, the firm may still gain some of the efficiencies offered by standardization by developing core platforms containing the essential technology and "grafting" variations on this basic platform.

    Answer: True Difficulty: Hard Page: 358

18. The core product--composed of the essential technology and all of its design and functional features--provides the platform upon which product variations can be added or deleted to satisfy local differences.

    Answer: True Difficulty: Easy Page: 358

19. The packaging component includes style features, packaging, labeling, trademarks, brand name, quality, price, and all other elements of a product's package.

    Answer: True Difficulty: Easy Page: 360

20. When entering a new foreign market, the America-First Corporation makes certain that strong warranties and guarantees are offered, adequate parts inventory is maintained, and appropriately trained service personnel are available. The firm is emphasizing the support services component of the product component model.

    Answer: True Difficulty: Hard Page: 362

21. The MOST important characteristic of a service is its intangibility.

    Answer: True Difficulty: Medium Page: 363

22. The America-First Corporation has built a chain a theme parks designed specifically to attract foreign tourists visiting the United States. The firm has joined the nation's largest export industry.

    Answer: True Difficulty: Hard Page: 363

23. A global brand is the worldwide use of a name, term, sign, symbol, design, or combination thereof intended to identify goods or services of one seller and to differentiate them from those of competitors.

    Answer: True Difficulty: Easy Page: 367

24. A successful brand is the most valuable resource a company owns.

    Answer: True Difficulty: Medium Page: 368

25. If an international firm must adapt its products to local market conditions, it is precluded from the successful use of global brands.

    Answer: False Difficulty: Medium Page: 368

26. While global brands can facilitate the introduction of new global products, their use involves significantly greater costs than are associated with the use of market-specific brands.

    Answer: False Difficulty: Medium Page: 368

# Chapter 12 Products and Services for Consumers

27. The brand serves as an external cue that allows the consumer to quickly associate both tangible and intangible values with the products to which it may be applied.

    Answer: True Difficulty: Medium Page: 368-369

28. The America-First Corporation produces a wide variety of products in many different countries. The firm may benefit from the country-of-origin effect by producing specific products in those countries best known or positively associated with such goods.

    Answer: True Difficulty: Hard Page: 369-370

29. At one time, the phrase "Made in Japan" conjured up images of cheap tableware and novelty items. The experience of Japan proves that quality products, when combined with effective marketing, can, over time, overcome negative stereotypes.

    Answer: True Difficulty: Hard Page: 372

30. As global brands have become more common, private brands have been driven from the global marketplace.

    Answer: False Difficulty: Medium Page: 372

**Multiple Choice Questions**

31. Firms that tend to emphasize cultural sensitivity are MOST likely to advocate:
    A) standardized products.
    B) differentiated products.
    C) global brands.
    D) global marketing programs.

    Answer: B Difficulty: Medium Page: 346

32. Global competition has:
    A) shortened product life cycles.
    B) focused on the importance of quality.
    C) emphasized innovation and competitive pricing.
    D) all of the above.

    Answer: D Difficulty: Medium Page: 346

33. A firm that is entering foreign markets for the first time is probably the BEST candidate for use of a:
    A) domestic market extension strategy.
    B) multidomestic market strategy.
    C) global market strategy.
    D) synergistic market strategy.

    Answer: C Difficulty: Medium Page: 346

34. The power in the global market is shifting to the:
    A) manufacturer.
    B) customer.
    C) wholesaler.
    D) retailer.

    Answer: B Difficulty: Medium Page: 346-347

35. Which of the following is MOST critical to success in international marketing?
    A) standardized products.
    B) differentiated products.
    C) global brands.
    D) quality products.

    Answer: D Difficulty: Medium Page: 347

36. Advocates of standardization believe that any differential advantage of a culturally adapted product will be offset by:
    A) price.
    B) quality.
    C) reliability.
    D) all of the above.

    Answer: D Difficulty: Medium Page: 347-348

37. In order to sell in many of its foreign markets, the America-First Corporation has had to modify its offerings. The MOST likely reason for these adaptations is:
    A) product homologation.
    B) cultural adaptation.
    C) sociological homoginization.
    D) psychological standardization.

    Answer: A Difficulty: Hard Page: 349

38. Product adaptations are often dictated by a new market's:
    A) legal/economic requirements.
    B) technological requirements.
    C) climatic requirements.
    D) any, or all, of the above.

    Answer: D Difficulty: Medium Page: 349

39. A product is BEST conceived as:
    A) a tangible entity.
    B) a bundle of satisfactions.
    C) an intangible entity.
    D) a revenue producer.

    Answer: B Difficulty: Easy Page: 350

40. EC green marketing regulations are MOST burdensome with regard to:
    A) advertising claims.
    B) product quality standards.
    C) recycling of packaging materials.
    D) branding and logo standards.

    Answer: C Difficulty: Medium Page: 350

41. The acceptance of a product by foreign consumers is often affected by:
    A) cultural norms.
    B) cultural values.
    C) behavioral patterns.
    D) all of the above.

    Answer: D Difficulty: Medium Page: 352

42. Nestles' attempts to sell iced tea in England proved unsuccessful. The firm discovered the difficulty (impossibility) of changing strongly-held:
    A) price preferences.
    B) packaging preferences.
    C) cultural preferences.
    D) distribution methods.

    Answer: C Difficulty: Hard Page: 352-353

# Chapter 12 Products and Services for Consumers

43. The final judge of whether a product is "new" is the:
    A) manufacturer.
    B) engineer.
    C) inventor.
    D) consumer.

    Answer: D Difficulty: Medium Page: 354

44. The process by which an innovation spreads through a society is called:
    A) diffusion.
    B) distribution.
    C) innovating.
    D) marketing.

    Answer: A Difficulty: Easy Page: 354

45. The vast majority of services enter foreign markets by:
    A) direct export.
    B) electronic networks.
    C) licensing.
    D) piracy.

    Answer: C Difficulty: Medium Page: 364

46. The America-First Corporation is preparing to introduce a product that it has sold in the U.S. for several years into the Asian market. In considering possible adaptations such an introduction may require, the firm should be sure to include:
    A) production costs in the new markets.
    B) advertising costs in the new markets.
    C) the stage of the product life cycle in the new markets.
    D) managerial talent in the new country.

    Answer: C Difficulty: Hard Page: 354

47. In entering a foreign market, the America-First Corporation seeks to achieve as large a market share as possible as quickly as possible. The firm should carefully study the process of:
    A) distribution.
    B) diffusion.
    C) production.
    D) advertising.

    Answer: B Difficulty: Hard Page: 354-355

48. The diffusion of an innovation requires:
A) an innovation.
B) communication through appropriate channels over time.
C) members of a social system.
D) all of the above.

Answer: D Difficulty: Medium Page: 355

49. The goal of the marketer of an innovation is to:
A) speed widespread adoption.
B) delay competitive entry.
C) minimize the use of advertising.
D) avoid making a financial commitment.

Answer: A Difficulty: Medium Page: 355

50. The rate of diffusion of an innovation is affected by the:
A) degree of perceived newness.
B) perceived attributes of the innovation.
C) method used to communicate the innovation.
D) all of the above.

Answer: D Difficulty: Medium Page: 356

51. The America-First Corporation believes that customer perceptions of innovations are based on relative advantage, compatibility, complexity, trialability, and observability. The firm is evaluating potential innovations based on the:
A) number of innovations.
B) characteristics of innovations.
C) cost of innovations.
D) age of innovations.

Answer: B Difficulty: Hard Page: 356

52. The perceived marginal value of a new product as compared to an existing product is described by the term:
A) relative advantage.
B) complexity.
C) compatibility.
D) observability.

Answer: A Difficulty: Easy Page: 356

53. The America-First Corporation is convinced that the primary factor in the success of an innovation is the product's ability to "fit in" with acceptable behavior, norms, and values of the target society. The firm is focusing on the innovation's:
A) complexity.
B) observability.
C) relative advantages.
D) compatibility.

Answer: D Difficulty: Hard Page: 356-357

54. The majority of R&D expenditures and Internet innovations are found in:
A) the United States.
B) Japan.
C) South America.
D) the EC.

Answer: A Difficulty: Medium Page: 357

55. The America-First Corporation typically provides a large sampling program to support introductions of new soaps and shampoos. The firm is seeking to assure success by emphasizing the factor of:
A) observability.
B) complexity.
C) trialability.
D) compatibility.

Answer: C Difficulty: Hard Page: 357

56. The ease with which the benefits of an innovation can be communicated is related to the factor of:
A) observability.
B) complexity.
C) compatibility.
D) trialability.

Answer: A Difficulty: Easy Page: 357

57. The rate of diffusion of an innovation is POSITIVELY related to all of the following product characteristics EXCEPT:
A) compatibility.
B) observability.
C) complexity.
D) trialability.

Answer: C Difficulty: Medium Page: 357

58. In analyzing the characteristics of an innovation to be introduced into a foreign market, the international marketer must be especially concerned with the fact that the results may be "contaminated" by:
A) economic projections.
B) their self-reference criterion.
C) production difficulties.
D) distribution difficulties.

Answer: B Difficulty: Medium Page: 357

59. In the FINAL analysis, the only evaluation of an innovation that matters is the one made by the:
A) marketer.
B) foreign government.
C) foreign middleman.
D) foreign consumer.

Answer: D Difficulty: Medium Page: 357

60. The core component, packaging component, and support services component of a product offering are analyzed through the use of the:
A) Product Component Model.
B) Analysis of Product Characteristics.
C) Analysis of Distribution Problems.
D) Model of Innovative Competitiveness.

Answer: A Difficulty: Easy Page: 358

61. The physical product--the platform that contains the essential technology--and all its design and functional features is described by the product's:
A) support services component.
B) packaging component.
C) core component.
D) marketing mix component.

Answer: C Difficulty: Easy Page: 358

62. The America-First Corporation has decided to make significant capital investments in basic research to create new product technologies. The firm is focusing on which of the following parts of the Product Component Model?
A) the support services component.
B) the core component.
C) the packaging component.
D) the marketing mix component.

Answer: B Difficulty: Hard Page: 358

63. The America-First Corporation recognizes that while some homogeneity exists across cultures, local cultural differences also exist. The firm might best approach this problem by:
A) developing a standardized core platform capable of supporting variations.
B) developing totally standardized products.
C) developing totally adapted products.
D) developing culturally specific products.

Answer: A Difficulty: Hard Page: 358-359

64. The America-First Corporation is developing a global brand name and logo to identify all of the products it sells worldwide. The firm is focusing on which of the following parts of the Product Component Model?
A) the support services component.
B) the marketing mix component.
C) the core component.
D) the packaging component.

Answer: D Difficulty: Hard Page: 360-361

65. The America-First Corporation is the world leader in the marketing of genetically modified (GM) food. The firm is MOST likely to experience opposition in:
A) Japan.
B) Australia.
C) the European Union.
D) New Zealand.

Answer: C Difficulty: Hard Page: 362

66. The America-First Corporation routinely emphasizes guarantees, warranties, and post-sale service as part of the introduction of any innovation. The firm is focusing on which of the following parts of the Product Component Model?
A) the support services component.
B) the core component.
C) the marketing mix component.
D) the packaging component.

Answer: A Difficulty: Hard Page: 362

67. Services are characterized by:
A) intangibility.
B) inseparability.
C) heterogeneity.
D) all of the above.

Answer: D Difficulty: Easy Page: 363

68. According to the UN, the MOST popular tourist destination in the next century will be:
A) the United States.
B) China.
C) France.
D) Russia.

Answer: B Difficulty: Easy Page: 363

69. The America-First Corporation is a major exporter of services to the global market. The firm is likely to find the closest approximation to a single market for its offerings in:
A) South America.
B) the Pacific Rim.
C) the Baltic States.
D) the European Union.

Answer: D Difficulty: Hard Page: 365

70. The worldwide use of a name, term, sign, symbol, design or combination thereof intended to identify goods or services of one seller and to differentiate them from those of competitors is at the core of:
A) national branding.
B) generic branding.
C) global branding.
D) domestic branding.

Answer: C Difficulty: Easy Page: 367

71. The most valuable resource a company has is:
A) a successful product.
B) a successful brand.
C) "cutting-edge" technology.
D) flexibility of supply.

Answer: B Difficulty: Medium Page: 368

72. Any influence that the nation in which a product is manufactured has on a consumer's positive or negative perception of that product is described by the:
A) country-of-origin effect.
B) location-of-production effect.
C) manufacturing location effect.
D) production location effect.

Answer: A Difficulty: Easy Page: 369

73. The positive or negative attitude engendered by the country of origin is affected by:
A) the country.
B) the type of product.
C) the image of the company and its brands.
D) ALL of the above.

Answer: D Difficulty: Medium Page: 370

74. Country-of-origin stereotypes tend to be:
A) applied to all products produced in that country.
B) product specific.
C) based on factual product comparisons.
D) unfairly biased judgments.

Answer: B Difficulty: Medium Page: 370

75. Wal-Mart's promise to feature American-made products is an appeal to:
A) ethnocentrism.
B) stereotyping.
C) Japan-"bashing."
D) a desire for low-price/low-quality products.

Answer: A Difficulty: Hard Page: 371

76. Which of the following types of countries typically enjoy the highest quality image for their products?
A) newly emerging nations.
B) developing countries.
C) industrialized countries.
D) underdeveloped nations.

Answer: C Difficulty: Medium Page: 371

77. Which of the following nations is currently enjoying an almost "FADDISH" acceptance of the products produced by its manufacturers?
A) China.
B) Japan.
C) Korea.
D) the United States.

Answer: D Difficulty: Medium Page: 372

78. Which of the following countries has provided the MOST dramatic example of how superior product quality and effective marketing can overcome a negative image?
A) Japan.
B) Germany.
C) France.
D) the United States.

Answer: A Difficulty: Medium Page: 372

79. Manufacturers' brands are increasingly being challenged by private brands owned by:
A) agents.
B) governments.
C) retailers.
D) wholesalers.

Answer: C Difficulty: Medium Page: 372

80. The America-First Corporation is preparing to introduce some of its existing products into other countries. Which of the following attributes of its products is the firmMOST likely to have to alter to ensure successful introductions?
A) physical size.
B) materials.
C) psychological attributes.
D) basic functions.

Answer: C Difficulty: Hard Page: 372

**Fill in the Blank Questions**

81. The consumer defines quality along the dimensions of _______________ quality and _______________ quality.

Answer: market-perceived; performance Difficulty: Medium Page: 347

82. More than a physical item, a product is a bundle of _______________ the buyer receives.

Answer: satisfactions Difficulty: Medium Page: 350

83. Product _______________ leads to production economies and other savings that permit profits at prices that make products attractive to the global market.

Answer: standardization Difficulty: Medium Page: 350-351

84. The America-First Corporation is selling a number of products perceived as "mature" products in the United States in foreign countries in which they seen as innovations. The firm's experience shows that the _______________ must be considered in any plan to introduce domestic products overseas.

    Answer: product life cycle  Difficulty: Hard  Page: 354

85. Regardless of the nation in which a product is introduced, marketers must be concerned with the process of _______________, which determines how the innovation will spread through society.

    Answer: diffusion  Difficulty: Medium  Page: 354

86. The America-First Corporation is launching a full-scale study of the way in which new products spread through foreign societies. The firm is attempting to understand the international aspects of the _______________.

    Answer: diffusion process  Difficulty: Hard  Page: 354

87. The rate of acceptance for a product is affected by its _______________, _______________, _______________, _______________, and _______________.

    Answer: relative advantage; compatibility; complexity; trialability; observability  Difficulty: Medium  Page: 356-357

88. The America-First Corporation markets a wide range of "high-tech" products that would generally be considered to be radical innovations. The firm must try to reduce the perceived _______________ of its products to encourage diffusion.

    Answer: complexity  Difficulty: Hard  Page: 357

89. The domestic marketer's attempts to evaluate product perceptions of potential foreign adopters may be adversely affected by his or her _______________.

    Answer: self-reference criterion  Difficulty: Hard  Page: 357

90. Product adaptation is often dictated by the _______________, _______________, _______________, _______________, and _______________ requirements of the local market.

    Answer: legal; economic; political; technological; climatic  Difficulty: Medium  Page: 357

91. The _______________ is the physical product, or essential technology, with all its design and functional features.

    Answer: core component  Difficulty: Easy  Page: 358

# Chapter 12 Products and Services for Consumers

92. The America-First Corporation pays particular attention to branding, coloration, and labeling of its foreign brands. The firm is focusing on the ______________ component of its products.

    Answer: packaging component  Difficulty: Hard  Page: 360

93. The America-First Corporation attempts to be sure that its products are backed by an adequate supply of spare and repair parts. The firm is focusing on the ______________ component of its effort.

    Answer: bills of lading  Difficulty: Hard  Page: 362

94. _____ are the LATEST problem to be faced by firms engaged in global marketing.

    Answer: Transborder data flows  Difficulty: Medium  Page: 365

95. The America-First Corporation has had a major problem with the theft of its intellectual property in China. The firm's "best" defense under international treaty may be found in the TRIPs portion of the _______ Agreement.

    Answer: GATT  Difficulty: Hard  Page: 366

96. The America-First Corporation routinely adapts its domestic products for sale abroad. The firm is following a(n) ______________ strategy.

    Answer: multidomestic market  Difficulty: Hard  Page: 366

97. A(n) ______________ brand is defined as the worldwide use of a name, term, symbol, design, or combination thereof intended to identify the goods or services of one seller and to differentiate them from those of competitors.

    Answer: Global  Difficulty: Easy  Page: 367

98. The ______________ is defined as any influence that the country of manufacture has on a consumer's positive or negative perception of a product.

    Answer: country-of-origin effect  Difficulty: Easy  Page: 369

99. The America-First Corporation is a major exporter of computer software and Internet technology. The firm is likely to benefit from the favorable _____ effects.

    Answer: country-of-origin  Difficulty: Hard  Page: 369

100. The America-First Corporation is concerned about the increasing competition its national brands are facing from retailer-owned brands in its retail outlets. The firm's competition is coming from ______________ brands.

    Answer: private  Difficulty: Hard  Page: 372

# Chapter 12 Products and Services for Consumers

## Essay Questions

101. Why is it important to conceive of a product as a "bundle of satisfactions" received by the consumer?

Answer:
The marketer has only one "product" to sell and the consumer is only interested in buying one "product"--SATISFACTION. The marketer must understand that the consumer has no loyalty to any specific firm. He or she will buy that offering they perceive as best, providing the satisfactions they desire are at a price they are willing to pay. The marketer MUST understand customer desires and provide continually better satisfactions in a dynamically competitive global marketplace.

Difficulty: Hard Page: 350-354

102. Why should the marketer be concerned with attempts to classify innovations according to their "degree of newness"? What role does this stage in the product life cycle play?

Answer:
The rate of diffusion of a product innovation is affected by the consumer's perception of the amount of newness it involves. The marketer should understand that these perceptions are related to the perceived amount of disruption its acceptance may entail. It is necessary to understand the sources of concern associated with a potential innovation--and devise strategies to overcome problems and build on strengths. An international marketer must realize that a product previously sold in his or her domestic country is likely to be further along in its life cycle--and face quite different marketing problems than it would face in its introduction in a foreign market. The real value of both of these tools lies in their potential to keep the marketer focused on the desires of the customer they seek to serve.

Difficulty: Hard Page: 354-356

103. Briefly discuss the basic characteristics of innovations. How do these characteristics relate to the rate of diffusion?

Answer:
Relative advantage relates to the perceived marginal value of the new product as compared to the old. Compatibility refers to the "fit" the new product has with acceptable behavior, norms, and values. Complexity refers to the difficulty involved in understanding and/or using the product. Trialability relates to the perceived economic and/or social use associated with adopting the product. Observability refers to the ease with which the product's benefits can be communicated. The rate of diffusion is positively related to relative advantage, compatibility, trialability, and observability--and negatively with complexity. The rate of diffusion is also affected by such external factors as degree of perceived newness and the method used to communicate the idea.

Difficulty: Hard Page: 354-357

# Chapter 12 Products and Services for Consumers

104. Briefly discuss the three basic components of a product. Describe the significance of each.

Answer:
The core component consists of the physical product--the platform that contains the essential technology and all of its design and functional features. This platform determines the basic offering and sets limits on the product variations that may be possible. This component is typically the most costly to modify. The packaging component includes the style and all of the elements of protection/promotion provided by the package. The package identifies the product and projects the images that may encourage purchase. Packaging is extremely important in countries such as Japan. The support services component includes all those activities and elements designed to reassure the customer prior to purchase and overcome post-purchase problems. Taken together, those components create the "bundle of satisfactions" offered to the consumer.

Difficulty: Hard Page: 358-362

105. Why is a global brand the firm's "most valuable asset"? What is the most recent challenge faced by global brands?

Answer:
All brands serve to identify the goods of a specific manufacturer and to differentiate them from those of competitors. Global brands extend the ability of brands to communicate positive product images to the worldwide market by associating the product with firms and nations that signify quality and value. Once a positive image is created, the introduction of new products is greatly facilitated. Within all markets, however, global brands are facing increasing competition from private brands associated with "local" retailers who are known by, and close to, the consumer--and who often control shelf space and local promotion.

Difficulty: Hard Page: 368-373

# Chapter 13 Products and Services for Businesses

## True/False Questions

1. Product adaptation is even more critical to the successful marketing of industrial goods than for consumer goods.

   Answer: False Difficulty: Medium Page: 376

2. The most rapidly growing sector of U.S. international trade today consists of business and consumer services.

   Answer: True Difficulty: Medium Page: 377

3. The first and foremost motive of the industrial goods buyer is to make a profit.

   Answer: True Difficulty: Medium Page: 377

4. The MOST significant factor affecting the industrial goods market is typically the degree of industrialization existent in the target country.

   Answer: True Difficulty: Medium Page: 379

5. The America-First Corporation produces and markets specialized and heavy capital equipment to firms worldwide. The firm's customers will tend to be concentrated in well-industrialized nations.

   Answer: True Difficulty: Hard Page: 380

6. Japan, the United States, Germany, and other nations that have reached the stage of complete industrialization have no need to import technology or industrial goods from other nations.

   Answer: False Difficulty: Medium Page: 380

7. Success in a fiercely competitive global market for industrial goods depends on building an edge in science and technology.

   Answer: True Difficulty: Medium Page: 380

8. The Japanese are currently dominant in the development of new technology.

   Answer: False Difficulty: Medium Page: 381

9. The America-First Corporation has sold technology to Mexico's Telefonos de Mexico for decades. With privatization, however, the firm can expect its exports to drop significantly because private enterprise cannot hope to match the economic power of state-owned enterprises.

   Answer: False Difficulty: Hard Page: 381

10. Cultural barriers are much more important to the seller of services than to marketers in the merchandise trade.

    Answer: True Difficulty: Medium Page: 382

11. In order for a product to be considered "high quality," it must exceed performance expectations.

    Answer: False Difficulty: Medium Page: 382

12. Effective competition in global markets means that over-engineered and overpriced products must give way to products that meet the specifications of the consumer at competitive prices.

    Answer: True Difficulty: Medium Page: 383

13. The international sale of industrial products is greatly hampered by the lack of universal standards.

    Answer: True Difficulty: Medium Page: 383

14. The United States has been among the leaders in the acceptance of the metric system of measurement for industrial goods--although conversion has been slow in the domestic consumer goods sector.

    Answer: False Difficulty: Medium Page: 385

15. The United States is the only major nation in the world that is not on the metric system.

    Answer: True Difficulty: Medium Page: 385

16. ISO 9000 standards are developed for individual products to assure that every product will conform to international quality standards.

    Answer: False Difficulty: Medium Page: 386

17. The America-First Corporation is seeking ISO 9000 certification. The firm will be subjected to an independent, external audit of the ability of its quality control system to meet published quality standards.

    Answer: True Difficulty: Hard Page: 387

18. ISO 9000 certification became a requirement for EC market access under the EC Product Liability Directive.

    Answer: False Difficulty: Medium Page: 387

19. If a company practices total quality management (TQM), the system probably meets ISO 9000 standards--and does not have to undergo an audit to be awarded ISO 9000 certification.

Answer: False Difficulty: Medium Page: 387

20. The America-First Corporation is preparing to enter the South Korean market. The firm is determined to ensure success by offering high-quality products at competitive prices. America-First must also be prepared to offer world-class installation and repair services.

Answer: True Difficulty: Hard Page: 388

21. Unfortunately, many American firms seem to operate according to a Selling Philosophy--and tend to overlook the customer's post-sales needs for service.

Answer: True Difficulty: Medium Page: 388

22. The intangibility that characterizes the services market ensures that the protectionism that plagues the industrial goods market will have little effect on the services sector.

Answer: False Difficulty: Medium Page: 391

23. Many firms that enter international trade by simply following existing multinational clients eventually evolve into market seekers who actively seek customers for their customers worldwide.

Answer: True Difficulty: Medium Page: 391

24. The America-First Corporation is a major seller of services in the international market. Unlike sellers of tangible products, the firm does not have to worry about the problem of protectionism.

Answer: False Difficulty: Hard Page: 391

25. The America-First Corporation is heavily engaged in the international provision of financial information and real-time stock quotes worldwide. The firm is especially sensitive to any restrictions on transborder data flows.

Answer: True Difficulty: Hard Page: 392

26. The America-First Corporation is attempting to improve its international promotional efficiency. The firm should become an aggressive participant in international trade shows.

Answer: True Difficulty: Hard Page: 393

27. Trade shows play a much more important role in international marketing than they have ever played in the United States.

Answer: True Difficulty: Medium Page: 393

# Chapter 13 Products and Services for Businesses

28. American firms spend a much higher proportion of their promotional budgets on trade shows than do their European counterparts.

    Answer: False Difficulty: Medium Page: 393

29. The America-First Corporation is seeking a way to reach potential customers that may never be contacted by its sales force. The firm should consider the use of trade shows for this purpose.

    Answer: True Difficulty: Hard Page: 394

30. Relationship marketing, although adequate for consumer goods marketing, is not sufficient for the needs of international marketing.

    Answer: False Difficulty: Medium Page: 396

### Multiple Choice Questions

31. Which of the following types of products is <u>BEST</u> suited to the use of a standardized marketing program and/or marketing mix?
    A) consumer goods.
    B) industrial goods.
    C) Fads.
    D) specialty goods.

    Answer: B Difficulty: Medium Page: 376

32. Which of the following is the <u>LARGEST</u> component of the global services sector?
    A) legal services
    B) travel
    C) financial services
    D) entertainment

    Answer: B Difficulty: Medium Page: 376

33. The <u>MAIN</u> product(s) sold to the global market by the United States is(are):
    A) machinery.
    B) legal services.
    C) entertainment.
    D) technology.

    Answer: D Difficulty: Medium Page: 376

# Chapter 13 Products and Services for Businesses

34. Which of the following are purchased for use in the production of other goods and services?
    A) specialty goods.
    B) consumer goods.
    C) shopping goods.
    D) industrial goods.

    Answer: D Difficulty: Easy Page: 376-377

35. The most-rapidly growing sector of U.S. international trade today consists of:
    A) specialty goods and services.
    B) shopping goods and services.
    C) industrial goods and services.
    D) consumer goods and services.

    Answer: C Difficulty: Medium Page: 377

36. The America-First Corporation has noticed that sales for its industrial products are much more volatile than for it's consumer goods. This is because the industrial market is characterized by:
    A) derived demand.
    B) low price competition.
    C) little protectionism
    D) low brand name recognition.

    Answer: A Difficulty: Hard Page: 378

37. All of the following are MAJOR considerations in the purchase of industrial goods EXCEPT:
    A) cost.
    B) durability.
    C) style.
    D) performance.

    Answer: C Difficulty: Medium Page: 379

38. Which of the following provides the BEST gauge of a foreign nation's potential as a market for industrial goods?
    A) the population of the country.
    B) the raw materials stocks of the country.
    C) the stage of industrialization attained.
    D) the nation's import/export regulations.

    Answer: C Difficulty: Medium Page: 379

39. The America-First Corporation is a major exporter of expensive construction equipment to countries that are using these goods to exploit raw materials and produce the agricultural goods that form the basis for the export business. The firm is primarily selling to nations that are in the:
A) preindustrial or commercial stage.
B) primary manufacturing stage.
C) industrialization stage.
D) well-industrialized stage.

Answer: A Difficulty: Hard Page: 379

40. Nations that focus on the importation of machinery and other industrial goods intended for the partial processing of raw materials and resources for export are MOST likely to be in which of the following stages of industrialization?
A) preindustrial stage.
B) primary manufacturing stage.
C) industrialization stage.
D) well-industrialized stage.

Answer: B Difficulty: Easy Page: 379

41. The growth of manufacturing facilities for nondurable and semi-durable goods is the hallmark of the:
A) preindustrial stage.
B) commercial stage.
C) primary manufacturing stage.
D) industrialization stage.

Answer: D Difficulty: Easy Page: 380

42. The production of capital goods and durable consumer goods are FIRST emphasized during the:
A) preindustrial stage.
B) well-industrialized stage.
C) primary manufacturing stage.
D) commercial stage.

Answer: B Difficulty: Easy Page: 380

43. South Korea is one of the NEWEST nations to enter the:
A) well-industrialized stage.
B) precommercial stage.
C) complete industrialization stage.
D) commercial stage.

Answer: A Difficulty: Medium Page: 380

44. The America-First Corporation exports primarily to Japan and Germany. The firm's clients are located in nations that are in the:
A) well-industrialized stage.
B) preindustrial stage.
C) complete industrialization stage.
D) commercial stage.

Answer: C Difficulty: Hard Page: 380

45. Success in the fiercely competitive global market for industrial goods depends on building an edge in:
A) regulations to protect the domestic market.
B) science and technology.
C) vital raw materials stocks.
D) global promotion networks.

Answer: B Difficulty: Medium Page: 380

46. Demand for technologically advanced products will be spurred by:
A) expanding economic and industrial growth in Asia.
B) the break-up of the Russian Empire.
C) the privatization of government-owned industries.
D) all of the above.

Answer: D Difficulty: Medium Page: 381

47. South Korea, Taiwan, and Singapore are prime examples of NICs, which:
A) are not capable of using modern technology.
B) are major creators of technology who specialize in pushing applications to the highest levels of efficiency.
C) are efficient users of technology, but not major contributors to new technology.
D) are major exporters of cutting-edge technology.

Answer: C Difficulty: Medium Page: 382

48. The consumer's perception of quality is affected by:
A) the level of technology reflected in the product.
B) compliance with standards that reflect customer needs.
C) competitive pricing and post-sale service.
D) all of the above.

Answer: D Difficulty: Medium Page: 382

49. The America-First Corporation ALWAYS seeks to sell the most technologically sophisticated products to all of its foreign markets. Unfortunately, in many of the world's less-developed nations, the firm has lost business to foreign firms that sell less sophisticated products. The firm may have forgotten that:
A) price is the most important factor in foreign trade.
B) quality is defined by customer needs and use patterns.
C) foreign manufacturers often employ bribes.
D) the quality of American-made goods is suspect around the world.

Answer: B Difficulty: Hard Page: 382

50. A quality product:
A) perfectly matches the buyer's needs and expectations.
B) consistently exceeds the buyer's needs and expectations.
C) offers "average" performance at a "discount" price.
D) is defined by conformity to the firm's internal quality control standards.

Answer: A Difficulty: Medium Page: 382-383

51. Which of the following international groups is dedicated to developing universal standards for several key industrial sectors?
A) the Global Harmonization Task Force.
B) the Universal Standards Committee.
C) the Metric League.
D) the U.S. Chamber of Commerce.

Answer: A Difficulty: Medium Page: 384

52. The America-First Corporation has announced that the firm will conform to measurement requirements used by the EU and the majority of its world customers. The firm is preparing to shift to the:
A) English measurement system.
B) inch-pound measurement system.
C) metric measurement system.
D) Japanese Ito measurement system.

Answer: C Difficulty: Hard Page: 385

53. Which of the following international trade problems can the United States resolve UNILATERALLY?
A) the lack of universal manufacturing standards.
B) the need for universal tariff reductions.
C) the need for international standards for protection of intellectual property.
D) the lack of acceptance of the metric system of measurement.

Answer: D Difficulty: Medium Page: 385

54. Which of the following is typically the least important factor in determining which industrial good will be purchased?
   A) product quality.
   B) price.
   C) style/features.
   D) timely delivery.

   Answer: C Difficulty: Medium Page: 385-386

55. ISO 9000:
   A) applies, individually, to specific products.
   B) refers to the registration and certification of a manufacturer's quality system.
   C) guarantees that a firm produces a "quality" product.
   D) is another term for the Malcolm Baldrige Award.

   Answer: B Difficulty: Easy Page: 387

56. The ISO 9000 approach:
   A) describes three quality system models.
   B) defines quality concepts.
   C) provides guidelines for using international standards in quality systems.
   D) all of the above.

   Answer: D Difficulty: Medium Page: 387

57. The EU has sought to put pressure on all companies to acquire ISO 9000 certification through the:
   A) *EU Product Liability Directive.*
   B) *Universal Product Certification Code.*
   C) Global Harmonization Task Force.
   D) *Global Standardization Directive.*

   Answer: A Difficulty: Medium Page: 387

58. The America-First Corporation is concerned with the level of liability a defective product may generate in the EU. The firm can best reduce this risk by:
   A) adopting the metric system of measurement.
   B) obtaining ISO 9000 certification.
   C) obtaining Malcolm Balrige certification.
   D) joining the Global Harmonization Task Force.

   Answer: B Difficulty: Hard Page: 387

# Chapter 13 Products and Services for Businesses

59. The America-First Corporation would like to acquire ISO 9000 certification. The firm's prospects for a successful audit should be improved by the fact that it already practices:
   A) statistical quality control.
   B) process control.
   C) total quality management.
   D) quality process management.

   Answer: C Difficulty: Hard Page: 387

60. American firms frequently lose foreign-market contracts because foreign competitors:
   A) always offer lower prices.
   B) always offer higher quality.
   C) typically have better advertising programs.
   D) typically offer better service.

   Answer: D Difficulty: Medium Page: 388

61. The America-First Corporation exports the most advanced technical equipment available to China. Considering the fact that China's work force is not highly technically proficient, the firm should include in its "package":
   A) liberal spare parts allotments.
   B) technical training.
   C) American operators.
   D) instructions to guide unionization.

   Answer: B Difficulty: Hard Page: 389

62. The fact that many types of machine tools use up to five times their original value in replacement parts over their life means that there is an extremely profitable:
   A) aftermarket.
   B) new/replacement machine market.
   C) competitive technology market.
   D) pre-market.

   Answer: A Difficulty: Hard Page: 389

63. The America-First Corporation promises next day delivery of any replacement part needed for any of the products it sells in any foreign market it serves. The firm's recognition of the importance of rapid delivery is part of a trend that has driven the growth of:
   A) rail delivery.
   B) motor truck transportation.
   C) air freight.
   D) water freight.

   Answer: C Difficulty: Hard Page: 390

64. The America-First Corporation has stated that its PRIMARY objective is to serve its domestic customers. If the firm should enter international trade, it will probably do so as a:
A) market seeker.
B) market expander.
C) client follower.
D) global marketer.

Answer: C Difficulty: Hard Page: 391

65. The America-First Corporation did not really plan to enter international marketing-it merely continued to serve its domestic customers as they moved abroad. The firm would be BEST described as a:
A) market seeker.
B) global marketer.
C) client follower.
D) service marketer.

Answer: C Difficulty: Hard Page: 391

66. Firms that actively pursue worldwide customers are called:
A) client followers.
B) growth marketers.
C) exporters.
D) market seekers.

Answer: D Difficulty: Easy Page: 391

67. Which of the following is the LEAST attractive method for selling services internationally?
A) franchising.
B) licensing.
C) direct investment.
D) exporting.

Answer: D Difficulty: Medium Page: 391

68. Today, the great majority of international marketers are:
A) market seekers.
B) client followers.
C) exporters.
D) importers.

Answer: A Difficulty: Medium Page: 391

69. The MOST serious threat to the continued expansion of international trade in services is:
 A) control of transborder data flows.
 B) protectionism.
 C) protection of intellectual property.
 D) licensing.

 Answer: B Difficulty: Medium Page: 391

70. The protection of intellectual property was MOST enhanced by the:
 A) GATT Agreement.
 B) Global Harmonization Task Force.
 C) International Copyright League.
 D) World Trade Congress.

 Answer: A Difficulty: Medium Page: 392

71. The focus of relationship marketing is:
 A) price.
 B) service and long-term benefits.
 C) an immediate sale.
 D) short-term profitability.

 Answer: B Difficulty: Medium Page: 392

72. The America-First Corporation is heavily involved in marketing international communications systems. The firm would be MOST concerned with:
 A) protectionism.
 B) intellectual property protection.
 C) control of transborder data flows.
 D) competition.

 Answer: C Difficulty: Hard Page: 392-393

73. The PRIMARY vehicle for doing business in many foreign countries is:
 A) television advertising.
 B) direct mail.
 C) catalogs.
 D) the trade show.

 Answer: D Difficulty: Medium Page: 393

74. In many foreign countries, the trade show is the most important vehicle for:
 A) selling products.
 B) reaching prospective customers.
 C) contacting/evaluating potential agents/distributors.
 D) all of the above.

 Answer: D Difficulty: Medium Page: 393

75. Which of the following marketing vehicles has traditionally been the most important means of reaching potential customers in Europe?
    A) television.
    B) direct mail.
    C) trade shows.
    D) catalogs.

    Answer: C Difficulty: Medium Page: 393

76. Most U.S. service firms INITIALLY enter international markets for all of the following reasons EXCEPT:
    A) to serve their U.S. clients.
    B) to seek customers worldwide.
    C) to serve business travelers.
    D) to serve tourists abroad.

    Answer: B Difficulty: Medium Page: 393

77. The market for industrial goods is best described as a:
    A) seller's market.
    B) distributor's market.
    C) direct market.
    D) buyer's market.

    Answer: D Difficulty: Medium Page: 396

78. The unique characteristics of the industrial goods market make it ideally suited to:
    A) relationship marketing.
    B) technical marketing.
    C) mass marketing.
    D) ISO-marketing.

    Answer: A Difficulty: Medium Page: 396

79. The America-First Corporation views the provision of "World-Class Service" as the key to long-term profitability derived from a growing group of loyal customers. The firm is practicing:
    A) relationship marketing.
    B) sales orientation.
    C) social responsibility.
    D) quality marketing.

    Answer: A Difficulty: Hard Page: 396-397

80. Relationship marketing will be MOST important in which of the following global markets?
   A) Europe.
   B) Russia.
   C) Asia.
   D) the United States.

   Answer: C Difficulty: Medium Page: 397

**Fill in the Blank Questions**

81. The buyer of industrial goods is seeking ______________, while the individual consumer seeks ______________.

   Answer: profit; satisfaction Difficulty: Easy Page: 377

82. Unlike consumer goods, industrial goods and services face ________________--demand dependant on another source.

   Answer: derived demand Difficulty: Medium Page: 378

83. The buyer of industrial products places high value on ______________, ______________, ______________, _________, and ______________.

   Answer: service; dependability; quality; performance; cost Difficulty: Medium Page: 379

84. The traditional stages of economic development reflect a(n) ______________ orientation.

   Answer: production Difficulty: Medium Pagc: 379

85. Countries that are primarily based on the exploitation of raw materials and agricultural products are said to be in the ______________ or ______________ stage.

   Answer: pre-industrial; commercial Difficulty: Easy Page: 379

86. The America-First Corporation focuses its attention on customer nations that must import specialized and heavy capital equipment to support domestic industry. The firm sells PRIMARILY to ______________ economies.

   Answer: well-industrialized Difficulty: Hard Page: 380

87. Japan, the United States, and Germany are examples of nations BEST described as ______________ economies.

   Answer: completely industrialized Difficulty: Medium Page: 380

## Chapter 13 Products and Services for Businesses

88. Increasingly, _______________ provides the edge in international competition.

Answer: technology   Difficulty: Medium   Page: 381

89. The industrial buyer's decision is based on a(n) _______________ relationship.

Answer: price-quality   Difficulty: Medium   Page: 382

90. The America-First Corporation strives to provide products whose design reflects the needs and expectations of the buyer—no more, no less. The firm is attempting to produce the "international" perception of a(n) _______________ product.

Answer: quality   Difficulty: Hard   Page: 382

91. A major problem facing an international seller of industrial products stems from the lack of _______________.

Answer: universal standards   Difficulty: Medium   Page: 383

92. The America-First Corporation is seeking to gain international acceptance for its products while minimizing potential liability. The firm should seek to achieve _______________.

Answer: ISO 9000 certification   Difficulty: Hard   Page: 387

93. While ISO 9000 is generally voluntary, the EU tries to "pressure" all companies to become certified through its _______________.

Answer: Product Liability Directive   Difficulty: Medium   Page: 387

94. The America-First Corporation produces a superior product, but often loses sales to Japanese competitors. In order to reverse this trend, the firm should probably improve _______________.

Answer: After-sales service   Difficulty: Hard   Page: 388

95. As technology continues to advance, _______________ will become more important as a sales tool.

Answer: customer training   Difficulty: Medium   Page: 389

96. The most serious threat to the continued expansion of international services trade is _______________.

Answer: protectionism   Difficulty: Easy   Page: 391

97. The America-First Corporation conducts much of its business, both at home and abroad, via the Internet. The firm will be very concerned with any attempts to regulate _______________.

Answer: transborder data flow Difficulty: Hard Page: 392

98. The America-First Corporation has had some difficulty in promoting its products in foreign lands. The firm should probably seek to make greater use of _______________.

Answer: trade shows Difficulty: Hard Page: 393

99. The most recent form of trade shows uses the Internet to present large, relatively inexpensive _______________.

Answer: virtual trade shows Difficulty: Medium Page: 394

100. The America-First Corporation seeks to force long-term, positive transactions with their customers. The firm has accepted the concept of _______________.

Answer: relationship marketing Difficulty: Hard Page: 396

**Essay Questions**

101. What are the MAJOR attributes of product quality? How can a product that exceeds performance expectations be considered to be of poor quality?

Answer:
The only evaluation of quality, and the attributes that compose it, that matters is the evaluation done by the customer. Generally, the customer measures quality by comparing the product's actual or perceived performance against performance expectations. Supplier dependability and timely delivery are also important. Price is usually related to performance capability. Therefore, a product that offers more capacity than is required will tend to be perceived as too costly--and of poor quality.

Difficulty: Hard Page: 382-383

102. How is product design related to quality? What is the role of TQM in this relationship?

Answer:
The task of product design is to create the appropriate level of performance capacity for a specific customer/user who exists within a specific environment--and to do so at an acceptable price. The key to success is the ability to understand, and satisfy, customer needs within the customer's environment and constraints. TQM provides a guiding philosophy for maintaining that essential balance.

Difficulty: Hard Page: 382-383

# Chapter 13 Products and Services for Businesses

103. Why would universal standards be helpful to the global marketing of industrial goods? What is ISO 9000--and how can this development assist in resolving the problem of universal standards?

Answer:
Industrial goods are typically used with, and must be compatible with, other industrial goods if they are to perform profitably. Unfortunately, each country has developed its own maze of standards--making compatibility difficult within a country and often impossible between countries. The U.S. has complicated its problems by not switching to the metric system of measurement used by most of the world. ISO 9000 is an attempt to assure that the quality SYSTEMS used by individual manufacturers will be capable of producing goods at a level consistent with some universally acceptable standards. Those firms that pass an external audit of their quality system are certified as being in compliance--and their products will typically be more readily accepted by world customers.

Difficulty: Hard   Page: 383-388

104. Briefly discuss the role, problems, and promises of the global services market.

Answer:
Services—from installation, user training, parts, and repair—are increasingly a major factor in successful global marketing. By nature, they are difficult to standardize and may exhibit wide variation in quality. However, the service market is often more profitable than the products they support—and often generate a highly profitable aftermarket.

Difficulty: Hard   Page: 388-393

105. What is relationship marketing? Why are industrial goods "ideally" suited to this approach to marketing?

Answer:
Relationship marketing focuses on the creation of mutually beneficial, long-term commercial interactions between sellers and their customers. Industrial goods, bought to produce other goods to be sold at a profit by their purchaser, are a "natural" for this approach. Their long life and high price promotes the customer-oriented production and post-sale service that lies at the heart of relationship marketing.

Difficulty: Hard   Page: 396-398

# Chapter 14 International Marketing Channels

## True/False Questions

1. In many markets, the MAJOR constraint to successful marketing is distribution.

   Answer: True Difficulty: Medium Page: 402

2. The channel of distribution is the path by which title to goods passes from the producer to the ultimate consumer or final user.

   Answer: True Difficulty: Medium Page: 402

3. Typically, an importer controls a fixed supply of goods and the marketing system develops around the philosophy of selling a limited supply of goods at high prices to a small number of affluent consumers.

   Answer: True Difficulty: Medium Page: 402

4. The Japanese distribution system has long been considered to be the most effective nontariff barrier to the Japanese market.

   Answer: True Difficulty: Medium Page: 404

5. The America-First Corporation is preparing to enter the Japanese market. The firm will find that once it "clears" Japanese tariff and standards barriers, Japan's short channels favoring direct distribution will greatly facilitate its entry.

   Answer: False Difficulty: Hard Page: 404

6. Japanese wholesalers typically act as agent middlemen and extend the manufacturer's control through the channel to the retail level.

   Answer: True Difficulty: Medium Page: 405

7. While U.S. firms complain about the difficulty of obtaining distribution in Japan, it is ironic to note that the Japanese distribution system seems to be the result of relationship marketing.

   Answer: True Difficulty: Hard Page: 406

8. The Japanese Large-Scale Retail Law was passed to facilitate the entry of modern, "mega-stores" into Japan's growing numbers of malls and shopping centers.

   Answer: False Difficulty: Medium Page: 406

9. Japanese businesspeople are uniformly opposed to any change in Japan's traditional distribution system.

   Answer: False Difficulty: Medium Page: 407

10. Japanese retailing may be going through a change similar to that which occurred in the United States after World War II.

    Answer: True Difficulty: Medium Page: 408

11. The America-First Corporation desires to open several of its new Ameri-Mart Super Centers in major Japanese cities. The firm believes that its direct distribution, low-cost approach will attract the Japanese consumer through low-price, one-stop shopping convenience. America-First is probably seeking a foothold in this market at the right time.

    Answer: True Difficulty: Hard Page: 408-409

12. Distribution, and the nature/functions of middlemen and channels, is one of the few universals in the field of international marketing.

    Answer: False Difficulty: Medium Page: 412

13. Generally, international retailing exhibits far less diversity than does international wholesaling.

    Answer: False Difficulty: Medium Page: 414

14. The America-First Corporation is preparing to sell its line of consumer cosmetics in Eastern Europe, Asia, Latin America, and other areas that have notably weak, or nonexistent, distribution systems. The firm is likely to have success with a direct distribution approach utilizing eager local entrepreneurs to take their products into the homes of local consumers.

    Answer: True Difficulty: Hard Page: 416

15. Catalog selling has proved to be an effective way for American firms to break through Japan's distribution system barriers.

    Answer: True Difficulty: Medium Page: 416

16. Unlike most marketing mix decisions, distribution and channel decisions may be easily changed.

    Answer: False Difficulty: Medium Page: 416

17. The America-First Corporation would like to have foreign offices staffed by locals in each of the foreign sites it serves. The firm may achieve this objective most economically by establishing "virtual offices" utilizing the Internet and global communications.

    Answer: True Difficulty: Hard Page: 418

18. The America-First Corporation prefers to "staff" its channels of distribution with merchant middlemen whenever possible. The firm prefers this option because it can exert more control over the activities of merchant, than agent, middlemen.

    Answer: False Difficulty: Hard Page: 418

19. The use of domestic, or home country, middlemen allows the international marketer to achieve maximum control of distribution in its foreign markets.

    Answer: False Difficulty: Medium Page: 419

20. Modern trading companies bear little, or no, resemblance to the international trading company concept.

    Answer: False Difficulty: Medium Page: 420

21. The America-First Corporation would like to enter the lucrative Japanese market. The firm is likely to find that Japanese trading companies offer the fastest, and least frustrating, means of breaking through that nation's barriers to entry.

    Answer: True Difficulty: Hard Page: 420

22. Norazi agents, unlike most agent middlemen, take title to the goods they sell.

    Answer: False Difficulty: Medium Page: 423

23. Foreign manufacturer's representatives take no credit, exchange, or market risk--but deal strictly as field sales representatives.

    Answer: True Difficulty: Medium Page: 425

24. Unlike most managing agents, compradors take title to the goods they sell.

    Answer: False Difficulty: Medium Page: 425

25. Although the middleman's functions cannot be eliminated, the cost of distribution may be reduced if duplicated functions can be minimized and all functions can be performed more efficiently.

    Answer: True Difficulty: Medium Page: 426

26. Generally, an inverse relationship exists between channel length and channel control.

    Answer: True Difficulty: Medium Page: 427

# Chapter 14 International Marketing Channels

27. Channels of distribution typically pose longevity problems.

    Answer: True Difficulty: Medium Page: 428

28. The America-First Corporation is in the process of selecting middlemen to represent the firm in China. The firm's major problems are likely to stem from the pricing of middlemen available.

    Answer: False Difficulty: Hard Page: 430

29. In selecting middlemen, emphasis is usually placed on actual or potential productivity.

    Answer: True Difficulty: Medium Page: 430

30. The extreme length of channels typically used in international distribution makes control of middlemen particularly difficult.

    Answer: True Difficulty: Medium Page: 431

**Multiple Choice Questions**

31. Which of the following is often the <u>MOST</u> critical and challenging task facing the international marketer?
    A) producing marketable products.
    B) creating effective advertising.
    C) forging aggressive/reliable channels of distribution.
    D) developing effective pricing.

    Answer: C Difficulty: Medium Page: 402

32. The distribution process involves:
    A) the physical handling and distribution of goods.
    B) the passage of title.
    C) buying and selling negotiations between channel members and the consumer.
    D) all of the above.

    Answer: D Difficulty: Easy Page: 402

33. Traditional channels in developing countries developed from economies with a strong dependence on:
    A) imported manufactured goods.
    B) domestic manufactured goods.
    C) exported manufactured goods.
    D) domestically assembled goods using foreign content.

    Answer: A Difficulty: Medium Page: 402

# Chapter 14 International Marketing Channels

34. The America-First Corporation is preparing to enter several markets that have long-depended upon the importation of foreign-made goods. The firm should expect that these markets will be characterized by:
    A) a large volume of competing goods.
    B) high prices aimed at a small group of affluent buyers.
    C) the existence of a strong buyer's market.
    D) long channel structures.

    Answer: B Difficulty: Hard Page: 402

35. In an import-oriented distribution system:
    A) distribution systems tend to be local in nature.
    B) demand exceeds supply.
    C) customers deal with a limited number of middlemen.
    D) all of the above.

    Answer: D Difficulty: Medium Page: 402

36. The Japanese distribution system is characterized by all of the following EXCEPT:
    A) a structure dominated by many small wholesalers dealing with many small retailers.
    B) laws that protect the retailer--the foundation of the system.
    C) channel control by retailers.
    D) a business philosophy shaped by a unique culture.

    Answer: C Difficulty: Medium Page: 404

37. Which of the following countries has the highest density of middlemen?
    A) the United States.
    B) Japan.
    C) Germany.
    D) China.

    Answer: B Difficulty: Medium Page: 404

38. The tradition of small retail stores in Japan is supported by:
    A) high population density.
    B) frequent trips to the store.
    C) an emphasis on service, freshness, and quality.
    D) all of the above.

    Answer: D Difficulty: Medium Page: 404

# Chapter 14 International Marketing Channels

39. Japanese manufacturers have maintained channel control, and blocked foreign access, by a variety of actions designed to support the existence and profitability of their middlemen over the long term. The loyalty of Japanese middlemen is largely a result of the Japanese version of:
    A) import marketing.
    B) sales orientation.
    C) relationship marketing.
    D) one-shot marketing.

    Answer: C Difficulty: Hard Page: 404-406

40. In Japan, competition from large-scale retail stores has been almost totally controlled by the:
    A) Large-Scale Retail Store Law.
    B) Chain Store Law.
    C) Distribution Management Law.
    D) Channel Composition Law.

    Answer: A Difficulty: Medium Page: 406

41. The America-First Corporation is preparing to locate a new Ameri-Mart Super Center in Tokyo. Before the firm can open the store, it must gain the approval of the:
    A) Ministry of International Trade and Industry.
    B) Retail Trade Ministry.
    C) Council of Retail Trade.
    D) Tokyo Dojo.

    Answer: A Difficulty: Hard Page: 406

42. Which of the following is designed to "pry open" the Japanese market for American companies?
    A) The Free Trade Act of 1994.
    B) The World Trade Imperative.
    C) The Structural Impediments Initiative.
    D) The Voluntary Trade Agreement Act of 1995.

    Answer: C Difficulty: Medium Page: 407

43. Which of the following nations has traditionally paid the highest prices in the world for the goods they buy?
    A) the United States.
    B) Japan.
    C) China.
    D) Germany.

    Answer: B Difficulty: Medium Page: 407

# Chapter 14 International Marketing Channels

44. In the World War II era in the United States, national manufacturers were allowed to set prices high enough to support small, inefficient retailers by:
    A) The Sherman Act.
    B) The Robinson-Patman Act.
    C) Fair Trade Laws.
    D) Daitenbo Laws.

    Answer: C Difficulty: Medium Page: 408

45. The hypermarket concept of retailing was developed in:
    A) the United States.
    B) Japan.
    C) England.
    D) France.

    Answer: D Difficulty: Easy Page: 409

46. Firms considering the use of the Internet for international marketing should consider:
    A) translation problems.
    B) the creation of "virtual offices".
    C) payment security issues.
    D) all of the above

    Answer: D Difficulty: Medium Page: 411-412

47. Which of the following types of goods typically has the shortest channel?
    A) low-price consumer goods.
    B) fads.
    C) industrial goods.
    D) shopping goods.

    Answer: C Difficulty: Medium Page: 413

48. The America-First Corporation has complained that Japanese manufacturers have used their economic power and influence to make it impossible for it to obtain distribution. The firm has encountered the phenomenon of:
    A) tariff barriers.
    B) blocked channels.
    C) boycotts.
    D) retail standards

    Answer: B Difficulty: Hard Page: 414

## Chapter 14 International Marketing Channels

49. Which of the following countries has the largest number of retail outlets?
    A) the United States
    B) Japan
    C) Canada
    D) India

    Answer: D Difficulty: Medium Page: 415

50. The America-First Corporation is preparing to enter several countries in which the domestic distribution system is either under-developed or nonexistent. The firm may BEST overcome this problem by:
    A) using direct marketing.
    B) selling to the nation's governments for redistribution.
    C) creating its own web of middlemen.
    D) buying out local middlemen.

    Answer: A Difficulty: Hard Page: 416

51. The America-First Corporation has been frustrated by the Japanese distribution system. The firm is seeking a way to crack that market without having to deal with local middlemen-and to do so at low cost. America-First should consider the use of:
    A) catalogs.
    B) Daitenbos.
    C) Kieretsus.
    D) distribution trusts.

    Answer: A Difficulty: Hard Page: 416

52. The America-First Corporation is seeking a low-cost low-risk means of building a presence in foreign markets. Which of the following may offer the best solution?
    A) corporate-owned retail outlets.
    B) country-specific catalogs.
    C) Internet web sites.
    D) keiretsus.

    Answer: C Difficulty: Hard Page: 416

53. Those middlemen who facilitate transactions, but do not take title to the goods they handle are called:
    A) merchant middlemen.
    B) transactional middlemen.
    C) agent middlemen.
    D) functional middlemen.

    Answer: C Difficulty: Easy Page: 418

# Chapter 14 International Marketing Channels

54. Middlemen who take title to the goods they handle are called:
    A) agent middlemen.
    B) merchant middlemen.
    C) transactional middlemen.
    D) functional middlemen.

    Answer: B Difficulty: Easy Page: 418

55. The America-First Corporation desires to retain as much channel control as possible. The firm should emphasize the use of:
    A) merchant middlemen.
    B) titled middlemen.
    C) franchised middlemen.
    D) agent middlemen.

    Answer: D Difficulty: Hard Page: 418

56. Which of the following types of middlemen assume the GREATEST amount of risk?
    A) manufacturer's agents.
    B) selling agents.
    C) merchant middlemen.
    D) brokers.

    Answer: C Difficulty: Medium Page: 418

57. The America-First Corporation has a small international volume--and is not willing to involve its own personnel or capital in the international function. The firm may achieve its goals by using a(n):
    A) export management company.
    B) international marketing department.
    C) global market division.
    D) franchise system.

    Answer: A Difficulty: Hard Page: 419-420

58. Which of the following types of external middlemen has the longest history in international trade?
    A) export management companies.
    B) complementary marketers.
    C) trading companies.
    D) foreign sales corporations.

    Answer: C Difficulty: Medium Page: 420

# Chapter 14 International Marketing Channels

59. The America-First Corporation is seeking to gain fast, easy access to the Japanese market--and assure an intensive degree of market coverage. The firm should probably employ:
A) complementary marketers.
B) Japanese trading companies.
C) its own international marketing department.
D) U.S. Export Trading Companies.

Answer: B Difficulty: Hard Page: 420

60. In several foreign countries, the America-First Corporation enjoys excess marketing capacity. The firm will often accept products produced by other manufacturers for distribution with its own goods in order to utilize this excess capacity and enhance its total offering. America-First is engaging in:
A) product piracy.
B) countertrading.
C) consensus marketing.
D) complementary marketing.

Answer: D Difficulty: Hard Page: 421

61. All of the following are prerequisites for successful piggybacking EXCEPT:
A) the product fits existing sales/distribution channels.
B) the product offers an attractive margin.
C) the product is totally unrelated to the firm's line.
D) the product is likely to succeed and be profitable.

Answer: C Difficulty: Medium Page: 421

62. The America-First Corporation often employs middlemen whose only function is to put potential foreign buyers in contact with the firm in return for a commission. The firm is using the services of a(n):
A) broker.
B) selling agent.
C) manufacturer's agent.
D) trading company.

Answer: A Difficulty: Hard Page: 420

63. The Webb-Pomerene Act of 1918 made it possible for American firms to join forces in export activities without being subject to the:
A) Clayton Act.
B) Robinson-Patman Act.
C) Miller-Tydings Act.
D) Sherman Act.

Answer: D Difficulty: Medium Page: 422

# Chapter 14 International Marketing Channels

64. Which of the following types of middlemen are distinguished by the fact that they specialize in "shady" or illegal transactions?
    A) brokers.
    B) Norazi agents.
    C) manufacturer's agents.
    D) selling agents.

    Answer: B Difficulty: Easy Page: 424

65. The America-First Corporation utilizes one manufacturer's representative for each country in which it operates. These firms provide aggressive sales representation, but take no credit, exchange, or market risk. America-First is using:
    A) brokers.
    B) Norazi agents.
    C) sole agents.
    D) trading companies.

    Answer: C Difficulty: Hard Page: 424

66. Which of the following types of foreign middlemen is a merchant middleman?
    A) foreign-country brokers.
    B) manufacturer's representatives.
    C) compradors.
    D) distributors.

    Answer: D Difficulty: Medium Page: 424

67. All of the following are characteristics of dealers <u>EXCEPT</u>:
    A) dealers sell industrial goods or durable consumer goods direct to customers.
    B) dealers often enjoy exclusive selling rights within specified geographic areas.
    C) dealers never take title to the goods they sell.
    D) dealers derive a large portion of their sales volume from the products of a single supplier.

    Answer: C Difficulty: Medium Page: 424

68. Which of the following is the <u>LEAST</u> likely means of dealing with government agencies?
    A) merchant middlemen.
    B) direct dealing.
    C) agent middlemen.
    D) brokers.

    Answer: A Difficulty: Medium Page: 426

69. Which of the following CANNOT be eliminated?
    A) middlemen.
    B) essential marketing functions.
    C) redundant activities.
    D) in-house sales forces.

    Answer: B Difficulty: Medium Page: 426

70. The America-First Corporation desires to maintain maximum control of its marketing program. The BEST way to do this would be to:
    A) employ agents.
    B) employ brokers.
    C) employ merchant middlemen.
    D) employ its own sales force.

    Answer: D Difficulty: Hard Page: 427

71. In the final analysis, the channel is ULTIMATELY controlled by:
    A) the manufacturer.
    B) the retailer.
    C) the consumer.
    D) the wholesaler.

    Answer: C Difficulty: Medium Page: 427

72. The fact that many middlemen are small and exhibit little loyalty to their suppliers contributes to the channel problem of:
    A) cost.
    B) coverage.
    C) character.
    D) longevity.

    Answer: D Difficulty: Medium Page: 429

73. Which of the following types of middlemen tend to be MOST loyal?
    A) dealers/distributors.
    B) selling agents.
    C) brokers.
    D) manufacturer's agents.

    Answer: A Difficulty: Medium Page: 429

# Chapter 14 International Marketing Channels

74. In selecting middlemen, emphasis is usually placed on:
    A) financial strength.
    B) actual or potential productivity.
    C) managerial stability and capability.
    D) the nature and reputation of the business.

    Answer: B Difficulty: Medium Page: 429

75. The America-First Corporation is preparing to enter a country in which neither it nor its products are known. Knowing that its chosen retailers will provide the key to market acceptance, the firm should emphasize the middleman's:
    A) financing strength.
    B) managerial stability.
    C) reputation.
    D) past productivity.

    Answer: C Difficulty: Hard Page: 429

76. The BEST way to select a middleman is through the use of:
    A) in-depth questionnaires.
    B) personal interviews.
    C) U.S. Chamber of Commerce lists.
    D) telephone interviews.

    Answer: B Difficulty: Medium Page: 430

77. The basis for evaluation of a middleman is typically:
    A) the potential productivity of the middleman.
    B) the middleman's reputation.
    C) performance relative to an agreed-upon sales minimum.
    D) managerial stability.

    Answer: C Difficulty: Medium Page: 430

78. Generally, initial middlemen contracts should be for:
    A) three years.
    B) an indefinite term.
    C) five years.
    D) one year.

    Answer: D Difficulty: Medium Page: 430

79. The single MOST essential means of motivating middlemen is the provision of:
    A) adequate margins or commissions.
    B) recognition.
    C) communication.
    D) technical assistance.

    Answer: A  Difficulty: Medium  Page: 430

80. International firms that initiate their own distribution systems are MOST likely to have done so in order to:
    A) minimize costs.
    B) maximize control.
    C) take advantage of market familiarity.
    D) ease market access.

    Answer: B  Difficulty: Medium  Page: 431

**Fill in the Blank Questions**

81. While the distribution process is central to the physical movement of goods, its MOST important function is the transfer of ______________.

    Answer: title  Difficulty: Medium  Page: 402

82. Unlike most systems, the Japanese distribution system is based on small ________________.

    Answer: retailers  Difficulty: Medium  Page: 404

83. The America-First Corporation is preparing to enter the European Common Market. The firm should emphasize cost-efficiency and low-price selling in anticipation of increased competition that should accompany the Common Market's acceptance of the ______________.

    Answer: Euro  Difficulty: Hard  Page: 404

84. Channel controls are maintained by ______________, ______________, ______________, and ______________.

    Answer: inventory financing; cumulative rebates; merchandise return; promotional support
    Difficulty: Medium  Page: 405-406

85. The difficulty most foreign firms face in Japan results from lack of access to desirable distributors—a prime example of ______________.

    Answer: blocked channels  Difficulty: Medium  Page: 407

86. The America-First Corporation has been frustrated by its experience with blocked channels in Japan. The firm may "get around" this problem by using _______________.

Answer: direct  Difficulty: Hard  Page: 407

87. _______________ middlemen do not take title and are paid by commission, while _______________ middlemen always take title and provide a wider array of services.

Answer: Agent; merchant  Difficulty: Medium  Page: 418

88. The America-First Corporation desires to expand its exports to foreign countries, but feels it must do so with the absolute minimum investment of cash and personnel. The firm will probably seek the assistance of a(n) _______________.

Answer: export management company  Difficulty: Hard  Page: 419

89. Over their long history, __________ have specialized in the accumulation and distribution of goods from many countries.

Answer: trading companies  Difficulty: Medium  Page: 420

90. The America-First Corporation often seeks complementary products from other suppliers to broaden its international offerings. The firm is employing the strategy of _______________.

Answer: piggybacking  Difficulty: Hard  Page: 421

91. _______________ agents are "unique" middlemen specializing in difficult, or illegal, transactions.

Answer: Norazi  Difficulty: Easy  Page: 423

92. The America-First Corporation routinely relies upon manufacturer's agents to represent the firm in its international markets. Typically, only one agent is used for each country. The firm representative in each country would be a(n) _______________.

Answer: sole agent  Difficulty: Hard  Page: 424

93. A(n) _______________ agent conducts business within a foreign nation under an exclusive contract arrangement with the parent company.

Answer: managing  Difficulty: Easy  Page: 424

94. While a(n) _______________ may be eliminated and channel costs reduced, someone must perform the necessary _______________ that firm had provided.

Answer: middleman; functions  Difficulty: Medium  Page: 426

95. The America-First Corporation prefers to employ direct distribution wherever possible. The firm is obviously willing to pay the higher _______________ required to achieve maximum channel _______________.

Answer: costs; control   Difficulty: Hard   Page: 426-427

96. Despite the form a channel of distribution may take, the ______ exercises ultimate control.

Answer: consumer   Difficulty: Medium   Page: 427

97. Without the combination of adequate _______________ and adequate _____________, a middleman cannot afford to give too much attention to a product.

Answer: margin; volume   Difficulty: Medium   Page: 430

98. The America-First Corporation is experiencing problems resulting from "secondary wholesaling" in many of its foreign markets. The firm is experiencing _______________ problems.

Answer: control   Difficulty: Hard   Page: 431

99. The _______________ is the newest form of direct marketing available to international firms.

Answer: Internet   Difficulty: Medium   Page: 431

100. The America-First Corporation is preparing to employ the Internet in its foreign markets. The firm should be prepared to deal with such special "web issues" as ____________. _______________, _______________, _______________, and _______________.

Answer: culture; translation; local contact; payment; delivery   Difficulty: Hard   Page: 434-436

**Essay Questions**

101. The channel of distribution allows the marketer to resolve major discrepancies between the manufacturer at one end of the channel and the consumer at the other. Discuss.

Answer:
Manufacturers would prefer to produce a large quantity of a limited number of products. Conversely, the consumer desires to purchase a wide variety of products in small quantities. The channel of distribution introduces middlemen to resolve the problem. Wholesalers buy in significant quantities--enabling them to deal directly with many manufacturers to build variety while reducing bulk. Retailers continue the process in their dealings with multiple wholesalers. As a result, the consumer can buy a wide variety of products at retail in small quantities.

Difficulty: Hard   Page: 402-403

# Chapter 14 International Marketing Channels

102. Briefly describe the Japanese approach to distribution and its impact on international trade. What, if anything, may cause this system to change?

Answer:
The Japanese system is characterized by a structure dominated by many small wholesalers and retailers, channel control by manufacturers, a business philosophy formed by a unique culture, and laws that protect the small retailer as the foundation of the system. Small retailers accommodate traditional concerns with quality, freshness, and convenience--which result in many trips to the store. The traditional system, in turn, is perpetuated by a culture based on loyalty, harmony, and friendship. Change will be driven by socio-economic changes that will cause the consumer to seek to save time and money. Such changes will cause small retailers to be replaced with larger, more efficient operations--which, in turn, will spawn widespread changes in the total distribution system.

Difficulty: Hard Page: 403-409

103. Why has direct marketing emerged as a rapidly growing method of distribution for firms engaged in international marketing?

Answer:
Direct marketing may be the only means of reaching consumers residing in countries that have insufficient and/or under-developed distribution systems. Not only does the approach allow access to the consumer, it does so by often allowing "locals" to realize their dreams of becoming an entrepreneur. The approach is also effective as a means of making an "end-run" around import barriers erected by such countries as Japan. Changing lifestyles, acceptance of credit cards, and improved postal and telephone services in many countries will assist in expanding this trend.

Difficulty: Hard Page: 409-412

104. Distinguish between agent and merchant middlemen. Why might an effective agent middleman literally work him/herself out of a job?

Answer:
Agent middlemen work on commission and arrange for sales in the foreign country, but do not take title to the merchandise. The fact that manufacturers retain title also means that they retain control. Merchant middlemen take title to the goods, assume the trading risks, and tend to be less controllable. If the agent middleman is successful in building volume, the commissions he earns may eventually exceed the cost of the firm using an in-house sales force. If the firm feels that its own sales force can perform in the market "prepared" by the agent and/or desires more control over distribution, the agent middleman may be replaced.

Difficulty: Hard Page: 418-419

# Chapter 14 International Marketing Channels

105. Briefly discuss the six basic goals of channel strategy.

Answer:
CHANNEL COST includes the initial cost of establishing the channel, and the commissions and/or margins required to maintain it. Cost should always be evaluated in terms of the channel's ability to provide ESSENTIAL functions. Capital requirements refer to the financial ramifications--such as the cash-flow pattern--associated with various options. Control relates to the manufacturer's ability to determine and enforce channel policy. Coverage refers to the channel's ability to achieve desired volume, market share, and penetration. Character relates to how well the channel "fits" market desires. Continuity refers to the likelihood that a channel may achieve longevity.

Difficulty: Hard  Page: 426-428

# Chapter 15 Exporting and Logistics: Special Issues for Business

## True/False Questions

1. Exporting is an indispensable part of all international business.

   Answer: True Difficulty: Easy Page: 443

2. Countries that have accepted the desirability of international marketing place no restrictions on the export or import of goods across their borders.

   Answer: False Difficulty: Medium Page: 443

3. Export regulations are <u>PRIMARILY</u> a means of generating revenue for the exporting nation through the imposition of tariffs.

   Answer: False Difficulty: Medium Page: 443

4. The America-First Corporation would like to enter the export business. The firm must apply for a special export license before it can legally sell any commodity to buyers in any foreign country.

   Answer: False Difficulty: Hard Page: 444

5. In recent years, the Department of Commerce has shifted increasing responsibility for the policing of export regulations to the exporting firm.

   Answer: True Difficulty: Medium Page: 444

6. The America-First Corporation is preparing to enter export trade for several products with several nations. The firm should become familiar with the *Commerce Control List*, published by the Department of Commerce.

   Answer: True Difficulty: Hard Page: 444

7. Exporters selling a "dual-use" product to a potential enemy may face legal action even if the professed reason for purchase is legal.

   Answer: True Difficulty: Medium Page: 444

8. The Export Control Classification Number (ECCN) consists of five characters that identify a product's category, product group, type of control, legal export price.

   Answer: False Difficulty: Medium Page: 446

9. Once an exporter has received a favorable advisory opinion from the BXA, it can be certain that it will be granted a license for the transaction in question.

   Answer: False Difficulty: Medium Page: 446

10. Prior to accepting any export transaction, the America-First Corporation is required to consult the Commerce Country Chart. The firm would not be allowed to conduct business with any nation listed on the CCC for any reason.

    Answer: False Difficulty: Hard Page: 447

11. An American firm is prohibited from making any shipment to any person located in any company or nation listed in the List of Denied Persons for any reason.

    Answer: True Difficulty: Medium Page: 447-449

12. The complexity of the Department of Commerce's attempts to minimize international terrorism through the use of such computerized programs as ELAIN, STELA, and ERIC has increased the time required to obtain an export license from an average of 14 to 46 days.

    Answer: False Difficulty: Medium Page: 449

13. In a world characterized by trade restrictions, the free and open market of the United States is unique.

    Answer: False Difficulty: Medium Page: 451

14. Besides tariffs, the most commonly encountered trade restrictions are nontariff barriers (NTBs).

    Answer: True Difficulty: Medium Page: 451

15. Unlike specific duties that levy a set charge per some specified unit of quantity, an ad valorem duty is based on a percentage of the determined value of imported goods

    Answer: True Difficulty: Medium Page: 451-452

16. Once an import license or even an exchange permit is obtained, it serves as a guarantee that the seller will be able to exchange local currency for the currency of the seller.

    Answer: False Difficulty: Medium Page: 452

17. The America-First Corporation faces both quotas and import licenses in many of the foreign nations in which it deals. The firm generally prefers to deal with import licenses because this approach provides greater flexibility than is available under the use of quotas.

    Answer: True Difficulty: Hard Page: 454

18. As the name implies, "voluntary agreements" are limitations on the quantity of goods that may be imported into a country that are entered into without duress.

    Answer: False Difficulty: Medium Page: 455

19. A foreign buyer would probably prefer that goods be quoted CIF since such quotas specify the cost of goods, including insurance and freight, to a specific overseas port of import.

    Answer: True Difficulty: Medium Page: 456

20. The America-First Corporation has just approved a purchase from an overseas supplier to be shipped to the port specified by the firm on a C&F basis. The seller will bear the cost of insurance in this transaction.

    Answer: False Difficulty: Hard Page: 456

21. The buyer assumes the largest portion of the total cost of importing goods sold under EX(port) terms.

    Answer: True Difficulty: Medium Page: 456

22. The America-First Corporation is actively engaged in export operations around the world. The firm is likely to prefer, and receive, most of its payments through letters of credit.

    Answer: True Difficulty: Hard Page: 457

23. The America-First Corporation has just begun export transactions with the China Far East Trading Company. The firm is <u>MOST</u> likely to encourage its new customer to the advantage of its open account option.

    Answer: False Difficulty: Hard Page: 459

24. The America-First Corporation is willing to offer long-term financing to its foreign customers, but would prefer to turn its sales into immediate cash. The firm can accomplish both goals by making forfaiting arrangements.

    Answer: True Difficulty: Hard Page: 459-460

25. The bill of lading is the most important document required to establish legal ownership and facilitate financial transactions.

    Answer: True Difficulty: Medium Page: 460

26. Wherever possible, the America-First Corporation uses Foreign-Trade Zones for the storage of goods shipped into countries utilizing quotas. The firm may hold goods in such facilities without penalty until a quota "opens up"—or, it may alter its products while stored in the FTZ to transfer the goods into product categories that are not covered by quotas.

    Answer: True Difficulty: Hard Page: 462

27. The use of maquiladoras was outlawed by mutual agreement between the United States and Mexico as part of the negotiations leading to NAFTA.

    Answer: False Difficulty: Medium Page: 463

28. When distribution is viewed in terms of total costs incurred, air freight may be a cheaper mode of transportation than water—even though air freight costs more.

    Answer: True Difficulty: Medium Page: 464

29. Containerization has played a major role in reducing the costs associated with shipping, handling, and breakage for both the ocean-going and rail modes of transportation.

    Answer: True Difficulty: Medium Page: 467-468

30. The savings in time and money made possible by the specialized knowledge, experience, and contacts of the foreign-freight forwarder provide the justification for the use even by firms that may have in-house specialists.

    Answer: True Difficulty: Medium Page: 469-470

**Multiple Choice Questions**

31. Export regulations are imposed to accomplish all of the following EXCEPT:
    A) to conserve scarce goods for home consumption.
    B) to control the flow of goods to actual enemies.
    C) to control the flow of goods to potential enemies.
    D) to provide tariff revenue.

    Answer: D Difficulty: Medium Page: 443

32. Export licensing controls apply to:
    A) exports of commodities and technical data from the U.S.
    B) U.S.-origin parts and components for foreign assembly.
    C) foreign products made from U.S.-origin technical data.
    D) all of the above.

    Answer: D Difficulty: Medium Page: 444

33. Most items requiring special permission or a license for exportation are under the control of the Bureau of Export Administration of the:
    A) Department of Commerce.
    B) Internal Revenue Service.
    C) Department of the Exterior.
    D) Department of State.

    Answer: A Difficulty: Medium Page: 444

34. The "exportability" status of an item is indicated by its description in the:
    A) Export Administration Regulations List.
    B) Commerce Control List.
    C) Contraband Control List.
    D) Department of the Interior Master List.

    Answer: B Difficulty: Medium Page: 444

35. The America-First Corporation is negotiating with Iraq for the export of uranium to be used for irradiation treatments in that nation's hospitals. The firm's proposed sale may be denied by the Department of Commerce on grounds that the transaction involves:
    A) a dual-use product.
    B) a hazardous product.
    C) a product that cannot be safely transported.
    D) an inherently unstable product.

    Answer: A Difficulty: Hard Page: 444

36. All regulations imposed by the Department of Commerce are published in the:
    A) Export Import Manual.
    B) Export Administration Regulations.
    C) Foreign Trade Procedures Source Book.
    D) International Trade Regulations Manual.

    Answer: B Difficulty: Medium Page: 444

37. Export control regulations are published in the:
    A) Commerce Blacklist.
    B) Commerce Export Limitations List.
    C) Commerce Control List.
    D) Commerce Regulatory Manual.

    Answer: C Difficulty: Medium Page: 444

38. The America-First Corporation would like to determine the exportability status of its products. In order to look its products up in the Commerce Control List, the firm must use the proper:
    A) Export Index (EI).
    B) Export Control Classification Number (ECCN).
    C) Department of Commerce Codex (DCC).
    D) Export Category Codex Number (ECCN).

    Answer: B Difficulty: Hard Page: 444

39. A product that could be used for military/strategic uses or commercial applications is called a(n):
A) dual-use product.
B) combined product.
C) regulated product.
D) end-use product.

Answer: A Difficulty: Easy Page: 444

40. The America-First Corporation creates security codes to safeguard information and data. The firm must comply with EAR regulations regarding:
A) scarce resources.
B) encryption.
C) coding.
D) privacy.

Answer: B Difficulty: Hard Page: 445

41. The ECCN consists of five characters that identify all of the following product characteristics EXCEPT:
A) product category.
B) product group.
C) type of encryption.
D) country group level.

Answer: C Difficulty: Medium Page: 445

42. The America-First Corporation exports firearms and munitions to various foreign countries for hunting and recreation use. Prior to export, the firm must determine the licensing requirements that may apply by consulting the:
A) Product Registry Index.
B) Commerce Country Chart.
C) Firearm Control List.
D) Country Commerce Registry.

Answer: B Difficulty: Hard Page: 447

43. No exports may be made to, or received by, any person or company appearing on the:
A) List of Denied Persons.
B) Country Commerce Index.
C) Export Exception List.
D) Importation Removal List.

Answer: A Difficulty: Medium Page: 447-449

44. The America-First Corporation is preparing to export to a new customer. As a final check prior to exportation, the firm must check to make sure that its new client does not appear on the:
A) No-Trade Index.
B) Federal Preclusion Table.
C) Country Commerce Index.
D) List of Denied Persons.

Answer: D Difficulty: Hard Page: 447-449

45. The America-First Corporation has just received authorization to submit its export license applications to the Department of Commerce electronically and receive the department's decisions via the same network. The firm has become part of the:
A) STELA system.
B) ELAIN system.
C) ApTRAC system.
D) DECTRAC system.

Answer: B Difficulty: Hard Page: 449

46. Foreign exporters may receive computer-voice updates on the status of their license applications by using the Department of Commerce's:
A) STELA system.
B) ELAIN system.
C) ApTRAC system.
D) DECTRAC system.

Answer: A Difficulty: Medium Page: 449

47. An exporter may submit commodity classification requests electronically to the Bureau of Export Administration by using:
A) ERIC.
B) STELA.
C) ELAINE.
D) ETHEL

Answer: A Difficulty: Medium Page: 449

48. Besides tariffs, the MOST frequently encountered trade restrictions are:
A) bills of lading.
B) nontariff barriers.
C) harmonization codes.
D) validated licenses.

Answer: B Difficulty: Medium Page: 451

49. Exchange permits, quotas, import licenses, boycotts, standards, and voluntary agreements are examples of:
A) harmonization codes.
B) validation procedures.
C) tariff barriers.
D) nontariff barriers.

Answer: D Difficulty: Easy Page: 451

50. Taxes or customs duties levied against goods imported from another country are called:
A) tariffs.
B) standards.
C) tributes.
D) exchange permits.

Answer: A Difficulty: Easy Page: 451

51. Tariffs based on a percentage of the determined value of imported goods are called:
A) monetary duties.
B) value-added duties.
C) ad valorem duties.
D) excess-value duties.

Answer: C Difficulty: Easy Page: 451-452

52. Tariffs set at a stipulated amount per unit weight or some other measure of quantity are called:
A) quantitative duties.
B) specific duties.
C) ad-valorem duties.
D) value-added duties.

Answer: B Difficulty: Easy Page: 452

53. The America-First Corporation always seeks to assure itself that sufficient foreign currency will be available to pay for its trade with other countries. To achieve this goal, the firm may apply for:
A) import licenses.
B) export licenses.
C) trade permits.
D) exchange permits

Answer: D Difficulty: Hard Page: 452

54. Which of the following is used by nations to ration the amount of their currency that will be made available for trade?
A) trade permits.
B) monetary duties.
C) exchange permits.
D) checking certificates.

Answer: C Difficulty: Easy Page: 452

55. Direct limitations on the quantity of certain goods that may be brought into a country during a specified period of time are set by the use of:
A) exchange limitations.
B) ad valorem duties.
C) quotas.
D) boycotts.

Answer: C Difficulty: Easy Page: 452

56. Which of the following is used to provide a flexible means of regulating the flow of exchange and the quantity of a particular imported commodity?
A) import licenses.
B) quotas.
C) boycotts.
D) ad valorem duties.

Answer: A Difficulty: Easy Page: 454

57. An absolute restriction against trade with a country, or trade of a specific good, is called a(n):
A) ad valorem prohibition.
B) boycott.
C) prohibitive quota.
D) import license.

Answer: B Difficulty: Easy Page: 454

58. Which of the following is the MOST restrictive form of trade limitations?
A) quotas.
B) standards.
C) boycotts.
D) import licenses.

Answer: C Difficulty: Medium Page: 454

59. The America-First Corporation is chafing under Japan's insistence that every unit of product the firm ships into Japan be tested by Japanese officials before it may be sold. America-First claims that Japan's use of standards in this manner amounts to a(n):
A) boycott.
B) import license.
C) prohibitive quota.
D) ad valorem duty.

Answer: A Difficulty: Hard Page: 454

60. Over the years, the U.S. government has persuaded Japan to limit its exports of automobiles to this country under threat of harsh import duties that might otherwise be enforced on Japanese goods. Japan's acceptance of these terms creates:
A) blackmail.
B) greenmail.
C) a voluntary agreement.
D) standardization.

Answer: C Difficulty: Hard Page: 455

61. The America-First Corporation is preparing to enter several new foreign markets. Prior to entry, the firm would like to make sure that it understands the current regulations and requirements it must meet in each potential new market. America-First should consult:
A) the *Department of Commerce Register.*
B) the *Foreign Trader Monthly.*
C) *Import Export News.*
D) *Overseas Business Reports.*

Answer: D Difficulty: Hard Page: 455

62. The America-First Corporation seeks to quote its prices in the most meaningful possible way for its foreign buyers. The firm is MOST likely to quote:
A) CIF.
B) C & F.
C) FAS.
D) FOB.

Answer: A Difficulty: Hard Page: 456

63. Under which of the following terms is the buyer responsible for the cost of loading onto the vessel, transportation, and insurance?
A) CIF.
B) FAS.
C) FOB.
D) EX.

Answer: B Difficulty: Easy Page: 456

64. The America-First Corporation had traditionally required its customers to pay ALL costs associated with the exportation of its products. The firm is utilizing which of the following terms of sale?
A) EX.
B) CIF.
C) FAS.
D) FOB.

Answer: A Difficulty: Hard Page: 456

65. Most American exports are paid through the use of:
A) open accounts.
B) letters of credit.
C) bills of exchange.
D) sight drafts.

Answer: B Difficulty: Medium Page: 457

66. Which of the following requires acceptance and payment upon presentation?
A) an arrival draft.
B) a date draft.
C) a sight draft.
D) an open draft.

Answer: C Difficulty: Easy Page: 459

67. The America-First Corporation requires access to large amounts of cash to finance some of its foreign clients. The firm may contact its bank to arrange for:
A) forfaiting.
B) open accounts.
C) bills of exchange.
D) factoring.

Answer: A Difficulty: Hard Page: 459-460

68. Which of the following is used to create statistical measures of the quantity of goods shipped abroad and to provide a means of determining whether regulations are being met?
A) consumer invoices.
B) bills of lading.
C) export declarations.
D) certificates of origin.

Answer: C Difficulty: Easy Page: 461

69. The MOST important document required to establish legal ownership and facilitate financial transactions is the:
A) export declaration.
B) bill of lading.
C) consular invoice.
D) certificates of origin.

Answer: B Difficulty: Easy Page: 461

70. A bill of lading serves as a:
A) contract for shipment between the carrier and shipper.
B) receipt from the carrier for shipment.
C) certificate of ownership or title to the goods.
D) all of the above.

Answer: D Difficulty: Medium Page: 461

71. The bill or statement for the goods sold is called a(n):
A) bill of lading.
B) consular certificate.
C) commercial invoice.
D) export declaration.

Answer: C Difficulty: Easy Page: 461

72. Areas within a country in which goods can be imported for storage and/or processing with tariffs and quota limits postponed until the products leave the designated area are called:
A) duty-free stores.
B) customs-privileged areas.
C) import-holding zones.
D) harbor havens.

Answer: B Difficulty: Easy Page: 462

73. The America-First Corporation has scheduled additional product shipments to several countries even though the firm has already reached its import quotas. The firm is planning to have the goods stored in special designated foreign locations until such time as quotas "open up". America-First is employing:
A) foreign trade zones.
B) harbor havens.
C) import-holding zones.
D) duty-free stores.

Answer: A Difficulty: Hard Page: 462

74. A request for a refund of a portion of the duties that had been paid on imports later reexported is called a(n):
A) rebate.
B) harmonization.
C) drawback.
D) residual payout.

Answer: C Difficulty: Easy Page: 462

75. Storing goods in a foreign trade zone allows the firm to:
A) take advantage of lower insurance costs.
B) temporarily conserve working capital.
C) realize significant savings on goods of materials rejected, damaged, or scraped.
D) all of the above.

Answer: D Difficulty: Medium Page: 462

76. The America-First Corporation routinely ships parts and processed materials for processing and assembly in its plants located in Mexican in-bond areas. The firm is able to take advantage of low Mexican labor rates and avoid import taxes on those products that are reexported to the U.S. or other foreign countries. The firm is using:
A) maquiladoras.
B) reexportation zones.
C) harbor havens.
D) harmonization zones.

Answer: A Difficulty: Hard Page: 462

77. The America-First Corporation is determined to minimize the total cost of its global distribution effort. The firm should adopt the concept of:
A) physical distribution.
B) logistics management.
C) containerization.
D) TQM.

Answer: B Difficulty: Medium Page: 464

78. Which of the following modes of international transportation has enjoyed the FASTEST rate of growth in recent years?
A) rail.
B) ocean shipping.
C) motor truck.
D) air freight.

Answer: D Difficulty: Medium Page: 464

79. A total systems approach to management of the distribution process is provided by the concept of:
A) logistics.
B) warehousing.
C) containerization.
D) harmonization.

Answer: A Difficulty: Easy Page: 464

80. The America-First Corporation frequently employs an outside specialist to handle the paperwork and export trade mechanics of its international trade. The firm also seeks expertise in routing, insurance, and freight consolidation. America-First is likely to employ the services of a(n):
A) automated freight handler.
B) foreign-freight forwarder.
C) commodity reshipper.
D) import/export harmonization agent.

Answer: B Difficulty: Hard Page: 469-470

**Fill in the Blank Questions**

81. _______________ regulations may be imposed to protect health, conserve foreign exchange, serve as economic reprisals, protect home industry, or provide revenue in the form of tariffs.

Answer: Import Difficulty: Medium Page: 443

82. The America-First Corporation is preparing to determine if it will need a license to export to its latest foreign clients. The firm should consult the _______________ for guidance.

Answer: Commerce Country Chart Difficulty: Hard Page: 447

83. If a person or company is listed in the _______________, no American exporter is allowed to sell to them.

Answer: List of Denied Persons Difficulty: Medium Page: 447-448

84. The America-First Corporation would like to obtain its export licenses as rapidly as possible. The firm may access the _______________ via the Internet to accomplish this goal.

Answer: Export License Application and Information Network Difficulty: Hard Page: 449

85. Exporters may use a touch-tone phone to check on the status of their license and classification applications through the _______________.

Answer: System for Tracking Export License Applications Difficulty: Medium Page: 449

# Chapter 15 Exporting and Logistics: Special Issues for Business

86. The ______________, a supplementary service to ELAIN, allows an exporter to submit commodity classification requests electronically to the Bureau of Export Administration.

    Answer: Electronic Request for Item Classification  Difficulty: Easy  Page: 449

87. While ______________ permit importing until a specified number is reached, ______________ limit quantities on a case-by-case basis.

    Answer: quota; import licenses  Difficulty: Medium  Page: 454

88. Japan has maintained a "closed market" by enforcing safety, health, and product quality ______________.

    Answer: standards  Difficulty: Easy  Page: 454

89. The America-First Corporation, a major producer of automobiles, has appealed to the U.S. government for relief from Japanese imports. The firm is hoping that the two governments may work out a(n) "______________" that will resolve the problem.

    Answer: voluntary agreement  Difficulty: Hard  Page: 455

90. Under the terms routinely used by the America-First Corporation, the firm's clients are responsible for loading the goods on the vessel and paying the costs of transportation and insurance. The firm is shipping ______________.

    Answer: FAS  Difficulty: Hard  Page: 456

91. Export ______________ opened in favor of the seller by the buyer handle most American exports.

    Answer: letters of credit  Difficulty: Easy  Page: 457

92. Under a(n) ______________, the buyer cannot alter credit terms in any way once they have been accepted by the seller.

    Answer: irrevocable letter of credit  Difficulty: Easy  Page: 457

93. The America-First Corporation expects its clients to pay for their goods immediately upon their receipt. The firm is employing ______________ drafts.

    Answer: arrival  Difficulty: Hard  Page: 459

94. Customers of long-standing or excellent credit reputation, may be allowed to buy on ______________.

    Answer: open account  Difficulty: Medium  Page: 459

95. In a(n) ______________ transaction, the seller makes a one-time arrangement with a bank or other financial institution to take over responsibility for collecting accounts receivable.

Answer: forfait  Difficulty: Medium  Page: 459-460

96. The most important document required for establishing legal ownership and facilitating financial transactions is the ______________.

Answer: bill of lading  Difficulty: Medium  Page: 461

97. Every international transaction requires a(n) ______________, or statement for the goods sold.

Answer: commercial transaction  Difficulty: Easy  Page: 461

98. A(n) "______________" is a request for a refund from the government of 99 percent of the duties paid on imports later reexported.

Answer: drawback  Difficulty: Easy  Page: 462

99. The America-First Corporation would like to take advantage of low-cost Mexican labor to assemble U.s. components in Mexico for reexport to the U.S. at favorable tariff rates. The firm may use ______________ for that purpose.

Answer: maquiladoras  Difficulty: Hard  Page: 462-463

100. The ______________, licensed by the Federal Maritime Commission, arranges for the shipment of goods as the agent for the exporter.

Answer: Foreign Freight Forwarder  Difficulty: Easy  Page: 469-470

**Essay Questions**

101. The recent push for free trade has reduced or eliminated many barriers to trade among and between countries. Should all barriers to free trade be eliminated?

Answer:
There are some valid reasons for trade regulations and/or limitations. Export regulations may be designed to conserve scarce goods for home use or to control the flow of strategic goods to actual or potential enemies. Import regulations may be imposed to protect health, conserve foreign exchange, serve as economic reprisals, protect home industry, or provide revenue in the form of tariffs.

Difficulty: Hard  Page: 443-444

# Chapter 15 Exporting and Logistics: Special Issues for Business

102. What functions are provided by the use of standards in international trade? How can the "legitimate" use of standards be "perverted" to have the effective impact of a boycott?

Answer:
Standards may be used legitimately to set minimum requirements deemed necessary to protect the health, safety, and product quality needs of specific countries or groups of countries. While such uses are certainly legitimate, their application may become so restrictive that no foreign manager can afford the cost of meeting them. This may occur when foreign-made goods are subjected to special requirements and tests, when testing must be done within the importing country and by its officials, and when each individual item must be tested.

Difficulty: Hard Page: 454

103. Why is the bill of lading generally considered to be the most significant single document in international trade? Distinguish between the two basic forms of these documents.

Answer:
Bills of lading are the most important document required to establish legal ownership and facilitate financial transactions. It serves as a contract for shipment between the carrier and shipper, as a receipt from the carrier for shipment, and as a certificate of ownership or title to the goods. A straight bill of lading is nonnegotiable and is delivered directly to a consignee. An order bill is a negotiable instrument. A clean bill of lading signifies proper packaging and no apparent damage on receipt. A foul bill of lading means the shipment was damaged when received and the damage was noted.

Difficulty: Hard Page: 460-461

104. How do foreign-trade zones (FTZs) facilitate international trade?

Answer:
Using a FTZ, goods may be imported and stored, even if subject to U.S. quotas. Once here, the goods may be simply held duty-free until quotas "open up" or combined with American-made goods and reexported free of quota restrictions and the necessity of using complex "drawbacks." In addition, FTZs free up working capital, lower insurance costs, allow significant savings on goods or materials rejected, damaged, or scrapped and exempt from duties the overhead and labor costs incurred in the FTZ.

Difficulty: Hard Page: 462

# Chapter 15 Exporting and Logistics: Special Issues for Business

105. Why "must" the international marketer treat the distribution problem within the context of a total system? What role might a foreign-freight forwarder play?

Answer:
Successful physical distribution requires the marketer to deal with a variety of transportation modes, options, and combinations as well as a bewildering array of rates, routes, regulations, middlemen, and storage alternatives. While each area is individually complex, the problem is further complicated by the fact that all areas are mutually interdependent. The only hope of achieving optimum results lies in understanding distribution interdependence and synergisms. A foreign-freight forwarder is a specialist in those matters. As an agent, this specialist works on a commission based on the cost savings he or she achieves.

Difficulty: Hard Page: 464-470

# Chapter 16 Integrated Marketing Communications and International Advertising

## True/False Questions

1. The goal of integrated marketing communications is to synergistically focus the elements of the promotional mix upon the goal of enhancing sales, image, or use.

   Answer: True Difficulty: Medium Page: 476

2. Unlike other parts of the promotional mix, the goal of sales promotion is ALWAYS short-term or immediate in nature.

   Answer: True Difficulty: Medium Page: 476

3. The America-First Corporation is very concerned with the creation and maintenance of a positive image and customer interactions. The firm can be expected to heavily emphasize the public relations component of its promotional mix.

   Answer: True Difficulty: Hard Page: 477

4. The America-First Corporation is preparing to introduce several new products in European markets. The firm would like to find a means of encouraging dealers to stock the product and reinforce the impact of its consumer advertising. The firm should consider the use of sampling for this task.

   Answer: True Difficulty: Hard Page: 477

5. The America-First Corporation has begun the process of creating an international advertising program. The development of effective messages for its various markets is likely to emerge as its most difficult task.

   Answer: True Difficulty: Medium Page: 479

6. Of all the elements of the marketing mix, decisions involving advertising are those most often affected by cultural differences among country markets.

   Answer: True Difficulty: Medium Page: 479

7. The America-First Corporation has not been able to establish recognizable global brand names. This failure will hamper the firm's desire to utilize global advertising campaigns.

   Answer: True Difficulty: Hard Page: 480

8. In practice, the linguistic, cultural, legal, and economic limitations on advertising in the global market renders standardization impossible.

   Answer: False Difficulty: Medium Page: 480

# Chapter 16 Integrated Marketing Communications and International Advertising

9. The America-First Corporation heavily relies on television advertising in all of its markets. To the firm, competing media and commercials would be "noise."

   Answer: True Difficulty: Hard Page: 480

10. The America-First Corporation is preparing a global promotional program. The firm would be well advised to employ product attribute/benefit segmentation in recognition of the fact that its global customers are buying satisfactions, not products.

    Answer: True Difficulty: Easy Page: 481

11. As European media coverage expands, failure to harmonize brand names, advertising, and promotion across Europe will lead to increasing confusion.

    Answer: True Difficulty: Medium Page: 482

12. The America-First Corporation has decided to attempt to create a uniform promotional package for use across European country markets. Potential cost savings were probably a major factor in this decision.

    Answer: True Difficulty: Hard Page: 482

13. Global market segmentation consists of the practice of finding homogeneous groups within each country in which a firm operates.

    Answer: False Difficulty: Easy Page: 482-483

14. Unlike Europe, Latin America is not well suited to use of a region-wide promotion program.

    Answer: False Difficulty: Medium Page: 483

15. Because advertising relies on perception, effective communication demands that there be a psychological overlap between the sender and the receiver.

    Answer: True Difficulty: Medium Page: 486

16. International marketers are likely to make costly mistakes in encoding advertising messages if they rely on their SRC instead of a firm base of market knowledge.

    Answer: True Difficulty: Medium Page: 486

17. The America-First Corporation heavily relies on comparative advertising in its domestic promotional efforts. The firm should expand this approach to its European and Asian markets.

    Answer: False Difficulty: Hard Page: 488-489

18. Language is one of the major barriers to effective communication through advertising.

    Answer: True   Difficulty: Easy   Page: 490

19. The America-First Corporation is preparing to market its instant soup in Japan. The firm should use the tag line "as easy as making rice" to reassure Japanese homemakers afraid of failure.

    Answer: False   Difficulty: Hard   Page: 492

20. American advertisers must understand the impact of culture on the way their messages may be perceived in foreign nations.

    Answer: True   Difficulty: Medium   Page: 492

21. In most foreign countries, media prices are susceptible to negotiation.

    Answer: True   Difficulty: Easy   Page: 495

22. The America-First Corporation is preparing to advertise its products in Turkish newspapers. The firm must be careful to consider the political stance of each paper as well as its coverage, readership, and cost.

    Answer: True   Difficulty: Hard   Page: 497

23. International consumer magazines have long enjoyed heavy use by international advertisers.

    Answer: False   Difficulty: Medium   Page: 497

24. Consumers in countries that have traditionally had only commercial-free, government-owned television do not like or want commercial stations and their advertising messages.

    Answer: False   Difficulty: Medium   Page: 500

25. Foreign governments have been uniformly enthusiastic in their acceptance of satellite and cable TV.

    Answer: False   Difficulty: Medium   Page: 502

26. The ability of satellites to cover a wide geographic region with a uniform message is BOTH their greatest advantage AND disadvantage.

    Answer: True   Difficulty: Medium   Page: 502

27. Media limitations in some countries have caused some advertisers to create their own media.

    Answer: True   Difficulty: Medium   Page: 504

28. While the Internet is emerging as a vital force in America, it holds little promise as a viable advertising medium in foreign countries.

Answer: False Difficulty: Easy Page: 504

29. The International Advertising Association was formed to fight the trend toward global regulation in the United Nations and the World Court.

Answer: False Difficulty: Medium Page: 508

30. Generally, the multinational advertising agency with local branches is the best choice for the international marketer because it combines the sophistication of a major agency with local representation.

Answer: True Difficulty: Medium Page: 506

**Multiple Choice Questions**

31. The disparate components of a firm's promotional program are coordinated to provide a synergistic impact under the aegis of:
A) the World Trade Association.
B) integrated marketing communications.
C) multinational marketing.
D) global marketing.

Answer: B Difficulty: Medium Page: 476

32. The America-First Corporation is preparing to launch a sampling program to introduce its new products in Europe. The firm's introduction strategy relies heavily upon the use of:
A) advertising.
B) sales promotion.
C) personal selling.
D) publicity.

Answer: B Difficulty: Hard Page: 476

33. Short-term efforts directed to the consumer and/or retailer to encourage trial, use, immediate purchase, store patronage, inventory stocking—or to enhance the impact of the other components of the promotional mix form the basis of:
A) advertising.
B) publicity.
C) sales promotion.
D) personal selling.

Answer: C Difficulty: Easy Page: 476

34. McDonald's sponsorship of Ronald McDonald Houses (which provide a free place to stay for parents of cancer patients) would be BEST described as a component of that firm's _______ program.
A) advertising.
B) sales promotion.
C) personal selling.
D) public relations.

Answer: D Difficulty: Hard Page: 477-478

35. Which of the following components of the marketing mix is MOST often affected by cultural differences among country markets?
A) product
B) price
C) distribution
D) advertising

Answer: D Difficulty: Medium Page: 479

36. Firms using a standardized advertising program are MOST likely to follow a:
A) domestic marketing strategy.
B) global marketing strategy.
C) multi-domestic marketing strategy.
D) multinational marketing strategy.

Answer: B Difficulty: Medium Page: 479-480

37. Firms involved in international marketing may employ:
A) standardized products and standardized messages.
B) adapted products and adapted messages.
C) a mixture of standardized and adapted products and messages.
D) any, or all, of the above.

Answer: D Difficulty: Medium Page: 481-482

38. The decision to standardize or modify advertising messages across countries should be based on:
A) buying motives.
B) media costs.
C) product price.
D) message length.

Answer: A Difficulty: Medium Page: 481-482

# Chapter 16 Integrated Marketing Communications and International Advertising

39. The America-First Corporation operates in a variety of countries. Some of the firm's markets share similar buying motives, but others respond to quite different appeals. America-First should probably use:
    A) standardized advertising.
    B) advertising adapted to each market.
    C) only sales promotion.
    D) augmented media.

    Answer: B Difficulty: Hard Page: 482

40. Brands that carry the same name, same design, and same creative strategy everywhere in the world are called:
    A) global brands.
    B) name brands.
    C) creative brands.
    D) designer brands.

    Answer: A Difficulty: Easy Page: 482

41. In many of its global markets, the America-First Corporation is faced with the problem of getting consumers who are loyal to domestic brands to try their product. The firm can <u>BEST</u> achieve this goal through a program of:
    A) sampling.
    B) aggressive advertising.
    C) price reductions.
    D) comparative advertising.

    Answer: A Difficulty: Hard Page: 477

42. Promotional activities are basically a(n):
    A) adaptive process.
    B) propaganda process.
    C) communications process.
    D) legal process.

    Answer: C Difficulty: Easy Page: 479

43. Under a strategy of standardization, ads must be:
    A) totally identical in all countries.
    B) produced in a single language.
    C) country or culturally neutral.
    D) consistent over time.

    Answer: C Difficulty: Medium Page: 480

# Chapter 16 Integrated Marketing Communications and International Advertising

44. Which of the following marketing strategies is based on the practice of aiming products and advertising toward a worldwide market--using a standardized approach whenever possible?
    A) an expansionist strategy.
    B) a multidomestic strategy.
    C) a domestic strategy.
    D) a global strategy.

    Answer: D Difficulty: Easy Page: 482

45. One important reason for uniform promotional packaging across country markets is the possibility for:
    A) language homogenization.
    B) cost savings.
    C) cultural homogenization.
    D) cost averaging.

    Answer: B Difficulty: Medium Page: 482

46. The identification of homogeneous market segments across groups of countries is at the core of:
    A) regional market segmentation.
    B) world homogenization.
    C) global leveling.
    D) the new world order.

    Answer: A Difficulty: Easy Page: 482

47. Consumers having more similarities than differences in their needs, wants, and buying behavior--even though they live in different countries--are described as:
    A) world citizens.
    B) a regional market segment.
    C) homogenized nations.
    D) "blurred" culture.

    Answer: B Difficulty: Easy Page: 482

48. The America-First Corporation sells to a small "niche" of consumers in many different nations whose needs can be satisfied with essentially the same product. While no one market produces a great deal of profit for the firm, it realizes significant profits from total sales to those "niches." America-First is making profitable use of:
    A) regional market segments.
    B) world citizens.
    C) multidomestic segments.
    D) market expansion.

    Answer: A Difficulty: Hard Page: 482

# Chapter 16 Integrated Marketing Communications and International Advertising

49. In selling to its European markets, the America-First Corporation employs a single visual component accompanied by a standardized text carefully translated into individual languages. The firm is using a:
    A) Pan-European promotional strategy.
    B) Multinational promotional strategy.
    C) Multidomestic promotional strategy.
    D) Systematic promotional strategy.

    Answer: A Difficulty: Hard Page: 482-483

50. In which of the following areas does the existence of a common language MOST favor region-wide promotion programs?
    A) Europe.
    B) Asia.
    C) Africa.
    D) Latin America.

    Answer: D Difficulty: Medium Page: 483

51. International communications may fail due to:
    A) media inadequacies.
    B) cultural barriers.
    C) failure to understand the market.
    D) all of the above.

    Answer: D Difficulty: Medium Page: 483

52. During which of the following stages of the communication process is the source's message translated into symbols for transmission to the intended receiver?
    A) decoding.
    B) noise.
    C) encoding.
    D) feedback.

    Answer: C Difficulty: Easy Page: 486

53. The America-First Corporation is always concerned about the potential distractions/confusion that may be caused by competitive messages. The firm views the activities of its competitors as:
    A) noise.
    B) feedback.
    C) argumentation.
    D) filtering.

    Answer: A Difficulty: Hard Page: 486

# Chapter 16 Integrated Marketing Communications and International Advertising

54. The encoding process suffers if the marketer relies on his or her:
    A) in-house advertising agency.
    B) self-reference criterion.
    C) encoding bias.
    D) noise filters.

    Answer: B Difficulty: Medium Page: 486

55. Effective advertising communication in the international market must ALWAYS overcome barriers associated with:
    A) bans on comparative advertising.
    B) the taxation of media.
    C) cultural differences.
    D) prohibitions of nudity.

    Answer: C Difficulty: Medium Page: 486

56. Decoding problems are GENERALLY created by:
    A) noise.
    B) media inefficiency.
    C) competitive sabotage.
    D) improper encoding.

    Answer: D Difficulty: Medium Page: 487

57. The America-First Corporation favors the use of comparative advertising. The firm would encounter legal problems should it attempt to employ this approach in any of the following countries EXCEPT:
    A) Germany.
    B) Belgium.
    C) Luxembourg.
    D) the United Kingdom.

    Answer: D Difficulty: Hard Page: 488

58. The problems caused for international advertisers by language differences include:
    A) different languages between/within countries.
    B) different dialects within countries.
    C) linguistic nuance and vernacular.
    D) all of the above.

    Answer: D Difficulty: Medium Page: 490

## Chapter 16 Integrated Marketing Communications and International Advertising

59. The international advertiser must be a student of culture because the culture of a nation has a major impact on:
    A) the way a message is perceived.
    B) the cost of media.
    C) the variety of media available.
    D) the number of available customers.

    Answer: A Difficulty: Medium Page: 492

60. The America-First Corporation is preparing to offer its line of coffees in Japan. The firm will probably be MOST successful selling:
    A) drip-grind coffee.
    B) instant coffee.
    C) expresso-grind coffee.
    D) coffee-liquor.

    Answer: B Difficulty: Hard Page: 493

61. A small budget may be BEST overcome through the use of:
    A) large media schedules.
    B) creative messages.
    C) low-interest loans.
    D) low-cost media and insertion times.

    Answer: B Difficulty: Medium Page: 493

62. In most foreign countries, media prices are:
    A) fixed.
    B) susceptible to negotiation.
    C) quoted from standardized rate cards.
    D) set by the government.

    Answer: B Difficulty: Medium Page: 495

63. The attractiveness of global television is diminished to some degree by the frequent lack of:
    A) standardized rate cards.
    B) media research.
    C) government regulation.
    D) advertising agencies.

    Answer: B Difficulty: Medium Page: 496

# Chapter 16 Integrated Marketing Communications and International Advertising

64. The America-First Corporation is preparing an advertising campaign for the Japanese market. Given this market's media preferences, the firm's media selection should emphasize:
 A) print media.
 B) radio.
 C) television.
 D) billboards.

 Answer: C Difficulty: Hard Page: 497

65. In most countries, the major entertainment media are:
 A) radio and television.
 B) magazines.
 C) newspapers.
 D) billboards.

 Answer: A Difficulty: Medium Page: 497

66. Television and radio advertising may be available in international markets on a:
 A) competitive commercial broadcasting basis.
 B) commercial monopoly broadcasting basis.
 C) noncommercial broadcasting basis.
 D) any, or all, of the above.

 Answer: D Difficulty: Medium Page: 497

67. The America-First Corporation is preparing to buy advertising time on radio and television stations in several foreign countries. The firm will have the <u>LEAST</u> difficulty in making its purchases in countries that have:
 A) a noncommercial broadcasting system.
 B) a commercial monopoly broadcasting system.
 C) a competitive commercial broadcasting system.
 D) any of the above.

 Answer: C Difficulty: Hard Page: 497

68. The government establishes the rules that control the ability of radio and television stations to accept advertising under which of the following systems?
 A) a noncommercial broadcasting system.
 B) a commercial monopoly broadcasting system.
 C) a competitive commercial broadcasting system.
 D) all of the above.

 Answer: B Difficulty: Medium Page: 497-499

# Chapter 16 Integrated Marketing Communications and International Advertising

69. Which of the following is <u>MOST</u> resistant to the acceptance of radio or television commercials?
    A) noncommercial broadcasting systems.
    B) commercial monopoly broadcasting systems.
    C) competitive commercial broadcasting systems.
    D) all of the above are equal in this regard.

    Answer: A Difficulty: Medium Page: 500

70. The most popular commercial vehicles in the world are television programs produced in:
    A) France.
    B) Britain.
    C) Germany.
    D) the United States.

    Answer: D Difficulty: Medium Page: 502

71. Broadcasting will become a more feasible vehicle for advertising in Europe with increases in:
    A) the availability/use of cable and satellites.
    B) privatization of government-owned stations.
    C) the EC's attempts to harmonize broadcasting laws.
    D) all of the above.

    Answer: D Difficulty: Medium Page: 502

72. The America-First Corporation would like to target the large, and growing Hispanic market. The firm should utilize:
    A) Star TV.
    B) Univision.
    C) RTV.
    D) Chile TV.

    Answer: B Difficulty: Hard Page: 502

73. Which of the following media is especially useful in countries with high illiteracy rates?
    A) magazines
    B) direct mail
    C) newspapers
    D) billboards

    Answer: D Difficulty: Medium Page: 504

# Chapter 16 Integrated Marketing Communications and International Advertising

74. The America-First Corporation is preparing to sell to business buyers in the Ukraine. The firm should probably rely most heavily on:
A) direct faxing.
B) direct mail.
C) radio.
D) television.

Answer: A Difficulty: Hard Page: 504

75. The America-First Corporation is looking for a fast, efficient media for its global business-to-business campaign. The firm should investigate:
A) direct mail.
B) catalogs.
C) the Internet.
D) billboards.

Answer: C Difficulty: Hard Page: 504

76. Direct mail is NOT a feasible medium in:
A) Japan.
B) Southeast Asia.
C) Chile.
D) Britain.

Answer: C Difficulty: Medium Page: 505

77. The America-First Corporation is launching a pan-European campaign through its new multinational advertising agency. Given a choice, the firm would prefer to pay the agency?
A) the traditional 15% commission.
B) on a reward-by-reward basis.
C) according to a media-based variable rate.
D) through a kickback system.

Answer: B Difficulty: Hard Page: 506

78. Which of the following alternatives offers the best compromise for attaining a sophisticated, coordinated worldwide campaign with market knowledge of individual foreign countries?
A) a local domestic agency.
B) a company-owned agency.
C) a global agency with local branches and joint ventures.
D) a boutique agency.

Answer: C Difficulty: Medium Page: 506

# Chapter 16 Integrated Marketing Communications and International Advertising

79. Which of the following advertising media are MOST likely to be forbidden by government edict to accept some advertising materials?
    A) magazines.
    B) billboards.
    C) radio and television.
    D) newspapers.

    Answer: C  Difficulty: Medium  Page: 507-508

80. Which of the following media is generally the LEAST regulated medium in most markets?
    A) the Internet.
    B) television.
    C) satellite TV.
    D) radio.

    Answer: A  Difficulty: Medium  Page: 509

## Fill in the Blank Questions

81. _______________ consists of a variety of activities designed to supplement advertising and personal selling.

    Answer: Sales promotion  Difficulty: Medium  Page: 476

82. The America-First Corporation has been plagued by rumors of poor quality. The firm is likely to respond via a strong, positive _____ campaign.

    Answer: public relations  Difficulty: Hard  Page: 477

83. The global _____ business is growing faster than the global ______.

    Answer: advertising; economy  Difficulty: Easy  Page: 479

84. The MOST difficult step in the creation of international advertising campaigns involves the attempt to create effective ______.

    Answer: messages  Difficulty: Easy  Page: 479

85. If regional differences between markets are emphasized, advertising messages will be _______________; if similarities are emphasized, messages will be _______________.

    Answer: customized; standardized  Difficulty: Medium  Page: 480

# Chapter 16 Integrated Marketing Communications and International Advertising

86. The America-First Corporation seeks to standardize its advertising messages as much as possible—employing customized adaptations only where necessary. The firm's advertising approach is part of a(n) _______________ marketing strategy.

    Answer: global   Difficulty: Hard   Page: 480

87. The America-First Corporation is attempting to identify market segments whose needs, demographics, and purchase behavior are similar regardless of the country in which they may reside. The firm is employing _______________.

    Answer: global market segmentation   Difficulty: Hard   Page: 480

88. Promotional activities are basically a(n) _______________ process.

    Answer: communication   Difficulty: Easy   Page: 483

89. The marketer is most likely to misread market needs if he or she relies too heavily on his or her _______________.

    Answer: self-reference criterion   Difficulty: Medium   Page: 486

90. As far as the consumer is concerned, the "true" meaning and impact of an advertising message is established during the _______________ stage of the international communications process.

    Answer: decoding   Difficulty: Hard   Page: 488

91. In selecting international advertising media, the America-First Corporation attempts to pick those that are less used by its competitors. The firm is attempting to minimize _______________.

    Answer: noise   Difficulty: Hard   Page: 488

92. Cultural diversity affects the way in which advertising is _______________ in various nations—each of which will act as if its interpretation is correct.

    Answer: perceived   Difficulty: Medium   Page: 492

93. In the face of small budgets, production limitations, poor equipment, and poor material, _______________ becomes even more critical.

    Answer: creativity   Difficulty: Medium   Page: 493

## Chapter 16 Integrated Marketing Communications and International Advertising

94. In its initial attempts to buy media time in foreign countries, the America-First Corporation was surprised to find that rate cards were almost nonexistent. The firm will discover that most media prices are set by _______________.

    Answer: negotiation  Difficulty: Hard  Page: 495

95. The usefulness of international media is diminished as a result of the lack of accurate _______________ available.

    Answer: media research  Difficulty: Medium  Page: 496

96. While it does not rank first in cable, satellite, or Internet penetration, _______________ is a strong second in all three categories.

    Answer: Germany  Difficulty: Medium  Page: 501

97. The America-First Corporation would like to reach as many Hispanic customers, with as much impact as possible, around the world. The firm might employ _______________ and _______________, the two leading Latin-American satellite TV networks, for this purpose.

    Answer: Univision; Televisa  Difficulty: Hard  Page: 502

98. The _______________ is the latest, and LEAST regulated, addition to the global advertising arsenal.

    Answer: Internet  Difficulty: Medium  Page: 504

99. Increasingly, global advertising is being handled by _______________ advertising agencies.

    Answer: global  Difficulty: Medium  Page: 506

100. In the international, as well as the domestic arena, advertising agencies would prefer that advertisers by subject to _______________ rather than face government intervention.

    Answer: self-regulation  Difficulty: Medium  Page: 508

# Chapter 16 Integrated Marketing Communications and International Advertising

## Essay Questions

101. What is sales promotion? What role does it play in international marketing?

Answer:
Sales promotion is a "catch-all" promotional category that encompasses all activities other than advertising, personal selling, and publicity. Sales promotion is used to assist, and enhance, the effectiveness of the other elements of the promotional mix. In international marketing, sales promotion may be even more critical. Sampling and demonstrations are especially important in dealing with consumers who are not only unfamiliar with the product--but may also be unfamiliar with the CONCEPT of the product.

Difficulty: Hard Page: 476-477

102. Briefly identify the basic steps in the creation of an advertising campaign. Which is the MOST difficult to achieve in international advertising? Why? What TWO roles are played by goals in this process?

Answer:
The process consists of: (1) marketing research; (2) settings goals; (3) message creation; (4) selecting media; (5) budgeting; (6) execution; and (7) evaluation of results. The creation of an effective message(s) is the most difficult task as a result of the cultural, legal, economic, linguistic, infrastructure (and other) diversity faced in the global market. The marketer's own SRC can compound these problems. Goals serve as “targets” during planning and implementation and “standards” of performance for the evaluation of results which should guide the next iteration of the process.

Difficulty: Hard Page: 479-480

103. What role does market segmentation play in the implementation of a global marketing strategy?

Answer:
Global marketing attempts to create world, or global, brands and/or standardized advertising. In order for these strategies to work, the marketer must be sure that there are a sufficient number of consumers having similar needs, wants, and behaviors to produce a profitable level of sales across their international markets. The task of l market segmentation is to identify those consumers who are homogeneous in those characteristics and behavior critical to the success of the marketer's offering. Since satisfaction is the goal of the consumer regardless of location, global marketers are well advised to employ product attribute and benefit segmentation in this effort.

Difficulty: Hard Page: 481-483

# Chapter 16 Integrated Marketing Communications and International Advertising

104. Briefly describe the communications process. Why is perception so important to the success of this process?

Answer:
The communications process consists of the SOURCE, the marketer, who must ENCODE his/her message in appropriate symbols for transmission to the receiver by some CHANNEL that will allow the consumer, or RECEIVER, to DECODE the message and provide FEEDBACK regarding its effectiveness through reactions to the message. NOISE, distractions that create confusion and generate misunderstandings, bedevils the process at every stage. PERCEPTION, the process by which we give meaning to stimuli, is critical to the process. The marketer plans his/her strategy, selects media, and creates messages based on his/her perception of the consumers' needs, wants, behaviors--and the culture in which they live. The consumers' perception of the marketer's offering, reputation, and country-of-origin determines how they will respond to it.

Difficulty: Hard Page: 485-488

105. Briefly describe the three basic options facing the international marketer selecting an advertising agency. Which option is generally preferred? Why?

Answer:
The basic options include use of a local domestic agency, company-owned agency, or multinational advertising agency with local branches. Local domestic agencies offer the best understanding of local culture, but tend to lack sophistication and create coordination problems in worldwide campaigns. The company-owned agency offers control--but may preclude effective local input when it is located out of the host country. The multinational agency with local branches retains the advantage of sophistication--while allowing significant local input and facilitating international coordination. This last approach is currently preferred as the best answer--although a compromise--to the unique problems of international advertising.

Difficulty: Hard Page: 505-507

# Chapter 17 Personal Selling and Sales Management

## True/False Questions

1. To most consumers, the salesperson IS the company.

   Answer: True   Difficulty: Easy   Page: 514

2. The successful salesperson must be a product/market expert, communications specialist, psychologist, sociologist, and anthropologist.

   Answer: True   Difficulty: Medium   Page: 514

3. The keystone of effective relationship marketing is communication.

   Answer: True   Difficulty: Easy   Page: 514

4. The task of managing the sales force begins with its design.

   Answer: True   Difficulty: Medium   Page: 514

5. The largest personnel requirement abroad for most companies is the sales force.

   Answer: True   Difficulty: Medium   Page: 516

6. The America-First Corporation markets highly sophisticated, technical products to Chinese manufacturers. The firm should probably utilize an expatriate sales force to assure that the product is properly explained, installed, and maintained.

   Answer: True   Difficulty: Hard   Page: 516

7. The America-First Corporation operates in Latin-America and the Orient. The firm will find a rich source for its foreign sales force needs among recent immigrants.

   Answer: True   Difficulty: Hard   Page: 517

8. The number of domestic personnel assigned to foreign posts by U.S. firms has dramatically increased in recent years.

   Answer: False   Difficulty: Medium   Page: 517

9. Local nationals provide a better understanding of a foreign culture, a "guide" through local laws, and a sales force that costs less to maintain than expatriates.

   Answer: True   Difficulty: Medium   Page: 517-518

10. The development of TCN executives reflects not only a growing internationalization of business, but also acknowledges that personal skills and motivations are not the exclusive property of one nation.

    Answer: True   Difficulty: Medium   Page: 520

11. The characteristics of maturity, emotional stability, and breadth of knowledge are critical to the success of an international salesperson.

    Answer: True   Difficulty: Medium   Page: 520-521

12. The America-First Corporation is proud of the technical training provided its sales force. The firm must also provide cultural empathy orientation to ensure success.

    Answer: True   Difficulty: Hard   Page: 522-523

13. It is possible to employ a checklist of desirable personal characteristics to select international salespersons that will be successful.

    Answer: False   Difficulty: Medium   Page: 523

14. Unlike products, management concepts and practices are universal and may be successfully utilized in all cultures.

    Answer: False   Difficulty: Medium   Page: 523

15. The American view of the individual as the "master of his/her own destiny" is accepted in all but the mot socialistic of the world's cultures.

    Answer: False   Difficulty: Medium   Page: 528

16. The concept of the corporation as an instrument for social change is a socialistic philosophy that is completely foreign to the United States.

    Answer: False   Difficulty: Medium   Page: 524

17. The America-First Corporation strongly believes that rewards should be based on individual merit and worth. The firm's philosophy will be universally welcomed—especially in those nations in which family affiliation had traditionally afforded an "unfair" advantage.

    Answer: False   Difficulty: Hard   Page: 524

18. The American practice of shared decision making is <u>MOST</u> consistent with the management practices of the Middle East.

    Answer: False   Difficulty: Medium   Page: 525

19. The American acceptance of—indeed, preference for—change is a characteristic that is only matched by the philosophy of Japan.

Answer: False Difficulty: Medium Page: 525

20. The use of the Internet enables firms to efficiently employ completely standardized training materials and approaches throughout the world.

Answer: False Difficulty: Medium Page: 526-528

21. Merit pay increases are the single most important sales force motivation tools in BOTH Japan and the United States.

Answer: True Difficulty: Medium Page: 528

22. The America-First Corporation provides excellent pay and benefit packages to encourage its best domestic managers to accept foreign postings. The firm may find that these same programs may make repatriation more difficult.

Answer: True Difficulty: Hard Page: 529

23. The IBM experience proved the impossibility of creating a global sales force compensation plan.

Answer: False Difficulty: Medium Page: 530

24. The America-First Corporation had hired many local nationals for sales duties in Japan. The firm may expect greater problems related to motivating poor performers than it had encountered at home.

Answer: True Difficulty: Hard Page: 532

25. Generally, a firm must pay $300,000 to $600,000 per year to support a domestic manager and his or her family in a foreign assignment.

Answer: True Difficulty: Medium Page: 533

26. Once an expatriate accepts a foreign assignment, it is virtually certain that they will complete the full term of their assignment.

Answer: False Difficulty: Medium Page: 533

27. It is quite common for a returning expatriate manager to experience as much "culture shock" upon returning home as they had experienced in their foreign posting.

Answer: True Difficulty: Medium Page: 535

28. A good sense of humor is vital to the process of developing, and employing, cultural skills.

    Answer: True Difficulty: Medium Page: 537

29. The CEO of the 21st Century must have a multi-environment, multi-country, multi-functional, and maybe even multi-company, multi-industry experience.

    Answer: True Difficulty: Medium Page: 538

30. The ability to speak a second language, even if one's job does not currently require it, is an indication of a person's willingness to accept and adapt to another culture.

    Answer: True Difficulty: Medium Page: 540

**Multiple Choice Questions**

31. International sales forces are drawn from:
    A) expatriates.
    B) local-country personnel.
    C) third-country nationals.
    D) all of the above.

    Answer: D Difficulty: Medium Page: 514

32. Relationship marketing is built on:
    A) effective negotiations.
    B) effective communication.
    C) global treaties.
    D) United Nations agreements.

    Answer: B Difficulty: Medium Page: 514

33. The first step in managing a sales force begins with:
    A) its design.
    B) hiring the sales force.
    C) sales training.
    D) sales compensation.

    Answer: A Difficulty: Medium Page: 514

# Chapter 17 Personal Selling and Sales Management

34. Which of the following types of products are MOST likely to require American firms to employ expatriates for their sale?
A) high-technology products.
B) services.
C) low-technology products.
D) insurance.

Answer: A Difficulty: Medium Page: 516

35. The largest personnel requirement abroad for most companies is:
A) production workers.
B) the sales force.
C) advertising executives.
D) warehousemen.

Answer: B Difficulty: Medium Page: 516

36. The America-First Corporation is preparing to staff its foreign sales force. Assuming the firm follows world trends, the firm will place LESS emphasis on:
A) expatriate personnel.
B) local nationals.
C) Third-country nationals.
D) cultural diversity.

Answer: A Difficulty: Hard Page: 516

37. The America-First Corporation specializes in the global sale of highly technical products that require an extensive background of information and applications knowledge. The firm's sales force will probably emphasize the use of:
A) local nationals.
B) expatriates.
C) Third-country nationals.
D) nomadic citizens.

Answer: B Difficulty: Hard Page: 516

38. Increasingly, global sales forces are being recruited from:
A) local nationals.
B) expatriates.
C) Third-country nationals.
D) members of the fourth estate.

Answer: A Difficulty: Medium Page: 517

39. The America-First Corporation feels that it must form its sales force from local nationals in high-context nations. The firm is most likely to follow this policy in:
A) Italy.
B) Great Britain.
C) Japan.
D) Brazil.

Answer: C Difficulty: Hard Page: 518

40. The America-First Corporation is preparing to enter several high-context countries. In recruiting its foreign sales force, the firm would be well-advised to emphasize:
A) advertising.
B) employment agencies.
C) personal referrals.
D) the Internet.

Answer: C Difficulty: Hard Page: 519

41. An expatriate from one country who works for a foreign company in another country is called a(n):
A) multi-national.
B) Third-country national.
C) resident alien.
D) displaced national.

Answer: B Difficulty: Easy Page: 519

42. The America-First Corporation requires a sales force knowledgeable of several languages and cultures. The firm is likely to emphasize the recruitment of:
A) expatriates.
B) local nationals.
C) Third-country nationals.
D) displaced nationals.

Answer: C Difficulty: Hard Page: 520

43. Which of the following is the <u>PRIME</u> requirement for expatriate and Third-country personnel?
A) emotional stability.
B) product knowledge.
C) language skills.
D) maturity.

Answer: D Difficulty: Medium Page: 520

44. Given the traits needed by a successful "global" salesperson, the MOST effective recruiting approach will emphasize:
   A) pencil and paper tests.
   B) psychological screening.
   C) referrals.
   D) biographical information.

   Answer: C  Difficulty: Medium  Page: 523

45. The America-First Corporation proudly affirms that any employee can rise through the ranks to become president—if they are intelligent and willing to work hard. The firm's statement is based on:
   A) shared decision making.
   B) independent enterprise as an instrument for social action.
   C) the "master of destiny" concept.
   D) objective analysis.

   Answer: C  Difficulty: Hard  Page: 524

46. Persistence, hard work, a commitment to fulfill expectations, and effective use of time is the key to personal success according to the concept of:
   A) master of destiny.
   B) objective analysis.
   C) shared decision making.
   D) independent enterprise.

   Answer: A  Difficulty: Easy  Page: 524

47. Corporate "loyalty" is based on:
   A) the concept of independent enterprise.
   B) shared decision making.
   C) the concept of "master of destiny."
   D) merit selection

   Answer: A  Difficulty: Medium  Page: 524

48. The legal view of the corporation as an "entity" with rules and a continuity of existence is based on which of the following concepts?
   A) merit selection.
   B) master of destiny.
   C) independent enterprise.
   D) shared decision making.

   Answer: C  Difficulty: Medium  Page: 524

49. The reward and punishment system used in American corporations is based on which of the following concepts?
    A) independent enterprise.
    B) merit selection.
    C) master of destiny.
    D) shared decision making.

    Answer: B Difficulty: Hard Page: 524

50. The America-First Corporation strongly believes in the collection and use of marketing research data in creating, executing, and controlling its marketing program. The firm's behavior is an expression of acceptance of which of the following concepts?
    A) merit selection.
    B) shared decision making.
    C) master of destiny.
    D) objective analysis.

    Answer: D Difficulty: Hard Page: 525

51. The America-First Corporation encourages managers at the lowest levels in the firm to make operating decisions. The firm's actions are MOST consistent with which of the following concepts?
    A) merit selection.
    B) wide sharing of decision making.
    C) objective analysis.
    D) independent enterprise.

    Answer: B Difficulty: Hard Page: 525

52. The TQM philosophy is MOST consistent with which of the following basic American business concepts?
    A) the never-ending quest for improvement.
    B) widespread decision-making.
    C) objective analysis.
    D) merit selection.

    Answer: A Difficulty: Medium Page: 525

53. The America-First Corporation is preparing a motivation plan for its Japanese sales force. The firm's bonus system should be based on:
    A) group effort.
    B) individual effort.
    C) corporate-wide sales.
    D) fixed, recurrent dates.

    Answer: A Difficulty: Hard Page: 528

# Chapter 17 Personal Selling and Sales Management

54. Which of the following types of sales force motivation is MOST important to both Japanese and Americans?
    A) job security.
    B) merit increase in pay.
    C) promotion.
    D) personal growth and development.

    Answer: B Difficulty: Medium Page: 528-529

55. In Europe, fringe benefits may be as high as:
    A) 95 percent of salary.
    B) 80 percent of salary.
    C) 75 percent of salary.
    D) 60 percent of salary.

    Answer: D Difficulty: Easy Page: 529

56. The America-First Corporation does not normally allow families to accompany their salespeople to foreign posts. The firm is likely to pay a premium under such conditions called a(n):
    A) separation allowance.
    B) family plan.
    C) spousal plan.
    D) fringe payments.

    Answer: A Difficulty: Hard Page: 530

57. A firm's compensation program can be used to:
    A) recruit personnel.
    B) develop personnel.
    C) motivate/retain personnel.
    D) all of the above.

    Answer: D Difficulty: Medium Page: 530

58. The America-First Corporation is attempting to minimize compensation costs in its foreign sales efforts. In order to accomplish this goal, the firm will try to limit its use of:
    A) Third-country nationals.
    B) expatriates.
    C) local nationals.
    D) resident aliens.

    Answer: B Difficulty: Hard Page: 530

59. A successful global compensation plan should include all of the following EXCEPT:
   A) involvement of reps from key countries.
   B) allow local managers to set the mix between base and incentive pay.
   C) a generally designed plan that all local offices must follow.
   D) consistent performance measures.

   Answer: C Difficulty: Medium Page: 532

60. The motivation of "poor performers" is MOST difficult in:
   A) the United States.
   B) England.
   C) Japan.
   D) Germany.

   Answer: C Difficulty: Medium Page: 532

61. The primary motivation tool used by American sales managers is:
   A) the incentive system.
   B) the corporate culture.
   C) public recognition.
   D) group rewards.

   Answer: A Difficulty: Medium Page: 532

62. Estimates of the cost of sending and supporting a manager and his/her family in a foreign assignment range from:
   A) 50 to 200 percent of base salary.
   B) 150 to 400 percent of base salary.
   C) 200 to 600 percent of base salary.
   D) 400 to 800 percent of base salary.

   Answer: B Difficulty: Medium Page: 533

63. Which of the following concerns are MOST often mentioned as reasons for refusing a foreign assignment?
   A) career and family.
   B) pay differences and fringe benefits.
   C) culture shock and loss of citizenship.
   D) discrimination and ethnocentrism.

   Answer: A Difficulty: Medium Page: 533

64. Which of the following is the MOST common reason for an expatriate to return home prior to the scheduled end of a foreign assignment?
    A) low pay.
    B) unsatisfactory fringe benefits.
    C) discrimination on the job.
    D) unsuccessful family adjustment.

    Answer: D Difficulty: Medium Page: 534

65. The America-First Corporation is determined to reduce its rate of early expatriate returns from foreign assignments. Which of the following probably offers the BEST means of accomplishing this goal?
    A) special "hardship" pay.
    B) family screening.
    C) high fringe benefits.
    D) generous moving allowances.

    Answer: B Difficulty: Hard Page: 534

66. According to current thinking, problems arising after an expatriate returns home can be minimized by:
    A) increasing the pay for foreign assignment.
    B) increasing moving allowances.
    C) increasing fringe benefits.
    D) decreasing benefits for foreign assignments.

    Answer: D Difficulty: Medium Page: 535

67. Companies that have the LEAST amount of attrition among expatriates returning from abroad are those which:
    A) pay the highest salaries for foreign assignments.
    B) provide personal career planning for the expatriate.
    C) allow the most generous moving allowances.
    D) provide readjustment bonuses.

    Answer: B Difficulty: Medium Page: 535

68. The America-First Corporation is determined to reduce the rate of attrition among returning expatriates. Which of the following should the firm consider as part of such a program?
    A) the use of mentors.
    B) reassigning expatriates to meaningful positions.
    C) offering a written job guarantee.
    D) all of the above are useful.

    Answer: D Difficulty: Hard Page: 536

69. Most expatriate failures are caused by:
    A) poor sales techniques.
    B) a lack of technical expertise.
    C) failure to understand cultural differences and their impact on management skills.
    D) poor compensation.

    Answer: C Difficulty: Medium Page: 536

70. People with cultural skills can:
    A) communicate respect, regard, and interest in other peoples and their culture.
    B) display empathy.
    C) recognize and control their SRC.
    D) all of the above.

    Answer: D Difficulty: Medium Page: 537

71. Executives in the 21st century are likely to have a background that is:
    A) multi-environmental.
    B) multi-cultural.
    C) multi-country.
    D) all of the above.

    Answer: D Difficulty: Medium Page: 538

72. In today's international environment:
    A) training is an exercise in futility.
    B) training must be continuous.
    C) training is not needed if good people are hired.
    D) training is no longer cost efficient.

    Answer: B Difficulty: Medium Page: 538

73. Which of the following countries has avoided the need for high foreign service "premiums" by the simple expedient at making foreign service a requirement for promotion?
    A) Japan.
    B) America.
    C) England.
    D) Germany.

    Answer: A Difficulty: Medium Page: 538

74. The America-First Corporation is attempting to upgrade the quality of its international sales force. One of the BEST ways to do this is to:
A) send new hires to school.
B) require foreign postings for new hires.
C) provide Internet access for all employees.
D) require new hires to learn a foreign language.

Answer: B Difficulty: Hard Page: 538

75. Foreign postings are MOST important in the training of managers who:
A) will be developing strategy.
B) have been with the firm the longest amount of time.
C) have become bored in their jobs.
D) deserve a reward for past service.

Answer: A Difficulty: Hard Page: 538

76. The America-First Corporation has been involved in foreign trade for some time. The firm is MOST likely to perceive itself as a global business when:
A) it sells more than one million dollars of goods abroad.
B) it hires its first global manager.
C) foreign revenues exceed domestic revenues.
D) the firm establishes a foreign sales force.

Answer: C Difficulty: Hard Page: 538

77. The first truly "global school" transcending national historical, linguistic, and cultural lines was established by the:
A) Union of Soviet Republics.
B) European Community.
C) United States of America.
D) Pacific Rim Consortia.

Answer: B Difficulty: Medium Page: 539

78. Traditionally, the language of international business has been:
A) French.
B) German.
C) Italian.
D) English.

Answer: D Difficulty: Easy Page: 540

79. The fact that many foreign nationals prefer to buy from salespeople who speak their language is MOST likely to be a problem for salespeople from:
A) Japan.
B) Britain.
C) America.
D) France.

Answer: C Difficulty: Medium Page: 540

80. The ability of an individual to speak a second language is, at minimum, an indication of a person's:
A) ability to learn.
B) willingness to get involved in another culture.
C) willingness to accept authority.
D) willingness to travel.

Answer: B Difficulty: Medium Page: 540

**Fill in the Blank Questions**

81. Traditionally, the international sales forces of American firms have been composed of ________________.

Answer: expatriates Difficulty: Easy Page: 514

82. Effective communication is at the core of ______________ marketing.

Answer: relationship Difficulty: Medium Page: 514

83. Global sales forces are drawn from ______________, ________________, and ________________.

Answer: expatriates; local nationals; Third-country nationals Difficulty: Medium Page: 514

84. The America-First Corporation feels that its foreign sales force should be familiar with the language, law, culture, and habits of the nations in which they serve. The firm is likely to recruit primarily from ________________.

Answer: local nationals Difficulty: Hard Page: 517-518

85. A(n) ______________ is an expatriate from their own country who works for a foreign company in yet another country.

Answer: Third-country national Difficulty: Easy Page: 519

86. Traditionally, American workers have believed that they are the ______________ and responsible for their own success.

    Answer: Masters of their own destiny  Difficulty: Medium  Page: 524

87. Because they must typically work more independently than their domestic counterparts, foreign sales personnel must demonstrate a great deal of ______________.

    Answer: maturity  Difficulty: Medium  Page: 525

88. The America-First Corporation is a strong believer in the use of market research in the shaping of international strategy. The firm's behavior is based on the American belief in ______________.

    Answer: objectivity  Difficulty: Hard  Page: 525

89. International training has been facilitated by the growth of, and access to, the ______________.

    Answer: Internet  Difficulty: Medium  Page: 526

90. In spite of cultural differences worldwide, salespeople everywhere agree that ______________ are the most effective form of motivation.

    Answer: merit pay increases  Difficulty: Medium  Page: 529

91. The America-First Corporation routinely pays premiums to expatriates who take short-term foreign postings without their families. The firm is paying a(n) ______________.

    Answer: separation allowance  Difficulty: Hard  Page: 530

92. The primary control system favored by American managers is the ______________.

    Answer: incentive system  Difficulty: Easy  Page: 532

93. The <u>MOST</u> frequently monitored reasons for a manager to refuse a foreign assignment involve concerns for ______________ and ______________.

    Answer: career; family  Difficulty: Medium  Page: 533

94. The America-First Corporation is attempting to improve the morale of its expatriate sales force by providing cultural training. To have its greatest positive impact, this training should include the salesperson's ______________.

    Answer: family  Difficulty: Hard  Page: 534

# Chapter 17 Personal Selling and Sales Management

95. A returning expatriate is MOST likely to resign after returning from a foreign posting as a result of _______________ concerns.

    Answer: career-related  Difficulty: Medium  Page: 535

96. Attempts to develop cultural awareness is MOST inhibited by the salesperson's _______________.

    Answer: self-reference criterion  Difficulty: Medium  Page: 536

97. Tomorrow's executives may begin their careers in _____, move to ______, and then _______ with international assignments to gain success.

    Answer: research; marketing; finance  Difficulty: Medium  Page: 538

98. The America-First Corporation is strongly committed to preparing its global sales force. In today's environment, the firm must provide _______________ training.

    Answer: continual  Difficulty: Hard  Page: 538

99. Firms typically perceive themselves as a global organization when foreign exceeds domestic _______________.

    Answer: sales revenues  Difficulty: Medium  Page: 538

100. American firms have probably been harmed by the traditional acceptance of _______________ as the language of business.

    Answer: English  Difficulty: Medium  Page: 540

**Essay Questions**

101. What is relationship marketing? What impact does the popularity of this concept have on the selection and training of the global sales force?

    Answer:
    Relationship marketing emphasizes the creation of long-term interactions between the firm and its customers. The basis of such relationships must be effective communication. Effective communication, in turn, is based on a knowledge of a foreign country's language and culture. Foreign nationals have a distinct advantage in these important areas, and have accordingly become an increasingly popular source for the international sales force. Expatriates must strive to gain these skills through training and experience if they hope to compete in this arena.

    Difficulty: Hard  Page: 514

# Chapter 17 Personal Selling and Sales Management

102. Identify the three recruitment sources available for staffing an international sales force. Briefly discuss their relative advantages and disadvantages.

Answer:
The international sales force may be composed of expatriates, local nationals, and/or third-country nationals. Expatriates may possess a better technical background and a superior knowledge of the firm and its products. They are a "proven" asset--and may bring some status to the force. However, expatriates may come at a high cost, face cultural and legal barriers, and may resist foreign assignments. Local nationals, currently the preferred group, offer cultural/legal knowledge--and are less expensive than expatriates. Locals may require training in technical material and company/product knowledge. Third-country nationals--expatriates from one country working for a foreign-owned firm in yet another country--bring the broadest international experience--but, will require training in the firm's products and procedures.

Difficulty: Hard Page: 516-520

103. Briefly discuss the seven cultural norms that tend to guide U.S. cultural and managerial behavior. Why are these "norms" significant in international negotiations?

Answer:
The MASTER OF DESTINY philosophy holds that the individual controls his/her own future through hard work, persistence, and a willingness to fulfill expectations. According to the INDEPENDENT ENTERPRISE concept, employees are dedicated to serving the organization and assuring its survival. The idea that PERSONNEL ARE SELECTED ON MERIT encourages hard work and provides a basis for expectations. The desire to BASE DECISIONS ON OBJECTIVE ANALYSIS supports the use of, and reliance on a scientific approach and research for decision making. WIDE SHARING IN DECISION MAKING supports the use of delegation, bottom-up management, and teams. The NEVER-ENDING QUEST FOR IMPROVEMENT supports TQM and other means of improving performance. These cultural norms are major factors in the SRC phenomenon that often causes American managers to misinterpret the behavior of foreign nationals. COMPETITION has been considered essential for efficiency, improvement, and regeneration since the time of Adam Smith.

Difficulty: Hard Page: 523-526

104. How can the international firm BEST select, train, and motivate expatriates to maximize the likelihood of success in foreign assignments?

Answer:
Candidates for international assignment must bring maturity, emotional stability, and wide-ranging business and cultural knowledge to the position. The firm must build on this adaptability and innate cultural empathy by providing specific knowledge of the culture, legal system, and behaviors of the host country. Motivation includes, but is not limited to, financial incentives. The expatriate needs understanding, continual communication, and strong reassurance of the importance of the assignment. From the outset, assurances must be given that the expatriate will experience long-term career benefits.

Difficulty: Hard Page: 526-533

105. Why is language proficiency important to the international marketer? Why is fluency preferable to simply using an interpreter?

Answer:
The foreign national who takes the time required to learn the language of the host country has DEMONSTRATED his/her appreciation of the culture and their willingness to expend effort in order to develop a fuller appreciation of it. Fluency also indicates that the person sees the assignment as a long-term position of importance to his/her career. A knowledge of the language of a country aids the expatriates' attempts to develop an understanding of the full culture and appreciate the subtle behaviors important in it. The use of interpreters demonstrates that the expatriate is either new to the culture--or, worse, is not interested in it. Furthermore, the interpreter is another "filter" in the communication process that may deliberately or innocently introduce misunderstandings.

Difficulty: Hard Page: 540

# Chapter 18 Pricing for International Markets

## True/False Questions

1. The product's price must accurately reflect the consumer's perceptions of the quality and satisfactions offered by the product.

   Answer: True   Difficulty: Medium   Page: 544

2. Profit is, by far, the MOST important pricing objective.

   Answer: True   Difficulty: Easy   Page: 545

3. The America-First Corporation occasionally imports products from distributors in Germany and resells them to Japanese distributors who are not part of the manufacturer's regular distribution system. The firm is engaged in parallel importing.

   Answer: True   Difficulty: Hard   Page: 545

4. The possibility of a parallel market occurs whenever price differences are less than the cost of transportation between the two markets involved.

   Answer: False   Difficulty: Medium   Page: 545

5. The practice of exclusive distribution often encourages parallel and "gray" markets.

   Answer: True   Difficulty: Medium   Page: 547

6. "Diverters" are gray market entrepreneurs who buy products at retail prices, usually during sales, and resell the goods to foreign buyers.

   Answer: True   Difficulty: Easy   Page: 547

7. The America-First Corporation is determined to increase its market share in international markets. The firm should vigorously encourage gray markets as part of the strategy for achieving that goal.

   Answer: False   Difficulty: Hard   Page: 548

8. Firms that employ full-cost pricing may gain a competitive advantage in international markets--at the risk of being charged with dumping.

   Answer: False   Difficulty: Medium   Page: 549

9. Because penetration pricing requires the marketer to accept lower margins, it can never produce the profit volume that can be delivered by the skimming approach.

   Answer: False   Difficulty: Medium   Page: 550-551

# Chapter 18 Pricing for International Markets

10. Generally, price differences between the domestic country and the importing country is the result of the costs associated with exporting the product from one country to another.

    Answer: True Difficulty: Hard Page: 551-552

11. Import tariffs and foreign taxes lead to significant price escalation in international markets.

    Answer: True Difficulty: Medium Page: 528

12. Ad valorem duties are levied as a flat charge per physical unit imported.

    Answer: False Difficulty: Easy Page: 552

13. In order to penetrate foreign markets, the America-First Corporation occasionally prices some products at, or below, their replacement cost. In those countries characterized by high inflation and slow payment, the firm will probably incur significant losses.

    Answer: True Difficulty: Hard Page: 553

14. Freely floating exchange rates have greatly simplified the process of predicting the net profit or loss to be associated with international transactions.

    Answer: False Difficulty: Medium Page: 554

15. At least in the short run, a "weak" dollar is beneficial to U.S. exporters.

    Answer: True Difficulty: Medium Page: 554

16. When the value of the dollar is weak, companies generally employ cost-plus pricing.

    Answer: True Difficulty: Medium Page: 554

17. Generally, foreign channels are shorter, and middleman margins are lower, than in the United States.

    Answer: False Difficulty: Medium Page: 555

18. Cost containment is especially critical for firms attempting to participate in the growth of markets around the world.

    Answer: True Difficulty: Medium Page: 556

19. The America-First Corporation is seeking to eliminate unnecessary features, and even lower the quality, of some of the products it sells abroad. If these actions can be implemented without damaging customer satisfaction, the firm will gain the benefits of lower prices and reduced ad valorem tariffs.

    Answer: True Difficulty: Hard Page: 557-558

20. The way in which a product involved in international trade is classified can have a major impact on the amount of tariffs that must be paid.

    Answer: True  Difficulty: Medium  Page: 558

21. Reducing the length of foreign channels may generate both better control and lower costs through eliminating markups and reducing value-added taxes paid.

    Answer: True  Difficulty: Medium  Page: 558

22. An FTZ is a tax-free enclave that is not considered to be a part of the country as far as import regulations are concerned.

    Answer: True  Difficulty: Easy  Page: 559

23. The America-First Corporation seeks to lower, or avoid, tariff impacts by shipping products unassembled, modifying goods to "fit" cheaper categories, and/or employing local labor or materials whenever possible. The firm should make extensive use of foreign trade zones in every foreign market in which they are available.

    Answer: True  Difficulty: Hard  Page: 560

24. The term "dumping" refers to the practice of selling goods in a foreign market for less than their cost in the country of origin--or for less than they cost to produce.

    Answer: True  Difficulty: Easy  Page: 560

25. Antidumping and countervailing duties are used to offset the impact of discriminatory pricing, kickbacks, and model-year discounts.

    Answer: True  Difficulty: Medium  Page: 560

26. By definition, countertrade transactions include only non-cash purchases.

    Answer: False  Difficulty: Easy  Page: 562

27. The America-First Corporation has agreed to sell a motorcycle plant to Romania in return for cash and a specified amount of the plant's output. The firm has negotiated a product buyback agreement.

    Answer: True  Difficulty: Hard  Page: 565

28. A proactive countertrade strategy is the most effective strategy for global companies that market to exchange-poor countries.

    Answer: True  Difficulty: Easy  Page: 567

29. Administered pricing relates to attempts to establish prices for an entire market.

    Answer: True Difficulty: Easy Page: 569

30. The Trans-Atlantic Conference Agreement proved that shipping cartels can have little or no impact on international trade or pricing.

    Answer: False Difficulty: Medium Page: 571

**Multiple Choice Questions**

31. Firms that view pricing as a static element in a business decision:
    A) tend to export only excess inventory.
    B) place a low priority on foreign business.
    C) view export sales as passive contributions to sales volume.
    D) all of the above.

    Answer: D Difficulty: Medium Page: 545

32. The <u>MOST</u> important pricing objective is:
    A) return on investment.
    B) market share.
    C) total profit.
    D) sales volume.

    Answer: C Difficulty: Medium Page: 545

33. Parallel imports are the basis of:
    A) the gray market.
    B) counterpurchasing.
    C) countertrading.
    D) barter.

    Answer: A Difficulty: Medium Page: 545

34. The practice of purchasing products from distributors in one country and selling them to distributors who are not part of the manufacturer's regular distribution system is called:
    A) counterpurchasing.
    B) countertrading.
    C) parallel importing.
    D) bartering.

    Answer: C Difficulty: Easy Page: 545

# Chapter 18 Pricing for International Markets

35. Parallel importing may be encouraged by:
    A) variations in the value of currencies between countries.
    B) restrictions on market supply in a country.
    C) restrictions created by import quotas and tariffs.
    D) all of the above.

    Answer: D Difficulty: Medium Page: 545-546

36. The DOMESTIC policies of which of the following countries have led to the growth of a powerful parallel, or gray, market that can undercut the prices of domestic retailers?
    A) the United States.
    B) Japan.
    C) England.
    D) France.

    Answer: B Difficulty: Medium Page: 546

37. Jon Perch and his associates routinely purchase high-price, high-status goods during sales at authorized retail outlets for resale to foreign buyers. Jon would be BEST described as a:
    A) diverter.
    B) privateer.
    C) barterer.
    D) pirate.

    Answer: A Difficulty: Hard Page: 547

38. The America-First Corporation, a major marketer of CDs, has noticed a sharp increase in the number of individuals buying its goods on the gray market. This phenomenon is PRIMARILY a result of the growth of the:
    A) price harmonization strategy.
    B) internet.
    C) brand harmonization strategy.
    D) European Common Market.

    Answer: B Difficulty: Hard Page: 548

39. Under which of the following pricing approaches is the marketer concerned only with the marginal or incremental cost of producing goods to be sold in foreign markets?
    A) skimming pricing.
    B) penetration pricing.
    C) full cost pricing.
    D) variable cost pricing.

    Answer: D Difficulty: Easy Page: 549

40. Which of the following pricing approaches is MOST likely to open a firm to charges of dumping?
A) skimming.
B) full-cost pricing.
C) variable-cost pricing.
D) barter.

Answer: C Difficulty: Medium Page: 549

41. The America-First Corporation is preparing to market its high-status, high-quality, high-tech products to wealthy citizens of the world's most developed nations. The firm isMOST likely to employ:
A) penetration pricing.
B) skimming pricing.
C) variable-cost pricing.
D) gray market pricing.

Answer: B Difficulty: Hard Page: 550

42. Market segments that are relatively price-insensitive and willing to pay a premium for quality and/or be the first to obtain a high-status, new product are PRIME prospects for:
A) penetration pricing.
B) variable-cost pricing.
C) skimming pricing.
D) one market pricing.

Answer: C Difficulty: Medium Page: 550

43. The America-First Corporation views pricing as a tool for achieving long-term profits, building market share quickly, and delaying/precluding competitive entry. The firm is MOST likely to favor:
A) penetration pricing.
B) skimming pricing.
C) prestige pricing.
D) gray-market pricing.

Answer: A Difficulty: Hard Page: 550-551

44. Tariffs, complex distribution systems, and value-added taxation contribute to the phenomenon of:
A) price stagnation.
B) price stabilization.
C) price escalation.
D) price rationalization.

Answer: C Difficulty: Medium Page: 552

# Chapter 18 Pricing for International Markets

45. The disproportionate difference in price between the exporting country and the importing country is called:
    A) price escalation.
    B) price stabilization.
    C) price stagnation.
    D) price rationalization.

    Answer: A Difficulty: Easy Page: 552

46. In several of the countries served by the America-First Corporation, imported goods are taxed on a per unit basis AND on the basis of their value. These nations are utilizing:
    A) ad valorem tariffs.
    B) specific tariffs.
    C) compound tariffs.
    D) unit tariffs.

    Answer: C Difficulty: Hard Page: 552

47. Which of the following discriminates MOST against foreign goods?
    A) retail sales taxes.
    B) excise taxes.
    C) turnover taxes.
    D) tariffs.

    Answer: D Difficulty: Medium Page: 552

48. Price escalation is caused by:
    A) shipping, insurance, and packing costs.
    B) tariffs, special taxes, and exchange rate fluctuations.
    C) longer channels, higher margins, and administrative costs.
    D) all of the above.

    Answer: D Difficulty: Medium Page: 552-553

49. The threat posed by spiraling inflation is especially significant for firms selling in:
    A) Japan.
    B) Latin America.
    C) Germany.
    D) France.

    Answer: B Difficulty: Medium Page: 553

50. The weakening of the U.S. dollar:
    A) aided U.S. exporters.
    B) aided U.S. importers.
    C) aided foreign exporters.
    D) had no impact on foreign trade.

    Answer: A Difficulty: Medium Page: 554

51. Firms located in countries that have a WEAK currency should engage in all of the following practices EXCEPT:
    A) stress price benefits.
    B) countertrade with other weak currency nations.
    C) shift sourcing and manufacturing to the domestic market.
    D) conduct cash-for-goods trade.

    Answer: B Difficulty: Medium Page: 554

52. The America-First Corporation feels that price escalation is the prime barrier it faces in its efforts to expand foreign markets. The firm will probably seek to offset this threat through a vigorous program of:
    A) cost containment.
    B) gray marketing.
    C) parallel exporting.
    D) reverse tariffs.

    Answer: A Difficulty: Hard Page: 554

53. Costs may be reduced by:
    A) lowering the cost of goods.
    B) lowering tariffs.
    C) lowering distribution costs.
    D) all of the above.

    Answer: D Difficulty: Medium Page: 557-558

54. The America-First Corporation carefully studies the tax structures of each of its client countries and is careful to describe its products in terms that would place them in one of the more "favored" categories. The firm is trying to reduce the costs of international marketing by:
    A) lowering the cost of goods.
    B) lowering distribution costs.
    C) lowering tariffs.
    D) lowering margins.

    Answer: C Difficulty: Hard Page: 558

# Chapter 18 Pricing for International Markets

55. Shortening foreign channels of distribution may cut costs by reducing total middleman markups and:
    A) cumulative value-added taxes.
    B) isolationist tariffs.
    C) specific tariffs.
    D) margin taxes.

    Answer: A Difficulty: Medium Page: 559

56. The use of FTZs allows greater control over:
    A) taxes.
    B) duties.
    C) surcharges.
    D) all of the above.

    Answer: D Difficulty: Medium Page: 559

57. A tax-free enclave that is not considered to be part of the country as far as import regulations are concerned is called a:
    A) MNC.
    B) SRC.
    C) FTZ.
    D) NEC.

    Answer: C Difficulty: Easy Page: 559

58. The America-First Corporation is determined to employ FTZs whenever possible as part of its cost containment program. The FTZ can save the firm money by:
    A) providing a place for assembly of goods shipped disassembled.
    B) allowing the firm to use cheaper foreign labor.
    C) allowing the firm to use local content.
    D) all of the above.

    Answer: D Difficulty: Hard Page: 560

59. Products sold below their cost of production or below their cost in the domestic market are said to have been:
    A) gray marketed.
    B) dumped.
    C) free-traded.
    D) free-zoned.

    Answer: B Difficulty: Easy Page: 560

60. Countries have attempted to get around anti-dumping legislation by using:
    A) kickbacks.
    B) subsidies.
    C) model-year discounts.
    D) all of the above.

    Answer: D Difficulty: Easy Page: 560

61. Companies that are found guilty of dumping are typically:
    A) barred from trading in the harmed market again.
    B) charged countervailing duties.
    C) required to fire the offending executives.
    D) forced to sell off the offending divisions.

    Answer: B Difficulty: Medium Page: 560

62. The America-First Corporation has charged one of its Japanese competitors with dumping. The firm claims that its rival lists prices at the same level as the domestic Japanese price, but provides under-the-table payments to importers that make the actual price paid much lower. If the charge is true, the Japanese firm is using:
    A) model-year discounts.
    B) government subsidies.
    C) kickbacks.
    D) countervailing duties.

    Answer: C Difficulty: Hard Page: 561

63. All of the following are advantages of leasing EXCEPT:
    A) allows access to a large segment of nominally financed foreign firms.
    B) attracts buyers in nations characterized by spiraling inflation.
    C) eases the problem of selling new, experimental equipment.
    D) provides stable revenue flows.

    Answer: B Difficulty: Medium Page: 562

64. The attractiveness of leasing is REDUCED by:
    A) currency devaluations.
    B) the threat of expropriation.
    C) political instability.
    D) all of the above.

    Answer: D Difficulty: Medium Page: 562

# Chapter 18 Pricing for International Markets

65. The DIRECT exchange of goods between the parties in a transaction is the hallmark of:
    A) compensation deals.
    B) barter.
    C) counterpurchase.
    D) buy-back.

    Answer: B Difficulty: Easy Page: 563

66. Payments are made in both goods and cash under a:
    A) compensation deal.
    B) barter.
    C) counterpurchase.
    D) buy-back.

    Answer: A Difficulty: Easy Page: 564

67. Which of the following is probably the MOST frequently used form of countertrade?
    A) barter.
    B) buy-backs.
    C) compensation deals.
    D) offset trades.

    Answer: D Difficulty: Medium Page: 564

68. The America-First Corporation has agreed to sell goods to another firm for cash contingent upon their purchase of a like value of goods from that firm within the next six months. The firm has entered into:
    A) barter arrangements.
    B) a buy-back contract.
    C) counterpurchase trade.
    D) a compensation deal.

    Answer: C Difficulty: Hard Page: 564

69. The America-First Corporation has just sold plant and equipment to China for cash. Under the terms of the deal, America-First has agreed to purchase a set amount of the plant's output. The firm has entered into a(n):
    A) barter arrangement.
    B) buy-back agreement.
    C) compensation deal.
    D) offset trade.

    Answer: B Difficulty: Hard Page: 565

70. Countertrade is MOST important for firms that sell to:
A) Japan.
B) the United States.
C) Eastern Europe.
D) Italy.

Answer: C Difficulty: Medium Page: 567

71. All of the following are reasons for purchasers to impose countertrade obligations EXCEPT:
A) to preserve hard currency.
B) to improve the balance of trade.
C) to gain access to new markets.
D) to lower the prices of exported goods.

Answer: D Difficulty: Medium Page: 567

72. Given recent trends, which of the following nations might have a strong reason to impose countertrade obligations on Japan?
A) the United States.
B) Germany.
C) Britain.
D) Italy.

Answer: A Difficulty: Medium Page: 567

73. The CRITICAL factor in a countertrade negotiation is:
A) obtaining government permission for the deal.
B) determining the value of, and demand for, the goods offered.
C) selecting the country with which to partner.
D) approving the exchange to be used.

Answer: B Difficulty: Medium Page: 567

74. The America-First Corporation would like to minimize the tax liabilities of some of its extremely profitable foreign subsidiaries. The firm is MOST likely to seek to accomplish this goal by "manipulating":
A) barter arrangements.
B) counterpurchase deals.
C) transfer pricing.
D) offset trading.

Answer: C Difficulty: Hard Page: 567

# Chapter 18 Pricing for International Markets

75. The objective(s) of intracompany pricing systems include:
    A) maximizing profits for the total corporation.
    B) facilitating parent-company control.
    C) allowing all of the firm's managers an adequate basis for maintaining, developing, and receiving credit for their own profitability.
    D) all of the above.

    Answer: D Difficulty: Medium Page: 568

76. Which of the following forms of intracompany transfer pricing is MOST acceptable to tax authorities and foreign divisions?
    A) local manufacturing cost plus a standard markup.
    B) most efficient producer plus a standard markup.
    C) negotiated prices.
    D) arm's-length pricing.

    Answer: D Difficulty: Medium Page: 568

77. In international marketing, price-fixing may be accomplished through:
    A) licensing.
    B) cartels.
    C) trade associations.
    D) all of the above.

    Answer: D Difficulty: Medium Page: 570

78. Which of the following methods of administered pricing is LEAST acceptable to most nations of the world?
    A) licensing.
    B) cartels.
    C) trade associations.
    D) free trade zones.

    Answer: B Difficulty: Medium Page: 570-571

79. Cartels accomplish ALL of the following EXCEPT:
    A) eliminates cut-throat competition.
    B) lowers consumer prices.
    C) "rationalizes" business.
    D) encourages technical progress.

    Answer: B Difficulty: Medium Page: 571

80. The America-First Corporation has been most frustrated by governmental price-fixing in its international activities. The firm has probably encountered its greatest frustration in:
    A) Great Britain.
    B) Brazil.
    C) Germany.
    D) Japan.

    Answer: D Difficulty: Hard Page: 572

## Fill in the Blank Questions

81. The most important pricing objective, by far, is _______________.

    Answer: profit Difficulty: Easy Page: 545

82. The America-First Corporation has been frustrated by the activities of unauthorized wholesalers who buy their goods in low-price markets and undersell the firm in its prime markets. The firm is facing competition from the _______________.

    Answer: Gray market Difficulty: Hard Page: 545

83. Ironically, the use of _______________ distribution to maintain high margins and prices encourages the growth of parallel importing.

    Answer: exclusive Difficulty: Medium Page: 547

84. Under _______________ pricing, the firm is concerned only with the marginal or incremental cost of producing goods to be sold in foreign markets.

    Answer: variable-cost Difficulty: Medium Page: 549

85. The America-First Corporation specializes in selling high-fashion items to price-insensitive niche markets around the world. The firm is <u>MOST</u> likely to employ _______________ pricing.

    Answer: skimming Difficulty: Hard Page: 550

86. The America-First Corporation routinely uses pricing to reach the mass market quickly and discourage competitive entry. The firm is most likely to employ _______________ pricing.

    Answer: penetration Difficulty: Hard Page: 550

87. A(n) _______________ duty consists of both a specific and an ad valorem tariff.

    Answer: compound Difficulty: Easy Page: 552

# Chapter 18 Pricing for International Markets

88. Price escalation may be reduced by lowering the cost of _______________, lowering _______________, and lowering _______________ costs.

    Answer: goods; tariffs; distribution  Difficulty: Medium  Page: 553

89. The America-First Corporation would like to postpone the payment of duties until its exported parts and components have been assembled inside its foreign markets and are ready for sale. The firm will emphasize the use of _______________.

    Answer: Free Trade Zones (FTZ)  Difficulty: Hard  Page: 559

90. Selling goods in a foreign country below their cost of production or their price in the home market is termed _______________.

    Answer: dumping  Difficulty: Easy  Page: 560

91. A(n) _______________ duty may be imposed on foreign goods benefiting from subsidies in production, export, or transport.

    Answer: countervailing  Difficulty: Medium  Page: 560

92. The America-First Corporation suspects that its Japanese competitors are providing secret payments to importers to avoid dumping charges. If true, the firm is facing the use of _______________ by its competitors.

    Answer: kickbacks  Difficulty: Hard  Page: 560

93. An important selling technique to alleviate high prices and capital shortages for capital equipment is the _______________ system.

    Answer: leasing  Difficulty: Medium  Page: 562

94. Countertrade includes: _______________, _______________, _______________, and _______________ transactions.

    Answer: barter; compensation deals; counterpurchase; buy-back  Difficulty: Medium  Page: 563

95. _______________ involve payment in goods and in cash.

    Answer: compensation deals  Difficulty: Easy  Page: 564

96. The America-First Corporation often buys from a foreign seller with the understanding that the firm will purchase goods of a similar value from it by a specified date. The firm is employing _______________.

    Answer: counterpurchase (offset trade)  Difficulty: Hard  Page: 564

# Chapter 18 Pricing for International Markets

97. ______________ pricing refers to the prices of goods shipped from a firm's operations or sales units in one country to its units elsewhere.

    Answer: Transfer Difficulty: Easy Page: 567

98. ______________ pricing refers to attempts to establish prices for an entire market.

    Answer: Administered Difficulty: Easy Page: 569

99. The ______________ is the form of price-fixing arrangement most directly associated with international marketing.

    Answer: cartel Difficulty: Medium Page: 570

100. The America-First Corporation is heavily dependent on trans-oceanic shipping. The firm is likely to find itself subject to price-fixing agreements under the control of shipping ______________.

    Answer: cartels Difficulty: Hard Page: 571

**Essay Questions**

101. Describe the practice of parallel importing. What factors lead to its use?

    Answer:
    Parallel imports develop when importers buy products from distributors in one country and sell them to distributors in another country who are not part of the manufacturer's distribution system. The practice is lucrative when wide margins exist between prices for the same product in different countries. This can arise as a result of currency fluctuations, deliberate restrictions in supply, supply restrictions due to quotas and tariffs, or price controls. The possibility of a parallel market occurs whenever price differences are greater than the cost of transportation between two markets. Designer or status products are prime candidates for the practice.

    Difficulty: Hard Page: 545-549

# Chapter 18 Pricing for International Markets

102. Briefly discuss the basic approaches to international pricing. What advantages/disadvantages are offered by each?

Answer:
International firms tend to focus on full-cost or variable-cost pricing, penetration pricing, and skimming pricing. Full-cost pricing ensures that all costs are covered in each market--and the firm's typical margin is maintained. This policy guards against losses, but may reduce competitiveness. The variable-cost approach is often employed by firms that view any foreign sale as a bonus. The approach enhances competitiveness, but may lead to charges of dumping. Penetration pricing refers to the practice of pricing "low" in the acceptable range of prices to discourage/preclude competition and/or build market share. Because unit margins are small, high volume is required for breakeven--and profitability. Skimming employs a high price to generate high margins in order to cover R & D costs quickly and return rapid profits while competitive products are scarce. While this approach also facilitates correcting an initial pricing mistake, it also tends to attract competition.

Difficulty: Hard Page: 549-551

103. What causes international price escalation? How can the international firm fight this problem?

Answer:
Price escalation in international trade is triggered by shipping costs, insurance, packing, tariffs, longer channels of distribution, higher middlemen margins, special taxes, administrative costs, and exchange-rate fluctuations. The process is "attacked" by lowering the cost of goods through reducing the cost of manufacturing, eliminating "unnecessary" product features or functions, and, perhaps, reducing "quality." Reduced product value will also result in reduced ad valorem tariffs. Tariffs may be reduced by having goods reclassified into lower tariff categories, modifying the product, performing assembly in market countries, or adding local content. Shorter channels reduce margin costs and may reduce value-added tax payments. Many of the strategies outlined may be implemented through skillful use of a foreign trade zone.

Difficulty: Hard Page: 551-560

104. What is dumping? How might the practice be "hidden"? What remedies are available?

Answer:
Dumping refers to the practice of selling goods in another country for less than their cost of manufacture--or, in some cases, for less than they are sold for in the country of origin. Dumping is used to gain market share--and, perhaps, drive domestic competitors out of business. Because of the real possibility of harm, many nations employ special import duties, or countervailing tariffs, to reduce or eliminate the price advantage of foreign producers. Dumping may be "hidden" by the use of government subsidies, kickbacks secretly given to buyers, or pseudo model-year discounts.

Difficulty: Hard Page: 560-562

105. What is countertrading? How can it be accomplished? Why has the practice become more significant to the international marketer?

Answer:
Countertrading is the practice of paying for goods partially, or fully, with other goods. Barter is the traditional practice of directly exchanging goods for goods. Compensation deals involve BOTH cash and goods as payment in the transaction. Counterpurchases, or offset trades, use reciprocity contracts to require firms to engage in stipulated transactions under stipulated terms within a stipulated period. Buy-back agreements require the sellers of capital goods and installations to purchase some portion of that plant's output. Countertrade provides an effective, often the only, means of gaining entry to emerging markets and NICs.

Difficulty: Hard Page: 562-567

# Chapter 19 Negotiating with International Customers, Partners, and Regulators

## True/False Questions

1. The implementation of international marketing strategy is typically accomplished through negotiation.

   Answer: True Difficulty: Medium Page: 576

2. The America-First Corporation is preparing to enter negotiations with a potential Japanese partner. The firm's representatives should consider the impact of the culture of their Japanese hosts—but strive to understand them as individuals as well.

   Answer: True Difficulty: Hard Page: 578

3. On every point of the negotiation scale, Japan is at, or near, the extreme position.

   Answer: True Difficulty: Medium Page: 578

4. Where language differences are the most obvious obstacles to international negotiations, other, more subtle, factors probably pose greater barriers to success.

   Answer: True Difficulty: Medium Page: 579

5. Generally, "side conversations" carried on by foreign negotiators in their native tongue are indications of attempts to hide facts, mislead, or deceive those who do not speak that language.

   Answer: False Difficulty: Medium Page: 579

6. Spaniards and Japanese are especially hesitant to provide information in negotiations.

   Answer: True Difficulty: Medium Page: 579

7. Japanese negotiators use less facial gazing and touching than any other nationality—while using the word "no" and periods of silence more than any other group.

   Answer: False Difficulty: Medium Page: 579

8. The America-First Corporation is preparing for negotiations with potential Korean partners. Because the firm has successfully negotiated with Japanese firms, America-First can be assured that the same approaches will be equally successful with the Koreans.

   Answer: False Difficulty: Hard Page: 582

9. Chinese negotiators are characterized by their heavy use of questions and information-exchange tactics.

   Answer: True   Difficulty: Medium   Page: 582

10. While Russians are, geographically, Europeans, their negotiation style is most similar to the Japanese.

   Answer: True   Difficulty: Medium   Page: 582

11. German negotiators, as might be expected, are highly aggressive questioners who provide little self-disclosure

   Answer: False   Difficulty: Medium   Page: 582

12. British negotiators are more similar to their American counterparts than those of any other nation.

   Answer: True   Difficulty: Medium   Page: 582

13. French, Spanish, and Brazilian businesspeople are the most aggressive of all negotiators.

   Answer: True   Difficulty: Medium   Page: 583

14. The America-First Corporation is preparing for a series of international negotiations. While each national group may exhibit some differences in style, America-First can be certain that all of these professional businesspeople will objectively separate the facts of the situation from the personalities of the negotiators.

   Answer: False   Difficulty: Hard   Page: 584

15. The fact that Americans find it difficult to understand the Japanese practice of giving complete deference to the needs and wishes of buyers goes far in explaining the loss of customers to Japanese competitors suffered by many American firms.

   Answer: True   Difficulty: Hard   Page: 584

16. Foreign competitors have learned to use the impatience of American business people as a powerful negotiating tool.

   Answer: True   Difficulty: Medium   Page: 585

17. American negotiators tend to employ a sequential approach while Asians prefer a holistic approach to negotiations.

   Answer: True   Difficulty: Medium   Page: 586

## Chapter 19 Negotiating with International Customers, Partners, and Regulators

18. The America-First Corporation is preparing for negotiations with a Japanese client. The firm should understand that the Japanese are likely to view negotiations as a means of creating mutually beneficial, long-term relationships rather than a short-term, problem-solving exercise.

    Answer: True Difficulty: Hard Page: 587

19. In addition to the skills needed by all international managers, successful negotiators must be willing to use team assistance, develop listening skills, and enjoy influence at headquarters.

    Answer: True Difficulty: Medium Page: 588

20. The single most important activity in negotiations is listening.

    Answer: True Difficulty: Medium Page: 588

21. The America-First Corporation is preparing to enter negotiations with a potential Japanese client. The firm must be careful to exclude women from their negotiating team.

    Answer: False Difficulty: Hard Page: 588

22. Ford Motor Company was one of the first, and most successful, firms to provide employees with practical negotiation training for Japan as well as Korea and the People's Republic of China.

    Answer: True Difficulty: Medium Page: 590

23. Preparation and planning skills are among the greatest advantages American negotiators typically bring to the table.

    Answer: False Difficulty: Medium Page: 591

24. The America-First Corporation is known worldwide as a leader in technology. The firm's use of the Internet and video conferencing as a negotiation tool will be understood and accepted by all the firms with which it deals.

    Answer: False Difficulty: Hard Page: 592

25. Because no business matters are discussed during the non-task sounding phase of negotiation, it is merely a social obligation that should be quickly disposed of.

    Answer: False Difficulty: Medium Page: 594

26. Americans too often rely on the legal system to "undo" mistakes resulting from a failure to take enough time to understand a customer or vendor.

    Answer: True Difficulty: Medium Page: 595

27. Unlike Americans, Japanese negotiators insist on a clear separation between task-related information exchange and persuasion.

    Answer: False Difficulty: Medium Page: 596

28. Frequently, the most powerful persuasive tactic is asking more questions.

    Answer: True Difficulty: Medium Page: 598

29. High-context cultures are especially likely to rely on legal systems to settle disputes.

    Answer: False Difficulty: Medium Page: 599

30. The America-First Corporation has just signed a contract with a major Chinese firm. The firm can be sure that the Chinese firm will insist on enforcing even the minutest detail of the contract.

    Answer: False Difficulty: Hard Page: 599

**Multiple Choice Questions**

31. Face-to-face negotiations are MOST important in which of the following phases of international marketing?
    A) implementation.
    B) product development.
    C) pricing.
    D) distribution development.

    Answer: A Difficulty: Medium Page: 576

32. The MOST important outcome of the initial negotiation is:
    A) the pricing agreement.
    B) the financial terms to be applied.
    C) the delivery terms enforced.
    D) trust and cooperative spirit established between the parties.

    Answer: D Difficulty: Medium Page: 577

33. The most difficult factor in international negotiations derive from:
    A) travel problems.
    B) cultural differences.
    C) language differences.
    D) legal system differences.

    Answer: B Difficulty: Medium Page: 577

# Chapter 19 Negotiating with International Customers, Partners, and Regulators

34. In terms of its position vis-à-vis negotiation position and strategy, theMOST distinctive nation is:
    A) Russia.
    B) China.
    C) Japan.
    D) England.

    Answer: C Difficulty: Medium Page: 578

35. The America-First Corporation is preparing for its first negotiations with a foreign client. While the firm is nervous at the prospect, it will probably have the least difficulty with which of the following areas?
    A) nonverbal behaviors.
    B) language.
    C) values.
    D) thinking and decision making processes.

    Answer: B Difficulty: Hard Page: 578

36. Which of the following factors exerts the most subtle, but most important, influence on international negotiations?
    A) language.
    B) nonverbal behaviors.
    C) values.
    D) thinking and decision-making processes.

    Answer: D Difficulty: Medium Page: 578

37. Which of the following nations are considered the WORST in language skills?
    A) the United States.
    B) Australia.
    C) England.
    D) Germany.

    Answer: B Difficulty: Medium Page: 579

38. American negotiators are MOST disturbed by which of the following practices of foreign negotiators?
    A) frequent "side conversations" in their native tongue.
    B) long periods of silence.
    C) direct gazing.
    D) frequent interruptions.

    Answer: A Difficulty: Medium Page: 579

# Chapter 19 Negotiating with International Customers, Partners, and Regulators

39. Regardless of the culture represented, the majority of statements made during negotiations tend to be:
    A) threats.
    B) recommendations.
    C) information exchanges.
    D) promises.

    Answer: C Difficulty: Medium Page: 579

40. The America-First Corporation is preparing for its first negotiations with a Japanese client. The firm should be prepared for:
    A) frequent periods of silence.
    B) little self-disclosure.
    C) little facial gazing.
    D) all of the above.

    Answer: D Difficulty: Hard Page: 579

41. Which of the following tend to employ the least aggressive style of negotiating?
    A) Japan.
    B) France.
    C) Germany.
    D) Russia.

    Answer: A Difficulty: Medium Page: 582

42. Which of the following are MOST likely to rely on commands or punishments as negotiating tools?
    A) Japanese.
    B) Russians.
    C) Koreans.
    D) Chinese.

    Answer: C Difficulty: Medium Page: 582

43. All of the following statements about the negotiating style of the Koreans are trueEXCEPT:
    A) Koreans rely heavily on punishments and commands.
    B) Koreans are likely to interrupt.
    C) Koreans frequently say "no".
    D) Koreans employ silence frequently.

    Answer: D Difficulty: Medium Page: 582

# Chapter 19 Negotiating with International Customers, Partners, and Regulators

44. Which of the following is MOST likely to employ information-exchange tactics in negotiation?
    A) Japanese.
    B) Chinese.
    C) Russians.
    D) Spanish.

    Answer: B Difficulty: Medium Page: 582

45. The America-First Corporation is preparing to deal with an unusually high volume of questions in their upcoming negotiations with a foreign client. The firm is PROBABLY in negotiations with the:
    A) Japanese.
    B) Koreans.
    C) Chinese.
    D) French.

    Answer: C Difficulty: Hard Page: 582

46. Aside from their heavy use of questions and information—exchange tactics, the Chinese negotiation style is most like that of the:
    A) Japanese.
    B) Koreans.
    C) Germans.
    D) Taiwanese.

    Answer: A Difficulty: Medium Page: 582

47. Of all Asians, which of the following ask the least questions and provide the most information?
    A) Japanese.
    B) Chinese.
    C) Koreans.
    D) Taiwanese.

    Answer: D Difficulty: Medium Page: 582

48. The Russian negotiating style is most similar to that of the:
    A) Germans.
    B) Japanese.
    C) French.
    D) Spanish.

    Answer: B Difficulty: Medium Page: 582

# Chapter 19 Negotiating with International Customers, Partners, and Regulators

49. Which of the following groups is LEAST likely to ask questions?
    A) Chinese.
    B) Russians.
    C) Germans.
    D) Spanish.

    Answer: C Difficulty: Medium Page: 582

50. The America-First Corporation is preparing to conduct negotiations with a variety of national groups. The firm is likely to be MOST comfortable with negotiators from:
    A) China.
    B) Russia.
    C) France.
    D) England.

    Answer: D Difficulty: Hard Page: 582

51. Which of the following tends to be most likely to employ commands in negotiations?
    A) Spanish.
    B) Japanese.
    C) Chinese.
    D) Russians.

    Answer: A Difficulty: Medium Page: 583

52. Of all nationalities, the MOST aggressive negotiation style is employed by the:
    A) Chinese.
    B) Russians.
    C) French.
    D) English.

    Answer: C Difficulty: Medium Page: 583

53. The highest number of commands were used by the:
    A) Brazilians.
    B) Japanese.
    C) Chinese.
    D) Americans.

    Answer: A Difficulty: Medium Page: 583

# Chapter 19 Negotiating with International Customers, Partners, and Regulators

54. The negotiating style of which of the following groups is most like that of Americans?
    A) Brazilians.
    B) Mexicans.
    C) French.
    D) Germans.

    Answer: B Difficulty: Medium Page: 583

55. Which of the following used the lowest percentage of aggressive persuasive tactics?
    A) French-speaking Canada.
    B) French.
    C) Russians.
    D) English-speaking Canada.

    Answer: D Difficulty: Medium Page: 583

56. The America-First Corporation insists on keeping its negotiations objective. The firm's approach is MOST likely to appeal to negotiations from:
    A) Britain.
    B) Spain.
    C) Japan.
    D) China.

    Answer: A Difficulty: Hard Page: 583

57. Which of the following groups are BEST at the task of maximizing joint profits?
    A) Americans.
    B) Japanese.
    C) British.
    D) Germans.

    Answer: B Difficulty: Medium Page: 584

58. Of all nationalities, which is most likely to give complete deference to the needs and wishes of buyers?
    A) Americans.
    B) British.
    C) Germans.
    D) Japanese.

    Answer: D Difficulty: Medium Page: 584

## Chapter 19 Negotiating with International Customers, Partners, and Regulators

59. The most impatient and time-conscious nation in the world is:
    A) America.
    B) Japan.
    C) Britain.
    D) Germany.

    Answer: A  Difficulty: Medium  Page: 585

60. The Japanese are adept at using "silent periods" and other delaying tactics to "force" their negotiating opponents to make mistakes and/or concessions. With which of the following groups is this tactic MOST likely to be effective?
    A) Chinese.
    B) Americans.
    C) Mexicans.
    D) Germans.

    Answer: B  Difficulty: Hard  Page: 585

61. The Japanese approach to negotiation is BEST described as:
    A) holistic.
    B) opportunistic.
    C) confrontational.
    D) highly structured.

    Answer: A  Difficulty: Medium  Page: 586

62. The America-First Corporation is preparing to negotiate with a potential Japanese client. The firm should understand that the Japanese are likely to view the negotiations as:
    A) a sequential progression of decisions.
    B) a problem-solving activity.
    C) a zero-sum game.
    D) an opportunity to develop a long-term relationship for mutual profit.

    Answer: D  Difficulty: Hard  Page: 587

63. The SINGLE most important negotiation activity is:
    A) a willingness to use teams.
    B) facility with the "opposition's" language.
    C) the ability to listen.
    D) interaction with top executives.

    Answer: C  Difficulty: Medium  Page: 588

# Chapter 19 Negotiating with International Customers, Partners, and Regulators

64. The America-First Corporation has decided to develop a formal training program for all of its executives who will deal with Japan. The firm is seeking to emulate the successes pioneered by:
    A) General Motors.
    B) Ford Motor Company.
    C) Chrysler Corporation
    D) Peugeot Motors.

    Answer: B Difficulty: Hard Page: 590

65. Power in negotiations is best measured by:
    A) the best alternative to a negotiated agreement.
    B) the relative size of the negotiating teams.
    C) the physical accommodations provided.
    D) the location selected for negotiations.

    Answer: A Difficulty: Medium Page: 591

66. In order to preclude the possibility of giving away too much, negotiations should prepare:
    A) talking points.
    B) "escape doors."
    C) concession strategies.
    D) team assignments.

    Answer: C Difficulty: Medium Page: 591

67. Which of the following tends to prefer a "cumulative" approach to negotiations?
    A) Japanese.
    B) Chinese.
    C) British.
    D) Russians.

    Answer: D Difficulty: Medium Page: 592

68. Activities designed to allow participants to get to know each other and, hopefully, establish a rapport are best described as:
    A) persuasion.
    B) non-task sounding.
    C) task-related information exchanges.
    D) concessions and agreement.

    Answer: B Difficulty: Easy Page: 593

# Chapter 19 Negotiating with International Customers, Partners, and Regulators

69. The need and preferences of the negotiating parties are discussed during which of the following stages?
    A) persuasion.
    B) non-task sounding.
    C) task-related information exchange.
    D) concessions and agreement.

    Answer: C Difficulty: Medium Page: 593

70. The America-First Corporation is preparing to enter negotiations with several potential clients. The firm will place the LEAST emphasis on which stage of negotiations?
    A) non-task sounding.
    B) concessions and agreement.
    C) task-related information exchange.
    D) persuasion.

    Answer: D Difficulty: Hard Page: 595

71. Which of the following stages of the negotiation process is given the LEAST emphasis by Americans?
    A) non-task sounding.
    B) concessions and agreement.
    C) task-related information exchange.
    D) persuasion.

    Answer: A Difficulty: Medium Page: 595

72. American negotiators too often rely on the legal system to "undo" mistakes made in deciding whom to trust during which of the following stages of the negotiation process?
    A) non-task sounding.
    B) task-related exchange of information.
    C) persuasion.
    D) concessions and agreement.

    Answer: A Difficulty: Medium Page: 595

73. Which of the following stages in the negotiation process is the MOST important to the Japanese?
    A) non-task sounding.
    B) task-related exchange of information.
    C) persuasion.
    D) concessions and agreement.

    Answer: B Difficulty: Medium Page: 597

# Chapter 19 Negotiating with International Customers, Partners, and Regulators

74. For Americans, the MOST important phase of the negotiation process is:
    A) non-task sounding.
    B) task-related exchange of information.
    C) persuasion.
    D) concessions and agreement.

    Answer: C Difficulty: Medium Page: 597

75. Which of the following groups is LEAST likely to employ intense questioning as a tactic during the information exchange phase of the negotiation process?
    A) Japanese.
    B) Russians.
    C) Chinese.
    D) Americans.

    Answer: D Difficulty: Medium Page: 598

76. The MOST effective tactic of persuasion is generally:
    A) the use of threats.
    B) expressions of anger or frustration.
    C) the polite use of questions.
    D) emotionally charged dialogue.

    Answer: C Difficulty: Medium Page: 598

77. The America-First Corporation is preparing to negotiate with firms from China, Brazil, and Spain. Assuming that each firm has a clear idea of the appropriate value of the deal, which of the following negotiating teams will make an initial offer CLOSEST to their desired outcome?
    A) the Chinese.
    B) the Americans.
    C) the Spanish.
    D) the Brazilians.

    Answer: B Difficulty: Hard Page: 599

78. Which of the following groups are MOST likely to offer early concessions in order to encourage reciprocity?
    A) Americans.
    B) Japanese.
    C) Chinese.
    D) Koreans.

    Answer: A Difficulty: Medium Page: 599

# Chapter 19 Negotiating with International Customers, Partners, and Regulators

79. Foreign negotiators, especially those from Asia, are likely to have difficulties with which of the following American contract practices?
    A) tight, detailed, legalistic wording.
    B) the assumption of enforcement.
    C) lack of "signing ceremony".
    D) all of the above.

    Answer: D Difficulty: Medium Page: 599

80. The America-First Corporation has just concluded negotiations, and signed an agreement, with an oriental client. The firm should now:
    A) engage a lawyer to enforce the contract.
    B) follow-up the signing with periodic, friendly contacts.
    C) respect client privacy by leaving the client alone.
    D) sign the contract to certified mail to underscore its importance.

    Answer: B Difficulty: Hard Page: 600

**Fill in the Blank Questions**

81. Cultural differences cause problems in international negotiations in the areas of _______________, _______________, _______________, and _______________.

    Answer: language; nonverbal behaviors; values; thinking and decision-making processes
    Difficulty: Medium Page: 578

82. The least aggressive, or most polite, style of negotiation is generally followed by the _______________.

    Answer: Japanese Difficulty: Medium Page: 582

83. The <u>MOST</u> aggressive of all national groups with respect to negotiating style are the _______________.

    Answer: French Difficulty: Medium Page: 583

84. Generally, _______________ fall in the mid-range on most negotiation criteria—although they are the least likely of all groups to interrupt.

    Answer: Americans Difficulty: Medium Page: 583

85. The core American values--_______________, _______________, _______________, and _______________--often cause misunderstandings and bad feelings in international business negotiations.

    Answer: objectivity; competitiveness; equality; punctuality Difficulty: Medium Page: 583

# Chapter 19 Negotiating with International Customers, Partners, and Regulators

86. The America-First Corporation routinely seeks to keep personal considerations out of its business negotiations. The firm's insistence on ______________ may cause problems in negotiations with Chinese or Hispanic firms.

    Answer: objectivity   Difficulty: Hard   Page: 583

87. As a result of the American values of ______________ and ______________, American negotiators have difficulty understanding the Japanese practice of giving complete deference to the needs and wishes of the buyer.

    Answer: competitiveness; equality   Difficulty: Medium   Page: 584

88. The America-First Corporation finds the slow pace of Asian negotiators extremely frustrating. The Asians probably know that the American fixation on ______________ can be a most effective means of obtaining concessions.

    Answer: time   Difficulty: Hard   Page: 584-585

89. Generally, Westerners employ a(n) ______________ approach to negotiations while Orientals are more likely to use a(n) ______________ approach.

    Answer: sequential; holistic   Difficulty: Medium   Page: 586

90. The American tradition of independence is often a barrier to the willingness to use a(n) ______________ approach in negotiations.

    Answer: team   Difficulty: Medium   Page: 587

91. There is general agreement that a good negotiator will excel in ______________ for any upcoming negotiation.

    Answer: preparation and planning   Difficulty: Medium   Page: 591

92. The America-First Corporation is attempting to assess the relative power enjoyed by itself and its rival in its current negotiations. The firm may use the notion of the ______________ for this purpose.

    Answer: best alternative to a negotiated agreement   Difficulty: Hard   Page: 591

93. Traveling to a competitor's home turf is considered a disadvantage because ______________ is often a surrogate for the relative power of the parties.

    Answer: location   Difficulty: Medium   Page: 591

# Chapter 19 Negotiating with International Customers, Partners, and Regulators

94. While Americans prefer to get everyone involved at the same time to "hammer out an agreement, the Japanese tend to prefer a series of _______________ agreements in advance of a mass meeting and Russians try to reach a final agreement through a(n) _______________ approach.

    Answer: individual; cumulative  Difficulty: Medium  Page: 592

95. The physical arrangement of rooms can be critically important in _______________ cultures.

    Answer: high-context  Difficulty: Medium  Page: 592

96. The America-First Corporation has always been impatient with the insistence of Japanese clients on having a series of social gatherings prior to the onset of actual negotiations. The Japanese consider such meeting a useful means of accomplishing _______________.

    Answer: non-task sounding  Difficulty: Hard  Page: 594

97. Ideally, _______________ involves two-way communication that clarified the initial beliefs, positions, and goals of the participants.

    Answer: task-related information exchange  Difficulty: Easy  Page: 596

98. To the American, the _______________ phase of the negotiation process is the most important portion of the activity.

    Answer: persuasion  Difficulty: Medium  Page: 597

99. Generally, reaching an agreement requires both sides to make _______________.

    Answer: concessions  Difficulty: Easy  Page: 599

100. Americans tend to view the end product of negotiations as a(n) _______________ subject to legal enforcement, while foreigners emphasize the creation of a mutually beneficial, long-term _______________.

    Answer: contract; relationship  Difficulty: Hard  Page: 599

# Chapter 19 Negotiating with International Customers, Partners, and Regulators

## Essay Questions

101. Identify the four types of problems that may derive from cultural differences. Compare and contrast the impact and importance of these factors for international negotiations?

 Answer:
 Cultural differences can generate problems related to behavior, values, and thinking and decision-making processes. Language is the most obvious, and easily addressed, source of confusion. The other, less obvious and more subtle, factors require an increasingly sophisticated understanding of culture. While, more subtle, each level of influence has an increasingly important impact on the results of negotiations.

 Difficulty: Hard Page: 578-579

102. Of what use are national behaviors and negotiating tendencies to the international businessperson? How should these "negotiation aids" be used?

 Answer:
 Stereotypes are useful in preparing the negotiator to prepare/train for a variety of negotiating styles that he or she might encounter. While each stereotype is, admittedly, just that—their use as a means of assisting negotiators in identifying and reacting to a variety of styles is significant. Ideally, of course, the negotiator will get to know their specific "opponents" and modify their reactions as needed on a tailored basis.

 Difficulty: Hard Page: 579-583

103. What values tend to characterize the American negotiator? How do these values differ from those of other nations?

 Answer:
 American negotiators tend to hold the values of objectivity, equality, competitiveness, and punctuality very strongly. These values can be a source of confusion and frustration for foreign negotiators—and a problem for Americans. Americans insist on objectivity—but foreigners do not separate facts from emotion or people from situations. Americans tend to be highly competitive from situations. Americans tend to be highly competitive while treating competitors and customers as equals—foreigners are more willing to award preferences. Americans are extremely time conscious—and often find that their impatience is used against them to obtain early concessions.

 Difficulty: Hard Page: 583-586

# Chapter 19 Negotiating with International Customers, Partners, and Regulators

104. Briefly contrast American and Oriental decision-making processes. How does this difference in thinking impact the effectiveness of the American negotiator?

Answer:
American negotiators tend to view negotiation as a problem to be broken up into parts and dealt with in a logical, sequential fashion. Other cultures, especially Orientals, tend to take a more holistic, less structured approach. The American is typically frustrated by the chaos of the holistic approach, impatient with the time taken, and unprepared for often abrupt conclusions. As in boxing or war, an off-balance adversary is more easily defeated.

Difficulty: Hard   Page: 586-587

105. Briefly describe the basic phases that comprise the negotiation process. Why are these stages significant?

Answer:
Regardless of cultural background, negotiations may be broken into non-task sounding, task-related information exchanges, persuasion, and concessions and agreement phases. Non-task sounding, although almost ignored by impatient Americans, offers the opportunity to size up, and develop a strategy to succeed with, one's opponent. During task-related information exchanges, both sides lay out and clarify initial positions and indicate desired outcomes. This stage also tends to be more significant to foreigners than Americans. Americans emphasize the persuasion stage on the promise that changing minds is the goal of negotiation. Americans seeking a quick resolution through reciprocity make concessions throughout the process—foreigners make few concessions until the end of the process. Americans view the resulting agreement as an enforceable contract—foreigners emphasize mutually beneficial long-term relationships.

Difficulty: Hard   Page: 592-600

### Exploration Connection:
### Interpreting diagrams

The atmosphere changes as you move away from Earth. For about 80 kilometers (50 miles) the mixture of gases stays about the same. What are those gases?

Scientists divide the atmosphere into four main layers. The troposphere starts at the surface and rises about 16 kilometers (10 miles) at the Equator. Near the North and South poles, the troposphere rises about 6.5 km (4 miles). All weather happens in the troposphere.

The stratosphere comes next. Find the stratosphere on the diagram. How high above Earth does it rise? There is almost no water or dust at this height.

Have you ever seen a shooting star? Meteors are rocks that fall from space and burn in the mesosphere. Beyond this layer is the thermosphere, which rises from about 200 km (125 mi) to as much as 500 km (311 miles) above Earth.

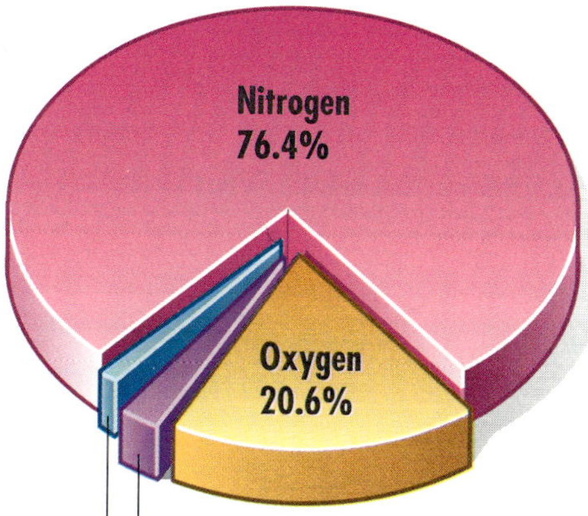


▼ There are no dividing lines between layers of the atmosphere. Which layer of the atmosphere surrounds you right now? Which layer is thinnest?

**LAYERS OF THE ATMOSPHERE**

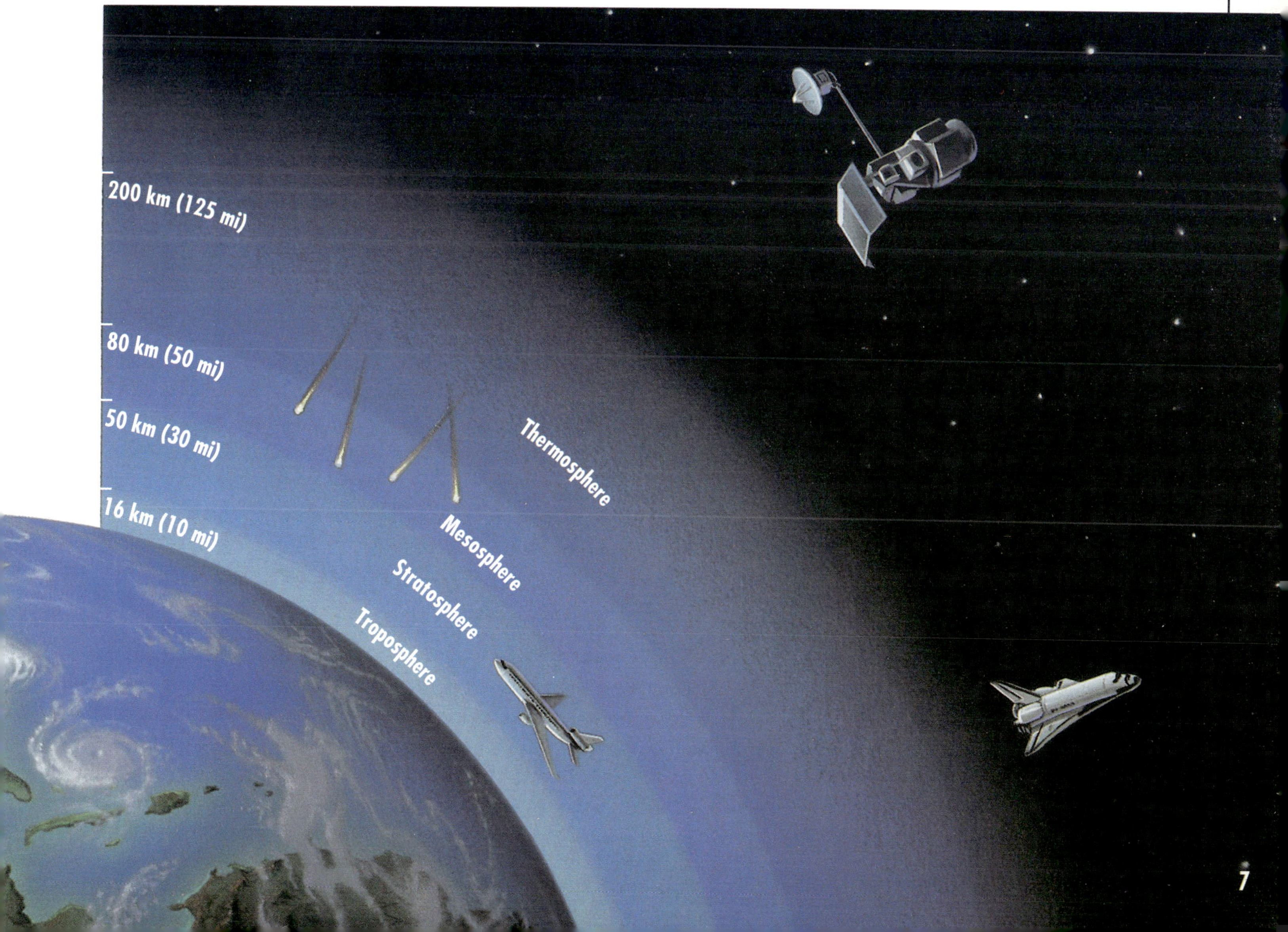

You know that you can't see air, but you've seen how air takes up space. When you push against most substances, you can feel them push back. If you push against your desk, you'll feel the desk press back against your hand. Even if your desk is on wheels and rolls away at your touch, you'll still feel a push. What happens when you push against air?

## Exploration: Push the air.

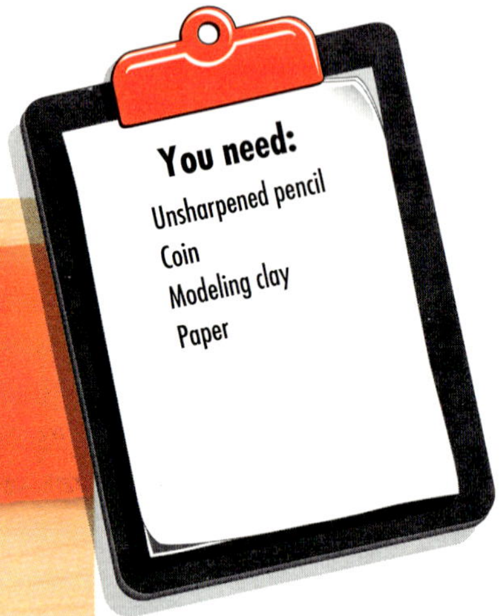


❶ Place the pencil on your desk with about 4 cm sticking out beyond the edge of the desk. Attach the coin to the end of the pencil on the desk with a small ball of modeling clay.

❷ With your finger, tap down on the end of the pencil sticking out. What happens? Record your observations.

❸ Put the pencil back in the same place and remove the coin. Lay a sheet of paper over the part of the pencil that's on the desk.

❹ Repeat step 2. What happens? Record your observations. What happens if you push the pencil down slowly?

❺ Pick up the paper and the coin. Compare their eights. Record your observations.

### Interpret your results.

- What happened to the pencil when you hit it in step 4? How did air affect the paper?
- What happened to the air around the sheet of paper when you pushed down slowly on the pencil?
- What would happen if you did the same Exploration using a yardstick and an open newspaper? **Try it!**

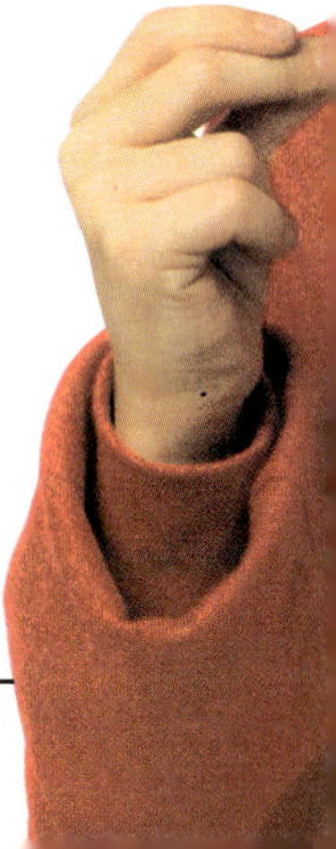

## Closer to Home: Tuning in the airwaves

When you tune in an AM radio station, how does the sound get to you? Sound moves through the air as vibrations. When these vibrations reach your ears you hear them as sound. At a radio station, sounds are changed into electrical signals that can travel through the air as radio waves.

Radio waves aren't sound waves. You can't hear them. They travel in straight lines through the atmosphere until they meet a radio. The radio picks up the electrical signal and changes it back into sound that you can hear.

Since radio waves only travel in straight lines, your radio would have to be in a straight line from the station to pick up a signal, if it weren't for the air high in the atmosphere. Radio waves hit that air and bounce back from high above Earth. At night, that air moves farther away. Radio waves coming from Earth at night travel higher and bounce farther than waves during the day.

- Why do some radio stations come in best at night?

**Think!**

**Why isn't an empty bottle really empty when you pour the liquid out of it? How could you make it truly empty?**

LESSON 3

# How Do You Know the Atmosphere Has Weight?

You can't see the air that makes up the atmosphere, but it's there. You've seen that air takes up space and pushes back when it's pushed. Air doesn't weigh a lot, but it isn't weightless. Where is the heaviest part of the atmosphere?

## Exploration:

### Investigate weight and pressure.

**You need:**
- Plastic tube
- Tape
- Ruler
- Pencil
- Modeling clay
- Pipe cleaner
- Scissors
- Cardboard
- Pennies

❶ Stick a strip of tape on the side of the tube from top to bottom. Mark the tape every centimeter. Push the tube into a piece of clay to make it stand.

❷ Wrap the pipe cleaner around a pencil to make a tight spring. Put the spring into the tube.

❸ Cut a circle of cardboard to fit inside the tube. Tape it to the spring. Mark the side of the tube to show where the cardboard rests.

❹ Put five pennies on the cardboard in the tube. Mark the side of the tube to show the level of the pennies. What's happening to the spring? Record your observations.

❺ Add more pennies, marking the side of the tube after each five pennies. Record your observations.

#### Interpret your results.

- How does adding weight to the cardboard affect the spring?
- The extra weight put more pressure on the spring. How would you describe pressure?
- How do you think air higher in the atmosphere affects air closer to Earth?

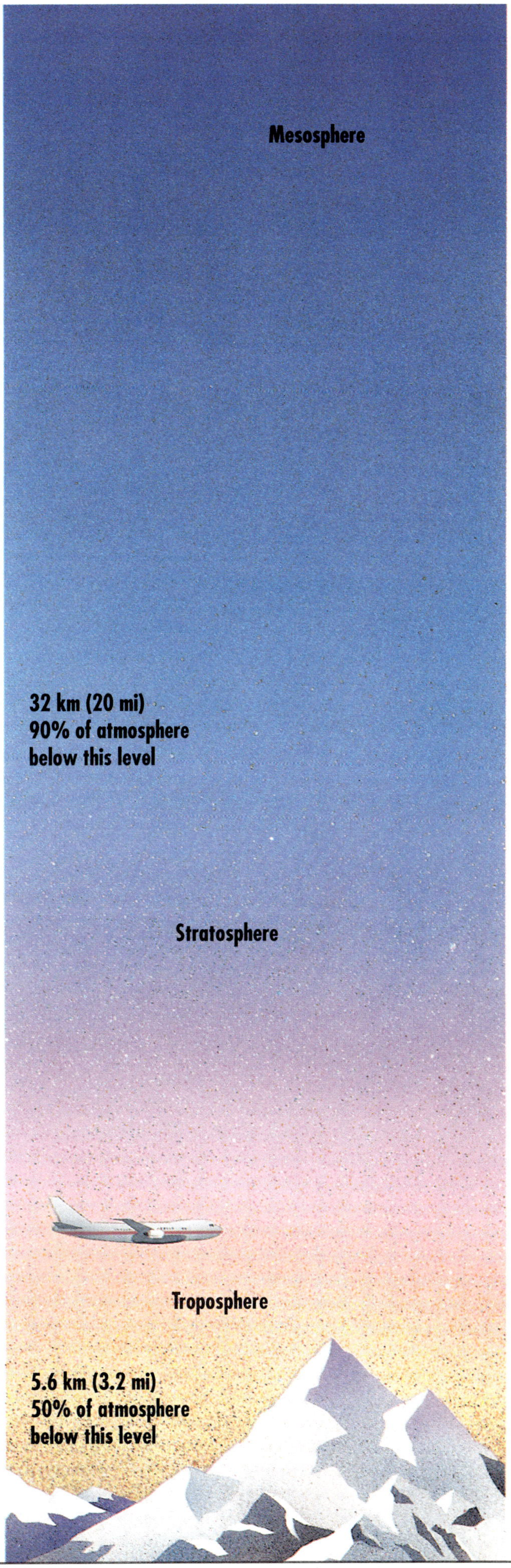


**Exploration Connection:**
**Interpreting diagrams**

Imagine a stack of six bathroom scales. If each scale weighs 22 pounds, the scale on top of the pile would read 0. What would the second scale read? Which scale would show the highest reading? What would it be? There's a spring inside a bathroom scale. Weight presses the coils of the spring closer together.

The atmosphere is like the pile of scales. Air is made of unbelievably tiny particles. The particles at the top of the atmosphere are far apart. They don't have as much weight sitting on them, so they can spread out. Air particles at the bottom of the atmosphere are pressed close together by the weight of all the air above them. Look at the diagram. Suppose you compared a bottle of air from the troposphere with a bottle of air from the thermosphere. Which bottle would weigh more? Which bottle would have more air particles in it?

▶ Where is the air most closely packed? Do you think air pressure is higher at the top of a mountain or in the valley below?

You've seen what happens when you push against air. Air also pushes against you. Imagine the column of air directly over your head—500 kilometers (300 miles) high. That column puts about half a ton of weight on the top of your head. Why doesn't it smash you flat?

## Exploration:

### Observe air pressure in action.

❶ Put the cardboard on top of the cup. Press down and turn the cup over. Take your hand away from the cardboard. What happens?

❷ Fill the cup to the brim with water. Put the cardboard on top again.

❸ Hold the cup over the pan. Press down on the cardboard and turn the cup upside down.

❹ You're going to take your hand away from the cardboard. What do you predict will happen? Take your hand away. What happens? Record your results.

### Interpret your results.

- What pushed against the cardboard when there was no water in the cup?
- In step 4, which was greater: the pressure of the water pushing down on the cardboard or the pressure of the air pushing up on the cardboard from below. How do you know?
- What did you learn about air pressure?

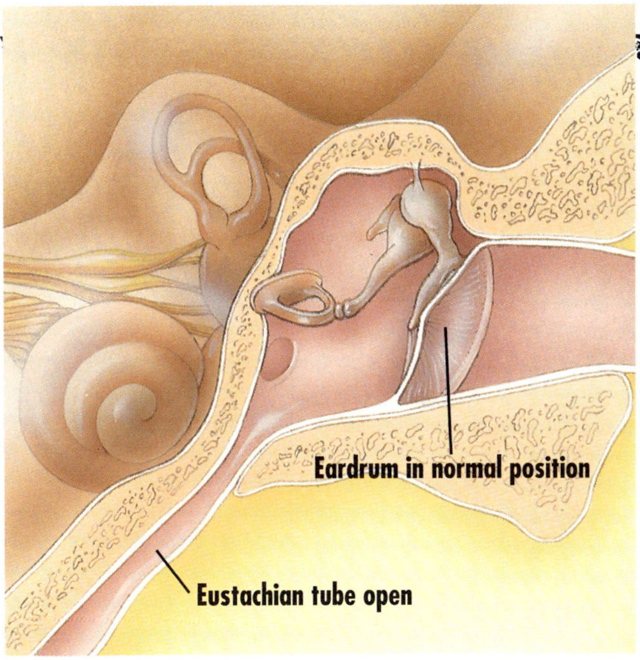


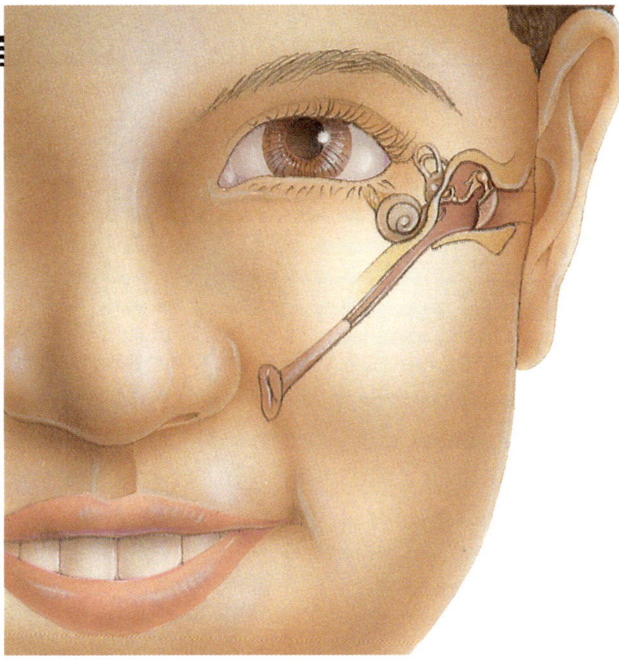

## Closer to Home: Air pressure in your ears

If you've ever ridden a fast elevator going down, you've probably felt your ears pop. What does ear-popping have to do with air pressure?

Air flows into a tube—called a Eustachian tube—between your eardrum and the back of your mouth. The pressure of that air is usually the same as the pressure of the air outside your eardrum.

If you walk down the stairs slowly, your breathing helps your Eustachian tubes adjust your ears to the change in air pressure. If you go down quickly in an elevator—closer to Earth's surface—the increasing air pressure outside your head pushes on your eardrum. You may feel this push as a funny change in the way you hear sounds. When the pressure is released, your ears pop—making the air pressure inside and outside your ears equal again.

- Yawning helps open the tubes between your ears and the back of your mouth. How do you think this helps make your ears pop?
- If you ride a fast elevator going up, your ears will also pop. How does what you know about air pressure explain this?

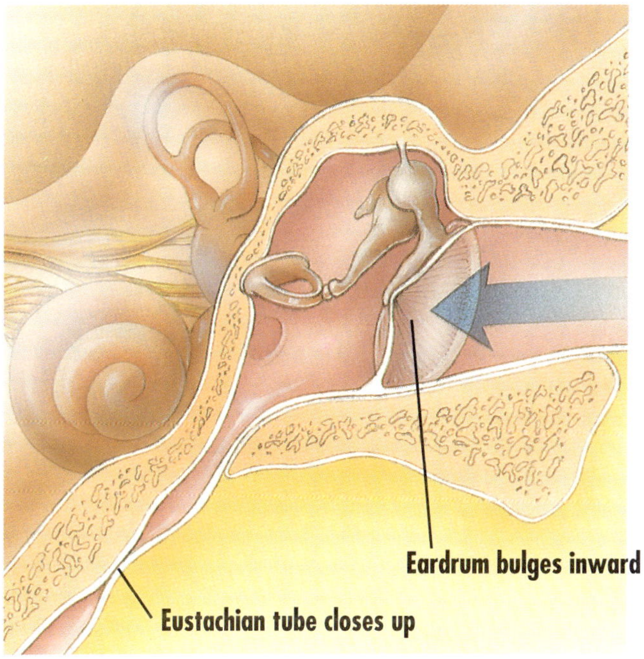


**Think!**

**In the upper part of the troposphere, air particles are farther apart than air particles close to Earth's surface. How do you think this might affect your breathing?**

LESSON 4

# How Does the Sun Affect the Atmosphere?

The sun is about 150 million kilometers (93 million miles) from Earth. The atmosphere acts as a shield, keeping some of the sun's energy from getting to Earth's surface. However, Earth's atmosphere doesn't block light energy. How do you think light energy affects the atmosphere? How do you think the atmosphere affects light energy?

## Exploration:
## Make an atmosphere model.

**You need:**
- Black paper
- Scissors
- 2 shoeboxes
- Tape
- Marker
- 2 thermometers
- Plastic wrap
- Lamp

❶ Line both boxes with black paper. Label the boxes "1" and "2." The boxes represent Earth's surface.

❷ Put a thermometer in each box. Record the temperature.

❸ Cover box 1 with plastic wrap and hold it in place with tape. The plastic wrap represents the atmosphere. Put both boxes under the lamp, which represents the sun.

❹ After 15 minutes, record the temperature in each box.

### Interpret your results.

- Earth's surface absorbs light energy and changes it to another form of energy. What form? How do you know?
- Based on your model, how do you think the atmosphere affects the second form of energy?

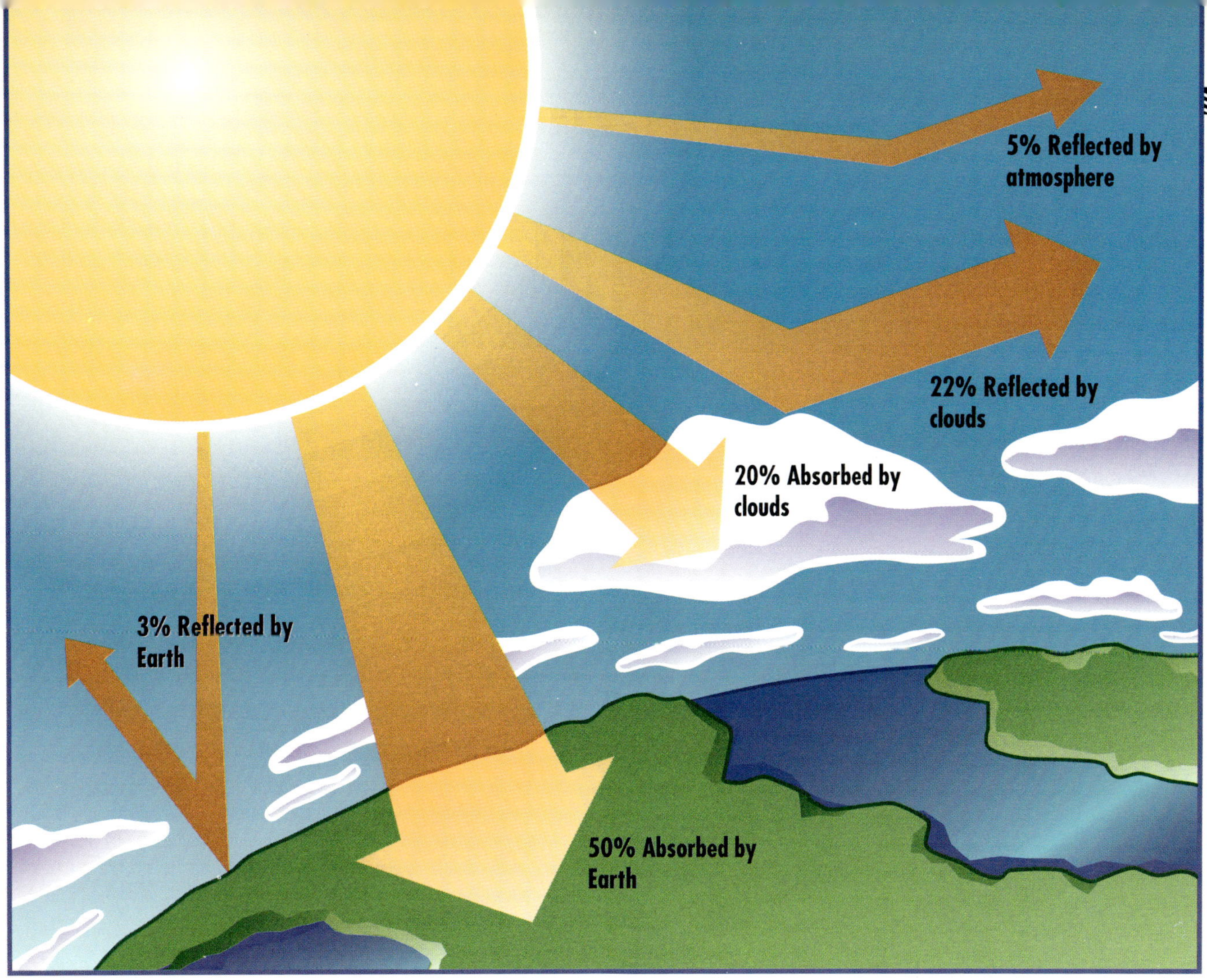


▲ Clouds do for Earth what winter clothes do for people. What is that?

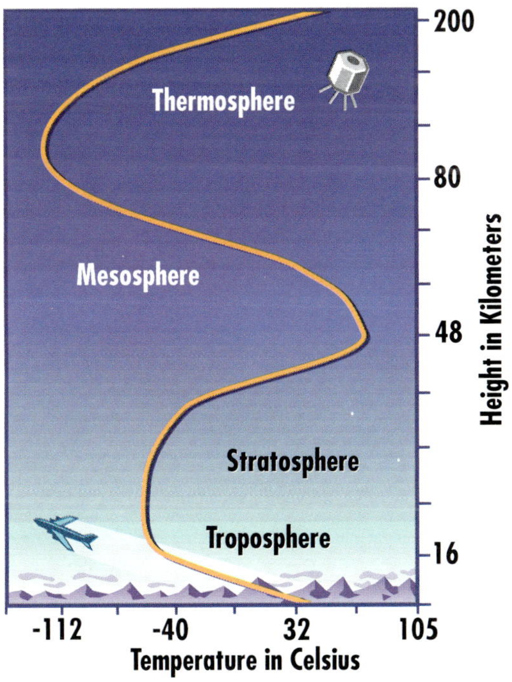


▲ Different layers of the atmosphere have different temperatures.

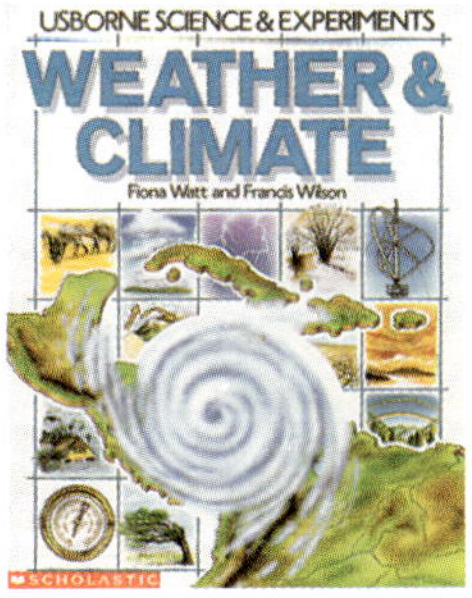


## Exploration Connection: Using reference books

Look at the diagram above. How much of the sun's energy gets to the surface of Earth? What happens to the sun's rays when they hit clouds?

You've seen some of the ways the atmosphere changes as you move away from the surface of Earth. What happens to temperature as you go higher in the troposphere? Why do you think some very high mountains have snow on them all year round?

Look at the graph. What happens to the temperature as you go above the troposphere into the stratosphere? At what point does the temperature of the stratosphere begin to get lower? What part of the atmosphere has the highest temperatures? To learn more about what happens to the sun's energy in Earth's atmosphere, turn to pages 4–7 in *Weather & Climate.*

## Closer to Home: Protect yourself.

Have you ever seen someone with a bad sunburn? Sunburned skin feels so hot that it hurts to put on a T-shirt. If the burn is really bad, the skin might blister and peel. It's not the sunlight you can see that burns your skin; it's other solar energy you can't see. That energy is ultraviolet (UV) rays.

Oxygen is one of the gases in the atmosphere. When oxygen comes in contact with UV rays, it changes into another form of oxygen called ozone. Ozone absorbs UV rays.

Until recently, there was enough ozone in the stratosphere to absorb most UV rays before they reached Earth. Since the late 1970s, however, more UV rays have been getting through. Air pollution has destroyed a lot of the ozone in the atmosphere.

Too much UV radiation can damage your eyes. It can also cause skin cancer. Look at the diagram. UV rays reach into the top layers of unprotected skin. They can damage a layer of cells under the surface of the skin. Sunblock lotion and sunscreen lotion can help protect those cells.

When UV rays hit sunblock they bounce off again. Sunscreen contains a chemical that absorbs UV rays and prevents them from damaging your skin cells. People can best protect themselves by preventing more damage to the ozone layer.

You'll find out more about holes in the ozone layer in Lesson 13.

- How could you protect yourself if you had no sunscreen?

▲ UV rays can move through clouds, but most UV rays don't pass through clothes.

► Sunscreen lotions absorb UV rays that cause a sunburn.

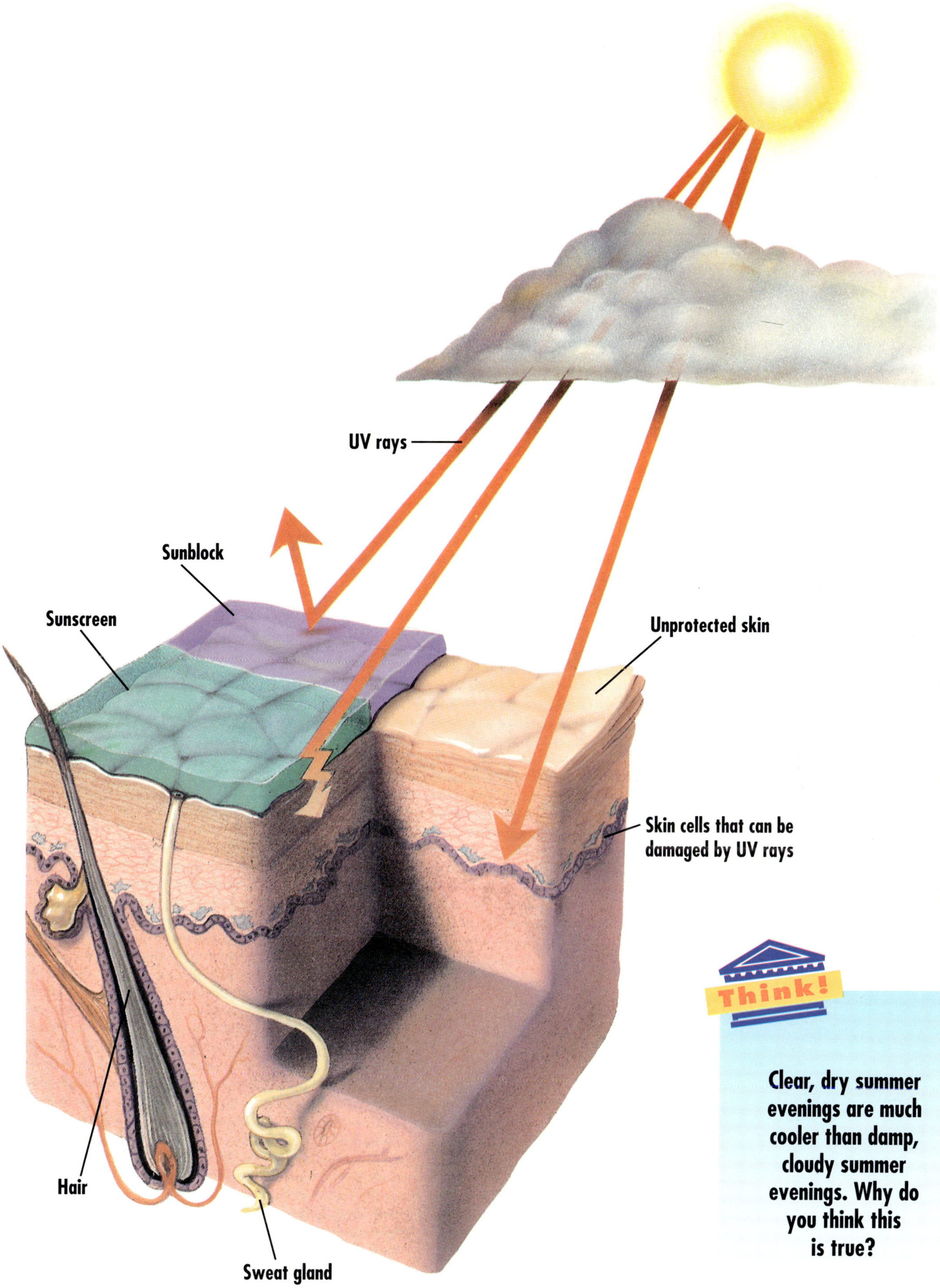


**Think!**

**Clear, dry summer evenings are much cooler than damp, cloudy summer evenings. Why do you think this is true?**

LESSON 5

# How Do Clouds and Rain Form?

The water in the raindrop sliding down your windowpane has fallen millions of times. It dripped from the tip of an icicle. It slid off wet green leaves in a rain forest. It flowed in an ocean current. Water evaporates, changing to water vapor, a gas that rises in the atmosphere and forms clouds. How do you think clouds form from water vapor?

## Exploration: Make a cloud.

❶ Cut the top off the bottle. Pour a cupful of hot water into the bottle.

❷ Put ice in the shallow pan. Cover the top of the bottle with the pan.

❸ Watch the inside of the bottle. What's happening? Check the bottom of the pan. What do you find? Record your observations.

❹ Repeat the experiment. This time put warm water instead of ice in the pan. Record your observations.

### Interpret your results.

- You just made a model of a cloud. What caused the cloud to form?
- When did liquid water change to water vapor? When did water vapor gas change back to liquid water?
- What do you think would have happened if you used very hot water instead of warm water in the pan? **Try it!**

▲ Clouds look different because they form under different conditions. The word *nimbus* means "rain cloud," and nimbus clouds are dark gray. The word *alto* means "high."

## Exploration Connection:
### Interpreting diagrams

It takes more than water vapor to make a cloud. Water vapor in the atmosphere becomes a cloud when it cools and comes into contact with tiny particles of dust. The troposphere is full of dust particles. Every cloud you see is a combination of dust and water droplets or ice.

The diagram shows different kinds of clouds. Find the three basic kinds of clouds—cirrus, cumulus, and stratus. Describe the basic shape of each. You'll often see clouds that look like combinations of these clouds. Is it cloudy outdoors right now? What kinds of clouds do you see?

Water freezes at 0° C (32° F). Water vapor turns into ice crystals in the cold upper troposphere. What kinds of clouds do you think are formed of ice crystals? What do you think might happen to the ice crystals as they fall toward Earth?

Rain or shine, there's always water in the air. Water vapor is invisible, and air containing water vapor is so light that it's squeezed upward by the air around it. What happens after water vapor condenses—changes back to liquid water?

## Exploration:
## Observe the water cycle.

❶ Cut the milk carton in half across the middle. Cut this piece in half again by following the seams. Form a boat-shaped "cloud" out of these halves, and tape them together.

❷ Cut an opening in the plastic bottle so that the cloud sits in it. Remove the cloud.

❸ Steady the bottle with four pieces of clay. Set another piece of clay inside, and set a cup of soil on top of it. Place two cups of hot water near the uncapped end of the bottle.

❹ Tape the cloud in place. Fill the bag with ice cubes and place it inside the cloud.

❺ Place your experiment in the sun or under a lamp. After three hours, record your observations.

### Interpret your results.

- What happened to the water and soil in the cups?
- What do you think would happen if you moved the cups farther apart? closer together?
- What do you think might happen if you put a top on the end of the bottle? **Try it!**
- What did you learn about the way water cycles back and forth from Earth's surface to the atmosphere?

▲ Even when it's sunny on the mountaintop, fog can fill the valley below.

## Closer to Home: Fog

If you've been outside on a foggy day, you've walked in a cloud. Fog is nothing more than a very low cloud. On clear nights the ground gets cool. When warmer air flows over this cool ground, its water vapor condenses in small, light droplets to form fog.

If fog is small water drops, why doesn't fog fall to the ground as rain? Actually, fog is falling all the time, but fog particles are so small that they fall slowly.

There are many different types of fog. Ground fog is the kind you've probably touched. It doesn't usually get more than 100 meters (328 feet) thick. Valley fog can cover entire valleys and can be more than 500 meters (1,500 feet) thick. Ice fog is similar to ground fog, but it's made of tiny ice particles.

- A bright, hot sun can make ground fog disappear. How do you think this happens?
- Why do you think fog usually lasts longer in the winter than in the summer?

▲ Rain evaporates slightly as it falls. Can you see the rain and the fog?

**Think!**

**Under what conditions will high clouds form? Under what conditions will low clouds form?**

LESSON 6

# How Does Wind Form?

Warm, moist air meets cool air and it rains on your picnic. You've seen how temperature differences cause water vapor to change into rain. Temperature differences also help cause wind. Lighter air rises and heavier air flows in underneath the lighter air. Which kind of air do you think is heavier, warm air or cool air?

## Exploration:
### Make a model of cool and warm air.

❶ Place the plastic bottle on its side, steadied by lumps of modeling clay. Cut an opening in the bottle as shown in the picture.

❷ Cut the cardboard to make a wall in the middle of the bottle. Use clay to seal any gaps between the cardboard and the bottle. Check the seal by pouring water in one side. Pour the water out.

❸ Add two drops of blue food coloring to 240 cc of cool water in one cup. Put 240 cc of warm water in the second cup.

❹ Pour the cool blue water into one side of the wall. Pour the warm water into the other side.

❺ Pull the cardboard wall slowly out of the water. How do the two types of water mix? Record your observations.

### Interpret your results.

- Your model shows how warm air and cool air act in the atmosphere. Which air is heavier—warm or cool?
- Which type of air would be more likely to rise—warm air or cool air?
- What do you think happens when warm air and cold air come together?

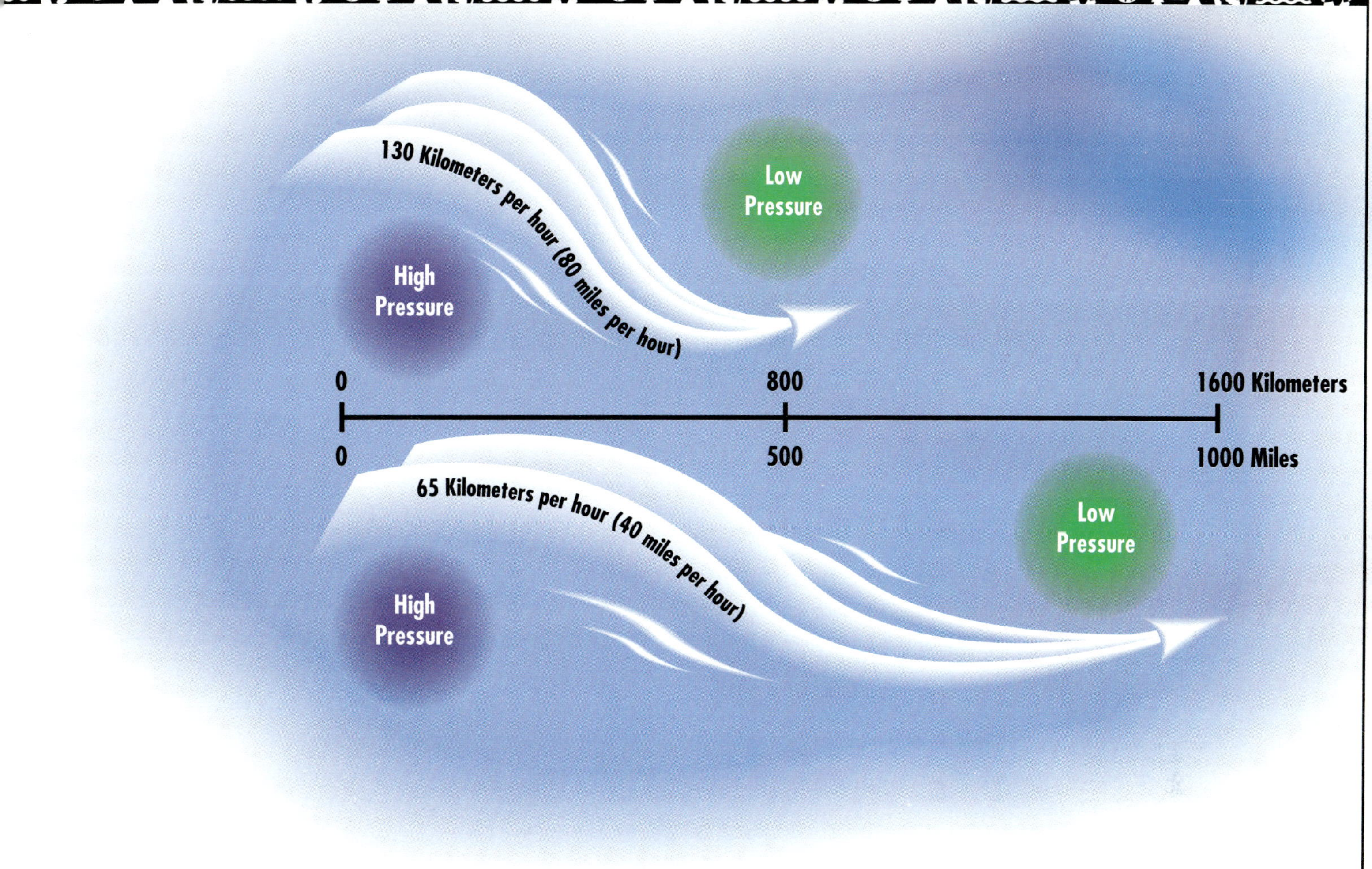


▲ Air moves from a high-pressure area into a lower-pressure area. If the two areas are close together, the air will move fast.

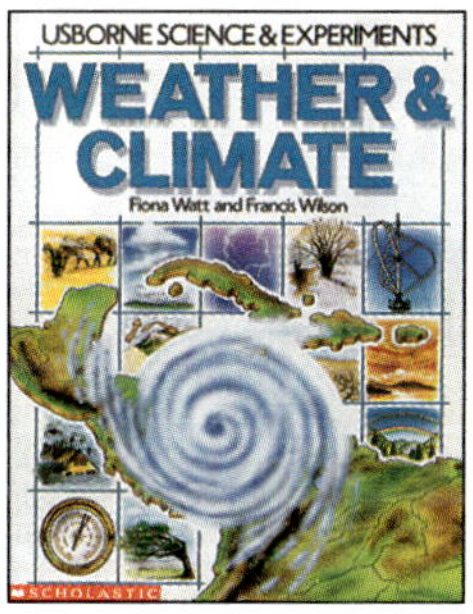


## Exploration Connection: Using reference books

An area where the air is heavy is a high-pressure area. An area where air is light and rises is a low-pressure area. Which area is warmer?

Think about what happens when you sit on a cushion filled with air. Your weight pushes the air in the cushion out of your way. High pressure pushes air away. You've felt this movement when the wind blows.

Look at the diagram. Do winds blow faster when the high- and low-pressure areas are close together, or when they are far apart? What do you think happens when an air mass with high pressure moves closer to an air mass with low pressure? What do you think happens if they move farther apart? To find out more about how air pressure affects the weather, read pages 10–11 in *Weather & Climate.*

You've seen how temperature and pressure differences make air move. To find out more about what's happening in the atmosphere, you can measure the speed of the wind. How strongly do you think the wind is blowing today?

## Exploration:
## Make a wind gauge.

❶ Cut from cardboard the half-circle shape shown on ThinkMat 6. This shape is your base. Glue the shape from your ThinkMat to the base.

❷ Tape your base to the ruler as shown below.

❸ Tie the thread to the base as shown. Staple the other end of the thread to the plastic foam ball.

❹ Take your wind gauge outside. Hold the gauge by the end of the ruler and face straight into the wind. Hold the gauge level. Note the wind speed every 30 seconds for 5 minutes. Make an *X* in the correct box on your LabMat.

### Interpret your results.

- What was the highest wind speed you recorded? the lowest?
- How could you find out the average wind speed?
- How often do you think wind speed changes? Use your data to explain your answer.

## Closer to Home:
## The chill is in the wind.

You might wish for a cool breeze on a hot day, but when the temperature drops, the wind makes you feel even colder. It's not just your imagination. The combination of wind speed and temperature is called the wind-chill factor. You may have heard about it on weather reports.

Your body makes its own heat. When the wind isn't blowing, the air close to you is warmed by your body heat. When the wind rushes past, it carries that warmth away. You feel colder as the wind blows faster.

Look at the table. Find the temperature in the top row. Now read down the column until you match it with the wind speed shown in the first column on the left. If the temperature is –12° C and the wind is blowing at 32 km per hour, the wind-chill factor will make it feel like it's –31° C.

- What would it feel like if the wind speed were 48 kph with a temperature of 12° C?
- How do you think wind affects how you feel on a hot day?

▼ You know how to use a thermometer to find out how cold it is outside. But to find out how cold it *feels*, you'll need to know the wind speed, too.

**WIND CHILL FACTOR**

WIND

| Kilometers per hour | Temperature in Degrees Celsius | | | | | | |
|---|---|---|---|---|---|---|---|
| | -1° | -4° | -7° | -9° | -12° | -15° | -18° |
| 24 | -13° | -17° | -21° | -24° | -28° | -32° | -35° |
| 32 | -16° | -19° | -23° | -27° | -31° | -35° | -39° |
| 40 | -17° | -22° | -26° | -30° | -34° | -38° | -42° |
| 48 | -19° | -23° | -28° | -32° | -36° | -41° | -45° |

**Think!**

**What do you think happens to wind when it comes into contact with water? with a building or a mountain?**

# How Do Storms Form?

As water evaporates, it gains heat. When water vapor condenses, it gives off that heat and warms the air around it. These changes cause temperature and pressure differences in the air. What do you think happens when these differences are very big?

## Exploration:
## Watch air pressure at work.

❶ Fill the container about three-quarters full of hot water.

❷ Take the cap off the plastic bottle and hold the bottle up to its neck in the hot water for three minutes.

❸ While the bottle is still in the container, screw the cap on tight.

❹ Take the bottle out of the water and set it on your desk. Record your observations.

### Interpret your results.

- Explain why the bottle changed.
- How was the air inside the bottle different from the air in the room?
- Explain why you would have gotten different results if the cap had not been put on the bottle before you removed it from the hot water.
- During a storm, the wind blows hard and rain falls heavily. How does the bottle show you where air pressure is greatest?

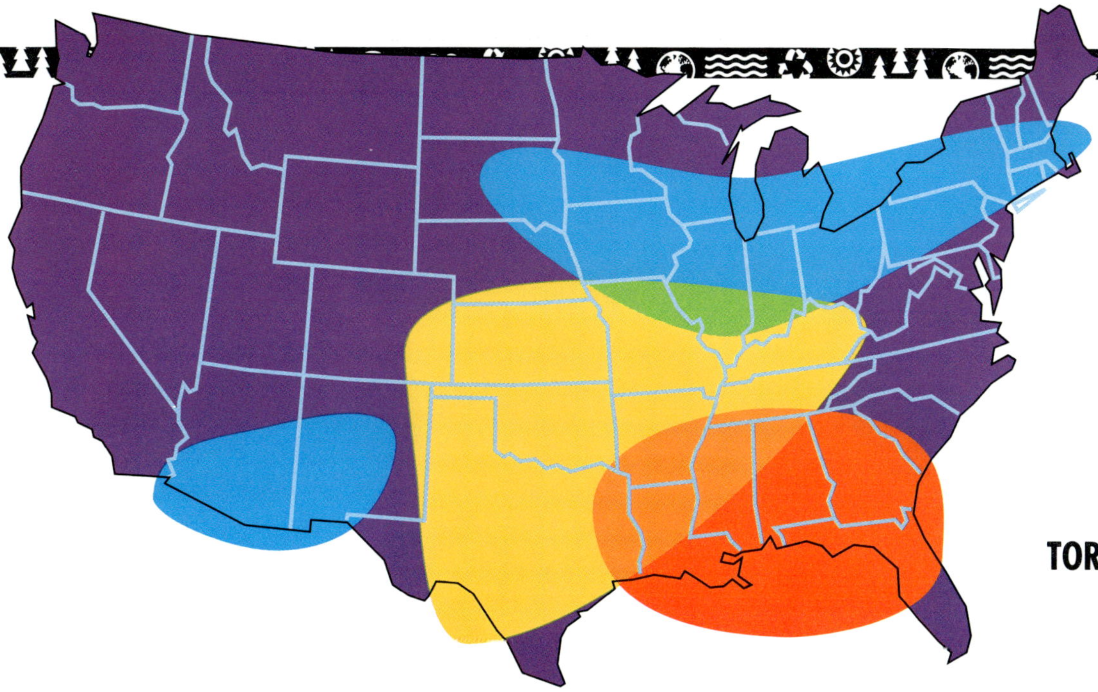


▼ Some tornadoes have winds as fast as 483 kilometers per hour (300 miles per hour).

## Exploration Connection: Using reference books

Sometimes a strong, fast column of rising warm air starts spinning. If it forms a tube of air that hangs from the cloud like an elephant's trunk, it's called a tornado. A tornado acts like a vacuum cleaner, sucking in air at the bottom and whirling it upwards, picking up anything in its path. Tornadoes can lift railroad cars, smash houses, and ruin whole towns in a matter of seconds.

No one knows why tornadoes form in some storms and not in others. The map above shows when and where tornadoes are most likely to strike. During what months of the year are you likely to hear about tornadoes in the news? When would you be surprised to hear about a tornado? To find out how scientists learned about how violent storms work, read pages 61–64 in *The Sierra Club Book of Weatherwisdom.*

## Closer to Home: Lightning and thunder

It all starts with storm clouds. Look back at the diagram of clouds on page 19 in Lesson 3. Giant cumulonimbus clouds can billow up, reaching a height of 16 kilometers (10 miles). Sometimes they even push their way into the stratosphere. Warm air rising inside the cloud carries water vapor up from Earth's surface. At the same time, condensed droplets join together and fall as rain. All the different forces in motion cause high winds and lightning.

Scientists have figured out what happens when a bolt of lightning appears in the atmosphere, but they're still trying to figure out how the electric charge builds up. Look at the diagrams to see what happens inside the cloud.

- Snowstorms almost never produce thunder and lightning. Can you think of a reason why? Explain.

▼ Particles with an electric charge zigzag from the cloud toward Earth.

▼ Particles with a different electric charge move upward from Earth.

◀ Lightning is hot. Its temperature can reach as high as 24,000°C (40,000°F). It is also fast. Lightning can move at 120,000 kilometers (75,000 miles) per second.

**Think!**

**A thunderstorm only lasts about an hour, but on a stormy day there could be hours of thunder and lightning. How would you explain that?**

▼ The two charges meet and a powerful electric current begins to flow between the cloud and Earth.

▼ Lightning's heat causes air to expand. Cooler air moves in. The air movement starts sound waves that you hear as thunder.

# How Do Weather Systems Move?

Masses of air move across the surface of Earth, pushing against each other. If Earth stood still, most surface winds would travel north and south in straight lines. But Earth rotates, turning in a complete circle on its axis once every day. The axis is an invisible line through Earth from the North Pole to the South Pole. How do you think Earth's rotation affects wind and weather?

## Exploration:

### Make a model of Earth's winds.

❶ Cut the box in half. Tape the halves together to form a square box.

❷ Poke a hole in the top and bottom of the box. Push the dowel through the center of the ball and then through the top and bottom of the box.

❸ The ball represents Earth. Draw its equator. Then cut a hole in the top of the box near the front of the ball. Tape plastic wrap over the front of the box.

❹ Use the eyedropper to put food coloring on your model of Earth's North Pole. Observe how it moves and the mark it leaves.

❺ Put more food coloring onto the ball, and observe its trail as you spin the ball rapidly clockwise.

### Interpret your results.

- Describe the path the drop took when the ball wasn't spinning. What kind of path did the drop take when the ball was spinning?
- What would happen if you spun the ball faster? **Try it!** What do you think would happen to Earth's winds if Earth rotated twice as fast?

## WORLD WIND PATTERNS

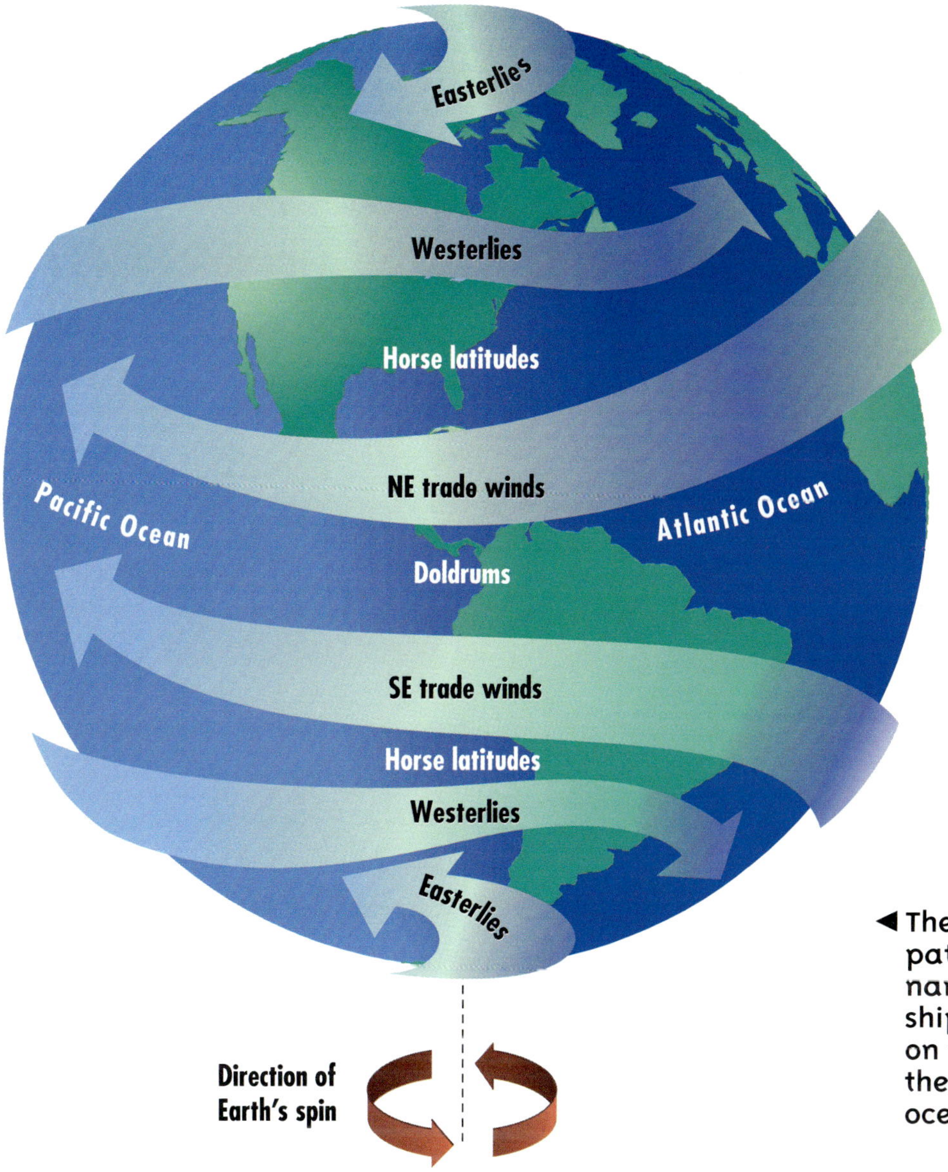


◀ The wind patterns were named when ships depended on winds to push them across the ocean.

### Exploration Connection: Using reference books

You've seen how Earth's spin affects some winds. The surface of Earth also affects winds. Water and land hold heat differently, and that difference has an effect on the weather.

When the sun comes up, land heats faster than water. When the sun sets, the land also cools off faster. Air masses with different temperatures and amounts of water vapor form next to each other. What happens when two of these air masses meet?

All these things happening at the same time cause global winds, the wind patterns shown in the diagram. What wind belt do you live near?

Most of the time, weather in the U.S. moves from southwest to northeast. Why? Look at the diagram again. Where do you think most of the rain that falls in the U.S. comes from? How does weather move in Alaska? To learn more about global winds, turn to pages 34–41 in *The Sierra Club Book of Weatherwisdom.*

In your last Exploration, you saw how Earth's spin affects its winds. Earth also orbits the sun. How does this yearly journey around the sun affect Earth's atmosphere?

## Exploration:
## Make a model of Earth's orbit.

❶ Write *1, 2, 3,* and *4* on four small sheets of paper. Put them on the table as shown in the photo.

❷ Move the ball to position 1. Tilt the north pole of the ball toward the classroom door. At all times make certain to keep the north pole tilted toward the door.

❸ Have a partner shine the flashlight at the ball. Mark a "1" on the part of the ball that gets the most direct light.

❹ Move the ball to position 2 and point the flashlight at it. Mark a "2" on the part of the ball that gets the most direct light. Repeat for positions 3 and 4.

### Interpret your results.

- Which area of the ball received the most direct sunlight in each position?
- Which area of the ball received the greatest amount of light in all four positions? the least amount of light?
- How does your model of Earth's orbit explain changes in season? How does it explain why parts of Earth are always warm or always cold?

Time: Midnight

Cold front

Warm front

Time: Noon

Cold front

Warm front

## Closer to Home: Tracking fronts

Winds push giant air masses across the surface of the earth until they run into other air masses. Then a shoving match begins. The place where this shoving match happens is called a front, and it can stretch for hundreds of miles. You can expect a change in weather when a front moves through—a good reason to keep track of fronts.

Warm fronts are masses of warm air that move forward against masses of cold air. Cold fronts are masses of cold air that move forward against masses of warm air. When a cold front moves through an area, the cold air pushes under the warm air, as shown above. Clouds and thunderstorms form.

When a warm front moves through an area, warm air slides over the cold air, creating a front with a gentle slope. You can see signs of the warm front as thin, wispy cirrus clouds form overhead. Look back at the diagram of clouds on page 19 of Lesson 5.

- What's the weather like where you are right now? Do you think you're under a high or a low pressure area, or under a moving front? How could you find out?

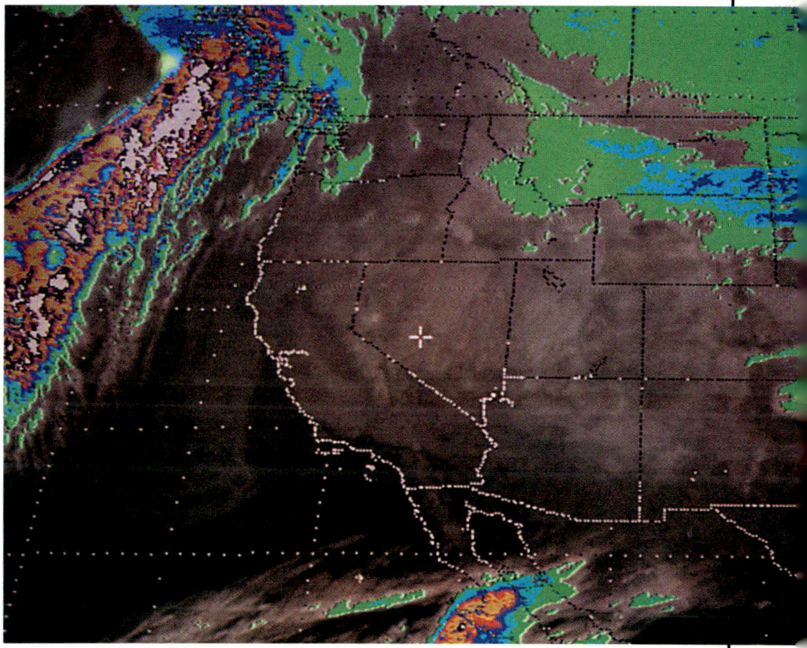

▲ TV weather maps that include radar data can help track the storms that form along a front. Where is the front in this map?

**Think!**

**Why would fronts make weather news?**

LESSON 9

# How Do People Predict Weather?

To make a quick prediction of the weather coming your way, look at the sky. What kinds of clouds do you see? Your wind gauge will tell you the speed of the wind. How do you think these observations could help you predict the weather?

## Exploration:
## Determine the direction of the wind.

**You need:**
- Cardboard
- Scissors
- Marker
- Tape
- Pen top
- Dowel
- Directional compass

❶ Cut out a circle of cardboard. Poke a hole in the center. Label it like the one in the photo.

❷ Cut out the wind vane shape from the cardboard. Tape the pen top to the middle of the wind vane as shown.

❸ Put the pen top onto the dowel. Make sure the wind vane can spin freely. Push the dowel through the hole in the direction disk, and then push the dowel into the ground.

❹ Use your compass to figure out which way north is. Move your direction disk until it lines up with your compass. Stand back and let the wind vane swing into position. Record the direction the wind is coming from.

❺ Record wind direction several times during the day. Has the wind changed direction?

### Interpret your results.

- If you recorded the wind direction every day for a year, from what direction do you think the wind would come most often?
- From what direction do you think most storms would come? Why?

## Exploration Connection: Using reference books

If you want to predict the weather, it helps to get the big picture. Weather forecasters put together details of what's happening at any one moment over a large area. Information from weather stations across the country is used to make weather maps.

Weather stations collect data on conditions at the surface of Earth, including temperature, air pressure, amount of water in the air, snowfall, rainfall, and wind speed and direction. Weather balloons float high in the troposphere. Instruments attached to the balloons record temperature, the amount of water in the air, and other measurements. How would information about conditions kilometers above the ground help in predicting weather fronts?

To learn more about weather maps and how they're made, turn to page 72 of *The Sierra Club Book of Weatherwisdom.*

▲ A barometer shows changes in air pressure. How could such a change help you predict weather?

◀ What kinds of measurements do you think would be taken at a weather field station like this one?

You've made instruments that show which way the wind is blowing and how fast it's moving. You can figure out when the weather is changing, but how do you know whether the front coming your way is warm or cold? How can you tell if air pressure is increasing or decreasing?

## Exploration:
## Make a barometer model.

❶ Cut off the neck of the balloon. Stretch the balloon tightly over the top of the cup. Secure it with a rubber band.

❷ Tape the straw to the stretched piece of balloon, as shown in the picture.

❸ Fold the cardboard to make a base, as shown. Tape the cardboard to the table. Draw a line on the cardboard 10 cm long. Make a mark on this line every 1/2 cm. Move the cup so the straw rests near this scale.

❹ Test the barometer. Add pressure by pushing down on the stretched balloon. Does the straw go up or down? Predict how the straw will move when air pressure increases and when air pressure decreases. Record your results.

❺ Check the straw's level at the same time each day. Record in the table whether the level rises, falls, or doesn't change. Record whether the weather is clear, cloudy, rainy, or snowy.

### Interpret your results.

- How did the level of the straw change when the air pressure increased? decreased?
- Think back on what you've discovered about air pressure and weather conditions. Make up a rule for predicting the weather using a barometer.

▲ These pictures were made by a satellite and a computer. They show the movement of a hurricane, the large yellow and red circle. How could these pictures help weather forecasters save lives?

## Closer to Home: How reliable are weather forecasts?

You can see weather reports on the news every night. First the forecasters tell you what's happening right then. Then they tell you what they predict will happen next. They might even forecast—predict—the weather for the next five days.

Predicting the weather is like doing detective work—you gather as much information as you can and then make some educated guesses. Even with the help of satellites and computers, forecasters know that predicting the weather isn't easy. That's why forecasters usually talk about what's *probably* going to happen in the atmosphere.

Suppose the forecast said there was a 70 percent chance of rain on Saturday. You carried your umbrella, but it never even drizzled. Was the forecast wrong? If there's a 70 percent chance of rain, what's the possibility that it won't rain? Forecasts are made for large areas. It may have rained nearby but missed you.

- Which weather report would you trust more: a forecast for tomorrow or a forecast for next week? Explain.
- Why do you think predicting weather is so hard?

**Think!**

**It's not raining where you are. However, it's raining hard only 100 kilometers (60 miles) away. What measurements would help you find out if this rain is likely to move across your area?**

LESSON 10

# How Do Volcanoes and Forest Fires Change the Atmosphere?

You've seen the role the water cycle plays in the troposphere. Other things carried by the air also affect weather patterns. Natural events, such as forest fires and volcanic eruptions, happen somewhere on Earth every year. How do you think they affect the atmosphere?

Dust and ash in the atmosphere bounce sunlight away from Earth. A volcano or forest fire can produce a thick layer of dust that can cool the air because less of the sun's energy gets to Earth.

More dust in the atmosphere means less light gets through, so it can also change the way you see. You can see farther when the atmosphere is clear. Fiery red and orange sunsets look great, but they're a sign of extra dust in the atmosphere.

▼ Mount Pinatubo in the Pacific erupted in 1991. What kinds of changes do you think the ash from the volcano could cause?

## WHERE VOLCANOES OCCUR

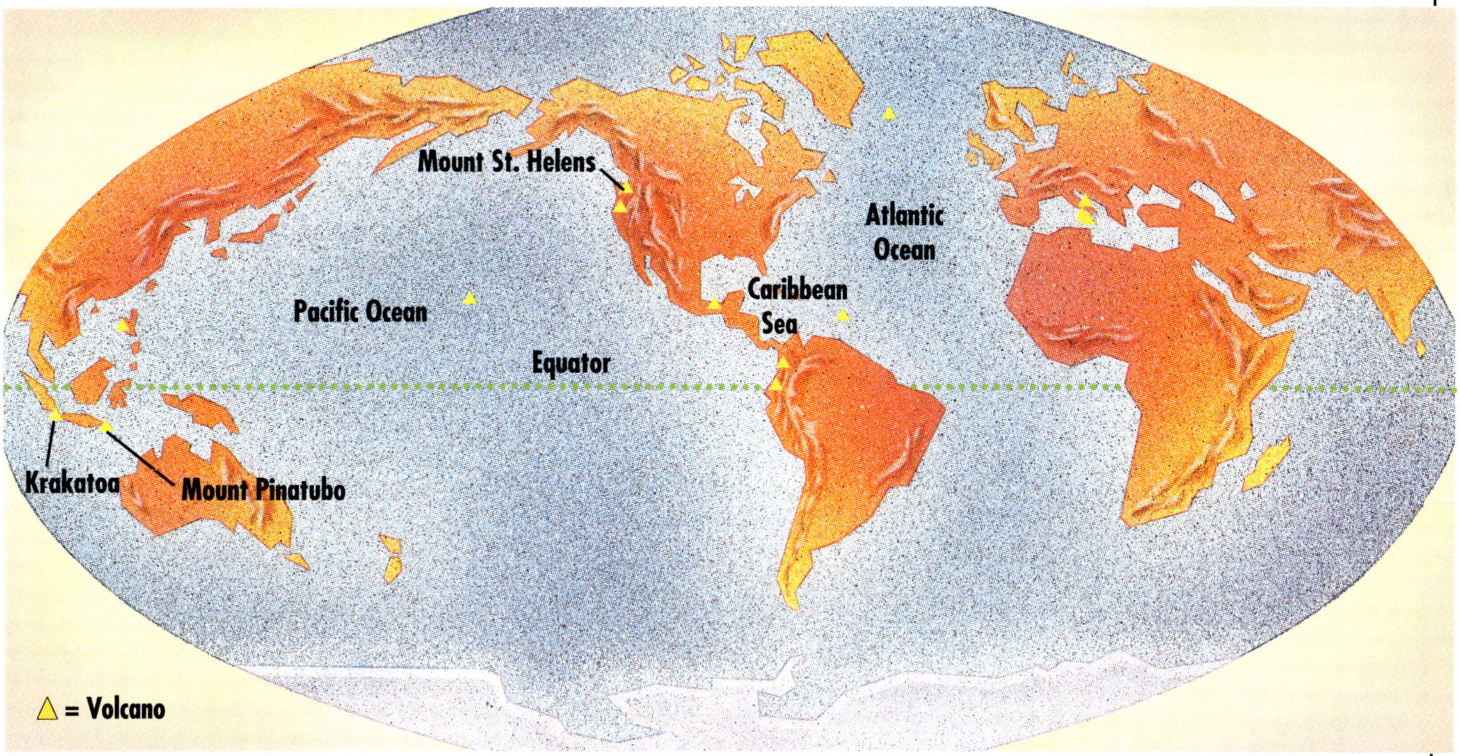

▲ Tons of ash from Mount Pinatubo settled slowly in the days after the eruption. Villages and fields were buried.

### Information Connection:
### Interpreting maps

Once in a while, the melted rock inside Earth pushes its way to the surface and a volcano erupts. Hot gases and melted rock can explode into the air with so much force that the rock is blasted into tiny particles of ash. If a volcano erupts straight up, the ash and gases can be blown miles into the stratosphere. The fast, strong winds that circle Earth can then carry them all around the globe.

That's what happened when Krakatoa erupted in 1883. This tiny island in the South Pacific blew tons of rock, dust, and ash about 80 kilometers (49 miles) straight up. Look at the map and find this famous volcano. Krakatoa is near the equator, where the sun's heat draws air upward. In two weeks, the cloud of dust and ash had circled the globe.

Now find Mount Pinatubo and the Caribbean Sea on the map. Three months after Pinatubo erupted in 1991, the amount of sunlight reaching the Caribbean had dropped by 30 percent.

## Closer to Home: Forest fires

There are some places where you can expect wildfires. In California fires burn 50,000 to 500,000 acres of land every year. Some of the plants that live there have oily sap. They can survive the dry, hot summers, but if they catch fire they explode into flame. Grasses grow thick during the spring rains, and then die. They dry into a thick layer of straw that burns fast, making a very hot fire.

Fires can start wherever there's fuel to burn. California has plenty of fuel, and a hot, dry wind that blows every year between mid-September and late October. This wind, called the Santa Ana, passes over the inland desert, losing moisture and gaining heat, and rushes toward the ocean to the west. It fans the flames and makes fighting the fires nearly impossible. Find the Santa Ana winds below.

Forests are also a natural storehouse of fuel for a fire. During a dry summer, dead trees and low brush in a forest can burst into flame wherever lightning strikes. Rain usually puts these fires out. But sometimes the combination of dry fuel, hot dry air, and strong winds is just right for a major forest fire.

In 1988 Yellowstone National Park was burned by several such fires at once. Lightning struck in two places. A worker dropped a lit cigarette in another place. On the worst day of the fire, more than 600 square kilometers (about 230 square miles) of forest burned. Clouds of smoke that looked like storm clouds rose into the atmosphere. Smoke blocked the sun and drifted far beyond the park.

Firefighters work hard to control fires like those in Yellowstone and California, many of which are caused by people. But long before humans learned how to start or put out a fire, prairies and forests burned every year. Both kinds of land recovered, as they have in Yellowstone and in California.

- Why might a rainy spring make big fires more likely in the late summer?
- Do you think forest fires should be allowed to burn as they did hundreds of years ago, or should all forest fires be put out?

▶ In 1992, several forest fires in Yellowstone National Park burned out of control.

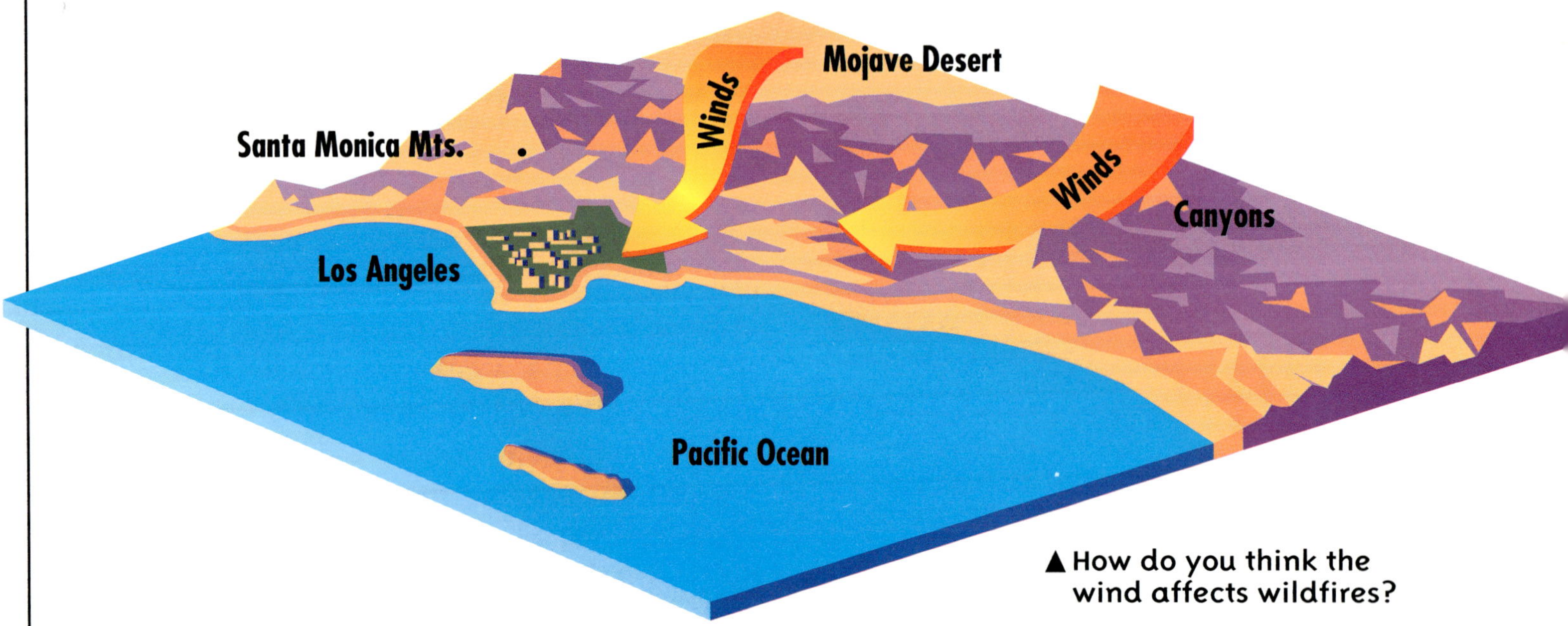


▲ How do you think the wind affects wildfires?

**Think!**

Which ash do you think is likely to travel farther—from a forest fire or from a volcano? Why?

LESSON 11

# How Do People Change the Atmosphere?

Do you ever get itchy eyes or feel the urge to sneeze even though you don't have a cold? Maybe it's something in the air. The wind carries pollutants, substances that make the air dirty. Pollutants don't just make things dirty; they cause health problems for living things. What kinds of pollutants does the wind carry in your area?

## Exploration:
### Measure air pollution.

**You need:**
- 3 index cards
- Black marker
- Petroleum jelly
- Plastic wrap
- Tape
- Hand lens

1. Color one half of each card black. Label the cards "1," "2," "3."
2. Spread a layer of petroleum jelly on one side of each card.
3. Cover card 1 with plastic wrap. Tape card 2 to a wall of the classroom. Tape cards 1 and 3 to a wall outdoors.
4. Wait one day. Then examine the cards with your hand lens. Record your observations.

### Interpret your results.

- Which card collected the most particles? the least particles? How would you explain the results?
- Did you find evidence of pollutants inside the building? Where do you think pollutants found indoors might come from?
- What kinds of pollutants could you identify?

▼ A car engine gives off pollutants as it burns gasoline.

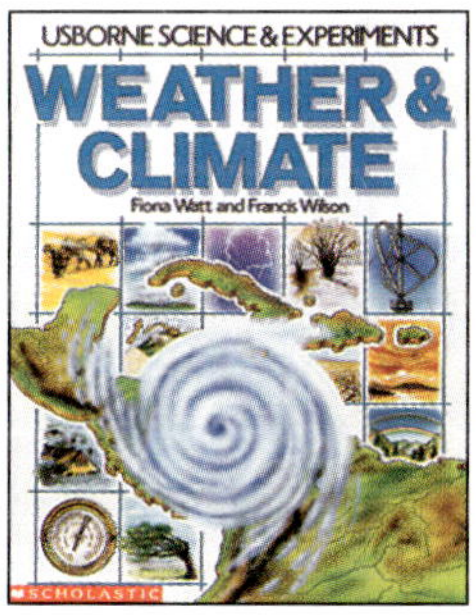


## Exploration Connection: Using reference books

Some of the pollutants you observed probably came from cars. If someone told you there was a fire burning in your school bus, you probably wouldn't get on the bus. But there's a fire burning in most buses, cars, and trucks on the road. Cars are one of the main causes of air pollution.

A car engine burns gasoline or diesel oil to release energy. That energy turns the car's wheels. All fire is the result of a reaction between oxygen and a fuel—gasoline, for example. A car engine uses oxygen as it burns gasoline, and gives off waste gases. The waste gases include carbon dioxide, water vapor, carbon monoxide, and other pollutants.

There are several ways to get where you want to go without burning up so much oxygen and leaving behind so many pollutants. Which do you think would burn more gasoline per person—a car with two people in it or a car with four people? How about a full bus? How about walking or riding a bike?

In many places there are ways to move many people. These ways of getting around are called public transportation. Public transportation includes buses, subways, trains, and ferries that run on a schedule. Most large cities depend on public transportation.

To find out more about pollutants in the atmosphere, read pages 40–41 in *Weather & Climate.*

## Closer to Home: Indoor air pollution

You can't get away from pollution by going inside and shutting all the windows. You can smell smoke and see dust, but some indoor pollutants are harder to detect. Chemicals in products like cleaners, bug sprays, and air fresheners give off gases. Some building materials, furniture, and carpets also add pollutants to the indoor air you breathe.

You can try to keep these pollutants out of your home. But fresh outdoor air may be the best defense against all kinds of indoor pollution.

While working on ways to keep the air in a space station clean, scientists discovered another way to clean indoor air. Certain plants, including the spider plant, actually remove pollutants from the air. All green plants use carbon dioxide (the gas you breathe out) and produce oxygen (the gas you breathe in), so they're useful whenever you're indoors with the windows shut. But a spider plant can also take up small amounts of air pollutants through its roots—and not let those pollutants go. All plants take in certain gases through their roots. But the roots of a few dozen spider plants can help clean up a houseful of indoor pollution.

- Some heaters and air conditioners recycle the same air over and over. Why do you think recycled air can make indoor pollution worse?
- In a cold climate, do you think indoor pollution would be better or worse during the winter? Explain.

► Some rooms in your home probably contain more sources of pollutants than other rooms.

SOURCES OF INDOOR POLLUTION

**Think!**

**Would using cars less often put an end to outdoor air pollution problems? Explain.**

LESSON 12

# How Does the Atmosphere Move Air Pollution?

A car burns gasoline and gives off pollutants. Rising air carries these and other pollutants high into the troposphere. Some pollutants combine with water vapor in the air, forming acid rain. How can you tell that there are pollutants in rain?

## Exploration:
### Test for acid.

**You need:**
- 4 plastic cups
- Marker
- Tape
- Graduated cup
- Vinegar
- Distilled water
- Spoon
- Bicarbonate of soda
- pH test strips

❶ Label one cup "vinegar," one cup "distilled water," and one cup "bicarbonate of soda."

❷ Pour 120 cc of each liquid into its labeled cup. In the cup marked "bicarbonate of soda," mix 120 cc of distilled water and 1 spoonful of bicarbonate of soda.

❸ Dip a test strip in each cup and compare it to the chart your teacher gives you. Record your observations on your LabMat.

### Interpret your results.

- Based on the chart, which sample do you think is most like clean rainwater? acid rainwater?
- Acid rain begins as air pollution and ends as water pollution. In which form do you think it travels farthest? What carries it?

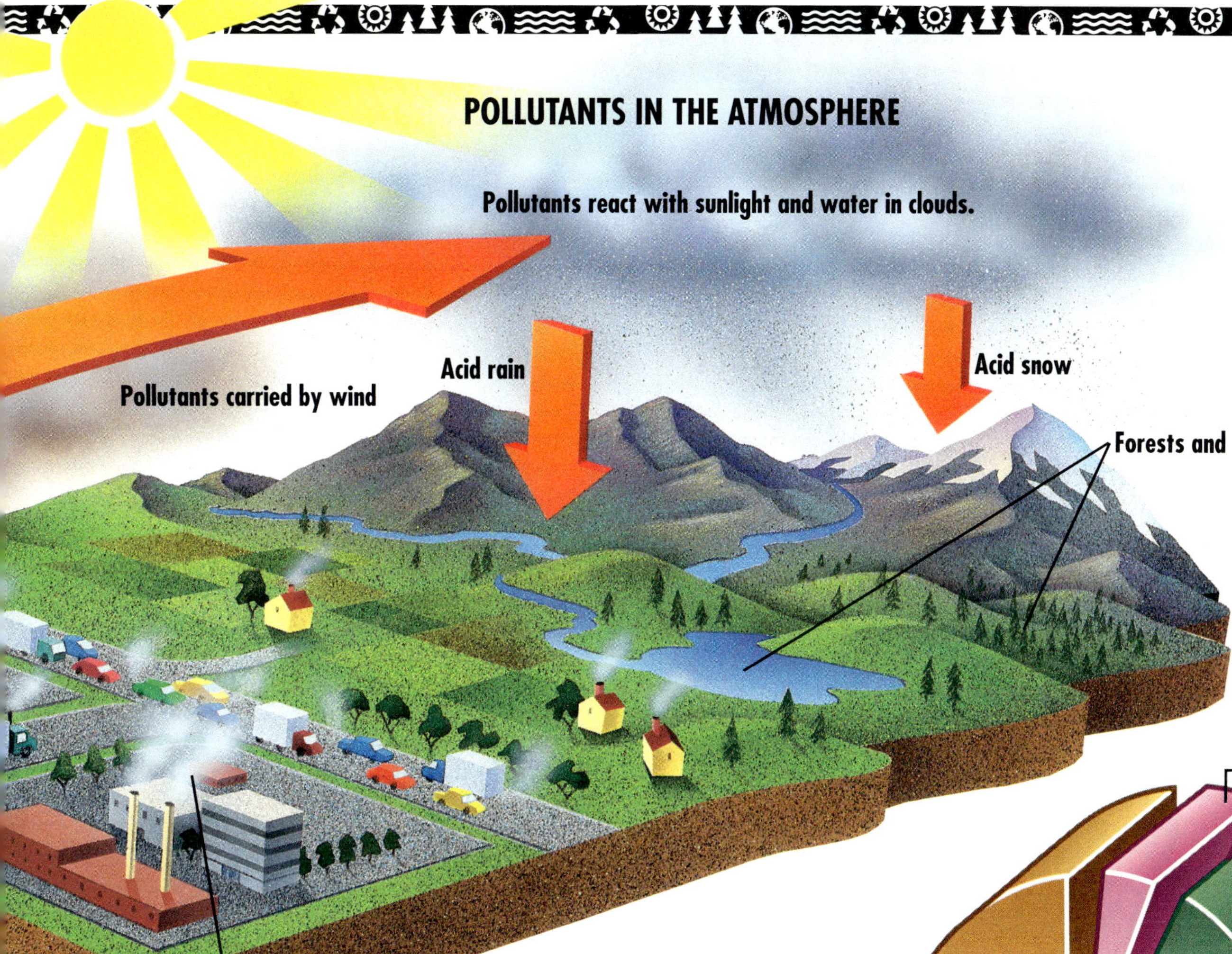


▲ After a journey through the atmosphere, sulfur dioxide and nitrogen oxides form acid rain.

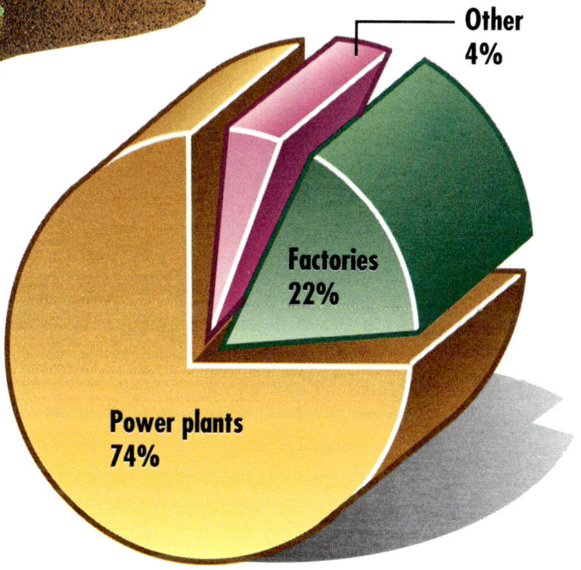


SULFUR DIOXIDE

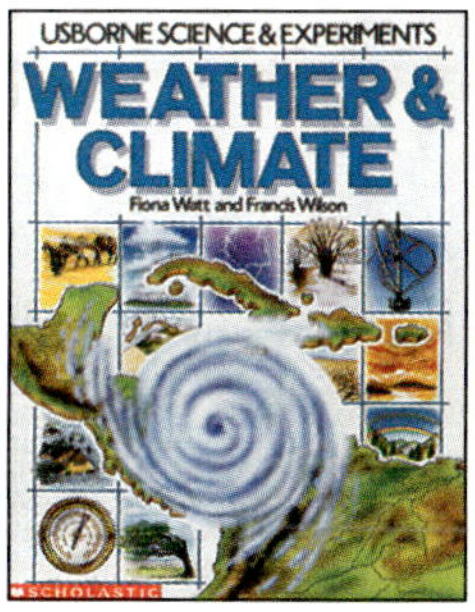


## Exploration Connection:
## Using reference books

The substances that turn to acids in the atmosphere are produced by burning fuels. Look at the pie graphs. Where do most sulfur dioxides come from? Where do nitrogen oxides come from? What else gives off a lot of nitrogen oxides?

Track the pollutants through the diagram. Where do they enter the air? Where do they end up? How do they get from the atmosphere back to Earth? What happens to the pollutants once they return to Earth? To find out more about pollution, read pages 40–41 of *Weather & Climate.*

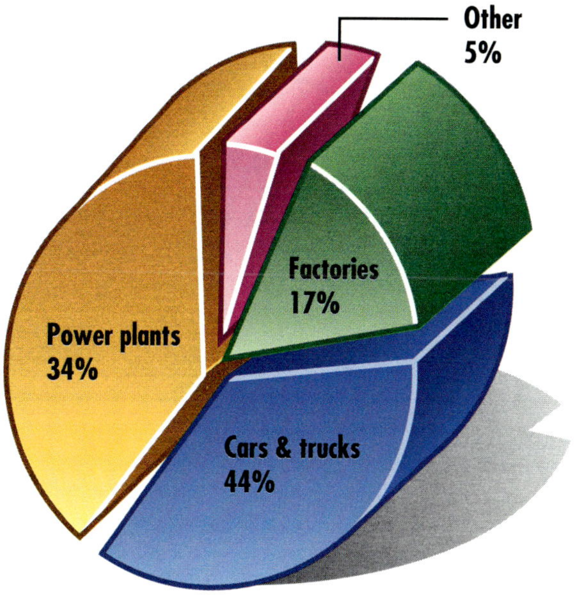


NITROGEN OXIDES

Go hiking in a wilderness area and you might come across a clear blue lake. It may look beautiful, but clear water is sometimes a sign of trouble. Tiny organisms that make lake water murky also provide food for fish and other living things. Acid rain can kill the fish in a mountain lake. How do you think acid rain affects growing plants?

## Exploration:
## Investigate the effect of acid on plants.

❶ Fill two cups with soil. Plant seeds about 2 cm deep in each cup. Label one cup "A" and the other "B."

❷ Fill another cup about half full of water. Test the amount of acid in the water with a test strip. Add vinegar to the water until it turns the test strip reddish orange. The reddish-orange color means that the water is a medium-strength acid.

❸ Water the seeds in cup A with tap water. Water cup B with the vinegar solution.

❹ Check the plants every day. Compare the growth of plants in cups A and B. Record your observations.

### Interpret your results.

- How did the acid water affect the growth of your plants?
- What do you think happens to plants in areas where acid rain falls?

## Closer to Home: What you can do about air pollution

Every time you ride in a car, cool a drink, or use any electricity made by burning fuel, you are using machines that put pollutants into Earth's atmosphere. Look at the chart. Which pollutants are related to heating? transportation? lighting?

Most electricity used in the U.S. is made in power plants that burn fuel. On a hot summer day in a big city, many people turn on their air conditioners. Air conditioners use lots of electricity. The power plants must make more electricity than on cooler days, and they do it by burning more fuel. What does that tell you about the amount of pollutants on a hot summer day?

**WHAT CAN YOU DO ABOUT AIR POLLUTION?**

| When You: | You Reduce: |
|---|---|
| • Walk or ride a bike<br>• Carpool<br>• Use public transportation | • Carbon dioxide nitrous oxides (from burning gasoline) |
| • Compost | • Methane (from landfills) |
| • Turn down the heat in winter<br>• Take shorter showers | • Carbon dioxide (from burning fuel for heat) |
| • Turn off lights<br>• Watch less television | • Carbon dioxide, sulphur dioxide, acid rain (from electrical power plants) |
| • Reuse and recycle | • Carbon dioxide, nitrous oxides (from transporting new products) |
| • Have air conditioners and refrigerators checked for leaks | • CFCs |

- From what you've learned about the atmosphere, what do you think happens to these pollutants when they enter the atmosphere?

**Think!**

**How does the atmosphere move pollutants from place to place?**

LESSON 13

# How Does Air Pollution Affect Living Things?

**You've seen how pollutants that move through the atmosphere can affect plants. Pollutants can also affect the gases that form the atmosphere. In Lesson 5 you read about how one gas, ozone, protects Earth from UV rays. In 1985 satellite photos showed that much ozone had disappeared from the stratosphere, leaving a "hole" through which UV rays could pass. It's not yet clear how changes in the ozone are affecting the atmosphere, but some scientists think the increase in UV rays is harming living things.**

For several years, scientists have been trying to understand why many frogs, toads, and other amphibians have been disappearing. Amphibians are animals that are born in water, but spend much of their adult life on land. In 1994 scientists said they'd found a clue to the vanishing amphibians.

Amphibians lay eggs, but unlike bird and reptile eggs, amphibian eggs have no shells. Many frogs and toads lay their eggs in sunny ponds, streams, and lakes. UV rays can damage the unprotected eggs so that they never hatch. Scientists compared the data on vanishing amphibians to the information on the thinning of the ozone in the atmosphere. Their theory is that many amphibian eggs are not surviving the increase in UV rays hitting Earth.

Dr. Andrew Blaustein was the leader of the amphibian study. He said that the Cascades frog and the Western toad could be "the canaries in the coal mine" for humans and Earth's ozone layer. He was talking about an old safety trick used by coal miners. Coal miners used to take canaries to work. These birds are more sensitive to dangerous mine gases than people are. When the birds became sick, the miners knew they had to get out of the mine. How could a yearly count of amphibians help warn humans of thinning of the ozone layer?

▲ Researchers tested how amphibian eggs survive in different kinds of light. Why do you think this part of the experiment was done outdoors?

▶ The Western toad has been affected by the thinning of the ozone layer.

## Information Connection:
### Interpreting graphs

Dr. Blaustein's team found their proof for the connection between the ozone layer and disappearing frogs by doing an experiment. They set out hatching tanks for ten kinds of amphibians at the edge of a mountain lake. They covered some of the tanks with plastic filters that remove UV rays from sunlight. The other tanks had no filters. Each type of egg was put in both kinds of tanks.

Look at the graph. Which kind of frog or toad egg hatched the most in the unfiltered tanks? the least? Which were most helped by the UV filter? How can you tell?

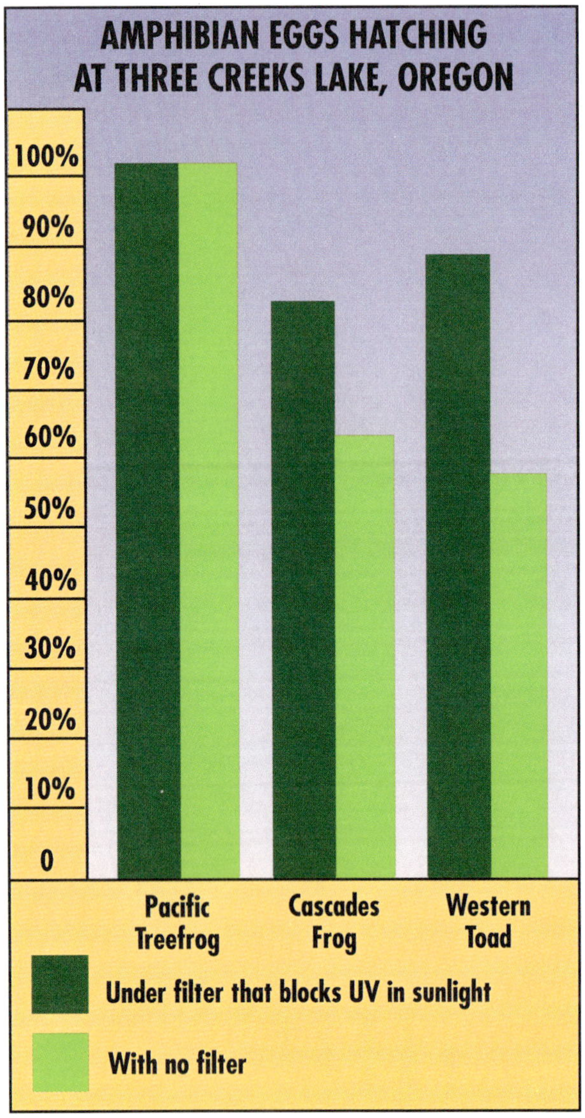


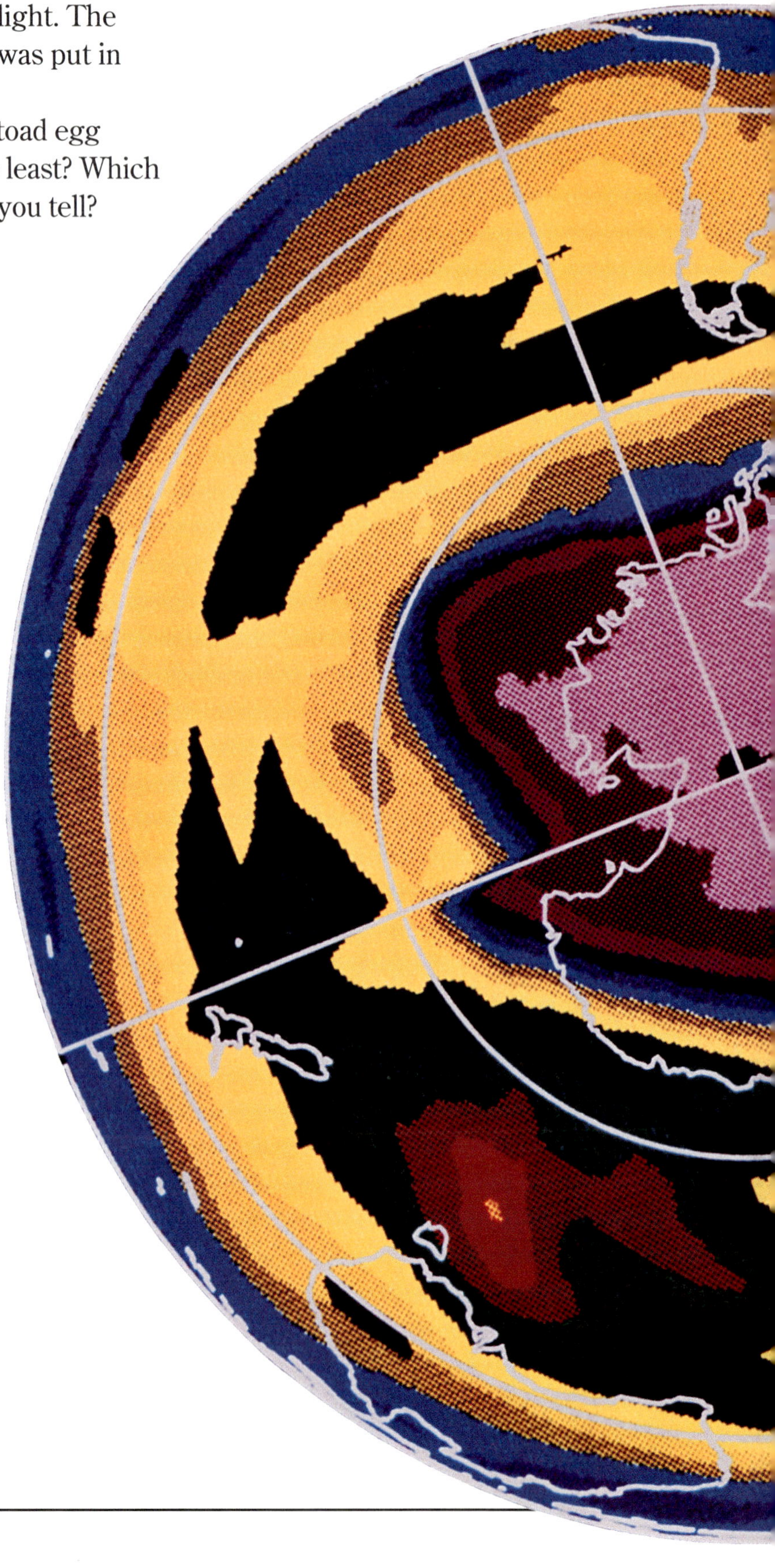

▼ This is a computer map of the Southern Hemisphere. The purple areas show where ozone is disappearing. The light purple area is the hole in the ozone layer.

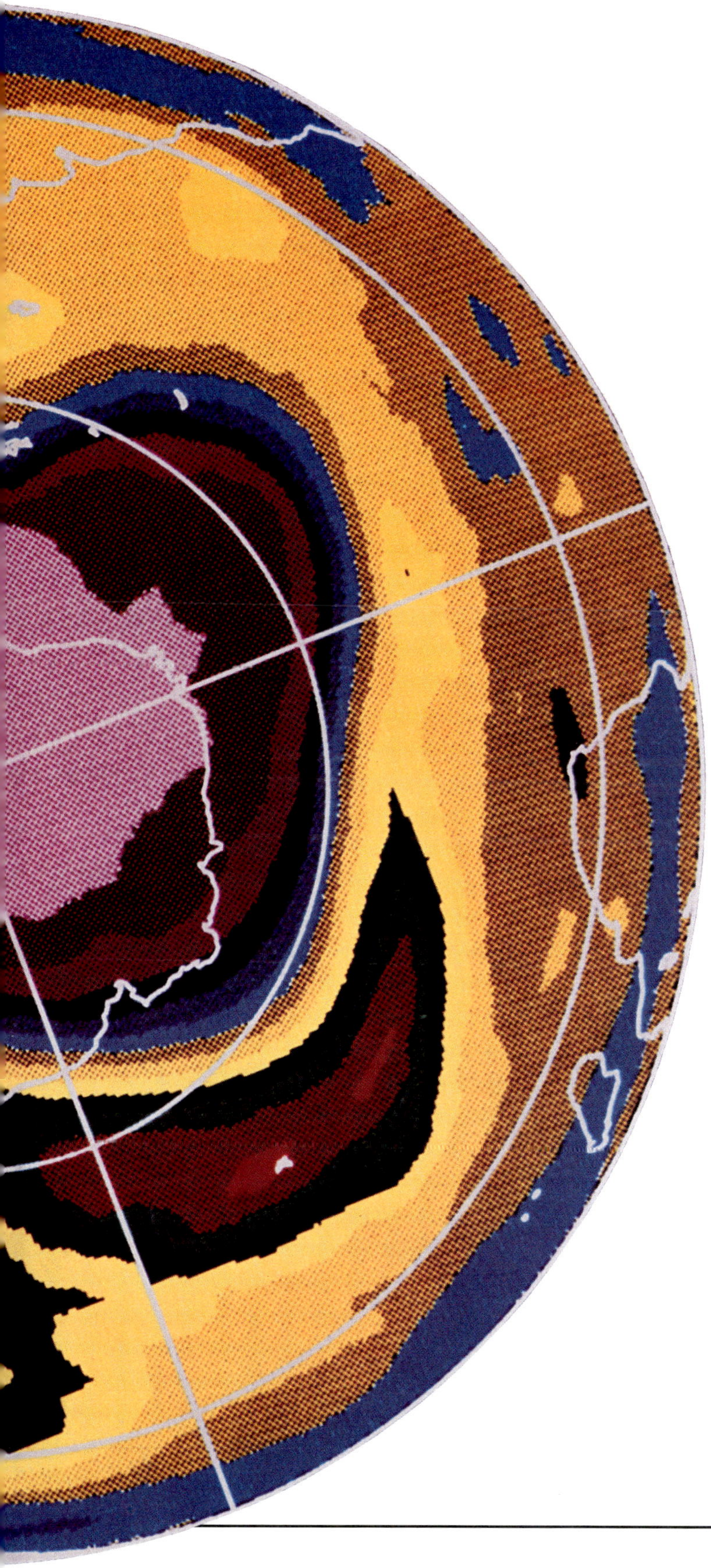

## Closer to Home: The "hole" in the ozone

You've seen how the thinning ozone may be affecting amphibians. The same gas, ozone, that protects you by blocking UV rays in the stratosphere can harm you if it's in the air you breathe. The amount of ozone in the stratosphere is decreasing. The amount in the troposphere is increasing. Scientists are still trying to figure out why.

Satellite photos showed the hole in the ozone that was letting more UV rays reach Earth. Scientists tried to figure out what else had changed that might have affected the gases of the atmosphere. The search led back to 1928, when a group of chemicals called CFCs were invented. At the time, chemicals used in cooling equipment, like refrigerators, were dangerous. CFCs worked well, seemed harmless, and made cooling easier.

Sixty years later people found out that CFCs weren't harmless after all. Once these chemicals enter the atmosphere, they move to the stratosphere and destroy ozone.

- For a long time people thought CFCs were harmless. Now CFCs are considered very dangerous. What does this tell you about the length of time it takes to determine if a substance will harm the atmosphere?

**Think!**

**Which do you think will be more difficult to fix—acid rain or the hole in the ozone layer? Why?**

LESSON 14

# How Could Greenhouse Gases Change the Atmosphere?

Gases that are good at trapping heat are called greenhouse gases. Carbon dioxide and water vapor are the most common greenhouse gases. How do you think polluting the atmosphere with more carbon dioxide might affect Earth?

## Exploration:
## Make a double-layered greenhouse.

**You need:**
- 2 thermometers
- Boxes from Lesson 4
- Tape
- Plastic wrap
- Black paper
- Lamp

❶ Place a thermometer in box 1 and box 2 from Lesson 4. Tape plastic wrap tightly over the top of box 1. The plastic wrap represents carbon dioxide in the atmosphere.

❷ Fold the black paper as shown in the picture. Tape the folded paper to box 1 and box 2 to make each box taller.

❸ Tape plastic wrap over the top of each box. You should now have two layers of plastic over box 1. Box 2 should have only one layer of plastic.

❹ Place both boxes under the lamp. After 15 minutes, record the temperature in each box.

### Interpret your results.

- How would you explain the changes you observed in step 4?
- Carbon dioxide holds heat in the atmosphere. What do you think might happen on Earth if too much carbon dioxide or other greenhouse gases are added to the atmosphere?
- How do you think greenhouse gases got their name?

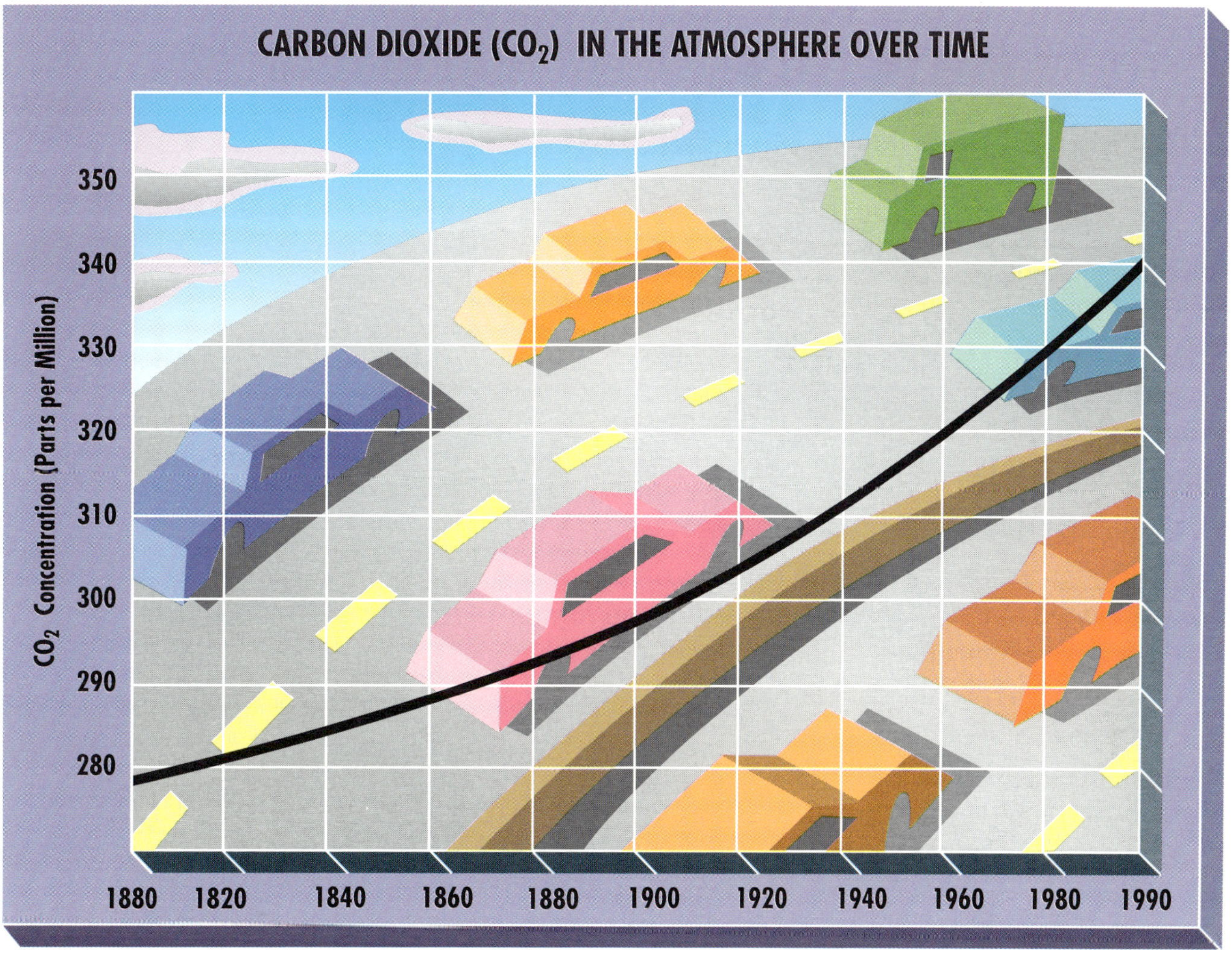


▲ Carbon dioxide levels in the atmosphere have been measured from a mountaintop in Hawaii since 1958. Air bubbles frozen in Antarctica have given scientists carbon dioxide data back to 1800.

**Exploration Connection:**

**Interpreting graphs**

By itself, carbon dioxide isn't a harmful gas. It doesn't hurt you to breathe carbon dioxide—as long as you have enough oxygen to breathe at the same time. Plants need carbon dioxide to grow.

The graph shows how the amount of carbon dioxide in the air is changing. What do you think is causing this change?

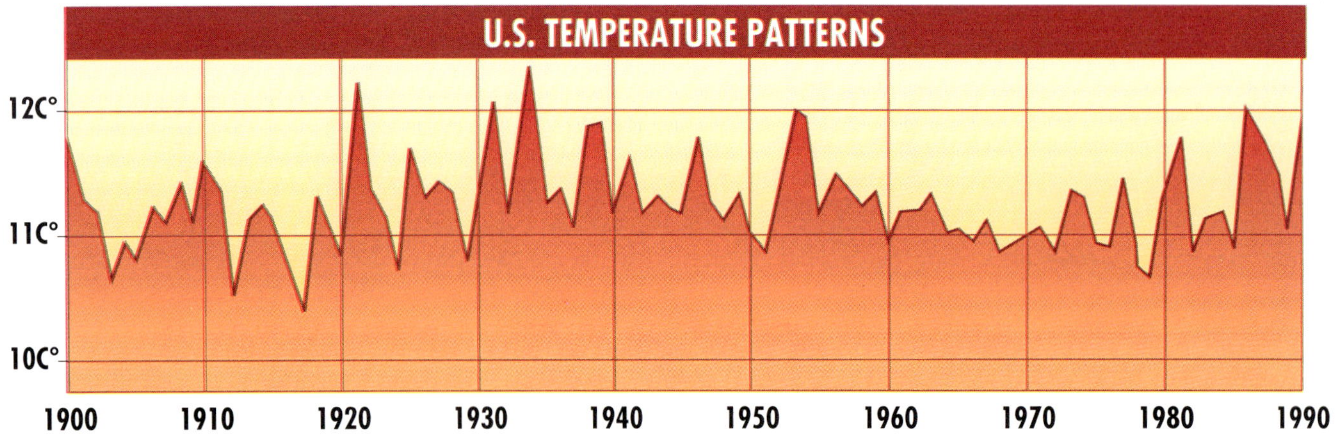


▲ Average U.S. temperatures. Do you see a change over the past 100 years?

## Closer to Home: Your weather and the greenhouse effect

Has the weather in your area ever surprised you? In 1988 there was an unexpected and severe drought in the midwest United States. The weather was hot and dry for months. Crops were ruined. In the summer of 1993 the same area had terrible floods. For months the rain didn't stop. Crops were ruined again. Look at the changes in the graph above. Some people think events like these are caused by greenhouse gases.

Scientists are sure that greenhouse gases do affect the weather. They're also sure that some greenhouse gases will be around for a while, as the bar graph shows. What they're not sure of is what the result will be. At first it seems simple—increasing the amounts of greenhouse gases will raise Earth's temperature by holding in more heat. Some people predict that most of the United States will become hot and humid all year long. As people study the situation, however, it becomes more confusing.

Look at the diagram on the next page. It shows one possible way greenhouse gases could change Earth. In this prediction the greenhouse gases started by raising temperatures, and ended up lowering them. Which will really happen? Scientists aren't sure.

- What do you think makes predicting the long-term effects of air pollution and greenhouse gases on the atmosphere so difficult?

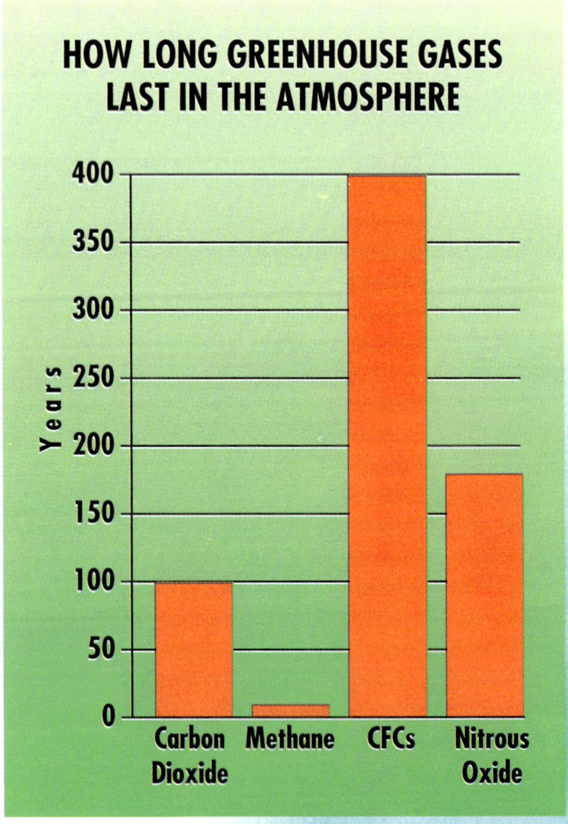

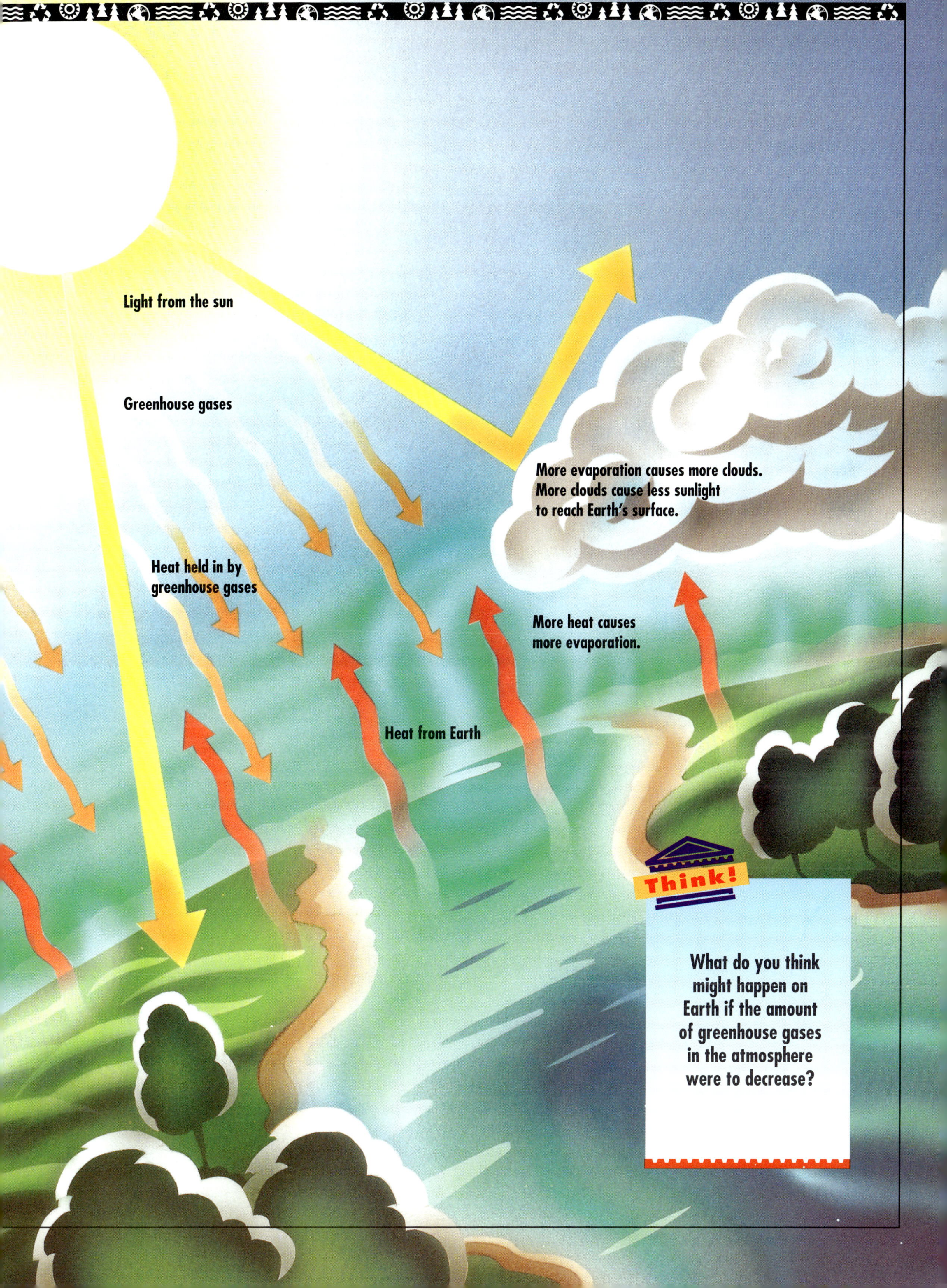


**Think!**

What do you think might happen on Earth if the amount of greenhouse gases in the atmosphere were to decrease?

# Identify Problems: Design an Atmosphere

When astronauts first landed on the moon, they got the chance to study it up close for the first time. If they had been able to stay longer, they might have learned even more. In order for scientists to remain on the moon, they would need many things, including a supply of air that would last throughout their stay.

15 In Lesson 15 you'll identify the problems you'd face in creating an Earthlike atmosphere for a space station on the moon.

16 In Lesson 16 you'll identify some possible solutions to those problems.

17 In Lesson 17 you'll design the atmosphere. Then you'll make a model based on your design.

You may also want to review the video.

**Problem:** The year is 2015. An international space agency wants to build a space station on the moon. Your team has been asked to design an important part of the life-support system—an atmosphere. You know what to expect: The moon has no air, no water, and no living things; its surface is covered with rocks and dust.

These questions will help you make a list of the problems you'll face while trying to design an Earth-like atmosphere to use on the moon:

1. How does Earth's atmosphere protect us? How does it provide enough oxygen for people to breathe?

2. What gases would you need to have in your atmosphere? Would you want water? Why? How will you clean and recycle the water? How will you keep the air free of pollution?

3. What kind of container will hold your atmosphere on the moon? How big will it be?

4. On the moon, it gets very hot during the two weeks of daylight and extremely cold during the two weeks of darkness. How could these temperature changes affect the way you design your atmosphere?

5. The pictures on these pages show some examples of atmospheres in closed spaces. As you study the pictures, ask yourself: What problems did the designers of these places solve?

◀ **Greenhouses** During the 1800s, English explorers brought plants home from all over the world. Many of these plants could not survive in a cool climate, so greenhouses were built to provide the right climate to grow plants all year round. Sunlight fills the greenhouse and warms the air inside. How can you heat your atmosphere on the moon?

▶ **Biosphere 2** Creating an Earthlike atmosphere isn't easy. Biosphere 2 was supposed to contain an atmosphere that could support life. Eight people lived inside it for two years. But researchers discovered that the biosphere had a leak. Why is it important that the container holding your atmosphere doesn't leak?

◀ **Vehicle Assembly Building (VAB)** Inside the VAB at the Kennedy Space Center, scientists built the giant rockets that carried the astronauts to the moon. The VAB was so big it was hard to heat the space evenly. Warm, moist air met pockets of cold air and formed clouds inside the building. Some people said that it even rained! How well would a big space work for your atmosphere on the moon?

**Think!**

**How are the problems the designers of these places faced like the problems you'll face?**

# Find Solutions: Design an Atmosphere

## Recycling isn't just for cans, bottles, and newspapers!

Recycling may be a new idea for humans, but it's an old one for our planet. The people who designed Biosphere 2 tried to copy—on a small scale—the natural recycling of gases that takes place in Earth's atmosphere.

NASA has been working on recycling water and air as a way of keeping people alive in space. As part of one NASA experiment, volunteers lived in a closed room. Any water they used for washing was saved. Urine was saved. Evaporated water was removed from the air. All the waste water then passed through a filter to remove particles. Then it was heated to kill germs. After more machines removed other particles, the water was safe for drinking again. And the volunteers said it tasted fine!

NASA has been thinking about recycling the air in the space station in the same way. For example, machines would remove carbon dioxide from the air when the levels got too high for human comfort.

You've just identified some problems that your team will face in designing an Earthlike atmosphere on the moon. You've also seen some examples of atmospheres in closed spaces. Now take a closer look at the greenhouse. Thinking about the solutions that the greenhouse designers came up with might help you find solutions to some of your problems.

1. Make a chart of the problems you listed in the last lesson. Beside each of your problems, try to list a similar problem that the greenhouse designers faced. You may not always be able to think of a matching one.

2. Next, study the diagram of the greenhouse. The greenhouse design allows people to control the temperature inside. How can you use some of these ideas to control the temperature of your atmosphere on the moon?

3. Greenhouses are made mostly of glass or plastic. Would either of those be a good material for the container that holds your atmosphere? Explain your thinking.

4. Plants take carbon dioxide from the air and give off oxygen. How could plants be helpful to your atmosphere on the moon?

5. Below each of the problems for your atmosphere, list any solutions you can think of.

## HOW A GREENHOUSE WORKS

### Other resources you can check:

- To find out more about how air, water, and food are recycled in nature: *One Small Square: Backyard,* by Donald M. Silver. W.H. Freeman and Company, 1993.
- To find out how people live in space: *The World Around Us: Space,* by Ian Ridpath. Kingfisher Books, 1991.

**Think!**

How can looking at the design of a greenhouse help you design an atmosphere in a closed space?

# Make Models: Design an Atmosphere

## Possible models for your atmosphere:

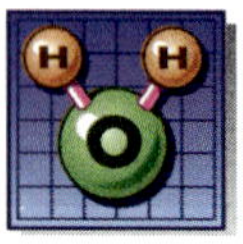

**Diagram** Look at the diagrams in Lessons 2, 3, 4, 11, and 14 to help you draw a large diagram of your atmosphere. Be sure to label the diagram to show your solutions.

**3-Dimensional Model** Use plastic jugs, plastic wrap, or any combination of materials to build a model of your atmosphere.

**Written Description** Write a letter from the moon to friends on Earth that carefully describes every detail of your atmosphere.

**Computer Graphics** Use a graphics program to design your atmosphere on the computer.

**Guided Tour** Give a speech about your atmosphere as though your team were taking a visitor on a guided tour of the space station.

You and your team have identified problems you'll face in designing an atmosphere for a space station on the moon. You've also identified possible solutions to some of those problems. Now you can try out your ideas.

1. Look over the chart of problems and solutions that you made. As a team, decide which is the best solution to each problem. Circle or highlight those solutions on your chart.

2. Now use those solutions to design an atmosphere that will keep people alive on the moon.

3. Make a model based on your design. Choose one of the kinds of models shown at the left. Pick the one that will best show your design.

4. Look at all the models your class has made. How did different teams solve the problem of designing an atmosphere? Did everyone think of the same problems? Were the solutions the same?

5. Describe what your model would have been like if you hadn't learned about the properties of Earth's atmosphere. How did doing the Explorations in this unit help you design your artificial atmosphere?

**Resources for designing your team's atmosphere:**

- Take a look at your journals and LabMats from the Explorations in the unit. They have information about how the atmosphere works.

- Refer to Lessons 1-14 of *Understanding the Atmosphere.*

- Check the reference books you've used in this unit for more information about how the atmosphere works.

- How did the Science Sleuths investigate the atmosphere to solve their problem?

- If you're unsure about where to start, try trading ideas with another team.

**Think!**

How did making a model of an atmosphere help you think of problems and solutions you missed before?

# FOR SCIENCE BROWSERS





## Sights Unseen

excerpt from *Life*

The stuff may sometimes seem a nuisance, but without it, all of humanity would be left high and dry.

It's everywhere, on everything. It can carry disease. It protects against the sun's rays. It is blowin' in the wind. It ranges in size from 1/25,000 of an inch up to 1/5,000 of an inch. Despite its lack of mass, it is a very big player in life on earth.

It is dust. The speck seen below is common house dust magnified 2,300 times.

Most dust is mineral matter, scraped from soil or rock and carried by the wind. House dust can comprise flecks of skin, such as the boulder at the center of this speck.

Perhaps the greatest paradox concerning dust, which we think of as dry, is its role in rainfall. Water drops will not form without solid matter to settle upon. Dust is the organizing principle for every raindrop, every snowflake.

Lastly: Dust lasts. As Cyril Blacktin noted in his 1934 book, *Dust,* a lot of today's dust existed before man did. Blacktin concluded: "All life is continuously surrounded by and enveloped by dust."

*—November, 1993*

© David Scharf/Peter Arnold Inc.

# Predicting Pounding Waves

by Neeraja Sankaran
from *SuperScience Blue*

© Charles Krupa/AP/Wide World

*Overflowing Oceans—This nor'easter hit the East Coast in December of 1992. Waves more than three times your height came crashing onto the beach. Some smashed right through houses and cars, and carried them out to sea.*

Winter winds can whip up some hard-hitting waves. So when a blasting nor'easter storm hits the Atlantic Coast, ocean waves can grow huge—and dangerous.

Nor'easters—named because the winds blow from the northeast—don't strike on a regular schedule. But thanks to two scientists, we now know when they're *most likely* to pound the coast: In February.

Robert Davis and Robert Dolan learned about nor'easters by looking at storms of the past 50 years. That way, they could tell not only when, but also how hard, the storms were likely to hit.

But Davis and Dolan had one problem. To measure the force of an ocean storm, you need to know wave height. And in the past, weather experts didn't always record wave height.

Luckily, the experts *did* record wind conditions. And scientists had already figured out how wind makes waves. So Davis and Dolan used this information to calculate wave heights.

To see how wind starts waves, try blowing across the top of a bowl of water. Your breath pushes down on the water, and ripples move out from that spot. Once ripples start, the wind smacks against their backs. That pushes them up into bigger waves.

What kinds of winds make the biggest waves?

- *Fast blowers:* Fast winds push hard, so waves get bigger.
- *Long lasters:* Waves start out small, and build up over time. So the longer the storm lasts, the bigger the waves get.
- *Far reachers:* Some winds blow in short spurts, and some sweep over long distances. Long-distance winds can really get behind a wave and build it into a wall of water!

Now Davis and Dolan know about wind *and* waves from the past 50 years. That helps people who live on the coast—or want to move there—know what to expect before the big waves start breaking!

*—February, 1994*

**Smart Tree!**
**A pine tree can be a good weather predictor. Its pine cones close up shortly before rain falls.**

# Mystery of the 300-Year Drought

by Christine Gorman
excerpt from *Time*

Paul J. Pugliese

Before the Han Dynasty, before Alexander the Great, even before Ramses, the first empire the world ever knew was built by a Mesopotamian ruler named Sargon of Akkad. He conquered dozens of cities and villages between the Tigris and Euphrates rivers more than 4,000 years ago, forcing them to pay tribute in wheat, barley, and silver. For a century the regime flourished until suddenly, mysteriously, it collapsed.

Now the mystery may have been solved by researchers from the U.S. and France. In last week's *Science,* they put forth evidence that the empire was undone by a combination of climatic catastrophes. First a volcanic eruption blanketed the region in ash. Then a drought, which lasted 300 years, crippled the farming communities on which the cities depended. The American and French researchers, led by Yale archaeologist Harvey Weiss, believe the drought was part of a major shift in weather patterns that affected the climate in many different areas of the globe 4,000 years ago. From Egypt to the Aegean to India, rainfall diminished and temperatures dropped.

By excavating the ancient Akkadian city of Shekhna in what is now Syria, Weiss and his colleagues determined that the urban center, once a thriving home for 10,000 people, was deserted for three centuries. One layer, which they dated to 2200 B.C., revealed the crumbling walls of a ghost town. It also provided some important clues about the weather. Weiss explains, "In a dry climate, you see very little earthworm activity and lots of loose silt, for example."

The pieces of the puzzle started falling into place after Marie-Agnès Courty, a geologist with the National Center for Scientific Research in Paris, painstakingly examined and sorted the soil samples from the roofs of the abandoned buildings under a microscope. She identified a thin veil of volcanic ash, one quarter of an inch thick, underneath 8 to 20 inches of silt. The layers showed no evidence of having been disturbed by earthworms and also showed patterns characteristic of soil that has settled after a dust storm. It looked like a volcano had erupted, perhaps in nearby Turkey, and a long drought had followed.

Wherever the researchers looked throughout the area, they found the same story: abandoned buildings and layers of volcanic ash and debris from fierce wind storms. After 300 years, when the rain returned, so did the people. A new empire, whose capital was Babylon, arose and fell. Today the region is flush once again with wheat fields.

Did the volcano cause the ancient drought? "That's unlikely," Weiss says. So, with one mystery solved, researchers find themselves trying to explain how a drought can persist for three centuries. *—August, 1990*

## What a Relief It Is

**by Jeffrey Brune**
**excerpt from *Discover***

In October 1989, 1,000 tons of limestone pellets fell like a hailstorm of antacid tablets onto 240 acres of the Woods Lake watershed in the Adirondack Mountains of New York. The pellets were dropped from low-flying helicopters in an effort to bring fast relief to an ecosystem soured by acid rain.

Five years earlier the fish in the lake had died when the water had turned too acidic. Biologists from Cornell initially attempted to treat the lake and restock it with brook trout, but the fish didn't last. Rains and melting snow in the spring brought pulses of acidity that killed off fish eggs and young fry.

So [Cornell] decided to go one step further and try liming the area draining into the lake. After the helicopters dumped the limestone, fall rains dissolved the pellets, washing the mineral into the streams and the soil. Acid levels in the lake dropped almost immediately. What's more, seasonal acid pulses in the following winter and spring were much less severe. While the effects of liming just the lake lasted about a year, Schofield thinks the watershed liming might last five years or longer. *—December, 1990*

Peter Spacek

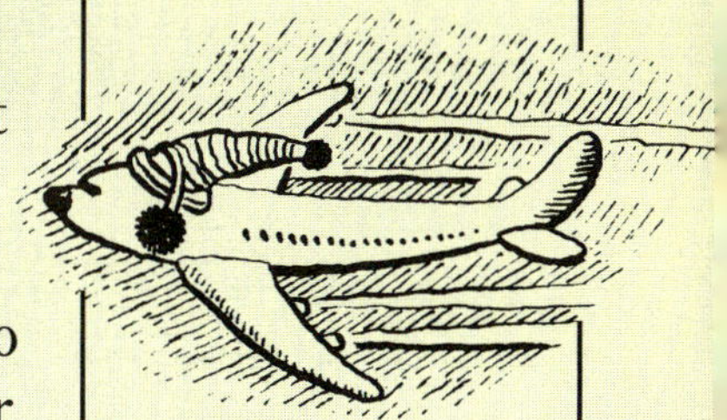

**Sky Lines**

**Have you ever noticed the white trails that high-flying jets leave behind? A jet trail is made of tiny ice crystals. Part of the exhaust from a jet engine is water vapor. Jets fly in the cold, thin air high above Earth, where the temperature is below freezing. The water vapor in jet exhaust freezes instantly in this cold air, forming a trail that can last for several hours.**

**Windblown**
**The windiest place in the United States is Mount Washington in New Hampshire, where the average wind speed is about 60 kilometers (36 miles) per hour. In 1934, the strongest gust of wind that ever hit Mount Washington blew past at an incredible speed of 372 kilometers (231 miles) per hour!**

# Icy Hike to School

by Gloria LaFay
from *National Geographic World*

There were no school buses. There were no crossing guards. When Motup, 11, and his sister Diskit, 8, attended boarding school in Leh, in northern India, they walked 14 days through the Himalayas to get there. The school lay 93 icy miles from their home in Tarang, a tiny village in this rugged mountain range. Relatives and friends accompanied the children along the frozen Zanskar River. It was the only route; snow blocked the roads. Could you brave such a trip? Read on.

Before Motup was old enough for school, his father traveled outside their village for the first time. The father was amazed. He had never seen a field of rice, for example, or a faucet. He wanted his son to learn about the world outside, too.

Since there were no schools in Tarang, Motup's father arranged for his son to attend school in Leh. Motup made his first trip there in 1986, when he was 8. Because traveling to and from school was so difficult, Motup stayed in Leh for long periods—once for three years. A group of adults brought him home along the frozen river. Motup shared his new knowledge of arithmetic, English, and biology with his parents. Within days they decided that Diskit

© Bob Grant/Comstock Inc.

should go to the school in Leh, too. So, during the 45-day period while the Zanskar remains frozen each year, Motup, then 11, and Diskit, then 8, joined their father and other adults on the icy hike along the river.

The surface of the winding Zanskar River constantly changed. If the sun raised the temperature slightly, the ice would become thin and break apart. The travelers had to test it with sticks at every step. If it broke, they could have plunged into waters so cold they would die.

At dawn each day Motup and Diskit awakened to temperatures of minus 35 degrees. Frost formed on their faces. The group members walked four hours before stopping for a meal of tea and cooked barley. They continued for another two hours, then found shelter for the night. Often they stayed on the river bank, where they built a fire. "Around a fire we could forget our worries," says Motup, "though the cold was cruel, and it was dangerous all the time."

After two weeks the band reached Leh. Diskit, who had never left her village, was amazed by the activity. The truck her father rented terrified her. She called it an "iron beast."

At the boarding school the children and their father met the principal for tea. They sat, not on the floor as at home, but on a sofa. No other students had come as far. It might be years before they could return to their family. "But in my village we are used to struggling," says Motup. "Here at school I can gain knowledge from books. Then I can help the people of my village."

Motup and Diskit made fast progress at the school in Leh. Now they attend a more advanced school in a city in northern India—and they're moving closer to their goal of helping out their village.

*—March, 1993*

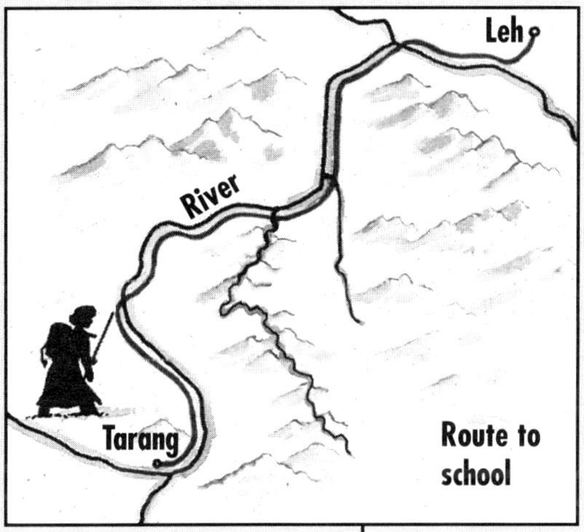


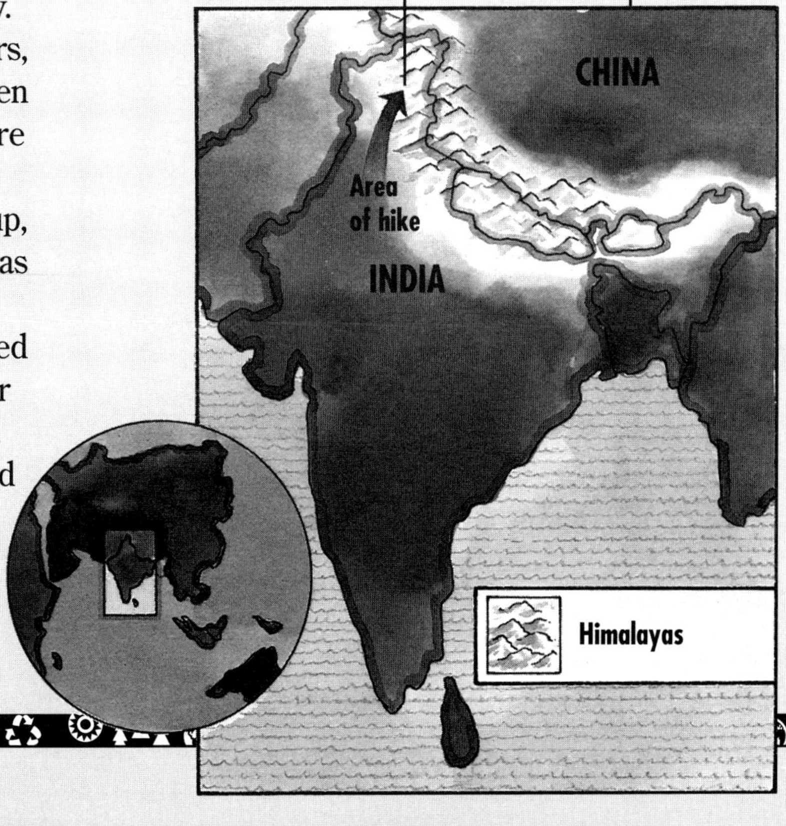


Barbara Leonard Gibson

**Read the Clouds**

**Clouds look white because the tiny water droplets that form them reflect the white light of the sun. Storm clouds look gray because they're so thick that very little sunlight passes through them.**

# GLOSSARY

## Concept vocabulary and other technical terms

**acid rain** [as' • id rān]: *n.* Rain containing high levels of sulfuric and nitric acid; it's caused mainly by the burning of fuels.

**altitude** [al' • tə • to͞od]: *n.* The height above any given point, especially above sea level.

**atmosphere** [at' • məs • fēr]: *n.* The air that surrounds Earth.

**barometer** [bə • rom' • ə • tər]: *n.* An instrument for measuring air pressure.

**condense** [kən • dens']: *n.* To change from a vapor or gas to a liquid.

**evaporate** [ē • vap' • ə • rāt]: *n.* To change into a gas or vapor.

**front** [frunt]: *n.* The forward edge of a moving mass of warm or cool air; the place where two air masses meet.

**gravity** [grav' • ə • tē]: *n.* The force by which two bodies attract each other, especially as shown by the tendency of objects to fall toward the center of Earth.

**greenhouse gases** [grēn' • hous gas' • əz]: *n.* Gases that absorb heat in the atmosphere.

**mesosphere** [mez' • ə • sfēr]: *n.* The layer of Earth's atmosphere just above the stratosphere, extending to about 80 kilometers (50 miles) above the surface of Earth.

**ozone** [ō' • zōn]: *n.* An unstable form of oxygen that is created when oxygen comes in contact with UV rays; ozone forms a protective layer in the stratosphere.

**pollutant** [pə • lo͞o' • tənt]: *n.* A substance, often a waste material such as smoke or dust, that spoils an environment.

**pressure** [presh' • ûr]: *n.* A push applied over a surface by something in contact with that surface.

**stratosphere** [strat' • ə • sfēr]: *n.* A layer of the atmosphere, beginning about 16 kilometers (about 10 miles) up, in which temperatures are more or less uniform and clouds are rare.

**thermosphere** [thûr' • mə • sfēr]: *n.* A layer of the atmosphere above the mesosphere, extending between about 200 kilometers (120 miles) and about 500 kilometers (310 miles) above the surface of Earth.

**troposphere** [trō' • pə • sfēr]: *n.* The layer of the atmosphere extending from Earth's surface to the stratosphere.

**UV rays** [yo͞o • vē rāz]: *n.* Invisible, high-energy rays from the sun that can damage unprotected eyes and skin; also called ultraviolet rays.

**water vapor** [wô' • tər vā' • pər]: *n.* Water in its gaseous form.

**wind-chill factor** [wind' • chil fac' • tər]: *n.* A temperature that is a measure of how cold the air feels to human skin, taking into account the chilling effect of the wind, as well as the actual air temperature.

| | | | | | |
|---|---|---|---|---|---|
| a | add, map | ī | ice, write | û(r) | burn, term |
| ā | ace, rate | o | odd, hot | yo͞o | fuse, few |
| â(r) | care, air | ō | open, so | ə | a in above |
| ä | palm, father | ô | order, jaw | | e in sicken |
| e | end, pet | o͝o | took, full | | i in possible |
| ē | equal, tree | o͞o | pool, food | | o in melon |
| i | it, give | u | up, done | | u in circus |

# INDEX

Page references in *italics* indicate illustrations, photographs, and tables.